D1286530

STUDIES IN ANTIQUITY AND CHRISTIANITY

The Roots of Egyptian Christianity
Birger A. Pearson and James E. Goehring, editors

The Formation of Q: Trajectories in Ancient Wisdom Collections
John S. Kloppenborg

Saint Peter of Alexandria: Bishop and Martyr
Tim Vivian

Images of the Feminine in Gnosticism
Karen L. King, editor

Gnosticism, Judaism, and Egyptian Christianity
Birger A. Pearson

Ascetic Behavior in Greco-Roman Antiquity
Vincent L. Wimbush, editor

The Institute for Antiquity and Christianity
Claremont Graduate School
Claremont, California

Ethiopian ('The Black") Moses
Courtesy of Father Antonious Henein, Holy Virgin Mary Coptic Orthodox Church of Los Angeles

STUDIES IN ANTIQUITY & CHRISTIANITY

ASCETIC BEHAVIOR IN GRECO-ROMAN ANTIQUITY
A SOURCEBOOK

Vincent L. Wimbush, editor

FORTRESS PRESS

MINNEAPOLIS

ASCETIC BEHAVIOR IN GRECO-ROMAN ANTIQUITY

Scripture quotations, unless otherwise noted, are from the Revised Standard Version of the Bible, copyright © 1946, 1952, and 1971 by the Division of Christian Education of the National Council of Churches.

Library of Congress Cataloging-in-Publication Data

Ascetic behavior in Greco-Roman antiquity / Vincent L. Wimbush,
    editor.
        p.   cm. — (Studies in antiquity and Christianity)
    Translations from Greek, Latin, Hebrew, Coptic, and Syriac.
    Includes bibliographical references and index.
    ISBN 0-8006-3105-6 (alk. paper) : $41.95
    1. Asceticism—History—Early church, ca. 30–600—Sources.
2. Asceticism—History—Sources. 3. Philosophy, Ancient—History-
-Sources. 4. Civilization, Greco-Roman—Sources. I. Wimbush,
Vincent L. II. Series.
BV5023.A73   1990
291.4'47'0901—dc20   90–44980
                                                           CIP

The paper used in this publication meets the minimum requirements of American National Standard for Information Sciences—Permanence of Paper for Printed Library Materials, ANSI Z329.48-1984. ∞™

Manufactured in the U.S.A.   AF 1–3105

94   93   92   91   90   1   2   3   4   5   6   7   8   9   10

Contents

PART ONE. Homily

Contributors

Joseph P. Amar
Associate Professor, Department of Classical and Oriental Languages
and Literatures
The University of Notre Dame, Notre Dame, Ind.

Robert Boughner
Associate Professor, Department of Classics, Philosophy, and
Religion
Mary Washington College, Fredericksburg, Va.

Michael H. Browder
Senior Pastor
First United Methodist Church, Hampton, Va.

David Bundy
Associate Professor of Christian Origins
Asbury Theological Seminary, Wilmore, Ky.

Virginia Burrus
Doctoral Candidate, Graduate Theological Union
Berkeley, Calif.

Elizabeth A. Castelli
Assistant Professor, Department of Religious Studies
The College of Wooster, Wooster, Ohio

Elizabeth A. Clark
John Carlisle Kilgo Professor of Religion
Duke University, Durham, N.C.

Gail Paterson Corrington
  Department of Religious Studies
  College of William and Mary, Williamsburg, Va.

Leah Di Segni
  Institute of Archaeology
  The Hebrew University of Jerusalem, Israel

Steven D. Fraade
  Mark Taper Professor of the History of Judaism, Department of
    Religious Studies
  Yale University, New Haven, Conn.

James E. Goehring
  Assistant Professor, Department of Classics, Philosophy, and Religion
  Mary Washington College, Fredericksburg, Va.

Paul B. Harvey, Jr.
  Associate Professor of Classics and History
  Pennsylvania State University, University Park, Pa.

Susan Ashbrook Harvey
  Assistant Professor of Religious Studies
  Brown University, Providence, R.I.

Yizhar Hirschfeld
  The Hebrew University of Jerusalem, Motza, Israel

David G. Hunter
  Assistant Professor of Theology
  College of St. Thomas, St. Paul, Minn.

Anitra Bingham Kolenkow
  Visiting Scholar, Dominican School of Philosophy and Theology
  Berkeley, Calif.

Michael O'Laughlin
  Instructor of Sacred Scripture, Bread of Life Scripture Ministry
  Archdiocese of Boston, Medford, Mass.

Teresa M. Shaw
  Doctoral Candidate, Duke University, Durham, N.C.

Michael D. Swartz
  Assistant Professor of Religious Studies
  University of Virginia, Charlottesville, Va.

Karen Jo Torjesen
  Associate Professor of Religion
  Claremont Graduate School, Claremont, Calif.

Joseph W. Trigg
  Rector, St. Patrick's Episcopal Church, Falls Church, Va.;
  Adjunct Professor, Virginia Theological Seminary, Alexandria, Va.

Leif E. Vaage
  Professor of New Testament
  ILAMP, Lima, Peru

Richard Valantasis
  Rector
  Church of St. John the Evangelist, Boston, Mass.

Kathleen O'Brien Wicker
  Professor of New Testament and Early Christianity
  Scripps College, Claremont, Calif.

Vincent L. Wimbush
  Associate Professor of New Testament
  School of Theology at Claremont;
  Associate Professor of Religion
  Claremont Graduate School, Claremont, Calif.

O. Larry Yarbrough
  Associate Professor of Religion
  The Middlebury College, Middlebury, Vt.

Robin A. Darling Young
  Assistant Professor of Theology
  The Catholic University of America, Washington, D.C.

Foreword

This sourcebook is a welcomed addition to the Institute's series of Studies in Antiquity and Christianity, the first major result of the Institute's Project on Ascetic Behavior in Greco-Roman Antiquity, directed by Vincent L. Wimbush. It brings together in English translation a number of widely scattered and quite divergent ascetic texts, a collection that both provides convenient access to material not readily available and directly and indirectly puts in focus one of the main long-range objectives of the project.

The term *askesis* does not in itself mean more than training or practice, a conscious or intentional posture toward one's world into which one works oneself, the exercise of one's self-understanding. The fact that asceticism, the various forms of abstinence usually associated with monasticism, is only one such way to relate to one's world suggests the broader context in which traditional asceticism is to be understood. The project seeks to penetrate that broader level behind asceticism.

Prior to and apart from monasticism, there was, of course, not only asceticism but also various ways of assuming a position toward one's world on the basis of one's self-understanding. This can be traced back to Christian beginnings in the cases of Paul, Jesus, and John the Baptist. As this already indicates, however, ascetic practice was then (as now) a much wider phenomenon, in the Judaism of Qumran and the Therapeutai, in Hellenistic-Roman religions and philosophical schools, and even in the way statesmen sought to understand and shape their world.

We live in a time when asceticism in the narrower sense less cogently lays its claim on us by and large but when understanding our world and assuming a stance that one then puts in practice is all the more urgently called for. It is for this that one is to listen in ascetic texts, to the extent they are to address us today. This sourcebook thus already trains the reader on the path to *askesis* in the modern world.

JAMES M. ROBINSON, *Director*
Institute for Antiquity and Christianity

Preface

This volume represents the collaborative efforts of more than two dozen members of the Society of Biblical Literature Group on Ascetic Behavior in Greco-Roman Antiquity. The interests of the group—reflected in the texts its members chose to translate—cut across the boundaries of Judaism, Christianity, and Hellenic philosophy and religion. This cross-religious, cross-philosophical presentation implicitly rejects some assumptions governing older models for the study of asceticism, for example, that early Judaism (in contrast to early Christianity) was "essentially" antiascetic or that Christian asceticism developed as a response to the moral depravity rampant in Roman paganism. Both the discoveries of new texts in the past half-century and recent scholarship on previously neglected documents mandate a revised approach to the topic. The popularity of such recent books as Michel Foucault's volumes on the history of sexuality in antiquity and Peter Brown's *The Body and Society: Men, Women, and Sexual Renunciation in Early Christianity* bespeaks a renewed interest in the issue—but an interest that evidences new assumptions and new methodologies.

The widened discussion pertaining to ancient asceticism is also suggested by the variety of languages from which the texts gathered here have been translated: Greek and Latin, with a modicum of Hebrew, no longer suffice for the study of late ancient asceticism. Coptic and Syriac are increasingly recognized as important for allowing us to enter the two vitally important centers of ascetic development, Egypt and Mesopotamia. This volume thus makes ample use of Coptic and Syriac materials that enrich our knowledge of late ancient asceticism.

A glance at the volume's contents reveals another notable feature of this collection: "high" theological treatises do not dominate. To be sure, the writings of philosophers and theologians are well represented in the pages that follow, but so are materials from the "lower" literary genres: the stories about and sayings of men and women deemed to be especially holy, sermons that were preached to ordinary Christians of little learning, magical texts, and documents that detail archaeological and papyrological discoveries. Materials such as these bring us closer to the social worlds of the average inhabitants of the Roman Empire than theological or philosophical treatises ever can by themselves. Thus, although asceticism often appears as an elite enterprise, the testimonies in this volume also let us glimpse the less than elite. Moreover, because asceticism's appeal was as strong for women as for men, several of the texts translated here offer us insights into women's lives and experience that are rare among strictly theological treatises of late antiquity.

The diversity of ancient ascetic behavior is clearly evident in these texts. The contributors to and editorial committee for the volume have wisely eschewed blanket pronouncements on "the meaning" of asceticism across the range of religions, philosophies, cultures, and centuries here represented. Yet, the wish of the contributors to this volume is that their efforts stimulate further discussion on the phenomenon of ascetic behavior in late antiquity.

ELIZABETH A. CLARK
John Carlisle Kilgo Professor of Religion
Duke University

Acknowledgments

Nearly thirty scholars from various fields and disciplines have for the past four years constituted the Project on Ascetic Behavior in Greco-Roman Antiquity, in connection with the Institute for Antiquity and Christianity (IAC) in Claremont and the Society for Biblical Literature (SBL) and the American Academy of Religion (AAR). Although I have taken upon myself the primary responsibility for the editing and final shape of the volume, it is very much the result of a collaborative effort.

So words of gratitude are due to many individuals, groups, and institutions for their assistance with the many tasks that were required for the completion and appearance of this volume:

To all members of the Project on Ascetic Behavior in Greco-Roman Antiquity for the lively discussions, friendships, and collegiality that inspired the volume and renewed the commitment of many to the scholarly life.

To Gail Paterson Corrington, James E. Goehring, Susan Ashbrook Harvey, and Robin A. Darling Young for their critical reading of contributions, constructive editorial recommendations, and general oversight work as the steering and editorial committee of the project.

To L. William Countryman and Ronald F. Hock for their thorough and critical reading of the entire manuscript. Their constructive recommendations and corrections helped the editor—and the manuscript—avoid many pitfalls.

To Elizabeth A. Clark, Gail P. Corrington, James E. Goehring, Susan A. Harvey, David G. Hunter, Teresa M. Shaw, and Michael D. Swartz for their suggestions for parts of the introduction for which they rank as experts.

To L. Zachary Maxey, my research assistant at Claremont Graduate School, for his thorough work in every phase of the project, including research, correspondence, editorial work, and assistance with the mini-conferences of the project.

To Kenneth Pomykala, also a research assistant, for his work in connection with the earliest phase of the project, especially his assistance at the earliest miniconferences.

To Sharon Engelstein, graduate student in art at Claremont Graduate School, for the map she provided; Richard Wright, graduate student in the Religious Studies Department at Brown University, for the abbreviations list and the index; and Paul Constas, graduate student at Catholic University, for the chronological tables.

To our hosts for the miniconferences held just before the national meetings of AAR/SBL—Abbot Armand Veilleux and the community of the Monastery of the Holy Spirit, November 1986, Conyers, Georgia; Father Richard Valantasis and the community at the Convent of the Sisters of St. Margaret, December 1987, Duxbury, Massachusetts; and the community at the Fullerton Cenacle, November 1988, Chicago—for their gracious and warm hospitality.

To the administration and board of trustees of the School of Theology at Claremont for their support of my research leave for the spring semester 1989, during which time—up to the birth of my daughter Lauren!—I was able to devote almost total (albeit nervous) attention to the volume.

To the late John Hollar of Fortress Press for his counsel and guiding hand.

To James M. Robinson, the staff, and Research Council of the Institute for Antiquity and Christianity for their support—financial, moral, and otherwise—throughout the life of the project.

To my family: my wife, Linda, for her encouragement; and my four-month-old daughter, Lauren, for her patience and understanding—most of the time.

September 1989
Cambridge, MA

Abbreviations

Abbreviations of biblical books are not given here. The ones used in this book are standard.

APOSTOLIC FATHERS

1–2 Clem.	*1–2 Clement*
Herm. Man.	*Hermas, Mandate(s)*
Her. Sim.	*Hermas, Similitude(s)*
Ign. *Eph.*	Ignatius, *Letter to the Ephesians*

TARGUMIC LITERATURE

Tg. Neb.	*Targum of the Prophets*
Tg. Onq.	*Targum Onqelos*
Tg. Ps.-J.	*Targum Pseudo-Jonathan*

ORDERS AND TRACTATES IN
MISHNAIC AND RELATED LITERATURE

(To distinguish the same-named tractates in the Mishna, Tosepta, Babylonian Talmud, and Jerusalem Talmud, an italicized *m.*, *t.*, *b.*, or *y.* is used before the title of the tractate.)

Ber.	*Berakot*
B. Qam.	*Baba Qamma*
Nazir	*Nazir*

Ned.   *Nedarim*
Ta῾an.   *Ta῾anit*

OTHER RABBINIC WORKS

Rab.   *Rabbah* (following abbreviation for biblical
                           book)

NAG HAMMADI TRACTATES

Gos. Thom.   *Gospel of Thomas*

CLASSICAL AND LATER CHRISTIAN
AUTHORS AND WORKS

Acta Sanct.   *Acta Sanctorum*

Ambrose
  Virg.   *De Virginibus*

Antiochus Monachus
  Hom.   *Pandecta scriptorae sacrae*, M.89,1428

Apoph. Patr.   *Apophthegmata Patrum*

Apuleius
  Met.   *Metamorphoses*

Aristotle
  Eth. Nic.   *Ethica Nicomachea*

Athanasius
  Virg.   *De Virginibus*
  Vit. Ant.   *Vita Antonii*

Augustine
  Civ. D.   *De Civitate Dei*
  Conf.   *Confessions*

Cassian, John
  Conf.   *Conferences*
  Inst.   *Institutes*

Cicero
  De Orat.   *De Oratore*

Fin.	*De Finibus*
Tusc.	*Tusculanae Disputationes*

Clement of Alexandria
Paed.	*Paedagogus*
Quis Div. Salv.	*Quis Dives Salvetur*
Strom.	*Stromata*

Cypr.	Cyprian
Ep.	*Epistles*

Cyril of Scythopolis
Vit. Euth.	*De Vitae Euthymii*

Democritus
Vorsokr.	H. Diels, *Fragmente der Vorsokratiker* (Berlin, 1922)

Didymus of Alexandria
Trin.	*De Trinitate*

Dio Chrysostom
Or.	*Orationes*

D.L.	Diogenes Laertius

Epictetus
Diss.	*Dissertationes*

Euripides
Ba.	*Bacchae*

Eusebius
Hist. Eccl.	*Historia Ecclesiastica*

Evagrius Ponticus
Ant.	*Antirrheticus*
or.	*de Oratione*

Florus
Epit.	*Epitome of Roman History*

Gr. Thaum.	Gregory Thaumaturgus
pan. Or.	*Panegyric for Origen*

Gregory of Nyssa
Virg.	*De Virginitate*
Vit. Mac.	*Vita Macrinae*

Hippocrates
Aph.	*Aphorismoi*

Hippolytus
   Haer.   *Refutatio omnium Haeresium*

Homer
   Il.   *Iliad*
   Od.   *Odyssey*

Horace
   Ep.   *Epistles*

Jerome
   Comm. in Isa.   *Commentarii in Isaiam Prophetam*
   De Vir. Ill.   *De Viris Illustribus*
   Ep.   *Epistles*
   Vit. Olmp.   *Vita Olympiadis*

John Chrysostom
   Virg.   *De Virginitate*

Josephus
   A.J.   *Antiquitates Judaicae*
   B.J.   *Bellum Judaicum*

Julian
   Or.   *Orationes*

Justin
   1 Apol.   *1 Apologia*

Lactantius
   Div. Inst.   *Divinae Institutiones*
   Mort. Persc.   *De Mortibus Persecutorum*

Lucian
   Demon.   *Demonax*
   Fug.   *Fugitivi*
   Nigr.   *Nigrinus*
   Peregr.   *De Morte Peregrini*
   Pisc.   *Piscator (The Dead Come to Life)*
   Pseudol.   *Pseudologista*
   Tox.   *Toxaris*
   Vit. Auct.   *Vitarum Auctio*

Marcus Aurelius
   Med.   *Meditations*

Methodius
   Symp.   *Symposium*

Origen
>   Cels.   *Contra Celsum*
>   Comm. in Matt.   *In Matt. Commentarius*
>   Hom. in Gen., Lv., Jer. *Homilies on Genesis, Leviticus, Jeremiah*
>   Mart.   *Exhortation to Martyrdom*

Palladius
>   Ad Laus.   *Ad Lausum*
>   Hist. Laus.   *Historia Lausiaca*
>   Prooem.   *Prooemium*

Paulus Orosius
>   Hist. Adv. Pag.   *Historiae Adversus Paganus*

Petronius
>   Sat.   *Satyricon*

Philo
>   Abr.   *De Abrahamo*
>   Conf. Ling.   *De Confusione Linguarum*
>   Congr.   *De Congressu Eruditionis Gratia*
>   Cont.   *De Vita Contemplativa*
>   Decal.   *De Decalogo*
>   Gig.   *De Gigantus*
>   Leg.   *Legatio ad Gaium*
>   Leg. All.   *Legum Allegoriae*
>   Migr.   *De Migratione Abraham*
>   Omn. Prob. Lib.   *Quod omnis Probus Liber sit.*
>   Op. Mund.   *De Opificio Mundi*
>   Prov.   *De Providentia*
>   Quaest. in Ex.   *Quaestiones in Exodum*
>   Quaest. in Gen.   *Quaestiones in Genesis*
>   Rer. Div. Her.   *Quis Rerum Divinarum Heres sit*
>   Sobr.   *De Sobrietate*
>   Som.   *De Somniis*
>   Spec. Leg.   *De Specialibus Legibus*
>   Vit. Cont.   *De Vita Contemplativa*
>   Vit. Mos.   *De Vita Mosis*

Philostratus
>   VA   *Vita Apollonii*

Plato
>   Ap.   *Apology*

Hi. I	*Hippias Major*
Leg.	*Leges*
Lys.	*Lysis*
Men.	*Meno*
Phd.	*Phaedo*
Phdr.	*Phaedrus*
Resp.	*Respublica*
Symp.	*Symposium*
Ti.	*Timaeus*

Plutarch

Aud. Poet.	*De Audiendis Poetis*
De def. or.	*De defectu oraculorum*
De Pyth. or.	*De Pythiae oraculis*
De vitand. alien.	*De vitando aere alieno*
Moral.	*Moralia*
Per.	*Pericles*
Quomod. adul.	*Quomodo adulescens poetas audire debeat*
Vit. illust.	*Vitae Illustrium Vivorum sine Parallelae*

Porphyry

Abst.	*De Abstinentia*

Quintillian

Inst. Orat.	*Institutionis Oratriae*

Sallust

Cat.	*Catilina*

Sozomen

Hist. Eccl.	*Historia Ecclesiastica*

Tertullian

Bapt.	*De Baptisma*

Vergil

Aen.	*Aeneid*
G.	*Georgics*

Xenophon

Symp.	*Symposium*

PERIODICALS, REFERENCE WORKS, AND SERIALS

ACW	Ancient Christian Writers
AfO	*Archiv für Orientforschung*

AJS Review	*Association for Jewish Studies Review*
AnBoll	Analecta Bollandiana
ARW	*Archiv für Religionswissenschaft*
ATR	*Anglican Theological Review*
AW	*Antike Welt*
Bessarione	*Publicazione Periodica di Studi Orientali*
BHO	*Bibliotheca Hagiographica Orientalis*, ed. Socii Bollandiani (Brussels, 1910)
BJRL	Bulletin of the John Rylands Library
BLE	*Bulletin de littérature ecclésiastique*
Cathedra	*Cathedra for the History of Eretz-Israel and Its Yishuv* (Hebrew)
CBQ	*Catholic Biblical Quarterly*
CH	*Church History*
Const. App.	*Constitutiones apostolorum*
CP	*Classical Philology*
CSCO	Corpus Scriptorum Christianorum Orientalium
CSEL	Corpus Scriptorum Ecclesiasticorum Latinorum
DACL	*Dictionnaire d'archéologie chrétienne et de liturgie*
Dict. Spir.	*Dictionnaire de Spiritualité*
DTC	*Dictionnaire de théologie catholique*
EO	*Echos d'Orient. Revue d'histoire, de géographie et de liturgie orientales*
Eretz	*Eretz Magazine*—A Quarterly from Israel
ESI	*Excavations and Surveys in Israel*
GCS	*Griechischen christlichen Schriftsteller*
GRBS	*Greek, Roman, and Byzantine Studies*
HTR	*Harvard Theological Review*
IDB	G. A. Buttrick (ed.), *Interpreter's Dictionary of the Bible*
IEJ	*Israel Exploration Journal*
ILAN	*Israel Land and Nature*
JAC	Jahrbuch für Antike und Christentum
JBL	*Journal of Biblical Literature*
JFSR	*Journal of Feminist Studies in Religion*
JHS	*Journal of Hellenic Studies*
JJS	*Journal of Jewish Studies*

JÖB	*Jahrbuch der Österreicheischen Byzantinischen*
JQR	*Jewish Quarterly Review*
JRS	*Journal of Roman Studies*
JSJ	*Journal for the Study of Judaism in the Persian, Hellenistic and Roman Period*
JTS	Journal of Theological Studies
LA	*Studii Biblici Franciscani, Liber Annuus*
LCL	Loeb Classical Library
Levant	*Journal of the British School of Archaeology in Jerusalem*
LTS	*La Terra Sancta*
Mus	*Muséon*
NHS	Nag Hammadi Studies
NovT	*Novum Testamentum*
NPNF	Nicene and Post-Nicene Fathers
OCA	*Orientalia Christiana Analecta*
OrChr	*Oriens Christianus*
PG	J. Migne, *Patrologia graeca*
PL	J. Migne, *Patrologia latina*
PO	Patrologia orientalis
Qadmoniot	*Quarterly for the Antiquities of Eretz-Israel and Bible Lands* (Hebrew)
RAC	*Reallexikon für Antike und Christentum*
RAM	*Revue d'Ascétique et de Mystiquae*
RB	*Revue biblique*
RBén	*Revue bénédictine*
RE	Pauly-Wissowa, *Realencyklopädie fur Protestantische Theologie und Vorarbeiten* (1916)
RGG	Religion in Geschichte und Gegenwart
RHE	*Revue d'historie ecclésiastique*
ROC	*Revue de l'Orient Chrétien*
RSR	*Recherches de science religieuse*
RSV	Revised Standard Version
SBLASP	Society of Biblical Literature Abstracts and Seminar Papers
SBLDS	Society of Biblical Literature Dissertation Series
SBLSP	SBL Seminar Papers
SBLTT	SBL Texts and Translations

SC	Sources Chrétiennes
SP	Studia Patristica
SubsHag	Subsidia Hagiographica, Société des Bollandistes
TAPA	*Transactions of the American Philological Association*
TDNT	*Theological Dictionary of the New Testament*
TextsS	Texts and Studies
TRE	*Theologische Realencyklopädie*
TS	*Theological Studies*
TU	Texte und Untersuchungen
VC	*Vigiliae Christianae*
ZDPV	*Zeitschrift des Deutschen Palästina-Vereins*

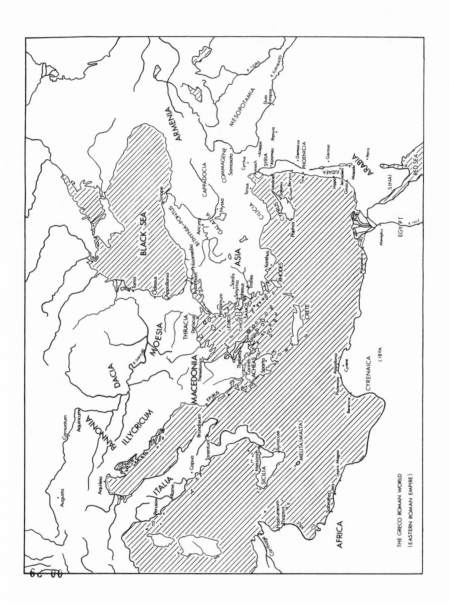

THE GRECO ROMAN WORLD
(EASTERN ROMAN EMPIRE)

Introduction

I

The size and scope of this volume require at the outset a clear statement of its intended purpose: to make accessible in English translation a number of interesting texts that will introduce the reader to a wide range of different types of ascetic piety as different understandings of, and responses to, the Greco-Roman world. As a collection of texts, the volume was not intended to be the definitive statement about or sourcebook for asceticism—not in Greco-Roman antiquity, much less in any other culture or period in history. The particular texts that follow should rather be considered representative of a number of *types* of ascetic piety in Greco-Roman antiquity. These types reflect more than anything else the expertise and range of interests of the group of twenty-six scholars who, along with others, constitute the Ascetic Behavior in Greco-Roman Antiquity Research Project, under the sponsorship of Claremont's Institute for Antiquity and Christianity and in connection with the Society of Biblical Literature (SBL) and the American Academy of Religion (AAR).

In the wide-ranging conversations that made up its several miniconferences, as well as its program units in connection with the national meetings of SBL and AAR, the Asceticism Group discovered that no one text, no one historical figure or group from antiquity, and no particular type of practice could adequately define or typify asceticism. The interplay of practice and motive and the seemingly infinite number of combinations and degrees of tension in the dynamic between practice and motive in different settings were found to be far too complex to allow any of us to be comfortable with generalizing the phenomenon from one focus or area of research.

The more we listened to each other, the clearer it became to all of us that an attempt to understand "asceticism" by beginning with the questions of origins or phenomenology was not productive. Our preliminary minimalist approach notwithstanding, we did, throughout our times together, caution ourselves against trying to evade altogether the "big questions" about asceticism. Over and over again, it became clear that in our translation and interpretation of texts we did indeed raise such questions: Why the odd, often antisocial practices? What statements were being made about the world and the self in engaging in such practices? Why were certain categories of persons attracted to certain kinds of practices? What were the consequences—personal, social, political—of such practices? Still, the collaborative effort that is the present volume was not to provide the final answers to these and other questions but first, through providing access to a diverse range of relevant texts, to enable ourselves and other researchers better to frame the questions and focus the issues and problems.

By providing a wide selection of texts with brief introductory essays, including information about the sociohistorical background, the volume represents a middle course between an attempt to be a comprehensive, definitive statement, on the one hand, and a minimalist, theory-free collection of texts, on the other. Each essay includes basic information about the text—authorship, approximate date of writing, literary genre, audience, and a summary description of the ascetic piety described, prescribed, and in one case (selection 10), proscribed in each text. This format for detailing basic information presumes the fundamental importance of knowledge of the sociopolitical background in order better to understand the important currents within the social world behind the text. Thus, we are able to argue that *ascetic behavior represents a range of responses to social, political, and physical worlds often perceived as oppressive or unfriendly, or as stumbling blocks to the pursuit of heroic personal or communal goals, life styles, and commitments.*[1] Moreover, the collection itself, in its diversity and organization, challenges the traditional but oft-denied assumption that asceticism is a single-issue, single-praxis phenomenon, corresponding to the traditional categories of scholarship ("Christian," "Jewish," "pagan," and the like). The members of the project, along with most other scholars, may not yet agree on what "asceti-

---

1. See W. O. Kaelber, "Asceticism," in Mircea Eliade, ed., *The Encyclopedia of Religion* (New York: Macmillan Co., 1987) 1.441–45, for comparativist discussion along similar lines.

cism" in Greco-Roman antiquity was or meant, but they are convinced that it cannot be understood without respect for differences in social setting, social status, geographical location, gender, literary expression, and motives. Thus, the translations and accompanying essays that follow evidence this respect.

II

Geographical location (e.g., Syria, Egypt), culture (e.g., Jewish, Greek, Roman), and religious cults and philosophical schools as somewhat translocal and transcultural phenomena have been chief among the traditional categories in the scholarly literature on ascetic piety in Greco-Roman antiquity. In the past decade or so, gender has also emerged as a major factor in research and generated its own set of methodological issues and questions. A very summary treatment of the emerging consensus in research in association with the most important of these categories is in order so that the usefulness of the present volume can be more clearly understood.

Philosophy

Greek philosophy supplied much of the language and conceptualization of the ascetic life style in Greek and Roman antiquity, especially for aristocratic males. The borrowing of the term *askesis* first among Greek philosophers and moralists from the athletic arena in order to convey the nature of the challenge of the philosophical or virtuous life was decisive for the history of asceticism in the West. "We become good by practice" (*ex askesios*), a fragment from Democritus (*Vorsokr.* 242), conveys well the application of the term in philosophical and moral discourse.[2]

The philosophical life style (*bios*), the virtuous life, was commonly understood to require forms of *askesis*—from physical withdrawal (*anachōrēsis*) from society and abstentions of various types among the Epicureans, Cynics, and radical Stoics to spiritual and psychological withdrawal into the self (*anachorein eis heauton*)[3] among the aristocratic Stoics, Peripatetics, and Neoplatonists. Focus was upon the cultivation of the ethical self, as the reemphasized ideals of *sophrosyne* and *enkrateia* demonstrated.

2. Cf. also Plutarch *Moral.* 76D; Lucian *Vit. Auct.* 7; *Tox.* 23.
3. Cf. Plato *Symp.* 174D as the *locus classicus* for the elucidation of the subject.

Apocalypticism and Gnosticism

The broadly defined movements of late antiquity referred to as "Apocalypticism" and "Gnosticism" often represented, in spite of their varied mythologies and social realities, a decidedly negative attitude toward "the world" and a corresponding response to "the world." Both movements attracted devotees who developed and held on to elaborate myths that sought to explain the origins and present nature of "this world" and its shortcomings and, most important, why so many were alienated from it or trapped in it. Such myths also legitimized the retreat from a world deemed evil and a prison. In varying degrees and in different times and contexts, vegetarianism, fasting, sexual continence, general dissipation of the body, political quietism, and even physical retreat from society and construction of an alternate social world characterized the ethic of these movements.

The loose grouping of different mythologies, theologies, and social realities that has continued to be known as apocalypticism and gnosticism seems to have represented an unstudied response on the part of some who defined themselves as outsiders, as enemies of the prevailing order. Ascetic behavior—at least that type that was rejection of the world—helped to articulate opposition to traditional political and cultural loyalties and ideologies in ways that were clear to insiders, but not immediately or easily understood by outsiders.[4]

Greek and Latin Christianity

In Greek and Latin Christianity, long before the beginnings of communal monasticism in the early fourth century, many held renunciation of sexual relations and abstemiousness in food, drink, and sleep as ideals. This was the case in spite of the efforts of some Greek and Latin Christians—especially those sensitive to the perceptions of respectable society—to restrain those who were perceived as radical in their renunciation of the world. Much care was taken by "establishment" Christians to distinguish their motives for renunciation from those of such radical groups as the "Gnostics" and Manichaeans.

One of the earliest and most important of such efforts in Christian

4. See Henry A. Green, *The Economic and Social Origins of Gnosticism* (SBLDS 77; Atlanta: Scholars Press, 1985); David Hellholm, ed., *Apocalypticism in the Mediterranean World and the Near East: Proceedings of the International Colloquium on Apocalypticism, Uppsala, August 12–17, 1979* (Tübingen: J. C. B. Mohr [Paul Siebeck], 1982); and Bentley Layton, *The Gnostic Scriptures* (Garden City, N.Y.: Doubleday & Co., 1987) for provocative discussion.

history is the apostle Paul's carefully stated response in 1 Corinthians 7 to the radical renouncers of the world in Corinth about whether celibacy should be a requirement for Christian existence. Paul clearly rejected the gnostic and apocalyptic contempt of the world. What he emphasized instead was uncompromised devotion to the Lord; he made no effort to sanction any particular life style as the only legitimate one for Christians. Among Greek and Latin "establishment" writers from the second century onward, 1 Corinthians 7 became a *locus classicus* for the articulation of the motive for Christian renunciation of the world.

Yet in Greek and Latin Christianity, even within "establishment" communities, more radical perspectives and rigorist life styles could be found. Among the Greeks (e.g., Gregory of Nyssa, John Chrysostom) was the tendency to stress the transience of life and the ever-present threat of death. Indifference to the world was deemed the appropriate response. In Latin Christianity, especially in North Africa, the rigorists (e.g., Tertullian, Cyprian of Carthage, Novatian of Rome) stressed the superiority of sexual renunciation. They sometimes took such radical interpretive and polemical positions that the charge of "Manichaeism" was leveled against them. Ambrose and Jerome were the most notable among rigorists who were so charged.[5]

Judaism

Ascetic behavior in ancient Judaism has until very recently generally been understood through Christian experiences and teachings. "Jewish asceticism" has sometimes been exaggerated and idealized; sometimes it has been thought to be an oxymoron, the result of foreign influence.

Recent scholarship has demonstrated the multiple motives among pious Jews for ascetic practices. Among the most important of motives was interest in meeting the demands of ritual and cultic purity. This was the case from the beginnings of the Temple piety through the Qumran experience, to the Mishnaic legal system, magic, and the mysticism of the talmudic period.

Ritual and cultic purity was understood to be necessary for rapprochement with God. Purity ensured protection of the Divine Presence from demonic contagion and rendered the individual worthy of being in

5. For general background discussion, see Peter Brown, *The Body and Society: Men, Women, and Sexual Renunciation in Early Christianity* (New York: Columbia University Press, 1988); and Robin Lane Fox, *Pagans and Christians* (New York: Alfred A. Knopf, 1987), esp. II.7. For discussion of 1 Corinthians 7, see Vincent L. Wimbush, *Paul the Worldly Ascetic: Response to the World and Self-Understanding According to 1 Corinthians 7* (Macon, Ga.: Mercer University Press, 1987).

God's presence. The Qumran community, as a "Temple community without a Temple," required a strict system of purity, not merely for "ethical" and "spiritual" benefits, but so that members of the community would be prepared, along with the angels, to take part in the eschatological war thought to be imminent, and to take their place in the restored Temple culture thought to be inevitable.

In Merkavah mysticism, self-denial was an important part of the preparatory rituals for the Angel of the Torah, with the result often that of induced mystical states. Midrashic legend often amplified biblical stories about the practices of the patriarchs, emphasizing their abstention from food and sex.[6]

Egypt and Syria

Egypt and Syria are distinguished as geographical and cultural areas that have long been the subject of much research on asceticism. In both areas asceticism was very much in evidence in very different social situations, religious and philosophical systems, and across the (Christian) spectrum from "heresy" to "orthodoxy."

Ascetic practice in Egypt exemplifies great diversity of expression and meaning. It was bound to no particular theological system, church, or social class. A range of practices, from the strict life of the desert hermit to communal asceticism (monasticism) to an urban philosophically influenced detachment from the world, existed concurrently in the third and fourth centuries.

The desert hermit (anchorite) is especially associated with Egypt. The hermit Anthony was made famous by the writings of Alexandrian archbishop Athanasius and Amoun of Nitria in lower Egypt. He and other hermits became the heroes and patrons of the lower classes. Complete detachment for the hermit was ever elusive; ironically, the more successful the hermit was in the effort to cultivate the self in isolation from the world, the more famous he became and the more crowds and disciples were attracted to him.

The other form of ascetic practice often associated with Egypt, cenobitic or communal monasticism, made its appearance in the fourth cen-

6. For full discussion of the issues, see Steven D. Fraade, "Ascetical Aspects of Ancient Judaism," in Arthur Green, ed., *Jewish Spirituality from the Bible to the Middle Ages*, vol. 13 of *World Spirituality* (New York: Crossroad, 1986) 253–88; Baruch Levine, *In the Presence of the Lord* (Leiden, Neth.: E. J. Brill, 1974); Jacob Neusner, *Idea of Purity in Ancient Judaism* (Leiden, Neth.: E. J. Brill, 1973); and Lawrence Schiffman, *Sectarian Law in the Dead Sea Scrolls* (Chico, Calif.: Scholars Press, 1983), esp. chap. 8.

tury in upper Egypt. Its origins are often attributed to Pachomius, but it is increasingly clear that this type of practice was already before the time of Pachomius in vogue among others within and beyond Egypt. The aim of such practice was to establish an alternative social world physically and psychically separate from the local dominant culture—both Christian and non-Christian. Within the alternative world, all persons shared in work, meals, and worship, reinforcing their difference from the outsiders. Such ascetic institutions flourished in Egypt and eventually became an integral part of the cultural, religious, and political landscape of the empire.

Ascetic practice in Syria has generally been associated with histrionics and idiosyncrasies and with the most extreme practices and motives. Certainly, ascetic behavior was in evidence in Syrian Christianity from its beginnings, again across the Christian spectrum from "heresy" to "orthodoxy," among the Gnostics, Marcionites, the Manichees, and "mainstream" Christians.

What characterized Syriac spirituality was the attraction to, and the attempt to imitate, heroic biblical models of piety, especially prophets and apostles (cf. Tatian; Odes of Solomon; *Acts of Thomas*). These heroic models in turn tended to produce certain images that provided Syrian Christians *justification* for embracing the rigorist life of renunciation, especially vegetarianism and celibacy. The image of Jesus as the Heavenly Bridegroom to whom every believer was wedded and the reimaging of the innocent Adam and Eve before the Fall, a state of existence every believer could realize through baptismal rites, were the two most important of such images.

The Syrians thought of the true believer as the "single one" or the "only begotten" (*ihidaya*), the celibate, single-minded in his or her devotion to God, namely, married only to the Heavenly Bridegroom. The ideal of the "single one" or "only begotten" notwithstanding, in earliest Syrian Christianity, unlike that of Egypt, ascetic piety was rarely practiced in isolation from a church or subchurch community. The fourth century shows much evidence for the existence of the Sons and Daughters of the Covenant (*Bnay/Bnat Qyama*), a group of elite laypersons living together in small, segregated households. These people were celibate and led lives of constant prayer and work in service of the church (Ephrem Syrus; Aphrahat the Persian).

Even when the institutional monasticism made its appearance in Syria in the late fourth and early fifth centuries, the monasteries were built within or very near cities. Yet, the tradition of the lay ascetic who lived a life of simplicity, celibacy, and prayer certainly continued even as institutional monasticism developed.[7]

Women

Scholars interested in antiquity in general and in the ascetic behavior of women in Greco-Roman antiquity in particular have noted that sources written by women are almost nonexistent. The need to rely upon the testimonies of (usually) aristocratic men places an enormous critical interpretive burden upon the contemporary scholar.

Recent studies have sought to establish the differences in meanings or social functions between male and female ascetic behavior in antiquity. The translation of more texts, inscriptions, and papyri and the employment of sociohistorical, sociological, and anthropological methods of inquiry have demonstrated the importance of the body as the locus of religious self-definition among men and women in antiquity.[8] Many scholars have argued that a woman's decision to remain a virgin or adopt a celibate life style was typically not merely a private religious choice but also a rejection of the traditional societal expectations of women.[9] For many women especially, the ascetic life seemed to offer the real possibility of new—and potentially liberating—social relationships, networks, and roles. This was, of course, in sharp contrast to the views of aristocratic male writers, many of whom regarded ascetic behavior on the part of women as a social aberration potentially disruptive of traditional mores and institutions.

7. See Brown, *Body and Society*; R. L. Fox, *Pagans and Christians* for general background discussion. For more detailed discussion, see A. Vööbus, *A History of Asceticism in the Syrian Orient* (vol. 1, CSCO 184/Sub. 14; vol. 2, 197/Sub. 17; vol. 3, CSCO 500/Sub. 81, Louvain: CSCO, 1958, 1988).

8. See Elizabeth A. Clark, ed., *The Life of Melania the Younger: Introduction, Translation, and Commentary* (Studies in Women and Religion 14; Lewiston, N.Y.: Edwin Mellen Press, 1984); Ross S. Kraemer, ed., *Maenads, Martyrs, Matrons, Monastics: A Sourcebook on Women's Religions in the Greco-Roman World* (Philadelphia: Fortress Press, 1988); and Sebastian P. Brock and Susan A. Harvey, eds., *Holy Women of the Syrian Orient* (Berkeley and Los Angeles: University of California Press, 1987).

9. See Ross S. Kraemer, "Ecstatics and Ascetics: Studies in the Functions of Religious Activities for Women in the Greco-Roman World" (Ph.D. diss., Princeton University, 1976); Elisabeth Schüssler-Fiorenza, "Response to 'The Social Functions of Women's Asceticism in the Roman East' by Antoinette Clark Wire" in Karen L. King, ed., *Images of the Feminine in Gnosticism* (Studies in Antiquity and Christianity; Philadelphia: Fortress Press, 1988) 324–28; and Antoinette Clark Wire, "The Social Functions of Women's Asceticism in the Roman East," in King, *Images of the Feminine*, 308–23.

III

This collection of texts does not necessarily contradict the consensus scholarship on ascetic behavior in any of the areas above. In its organization by *literary genre*, however, the collection cuts across these areas insofar as they are based on historical period, location, culture, and language. By dividing the texts into literary types, we hope to avoid the generalizations and artificialities of juxtaposition that are often a part of treatments that are strictly culture-, language-, or location-specific or limited to one period in history or to one author (e.g., "Christian," "Jewish," "Philosophical," "Syrian," "Classical Period"). Too often such treatments—in spite of the scholar's best efforts—claim too much about asceticism from one focus of research. Beginning with literary genre is wise because it begins with what is most basic to all the texts included— their resemblance to a recognizable type of literary expression. With literary genre as the order of categorization of the texts below, the reader will be challenged to suspend, even if briefly, the traditional categories of inquiry. This suspension, because it will represent recognition of an "odd" mix of texts—different languages, different authors, different cultures, different religious traditions, different social settings, different periods in history—will in turn allow the widest diversity of expressions of ascetic behavior to get a reading. Thus, the reader may be able to suspend thinking of "Christian" asceticism as a single phenomenon! To be sure, some literary expressions are wholly represented by Christian authors (cf. Part 1). With others, the reader may even be able to begin thinking of some "Christian" understandings and expressions of ascetic behavior as more similar to some non-Christian understandings and expressions than to other Christian expressions (cf. Parts 2 and 3). Beginning with a literary genre division helps make the discovery of diversity much less difficult. For the reader interested in exploring a particular type of expression in more depth, this volume will have provided a general introduction.

The twenty-eight texts in this volume are divided into five major parts corresponding to five literary types: (1) "Homily," (2) "Philosophical/ Theological Exhortation," (3) "Ritual/Revelation," (4) "Life and Teachings," and (5) "Documentary Evidence." Because introductory essays precede each text, no clarifying, introductory words about the substance of the texts are required here. It is important to make clear, however, that no criteria beyond *expression* (description, prescription—positive or negative) of some type of ascetic behavior and *origins* (even if from some remote geographical corner or chronological end) in the Greek and Roman worlds of antiquity were established for inclusion of a text.

Some clarifying words may be in order, however, regarding the literary categories used: Under "Homily" are included texts of exhortation toward different types of ascetic responses to the world with specifically Christian justification. Under "Philosophical/Theological Exhortation" are included texts that convey the rhetorical and moralistic challenges and visions of philosophers, moralists, and theologians. Under "Ritual/Revelation" are included texts that through the esoteric language of ritual, magical rites, or mysticism reflect the very *structure* of particular types of ascetic piety. Under "Life and Teachings" are included texts that tell the inspirational stories of the heroic and disciplined exploits and teachings of women and men of unusual imagination, strength of character, and resolve. Finally, under "Documentary Evidence" is included a diverse group of texts that purport to describe types of heroic behavior in communal settings and among individuals. A special contribution (selection 26) draws upon archaeological research as a way of documenting the institutional life and piety of the community referenced in the immediately preceding text (cf. selection 25).

In order to facilitate the fullest understanding of the texts that follow, as well as further research, a map of the Greco-Roman world (specifically, the regions of the ancient eastern Mediterranean basin during the time of the empire) has been provided (p. xxiii) on which some of the general settings in which texts were written have been pointed out. Also provided are regional chronological timetables (p. 465) that give dates for important events in the history of asceticism. They indicate where possible the approximate dates for the writing of the texts and/or the events described in the texts included in the volume. These will further help the reader to contextualize the ascetic piety being described or prescribed in any particular text. At the end of each text, a short list of suggested readings for further reading and research is included. The volume concludes with a list of suggested readings for general or survey works on asceticism.

IV

No grand common themes or theses were sought from the beginning of this project, nor are any to be proferred at this point. Even if it can safely be generally said about ascetic behavior that it represents abstention or avoidance and that "what one avoids, one condemns,"[10] one must nevertheless contend with the fact that in different settings and times ascetic behavior represented different expressions of and reasons for avoidance and condemnation. Such is the lesson that this collection of texts teaches.

This volume, then, should help to change the thinking of those who were convinced that asceticism can or must mean one thing. It should further be a valuable resource for students and scholars of Greco-Roman antiquity who are not yet convinced that the complex religious self-understandings and orientations of the period have been adequately accounted for, much less critiqued, in terms of their decisive influence in the social, political, and religious history of the West. In a comprehensive historical reconstructive effort (which this volume does not claim to be), different groups in different generations will have different emphases and perspectives. All should agree, however, as have the contributors to this volume, that it is imperative that we begin with the *sources*.

10. See Ramsay MacMullen, *Enemies of the Roman Order: Treason, Unrest, and Alienation in the Empire* (Cambridge: Harvard University Press, 1966) 50.

HOMILY

JACOB OF SERUG
Homily on
Simeon the Stylite

INTRODUCTION

Simeon the Stylite was one of the most notable ascetic figures in late antiquity. Born ca. 386 C.E. in northern Syria, Simeon became a monk in Telʿada in 403. There, and later again in Telneshe, he gained renown for his lengthy fasts and acts of self-mortification. Around 423 about forty miles east of Antioch, he mounted the first of three successively higher pillars and carved out his unique vocation as a stylite (from the Greek *stylos*, "pillar"). The final pillar, on which he spent roughly the last forty years of his life, was about forty cubits high (as much as sixty feet), topped by a small platform and railing to keep him from falling off. There Simeon pursued a life of continual prayer, exposed to the elements and tended by disciples. His daily schedule consisted of stationary prayer, genuflection, and attention to the crowds of pilgrims who flocked to see him. In 459, at the age of more than seventy years Simeon died. He was the first of what would become a long tradition of pillar saints: his imitators were still to be found in the mid-nineteenth century.

In the years following Simeon's death, the great Syrian homilist Jacob of Serug (ca. 449–521) came into prominence as a monk, *periodeutes* (traveling cleric), and finally Bishop of Batna (519–521), serving in the rural district of Serug that bordered on the Euphrates. Jacob was extraordinarily prolific: he is said to have composed 763 verse homilies, called *mīmrē*, of which over 300 survive. Jacob, standing in the tradition of Ephrem Syrus, was a powerful poet-preacher. He is known in Syriac tradition as the "Flute of the Holy Spirit." Among his surviving homilies is one devoted to Simeon the Stylite.[1]

---

1. *BHO* 1126.

Jacob's homily on Simeon assumes his audience already knows the saint's story and seems to depend upon the particular version of it told in the Syriac vita written by Simeon's disciples.[2] It focuses upon three specific aspects of the story.

After an extended opening prayer, Jacob turns to what is for him the central issue of Simeon's vocation: the pillar as the battleground on which the saint wages endless war against Satan and his forces. Jacob details the forms of Satan's assaults: terrifying apparitions of beasts, bugs, and snakes, whirlwinds, fog, and storms repeatedly assail the saint. Simeon is "an innocent dove," a "sweet-singing partridge" who yet prevails; he is David in the face of Goliath. Hence the very real physical trials of stylitism are treated as so many wiles of Satan to bring the downfall of God's chosen one. Simeon's "weapon" in response is simply the purity of his prayer—the continual chanting of the psalms.

Jacob turns next to the famous incident of Simeon's near death from a gangrenous ulcer on his foot. Once again, this is Satan's work. Simeon is tested, as Job had been on his dungheap, by the agony of physical illness. Alone among our sources, Jacob claims that Simeon survived by amputating his foot. The various hagiographies present Simeon's cure as miraculous. Perhaps Jacob's account is intended metaphorically, but the sense is the same—Simeon triumphs over the dreadful infection by the sheer willpower of his faith. In Jacob's homily, the incident becomes the occasion for a moving address by Simeon to his severed foot, praising its valiant work on God's behalf and comforting it with the assurance that in the resurrection they will again be reunited: a body and soul, healthy and inseparable, as he was created.

The last portion of the homily deals with Simeon's death. He preaches a final testament to his disciples, the heavenly hosts receive his soul as the Bride of Christ and escort her into heaven, and all creation joins the disciples in mourning the loss of this holy one.

Delivered some decades after Simeon's death, Jacob's homily was preached at the time when stylitism was emerging as a significant and widespread vocation in the monastic communities of the east. His images are striking not least because certain motifs familiar to the interpretation of this ascetic practice are noticeably absent. Jacob does not present it as an activity of penance or as punishment for sin. Again, he presents no conflict between body and soul, which are rather shown to

2. *BHO* 1121, 1124.

work in perfect harmony in the task of serving God. Further, Simeon is likened to Christ on the cross only at the moment of his death; the vocation is not presented as an imitation of the crucifixion (which is mentioned only at this one point). Instead, we are shown Simeon engaged in the battle against the Adversary. Here is the purpose of asceticism—the cosmic battle between good and evil. Despite Jacob's admiration for Simeon's endurance on the pillar, he makes it clear that Simeon's practice in fact consists of a single activity: the practice of prayer.

The present translation is based on the edition by P. Bedjan, *Acta Martyrum et Sanctorum* IV (Paris and Leipzig: O. Harrassowitz, 1894; repr. Hildesheim: G. Olms, 1968) 650–65; I have indicated the page numbers of this edition in the text.[3] [Ed.: Syriac transliterations in this volume follow a simplified system, for the sake of uniformity and readability.]

TRANSLATION

(650) A *mimrā*[4] of Mār[5] Jacob the Teacher,
on the holy Mār Simeon the Stylite

O Lord, grant that I may paint a picture filled with beauties about Simeon the chosen one, whose beauties are too high for the tongue. Through You I would speak of his victories, marveling, since but for You, the beauty of Your servant would be unspoken. For his sake, O Lord, speak abundantly in me, that I may speak of this athlete full of victories. I am Your flute: breathe into me Your Spirit, O Son of God. Let me give forth melodies filled with wonder about this beautiful one. May Your power move me, as wind moves a reed and sings thereby a sweet song in a loud sound. A reed does not have a sound filled with songs. It is shaken by the wind and sounds forth its melodies for its hearers. No

---

3. An Italian translation was published by I. Pizzi, "Omelia di San Giacomo di Sarugh in lode di San Simone Stilita Tradotta dal Siriaco," *Bessarione* ser. 3, vol. 4 (Rome, 1908) 18–29; and a German one by S. Landersdorfer, *Ausgewählte Schriften der syrischen Dichter, Cyrillonas, Baläus, Isaak von Antiochien und Jakob von Sarug* (Bibliothek der Kirchenväter 6; Munich: Kösel-Verlag, 1913) 387–405. I have consulted both in the course of the present translation. I am indebted to Professor Sidney H. Griffith and to Dr. Sebastian P. Brock for their help with the text; remaining problems are my own.

4. This *mīmrā* was composed in lines of Jacob's habitual twelve-syllable meter, with caesurae after the fourth and eighth syllables. See chap. 4 below.

5. *Mār* is the title formed from Syriac *māryā*, "lord" or "sir," used to address superiors and especially saints.

speaker has a word to say; if Your word does not move him, he does not speak. Through you, O Lord, may the mouth be moved to bring forth new melodies, full of wonder, and singing praises without disharmony.

Come, you who hear, suck the sweetness from this teaching, a kind sweetened to enlighten the soul by its taste. Come, take pleasure in the story of one beautiful man, whose history is mightier than the waves of the great sea. Come, take heed (651) and listen to his divine victories, more exalted than the tongue may speak. Come, enter, and sit down at this table full of good things, of a homily set like a feast to delight you. Come to the banquet whose supper leaves no waste; nor is the person heavy who enjoyed its provisions. Come, take freely the great immeasurable wealth, from the treasury not impoverished by those who partake of it. Come, discerning ones, pay attention in great silence, and I will give you a living word in a loud voice. The story of Simeon will become the occasion of all riches. But also for me and for you, the gain is for anyone who hears it. A good laborer is one who begins and ends successfully, and is not wearied by divine labor.

Satan called out to summon his troops, and he opened his mouth like the captain of hosts and commanded them. The Evil One said to his troops, "Behold, this is the time. Let us rise up for battle and not be weak, lest we fail. Put on a frightful appearance, and show a disguise, and with false visions go against him. Lift up heavy whirlwinds in the likeness of mountains. Let dust rise up, and let the color of the air be obscured. Let violent winds blow, and let the earth be moved; and like the voice of the sea let us make a great racket. Appear in the guise of horrible vermin and noxious snakes. Become birds and creeping things and crawl on the walls. The time is at hand: let us rouse (652) ourselves for battle. Let us rouse up combat and not be weak, lest we fail. It is easy for us now to attack him on his pillar, and let us shake him with fearful visions so that through them he will go astray."

Then a company of demons gathered, sons of the left hand, and they made a pact and gave hands and rose up for battle. The devils were divided one swarm after another, so that they might capture the fledgling eagle by their evil wiles. The snakes crept out from their holes to hiss at him, innocent dove who wove his nest on the rock. The basilisks vomited hateful venom that they might kill him, the partridge singing a sweet song from the mountaintop. Flocks of falcons gathered above the sparrow that they might catch him, but he flew up into the air and left them raging.

Troops of devils and demons assembled at the mountain, and like smoke they rose up beside him and darkened the air. The light of the sun was obscured by the mists, and the night was black and the darkness hateful and thick. Gusts of wind rose up, and dust ascended and veiled the mountains. The winds blew and uprooted rocks, and clouds piled up. Fire smoldered and as in a furnace the blaze went up, and it seemed even to have caught hold in the crags. Whirlwinds came and knocked the pillar, and its foundations shook. But the just man stood there as upon a rock unshaken. Violent winds assailed its joints and it quaked. And the pillar swayed, and lo! it would have fallen, but there was the just man singing. The mountains split asunder with the sound of it, but not in fact. And that steadfast man (653) did not abandon what was his or even look around at them.

The hateful ones appeared as snakes and creatures, but he did not lower his hands, which were stretched out to heaven. He sang against them what he had learned from the son of Jesse, and with the harp of David he made a joyful noise and said, "Like bees lo! these awful powers surrounded me, and suddenly they subsided in the likeness of a fire of thorns;[6] and they surrounded me on all sides like smoke. And in the name of the Lord I caused them to disappear, and they disappeared and vanished. I am about to be overthrown and to fall and perish, but the Lord helps me. And I have put them to shame and conquered them with the power of God."

And Satan saw that the truth won, and his tricks failed. And again he schemed that he would attack him with blows. And the crafty one went up and stood beside him on the pillar, keen to do harm. But the just man saw him and he knew at once that he was the Adversary, and he saw that he was excited and his countenance was fuming, and he understood that the master of Judas had come to lay hold of the servant of Jesus. And he said to him as also our Lord did to Iscariot, "Why have you come to stand here at this time?[7] I will not flee from the contest for which I am prepared. Why are you standing? Approach like Judas and do what is in your heart." And he was standing beside him like Judas beside our Savior. And the devils were standing like crucifiers and waiting for him.

And again, the Evil One was like Goliath as a type. And the demons who were with him were like Philistines, and the just man was like David.[8] And the crowd of the followers of Caiaphas arose and looked to see whether (654) his servant would betray Jesus as Judas had done.

6. Ps 118:12.
7. Matt 26:50.
8. 1 Sam 17:32ff.

There stood Goliath and unsheathed his sword, and David his sling. And the ranks were standing and looking at the contest to see who would win. And the corrupter approached and grabbed the true one. And like an athlete in a match he grabbed him and held on to throw him down. The blessed man slipped out of his grasp and turned and laid hold of him, and seized him with his hand and hurled him on the platform, and trampled on his neck. And while [Satan] was caught, he bit him in the foot and sank his teeth in. And as though he were a dog, [Simeon] kicked him and threw him from the pillar.

He fell like lightning and howled greatly and the just man heard the sound of the fall of that Satan, and he blew away like chaff. Goliath's master fell just like Goliath, and he became a laughingstock. And the one like David was standing like David and sang, "Blessed is the Lord who girt me with strength against the evil one. And he set my foot as though upon a rock and made firm my steps. He set my feet on high, upon a pillar, and trained my hands for war against the enemy.[9] He gave my lips new praise to speak, like the son of Jesse who conquered Goliath by the power of God. If you loose upon me a host of demons, I will not fear. For the company of the angels stands beside me and comforts me."

And when the Evil One was put to shame, and he stood embarrassed in the presence of truth, he did not stop continually contending with him. And he saw that [Simeon] was not stopping the glory of the gospel that he preached, "Turn from error toward God." He saw that the weary ox was not resting from his labor. (655) And he crippled him, so that he would leave off his field of labor without bringing it to completion. His foot developed a gangrenous putrescent ulcer, and harsh pain came and went through all his body. And fearful pains of death seized him, but he endured them. For he did not murmur, nor was he hindered from his labor.

He was struck like Job by Satan who struck Job,[10] and he was companion to Job who conquered the enemy: two athletes in two ages and two contests. They conquered the Evil One in the contest, he who had conquered in each of their own eras. One upon ashes and one upon a rock fought with him. And they prevailed over him, and by mortals he was shamed. The pillar was like the dungheap for the second Job. And instead of dirt, a soft element, there was hard rock. And the blessed man was struck by the hateful pain of a cruel arrow. But however much the

9. Ps 18:32–34.
10. Job 2:7.

Evil One afflicted him, that much his beauty increased. For good gold entered the crucible and manifested its beauty. And he gladdened his Lord, who had removed from him the hateful dross.

But when the affliction grew strong and acted mightily on the holy one, his flesh decayed and his foot stood exposed. He lifted his voice and the angels marveled at his fortitude, while he sang with the harp of David on his pillar, "My foot stands straight and does not bend.[11] For its Lord will sustain it that it may stand and support the burden of two. For lo, it bears the palace of the body like a pillar of that master-builder who fastens and supports it so that it will not be shaken. O Evil One, the hurt you are causing does not hurt me since it is sweet for me; you will tire yourself out as I am not going to leave my labor. (656) Increase the torment like a craftsman for good gold, so that I will grow bright, and as for you, your craftsmanship will have been exhausted. Strike me not only on the feet if you can: strike all my body and continue without boasting. A horse is not tamed without a bridle, so undertake to chastise the insolent one like savage youths would. Do not think that I am hindered by your blows, for I will not cease from the labor to which I have applied myself. The walls of a house are not shaken if it is set upon a rock, and waves and winds do not shake that which stands firm. For while you think you shake me, you will weary instead of me. You are weaving my crown, O shameful one, and you do not know it. This matter of the foot is nothing among your threats. Strike hard, as you did Job, whose companion I am. Your scourging is feeble and your struggle is weak and your battle is slack. And your contest is not, as they claim, vigorous, but is feeble and slack. He is cowardly who shrinks away from your contest. For you cannot even conquer one who is weak unless he is willing. For your blow is nothing for the one who knows about it. And he who does not give you his armor is not beaten. You conquer the weak, but you cannot boast about the strong. You test your strength on the one who is sick, not the healthy. Strike if you can, and rip up the flesh and tear apart the muscles. And if I say, 'Oh! Oh! It's enough!' then I am the loser. Every weak and flabby athlete grabs the feet. For what you have done is not of the strong (657) but of the feeble. Look, you are contending with a man with one foot. And if a lame man conquers you, you are worthy of ridicule."

But while the just man was smitten with pain and disease, his mouth never ceased giving praise. Satan wearied, but the just man did not

11. Ps 26:2.

weary nor rest nor fail, for as long as his strength came he prevailed, and his wages increased. And he watched his foot as it rotted and its flesh decayed. And the foot stood bare like a tree beautiful with branches. He saw that there was nothing on it but tendons and bones. And he took its weight and raised it and set it upon its companion. He saw that the wearied heifer could not bear the yoke, and he sought to unhitch her from her work, and he would labor with the one. The blessed man did a marvelous deed that has never been done before: he cut off his foot that he would not be hindered from his work. Who would not weep at having his foot cut off at its joint? But he looked on it as something foreign, and he was not even sad.

And as Satan was wallowing in blood and sprinkled with pus and covered in mucus, and the rocks were spattered, the just man nevertheless sang. While a branch of his body was cut off from its tree, his face was exuding delightful dew and comely glory. Then he said to it, "Go in peace until the resurrection. And do not grieve, for your hope will be kept in the kingdom." And even though all of him lived, his limb died and was cast before him. And the one foot bore the burden of the whole body. And while his limbs dripped with sweat and were spattered with blood, his sword was unsheathed and his bow drawn against (658) Satan.

But now the corpse of his foot was set before him and he was singing to it, and with the harp of David he was chanting comfort to it: "Why are you shaken and grieved since your hope is kept?[12] For again onto that tree from which you have been cut off you will be grafted. Go, wait for me until I come and do not grieve. For without you I will not rise up on the last day. Whether to the bridal chamber or to Gehenna I will walk on you. And whether to heaven or to the abyss, our way is one. We will be one when we are resurrected just as we have been, for death or life, for judgment or fire, or for the kingdom. I will not rise up from the grave and leave you. For with me you will be raised and I with you at the same moment. He for whom you have worked from your youth will not cheat you, but in return for your labor He will give you your wages and make you glad. Pray that I may see you and rejoice with you when we are raised. But together let us give thanks that He will give us strength to stand before Him."

Again he turned and prayed, and with groans he was weeping and imploring, "O Lord, grant strength to the foot that remains without its companion. Keep the one alive and strengthen the one until it comes to

12. Ps 42:5.

rest. It is bearing the weight of two, and it wants strength. See how the burden of the whole body is borne by the one alone. And if Your command does not come to it, it will be weakened. Its strength is diminishing, its labor is harsh, and its opponent is evil. And if Your grace does not help it, it will be defeated. It is alone and the weight of the body is too heavy for it. Support the weary one, for the burden of the two is placed on (659) its neck. Let not the temple of the body in which You dwell be shaken. For only one pillar is bearing it: make its base firm. Behold I work with one cow instead of a yoked team. Bestow strength that it may labor successfully with You. O Lord, may I not be shamed by the Evil One who thirsts for my ruin, he who would rejoice to see my feet failing at Your work. May he not boast that he has conquered Your servant and taken his armor. Give me a shield that I may go to meet his arrows and conquer his strength. Lord, judge my case with Satan who contends with me. Seize armor and stand up to fight against the Evil One. May his path, full of darkness and slippery spots, become dark, and where he has lain nets and snares upon the way to ensnare me. And may my soul rejoice like a tree with beautiful branches, for I have plucked and sent forth sweet fruits to the plowman of the field. With the strength from You I will conquer the strength of the enemy. For there is no [other] strength by which it is possible for me to prevail."

The blessed one was occupied with this labor for a very long time, while he was standing on one foot, and he did not weaken. It is marvelous to speak, that there should even be a way of life like this pillar! For his foot stood firm, that foot of the blessed man, and it was not shaken. Who would withhold this work from the discerning, but one whose heart is blind of understanding? One moment a man might stand still, but hours he could not. But that chosen one was standing up day and night on his one foot. Thirty and ten years he endured as one day, heat and cold and vigils and fasts, and the contest with the Evil One. Never have I seen (660) one who stood like this just man, nor in books have I seen a story like his. Righteous men fasted for generations for a known period of days, from thirty weeks and sixty, each according to his strength. But who would count the fasting of this angel in the body? For he is not comparable with men but with angels. Forty days the divine Moses fasted.[13] And also Elijah in his number of days fasted like Moses.[14] Of these two men, one shone and one was taken up. Who would say that this man was not equal to these just men?

13. Exod 24:18.
14. 1 Kgs 19:8.

But what shall I say about this fasting, this man who was a faster? I cannot paint the image of one whose beauty has overwhelmed me. Which one of his feats shall I tell, and which shall I leave out, because each one of them is higher and more exalted than its mate? If I tell of his fasting, lo! another beauty overtakes me. If I preach his vigil, I would be much too meager for his service. If I tell of his standing, lo! his other ascetic habits would go uncomprehended, if I marvel at his sufferings or his afflictions, at how amazing they are. If I reckon up his pains, the battles he fought are more valiant, since lo! he was contending with the Evil One for his soul every day. I would say how much his foot stood and he was not weakened, or about his mouth, how very long it was wearied with the gospel. I would say how long his pupils ran with continual tears of mourning, or how long he was patient with his hands stretched out. I would tell his battle with Satan, but I am not sufficient for it, since the time is short, the battle wondrous, and the contest great. The victorious one has conquered me; I shrink from in front of him, how beautiful he is, and I am not able to speak his beauties as they are. Like a painter I wished to paint him, but his beauty has conquered me. Like a hunter (661) I wished to capture him but he has flown away from me. While I am wanting to stretch out toward him, he has attained heaven. I am tarrying below, and he has been raised up.

Let us return then to the pillar, which is right here. For he did not leave it, all the while his own dwelling place was in heaven. I would speak now about his departure if I am able, and about the ending his Lord gave him if I can. I will reveal to his followers how he completed his course and fell asleep, and also how the weary heifer rested from its labor. At that moment when his end approached and his blessing arrived, his Lord revealed to him the day of his death just as to Moses.[15] It was made known to him as to the son of Amram concerning his separation, so that like Hezekiah he could command his sons concerning his inheritance.[16] The angels came down and spoke with him like Daniel.[17] And they showed him that he had come and arrived at the point where he could rest from his labor.

"Behold, evening has arrived and drawn near to relieve your toil, and also the steward carrying the denarius and waiting for you. Lo! the time has come for your labor to be relieved from exhaustion, and your soul will dwell in the treasury of life until the resurrection. Lo! the day has

---

15. Deut 32:49–50.
16. 2 Chr 30—32?
17. Dan 9:21ff; 10:5ff.

come for you to enter in order to rest from your work. And you will go to your reward, and take your stand as a successful man. It is time for you to go forth and come away from the world, to a place of light that has been prepared for you lo! from of old. Stand up, plowman, loose your yoke and take rest, for you are weary; for you have diligently labored your yoke of land with one ox. Stand up, sailor, go out from the sea and from its billows. Hold fast to your purse with (662) your yield and dwell in peace. Do not grieve that your body is a nest for pains, for with Lazarus you will dwell there with Abraham.[18] Do not grieve that your body is foul from afflictions, since its fragrance is sweet like spice and you will rest in it. Summon your disciples, and by your commandments make them firm, that they may be vigilant after your death as they were during your life. Say to creation, 'I have stood pledge for you before God. Do not again turn to Satan and my boast will not be ashamed.'" And how many things like these were told to the blessed man! An encampment of angels surrounded the mountain from all sides. The angels came down to praise the mortal and to receive him on their wings when he was to be taken up. The choirs from the house of Gabriel came down to bear in procession the chaste body that was the dwelling place of the Son of God.

He summoned his disciples as he was passing away and admonished them, just as our Savior when he has been raised to his twelve apostles. "The peace of Jesus I leave you,[19] O my disciples, that which he left us when he was taken up to the one who sent him. Farewell, and keep the commandments that you have learned from me. Do not be unmindful of me after my death, or of my admonitions. Farewell, church and priests in every place. May the cross of the Lord be the wall in your dwellings. Farewell, sick people who come to the name of Jesus, and just as the sick woman,[20] may there be respite from your afflictions. Farewell, vessel who has borne me a very long time. From now and henceforth, the standard of Jesus will be carried by you. Farewell, earth full of (663) every grief. Blessed is he who departs from you undefiled. How much I have been wearied on your behalf and I have endured sufferings! May the Evil One not lead you astray after me like the Daughter of Jacob. Or, as she did when Moses went away and she forged the golden calf,[21] will you, too, say, 'Because Simeon has gone, I will return to abominable

---

18. Luke 16:20ff.
19. John 14:27.
20. Luke 8:43–44?
21. Exod 32:4.

things'? If I depart, the Messiah lives, he whom you have loved. For just as to a man you betrothed yourself, cling to your betrothed. I would not be ashamed of you when the bridegroom your spouse calls you. For your sake, I would enter and see the bridal chamber and take pleasure in it. Remember me before him at every hour at his table, and when he calls you to enter in with him, remember me. See that you do not be unmindful of the sufferings he bore for your sake, of the gall and vinegar, the cross and nails and the sharpened sword. For your sake God died, while not dying. Do not again turn to the error of dead idols."

And for as long as these words were being spoken by the blessed man, the angels stood and waited for him to pass away. And he lifted up his eyes on high and let his tears fall, and stretched out his hands in the likeness of his Lord on Golgotha. He stretched out his right hand and blessed the earth and her inhabitants. And he made the sign of the cross and bowed his head and gave up his spirit. The angels hastened to receive at once the bride of light. And they raised up their voices to sing, and Satan trembled. There the heavenly watchers raised their voices in songs of new praise to Him who had chosen people more exalted than the angels. They prolonged (664) the anthem, and the mountains sang and the earth shook, while they were saying, "This is the one who called on the Lord and He heard him."[22] And they spread their wings and received his soul into their bosoms, for they saw the labor of this just man and his deeds. Their faces were gladdened for him at the moment of his death, as the watchers on high were gladdened in the presence of Daniel. They arrived at heaven and sang there, "This is the gate, by which the righteous enter as heirs of the new life." His spirit entered among the heavenly congregations. And the congregations shouted, "Come in peace, bride of light." She entered and bowed down before the dread judgment seat of the Son. And all of them shouted, "My Lord, receive the one who labored with you. Command her to enter the storehouse of life until the resurrection, when her beloved body is raised from dust."

The disciples saw that their master had fallen asleep, and gave voice; and the rocks in the walls wept with them and the mountains quaked. They embraced the pillar and gave voice like jackals. They wet the ground with their tears bitterly. The corpse was standing on the pillar and everyone was looking. And the congregation were thinking that he had in fact fallen asleep. Creation stood still and groaned in pain in

---

22. Ps 3:4; Jer 29:12.

response to his disciples, while they were saying to him, "Our father, you have left us like orphans. Where shall we go and with whom shall we seek refuge instead of you? Who like you will comfort us in our miseries? We left family and took refuge with you, O beautiful one. And you filled for us the place of family and siblings and father. Report of you went out in all places and we had heard about you, and when we came to (665) your fountain death stopped it up. We saw your light like a torch and came to visit it. And suddenly the breath of death breathed out and quenched its flame. Like a tree, beneath your shadow we took refuge, and death coming cuts you off suddenly and we have been scattered. In your great fortress we had been taking refuge from robbers, and death came and threw it down and it fell, and captivity came. Our sun set, and the light became darkened by which we were traveling, and lo! we have been led astray by stumbling blocks into a hateful place. Your sheepfold is weeping because the sound of your voice departs from it; the desert surrounds it and it resembles a house whose master has died. The rocks will grieve with us and also the high mountains, because of your departure, blessed father full of grace. The pillar upon which you stood day and night cries out in grief and sorrow because of your departure; let all the earth feel suffering with us at your departure, our chosen father, O lord Simeon, servant of Jesus. We are bereft of your converse, full of life; pray, our father, that you will be spiritually with us. Blessed be your spirit which has traveled this day to the house of life. And your body has rested from anxieties and harsh labors. Blessed be your spirit, our chosen father, full of victories, which has reached and arrived at that divine kingdom. The Son of God is He whom you have loved from your youth. May He in His mercy make us worthy, so that by your prayers we may find mercy."

SUGGESTED READINGS

Alwan, K. "L'homme, le ⟨⟨microcosme⟩⟩ chez Jacques de Saroug." *Parole de l'Orient* 13 (1986) 51–76.

Brock, S. P. *The Syriac Fathers on Prayer and the Contemplative Life.* Cistercian Studies 101. Kalamazoo, Mich.: Cistercian, 1987.

Delehaye, H. *Les Saints Stylites.* Sub. Hag. 14. Bruxelles, Belg.: Société des Bollandistes, 1923; reprint 1962.

Doran, R. *The Lives of Simeon Stylites.* Cistercian Studies 112. Kalamazoo, Mich.: Cistercian, 1990.

Drijvers, H. J. W. "Spätantike Parallelen zur altchristlichen Heiligenverehrung unter besonderer Berücksichtigung des Syrischen Stylitenkultus." *Göttingen Orientforschungen* 1, Reihe: Syriaca 17 (1978) 77–113.

Guinan, M. D. "Where Are the Dead? Purgatory and Immediate Retribution in James of Sarug." Symposium Syriacum 1972. *OCA* 197 (1974) 541–50.

Harvey, S. A. "The Sense of a Stylite: Perspectives on Simeon the Elder." *VC* 42 (1988) 376–94.

Lietzmann, H. *Das Leben des Heiligen Symeon Stylites.* TU 32.4. Leipzig: Hinrichs, 1908.

Peña, I., P. Castellana, and R. Fernandez. *Les Stylites Syriens.* Studium Biblicum Franciscorum Collection Minor 16. Milano: Franciscan Printing Press, 1975.

Sony, B. "L'anthropologie de Jacques de Saroug." *Parole de l'Orient* 12 (1984–5) 153–85.

Vööbus, A. *Handschriftliche Überlieferung der Memre-Dichtung des Ja'qob von Serug.* CSCO 334/Sub. 39; 335/Sub. 40. Louvain: CSCO, 1973.

Homily: On Virginity

INTRODUCTION

This anonymous homily on virginity was written in Greek, probably in Syria, in the early fourth century C.E.[1] The preacher addresses both parents and their children. His purpose is to persuade fathers and mothers to support and encourage their daughters and sons who desire to live at home in perpetual virginity and to convince young women and men that virginity is better than earthly marriage. The text is a valuable source for the history of early Christian asceticism, especially the practice of "familial asceticism" or "home monasticism" in the east.[2] These young virgins and continents have not entirely left "the world" but live at home under the supervision and discipline of their fathers. There is no mention of organized monastic institutions or solitary ascetic retreat to

1. David Amand de Mendieta and Matthieu-Charles Moons, "Une curieuse homélie grecque inédite sur la virginité adressée aux pères de famille." *RBén* 63 (1953) 18–69, 211–38. The text was established from four manuscripts of the ninth and tenth centuries, all of which attribute the homily to Basil of Caesarea. Amand and Moons have rejected the notion of Basil's authorship, basing their argument on the homilist's style and apparent lack of knowledge of eremitic or cenobitic monasticism (pp. 19, 234–35). They date the homily to the first half of the fourth century (p. 238). See also Concetta Aloe Spada, "Un'omelia greca anonima 'sulla verginità' (Rev. Ben. 63 [1953])," in Ugo Bianchi, ed., *La Tradizione dell'Enkrateia* (Rome: Ateneo, 1985) 622–23 for a discussion of the date. David Amand de Mendieta suggests that the homily probably comes from Syria ("La virginité chez Eusèbe d'Emèse et l'ascétisme familial dans la première moitié de IVe siècle." *RHE* 50 [1955] 818), and Arthur Vööbus argues likewise ("Syrische Herkunft der Pseudo-Basilianischen Homilie über die Jungfräulichkeit." *OrChr* 40 [1956] 69–77).

2. Before the rise and widespread availability of male and female monasteries, home monasticism would have been one very practical option for a woman who wanted to remain unmarried—provided that her parents were sympathetic. Otherwise, small groups of ascetic women might live together, or a woman might find companionship and security by living with a continent male in spiritual marriage.

the desert or wilderness. Further, although the preacher refers to various church functions, there is no hint of any ecclesiastical ceremony of consecration or public vow to virginity. The context is entirely familial.

The homilist focuses particularly on the roles of the father and virgin daughter. As head of the household, the father must become "priest of the Most High God" (20, 62, 63), encourage and oversee his child's dedication to virginity (18, 61), and maintain vigilant and strict discipline over his young "deposit of the Lord" (19–26). The virgin, who is the bride of Christ, is to be confined to her home and kept away from the sexually charged and dangerous company of men (27–37) in order that she will enter the nuptial chamber of Christ pure and undefiled (44).

The homilist also warns parents not to oppose their child's holy aspirations or try to force their child to marry—by such opposition the parents risk their own salvation (12–13). For their part, young virgins and continents are told to honor no one (including their mothers and fathers) more than God (112, 114). The virgin who encounters resistance from her parents should imitate Thecla, the holy virgin who defied her family and the world to follow Christ (99–101). The text thus reflects the possible conflicts between practical familial concerns of inheritance and descendants and ecclesiastical desires to maintain the corps of dedicated young virgins. There is no explicit description of the types of daily ascetic practices expected of the young believers. The preacher mentions the virgin's fasting (18), and he instructs the father to restrict the food of his son (63). There is also reference to scriptural study (44, 56, 58, 59), rejection of the world (81–89), and keeping the body and the soul pure and uncorrupted (13, 39, 58, 140, 152). The child's avoidance of sexual relations and earthly marriage in favor of chastity and betrothal to Christ is the central ascetic focus of the homily.

The Greek text translated here was edited by Amand and Moons and is found in *RBén* 63 (1953) 35–69.

TRANSLATION

I

[1] Because each one of us has received freedom of choice from God, "each one has authority over his or her own will," as holy Paul says in the first letter to the Corinthians.[3] [2] "And the one who has resolved in

---

3. 1 Cor 7:37.

his own heart to keep his [daughter as a] virgin, he will do well, so that the one who gives his daughter in marriage," he says, "does well, and the one who does not give her in marriage does better."⁴ [3] In order to express myself more clearly, for these issues compel me to speak, I will not hesitate to describe in detail the "good" and the "better," especially for those who wing their way⁵ toward God by means of a heavenly and spiritual love.⁶ [4] Chaste marriage is a "good," as it is instituted by God; but undefiled virginity is "better," because it is "better" than the "good," but they are not alien to each other. [5] For just as [many] fruits are found on trees, but only the sweet fruit turns away the axe, so our Savior says, "The axe is laid at the root of the trees."⁷ [6] "Every tree therefore that does not produce good fruit is cut down."⁸ [7] Paul condemns the transgression of the woman, in accordance with the example of Eve the first-formed, but he promises that there will be salvation [for her] through bearing children.⁹ [8] But he did not leave this promise without clarification: "if," he says, "they are steadfast in faith" and truth "and love and holiness and chastity."¹⁰ [9] Thus it is immediately clear: "if they are steadfast." But if they are not steadfast, they will be held liable for the charge of transgression.

II

[10] Let the father persuade his son, and the mother her daughter, to live in chastity for Christ, for the children are common to both of them. [11] But if someone wants to treat them gently rather than persuade them to the zeal for God, let [that parent] not be so bold as to hinder those who are eager to live in chastity, whether it happens to be a son or a daughter, a male slave or a female slave. [12] Do not rush to prevent the [daughter] who longs to live in chastity, lest you sow some enmity with Christ the true Bridegroom. [13] In that case, if nature should bring forth a soul that blossoms with the body in purity for the glory of Christ

---

4. 1 Cor 7:37–38.
5. The verb *pteroō* is often used in relation to spiritual ascent. See, for example, Clement of Alexandria *Strom.* 7.7; Plato *Phdr.* 246, 251, and 255c (on the "wings of the soul").
6. The author of the homily frequently uses the words *erōs* and *pothos*, which usually imply, especially in classical Greek, sexual passion and desire. He clearly intends to draw a contrast between heavenly, spiritual desire and earthly, physical passion (Amand and Moons, "Une curieuse homélie grecque," 35 n. 5).
7. Actually, according to Matt 3:10, these are the words of John the Baptist.
8. Matt 3:10.
9. 1 Tim 2:14–15.
10. Ibid. The homilist's citation is inexact.

and is turned toward him, but the father—who together with the mother is nailed into the earth—does not assist the child who is blossoming for the glory of Christ, and if nevertheless the child, nourished on the pure air of chastity and watered with the dew of the good promise, appears before the Master truly virginal and pure and without stain, [then] the child will be glorified above honor, because she grew into a bunch of grapes amid thorns and briers, but those who begat her bring upon themselves condemnation instead of glory. [14] This is why, therefore, your daughter wants to remain a virgin for Christ. [15] You ought to rejoice; but do not assent to it immediately. [16] [At first], do not offer the [feelings] in your heart, but the [words] from your lips.[11] [17] For this inquiry [into her intentions] is honorable in the beginning, not because you are consumed with jealousy, but because you fear her fall, lest you shame the Bridegroom. [18] Then, if you see that her steps are honorable, her movements well ordered, [and] her eye respectful; [if you discern] what her intention is, of what type her desire is, whether human or heavenly, and of what intensity her fasts and all of her piety in Christ; if you observe a heavenly passion stirred up without pretension, then by all means lead her into the nuptial chamber of the Child of God, the faultless and undefiled Bridegroom. [19] Henceforth let the father watch over the temple of God.[12] [20] Become a "priest of the Most High God."[13] [21] Do not allow anything wicked to approach the pure temple. Do not look down on her because you have begotten her, but because you have a deposit of the Lord [entrusted to you], you must not be negligent. [22] Watch yourself; do not get drowsy, lest you lose the deposit of the Heavenly King. [23] Do not be careless while guarding her, lest you be despondent after losing her; do not laugh at [your responsibility], lest you mourn [your failure]. [24] Even if she should suffer, it is better for her to suffer for the sake of Christ. [25] For if someone does not oppress the child, she will not learn the highest goods; yet [the father] is not provoked by anger, but moved by a parental and loving affection. [26] Do not disregard [your deposit] simply because you have her [now], but be fearful while you guard her so that you will have her [later]. [27] Let no man enter your home; for the Devil's snares are many. [28] Do not display your deposit to any man; for envy is every-

---

11. For other examples of the contrast between the things in the heart and on the lips, see Isa 29:13; Matt 15:8; 2 *Clem.* 3.4–5; and *Herm. Man.* 12.4.4.

12. Cf. 1 Cor 3:17.

13. Heb 7:1.

where. [29] Zealously prevent her conversation[14] with men, for it was by means of conversation that, in Genesis,[15] the first-formed man fell with Eve. [30] Even if the conversation is useful, nevertheless the Useless One[16] is playing a trick. [31] For he is clever in evil ways; he does not inflict his poisons straightforwardly, but he escapes notice while mixing the bile with honey. [32] Just as one is entrapped by the lips of an unchaste woman, in the same way the words of a licentious man anoint the throat like honey in the beginning, but the end results are more bitter than bile, sharper [and] more terrible than a double-edged sword. [33] Even if his appearance is chaste and his words pious, do not trust him, but fear him. For each one of the two sexes has grown from the same seeds, and it is impossible to root out the plant of lust unless a chaste disposition extinguishes it. [34] Do not send your prisoner off on the occasion of an all-night vigil as if you were [simply] allowing her to go to church. [35] May she no longer extinguish the lamp of chastity when she lights the lamp for a vigil. [36] Do not [you, the daughter,] be taken away under the pretext of assemblies, lest you be carried off by your companions and remain out of the company of the saints. [37] Let her not go out of the house [for funerals] because some persons have died, as she herself might be found dead. [38] And watch out for the lasciviousness[17] within her—for the Malicious One is everywhere—as well as her laughter, her temper, her anger, her oaths, her idle words, and the rest of the passions of the flesh. [39] Do not concede anything at all to her, so that no defilement comes to the undefiled one. [40] Cultivate your young plants, that you may reap the sheaves. [41] Learn what it is that you have, that you may also know how to guard the sanctuary [dedicated] to God, temple of Christ, pure altar to the King, Holy Spirit become flesh, pure members of Christ, amulet of the law, student of the Gospels, pride of the church of God, triumph over Eve's transgression, revocation of banishment, reconciliation with humanity, bride of the Heavenly King, pledge of life. [42] Your deposit is herself the cause of such great deposits; therefore, do not care for her negligently, so that you may become her partner in perfection. [43] Let this passage from Holy Scripture echo

14. Homilia—also "association" or "intercourse"—may imply sexual relations (see Aloe Spada, "Un'omelia," 610).

15. Or "in the beginning."

16. I.e., the Devil.

17. The word here is koitē, which normally means "bed" or "marriage bed," but can also mean "lasciviousness" (Rom 13:13), which seems to make more sense in the context of this sentence, especially with esō ("inside," "inner," "within"), and with the list of the "passions of the flesh" that follows.

[in your ears]: "better is a life without children, but with virtue,"[18] and also the words spoken to holy Mary by the angel: "Hail, you who have received grace, the Lord is with you."[19] [44] And gathering up flowers similar to these from the seeds and benefits of Holy Scripture—[that is] the precepts that glorify chastity—and weaving a pure crown with the words of chastity, set it before her, so that, longing for these things, she may enter eagerly into the undefiled nuptial chamber of Christ and gather there with the wise virgins, and so that you who engendered her may reap [the reward of] the bridal chamber of the Kingdom, and she may receive the crown of immortality.

III

[45] If she does not want to remain a [virgin], however, no one should force her and no one should blame her. [46] But she will blame herself, when pains come to her and temporal [pleasures][20] escape her, when the pains of childbirth do battle with her, when she makes "a wailing like the dragons and a mourning like the daughters of the owls."[21] [47] For she has drawn the judgment of the Lord upon herself, which He pronounced against Eve in Genesis: "I will greatly multiply your pains" and your suffering in childbirth, and "in sorrow you will bear children."[22] [48] For she has ignored the saying, "Hail, you who have received grace."[23] [49] And although she holds in her arms the temporal husband in whom she has sought refuge, even the recourse that she has in him becomes far removed from her. [50] She will blame herself, when her daughter dies and her son falls ill, when another misery threatens with her preceding misery, and groaning will follow after groaning. [51] She will blame herself, when her husband is away and yet sorrows dwell with her, and the things necessary [for the household] are not there; when her husband is slow in his absence and grief takes root in her; when, after watching many roads, the tears come pouring down; when the angel claims the death of her beloved husband before her own death; when she runs up one street and down the other crying out in sorrow with her hair hanging loose, even if she is delicate and barefoot, and even if she encounters streams, the urgency of her grief [causes her] not to notice;

18. Wis 4:1.
19. Luke 1:28.
20. The editors propose a small lacuna here in the text.
21. Mic 1:8.
22. Gen 3:16. The citation is inexact.
23. Luke 1:28.

when she tears out her curls and beats her own breast; when she entwines her fingers and puts them around her knees and falls to the ground; when her breath is intermittent while she sobs and she opens up her eyes; when she curses the day and she measures out dust onto her head; when she sprinkles ashes from the hearth, thus defiling her head, which was once crowned with fruit and sprinkled with lilies. [52] And she will blame herself, when a robe of mourning replaces her bridal garment. [53] And perhaps a second mourning will be engaged to her [present] mourning, because of a second marriage. [54] Even if she should avoid [remarriage], a spirit that is troubled and full of the many groans of widowhood will be more than enough and sufficient for her. [55] Then, when this miserable woman has finished all of these things, or rather when she herself has been utterly finished, she leaves this very painful life. [56] And there [above] she will quickly have other pains and more moaning when she sees holy virgins clothed in the garments of immortality, holding in their hands the Psalter that is engraved in their hearts, singing the triumphant hymn of virginity, and wearing on their temples the wreaths of immortality in return for which they renounced the human groaning here [below], dancing in front of Christ under the leadership of the angels, with delight arising in the merriment. [57] When Christ the Bridegroom shows them affection—while she sighs deeply with groans—then she will blame herself again, then she will strongly regret her past actions and her repentance will be in vain.

IV

[58] Let [the parents] not only persuade those of the female sex to live in chastity, but let them also not be remiss in persuading the males to sanctify their own bodies; therefore, let them pluck the strings of Holy Scripture [and chant]: "Blessed is the man for whom the name of the Lord is his trust";[24] and, "Blessed are the blameless";[25] and, "The unmarried man is anxious about the affairs of the Lord";[26] and, "Blessed are the continent ones, for God will speak to them";[27] and that "corruption will

---

24. Ps 40:4.
25. Ps 119:1.
26. 1 Cor 7:32.
27. "*Acts of Paul and Thecla*" 5, in Edgar Hennecke and Wilhelm Schneemelcher, *New Testament Apocrypha* (trans. R. McL. Wilson; Philadelphia: Westminster Press, 1965) II:354. It is significant that our homilist cites from the beatitudes of the apocryphal *Acts of Paul*, which places heavy emphasis on absolute continence, and regards this passage as "Holy Scripture."

not inherit incorruption";[28] and that "the one who sows to the spirit will
reap everlasting life";[29] and that "those who are in the flesh are unable to
please God";[30] and "decorum and devotion to the Lord without distraction";[31] and that "it is good for a man to remain as he is";[32] and that
which the Lord said to the prophet Jeremiah: "You shall not take a wife,
nor shall you have sons or daughters in this place";[33] and the word of the
Lord who says to the prophet Isaiah: "Let not the eunuch say, 'I am a dry
tree,' for thus says the Lord to the eunuchs: 'those who choose the things
which I desire,'" so as to keep their own hands from doing injustice, and
who do not think of evil things against the Lord, "'I will give them,' He
says, 'in my house a notable place and within my walls a better [name]
than sons and daughters'";[34] and also these words proclaimed out loud
by the Lord Himself in the Gospels: "There are eunuchs who have made
themselves eunuchs for the sake of the Kingdom of Heaven."[35] [59]
Indeed let the soul of the young son be all the more firmly supported by
Holy Scripture. [60] But if [the fathers] also describe the miseries of
marriage to their sons in order to turn away the passions of the flesh,
thus overthrowing—by means of heavenly desire—the temporal and
frenzied desire of the flesh that passes away like a flower of the grass,[36]
then they will extinguish the bitterness of [earthly] sweetness, having
conquered by means of a chaste argument.

V

[61] Therefore, father, talk with your son for the purpose of reducing
the vigor of the young male. Then if you should see that his faith is
unbroken, that his attitude does not appear agitated or weak, or unruly
due to licentiousness in the flesh, but rather his faith operates by the fear
of God,[37] then imitate the patriarch, become a new Abraham who offers
his young Isaac; send away the ass and the young slaves, that is to say,
the temporal activity of this world, and lay the [sacrificial] wood upon

28. Or "immortality." 1 Cor 15:50.
29. Gal 6:8.
30. Rom 8:8.
31. 1 Cor 7:35. The full verse reads: "I say this for your own benefit, not to lay a
snare for you, but for the purpose of decorum and devotion to the Lord without
distraction."
32. 1 Cor 7:26.
33. Jer 16:2.
34. Isa 56:3–5. The citation is inexact.
35. Matt 19:12.
36. Cf. Isa 40:6; Jas 1:10.
37. Cf. Gal 5:6.

him,[38] that is to say, the cross. [62] In keeping with this image, you yourself lead your own young Isaac to the mountain, offering a living sacrifice to the living God,[39] so that you also may become a "priest of the Most High God"[40] by offering praise to God; "for God is well pleased with such sacrifices,"[41] [and] such priests serve God. [63] Bind [your son] hand and foot, and do not allow him easy access to food, in order that his fattened flesh will not kick,[42] and lest, because he has nourished the strength of the body and not of the soul with excessive food and drink—which are harmful—he should kick, leaping up, and refuse to accept the wood of the cross, or perhaps break apart the altar. [And bind your son] in order that with hope you may also have other hopes, that you may be both father and "priest of the Most High";[43] and if you offer prayers for him, you will demonstrate your affection. [64] For thus did Job, the servant of God, who as you know sacrificed a calf every year in regard to his sons' thoughts, saying, "It may be that my sons have had evil thoughts about God."[44] [65] And if the mother should make tunics for her son, let her not be at all irritated; for, as it is written in the first Book of Kings, Anna the servant of God made double cloaks each year for holy Samuel, her son.[45] [66] And the King will certainly labor to honor in return those who have honored His own soldiers.

VI

[67] Paul has taught that parents should lay up treasure for their children. [68] What is the treasure? It is to bring them up "in the discipline and admonition of the Lord."[46] [69] For this is truly the good treasure, the property of the one who has it, which "no thief approaches and no moth destroys,"[47] and which is not the temporal wealth of this world, [bringing] to people [only] scandal, trouble, and fighting. [70] For often the one who possesses [wealth] loses life itself because of it, as we have often both heard and seen the result with our own eyes—such is truly the case. [71] Therefore, let the parents lay up treasure for their

38. Cf. Gen 22:5–6.
39. Cf. Rom 12:1.
40. Heb 7:1.
41. Heb 13:16.
42. Cf. Deut 32:15.
43. Heb 7:1.
44. Job 1:5.
45. 1 Sam 2:19.
46. Eph 6:4.
47. Luke 12:33.

own children, supplying them with the things that are pleasing to God. [72] And if some other person should be eager to do this for God, only in the name of a disciple, and drawing and pouring a cup of cool water he or she should offer it to the disciple of Christ,[48] that person will be the heir to the divine Kingdom. [73] Therefore, let all those who love Christ be eager to provide useful things [to His disciples]. [74] But let it not be supposed by any correctly thinking persons that there is anything more useful than the salvation of the soul. [75] There are many things that bring about salvation for the soul, even so much as two small coins[49] and so much as a good word, which is better than a gift.[50] [76] For this genuine free choice, coming from an honest intention, is more acceptable to the benevolent God than the blood of sacrifices.[51] [77] Indeed, often our ears ring with the testimony of the all-wise God to David, which was spoken through holy Samuel in the beginning [of David's life], that "People look at the face, but God looks into the heart,"[52] above all into [the hearts] that are lifted up on the wings of a perfect heavenly desire.

VII

[78] Let the virgins enter, therefore; for there is need of them in the Kingdom, but there is need of *wise* virgins. [79] For [the Bridegroom] was not unjust when he shut the virgins of whom you have heard out [of the bridal chamber];[53] because they had no oil, due to their negligence, they were not capable of the "good," [that is] to enter and greet Him, nor did they strive for the "better," [that is] to be watchful. And because of this they have not been called "brides," and they have not reached the incorruptible nuptial chamber, and they have not stretched out their bridal bedcurtain; and because of this they have not received the crown of the Kingdom of the Heavens, and they have not kept company with the immortal Bridegroom, as they have not attained to Him. [80] This is why it has been said, "there is need of wise virgins." [81] If you live a virgin life for Christ, do not [live] as you desire, but as the one for whom you are a virgin desires. [82] Do not desire the same things as those who set their minds on worldly affairs. [83] For how will the one who has

48. Cf. Matt 10:42.
49. Cf. Luke 21:2.
50. Cf. Sir 18:17.
51. 1 Sam 15:22.
52. 1 Sam 16:7.
53. See Matt 25:1–14 for the parable of the wise and foolish virgins.

deadened his or her earthly members, which are sinful, be among those who do not submit to the truth? [84] What are you, who have been crucified to the world,[54] looking for with those who live according to the world and take pleasure in the world? [85] "No one," says [Paul], "who is a soldier gets entangled in the affairs of [civilian] life—in order to please the one who enlisted him—and no [athlete] is crowned unless he competes according to the rules."[55] [86] You have been buried with Christ in baptism; why do you reason as if you still lived in the world? [87] You have crossed the Jordan; do not turn back toward Egypt. [88] That is, you have left the world for the spirit; do not let earthly thoughts again darken your spirit, which has attained to heaven in order to be illuminated. [89] Do not let your exterior appearance be Jerusalem, but your character Egyptian.[56] [90] Watch out that you do not cover the interior wolf in sheep's clothing,[57] and do not crown the thistle with pomegranate flowers. [91] The clothing is lifted, the character of the sheep is sought. [92] The leaves fall off, the grapes are sought. [93] The flowers fall from the outside, the [true] character appears—for the nature of the thistle manifests itself. [94] Thus there is need not of virgins in body [only], but there is need of honest characters. [95] The flowers do not nourish the farmer—it is the fruit that gives him pleasure. [96] Consider my position to be thus also on all other subjects; for it is not necessary to discuss them in detail. [97] Indeed, in the opinions springing up in the minds of wise people, subtlety of argument is considered a burden. [98] I beseech you, therefore, not to assume an exterior appearance, but prefer action to appearance, lest some people, whose outward actions otherwise appear proper, should be discovered by us to be in fact indecent in their actions.

VIII

[99] Often when a daughter yearns to strive for higher things, the mother, concerned for her children or misled by their imagined temporal beauty, or perhaps consumed by jealousy, tries to make her daughter a child of this age and not the one espoused to God. [100] All wicked things imaginable set traps [for you]; but do not flinch in fear, my child!

54. Cf. Gal 6:14.
55. 2 Tim 2:4–5.
56. Jerusalem here symbolizes the heavenly kingdom or paradise, whereas Egypt, in contrast, symbolizes bondage to the material, sexual, corruptible world of sinful pleasures and grievous suffering.
57. Cf. Matt 7:15.

Lift your eyes upward to where your Beloved is; follow in the footsteps of that famous one who has gone before you and of whom you have heard: Thecla. [101] Although what I have said is off the subject, even if Theocleia is troubled and Thamyris laments, even if Alexander overtakes you, even if the judge threatens you, let nothing extinguish your love.[58] [102] For it is profitable for young people to be crucified with Jesus Christ. [103] "Who will separate" those who love him "from the love of Christ?"[59] [104] Neither "oppression," nor "distress," nor judges, nor orators, nor sword, "nor any other creature will be able to separate us from the love of Christ."[60] [105] But even if you should be deprived of your parents, nevertheless you are not deprived of God. [106] And if you should forget your father's house, nevertheless "the king will desire your beauty."[61] [107] Come then, indeed, whether you are rich or unknown, whether you are a day laborer or poor. [108] Be courageous, come; for the Bridegroom Jesus Christ does not love beauty that fades away, nor does He turn away from poverty. [109] For lowly and great, the same grace summons both, but it puts their free choice to the test, and in this way it receives those who are fully armed with virtue, by means of a chaste disposition. [110] It is this way also in the case of a son who is eager to consecrate his body; the father stirs up enmity against his own child if he is not able to understand such a virtuous achievement. [111] He regards as foolishness what is, according to Holy Scripture, wise in the eyes of God.[62] [112] But do not give up, O young man! Do not honor your mortal father or mother or anyone else more [than God]. [113] As it is written in the Gospel, Jesus has declared worthy of Him those whom He calls: "Leave your boat, leave your father and your fishing nets,"[63] even if there are many expectations in life, even if Zebedee is upset. [114] Honor nothing more than God, or rather more than your own salvation, so that you also might be with John, bearing the dignity that shares his throne.[64] [115] For thus God has promised those who have left father,

58. See *Acts of Paul and Thecla*. Theocleia is Thecla's mother who is distressed when Thecla decides to break off her engagement to Thamyris and follow Paul, the Christian preacher of the virgin life. Alexander is a politically and physically powerful man who lustfully attacks Thecla on the street. When she successfully fights off his advances and publicly humiliates him, even knocking the crown off his head, he brings her before the judge. It is clear that our preacher assumes that his audience is quite familiar with the details of this very popular story.
59. Rom 8:35.
60. Rom 8:35, 39. The citation is inexact.
61. Cf. Ps 45:10–11.
62. Cf. 1 Cor 3:19.
63. Cf. Matt 4:18–22.
64. Cf. Matt 19:28–29.

mother, siblings, lands, and homes that they will be seated on twelve thrones in the Kingdom of Heaven.[65]

IX

[116] This is what He has said to virgins; this is what He has said to those who listen; for He Himself included all people, and all people "are for Him"[66] in order to be united [in Him]. [117] He has not commanded these things only to those who live as virgins, but He also said: "Whoever has left" wife, "children," and the rest "will inherit many times over and eternal life."[67] [118] He has not said this in order to separate [husband and wife], but He has spoken to those who have [spouses], that they might "live as though they had none," because the time "has grown short";[68] therefore He is not breaking the marriage bond, but sowing [the seeds of] chastity, in order to choke out incontinence. [119] Even when we bear the marks of Christ,[69] and yet it is only in word that we reject divorce, then probably it is in vain that some of us come together in the church.[70] [120] And I will not leave this claim unattested. [121] Come now, we will present examples from the Gospel. [122] [The Lord] has compared His Kingdom to a net that has been cast into the world and has gathered many [fish] of all kinds.[71] [123] When [you pull the net] onto the shore, He says, pick out the good fish but throw out the rotten ones.[72] [124] He Himself says, "Many are called, but few are chosen";[73] "few," not because of the one who chooses, but because [there are few]

---

65. Ibid.
66. Cf. Rom 11:36.
67. Matt 19:29. The citation is inexact.
68. Cf. 1 Cor 7:29.
69. Cf. Gal 6:17.
70. The meaning of this sentence is not immediately clear. The homilist has been arguing that Christ did not advocate the dissolution of already-existing marriages but that married Christians should nevertheless live in chastity. In this sentence he claims that if some Christians reject the dissolution of the marriage bond in word only—that is, if they in fact break that bond through divorce—they will not be received into the Kingdom (see sentences 122–125).
The editors of the Greek text feel compelled to add the word "not" to this sentence, so that it reads, "And when we do *not* bear the marks of Christ. . . ." Because, however, bearing the marks (*ta stigmata*) of Christ can refer to the mark or "seal" of baptized Christians in general (e.g., Clement of Alexandria *Excerpts from Theodotus* 86.2–3), the sentence makes sense as it stands. Even if one is a baptized Christian and gathers with others in the church, one's entrance into the kingdom is not thereby simply assured (see sentence 125).
71. Matt 13:47.
72. Ibid.
73. Matt 22:14.

chosen ones to be found. [125] For just as many grains are gathered on the threshing floor, but few are put into the storage house, so also many of us are gathered in the church, but few will be brought into the Kingdom. [126] For the cargo ship headed for the Kingdom proceeds and steers through the passable places, and the north winds do not play [with it].[74] [127] The ship does not refuse to receive anyone out of malice, but whatever is too light in weight is carried away [by the wind]. [128] Therefore, do not be too light, lest you become like the chaff that is thrown out. [129] No one is able to escape [God's] notice. [130] For the winnowing shovel is in the hand of God who clears the threshing floor; God mixes the grain with the other grains; the chaff is separated off by the discrimination of the wind,[75] and is delivered to the fire, as you have heard.[76] [131] And in another place in the Gospel we see the exact nature of our point of inquiry. [132] The king came in, [the passage] says, to see the guests reclining at table, and he found one who seemed to be hidden.[77] [133] The king spoke [to him]. [134] The man suffered as he listened to [the king's reproach], because what he said to him was severe. [135] I hesitate to utter the words with my own mouth, and because of this I will not repeat them in my homily. [136] But those [of you] who are eager for knowledge are familiar with the fearful words [addressed] to that guest and to those of similar character. [137] The feast was not inferior, but the guest was unworthy of the feast. [138] The king was not jealous, but the one who came in [secretly] did not make himself worthy, as he reclined at the table although he was wicked. [139] May no one, therefore, suffer this [reproach], may no one be wicked, lest you be silenced. [140] So, you who wish to live piously, put to silence the appetites of the flesh. [141] Indeed, Paul entreats us to flee youthful desires.[78]

---

74. The image of the church as the ship of life and salvation that departs this world of sin, corruption, and death and carries its cargo of believers through dangerous waters to the safe harbor of the Kingdom is common in patristic literature. See, for example, Hippolytus *Refutation* 7.1 and *Treatise on the Antichrist* 59; Clement of Alexandria *Exhortation to the Greeks* 12; and Maximus of Turin *Sermon* 37.

75. Or, "the spirit."

76. Matt 3:12.

77. Matt 22:11–13. These verses appear in the context of the parable of the king's marriage feast for his son, and read, "But when the king came in to look at the guests, he saw there a man who had no wedding garment; and he said to him, 'Friend, how did you get in here without having a wedding garment?' And he was speechless. Then the king said to his servants, 'Bind him hand and foot, and cast him into the outer darkness; there will be weeping and gnashing of teeth.'"

78. 2 Tim 2:22.

X

[142] I did not want to burst out in this manner, but I am compelled thus to speak, in order that you who have heard the severe [reproach] may flee suffering. [143] And when is it necessary to flee? [144] "Now is the day of salvation."[79] [145] Those of you who desire to be with Christ, you know that the time is coming when "no one is able to work."[80] [146] The night is coming when "each person will receive according to what he or she has done while in the body."[81] [147] The day is coming when no one is able to put off until tomorrow. [148] For "in death there is no one who remembers you, and in Hades who will praise you?"[82] [149] If, therefore, brothers and sisters, this is the sentence, and we cannot disregard it—or rather if we disregard it there is no hiding—"let us come before His presence with thanksgiving."[83] [150] Let us come before Him, lest we be surpassed. [151] Let us conquer evil with virtues,[84] lest we be found among the evil. [152] "Let us purify ourselves of every defilement of flesh and spirit,"[85] in order that, appearing pure before the Pure One, we may receive the pure crown through Jesus Christ our Lord, through whom be glory to the Father from ages to ages. Amen.[86]

SUGGESTED READINGS

Greek Text

Amand de Mendieta, David, and Matthieu-Charles Moons. "Une curieuse homélie grecque inédite sur la virginité, adressée aux pères de famille." *RBén* 63 (1953) 18–69, 211–38. The Greek text of the homily is found on pages 35–69.

Related Primary Texts

E. M. Buytaert, ed. Eusebius of Emesa. "Homilies 6 and 7." In *Eusèbe d'Emèse: Discours conservés en latin*, I:151–95. Spicilegium Sacrum Lovaniense 26. Louvain, Belg.: Spicilegium Sacrum, 1953.

Lebon, J., ed. and trans. "Athanasiana Syriaca I: 'Un Λόγος περὶ παρθενίας attribué à saint Athanase de Alexandrie.'" *Mus* 40 (1927) 205–48.

79. 2 Cor 6:2.
80. John 9:4.
81. 2 Cor 5:10.
82. Ps 6:5.
83. Ps 95:2.
84. Cf. Rom 12:21.
85. 2 Cor 7:1.
86. I am grateful to William Beardslee and Bernadette Brooten for their helpful suggestions concerning difficult passages.

Lefort, L.-Th., ed. and trans. "Saint Athanase: Sur la virginité." *Mus* 42 (1929) 197–275.

von der Goltz, Eduard, ed. *Pseudo-Athanasius. "De virginitate."* TU 29 (2a). Leipzig: Hinrichs, 1905.

Wilson, R. McL., trans. *"Acts of Paul and Thecla,"* in *New Testament Apocrypha*, edited by Edgar Hennecke and Wilhelm Schneemelcher, II:353–64. Philadelphia: Westminster Press, 1965.

Useful Secondary Studies

Aloe Spada, Concetta. "Un'omelia greca anonima 'sulla verginità' (Rev. Ben. 63 [1953])." In *La Tradizione dell'Enkrateia*, edited by Ugo Bianchi, 603–23. Rome: Ateneo, 1985.

Amand de Mendieta, David. "La virginité chez Eusèbe d'Emèse et l'ascétisme familial dans la première moitié de IVe siècle." *RHE* 50 (1955) 777–820.

Aubineau, Michel. "Les écrits de saint Athanase sur la virginité." *RAM* 31 (1955) 140–73.

Elm, Susanna K. "The Organization and Institutions of Female Asceticism in Fourth-Century Cappadocia and Egypt." D. Phil. dissertation, University of Oxford, 1986.

Vööbus, Arthur. "Syrische Herkunft der Pseudo-Basilianischen Homilie über die Jungfräulichkeit." *OrChr* 40 (1956) 69–77.

ORIGEN
Homily I on Ezekiel

INTRODUCTION

Origen (ca. 185–ca. 253 C.E.) preached this homily to the church at Caesarea in Palestine around 240.[1] Its parenetic tone and its diatribe style, often with hypothetical dialogues (see § 2), typify Origen's homilies. As in all his work, he presupposes that Christ is personified in and speaks through the characters of the Old Testament (5) and that all scripture is directed toward the actual spiritual needs of believers (4).[2] Ezekiel represents Christ (4) and the captivity of the Jews in Babylon is our captivity to sin (3). Having limited time (9) and speaking to an audience composed largely of simple Christians unprepared for advanced doctrine (3), Origen does not attempt a full exposition of the biblical text.

Origen exhorts his hearers to choose spirit over fire (13), that is, to embrace the opportunity God provides in this earthly life to obtain purification through prayer, study, and self-discipline. They can thus undergo the inevitable purification from sin, which will be much slower and more painful if delayed beyond this life. Origen presupposes the theological system set forth in *On First Principles*: souls fell from their original union with God, symbolized by Adam's expulsion from Paradise (3), and are reunited with God by accepting the teaching of God's

1. For this dating, see Pierre Nautin, *Origene: sa vie et son oeuvre* (Paris: Gabriel Beauchesne, 1977) 389–409. But see also David J. Halperin, *The Faces of the Chariot: Early Jewish Responses to Ezekiel's Vision* (Tübingen: J. C. B. Mohr [Paul Siebeck], 1988) 337–38. David Halperin's assistance with this translation is much appreciated.

2. See Karen J. Torjesen, *Hermeneutical Procedure and Theological Method in Origen's Exegesis* (Berlin: Walter de Gruyter, 1986).

word united with a human being in Jesus Christ (5, 10). He is especially concerned to uphold, against the Marcionites, the identification of Jesus' God and Father with the Creator-God of the Old Testament (4).

A remarkable feature of this homily, demonstrated by David J. Halperin, is its dependence on *Shavu'ot* preaching on Ezekiel's "chariot" vision, which Origen evidently heard in the Greek-speaking synagogues of Caesarea. Details from such preaching include the reference to a plurality of heavens (7), the connection between Ezekiel's vision and the ascension imagery of Ps 68:19 (6), the vivid description of the descent of guardian angels (7), the statement that Ezekiel saw the vision with the eyes of his flesh while the people of Israel saw them with the eyes of their hearts (8), and the ironic reading of "and I was in the midst of exile" (5). Origen was also aware of rabbinic comparison of the Babylonian exile to Adam's expulsion from Paradise (3).[3] He Christianizes these themes and integrates them into his own theology. This work thus attests to the creative adoption of Jewish homiletical themes in a Christian ascetic context.

Although he shared with the church of his time a veneration of martyrdom, Origen made ascetic discipline and study a new ideal of Christian life. After undergoing as a young man a conversion to a life based on the gospel precepts, he rejected pagan literature, sought to mortify his appetites, and adopted utter simplicity of dress (even going barefoot).[4] He tempered but never abandoned this manner of life. Here he tells his lay audience that "we have been freed by Christ from the affairs of the world" (16) and depicts God as particularly concerned to cleanse them from "works of generation and lust" (3). Origen chafed at the constraints of lay life in other works. He taught, against Clement of Alexandria, that Jesus' advice to the rich man to sell all that he had should be followed literally; he quoted Luke 14:26 to Ambrosius on the need to hate family; he warned against praying near the conjugal bed; and he only grudgingly allowed widows to remarry. He warned Christian women that the incestuous union of Lot's daughters with their father, undertaken to repopulate the world when they mistakenly thought that they alone remained, was better than legitimate marital relations undertaken for pleasure.[5] We know from the *Panegyric* attrib-

---

3. David J. Halperin, "Origen, Ezekiel's Merkabah, and the Ascension of Moses," *CH* 50 (1981) 261–75, and *Faces of the Chariot*, 322–56.
4. Eusebius *Hist. Eccl.* 6.3.9–12.
5. Origen *Comm. in Matt.* 19.18; *Mart.* 37; *On Prayer* 31.4; *Hom. in Jer.* 20.4; and *Hom. in Gen.* 5.4.

uted to Gregory Thaumaturgus that moral and ascetic formation was integral to Origen's teaching.[6]

The Greek text of this homily survives only in fragments. The translation is from Jerome's Latin translation in the edition of W. A. Baehrens (*GCS* 30, *Origenes* 8:319–40).

TRANSLATION

1. Not everyone who is a captive undergoes captivity on account of sin. Even when the whole population of the Jews was abandoned by God on account of its sin and underwent captivity—seized by Nebuchadnezzar, ejected from the holy land, and led into Babylon[7]— a few righteous were among the people. These did not undergo captivity on account of their own guilt, but so that the sinners oppressed by the yoke of captivity would not be bereft of aid. Let us just suppose that the sinners had been taken to Babylon but the righteous had remained in their original homes; in that case, the sinners could never have found any remedy. Because God is gentle, kind, and a lover of humanity, he has tempered the chastisements with which sinners are punished with the mercy of his visitation. In that way he does not oppress the wretched with penalties that are too severe. Our God always acts this way. He torments the guilty, but does so with the gentleness of a merciful father.

If you wish to confirm the truth of what we say, examine the events in Egypt during the famine.[8] If God had wished to kill so many Egyptians, and to punish them with a tormenting seven-year famine, he could certainly have done so. In that case Joseph would not have gone down into Egypt, Pharaoh would not have dreamed about the things that were to happen in Egypt, and it would not have been revealed by the chief cupbearer that there was someone held in prison who could interpret the king's dream. Now, this instance plainly proves that God punishes as a father. On account of his gentleness he spares Israel, and he even spares the Egyptians, who are strangers to him. This is beyond doubt. They experience the work of a good God when Joseph goes down into Egypt, when Pharaoh is warned by dreams, when the chief cupbearer points out the interpreter, and when the interpreter explains the dream. These events make it possible for famine to be avoided by storing

6. Gr. Thaum. *pan. Or.* 7.93–99 and 9.115–121.
7. Cf. Jer 24:1.
8. Cf. Gen 39; 41.

produce during a time of plenty. Such considerations make it obvious that the heretics are wrong to condemn the Creator for immoderate wrath. We could easily cite many more cases to prove what I have said. Nonetheless, rather than give the appearance of digressing, I shall proceed to the topic at hand. That topic is to explain the people of Israel's being led into captivity on account of their sins.

2. So that no one may think that sinners handed over by God are no longer governed by him—that once led away into captivity they are beyond his direction and do not deserve his mercy—let us examine diligently the passage just read. Daniel did not sin, and Hananiah, Azariah, and Mishael were without sin, and yet they were made captive, so that, being where they were, they might console the captive people. Thus, by their exhortation, they could restore the penitent to Jerusalem after their temporary chastisement. Even though distressed by seventy years of bondage, they did in fact return to their own homes because the prophets' holy word upheld their otherwise dispirited souls. Those four, indeed, were not the only prophets who were in captivity. Ezekiel was one, and Zechariah the son of Berechiah, who prophesied in the time of captivity under King Darius.[9] We also find Haggai, and many other prophets who prophesied in those times. This shows that God does not just punish sinners, but tempers punishment with mercy.

In case you doubt that God acts this way, listen to their voices, the lamentations of those who are patient. How piously do they testify to God's forbearance even in their suffering: "We have eaten the bread of tears, and we have drunk in tears and in measure."[10] It does not say simply "in tears," but "in tears and in measure." Balance characterizes God's mercy. If sinners did not need to be threatened with torment in order to turn from their ways, God, merciful and kindly as he is, would not use punishment to chastise the wicked. Nevertheless, a devoted father corrects his son so that he may learn, and a perspicacious teacher assumes a stern face to chastise a lazy pupil, concealing his affection so as not to lose his effectiveness. Look at what Solomon, the wisest man of all, admires in God's correction: "My son, do not be fainthearted in God's discipline, nor fail under his chastisement, for the Lord disciplines him whom he loves, and he scourges each son whom he accepts."[11] There is no son, as the Apostle says, who is not punished by his father. And to this he marvelously added, saying: "Persevere in discipline. God

9. Cf. Zech 1:1.
10. Ps 79:6 (LXX).
11. Prov 3:11–12.

is treating you as sons. For what son does a father not correct? For him whom he loves, God corrects, and he scourges every son whom he accepts. If you are not subject to discipline, in which all have participated, you are bastards and not sons."[12]

Perhaps someone, offended by the very word "wrath," will denounce God for it. To that person we respond that God's wrath is not so much wrath as a necessary procedure. Listen, this is the purpose of God's wrath. It is to chastise, to discipline, to amend: "O Lord, do not chastise me in your wrath, and do not discipline me in your indignation."[13] He who speaks this way knows that the wrath of God is not unsalutary; it is employed to heal the sick and to amend those who despise his word. That is why he prays not to be amended by such remedies, not to recover his original health by means of the remedial treatment of punishment. It is as if a slave, while being scourged, should pray his master, promising him that he will do what he is ordered to do without being whipped, saying, "O Lord, do not chastise me in your wrath, and do not discipline me in your indignation." Everything that is from God is good, and we deserve correction. Hear what it says: "I shall correct them in the hearing of their afflictions."[14] Therefore, let us hear those things that concern affliction, so that we may be amended. Indeed, it is written in the curses of Leviticus: "If after these things they do not obey, nor are turned back toward me, I shall appoint seven plagues on account of their sins. If after this they will not turn back, I shall amend them."[15] All those things that seem bitter to us serve as means of instruction and healing. God is a physician, God is a father; he is not a harsh master, but a lenient one.

When you come to those whose punishments are vividly described in scripture, compare scripture to scripture, as the Apostle instructs.[16] You will find that he is most sweet, just where he is considered most bitter. It is written in the Prophets: "He does not avenge himself twice in the same matter in judgment."[17] He avenged himself once in judgment by the flood; he avenged himself once in judgment against Sodom and Gomorrah; he avenged himself once in judgment against Egypt and 600,000 Israelites. Do not think that God would exact vengeance upon sinners with such punishment, if they were yet to receive torment upon

12. Heb 12:7–8.
13. Ps 6:1.
14. Hos 7:12.
15. Lev 26:27–28.
16. 1 Cor 2:13.
17. Nah 1:9.

torment after death; they are punished in the present so as not to be punished afresh in the future. Understand the poor man in the gospel; he is oppressed by filth and penury, and later on he rests in Abraham's bosom.[18] He received his evils during his life.[19] Where do you learn that those who perished in the flood received their evils in life? Where is it known whether or not Sodom and Gomorrah had their evils restored to them in their life? Hear the witness of the scriptures. Do you want to learn the testimony of the Old Testament? Do you want to be taught that of the New? "Sodom shall be restored to its old state."[20] And up to now you have doubted that God did well in punishing the Sodomites? "It shall be more bearable for the land of Sodom and Gomorrah on the day of judgment."[21] Therefore, God is kind, God is merciful. "He makes his sun to rise" truly "upon the good and the evil and he makes it to rain" truly "upon the just and the unjust,"[22] and not just that sun that we see with our eyes, but also that sun that is perceived by the eyes of the mind. I have been evil, but the sun of righteousness has risen[23] upon me. I have been evil, but the rain of righteousness has come upon me. The goodness of God is even in those things that are thought to be evil.

3. This explains why the prophet was in the captivity.[24] Now contemplate the vision he received in order to alleviate the sorrows of captivity. Looking about him below, he saw oppression, but lifting up his eyes he perceived the heavens opened, he discerned heavenly matters disclosed, he saw the likeness of the glory of God. What he saw were the four living creatures that are the subject of much discussion because they are hard to interpret. He perceived a chariot of the four living creatures with wheels within its wheels. That chariot of the four living creatures is fiery, but not entirely so, only from the middle to the feet. From the middle up to the top, it glowed with the splendor of amber. This shows that God is not all torment; he is refreshment as well. He punishes sinners with those ministrations symbolized by the lower parts of the vision. The prophet, however, did not see fire in the head, or in parts of the body above the waist. God is fiery, but only from the waist to the feet, an indication that those who participate in generation require fire. That is because the parts below the waist symbolize sexual

18. Luke 16:22.
19. Luke 16:25.
20. Ezek 16:55.
21. Matt 10:15.
22. Matt 5:45.
23. Mal 4:2.
24. Ezek 1:5; 2:1.

intercourse. Thus, Levi was still in the loins of his father Abraham, when Melchizedek met him,[25] and it is said in the Psalm: "Of the fruit of your loins shall I place on my throne."[26] God is fiery from the waist down; works of generation and lust are chastised by the torments of Gehenna.

Although God is fiery, he is not entirely so. His upper parts are of amber. Amber is not only more precious than silver, it is more precious than gold. Scripture, of course, uses amber to portray splendor, not because God really is amber. By the same token, just as God is not actually amber, he is not actually fire from his waist down to his toes. This fire consumes, but what it consumes is not mentioned. This is so that you may seek to find out what is consumed by God's fire. "Our God is a consuming fire";[27] what does this fire consume? Not the wood that we see, not sensible hay, not the stubble we look at, but if you should build upon the foundation of Jesus Christ, works of sin are wood, works of sin are hay, inferior works of sin are stubble.[28] The fire comes and it tries all these things. What is this fire, which the law announces, and concerning which the gospel is not silent? "Whosoever's works, of what sort they are, the fire shall prove."[29] Tell us, Apostle, what is this fire that proves our works? What is this fire, a fire so wise that it preserves my gold, so wise that it makes my silver gleam more splendidly, so wise that it leaves unharmed the precious stone in me even as it consumes so many of my evil deeds, those things in me which I have built with wood, hay, and stubble? What is this fire? "I have come to send fire upon the earth, and how I wish that it were already kindled."[30] Jesus Christ says, "how I wish that it were already kindled." This is because he is good, and he knows that if this fire is kindled, wickedness will be consumed. It is written in the prophets: "He has consecrated him in blazing fire, and it has devoured wood like hay"[31] and again "The Lord of Hosts sends forth reproach in your honor, and in your glory a blazing fire is kindled."[32] These mean that, so that you may be glorified, he sends forth fire against your sinful works.

Do you wish to learn from the prophet that the torments of a good God are to the benefit of those who undergo them? Listen to the same

25. Heb 7:10.
26. Ps 131:11.
27. Heb 12:19.
28. Cf. 1 Cor 3:12.
29. 1 Cor 3:13.
30. Luke 12:49.
31. Isa 10:17.
32. Isa 10:16.

prophet saying, "You have coals of fire. Sit upon them. They are to be for your assistance."[33] It is best to hide this, and not publicize it, but the heretics impel us to make public things that ought to be concealed. They are best kept hidden from those who are still babes as far as the age of their soul is concerned, who require the teacher's rod. These are people who do not seek goodness unless they are chastised by threats and fears. It is only by such bitter remedies that they can be prevented from wounding themselves by sinning. That is why God's mysteries are always somewhat veiled for the sake of the spiritually immature. "How great are the multitude of your delights, O Lord, which you hide from those who fear you."[34] The God of the Law and the Prophets hides the multitude of his goodness, not from those who love him, but from those who fear him. Such persons are children. They cannot profitably learn that they are loved by the father. To do so would injure them, because they would only despise God's goodness.

Therefore, when you hear of the captivity of the people, believe that it did indeed happen according to the historical narrative, but then go on to understand that story as a sign of something else. Following that sign you will discover the mystery. You, if you call yourself a believer, when you experience peace—Christ indeed is our peace[35]— inhabit Jerusalem. If you then sin, God's visitation leaves you, and you are handed over captive to Nebuchadnezzar, and so led captive into Babylon. When then your soul is troubled by vices and disturbances, you are taken into Babylon. ("Babylon" means "confusion.") If you then do penance, and if, with a genuine, heartfelt conversion, you beseech God's mercy, Ezra will be sent to you and he will lead you back and cause Jerusalem to be rebuilt. "Ezra" means "helper"; he is the supporting word sent to you so that you may return to your fatherland.

This is a mystery that is spoken of by Daniel in a riddle and narrated by the Apostle in a way that equally hides and reveals: "In Adam we all die, and in Christ we all are made alive."[36] Adam was indeed in Paradise, but the serpent caused his captivity, and brought it about that he was expelled from Jerusalem or Paradise, and entered into this place of tears.[37] The serpent is an enemy, contrary to the truth, but he was not originally created so. He did not originally crawl about upon his breast

33. Isa 47:14–15.
34. Ps 30:20.
35. Eph 2:14.
36. 1 Cor 15:22.
37. Judg 2:5 (LXX).

and belly. He was not accursed from the beginning. Just as Adam and Eve did not sin right when they were created, so the serpent was not a serpent during the time when he dwelt in the paradise of delights.[38] Later, having fallen, he deserved, on account of his sins, to hear: "You were born a seal of resemblance and a crown of beauty in the paradise of God. Until iniquity was found in you, you walked blameless in all your ways."[39] That is why he remembered Job, because he was proud in the sight of Almighty God.[40] Indeed, "The morning star fell from heaven. He who arose in the morning is trampled beneath the earth."[41] See how the words of the prophets harmonize with those in the gospels. The prophets said, "The morning star fell from heaven. He who arose in the morning is trampled beneath the earth." Jesus said, "I have seen Satan falling from heaven like lightning."[42]

What difference does it make whether it is lightning or the morning star that fell from heaven? Insofar as our subject is concerned, they agree completely—he fell from heaven. God, you notice, did not cause his death[43] or treat him at all maliciously; he allows a free will in angels as well as men. This must be understood: by freedom of will some ascend to the summit of goodness while others descend to the depth of wickedness. You, as a matter of fact, why do you not exercise your will? Why do you consider it so tedious to advance, to labor, to contend, to work out your own salvation? Would you be happier sleeping, would you like to be utterly undisturbed so that you could always be comfortably relaxing? "My Father," Jesus says, "works and I work."[44] Why do you not like to work, even though you were born for work? Do you not wish your work to be righteousness, wisdom, and chastity? Do you not wish your work to be courage and all the other virtues? That is why you are led away into captivity and you deserve the torment of slavery on account of your sins. But Jesus Christ comes to preach release for the captives and sight for the blind.[45] To those who are in chains he cries, "Come out," and to those who dwell in darkness he says, "See." We are the ones who are in the chains of sins, and we often dwell in darkness, fighting against the rulers of darkness of this world.[46] Jesus comes, announced by

38. Cf. Gen 2:8.
39. Ezek 28:12–15.
40. Cf. Job 1.
41. Isa 14:12.
42. Luke 10:18.
43. Wis 1:13.
44. John 5:17.
45. Luke 4:19.
46. Eph 6:12.

the voices of all the prophets, saying to the bound, "Go out," and to those who are in darkness, "Look around you."

4. If you want to hear Ezekiel, the son of man, preaching in captivity, understand him as a type of Christ. "Behold it came to pass," he says, "in the thirtieth year, in the fourth month, in the fifth day of the month, I was in captivity by the river Chebar, and the heavens were opened."[47] By the river Chebar, when he was thirty years old, Ezekiel saw the heavens opened. And the Lord Jesus Christ was beginning his ministry, about thirty years old, by the river Jordan, when the heavens were opened.[48] Ezekiel is addressed "son of man" throughout his prophecies. But who is the son of man, if not my Lord Jesus Christ? The heretics will answer me that his birth is delusory, an apparition. Why, then, was he called "son of man"? I claim that he was the son of man, because he who assumed human sufferings had to undergo birth before suffering. For he could not have undergone human feelings, words, customs, the cross, and death, if he had not experienced a human beginning. Those who take away his birth take away his passion. To put it simply, for them Jesus was not crucified. Now you do, in fact, confess the cross, and you do not blush to preach him crucified even though it is a scandal to the Jews and foolishness to the Gentiles,[49] and a scandal more on account of death than on account of suffering. Nonetheless, you are ashamed to confess his birth. It is certainly no greater scandal for Jesus to have been born than for him to have died. If you are going to allow a scandal in the Christian faith, why do you fear the lesser, when you are bold to proclaim the greater? You have all the less reason to because we do not believe his birth to be from man and a woman sleeping together,[50] but as the prophet so eloquently said: "Behold, a virgin shall conceive in her womb, and bear a son, and you shall call his name Emmanuel."[51] "Emmanuel" is not just a name; it also signifies the thing itself. At Jesus' advent we can say, "The Lord is with us."[52]

Thus it is not by chance that Ezekiel prophesied in his thirtieth year; even his name is a figure of Christ. "Ezekiel" means "power of God," but no one is the power of God, except Jesus Christ. Also it is written that he was the son of Buzi, which means "held in contempt." If you encounter the heretics and hear them rejecting the Creator, counting him for

47. Ezek 1:1.
48. Luke 3:21, 23.
49. Cf. 1 Cor 1:23.
50. Wis 7:2.
51. Isa 7:14.
52. Matt 1:23.

naught, even indicting him of crimes, you will see that my Lord Jesus Christ is the son of the one who is, in their opinion, a most contemptible Creator. What if someone should object, someone who does not want us to interpret the prophecy in a way that makes it relevant to us? I would ask that person why it is in fact recorded in scripture that, in the thirtieth year of Ezekiel's life, the heavens were opened and he saw those visions that are contained in his book. What difference does the number of years make to me, except this, that I learn that in their thirtieth years the heavens were opened to both the Savior and the prophet, and, comparing spiritual things to spiritual, I recognize that all of the things that are written are words of the same God? Indeed "words of the wise are as goads, and like nails fastened deeply, since they are given as collections by one shepherd."[53]

I am also investigating insofar as I am capable the meaning of "in the fourth month on the fifth day of the month." Pray to God that I may be able to understand just what his scriptures mean. The Jews are just beginning a new year [with Rosh Hashana in the fall, according to the postbiblical Jewish calendar], and their first month is counted from the beginning of the new year. Nevertheless, the Passover is celebrated at the new year according to a different calendar—"This will be for you the beginning of months of the months of the year."[54] From the present Jewish new year, count four months with me and realize that Jesus was born in the fourth month of the new year. It is, after all, in the month called January by the Romans that we celebrate the baptism of Jesus. This is the fourth month of the new year according to the Hebrew calculation! In addition, Jesus assumed a body consisting of the four elements of the world, and also received the human senses. That may be why the vision was observed in the fourth month and in the fifth day of the month.

5. *"And I was in the midst of captivity."*[55] The words "and I was in the midst of captivity" are, it seems to me, spoken ironically. "Even I," as if a prophet should say in history, "Even I, who took no part in the sin of the people, I was in the midst of captivity." By the same token, allegorically, Christ could say, "even I came to a place of captivity, I came to those limits, where I served, where I was detained as a captive." This is the way our Savior speaks in the persona of the prophets. He is indignant at those of us who think that we believe in him. He says indeed to his

53. Eccl 12:11.
54. Exod 12:2.
55. Ezek 1:1.

Father: "What usefulness is there in my blood, when I am descending into corruption? Can the dust ever confess to you, or proclaim your truth?"[56] I find also another voice in the same way, which in the role of our Savior speaks by a prophet who sought souls full of righteousness, full of divine interpretations, full of holy fruits, who sought the true grapes on the true vine[57] but found instead all kinds of sinners, barren of good works. He therefore said: "Woe is me because I am made like one who gathers stubble in the harvest, and stalks in the vintage, which do not even have the first grapes that ought to be eaten."[58] Woe is me. The voice that said "woe is me" is not the firstborn of all creation;[59] it is not the voice of divinity, but of the human soul that he assumed. Consequently, there follows: "Woe is me, my soul, because it has perished returning to the earth, and it is not possible for it to improve among men. All are judged in blood, each one sorely distresses his neighbor."[60] These things are called to mind by the prophet's saying, "And I was in the midst of captivity by the river Chebar," which is interpreted "heaviness." But the river of this world weighs heavily, as it says elsewhere in a sacred way. According to the simple, this narrates history, but to those who really hear the scriptures spiritually, it signifies the soul, which encounters storms in this life: "By the waters of Babylon there we sat down and wept when we remembered Zion, in the willows in the midst of it we hung up our musical instruments, because there they who had taken us captive asked us the words of songs."[61] These are the rivers of Babylon, beside which we sit and remember our heavenly country. They wail and weep, where they hung up their musical instruments, in the willows of the law and the mysteries of God. It is written in a certain book that all who believe receive a willow crown,[62] and in Isaiah it is said: "It has arisen as hay in the midst of water, and a willow beside flowing water."[63] In addition, in the feast of God, when tabernacles are built, willow branches constitute the frame for the tabernacle.[64]

6. *"Beside the river Chebar"*—beside this most heavy river, the world— *"And the heavens were opened."* The heavens were closed, and at the

56. Ps 29:19.
57. John 15:1–5.
58. Mic 7:1.
59. 1 Cor 1:15.
60. Mic 7:2.
61. Ps 136:1–3.
62. *Her. Sim.* 8.2.1.
63. Isa 44:4.
64. Cf. Lev 23:40.

Christ's appearance they were opened. When they were drawn back, the Holy Spirit came upon him in the form of a dove.[65] For it could not be with us, unless first it descended to the sharer of its nature [the incarnate Christ]. Jesus ascended on high, led captivity captive, received gifts for men. He who descended is he who ascended through all the heavens that all things might be fulfilled. And he gave some to be apostles, others prophets, other evangelists, others pastors and teachers for the perfection of the saints.[66]

7. *"The heavens were opened."* It was not enough for one heaven to be opened; many were opened, so that angels descended not from one, but from all the heavens to those who were to be saved, the angels who ascended and descended upon the son of man,[67] and they came to him and ministered to him.[68] However, the angels descended, because Christ had already descended, fearing to descend before the Lord of powers [= Lord of Hosts][69] had obtained beforehand every power and every thing. However, when they saw the prince of the heavenly host[70] sojourning in earthly places, then they entered by the open way following their lord and being subject to his will who distributed them as guardians of believers in his name.

You, who yesterday were under a demon, are today under an angel. "Do not," the Lord says, "despise one of the least of these" who are in the church. "Truly I say to you, that in heaven their angels always behold the face of my Father who is in heaven."[71] The angels serve you for your salvation; they are dedicated to the ministry of the Son of God and say among themselves: "If he descended, and descended in the body, if he had taken upon himself mortal flesh, and endured the cross, and died for men, shall we stay quietly, shall we spare ourselves? See! let all of us angels descend from heaven." That is why a multitude of the heavenly host were glorifying and praising God when Christ was born.[72] All things are full of angels. Come, angel, sustain with a word one converted from original error from the teaching of demons, from wickedness speaking in depth,[73] and, while sustaining him, as a good physician keep

65. Matt 3:16.
66. Ps 66:19; Eph 4:10–12.
67. John 1:15.
68. Matt 4:11.
69. Ps 47:9.
70. Josh 5:14.
71. Matt 18:10.
72. Luke 2:13.
73. Ps 72:8.

him healthy and train him. He is a baby.[74] Today he is born, an old man becoming a child again. Uphold him by bestowing on him the baptism of second birth[75] and summon your companions in ministry, so that such persons who were once deceived you may now instruct in the faith. "There is greater joy in heaven over one sinner who does penance than over ninety-nine righteous who have no need to do penance."[76] All creation exults, and those who are being saved rejoice together and applaud. For "with earnest expectation the creation awaits the revelation of the sons of God."[77]

Notwithstanding that those who say that the apostolic scriptures have been interpolated do not wish to admit in their books words by which Christ can be proved to be creator, nonetheless the whole creation awaits the sons of God, for them to be freed from sin, snatched from the devil's hand, and regenerated by Christ. Surely this is the time for us to touch some of these things where we are now. The prophet did not see a vision, but visions of God. Why did he see not one, but many visions? Hear the Lord promising and saying, "I have multiplied visions."[78]

8. *"On the fifth day of the month."* This is the fifth year of the captivity of King Jehoiachin. In the thirtieth year of Ezekiel's life, and in the fifth of the captivity of Johoiachin,[79] a prophet was sent to the Jews. It is not as if the most merciful Father were inattentive; he did not long leave the people unwarned. How much time went by? Five years since they began to serve as captives. At once the Holy Spirit descended; it opened the heavens, so that those who were oppressed by the yoke of captivity could see those things that were seen by the prophet. When, indeed, he said, "The heavens were opened," in some way they themselves perceived with the eyes of the heart what he himself saw also with the eyes of the flesh.

9. *"And the word of the Lord came to Ezekiel the son of Buzi, a priest."* The word of God who was in the beginning with God the Father[80] is God the Word, the word who makes those who believe gods.[81] If then he says that those to whom the word of God comes are gods, and scripture is not to be contradicted, all who receive the word of God are gods. Ezekiel

74. 1 Cor 3:1.
75. Titus 3:5.
76. Luke 15:7.
77. Rom 8:19.
78. Hos 12:10.
79. Ezek 1:2.
80. John 1:1.
81. John 10:35.

also was a god, because the word of God came to him: "I have said, 'You are gods, and all of you sons of the most high.' But truly you die as men, and you fall as one of the princes."[82] Where do you have such a promise in the New Testament? If it is appropriate to make distinctions in such a matter, and to say that there are gods who differ among themselves—even to suggest such a thing is, of course, impious, except when using language anagogically as we do—I can boldly assert that humanity is portrayed more favorably in the Old Testament than in the New. "I have said, 'You are gods, and all of you sons of the most high.'" It does not say, "Some of you are gods, and some of you are not," but, in fact, "you are all gods."

Nevertheless, if you sin, listen to what follows: "But truly you die as men." This is not the fault of the one who calls to salvation; he who invites us to be gods and to acquire a heavenly nature is not the cause of death. Rather, our sin and our crime are responsible for the words, "but truly you die as men and fall as one of the princes." There were many princes, and one of them fell. This is he of whom it is written in Genesis, "Behold Adam is made," not like us, but "like one of us."[83] Therefore, when Adam fell, he became like one.

10. *"And the word of God came to Ezekiel, the son of Buzi."* If you wish to understand this phrase as referring to the Savior, do not hesitate; that is its allegorical sense. The word of God came to him who was born of a virgin, and that is the man, the word always remaining in the Father,[84] so that the two might be made one,[85] and the man, whom he assumed in a mysterious way for salvation of all of humanity, would be associated with his divinity and the nature of the only begotten of God. *"The word of God came to Ezekiel, the son of Buzi, a priest, in the land of the Chaldeans."* The Chaldeans dispute concerning celestial events and cast horoscopes. "In the land of the Chaldeans" means, then, of those who take away fate, of those who explain the causes of everything on the basis of the revolution of the stars. Now this error, this perversity of mind, is signified figuratively by the land of the Chaldeans. *"In the land of the Chaldeans by the river Chebar. And the hand of God came upon me."* Both the Lord's word and his hand came to the prophet so that he might be adorned by both deeds and words. *"And I saw visions."* I skip over some things, as is appropriate, given the short time at my disposal.

---

82. Ps 81:67.
83. Gen 3:22.
84. Cf. John 1:1.
85. Cf. Eph 2:12.

Consequently, those things that I do say must suffice, even though I shall only take a tiny sip from the fullness of the vision.

10. *"I looked and, behold, a destructive wind had come from the north."* Consider diligently the number of things that are said: (1) A rising, or destructive, wind came from the north; (2) *"and great clouds were in it,* (3) *and splendor in its circuit,* (4) *and a blazing fire,* (5) *and in its midst like a vision of amber in the midst of the fire,* (6) *and light in it,"* (7) after this the likeness of four living creatures and a vision of them and a narration of the vision, and (8) *"and in the midst of the living creatures like coals of fire."* Who can interpret each of these things?

Who has that capacity for the Spirit of God that would enable him to elucidate these mysteries? Before they make accusations, those who accuse the Creator, the God of the prophets, ought first to understand what the prophets said. It is obvious that someone who makes a true accusation must know what he is talking about. If, in fact, the heretics are not even close to a divine understanding, how can they rationally accuse on the basis of what, we are convinced, is ignorance? Let them learn the meaning of this vision. First appears a destructive wind. Second, there are great clouds in the destructive wind. Third, there is splendor in the circuit of the destructive wind. Fourth, there is a blazing fire. Fifth, in its midst there is something like a vision of amber; this must be in the midst of the fire. Sixth, there is splendor in the amber.

I cheerfully confess that this sentence is said by a wise and faithful man, whom I often admire, for to speak truly of God is dangerous. Those things, indeed, that are said falsely about God are not so dangerous as those things that are true. If true statements are uttered inopportunely, they endanger the one who is speaking. A pearl is genuine, but if it is thrown to swine, it is trodden under their feet.[86] To illustrate, let us take an example from our common life. These gatherings, not just in Aelia [Jerusalem], not just in Rome or in Alexandria, but in all cities, resemble a net that holds all kinds of fish.[87] Not all the fish found in it can be good, so, of course, the Savior says: "When you take them out, and are seated on the shore, store those that are good in your bag, but throw away those that are bad."[88] It is thus necessary in the net of the whole church for there to be both good and bad. If the net, on the other hand, is interpreted to mean the world, what do we leave in God's judgment? According to another parable, both wheat and chaff are

86. Matt 7:6.
87. Matt 13:47.
88. Cf. Matt 13:48; John 21:11.

contained on one threshing floor, when the wheat is gathered into Christ's granary, and the chaff is separated by him "whose threshing fan is in his hand, and he shall cleanse his threshing floor, and he shall gather the wheat into the granary, but he shall truly consume the chaff with unquenchable fire."[89] Neither in this case do I hold that the threshing floor is the world, but rather that it is the congregation of Christian people. Just as one threshing floor is described, full of wheat and chaff, which is neither all wheat, nor, again, all chaff, so in the earthly churches there is some wheat, and there is some chaff. Certainly the wheat does not cause itself to be there, nor does the chaff, nor, for that matter, does either chaff or wheat choose to be such. Nevertheless, it is genuinely in your power to choose whether you will be chaff or wheat. These things ought to teach us that, whenever someone in our congregations sees a sinner, he should not be scandalized and say: "Look, a sinner is in the congregation of the saints! If this is permitted, if this is allowed, why may not I sin too?" While we are in the present age, that is, in the threshing floor and in the net, both good and evil are contained in it. When Christ comes, he will make a distinction, and that will be fulfilled which was said by the Apostle: "All of us must appear before the judgment seat of Christ, that each one may receive what is appropriate according to what he has done in the body, either good or ill."[90] In this prologue the soul is said to be hesitant about the interpretations of the visions and of two minds concerning which to keep silent about, which to mention, which to leave lightly touched, which ought to be more openly and which ought to be more obscurely expounded, so that we may, nonetheless, accomplish what we wish.

12. First, then, appears a destructive wind. What we said a little earlier, that our God is a consuming fire,[91] we shall repeat, adding that it is consistent with this testimony. How is God presented as a destructive wind? God is spirit [= wind][92] and appears as a destructive wind. What does he destroy in me and in my soul, if he is justly called a destructive wind? Evils assuredly. I am then aware of his goodness, because he has taken such things from me. Nor is there actually any imaginable limit to the resulting blessedness, when we are freed from such evils, because sinlessness is the beginning of happiness. Along the same line, in Jeremiah it is written (clearly all things written in the prophets vindicate

89. Luke 3:17.
90. 1 Cor 5:10.
91. Heb 12:29.
92. John 4:42.

God's mercy): "Behold I have given my words in your mouth. Behold I have set you over nations and kingdoms to uproot, and to undermine, and to destroy, and to raze, and to plant."[93]

God displays his kindness in giving words for uprooting. What, indeed, is it that must be rooted out and overthrown? It is any evil rooted in the soul, any heretical doctrine. These are what the prophetic word uproots and overthrows. I only wish that I might receive such a word, a word that would uproot the seeds of heretics and the teaching flowing from the spring of the devil, a word that would remove from the soul of one now first entering the church the weed of idolatry! "I have given my words in your mouth. Behold I have set you to uproot and to undermine." Plainly this is so that, if there is anything shoddily built, it may be demolished. How I wish I could demolish whatever Marcion has built in the ears of those deceived, to uproot, and to undermine and to destroy such things, as Jacob destroyed the idols.[94]

It is still necessary to destroy and to build; the heretics boldly destroy and subvert so much, and they turn away inattentive ears from the word that edifies and nourishes. Nor, for that matter, do they even wish to consider why it is that certain things that appear unpleasant to begin with afterwards appear pleasant. Why do we call them to mind now? So that it will be plain that God's word overthrows evil things, and builds excellent things, it uproots vices, like a good farmer, so that in the cleared field a fertile harvest of virtues may arise. This is enough about the destructive wind.

He first saw the destructive wind; then he saw a great cloud in it. When you are cleansed by the destructive wind so much that all evil is borne away from you, and that which is worthless in your soul is extracted, then you begin to enjoy the great clouds that are in the destructive wind. These clouds resemble the clouds that we read of in the gospel, from which issued a voice: "This is my beloved Son, in whom I am well pleased."[95] A destructive wind, then a great cloud in it, afterward a most splendid light in its circuit. Sin is taken away from you. A great cloud is given to you, so that it may drop rain upon your vineyard, according to another scripture that says, "I shall order the clouds, that they not rain upon that vineyard."[96] If, in this case, the cloud is ordered not to rain on a bad vineyard, by the same token, if you are a good vineyard, the cloud will undoubtedly rain upon you.

93. Jer 1:10.
94. Cf. Gen 35:5.
95. Luke 3:21.
96. Isa 5:6.

13. *"And brightness in its circuit. Then a blazing fire in the midst of it like a vision of amber."* God takes away evils from us in two ways, by spirit [= wind] and by fire. If we are good and attend to God's precepts, and if we study his words, he takes away our evils with spirit, according to the scripture: "If by the spirit you put to death the things of the flesh, you shall live."[97] But if the spirit does not actually take away evils from us, we must be purged with fire. Therefore, observe carefully the conjunction of details. The first conjunction is of the wind and the cloud; the second is of the wind and the light; the third of the amber and the brightness. The unpleasant details become more pleasant in context. If a wind arises, clouds immediately follow. If fire appears, light is linked with it. If amber precedes, there is brightness in its circuit. Indeed, we must be most harshly tried with fire as gold in the furnace and as amber.[98] And in this prophet whom we now expound, we have the Lord sitting in the midst of Jerusalem and smelting those who have become silver mixed with bronze, and iron, and tin, and lead and in a querulous voice pleading with those who have in themselves a mixture of base matter. "You have all," he says, "become one base mixture, on this account I shall remove you from out of the midst of Jerusalem."[99] When to the creation of God, which was originally good, we added, from our evil, vices and passions, then with the silver and gold we mix brass, tin, and lead. This makes a fire necessary for purgation. That is why we must take great care that, when we come to that fire, we may pass safely through it, like gold, silver, and precious stones,[100] or such things as, without fire, are adulterated. Let us not be consumed by the fire, but tested!

14. *"Behold, a destructive wind came out of the north."* There is a reason why this destructive wind came out of the north and later returned. It is, in fact, from the north that evils are kindled upon the inhabitants of the earth. The north wind, the one we call Boreas, is the most violent, and of the four corners of the sky, from which the winds are said to blow, the north is the source of the coldest and harshest. What is written in Numbers[101] concerning the order of the camps in Israel is consistent with this symbolism. Dan is at the farthest camp to the north. Judah is at the first camp to the east, and next to him is Reuben, afterwards Ephraem toward the west, and Dan, as we have said, on the northern edge.

97. Rom 8:13.
98. Wis 3:6.
99. Ezek 22:18–19.
100. 1 Cor 3:12.
101. Num 2.

Similarly a pot that is set over a fire is described[102] that is enkindled from the north. The north means figuratively an adverse power, which is Satan, who is truly the harshest wind.[103] Thus a destructive wind comes from the north, and great clouds in it. We have explained how vices are from it. *"And splendor in its circuit, and a blazing fire."* It could have said "consuming fire," but the Bible hesitates to name unpleasant things, and to describe its function, it speaks of splendor instead of penal force.

15. *"And in its midst as the likeness of four living creatures, this is the vision of them. There is a likeness of a man among them. And four faces of one, and four wings of one, and their legs were straight, and their feet were winged."*[104] Cherubim are interpreted "multitude of science," and whoever is full of science is made a cherub, whom God directs. But what do the four faces mean? Those who are to be saved bend the knee to the Lord Jesus and are enumerated threefold by the Apostle "that at the name of Jesus everything should bow, things heavenly, things earthly, and things infernal."[105] And those who are subject say: "Is not my soul subject to God? With him is my salvation,"[106] "and he must reign until he puts all his enemies under his feet."[107] What is the fourth? Heavenly, earthly, and infernal, these are just three. Obviously this: "Praise the Lord O heavens of heavens and let the waters which are above the heavens praise the name of the Lord."[108] All these things are directed by God, and are led by his majesty.

16. *"Wherever the wind went, the living creatures also went."* These living creatures have the likeness on them of a man, even though there are four faces. It is not said in the beginning that they have four faces, but that a human face stands out among four faces and has the chief position. As it is described, each is said to have a human face, and the face of a lion on the right among the four parts, the face of a calf on the left among the four, and the face of an eagle behind the four. Let us see therefore whether it signifies the tripartite soul, a matter of disputation in the opinions of others, in such a way that courage presides over the other quarters. The man stands for its rational part, the lion for its irascible part, the calf for its concupiscible part. Truly the spirit that presides for its aid is not to the right, like the man, or the lion, or to the

102. Cf. Jer 1:13.
103. Cf. Sir 43:20.
104. Ps 79:2.
105. Phil 2:10.
106. Ps 61:2.
107. 1 Cor 15:25.
108. Ps 148:4–5.

left, like the calf, but is placed above all three faces. The eagle, indeed, is named in another place. This means that the eagle stands for the governing spirit of the soul—I say the spirit of man who is in him. And thus all things are guided by the will of God, heavenly, earthly, and infernal, and those that are above the heavens. Let us all become cherubim[109] under God's feet, to whom wheels are attached, which follow under them. Let us not be turned under wheels ourselves, nor under the dominion of the age and such things, because now we have been freed by Christ's passion from affairs of the world. *"And wheels in the middle of wheels."*[110] If you consider how all things are resolved by contrary things occurring, either in those who are thought to err, or in those who are said to be alien to error, you see how there are wheels in the middle of wheels. For God rules over all and turns all things whatever way he wishes, in Christ Jesus, to whom belong glory and might for ever and ever. Amen.[111]

SUGGESTED READINGS

Bettencourt, Stephanus Tavares. *Doctrina ascetica Origenis, seu quid sit ratione animae humanae cum daemonibus.* Rome: Studia Anselmiana, 1945.

Bornemann, Friedrich Wilhelm Bernhard. *In investiganda monachatus origine quibus de causis ratio habenda est Origenis.* Göttingen: Vandenhoeck & Ruprecht, 1885.

Brown, Peter. *The Body and Society: Men, Women and Sexual Renunciation in Early Christianity.* New York: Columbia University Press, 1988.

Crouzel, Henri. *Origen.* Tr. A. S. Worrall. San Francisco: Harper & Row, 1989.

———. "Origène, précurseur du monachisme." In *Théologie de la vie monastique: études sur la tradition patristique,* 15–38. Paris: Aubier, 1961.

———. *Virginité et marriage chez Origène.* Bruges, Belg.: Desclée de Brouwer, 1963.

Völker, Walther. *Das Vollkommenheitsideal des Origenes: eine Untersuchung zur Geschichte der Frömmigkeit und zu den Anfängen christlicher Mystik.* Tübingen: J. C. B. Mohr (Paul Siebeck), 1931.

109. Ezek 10:9.
110. Ezek 1:16.
111. 1 Pet 4:11.

On Hermits
and Desert Dwellers

INTRODUCTION

The immense body of Syriac ecclesiastical literature that has come down to us attests to the vigorous catechetical, exegetical, and liturgical activity of Syriac-speaking Christianity. Beginning in the fourth century, Syriac authors created vast collections of both poetry and prose that testify to the beauty and vitality of the Syriac-speaking church. The metrical homily entitled "On Hermits and Desert Dwellers" takes up a pervasive theme in Syriac-speaking Christianity, namely, asceticism and the ascetic ideal as it is lived in the church.

Although both the title and closing lines of the homily ascribe the work to Ephrem the Syrian, Dom Edmund Beck, editor of the critical Syriac edition of the text, has rejected this attribution. In the eschatological perspective of the homily, the soul of the ascetic is spoken of as coming into full possession of the kingdom immediately upon death (cf. lines 304, 312, 328). However, in the authentic writings of Ephrem, full possession of the kingdom is only possible after the general resurrection (cf. line 351). The presence of this ambiguous eschatology, the homily's glorification of the deaths of the ascetics, and its generally panegyrical tone support Dom Beck's negative verdict. The genuine writings of Ephrem encourage an ascetic moderation and tolerance that would be difficult to reconcile with the excessive practices that the homily praises. One of Ephrem's more concise statements on the subject comes from the collection called *Contra Haereses* (45, 9–10), where he observes: "The law is divided into three parts for us: it allows for family, continence, and virginity; possessions, renunciation, and perfection."

Syriac authors distinguished between two categories of religious poetry: the *mīmrā* (plural *mīmrē*) and the *madrāshā* (plural *madrāshē*). When the strophes of a poem were gathered into stanzas, it was called a *madrāshā*, or "hymn." A freer arrangement of lines not gathered into stanzas was known as a *mīmrā*, or "metrical homily." The *mīmrē* of St. Ephrem the Syrian employ the pattern of 7 + 7 syllables per line, making him the eponymous ancestor of this widely copied syllabic pattern, which is identified by Syrian authors as *ēphrīmayā*.[1] The anonymous author of the metrical homily "On Hermits and Desert Dwellers" has employed this 7+7 syllabic pattern popularized by Ephrem.

The homily describes a transitional phase in the history of Syriac-speaking asceticism, away from a time when the ascetic ideal was lived within society and did not require flight from the world. Aphrahat the Persian Sage and Ephrem the Syrian are the two most famous witnesses to this early period of native Syrian asceticism referred to by scholars as "proto-monastic."[2] Neither flight from society nor excessive feats of mortification characterized this initial phase. Rather, early Syrian ascetics took either temporary or permanent vows of celibacy, while maintaining active roles in the life of the church. By the middle of the fourth century, western Syria began to feel the impact of Egyptian monasticism with its emphasis on the necessity of flight from the world and its pursuit of the solitary ascetic ideal. This fact would exercise a fundamental influence on the course of native Syriac-speaking asceticism.

The homily takes up a theme that is common in Syriac ascetic literature of this later period: radical and utter "renunciation" or "self-emptying" (Syr. *msharqūthā*), as Christ "emptied himself" (Syr. *nafsheh msharreq*) and took on the form of a slave (Phil 2:7). The heroes of this new model of ascetic life were Elijah and John the Baptist, who emptied themselves of the world to live solitary lives of mortification in the desert (cf. lines 37–44, 429–36). Although the homily's emphasis on escape from the world and its unreserved praise of ascetic excess have more in common with the Evagrian-inspired asceticism of Egypt than with the original spirit of native Syrian asceticism, this new and rigorous model of Christian perfection would irrevocably influence and alter the

---

1. Other prominent Syriac literary figures lent their names to the more successful syllable patterns. A pattern of five and five syllables is traditionally associated with the author Balâi, and hence five plus five meter is known to Syrians as *balâinayâ*. Likewise, a pattern of twelve plus twelve syllables, a meter popularized by Jacob of Serug, is known as *yaqabâyâ*. See chap. 1 above.

2. E. Beck, "Asketentum und Monchtum bei Ephraem," *OCA* 153 (1958) 341–62.

earlier, more moderate Syrian impulse. Here we view the beginnings of the tradition of astounding acts of mortification and self-denial with which asceticism in the Syriac-speaking east would come to be associated.

The text presented here is the version of the critical edition of Dom Edmund Beck in *Des Heiligen Ephraem des Syrers Sermones IV*. CSCO 334/Scr. Syr. 148. Louvain, Belg.: 1973. The abbreviated form of the full Syriac title is *mīmrā d-ʿal īhīdāyē w-madbrāyē wʿabīlē*.

TRANSLATION

Again, by the same Holy Mar Ephrem

A Homily

On Hermits and Desert Dwellers and Mourners,
Those Who Live on the Mountains and Plains,
in the Crags and Burrows of the Earth,
and Who Empty Themselves of Everything in This World

1   Whoever desires the things to come is not overwhelmed by what he sees,
so he will not burn the weeds on account of money.[3]

5   The discerning disdain everything, and give no thought to the world.
They wander through deserts and desolate places so they will not be stained by sin.

9   Those who are far wiser than the greedy who have wealth
leave their wealth to the greedy, for their treasure is in heaven.

13   They despised everything that distracts from the works of perfection,
and they loved the Lord of everything, who possesses everything.

17   No one who loved possessions has gone up to heaven in the flesh,
that the discerning should imitate them, and leave everything that does not last.

21   Those who emptied themselves are the ones who went up in the flesh,

3. Cf. Matt 13:30.

those who despised greed and deadened their bodies on earth,[4] so
they would not be stained by sin.

25   Justice placed both sides on the scale of truth;
it weighed the greedy down to earth,[5] while those who emptied
themselves flew to heaven.

29   That generation in Noah's days that was depraved and loved
money,
a flood killed them in anger, because they angered God.

33   Because Enoch pleased God,[6] he was taken off to paradise;
but dogs devoured Ahab who loved greed,[7] just as it is written.[8]

37   Elijah, who wandered in the desert, went up to heaven in a chariot;[9]
but Herod, who loved wealth, his wealth came to an end at death.

41   And John, who lived in the desert, became great in the kingdom.[10]
The discerning look to these, and choose the glorious.

45   The way of life of their companions lets them soar to heaven.
[They knew how] to gain their lives,[11] though to the world they
were dead,

49   in their death to worldly desire, so [God] would give them the life to
come.
They are a good example for us to follow after,

53   to fly and meet them on wings of renunciation.
They are people, clothed in flesh like us,

57   and for love of God, they went out to the desert like animals.
They have relatives and families, houses, property, and possessions,[12]

61   but they gave no thought to them, in order to set out for the
kingdom on high.

4. Cf. lines 247 and 463.
5. Cf. line 133.
6. Cf. Heb 11:5.
7. The author plays on the name "Ahab" and the Syriac verb *āheb*, "he loved." In
Syriac the phrase reads: "W-*āḥab dāḥeb*."
8. An apparent conflation of 1 Kgs 22:38 and 2 Kgs 9:36.
9. 2 Kgs 2:11.
10. Luke 7:28.
11. Cf. Matt 10:39.
12. Cf. line 378.

Those who wander in empty wastes, so they will not be stained by
   sin,

65   roam like animals, to be worthy of the joyous wedding feast.
     Those who graze on grass and roots instead of delicacies,[13]

69   and in place of lofty dwellings, live in lowly caves.
     Like birds they go up to live on rocky ledges.

73   It was about them the prophet proclaimed: "Let them cry out from
       the mountain tops."[14]
     They stretch out on the bare earth, rather than on beds,

77   and they rest their heads on rocks, rather than on soft cushions.
     They put the herbs they eat for food

81   on their knees, instead of on tables at meal-time.
     Instead of wine, they drink water;

85   instead of ointments and creams on their bodies, there is squalor.
     Their bodies become dark for the love of Christ.[15]

89   They substitute burlap and nakedness for silk;
     and instead of fine sandals, they walk barefoot.[16]

93   They see only animals instead of people;
     and instead of the families they left behind, angels come down to
       them.

97   Their bodies are temples of the Spirit,[17] their minds are churches;
     their prayer is pure incense, and their tears are fragrant smoke.[18]

101 Their groaning is like the oblation; their psalmody [like] joyous
       melodies.
     Their sighs are pearls, and their modesty is like beryl.

105 When their tears stream down, they banish harm from the earth;
     and when their petition is raised, it fills the world with assistance.

109 None of them is concerned about his survival, for they live in hope
       every moment.

13. Cf. line 385.
14. Isa 42:11.
15. Or: "Their bodies become dark for love of ointment." Cf. CSCO 335,23.
16. Cf. Matt 6:25; also lines 341–42.
17. Cf. 1 Cor 6:19.
18. Cf. lines 489–96.

And none of them is concerned about clothes,[19] for they are clothed in faith.

113 None of them is concerned about money, for their treasure is laid up in heaven.
And none of them is occupied with possessions, for their hope is entirely in paradise.

117 None of them bickers with another, for they possess nothing in creation.[20]
And no one quarrels with his neighbor, for love dwells with them.

121 None of them despises his companion, for there is perfect harmony among them.
Nor does one of them envy another, for they are not greedy for wealth.

125 None of them shows anger toward another, since they do not argue over possessions;
no one quarrels with his brother, for they do not care about property.

129 They are like spirits, though among mortals;
and like angels in heaven, though among men of earth.

133 They do not burden their bodies with love of the world and its possessions;
they did not forsake their desires to be choked by money.

137 They regard gold as garbage, and wealth as nothing;[21]
they forsook pleasure, and yoked their bodies to fasting.

141 They trampled Satan's head, and he cannot snare them in his nets.
And they shattered the yoke of sin, for it had no power over their bodies.

145 Satan is slain before them, for he could not slay them with what is his;
they subdued him and escaped, for they were not entangled in his snares.

19. Cf. Luke 12:22.
20. Or: "since they possess nothing in the wild."
21. Cf. Phil 3:8.

149 He cries out from their torments, for they escaped his traps;
     he moans from their tortures, for they torture him with their deeds.

153 He is tormented by them all the time, for they foil him with daily
        vigils;
     they humiliated him, and made themselves strong, for he is tor-
        mented by their prayers.

157 The desert, frightful in its desolation, became a city of deliverance
        for them,[22]
     where their harps resound, and where they are preserved from
        harm.

161 Desolation fled from the desert, for sons of the kingdom dwell
        there;
     it became like a great city with the sound of psalmody from their
        mouths.

165 Wherever one of them goes, peace reigns round about him,
     for an army of angels encamps with the one who loves God.

169 Though he lives by himself as far as the body can observe,
     in his heart he is secretly allied to the assemblies of the sons above.

173 When two dwell together, there is great love there;
     though they are two physically, they are of one will.

177 And when there are three, harmony abides there,
     for there is no division or deceit, only love and tranquility.

181 Wherever four dwell, the Holy Spirit dwells with them,
     for they are like one body, a spotless temple for God.

185 The commandment is fulfilled in them which our Lord taught in his
        Gospel:
     "Whoever wishes to find himself, will do away with himself here"
        with afflictions.[23]

189 They greatly afflict their bodies, not because they do not love their
        bodies,
     rather, they want to bring their bodies to Eden in glory.

---

22. The image of the desert turned into a city presents a striking parallel to a remark
in chapter 14 of Athanasius's *Vit. Ant.*: "And so, from then on, there were monasteries
in the mountains, and the desert was made a city by monks, who left their own people
and registered themselves for citizenship in heaven." See also line 163.
23. Cf. Luke 9:24; 17:33.

193 Winter and summer they bear the burden of their afflictions;
   in winter, cold and frost, and in summer, parching heat.

197 There is the one who has decided not to take shelter,
   and entirely entrusts himself [to God] against all dangers.

201 Another has vowed not to see people;
   he goes out to the desert waste to be there by himself.

205 They set out on the way with clear judgment, to be preserved from
   everything;
   this is why they love to be alone in the desert.

209 Since each of them is alone, they are preserved from every evil;
   no one can harm them with so much as a word.

213 Their mouth refrains from derision, and is filled every hour with
   praise;
   they refrain from frivolous words, and recite the psalms.

217 They refrain from slander; in its place they are filled with praise.
   They refrain from all harm, and attain profit.

221 They bear the burden of their hair, and the affliction of their
   clothing;
   some put on burlap, and some, straw mats.

225 Blood flows from their feet from going barefoot every day.
   Their bodies are afflicted by the filth that covers them.

229 Wherever one of them goes, he plants his cross and it becomes [his]
   church;
   and wherever the day ends, there is the temple of his rest.

233 His table is in front of him; he sets it everywhere.
   When he has the chance, he gathers small herbs, and eats.

237 He enjoys the herbs he picked in faith;
   he leaves the rest behind, and moves on from there,

241 because he heard the saying, "Do not be anxious about tomorrow."[24]
   They have no fear of sickness, for they thirst for hardship.

245 Neither are they troubled by death, for it is rest from their labors.
   Since they have died here in their lives, they are alive there in God.

24. Matt 6:34.

249 They recall what the angel said to Daniel,
    "Go to your land, and rest from your labor."[25] They trust that death
      means rest.

253 And since temporal death means rest for the righteous,
    they are scornful of death because it is subject to them like a slave.

257 What harm did death do to Elisha who went down to Sheol?
    While deep within death's lair, he snatched a dead man from its
      mouth.[26]

261 Since they entrust their spirits and bodies alike to God,
    they are not saddened by physical hardship.

265 If a hermit becomes sick, he has no companion to look after him.
    But because he entrusted himself to God, the power of heaven
      looks after him.

269 Since there is no one to prepare food for him, or to bring it to him
      when he is sick,
    he is comforted by the Holy Spirit, regains strength, and recovers.

273 And if the end comes, and the day of his death arrives,
    and he has not relied on mortals, he is buried by angels.

277 Wherever he ends his life, there also is his grave;
    like seeds in furrows, he is kept for resurrection day.

281 And if by chance he reaches the end in a cave,
    the cave will be his grave, honoring the treasure of his bones.

285 If he reaches the end in a cavern, his bones are kept there.
    Angels descend at all times to serve at the treasure of their bones.

289 And since they live in isolation, and do not come near one other,
    wherever one of them dies, there assistance abounds.[27]

293 One of them will be in a cave when he reaches his final day;
    and there is his joyful wedding chamber which remains until the
      resurrection.

297 Another will conclude his life on rocky cliffs;
    and his bones are kept there like brilliant beryl.

25. Cf. Dan 12:13.
26. 2 Kgs 13:21.
27. A reference to the intercessory role of the relics of the saints, even if the precise location of their resting place was unknown.

301 Another will meet his end and find rest while at prayer;
    and while sighing within, his soul soared to heaven.

305 The end comes to one, and he dies, at the time of service;[28]
    and with his mouth filled with praise, he departs to find rest from
        his labor.

309 One reaches the end and finds rest while eating;
    and from a table of herbs, he is summoned to the table of life.

313 Another reaches the end and dies while leaning against something;
    and there his corpse remains to resurrection day.

317 One will be walking along, and wherever he happens to be when
        he dies,
    there he finds his rest, and escapes the suffering.

321 They are preserved in hope, that hope in which they concluded
        their labors;
    and there is no one to close their eyes or bury their bones.

325 One placed his head on a rock and rested the sleep of peace.
    Another put his head between his knees, and his soul departed for
        that place.[29]

329 There is no weeping in their wanderings, and no grieving in their
        gatherings;
    the praises of the angels above surround them on every side.

333 There is no distress in their death, nor wailing at their departing;
    for their death is the victory with which they conquer the adver-
        sary.[30]

337 There is no sadness when they are sick, nor distress when they are
        afflicted;
    for their sickness brings strength, and their hardship intensifies the
        trial.

341 They are not adorned with [fine] clothes, for their clothing is faith;
    and their graves are unknown, for paradise is their resting place.

---

28. The Syriac word *teshmeshthā* used here signifies "divine service."
29. Beck suggests that lines 325–28 are out of context here and should more likely
follow line 304.
30. In Syriac, the devil is often referred to as "the adversary" or "the slanderer."

345 They are not carried aloft on biers, for their shroud is common dust.
     The place where each of them dies serves as his bier.

349 As soon as the soul of one of them leaves his limbs,
     it is carried away to the treasury of life, and is kept until the
     resurrection.

353 Their bones are in a desolate place, which becomes a dwelling place
     of angels;
     for wherever their bones are, angels minister there.

357 For ranks upon ranks of angels are dispatched to their tombs,
     to minister at the bones of those crowned with victory.

361 They saw the world as a sea, and everyone's ship battered;
     they escaped it, lest the storm harm them.

365 They cleverly flew over it, and their ships reached port;
     the winds that were with them in the wilderness made the waves
     surge.[31]

369 When the world became enslaved by wealth, they emptied them-
     selves of it;
     because it choked on money, they treated it with contempt and
     disdain, and scoffed at it.

373 Because gold is a pit, they quickly leaped over it,
     because possessions lead the foolish astray, they had none.

377 Because the greedy plunder the lands, they left what was their own
     and went forth.
     Against all dangers, they arm themselves with truth.

381 And against all evils, they secured faith.
     When they saw the world rejoicing, they preferred mourning.[32]

385 And when they saw delicacies in the world, they fed on roots,
     so that through their temporary hardship, they would be worthy of
     eternal blessings.

389 When they saw boasting in the world, they preferred humility,
     so that through their humility, they would become worthy of the
     dignity that does not end.

31. The large number of variant readings of lines 367–68 strongly suggests that the
Syriac has been corrupted beyond recognition.
32. Cf. John 16:20.

393 And when they saw attractions in the world, they clung to pure
     fasting,
     so that through their fasting, they would acquire wings, and soar to
     heaven on them.

397 And when they saw indecency in the world, they held to chastity;[33]
     so that the chastity of their bodies would entitle them to the king-
     dom.

401 And when they saw commotion in the world, they preferred restful
     stillness;
     so the evil one could not foil their efforts with so much as a word.

405 They saw hateful deceit in the world, and see, they cling to simple
     truth,
     so that the truth would achieve confidence for them at the resur-
     rection.

409 They saw lying and treachery in the world, and they preferred
     truth,
     so their truth would bring them to the high dignity of heaven.

413 And when they saw scheming in the world, they chose simplicity;
     and the saying was fulfilled in them, just as it is written. They
     became "like children."[34]

417 They heard the saying of the apostle who spoke of himself with
     sadness, saying:
     "I am crucified to the world, and the world is crucified to me with its
     attractions."[35]

421 Faced with all these cravings, they crucified their bodies,[36]
     tormenting them every day with every manner of hardship.

425 Likewise they learned from the ancients where honor was [to be
     found] for them;
     and when they were much reviled, they achieved wisdom.

---

33. The author employs the technical term for vowed chastity, *qaddīshūthā*, or
"holiness."
34. Cf. Matt 18:3.
35. Cf. Gal 6:14 and Luke 8:14.
36. Cf. Gal 5:24.

429 They saw that Elijah never suffered any misfortune from the wil-
      derness;
      but the moment he entered civilization, mad Jezebel pursued him.[37]

433 As long as John was in the desert, the crowds went out to greet
      him.[38]
      But he no sooner entered civilization, and Herod cut off his head.[39]

437 This is why they forsook and left a world full of danger,
      and made the wilderness their dwelling until they receive their
      rewards.

441 They found two advantages in that desolate place they went out to:
      they were preserved from transgressions, and from the insults of
      men.

445 There they are protected from wickedness and from mortal greed;
      there they are protected from treachery, and from ridicule and
      envy,

449 from fraud and from offensive arrogance.
      They become companions of the angels above; indeed, they re-
      semble them.

453 The angels in heaven have nothing, and only sing glory.
      Money does not detain them from the hour of service,

457 nor does anxiety keep them from the hour of prayer.
      They bear no burdens, for their minds are illumined.

461 Fatigue does not come near them, for they are anxious for the
      reward.
      They let their bodies[40] die to the world, so it could not harm them.

465 They put their trust in heaven, and their heart is entirely there.
      Their eyes are fixed; their hands reach out there.

469 They sent their labors there, and their dignity is there.
      See, this is why they live with the apostles in the heights above.

---

37. Cf. 1 Kgs 21.
38. Luke 3:7.
39. Matt 14:10.
40. Literally "members."

473 When they kneel in prayer, they moisten the ground with their
        tears.
        And when their groaning ascends, the angels in heaven rejoice.

477 One has chosen not to lie down, and so he stays awake honorably.
        Another has chosen not to sit, and so he stands innocently.

481 One has decided that a flippant word shall never leave his mouth.
        Yet another has decided to pronounce only the text of scripture.

485 They stay very late at service, and they rise early for service.
        The whole day and night, their occupation is the service.

489 Instead of incense, which they do not have, their purity is reconcili-
        ation.
        And instead of a church building, they become temples of the Holy
        Spirit.[41]

493 Instead of altars, [they have] their minds. And as oblations, their
        prayers
        are offered to the Godhead, pleasing him at all times.

497 The wilderness that everyone fears has become a great place of
        refuge for them,
        where assistance flows from their bones to all creation.

501 Civilization, where lawlessness prevails, is sustained by their pray-
        ers.
        And the world, buried in sin, is preserved by their prayers.

505 And earth, heaving with controversy, is upheld by their prayers;
        troubled with speculation, their vigil fills it with calm.[42]

509 Blessed is the one worthy of becoming a companion of these who
        have triumphed.
        Blessed is the one who loves them, and imprints their ways on
        himself.

41. Cf. 1 Cor 6:19.
42. "Controversy" (line 505, Syr. *drāshā,*) and "speculation" (line 507, Syr. *'uqqābā*) are
the standard Syriac terms used to characterize the theological methods of the Arians
who applied the principles of intellectual inquiry to the question of the nature of God.
Ephrem would say of them: "Those who speculate about your nature go astray" (*Hymns
on Virginity*, 31.1).

513 Blessed is the one who set out with them, and completed his course
in their labors.
Blessed is the one who does not deviate from the example of their
ways.

517 Blessed is the one who is not separated from them when they
inherit their promises.[43]
Blessed is the one who perfectly completed his course like them.

521 And we, my Lord, who loved those who loved your company,
do not separate us from their ranks when they are established in
your kingdom.

525 And as we relate their struggles with love to proclaim their victories,
make us worthy to receive unending joy with them.

529 And may our entire congregation, which has enjoyed the account of
the sons of light,
find mercy on the day of judgment through their prayers. Yes and
Amen!

**The End of the Homily by Mār Ephrem
On Hermits and Those Who Have Renounced the World.**

SUGGESTED READINGS

Beck, E. "Asketentum und Mönchtum bei Ephraem." *OCA* 153 (1958) 341–62.
———, ed. *Des Heiligen Ephraem des Syrers Sermones IV.* CSCO 334/Scr. Syr. 148; CSCO 335/Scr. Syr. 149. Louvain, Belg.: CSCO, 1973.
Brock, S. "Early Syrian Asceticism." *Numen* 20 (1973) 1–19.
———. *The Luminous Eye: The Spiritual World Vision of St. Ephrem.* Kerala, India, 1985.
Vööbus, A. *A History of Asceticism in the Syrian Orient,* vol. 1, CSCO 184/Sub. 14; vol. 2, 197/Sub. 17. Louvain, Belg.: CSCO, 1958; vol. 3, CSCO 500/Sub. 81. Louvain, Belg.: CSCO, 1988.

43. Cf. Luke 24:49.

PSEUDO-MACARIUS
THE EGYPTIAN
Homily IV

INTRODUCTION

The corpus of texts that has come down to us pseudonymously as those of Macarius the Egyptian, a fourth-century monk from the Egyptian desert, dates from the last quarter of the fourth century C.E. or the first quarter of the fifth, and appears to be originally from Asia Minor and written in Greek. These monastic sermons and letters are among the most influential popular and monastic writings on asceticism in Eastern Christianity and have had wide impact in Western Christianity in both Catholic and Protestant traditions. Although contemporary scholarship has tried unsuccessfully to identify the Pseudo-Macarian corpus as part of the Messalian or Euchites heresy of the fifth century, Eastern Christian scholars have not found any heretical tendency in the texts.

The sermon translated below is from the collection called the *Spiritual Homilies*. It was selected for two reasons: first, it serves as an exemplar of many literary ascetic themes and topics and their interrelationships; second, it demonstrates that metaphor was a primary means of transformation in Christian asceticism.

"Spiritual Homily IV" presents a complex network of themes, none of which is easily separable from the others. The following listing is not in any particular order:

1. There are two major allegories in the text, one of a scriptural reference (The Wise and Foolish Virgins as an allegory of the logical senses of the soul) and the other of a narrative of the person walking through the dangers of the world. Each allegorical situation elucidates complex patterns of ascetic behavior and attitudes.

2. The theme of the soul's yearning and desire for God recurs throughout the text. Such yearning, emerging from the Platonic tradition of ascent through *eros* from physical to spiritual beauty (*Symp.* 209 a–e), extends into such suggestive metaphors as spiritual marriage, entering the heavenly nuptial chamber with the heavenly Bridegroom, and mystic communion.

3. The theme of the problematic nature of living in the world pervades the text of the homily not only in its direct description in the allegorical narrative but also in the description of biblical figures who found destruction and an evil fate when they did not follow God. The origin of this problematic living rests in the evil promulgated in the mythical history of Adam and Eve. This primordial Fall of humanity is restored, however, in the soul entering the bridal chamber with the Bridegroom.

4. The ascetic program outlined here revolves about acquiring virtue in the soul. To be clothed in God means to have been clothed in virtue, and the ascetic life moves from virtue to virtue, until perfection is achieved.

These four themes point to only a portion of the many possible strands for understanding the asceticism promulgated by the homily. The relationship and interweaving of themes, moreover, redirects and redefines their signification.

After the themes, "Spiritual Homily IV" documents the ascetic transformation through metaphor. The metaphor of the person's problematic life in the world, for example, does more than simply describe an attitude toward the world because it also engages the reader in a certain experience of it. The forest full of fire, the thorn, implanted daggers, and deep waters create and define the dangers of living in the world. The metaphor recreates and restructures the physical world it attempts to describe, so that it forms and models the experience of the world. The world no longer appears as it seems but becomes spiritually and experientially dangerous. The reader (or hearer) of the homily becomes dramatically involved, and her or his understanding and attitude toward the world are remade. The metaphor then functions as a means of entering and mastering other views of the world. Finally, the metaphor as a means of ascetic transformation allows for different levels of analysis of one experience: the world, in the above metaphor, might be explored from the reason, emotions, reactions to problems, effects of certain bad behavior, effects of certain beneficial and careful behavior, and causality, without ever needing to address these issues theoretically or discursively. The metaphor, in asceticism, enables complex patterns of thought to be presented in their most complex state.

This translation is based on the critical edition of the text by Hermann Dörries, Erich Klostermann, and Matthias Kroeger (*Die 50 Geistlichen Homilien des Makarios*. Patristische Texte und Studien 4 [Berlin: Walter de Gruyter, 1964] 25–45).

TRANSLATION

1. We who desire to achieve with great precision the Christian manner of life ought above all to manage the intellectual and discriminating parts of the soul; so that we, acquiring scrupulously the discernment of the good and the bad and always discerning the passions contrary to nature as they are led to a clean nature, might live suitably and without stumbling; and so that we, using the critical part of the soul for an eye, might be strengthened enough not to make and to be implicated in a covenant with the evil principles and in this way, having been deemed worthy of divine gifts, we become worthy of the Lord. From visible things let us receive a model, for the body is like the soul, and the things of the body are like those of the soul, and the apparent are like the hidden.

2. Just as the body has the eye as a guide and it, seeing everything, guides the body toward rectitude, suppose with me that someone is passing through places filled with woods and thorns and mud, and in which fire jumps up and daggers are implanted in the earth, and there are both cliffs and deep waters. Now, the fierce, zealous, and agile person, having the eye as a guide, passes by those rugged places with complete attentiveness, while gathering up his tunic from every place by hand and foot lest it be ripped in the woods and thorns or disappear under the mud or be cut by the daggers. And the eye, because it is its light, guides the whole body lest it fall over cliffs, or drown in water, or be damaged by some rugged ground. The fierce and sagacious and totally sober person who passes by, girding up his tunic, being guided straightway by his eyes both protects himself unharmed and preserves the tunic of his garment unburnt and untorn. If one should be lazy, timid, careless, heavy, and frivolous while passing through such places, his tunic, flowing around on this side and that, is torn in the woods and thorns, or is burned by the fire because he does not courageously gather

his garment from every side, or is cut up by the implanted swords, or is soiled by the mire, and in general soon destroys the beautiful and new tunic of his garment through his inattentiveness, frivolousness, and timidity. But if he does not pay attention well and directly to the eye, he will also fall into a ravine or will be drowned in the water.

3. In the same manner also, the soul, wearing the clothing of the body as a beautiful tunic, having the discerning part as a corrector for the whole soul together with the body, passing through the woods and thorns and mire and fire and cliffs of life, that is, the lusts and desires after pleasure and the remaining strange things of this age, ought in every way with sobriety, courage, zeal, and attentiveness to gird up and protect herself and the tunic of the body, lest in some degree she is torn in the woods and thorns of the anxieties and endeavors and earthly distractions of the world and is burned by the fire of lust. In this way, [the soul] being [so] clothed averts the ear in order not to hear slander, the tongue not to speak vain things, the hands and feet from the pursuit of evil things.

4. For the soul has a will to avert and withhold the parts of the body from the worst sights, wicked and shameful hearing, improper discourse and from secular and wicked business. The soul also averts herself from mental distraction, protecting her heart so that her reasoning part would not wander in the world. And thus exercising, endeavoring, and gathering from every direction the parts of the body from evil things, she protects the beautiful tunic of the body untorn, unburnt, and unblemished. And because of her knowledgeable, intellectual, and discerning will, she will be protected with respect to all things by the power of the Lord, while she gathers herself with as much power as she has and turns away from every worldly desire, and thus she is helped by the Lord to be protected in truth from the aforementioned evils. For whenever the Lord sees someone nobly turning away from the pleasures of his life and the distractions and the material cares and earthly bonds, and the wandering of vain thinking, he gives his own assistance of grace, well preserving as undisturbed that soul that is passing through this present evil age. And in this way, the soul will craft heavenly praises from God and angels because she has protected well the tunic of her body and turning away as much as she is able from every desire in the world, and being helped by him, she will complete well the race of the course of this life.

5. If someone in this life walks frivolously and carelessly while not paying attention and does not of his own will turn away from every desire of the world and search only for the Lord in every desire, he

becomes entangled in the thorns and woods of this world, and the coat of his body is burned by the fire of desires, and is soiled by the mire of pleasures, and thus the soul is found to be without liberty on the day of judgment, not being able to maintain her garment spotless, but destroying it [the garment] by the deceits of this age. And so he becomes a castoff of the kingdom. What will God do to the personal will that has given itself over to the world and that is deceived by its pleasures or deluded by material wanderings? He gives assistance to the one who turns away from material pleasure and previous custom and to the one who draws his mind always toward the Lord by force both by denying himself and by seeking after the Lord alone. He preserves this one who protects himself from every side from the traps and snares of the wood of the world "who with fear and trembling works out his own salvation"[1] and carefully passes through the traps and snares and desires of this age, and he preserves the one who searches for the Lord's help and hopes to be saved by his grace.

6. As an explanation, behold: the five wise virgins, self-controlled and hastening, receiving the oil foreign to their own nature into the vessels of their hearts, namely, the grace of the spirit from above, were strengthened to enter along with the Bridegroom into the heavenly bridal chamber. But the others, the foolish virgins, who remained in their own nature, were not self-controlled and were not eager to receive the "oil of gladness"[2] in their vessels, because they were still in the flesh. But just as they went to sleep because of negligence, [they also were put to sleep because of] frivolity and lightheartedness and ignorance or even a false notion of righteousness. So they were shut out of the bridal chamber of the kingdom, because they were not able to be well pleasing to the heavenly Bridegroom. Because they were held back by a worldly bond and by some sort of earthly love [agapē], they did not give their whole love [agapē] and their whole sexually passionate love [erōs] to the heavenly Bridegroom, nor did they provide themselves with the oil. For in fact, the souls who search for the sanctification of the Spirit that is foreign to their nature bind fast all of their love [agapē] to the Lord, and there they live and there they pray and there they reason, having turned away from all things. Wherefore, they are worthy to receive the oil of heavenly grace and thus they are able to go never overthrown, at the end being well pleasing to the spiritual Bridegroom. The souls remaining

1. Phil 2:12.
2. Ps 44:8; cf. Rom 7:5.

in their own nature walk slowly in their discourse on the earth, reason on earth, and on earth their mind [*nous*] has its mode of life; and by their own consideration they think that they belong to the Bridegroom and that they were adorned by the righteousness of the flesh, but they have not been born again of the Spirit, not receiving the "oil of gladness."

7. The five reasonable senses of the soul, if they receive the grace from above and the consecration of the Spirit, truly succeed [in being] wise virgins, because they have received the wisdom of grace from above. And if they remain in their own natures alone, they are found [to be] foolish and make themselves known as children of the world, for they did not strip off the spirit of the world, even if by their own opinion they think that they are brides of the Bridegroom through some sort of false appearance and mien. Just as all the souls who are completely cleaving to the Lord have their thinking there, and there pray, and there walk, and there yearn for the love [*agapē*] of the Lord in this way contrarily, souls who have been bound in the love of the world and who prefer to have the earthly manner of life, walk there and there think, and there the mind dwells. Wherefore, they also succeed in being without orientation toward the good "purpose of the spirit."[3] So it is something foreign to our nature (I speak of course of the heavenly grace) needing to unite and to be fashioned together with our nature, so that we might be strengthened to enter together into the heavenly bridal chamber of the Lord's kingdom and to attain eternal salvation.

8. We have received something different from our nature, the evil of our passions, into ourselves "through the disobedience of the first human being."[4] And just as this evil is established as our nature by custom and great predisposition because of its strangeness to our [true] nature, the heavenly gift of the Holy Spirit, this evil must be expelled again and be restored to its primordial cleanliness. And if we do not receive that love of the Spirit from heaven now with great demand, entreaty, faith, prayer, and turning from the world, and let our nature defiled by evil cleave to love, which is the Lord, and be sanctified by that love of the Spirit; if we do not remain unthrown until the end, dwelling precisely in all of his commandments, we will not be able to gain the heavenly kingdom.

9. I wish to speak according to the power belonging to me a somewhat subtle and profound speech. So listen intelligently. The boundless,

---

3. Rom 8:6.
4. Rom 5:19.

unapproachable, and uncreated God embodied himself through an infinite and inconceivable goodness, and so to speak shrunk from his inaccessible glory to be able to be united with his invisible creations (the souls of saints and angels, I mean), so that they would be strengthened to participate in divine life. Each thing has a body according to its own nature: the angel, the soul, the demon. Because even if they are subtle [bodies], nevertheless in actual existence, and in distinctive mark, and in living image they are found [to be] subtle bodies according to the subtleness of their nature. Just as in actual existence this body is dull-witted, in the same way even the soul, being a subtle entity, embraces the eye through which it sees, the ear through which it hears, likewise the tongue through which it speaks; the soul is held together embracing the hand, and in general all the body and its parts through which the soul completes all of the pursuits of life.

10. In the same way also, the boundless and inconceivable God by his goodness diminished himself and assumed the parts of this body and encompassed himself away from his inaccessible glory, and being transformed through gentleness and love for humanity, he embodied himself and he mixed with and received the holy, well-pleasing, and faithful souls, and became among them as "one Spirit,"[5] according to Paul's saying; soul, so he says, to soul and actual existence to actual existence, so that the soul might be strengthened in its divinity to live and to breathe eternal life and to become a participant of incorruptible glory, if it is worthy of him and well pleasing. If out of nonexistence he made such a visible creation to exist in such great variety and diversity—and it did not exist before he created it—he desired and easily made from what did not exist gross and strong substances (namely, I mean earth, mountains, trees; you recognize such hardness in nature) and even intermediary waters and from them he commanded birds to be created and even more subtle things, fire, and winds, and things not visible to the eye of the body because of their subtlety.

11. How does the boundless and indescribable art of "the manifold wisdom of God"[6] create out of nothing the grosser and more subtle and softer bodies to be substantial by his will; how much more being himself does he transform, diminish, and assimilate himself as he wished and what he wishes through a marvelous goodness and inconceivable goodness, embodying [himself] progressively through the holy and worthy,

5. 1 Cor 6:17.
6. Eph 3:10.

faithful souls, so that the invisible one might be seen by them, and the untouched one might be touched according to the nature of the subtlety of the soul, and they would perceive his sweetness and might enjoy the goodness of the light of the unspeakable pleasure by the same experience? Whenever he wishes, he becomes a fire completely burning every indifferent and alien passion of the soul, for it is said, "Our God is a consuming fire."[7] Whenever he wishes, he becomes an ineffable and unspeakable rest, so that the soul might rest in the divine rest. Whenever he wishes, he becomes joy and peace, warming her and treating her well.

12. If even he wants to make himself like one of his creatures, through the exaltation and joy of the noetic creatures, such as Jerusalem, the city of light, or Zion, the heavenly mountain, he is able [so to make himself] all things as he wishes, as it is said, "And you have come to the mount Zion and the city of the living God, the heavenly Jerusalem."[8] Everything is easy and effortless for him who is transformed into that which he wishes by his worthy and faithful souls. Only let someone contend to become a friend and a person well pleasing to him, and through that trial and perception he will see heavenly goods and marvelous luxuriousness and boundless wealth of divinity, truly "which eye has not seen, and ear has not heard, and has not come into the heart of a human being,"[9] the spirit of the Lord that exists for the rest, the joy, the luxuriousness, and eternal life of the worthy souls. For the Lord embodied himself also for food and drink, as it is written in the gospel: "The one who eats this bread will live to eternity"[10] so that he might give rest unspeakably and completely fill the soul with spiritual joy; for he said, "I am the bread of life."[11] Likewise [he is transformed] into a drink of heavenly running water, as he said: "The one who drinks from the water which I will give to him, it will become in him a well of springing water for eternal life,"[12] "and we have all drunk," he said, "that drink."[13]

13. Thus to each one of the holy patriarchs he was seen as he wanted and as it was beneficial: in one way to Abraham, another to Isaac, another way to Jacob, another to Noah, Daniel, David, Solomon, to Isaiah, and to each one of the holy prophets; in some other way to Elias,

---

7. Deut 4:24; Heb 12:29.
8. Heb 12:22.
9. 1 Cor 2:9.
10. John 6:58.
11. John 6:35.
12. John 4:14.
13. 1 Cor 10:14; 12:13.

another way to Moses. And I think that Moses every hour on the mountain, in the forty-day fast, when he came to that spiritual table he reveled [in it] and enjoyed it. So to each one of the saints, he was seen as he wanted in order to give rest and save and lead [them] to the knowledge of God. Everything he wants is effortless for him; and as he wills, diminishing himself, he becomes embodied; and, becoming visible to those who would love him, he is transformed into an inapproachable glory of light; according to his great and ineffable love, he becomes manifest to the worthy ones by his power. Every soul who is deemed worthy in great desire and expectation and faith and love to receive that "power from on high,"[14] receiving the heavenly love of the Father and the heavenly fire of immortal life, is loosed in truth from every worldly love and freed from every bond of evil.

14. For just as iron, lead, gold, or silver when put on the fire is loosed from its hard nature to be changed into softness, and so long as it is in the fire it is loosed and changed from its natural hardness by the warming power of the fire; in the same way the soul, when denying the world and yearning for the Lord alone in much soul, will search both with labor and contestation, and having the uninterrupted expectation for him by hope and faith, and receiving that heavenly fire of the divinity and love of the Spirit, then in truth she is loosed from every worldly love and freed from every evil passion, and everything is made far from her, and she is changed from her natural habit and hardness of sin; and when all things are accounted superfluous, she is led toward only the heavenly Bridegroom whom she receives, resting in his warm and ineffable love.

15. I say to you that she will turn away from these much beloved brethren whom she has before her eyes, if they hinder her from that love, she turns so to speak, for the mystical and ineffable communion of the heavenly King is her life and rest. If love (*agapē*) separates father, mother, brothers from fleshly association and in the mind every [relationship] becomes more exterior for them, and if [the soul] would love [these relations], she would love [them] exteriorly, but she possesses all of her disposition [*diathēsis*] for the sake of her spouse [*synoikos*]: "Instead of this," he says, "the human being will leave his father and his mother and will be joined to his wife, and the two will become one flesh."[15] So if the love [*agapē*] of flesh destroys every love in this way, by

14. Luke 24:49.
15. Gen 2:24; Matt 19:5; Eph 5:31.

how much more shall as many as have been deemed worthy in truth of that holy, heavenly and beloved Spirit in truth be released to participate in every worldly love and everything shall appear superfluous to them by their being conquered by heavenly desire and by their being united to his wounding? They yearn there, they reason there, they live there; there their reasonings live, there the mind always has leisure, because it is conquered by the divine and heavenly love [erōs] and by spiritual desire.

16. Finally, O beloved brethren, because such a love lies before us and because so many promises are proclaimed to us by the Lord, let us cast off all of the fetters from ourselves, turn aside from every cosmic love, and surrender ourselves to that only good by searching and desiring, so that we might be strengthened to achieve that ineffable love of the Spirit concerning which the blessed Paul exhorts us to strive toward it, saying, "Pursue love,"[16] that we might be strengthened to be deemed worthy of the right hand of the Highest, out of the harshness of our mental confusion, and to come to spiritual gentleness and rest, because we are wounded by the erotic love of the divine spirit. For the Lord, feeling deeply, shows much kindness, whenever we shall completely turn around toward him, removing ourselves from all that opposes him. If, through great ignorance, childishness, and an evil predisposition, we turn away from the life and we place many shackles upon ourselves because we do not desire in truth to repent, still he shows great kindness toward us because he is long-suffering, that whenever we turn around we might come toward him, and that we might illuminate our inward human being, so that our faces will not be ashamed on the day of judgment.

17. Even if it appears difficult for us because of the harsh practice [ascēsis] of virtue, and especially because of the purpose and counsel of the adversary, behold, he feels deeply and is long-suffering awaiting our return, enduring our sins: he suffers, awaiting our repentance and when we fall he is not ashamed to receive us again, as the prophet said, "Is not the one who falls stood upright, or the one who has turned away, not turned back?"[17] Only let us be sober, acquiring good sense, and let us return immediately and truly search for assistance from him. He is ready to save us. For he awaits the fervent movement of our will toward him (as much as we are able), and the faith [arising] from a good purpose and desire. He himself works at the complete reform in us. Accordingly, beloved, as children of God who have stripped off every predisposition,

16. 1 Cor 14:1.
17. Jer 8:4.

indifference, and confusion to become ready and noble-minded, let us be eager to follow behind him, not delaying day after day beguiled by evil, for we do not know when the exodus from our flesh happens. The promises of Christians are so great and unspeakable that all of the glory and beauty of heaven and earth, and both the remaining adornment and variety of the universe, and the loveliness, wealth, and delicacy of visible things do not compare to the faith and wealth of our soul.

18. How then shall we not want, by so many exhortations and promises of the Lord, entirely to come to him, and to be established as those who have given themselves over to him, because we deny above all things even our own soul, according to the gospel; and shall we not want to love him alone and besides him no other? And behold all these things, and how much glory has been given! How many dispensations of the Lord came from the patriarchs and the prophets, how many promises were announced, how many exhortations, what compassion of the Master has come upon us from the beginning? And in the end through his own sojourn [among us] he showed his unspeakable goodness toward us through his crucifixion, so that we who have turned around might be transferred into life. And shall we not withdraw from our own wills and love of the world, and the predisposition and habit of evil things? Therefore, we show ourselves to be people of little faith, or even faithless. And behold he himself is merciful upon these with respect to everything, because he guards and cherishes us unseen, and because he does not hand us over as our sins deserve in the end to the evil and the deceit of the world, dismissing us to die, but we return to him when he looks away from these things because of his great goodness and patience.

19. But I fear lest ever the word of the Apostle be fulfilled toward us who are living with the contemptuous intent and who are led astray by our dispositions, saying: "Or do you presume upon the riches of his kindness and patience? Do you not know that God's kindness is meant to lead you to repentance?"[18] If we have beheld greater things in his patience, goodness, and forbearance, and if through our indifference and contempt we will be providing ourselves more sins and larger judgments, the saying will be fulfilled: "But by your hard and impenitent heart you are storing up wrath for yourself on the day of wrath when God's righteous judgment will be revealed."[19] With regard to the human race, God has employed a great, inexpressible goodness and an ineffable

18. Rom 2:4.
19. Rom 2:5.

patience, only let us desire to be self-controlled, and above all let us strive to return to him, so that we might be strengthened to achieve salvation.

20. If you wish to discover the patience and the great goodness of God, let us examine closely the God-inspired scriptures. Look at Israel, from whom the patriarchs [came], to whom the promises were established, "from whom is the Christ according to the flesh," to whom [belong] the worship and a covenant.[20] As much as they sinned, as often as they turned aside, he did not leave them to perish in the end, but for a temporary time he gave them over to education for their own benefit. Because he desired to soften the hardness of their heart through affliction, he turned around, he invited, and he sent prophets. And on so many occasions when they sinned and offended he was patient and he received those who converted with joy; and again when they turned aside, he did not leave, but rather he summoned them through the prophets to conversion. Frequently, when they turned away and were converted, he gladly endured them and received them kindly, up to the point at which they were found [to be] in the great trespass, namely, placing their hands upon the same Master, whom through traditions of the patriarchs and holy prophets they awaited as a redeemer, savior, king, and prophet. When he came, they did not receive him, but quite the opposite, after marking him with many things worthy of disgrace, they later exacted vengeance [from him] with a cross of death. Both in this great offense, and in their surpassing trespass, their sins were filled up, being exceedingly multiplied. And in this way, then, they were left in the end, when the Holy Spirit withdrew from there, when "the veil of the temple was torn,"[21] and thus their temple having been given over to the nations was utterly destroyed and laid waste, according to the judgment of the Lord: "There will not remain stone upon stone here, which will not be thrown down."[22] And thus at the end they were given over to the nations and they were scattered abroad in every land by the king, who then took them prisoner, being ordered never again to return to their own regions.

21. So this is how it is even now for each one of us; he, being good and gentle, waits, seeing how much each one offends, and he rests, waiting for the time when the no-longer-offending [person] will become sober and return, and receiving the one who returned from his sin in great love

20. Rom 9:4–5.
21. Mark 15:38.
22. Matt 24:2.

and joy. For thus it is said: "There is joy over one sinner who repents."[23] And again, "It is not the will of my Father that one of the least of these little ones be lost."[24] If some person upon whom the great goodness and patience of God has been placed does not proceed with vengeance upon the offenses of sins, whether [they are] hidden or manifest (because he sees and waits as for the repentance expected from God), that one, coming toward great disdain, adds sin upon sins, and joins indifference upon indifference, and builds offense upon offense. He fills the limit of sins, and he comes to such an offense at the end, above which he is no longer able to rise. He is shattered and in the end, having been given over to evil, he dies.

22. This is how it happened for Sodom. When they sinned greatly and did not later repent, they offended in this way, when upon the bad counsel of the angels they desired to perform upon them the act of lying with men, so that they no longer were repentant, and in the end they were rejected as unworthy. For they filled up the limit of sins and transgressed; therefore, they became fire-burned by the divine judgment. So it was also for Noah. When they had offended much and not repented, they reached such a level of sins that in the end the whole earth was destroyed. So also God was merciful upon the Egyptians who offended greatly and who sinned against the people of God. He would not inflict such plagues upon them that in the end they would die. Instead, he, being patient and waiting for them to come to repentance, brought to them the small blows of plagues for their education, conversion, and repentance. Those who have greatly sinned against the people of God and converted and again changed their conduct and settled into the ancient unbelief of the evil sect, and oppressed the people of God, later when God through many wonders led the people out of Egypt under Moses' leadership, they offended greatly, following hard behind the people of God. Therefore, also at the end, the divine judgment destroyed and killed them and drowned them in the water, not even judging them worthy of the visible life.

23. Israel likewise, as was said, when they had sinned and offended greatly, killing the prophets of God and doing many other bad things, God, resting and waiting for them to come to repentance, was patient. They offended in this way at the last, when crushed, they were no longer able to be raised: they placed their own hands upon the imperial

23. Luke 15:10.
24. Matt 18:24.

power. Therefore, even at the end the ones who were abandoned were cut off, and the prophecy, the priesthood, and the worship were taken from them and were given to the believing nations, as the Lord said, "The kingdom will be taken away from you and be given to a nation producing the fruits of it."[25] Until then God sustained them and he was patient and did not reject them, for he felt deeply about them, but when they filled up the limit of sins, and they abounded exceedingly, at the end those who were laying hands upon the imperial honor were left behind by God.

24. Beloved, we have gone through these things through many [examples] from scriptural reflections to demonstrate the necessity of our quick conversion and eagerness for the Lord who is merciful and who awaits our perfect separation from every evil thing and bad predisposition, and who receives those who have returned with great joy, in order that our contempt might not increase day by day, and that the given offenses might not increase upon us and bring down upon ourselves the wrath of God. Let us be eager, then, to come to him, returning in a true heart and not despairing of salvation, which very thing itself happens to be a knavery of evil things; by remembering the preceding sins it brings the human being into hopelessness and into looseness, contempt, and sluggishness, so that not returning and coming to the Lord, he might not find salvation, which the great goodness of the Lord has placed upon the human race.

25. If it appears to us as difficult and impossible to turn from many sins because we have been preoccupied (which, as we have already said, happens to be a pretext of evil and a stumbling block of our salvation), let us remember and look away from other things at how the Lord, when by his goodness he resided [with us], made the blind to see again, he cured the paralytics, he healed every illness, he raised the dead who were already dead and destroyed, he made the deaf to hear, he expelled a legion of demons from one human being and restored the one who had gone into such a madness. By how much more then, when the soul turns toward him and seeks mercy from him and when she needs his help, she will not return and aim at good cheer of insensibility, and the fixedness of every virtue, and the renewal of the mind, and change into a healthy and intelligent sight and reasoning of peace, reaching from the blindness and deafness and death of faithlessness and ignorance and fearlessness to the temperance of virtue and the cleanliness of heart, for

25. Matt 21:43.

the one who created the body, the same one also made the soul? And just as when he dwelled on earth, when those who came to him and searched the help and health from him by his goodness, and he furnished abundantly as each needed, as an only and good doctor, so also will he provide for the spiritual things.

26. If again he feels compassion for the dissolving and mortal bodies, and he acted readily and properly to each one who sought, by how much more [will he feel compassion] for the immortal and indissoluble and incorruptible soul who happens to be in the disease of ignorance [of the evil of unfaith and fearlessness and the remaining passions of sin], but who comes to the Lord, and who searches for assistance from him and who watches for his mercy, and who desires to receive the grace of the Spirit from him for her redemption and salvation and for the deliverance from every evil and every passion—will he not give more quickly and most readily the redemption of healing? According to his word: "By how much more the heavenly Father will avenge him who calls to him day and night," and continuing he says: "Yes, I say to you, he will avenge him speedily."[26] And again in another place, he exhorts: "Ask and it will be given to you; seek and you will find; knock and it will be opened to you; for everyone who asks will receive, and who seeks finds, and for the one who knocks it will be opened."[27] And going further, he puts forth: "How much more will our Father who is in heaven give the Holy Spirit to those who ask him?"[28] Amen I say to you, if even because he is his friend he will not give to him, because of his impudence, rising, he will give to him as much as he needs."[29]

27. Our asking impudently, incessantly, and indefatigably invites the support of his grace through all of these things. For he came on behalf of the sinners so that he might win them over to him and heal the ones who believed in him. Only let us separate ourselves from the evil predispositions as much as we are able, and let us hate the petty pursuits and the deceits of the world, and let us put to flight both the evil and the vain discourses and always cleave to him with as much power as we have. He readily gives his assistance to you. Toward this end, there is mercy-making, life-giving, healing of the incurable passions, and the performing of redemption for those who call upon him and willingly turn toward him from every worldly love as much as possible, and for those

26. Luke 18:7–8.
27. Matt 7:7–8; Luke 11:9–10.
28. Luke 11:13.
29. Luke 11:8.

who withdraw deliberately, and for those who draw their understanding away from the earth, and for those who are crucified with him in
their search and longings. This sort of soul, leading beyond all excesses,
resting upon nothing in the world, is worthy of assistance from him, still
expecting to be happy and to rest in his most good rest. And in this way
she achieves the heavenly gift through such a faith and she rests her
desires through grace in certainty, and at the end she serves in accordance with and in harmony with the Holy Spirit, and she daily improves
in the good, and remains on the road of righteousness and in the end she
perseveres unbending and without coupling with the evil part, and
grieving the grace in no one, she is found worthy of eternal salvation
with all of the saints, inasmuch as she behaves in imitation of them on
the earth as a partner and co-runner. Amen.

SUGGESTED READINGS

Desprez, Vincent, and Mariette Canévet. "Macaire (Pseudo-Macaire; Macaire-
    Syméon). *Dict. Spir.* 10 (1977) 20–43.
Dörries, H. *Die Theologie des Makarios/Symeon.* Göttingen: Vandenhoeck &
    Ruprecht, 1978.
————. *Symeon von Mesopotamien. Die Überlieferung der messalianischen "Makar-
    ios"-Schriften.* TU 55. Leipzig: Hinrichs, 1941.
Jaeger, Werner. *Two Rediscovered Works of Ancient Christian Literature: Gregory of
    Nyssa and Macarius.* Leiden, Neth.: E. J. Brill, 1965.
Meyendorff, John. "Messalianism or Anti-Messalianism? A Fresh Look at the
    'Macarian' Problem." In *Kyriakon. Festschrift Johannes Quasten,* edited by
    Patrick Granfield and Josef A. Jungmann, 2.585–90. Münster: Aschendorff,
    1977.
Pseudo-Macaire. *Oeuvres Spirituelles,* trans. Vincent Desprez. SC 275. Paris: Les
    Editions du Cerf, 1980.

PART TWO

PHILOSOPHICAL AND THEOLOGICAL EXHORTATION

AMBROSIASTER
On the Sin of
Adam and Eve

INTRODUCTION

"On the Sin of Adam and Eve" stands as Question 127 in a collection of 127 *Questions on the Old and New Testaments* (*Quaestiones veteris et novi testamenti*), once attributed to St. Augustine. This series of biblical discussions, as well as a lengthy commentary on the Pauline epistles (formerly ascribed to Ambrose), is generally accepted to have been written by the mysterious author now called Ambrosiaster.[1] Although the precise identity of this writer is unknown, a few important facts about him can be deduced from his writings.

First, it is firmly established that Ambrosiaster was writing at Rome during the pontificate of Damasus, that is, between 366 and 385 c.e. He refers to the church at Rome, "whose rector at present is Damasus," in his commentary on 1 Timothy.[2] His residence at Rome also is affirmed at several places in the *Quaestiones*.[3] A definite *terminus ad quem* for questions 6, 8, 10, 11, and 12 is the year 384, when Damasus submitted to Jerome five questions on the Old Testament that clearly are derived from Ambrosiaster's collection.[4] Another question, "De fato" (115), refers

1. The argument for the attribution of the *Quaestiones* to Ambrosiaster is found in A. Souter, *A Study of Ambrosiaster*. TextsS 7/4 (1905; reprint, Nendeln, Liechtenstein: Kraus, 1967). The Pauline commentary has been edited by H. Vogels in CSEL 81/1–3 (1966–69). The *Quaestiones* also exist in a longer collection of 150 (*PL* 35, 2215–2422).
2. CSEL 81/3, 270.
3. Q. 115 (CSEL 50, 323): *hic enim in urbe Roma*. Cf. also Q. 101, *De iactantia Romanorum levitarum* (CSEL 50, 193–98) and Q. 102, *Contra Novatianum* (CSEL 50, 199–224).
4. See Jerome, *Ep.* 35–36, and Souter, *Study of Ambrosiaster*, 173–74. On Jerome's knowledge of Ambrosiaster, see H. Vogels, "Ambrosiaster und Hieronymus," *RBén* 66 (1956) 14–19.

to a famine and other events that seem to have taken place after the year 382.[5] Because all of the *Quaestiones* may not have been collected during Ambrosiaster's lifetime and because some of the longer questions, such as "On the Sin of Adam and Eve," probably circulated separately, however, these dates can be used only approximately in regard to any particular *quaestio*. The years 382 to 384, however, seem to be a reasonable estimate of its date of composition.

Second, Ambrosiaster's writings reflect the knowledge and attitude of a Christian aristocrat. He frequently refers to the emperor, to high state officials, and to members of the senatorial order.[6] Ambrosiaster also was quite interested in Roman legal traditions and seems to have traveled widely, particularly in Africa and Egypt.[7] These considerations have led some scholars to suggest that Ambrosiaster might have held high office.

Third, Ambrosiaster was very likely a presbyter of the Roman church.[8] In favor of this view is the fact that he appears so knowledgeable about ecclesiastical customs, especially those regarding church office. Many of the *Quaestiones* appear to be homilies or sermons that address the audience in the second person.[9] Question 120 begins with words that seem to identify the speaker as a "priest" (*sacerdos*).[10] Even the present treatise, "On the Sin of Adam and Eve," concludes its defense of marriage with an explanation and confirmation of clerical celibacy. The sum of this evidence, although not conclusive, makes Ambrosiaster's clerical status appear most likely.

This treatise is of interest primarily because it represents the opposition of one influential Christian to the ascetic ideals spreading throughout the West in the late fourth century. Three aspects of Ambrosiaster's treatise are noteworthy. First, the disputes over the value of asceticism are, to a great extent, *exegetical* disputes. The texts in question are taken

---

5. Q. 115.49 (CSEL 50, 334): a famine in Italy, Africa, Sicily, and Sardinia, also mentioned by Ambrose and Symmachus. Cf. A. Souter, *The Earliest Latin Commentaries on the Epistles of St. Paul* (Oxford: Clarendon Press, 1927) 42.

6. See, for example, the illustration Ambrosiaster offers in sec. 36 of the present treatise. See further the discussion in Souter, *Study of Ambrosiaster*, 23–31, 174–78.

7. Souter, *Study of Ambrosiaster*, 178–83. Souter (179–80) concludes that Ambrosiaster "had held high office there, had been perhaps either *dux* or *comes Aegypti*."

8. A. Suiber, "Ambrosiaster," *TRE* 2 (1978) 357, says that Ambrosiaster's clerical status cannot be determined for certain. P. Brown, *The Body and Society. Men, Women and Sexual Renunciation in Early Christianity* (New York: Columbia University Press, 1988) 377, refers to him without discussion as an "anonymous Roman priest." L. Speller, "Ambrosiaster and the Jews," *SP* 17/1 (1982) 75, suggests that Ambrosiaster was "a presbyter who once hoped to be bishop."

9. For example, Q. 100 and Qq. 116–121.

10. Q. 120.1 (CSEL 50, 361): *Congruum est, fratres carissimi . . . dei sacerdotem et praepositum plebis Christi exhortari populum, sub cura sua positum, in doctrina sana.*

largely from the first three chapters of Genesis. Thus, the discussion of asceticism is inseparable from broader questions raised by the biblical story regarding the goodness of creation and the nature of sin. These issues were hotly debated in Ambrosiaster's day, and his positions sometimes contrast sharply with those of other Christian writers.[11]

Another related issue that Ambrosiaster faces directly in the present treatise is the validity of the Jewish scriptures, particularly the injunction to "increase and multiply." Ambrosiaster's defense of the goodness of procreation led him to uphold the essential harmony of the Jewish and Christian dispensations. Here again, not only does his position contrast with that of contemporary extremists, such as the Manichees, but it also contradicts the views of more "orthodox" Christian ascetics, such as Jerome.[12]

Finally, despite his vigorous defense of marriage and childbearing, Ambrosiaster strongly endorses the practice of clerical celibacy. His treatise, therefore, sheds light on the process by which the ascetic movement was gradually assimilated into mainstream Christianity and its hierarchy.

This translation has been prepared from the critical edition of Alexander Souter, *Pseudo-Augustini. Quaestiones veteris et novi testamenti CXXVII*, published in the Corpus Scriptorum Ecclesiasticorum Latinorum (Vienna, 1908) 399–416.

TRANSLATION

1. No one doubts, I think, that this world was made for the sake of the human race. Although the world consists of diverse substances, nonetheless it is one, having been furnished with many members, that out of their mutual interactions everything people need might be produced. For a home was made for the human race [and provided] with a yearly

---

11. See the important discussion in E. A. Clark, "Heresy, Asceticism, Adam, and Eve," in her *Ascetic Piety and Women's Faith* (Lewiston, N.Y.: Edwin Mellen Press, 1986). Unlike Ambrose and Jerome, Ambrosiaster accepts the possibility of physical sexual relations *before* the fall.

12. I have developed this point in my article: "*On the Sin of Adam and Eve*: A Little-Known Defense of Marriage and Childbearing by Ambrosiaster," *HTR* 82 (1989) 297–313. Numerous parallels can be drawn between this work of Ambrosiaster and other opponents of ascetic extremism, such as Jovinian, Helvidius, and Vigilantius. On Jovinian, see D.G. Hunter, "Resistance to the Virginal Ideal in Late-Fourth-Century Rome: The Case of Jovinian," *TS* 48 (1987) 45–64. On Vigilantius, see M. Massie, "Vigilance de Calagurris face à la polémique hieronymienne," *BLE* 81 (1980) 81–108.

produce, in order that each thing might come into being upon the earth according to its own species. In other words, created things possess this innate power to produce offspring of every kind on earth. For the beginnings were instituted in such a way that seed might be of use for the procreation of multiple species upon the earth.

2. That is why scripture testifies: "And God blessed them saying: Increase and multiply upon the earth."[13] In a similar way the human race also was blessed. We observe this idea in the law, for we see that it has been written, "The people increased and multiplied in Egypt."[14] For the human race was blessed by that same blessing by which those things created for its use were blessed, so that from the woman (just as from the sea),[15] the offspring of the human race might increase and multiply upon the earth. Just as seeds were to be improved by cultivation, so also the human race was to strive to direct its life toward attaining the Creator's favor, having achieved knowledge of him. In this way, all things were to make progress together for the praise and glory of the Creator.

3. And that these words signify nothing else, the facts themselves attest. For all created things have multiplied and improved upon the earth at God's command. For nothing could grow in a manner other than that which the will and blessing of God has decreed to the seeds. Therefore, how could something that receives its increase with God's blessing and favor be said to have come into being wrongly or not to be allowed? The tradition of this thing has remained in the synagogue and now is celebrated in the church. The result is that God's creature is joined by God's blessing and not by arrogant presumption, because the formula has been given this way by the Maker himself.[16]

4. But if someone thinks that [human generation] ought to cease, it ought to cease only when those things that have received a similar blessing to multiply have ceased. For if human generation ceases, to what end are those things born that have been blessed upon the earth? For the world cannot partly continue and partly cease. Either it operates as a whole or it comes to rest as a whole. Is a body useful, if some of its members thrive while others wither?

13. Gen 1:22.
14. Acts 7:17; cf. Gen 1:28.
15. Ambrosiaster refers to the second part of Gen 1:22: "Increase and multiply and fill the waters and the seas."
16. The preceding two sentences refer to the liturgical practice of a nuptial blessing. Cf. K. Ritzer, *Le mariage dans les églises chrétiennes du Ier au XIe siècles* (Paris: Les Editions du Cerf, 1970) 223.

5. Why, then, do some people call that which God has blessed a sordid and contaminated work, unless because they themselves in some way raise their hands against God? For they would not criticize this [work], unless they had wicked ideas about God, the Maker of the work. But because they are afraid to criticize God openly, they accuse him through the work that he has made. For when the work causes displeasure, the Maker is criticized.

6. But if people of this type would read—or, rather, if they would accept—the scriptures, they would remember that Balaam said: "Why should I curse the one whom God has blessed?"[17] For in vain is he accused, who is praised by the judge; indeed, that person accuses himself, who says that the one whom the laws defend is guilty. Who, then, are you, who think that you should condemn what has been blessed by the God of the law, unless you either deny that he is this God or accuse the scripture of being false?

7. Indeed, there are people who, while seemingly accepting the new, think that the old must be repudiated. But the new commandments delivered by Christ to the people do not differ from these [old ones]. Christ himself, when invited to a wedding, did not refuse to go, and not only did he illumine it with his presence, but he also provided what was lacking for joy.[18] For as scripture says, "wine gladdens the heart."[19] And in order to show that he did this according to the will of God his Father, when the Jews asked him whether a man was allowed to divorce his wife, among other things he made this response: "From the beginning God made male and female and said: For this reason a man will leave his mother and father and cleave to his wife, and they will be two in one flesh. And so they are no longer two but one flesh. Therefore, what God has joined, man should not separate."[20] That is why when asked to a wedding he went freely, lest he appear to invalidate what his God and Father had done. Furthermore, when he showed that the teaching of the old and the new law were in harmony, not only did he not prohibit marriage, but he also deigned to be present there, giving them testimony that God is the author of marriage. Thus he showed by a salutary precept that what God has joined ought to be neither prohibited nor separated.

17. Num 23:8.
18. Cf. John 2:1–11.
19. Ps 104:15; Ps 103 (RSV); cf. Sir 40:20.
20. Matt 19:4–6; cf. Gen 1:27; 2:24.

8. And because birth is good, when he was about to leave the world, he entrusted his mother to his disciple John.[21] For this reason, we, too, are taught through all the commandments of both the old and the new law to honor our parents, and unless we do this, as the law warns us, we will incur a curse.[22]

9. And so, what arrogant presumption is this? From what law has there come a prohibition against marriage when both the old and the new law appear to favor marriage in every respect? But we have read that "what is from outside is from the evil one."[23] Therefore, the apostle says that people like this, who prohibit marriage and teach abstinence from foods that God has created for consumption, have a *seared conscience*.[24] For they are said to act *out of hypocrisy*[25] because of hostility, with the result that they criticize the law that God has handed down.

10. Others, who strive for the same goal, raise their hands in opposition to the saving precepts and thus endorse the mandates of a wicked teaching. Because of this they are said to have a *seared conscience*. Because their minds have become corrupted, they know one thing but profess another. The Jews once did the same thing. Although they knew that the deeds of the Savior were works of the Holy Spirit, they said in jealousy that he cast out demons in Beelzebul, in order to turn the people away from faith in him.[26] Our present opponents display the same insanity. In order to pretend that they are lovers of chastity and the consecrated life, they also say that marriage should be condemned; they hope to be commended by this and to turn people away from the truth. Furthermore, in order to act as if they are zealous for abstinence, they teach that one should refrain from foods, in order thereby to show that they are hastening as aliens from earth to the heavenly realms. In this way, they mislead people's minds and then teach that illicit things are licit and condemn licit things, as if they were forbidden.

11. These are the snares of Satan, to turn matters upside down and, by introducing some novelty, as it were, to shut out the truth; but in the truth there is no novelty, as it is wholly eternal. Who does not see that this notion has been fabricated by the Adversary? For who would dare to criticize what God has made and what is no hindrance, except the Adversary of truth? In order to cloak his own impurity, he preaches

21. Cf. John 19:26.
22. Cf. Exod 20:12; Deut 5:16; Matt 15:4, 19; etc.
23. Matt 5:37.
24. 1 Tim 4:2.
25. 1 Tim 4:2.
26. Cf. Matt 12:24.

consecrated virginity, which he does not love, but, in this manner displaying such good intentions, as it were, he urges illicit things as if they were licit. For he commends himself in order to deceive more easily and in this way, after capturing the imprudent, he suggests [means] by which he may make them even worse sinners. In order to confer some benefit to his own cause, he persuades people to sin lavishly, seeking great comfort from this. As long as he reveals many [to be] accomplices in his crime, he considers it a small price to pay (although it is great), if he sees many with him in Gehenna. As long as these persons are conquered by vices, they will cause others to sin or even ignorantly maintain that [vices] should not be punished here.

12. What pernicious desire causes this deception? What shadow prevents the truth from being seen? For letters usually are misunderstood either when they are pronounced incorrectly or when they are improperly distinguished. But when the text says: "God made," and "He blessed what he made,"[27] who would dispute this? Who would doubt? Who would think that what he has heard blessed is cursed, unless he is animated by another spirit? Indeed, if this were said to be the word of a human being, perhaps one might think that some deceit were involved. But do you doubt when God is said to speak? Does God bless and you condemn?

13. "But perhaps Moses introduced this error in God's name!" The signs and wonders worked through Moses in Egypt should be enough for you; the miracles that were done at the Red Sea to liberate the children of Israel should persuade you. I have heard the magi confess that "here is the finger of God."[28] The apostle agrees, saying: "I do not want you to be ignorant, brothers, of the fact that all our fathers were under a cloud and all passed through the sea and all were baptized in Moses in the cloud and in the sea and all ate the same spiritual food and all drank the same spiritual drink. For they drank from the spiritual rock which followed; but the rock was Christ."[29] And why has the apostle said this? Here is the scripture in which we read that Christ our Lord said to the Jews: "If you believed Moses, you would also believe me, for Moses wrote about me."[30] Who would refuse to put faith in this harmony? Who would dare to say that what is one is in discord? Whose mind is so wicked as to argue that undivided charity is enmity? Behold,

27. Cf. Gen 1:21, 22.
28. Exod 8:15 (19).
29. 1 Cor 10:1–4.
30. John 5:46.

you have both the testimony of words and the example of miracles, which yoke your mind to the truth; as a result, you should not think that anything is true other than what the books of the catholic church contain.

14. Because, then, it has been proven that the same God, who now is our God, also was present in the old [dispensation], and because by many miraculous signs [it has been proven] that this God is true, it follows that his authority ought to be preferred. Therefore, even that which we consider difficult or perhaps absurd ought to be accepted and understood in a way other than we would normally view it, if it is commended by God, because we should trust God rather than ourselves. For our weakness and inexperience often judge harmful things to be useful and consider the false to be true. It is wicked even to suspect this of God, for it is not his nature to be able to be deceived. How much more ought one not to doubt when God speaks about marriage. For the matter is plain and simple!

15. Certainly, every person rejoices when he has reached a state of worthiness before God, and he believes himself to be improved when he gains further knowledge of the mystery of the Creator.[31] And yet, he would not have achieved this unless he had been born. Why, then, does he mourn for what he rejoices in and condemn what he boasts to have learned? For if he rejoices because he learns, and if he would not have learned if he had not been born, without a doubt it is good to be born, because the fruit of birth is knowledge of the truth. But if it is evil to be born, knowledge will not be good. For what benefit will knowledge convey, if birth is condemned? If it is useless or improper to be born, it is foolish that one who is to be damned should learn. But because no one is so feebleminded as to deny that knowledge of God benefits human beings, [knowledge] is both good and useful. For through this [knowledge] birth is improved, so that it may merit more than what was conferred on Adam, because believers will reign in heaven,[32] not on earth, in the paradise of God the Father, not in that place where Adam was ordered to labor in a bodily way.[33]

16. For if the Encenia was celebrated at Jerusalem, that is, if the feast of the dedication of the Lord's temple was observed, how much more ought we to celebrate the birthday of the human being, who is even

31. The Latin word *sacramentum* has been rendered here as "mystery." See sec. 16, where the expression *cognitum . . . mysterium* appears to be its equivalent. In sec. 19 the words *mysterii eius cognitione* seem to refer to a knowledge of the incarnation.
32. Cf. Rev 2:7.
33. Cf. Gen 2:15.

more the temple of God,[34] and whose hands have built a temple to give thanks to God![35] Indeed, our body is a better temple, because it has been constructed by the work of God, whereas that [earthly temple] was made by human labor. The former is under the hope of eternity, the latter under perdition. And so, whoever knows that he has been born as a result of God's decree, in order that he may give thanks and gain knowledge of his mystery,[36] ought to rejoice at his own birthday, seeing the benefit that comes from his own birth. On the other hand, those who abandon their Creator and attribute his glory to others truly ought not to have been born.[37] For their birth leads to punishment, although it is not birth that incurs judgment, but the will.

17. But who are you to forbid marriage? Perhaps Marcion,[38] as you think that the body was not made by God, but by the devil, and as you claim that the soul suffered a fall by some kind of error, so that it came to the shadowy regions in which the world now lies. How, then, can it be liberated from here, if generation is forbidden? For it was only after being born that you recognized your fall and, after exerting the effort, managed to return to the Father's abode, having been restored to your source. Finally, you say that you give thanks to Christ, through whom you rejoice to have achieved this knowledge. But notice, if you had not been born, [your] knowledge would have ceased and [your] liberation would not have progressed. And so, if you rejoice that your soul is liberated, look favorably on birth, for if you oppose birth, you are an enemy of souls.

18. Or, if you are Manicheus,[39] who rejects marriage as contrary, I ask you, if bodies were not born, how could the soul, which you claim was poured into the shadowy realms and clings to hylic things, be snatched from this place?[40] For you have it written in your books that it is liberated by being born, with the result that, after being taken from the moon, as

34. Cf. 1 Cor 3:16.
35. Cf. 2 Cor 5:1.
36. Cf. Col 2:2.
37. Cf. Rom 1:25; Isa 42:8.
38. Marcion of Sinope (died ca. 160 c.e.) taught at Rome and founded a Christian sect whose teachings rejected the Old Testament and its God and accepted only several Pauline letters and an abridged version of Luke as canonical.
39. Manicheus (otherwise known as Manes or Mani) was born ca. 216 c.e. near Seleucia-Ctesiphon, the capital of the Persian empire. He developed a religious system that blended Jewish-Christian and Gnostic elements, including a thorough cosmic dualism, an elaborate salvation myth, and a severe asceticism.
40. "Hylic things" (hylicis rebus), i.e., material things. Ambrosiaster intentionally uses the Greek word, probably because of its Gnostic overtones. Souter, Study of Ambrosiaster, 149, believes that Ambrosiaster has derived this term from his reading of Irenaeus: Adversus Haereses 1.1.9.

they depart from bodies, souls are handed over to the sun, which you claim is the god of your souls. For you rejoice when you are called "Manicheans." Indeed, by this very name you impugn your own liberation, because you would be utterly ignorant, if you had not been born. And so, it is quite apparent that you condemn marriage "out of hypocrisy."[41] For while you profess the consecrated life, you secretly pursue wickedness, something that has been condemned not only privately, but also by the edicts of the emperors.[42]

19. Hear now, O Catholic, while the gospel testifies that human birth is good. For when Symeon, a just man, wished to depart this life, thinking that an awareness of the Creator, without knowledge of this mystery, was sufficient for him, he was not permitted to have the full reward of his faith, until he had made progress in the knowledge of God. Finally, after taking the newborn Savior in his hands, "he blessed God and said: Now let your servant go in peace according to your word, for my eyes have seen your salvation."[43] It certainly is obvious that God's blessing lies in human birth, because that just man contemplating death received the response that he would not die before he had seen the Christ of the Lord.[44] For he had made such progress in his life that he was worthy to see even in the present life the liberator, whom he hoped [to see] after death. How, then, can it be said that birth was not a good for that man who was preserved in this life and not permitted to die until he had seen the fruit of his hope, so that he was certain that he was passing from life to life?

20. Indeed, if being born is evil, there would be no promise of paradise,[45] nor eternal life, nor the kingdom of heaven, but only the perdition of Gehenna as a punishment. In that case, a person who knew that he had been born for perdition would be afraid to give birth to another, because it would not be licit to produce something born illicitly.

21. But perhaps someone may say: "Indeed, the kingdom of heaven has been promised, but only to those who are faithful and who do good works." Precisely! And so you see that people become guilty, not be-

---

41. 1 Tim 4:2.
42. Ambrosiaster refers to the series of edicts against the Manichees that began with Diocletian's rescript of 297. Ambrosiaster cites Diocletian's edict in his commentary on 2 Tim 3:7 (CSEL 81/3, 312). Legislation against the Manichees was renewed several times during Ambrosiaster's lifetime. See *Codex Theodosianus* 16.5.3 (372), 7 (381), 9 (382), 11 (383), 18 (389), etc.
43. Luke 2:28–30.
44. Cf. Luke 2:26.
45. Cf. Luke 23:43.

cause they are born, but because they have acted wickedly. For the kingdom of heaven has not been promised to the unborn, so that those who will not receive it can attribute this to their being born. No, it has been promised to those who, after being born, act well. As a result, birth does not benefit one who acts wickedly, nor does it hinder one who acts well.

22. For birth is improved by those who are faithful and who do good works, but it is made worse by those who are unfaithful and who act wickedly. For birth is like the planting of a tree. If it is planted in good soil, it will become better and will be called good. But if it is planted in bad soil, it will become worse and will not be called good, but wicked. So, too, if good teaching is added to birth, it will produce good fruit; but if wicked teaching is added, it will produce bad fruit. Therefore, just as a tree necessarily takes on the character of the place where it is planted, so, likewise, those who are born necessarily take on the character of the place where they grow.[46]

23. But a different objection may be made: "If birth is beneficial, why is one reborn?" We would not be reborn, if birth were not beneficial. For to be reborn is to be made anew, and whoever is made anew is begun. Therefore, the possibility of rebirth does not impugn birth, but rather reforms it, and whatever is reformed is proven to have been well instituted from the beginning. So, then, because we are reborn, we are changed by our will and thereby achieve the expiation of the body, that we might be restored to the pristine state of Adam. Although the body was stained by the sin of the soul, once one's will is repaired and improved by faith, the body is cleansed. As a result, just as the body had been defiled by contempt of God, so by obedience it is cleansed so that it may flee the sentence given to Adam and be able to rise.

24. So then, if sin began from the soul, why is the nature of the body impugned? For bodily desire was not at the root of Adam's sin; rather, the soul, allured by hope of deity, transgressed God's commandment, so that it subjugated even its body to sin and people were born under sin.[47] Indeed, the body is no obstacle, as long as one obeys the law of God. Death is the only hindrance, but for this God's benevolence has promised a reward: because now the faithful are found devoted to the Creator, even though they are subjected to death and corruption on account

---

46. I have taken some liberties with this sentence. The subject of "take" and "grow" is literally "birth" (*nativitas*).
47. Cf. Gen 3:5.

of Adam's transgression, they will receive from the divine Judge more than what was granted to Adam.[48] As a result, in the future they will be glorious and will possess eternal life and will be called the adopted children of God, that their birth may become their reward.

25. Now let us return to the remainder of the reading. When the human beings were placed in paradise, they received these commands: "From every tree that is in paradise you may eat; but from the tree from which is discovered good and evil, you may not eat of it."[49] All the trees that he mentions bear fruit for creatures to eat. Therefore, they are called by the one name "trees," although they are understood to be varied in their fruits. Nevertheless, all are trees, and there is one kind of eating, although the things that are eaten are varied. For because he had created many trees with fruit for them to eat, as I said, from one tree he prohibited eating, so that they, who had received power over all things, might have reverence for the Creator in some measure. As long as one tree was set aside that they did not have permission [to touch], they were to be mindful of the law governing their creation.[50]

26. How was the type of sin to be determined from the sentence? This sentence was fitting for persons guilty of homicide, magic, adultery, and disreputable conduct. For example, when Achar, the son of Charmi, had sinned, he was condemned to be destroyed with his entire household.[51] How can the type of sin be determined from the sentence? One can see that it was a great sin, but not exactly the type of sin. Both Aman and the inhabitants of Sodom are known to have perished with all their households.[52] For so it happens that persons guilty of different crimes may be punished by one and the same kind of punishment. Therefore, the type of sin that Adam and Eve committed cannot be determined from the sentence that was given.

27. Although their sin was one, the man and the woman received their sentences individually, and it was the same in the case of the serpent. Not only did they not remain in the state in which they were created, but also suffering was added to them as punishment. For although all the cattle and living creatures had been subjected to the human beings, as we have read, the serpent rejected this order and, after circumventing them by a deceitful trick, subjected them to himself. For without a doubt

---

48. Cf. Rom 5:14.
49. Gen 2:16, 17.
50. On the unusual syntax of this passage, see E. Löfstedt, "Vermischte Beiträge zur lateinischen Sprachkunde," *Eranos* 8 (1908) 112–13.
51. Cf. Josh 7:25.
52. Cf. Add Esth 16:18; cf. Gen 19:24–25.

whoever seizes someone puts that person below himself. Therefore, lest his cunning prove to be effective, the serpent was called back by the sentence of God and reduced to a level below his original creation,[53] that he might not be superior to the human being. As a result, he grieved not only because he had derived no benefit from his shrewdness but also because his status had deteriorated. For although one reads that he was wiser than the other beasts,[54] after he deceived man, he became cursed by all the beasts of the earth.

28. After the sentence was delivered against the serpent, then the woman, whom he had made his ally in despising God's law, received her sentence. For its says: "I will multiply your sorrows and your groans; in pain you will bear children; you will turn to your husband and he will be your master."[55] No one would confirm what he himself reprehends. If children were allowed because [the woman] had unjustly made use of intercourse, then the unjust use would be all the more established. If you think that procreation originated when he said "in pain you will bear children," where will you put the words: "Increase and multiply"?[56] Know, then, that the only penalty that was added was the pain, because [intercourse] previously had been conceded as a joy. And in order that a greater and harsher penalty might always beset the woman, there is added the turning to the husband, so that she might be restored again to her previous state.

29. If the Lord condemned intercourse in his servants, why did he add: "You will turn to your husband"? No one establishes as a punishment that which he condemns, because the punishment should be contrary to what is condemned; it should never arise out of the offense, but rather out of its opposite. If [the crime and the punishment] were the same, no one would fear condemnation. Would anyone give as a sentence that which is an offense against the law? This would amount to a confirmation, not a punishment, of sin. Therefore, if a woman's turning to her husband [derives] from the fact that she had intercourse and not because . . . ,[57] the turning, which previously was allowed in a simple manner, I believe, is now imposed on her along with extreme servitude as a penalty. Because it was through the woman that the man was made subject and because without a doubt he was formerly in a superior

53. Cf. Gen 3:14–15.
54. Cf. Gen 3:1, 14.
55. Gen 3:16.
56. Gen 1:28. Ambrosiaster refers to the fact that the command to procreate occurs before the Fall in the Genesis narrative.
57. There is a lacuna at this point in the text.

position (for he followed her advice and believed that it would be bene-ficial, so that God's work appeared to be destroyed by the cunning of the serpent), God's order was restored by the sentence. Therefore, the woman returned to her condition of subjection and humility before the man, as it had been established, and she received the additional penalty in these words: "I will multiply your sorrows and your groans; in pain you will bear children; you will turn to your husband and he will be your master."[58]

30. Was it decreed otherwise than that a woman should be subject to the lordship of her husband? Therefore, it is clear that the woman was recalled to the state in which she had been created, but with an addition. That is why he says: "I will multiply your sorrows and your groans." Why "multiply"? He adds to that which is less; he does not create something that is nonexistent. Therefore, the previous statement, "Increase and multiply," does not commence at the [moment of] creating, but only when the creation, which had been granted, was ruined. To the woman is added pain in childbirth; a difficulty is imposed, but no new form of procreation is composed. For if it were correct to think that generation derived from this, then generation would exist more because of the will of the serpent than of the Lord. In that case, there truly would be, as he says, "a brood of vipers."[59] But if anyone thinks that he has been born in this way, let him notice what she deserved, namely, that because of her sin her pain in childbirth was multiplied. She, who was to have a small amount of pain from children, received an increase because of sin, because children are born in sorrow and groaning and those who are born are not produced without sadness.

31. Next, in third place, this sentence is issued against the man: "Since you listened to the voice of the woman and ate of the tree from which I had forbidden you to eat, from this you ate, the earth has been cursed in your works, and you will eat in sorrow from it all the days of your life; thorns and thistles it will produce for you," and so on.[60] Even this one, that is, Adam, is recalled to that state in which he had been made, but with a detriment. Previously he had been created to work the earth in a simple way, so that an effect might follow from his labor. But when he spurned God's commandment, believing that by the counsel of the serpent he would acquire something better than what God had made, he was called back to the original order, but with a defect in his labor. As a

58. Gen 3:16.
59. Matt 3:7.
60. Gen 3:17–18.

result, the earth, having been cursed not in respect to itself, but in respect to man's work, did not respond to him according to his labor. Thus it showed that God's intention could not be subverted and that no one could provide better than God. For no one can love the work of another more than the very one who made it, as the apostle says, because "no one hates his own flesh, but he nourishes it and cares for it, just as Christ does his church."[61]

32. Let us now look at what follows in the law, whether it agrees with the beginning. Abraham, because he was pleasing to God, among the many rewards that his faith received, was judged worthy of bearing a son, even though he was old.[62] How, then, can one criticize that which God appears to have granted because of merit? For because Abraham had done God's will, God fulfilled Abraham's will. This certainly would not have been fulfilled, if it were not harmless, nor would God fulfill a wicked or ignorant request, especially from someone who was pleasing to him; even a human being would not do that. And Anna, because she was sterile and loved God, sought to have a son and received one.[63] But if it had been contrary, she could have been warned by the one whom she loved not to ask for something wrong. And her most holy son Samuel produced children and yet did not lessen the merits of his righteousness. From the earliest age, he always increased, so that in his happy old age he was commended by the testimony of God.[64] And the priest Zacharias, a just man, bore a son in his old age by the will of God, and at his son's birth merited to prophesy.[65] Why, then, should one attack that which we have proved to be no obstacle? And who would deny that one should deem good that which harms no one?

33. And it will strengthen my case to say something here about the apostles. Certainly the holy John preserved his virginity. But it is equally certain that his codisciple Peter had a wife and children, and producing children did not prevent him from receiving primacy among the apostles.[66] How, then, can one condemn that which does not restrict merits?

34. This is why the apostle demonstrated that he who has a wife, if he keeps the commandments in other respects, can and should become a

61. Eph 5:29.
62. Cf. Gen 18:10; 21:2.
63. 1 Sam 1:11, 20.
64. Cf. 1 Sam 8:1.
65. Cf. Luke 1:57, 67ff.
66. Cf. Matt 8:14. Souter, *Study of Ambrosiaster*, 40, suggests that the reference to Peter "is doubtless derived from one of the 'Clementine' writings." He refers to the pseudo-Clementine *Recognitions*. Clement of Alexandria, *Stromateis* 3.52, also cites the example of Peter to support the value of marriage.

bishop.[67] But if [marriage] were forbidden, he certainly could not say that a sinner should become a bishop. And what is so patent as this? For the voice of the same apostle says: "Concerning virgins I have no command of the Lord."[68] Because the Corinthians were being disturbed by heretics who hypocritically taught that marriage should be condemned, they asked the apostle by letter whether it was lawful to marry or to divorce a wife.[69] Then the apostle taught that a woman ought not to leave her husband,[70] although he had the opportunity to say that marriage was entirely forbidden, if he had known that such teaching was correct. He showed that he could not teach what he knew had not been handed down to him.[71] Which of the disciples, therefore, would dare to teach what has not been handed down by the master, whom he may hear proclaiming: "I wish the young women to marry, to bear children."[72]

35. But perhaps someone may say, "If it is licit and good to marry, why are priests not allowed to have wives, that is, so that those who already are ordained are forbidden to have intercourse?" Who does not know that each individual has a law in respect to his own person and dignity? For there is that which is forbidden to everyone as an absolute and general rule; then there is that which is allowed to some and not to others; and there is that which is sometimes allowed, but sometimes not allowed. Fornication is always illicit for all; to conduct business is sometimes allowed and sometimes forbidden. For example, before someone becomes a cleric, he is allowed to conduct business; but after he has become one, it is forbidden. And a Christian is allowed sometimes to have intercourse with his wife, but sometimes it is forbidden. For example, because of a day of procession intercourse sometimes is forbidden, because even from licit things one should abstain, in order to be able to obtain more easily what one asks for. That is why the apostle says: "By agreement, abstain for a time, that you may be free for prayer."[73] For even according to the law it was forbidden to be killed or

---

67. Cf. 1 Tim 3:2.
68. 1 Cor 7:25. Cf. Ambrosiaster's commentary on 1 Cor 7:27 (CSEL 81/2, 81): "[Paul] denies that he has received a command regarding virgins, because the author of marriage could not have decreed anything against marriage, lest he impugn his own original creation."
69. Cf. 1 Tim 4:2; 1 Cor 7:1.
70. Cf. 1 Cor 7:10.
71. Cf. 1 Cor 7:10, 12.
72. 1 Tim 5:14. In his commentary on this verse (CSEL 81/3, 283), Ambrosiaster praises the merits of married women over the vices of those virgins who "sin under a pious profession."
73. 1 Cor 7:5.

to quarrel during a fast, but it is allowed later, because greater reverence is owed to matters that concern God.[74]

36. Is everything that is allowed in the presence of others allowed before the emperor? How much more is this the case in matters that concern God! For this reason, it is fitting that his high priest should be purer than others, for he appears to bear the person of God himself. He is God's representative, so that what is allowed to others is not allowed to him, because he must act each day in the place of Christ, either praying for the people, or making an offering, or anointing. And not only is it forbidden for him, but also for his minister, because [the minister] also ought to be cleaner, as he ministers holy things.[75] Just as in comparison with a lamp, shadows are not only obscure but also sordid; but in comparison with the stars, a lamp is darkness; but in comparison with the sun, the stars are cloudy; but in comparison with the brightness of God, the sun is night; so those things that are licit and clean for us are, so to speak, illicit and unclean in respect to the dignity of God. For although they are good, nonetheless they are not suited to the person of God. Is not the tunic of an ordinary man, although it is clean, still sordid and illicit for an emperor? Likewise, is not a Saxon's tunic unbefitting a Roman senator?[76] For this reason, the high priests of God ought to be purer than other people, because they also bear the person of Christ, and they ought to be cleaner ministers of God. For no one ministers to the emperor who is not carefully prepared; and so, they minister garbed in bright, clean garments.[77] But because God is the brightest in nature, it is fitting that his ministers be clean, more in nature than in clothes.

SUGGESTED READINGS

Callam, D. "Clerical Continence in the Fourth Century: Three Papal Decretals." *TS* 41 (1980) 3–50.

Clark, E. A. *Ascetic Piety and Women's Faith. Essays on Late Ancient Christianity.* Lewiston, N.Y.: Edwin Mellen Press, 1986.

Gordini, G. D. "L'opposizione al monachesimo a Roma nel IV secolo." In *Dalla chiesa antica alla chiesa moderna,* edited by M. Fois, et al. Rome: Università Gregoriana Editrice, 1983.

74. Cf. Isa 58:3–4.

75. The "minister" in question is probably the deacon.

76. The word *saxonicia* does not appear in any of the standard lexica or thesauri. I have translated it here as an adjective in agreement with the word *tunica* from the previous sentence. Ambrosiaster may have in mind legislation of Gratian, Valentinian, and Theodosius (Jan. 12, 382), which prescribed the proper garb for a Roman senator: *Codex Theodosianus* 14.10.1

77. Cf. Rev 19:14.

Martini, C. *Ambrosiaster. De auctore, operibus, theologia.* Rome: Pontificium Athenaeum Antonianum, 1944.

Pietri, C. "Le mariage chrétien à Rome." In *Histoire veçue du peuple chrétien,* edited by J. Delumeau. Rome: Privat, 1979.

Souter, A. *A Study of Ambrosiaster.* TextsS 7/4. Cambridge: Cambridge University Press, 1905; reprint Nendeln, Liechtenstein: Kraus, 1967.

Cynic Epistles
(Selections)

INTRODUCTION

The following selection of letters is made from a group of pseudon-
ymous compositions referred to as the Cynic epistles. The first set (A) is
taken from those attributed to Crates, the second (B) from those ascribed
to Diogenes. Although we are quite sure that neither the historical
Crates nor the historical Diogenes wrote what here bears their names,[1]
we do not know beyond the most general suppositions who exactly is
responsible for them,[2] nor where the letters were first written.

All of the letters belong to the Augustan age. Those attributed to
Crates are generally thought to date from the first or second century C.E.
A number of them were written in response to and, thus, after those of
Diogenes. The latter are perhaps from the first century B.C.E. or before
(although the last two printed here are from a later period, perhaps the
second century C.E. or a subsequent date).

All of the letters selected discuss in different ways specific aspects of
the Cynics' way of life, the rigor of which was understood by them as
part of "training" (*askēsis*) for happiness. Thus, they describe, typically in
some detail, what the aspiring philosopher should and/or should not do
in accordance with this vision. Instructions and explanations are given

---

1. The historical Diogenes was born in Sinope at the end of the fifth century B.C.E.,
became a disciple of Antisthenes in Athens, and died in Corinth in the 320s. For further
details, see D.L. *Vitae* 6.20–81. Crates of Thebes, disciple of Diogenes and husband of
Hipparchia, was at his peak between 328 and 324 B.C.E. (= 113th Olympiad; see D.L.
Vitae 6.87). For further details, see D.L. *Vitae* 6.85–93, 96–98.
2. In fact, more than one person seems to have authored each set of letters.

about whom (not) to emulate. Stories are told, relating how some new bit of wisdom was acquired or demonstrated. There is, finally, the occasional polemic against persons whose opinion on these matters begged to differ.

It was thought at one time that the letters were written as rhetorical school exercises—in the case of Pseudo-Diogenes, "the work of three or four untalented rhetoricians who were content, for the most part, to reproduce or develop the themes of the Stoic diatribe." Scholars now believe that they rather represent a certain mode of propaganda, "to justify the Cynic modus vivendi and perhaps to offset the picture of the Cynics we find in such authors as Lucian."[3]

The type of asceticism in view in the letters is, for lack of a better term, "ethical" (versus cultic or "religious"). The purpose of its practice was not so much to attain greater intimacy with the divine as to break the shackles of dependency and conformity that the normal, that is, normative, culture imposed upon the ordinary citizen.[4] As a type of asceticism, it has been called "social protest."[5] However, I prefer the term "ethical" so as to reflect the fact that a different ethos is here proposed. In Greco-Roman antiquity, this "inner-worldly" asceticism often represented a certain political posture, directed against cultural traditions for the sake of social transformation. Achievement of the latter in the individual person was called "virtue." (See the introduction to selection 11 for more discussion.)

The text on which the following translations are based can be found in A. J. Malherbe, ed., *The Cynic Epistles* (see n. 3), which reprints the critical edition of R. Hercher, *Epistolographi Graeci* (Paris: Firmin-Didot, 1873).

---

3. See A. J. Malherbe, ed., *The Cynic Epistles* (Missoula, Mont.: Scholars Press, 1977) 17.

4. Cf. Walter O. Kaelber, "Asceticism," in Mircea Eliade, ed. *The Encyclopedia of Religion* (New York: Macmillan & Co., 1987) 1:441: "The term [asceticism], when used in a religious context, may be defined as a voluntary, sustained, and at least partially systematic program of self-discipline and self-denial in which immediate, sensual, or profane gratifications are renounced in order to attain a higher spiritual state or a more thorough absorption in the sacred."

5. See Vincent L. Wimbush, "Renunciation Towards Social Engineering (An Apologia for the Study of Asceticism in Greco-Roman Antiquity)," *Occasional Papers of the Institute for Antiquity and Christianity* 8 (1986) 5.

TRANSLATION

A. PSEUDO-CRATES

1. To my disciples:[6] Practice[7] needing little, for this is nearest to God, while the opposite is farthest away. And you, being halfway between the gods and unthinking[8] animals, will be able to become like the better kind and not the worse.

2. To the youth:[9] Get used to washing yourselves with cold water, to drinking water, to eating by the sweat of your brow, to wearing a coarse cloak,[10] to being worn out[11] on the ground; and the baths will never be closed to you nor shall the vineyards and flocks be fruitless and the delicatessens and bed-stores go bankrupt, as happens to those who have acquired the habit, for example, of washing themselves with hot water or drinking wine and eating though they do not toil[12] and wearing purple and resting on a bed.

3. To Patrocles:[13] Do not call Odysseus the father of the Cynic way of life,[14] who was the biggest softy[15] of the whole troop[16] and always put pleasure first before anything else, just because he once put on the outfit of a Cynic.[17] For clothes do not make a Cynic, but the Cynic the clothes—which was not the case with Odysseus.[18] First, he always suc-

6. Epistle 11 in Malherbe, *Cynic Epistles*.
7. The verb here is *askeō*, from which we get the English term "asceticism."
8. The adjective is *alogos*, i.e., without *logos*. The problem of how to translate this and all affiliated terms has been handled here and elsewhere by consideration of the context.
9. Epistle 18 in Malherbe, *Cynic Epistles*.
10. I.e., a *tribōn*.
11. I.e., sleeping.
12. Toil (*ponos*) was one of the basic characterizations of the Cynic way of life. See, for example, Pseudo-Crates 4, 15; and Dio Chrysostom *Or.* 7.66.
13. Epistle 19 in Malherbe, *Cynic Epistles*.
14. Cf. D.L. *Vitae* 6.103.
15. For a discussion of Cynic views on being "soft," see Leif E. Vaage, "Q: The Ethos and Ethics of an Itinerant Intelligence" (Ph.D. diss., The Claremont Graduate School, 1987) 552–71.
16. I.e., the Achaian army to which Odysseus belonged, whose attack on Troy is the setting of Homer's *Iliad*.
17. Specifically, when he disguised himself as a beggar upon his return to Ithaca. The outfit of a Cynic had somewhat the character of a uniform. Its standard features were (1) a coarse cloak (*tribōn*); (2) a beggar's bag (*pēra*); (3) a staff (most often, *baktēria*); and (4) bare feet. Julian *Or.* 6.200D (cf. Pseudo-Crates 33.2) calls the first three the *gnōrismata* or "identifying marks" of the Cynic philosopher. Long hair and a beard plus a filthy appearance were also not uncommon.
18. This was a topic of some debate. See, e.g., Lucian *Pisc.* 31; *Fug.* 20; and Pseudo-Diogenes 15.

cumbed to sleep as well as food. He sang the praises of the sweet life, never did anything without invoking God and Lady Luck,[19] begged from everyone—even the poor—and took whatever anyone gave him.[20] Rather, cite Diogenes, who put on Cynic clothing not just once but his whole life, who bettered both toil and pleasure, who begged—although not from the poor—who gave up every necessity, who had confidence in himself,[21] who never prayed that he would be honored for being pitiable but for being noble[22] and trusted reason[23] instead of guile and bow,[24] who was courageous not only when facing death but manly[25] when practicing[26] virtue. And it will be possible for you to follow not Odysseus's but Diogenes's lead, who, both when he was living and having died, set many persons free from vice for virtue through the sayings that he left us.[27]

19. The Cynics sharply questioned popular religious practice and other superstitions. See, e.g., Pseudo-Heraclitus 4; Julian *Or.* 6.199A; D.L. *Vitae* 6.28, 37, 39, 42, 59. See also A. J. Malherbe, "Pseudo Heraclitus, Epistle 4: The Divinization of the Wise Man," *JAC* 21 (1978) 50–51; idem, "Self-Definition among Epicureans and Cynics," in *Self-Definition in the Greco-Roman World* (Philadelphia: Fortress Press, 1982) 57–58; and L. Vaage, "The Woes in Q (and Matthew and Luke): Deciphering the Rhetoric of Criticism," *SBLASP* (ed. D. J. Lull; Decatur, Ga.: Scholars Press, 1988) 582–607.

20. The Cynics begged as a rule, but within certain guidelines. See, for example, Pseudo-Crates 26, 27; Pseudo-Diogenes 10, 34; Epictetus *Diss.* 3.22.10; D.L. *Vitae* 6.38, 46, 56, 59; further, Vaage, "Q: Ethos and Ethics," 328–33. Specifically, they were advised not to beg from everyone: cf. Pseudo-Crates 2, 17, 22, 36; Pseudo-Diogenes 38; Lucian *Demon.* 63; D.L. *Vitae* 6.67.

21. Specifically, he had the Cynic virtue of "boldness" (*parrēsia*). Concerning this particular virtue of the Cynics, see, e.g., Dio Chrysostom *Or.* 77/78.37, 45; Epictetus *Diss.* 3.22.19, 93–106; Lucian *Pisc.* 29–37; *Demon.* 3; Pseudo-Socrates 1 (12); Julian *Or.* 6.201A; and Malherbe, "Self-Definition," 56.

22. The term is *semnos*. The Cynics often characterized their way of life in terms of kingship or their possession of a certain kingdom. See, for instance, Julian *Or.* 6.195B; further, R. Höistad, *Cynic Hero and Cynic King: Studies in the Cynic Conception of Man* (Lund, Swed.: Carl Bloms, 1948); L. Vaage, "The Kingdom of God in Q," forthcoming in *Forum.* This included, then, taking on other sorts of kings, especially tyrants, and their kind of rule. See, for instance, Dio Chrysostom *Or.* 1–4; Epictetus *Diss.* 1.24.15–19, 25.21–22; Pseudo-Anacharsis 7; Pseudo-Diogenes 23, 34; further, J. M. C. Toynbee, "Dictators and Philosophers in the First Century A.D.," *Greece and Rome* 13 (1944) 43–58.

23. I.e., *logos*.

24. Odysseus was famous for both his cunning and his marksmanship. In Homer's *Odyssey*, the "man of many turns" demonstrates repeatedly his talent for ruses and deceptions. Classical Greek writers presented him sometimes as an unscrupulous politician.

25. The term is *andreia*. It is apparent that for the Cynics to follow their way of life meant "being a real man." Its contrary was to become "womanish" (cf. Pseudo-Crates 14). The conception is clearly sexist and, for Greco-Roman antiquity, quite conventional.

26. The verb, again, is *askeō*.

27. Cf. other collections of sayings from antiquity similarly thought to be instructive and salvific that may be found in John S. Kloppenborg, *The Formation of Q: Trajectories in Ancient Wisdom Collections* (Philadelphia: Fortress Press, 1987) 329–41.

4. To Metrocles:[28] After you left us to go home, I went down to the young men's palaestra[29] and having oiled up,[30] proceeded to run. But the young men, once they spotted me, were laughing at me, while I, in order not just to give up exercising, encouraged myself, saying, "Crates, you toil on behalf of your eyes, on behalf of your head, on behalf of your ears, on behalf of your feet." Well, they overheard me saying these things and no longer made merry but, trying it out, also began to run themselves. And from that moment on, they no longer merely oiled up but actually exercised and thus did not lead lives prone to illness like before. They then felt grateful to me as the cause of their health and would not let me go, but followed me wherever I strolled, listening to and imitating whatever I said and did.[31]

I have written you this so that you too do not run off by yourself but rather, where the young men spend their time, for whom we ought to show some concern, because deeds teach hardiness more quickly than talk, something found only in the philosophy of Diogenes.[32]

5. To Hipparchia:[33] Women are not by nature worse than men. Indeed, the Amazons, who wrought such impressive deeds, fell short of men in nothing.[34] If, then, you recall these things, do not prove less than they. For you would not persuade us that you are going to pieces in your own home. But what a disgrace after having distinguished yourself by shar-

28. Epistle 20 in Malherbe, *Cynic Epistles.*
29. The palaestra was for young persons what the gymnasium was for their elders. There were typically, at least in sufficiently large cities, several such institutions, distinguished according to age group and occasionally on the basis of sex. They were essentially sports grounds, generally square, surrounded by colonnades, in which the necessary services were set up, namely, cloakrooms, washstands, and training and massage rooms. At the side was a track for footraces. See H.-I. Marrou, "Education, History of," in Phillip W. Goetz, ed., *The Encyclopaedia Britannica: Macropaedia* (Chicago: University of Chicago Press, 1985). Cf. H.-I. Marrou, *Education in Antiquity* (Madison: University of Wisconsin Press, 1982).
30. The custom in Greco-Roman society was to spread (olive) oil on oneself before exercising.
31. The attraction of disciples by the Cynics is referred to and discussed occasionally in Cynic literature. See Pseudo-Diogenes 2, 38; D.L. *Vitae* 6.94; cf. Pseudo-Diogenes 31; D.L. *Vitae* 6.36.
32. Regarding the letter as a whole, cf. D.L. *Vitae* 6.91f.
33. Epistle 28 in Malherbe, *Cynic Epistles.* Hipparchia is the archetypal female Cynic. See D.L. *Vitae* 6.96–98; and further, L. Paquet, *Les cyniques grecs* (Ottawa: Éditions de l'Université d'Ottawa, 1975) 120–21. There is no way to know how many other women, if any, followed her lead.
34. The Amazons were legendary female warriors. The myth of the Amazons is believed to be a variant of the familiar folktale of a distant land where everything is done the other (wrong) way around. Thus, the Amazons as women fight, which was usually the occupation of men. See *Encyclopaedia Britannica: Micropaedia*, 1986 ed., s.v. "Amazon."

ing this Cynic way of life with your husband, both at the gates[35] and vis-à-vis wealth,[36] now to change your mind and halfway down the pike, turn back!

6. To the same woman:[37] Our philosophy is called Cynic not because we are indifferent[38] to everything, but because we aggressively endure what others, due to being soft or general supposition[39] find unbearable. So it is for this reason and not the former that they have called us Cynics.[40] Stay, therefore, and continue as a Cynic—for you are not by nature worse than we are, for neither are female dogs worse than male—in order that you also might be freed from Nature,[41] as all either because of law[42] or due to vices, live as slaves.

7. To the same woman:[43] I have sent you back the cloak[44] you sent me after weaving it, because it is forbidden those who live by hardship to wear such things; and so that I can stop you from doing this, into which you have launched so eagerly, so that you might appear to most like someone who loves her man. Now if I had married you for this kind of thing, what you are doing would be very fine indeed and through these things, you would have proven yourself to me. But if I married you on account of philosophy, which you yourself looked for, let such eager pursuits go their way; try, rather, to be of service to the life of human beings for their betterment.[45] For this is what you learned both from me and from Diogenes.[46]

35. Cf. D.L. *Vitae* 6.97 (*kai en tō phanerō synegineto*).

36. Crates was famous for the abnegation of his previous, considerable wealth: see, e.g., D.L. *Vitae* 6.87. Hipparchia rejected all other suitors, despite their wealth, noble birth, and good looks, to choose Crates as her husband (See D.L. *Vitae* 6.96).

37. Epistle 29 in Malherbe, *Cynic Epistles*.

38. I.e., *adiaphorein*.

39. I.e., *doxa*. Conventional opinion was one of the principal targets of the Cynics' critique. In their opinion, what for most of the members of civil society was "common sense" represented instead basic errors of assumption, if not a covert, corporate conspiracy of self-delusion.

40. A considerable discussion emerged about being called a Cynic, i.e., a "dog." Clearly the connotations were not especially positive. It is difficult to see how it could have been otherwise. Attempts were made, however, such as this one and some even more imaginative, to revindicate the title. See, further, Pseudo-Crates 16; Pseudo-Diogenes 2, 7, 44; D.L. *Vitae* 6.61.

41. This phrase is difficult to understand, insofar as the Cynics generally claimed to be following nature. Cf. Pseudo-Diogenes 36, 42; D.L. *Vitae* 6.22, 38.

42. Law (*nomos*) was, for the Cynics, just another form of conventional opinion (*doxa*). Any claims of a less relative foundation for it were rejected as deceptive (cf. Pseudo-Crates 5).

43. Epistle 30 in Malherbe, *Cynic Epistles*.

44. I.e., *exōmis*.

45. Among other things, the Cynics could describe themselves as pedagogues of humanity.

46. Another version of this letter is Pseudo-Crates 32; cf. D.L. *Vitae* 6.98.

8. To the same woman:[47] Reason[48] is the soul's guide, a beautiful thing, and human beings' greatest good. Seek, therefore, by whatever means to get it. For you will have yourself a happy life and a valuable possession. And seek out wise men, even if you have to go to the ends of the earth.

9. To the same woman:[49] I just learned that you gave birth and easily. For you told us nothing about it. But thanks be to God and to you. You are persuaded, I guess, that toiling is the reason why you did not toil. For you would not have given birth so very easily, unless you were toiling just like an athlete[50] while you were pregnant. Now, most women when they are pregnant go to pieces; and when they give birth, those who happen to come out of it alive have babies that are born sickly. But having demonstrated that that which had to come has arrived, take care of this little pup of ours. And you will do so, if you go at it with determination, as is your wont.

Let, therefore, his bath be cold, his swaddling clothes a coarse cloak, his food as much milk as is, in fact, not too much. You should lull him to sleep in a tortoise shell. For they say that this makes a difference also against childhood diseases. Whenever the time comes for him to speak or walk about, having decked him out not with a sword, as Aethra did Theseus,[51] but with a staff and a coarse cloak and a beggar's bag, which are able to defend human beings rather more than swords,[52] send him off to Athens. As for the rest, I will concern myself with rearing a stork for my old age instead of a dog.[53]

10. To Aper, greetings.[54] The oracle of the ancients, most honorable

47. Epistle 31 in Malherbe, *Cynic Epistles.*
48. I.e., *logos.*
49. Epistle 33 in Malherbe, *Cynic Epistles.*
50. The regimen of athletes could serve, like here, as a model or metaphor of the Cynic way of life. But athletes also represented at times the precise opposite, embodying exactly what the Cynic strived not to be. See, for example, Pseudo-Diogenes 31; D.L. *Vitae* 6.49.
51. In Greek mythology, the legend is that Aegeus, king of Athens, being childless, was allowed by Pittheus, king of Troezen, to have a child by Pittheus's daughter. Her name was Aethra; the child was called Theseus. When Theseus reached manhood, Aethra sent him to Athens. Along the way, he was forced to overcome a series of obstacles and dangers.
52. For a discussion of Cynic views on self-defense, see Vaage, "Q: Ethos and Ethics," 402–30.
53. The precise point of this sentence is unclear, partly because it is difficult to know if the first-person plural, used here in Greek, is intended literally to mean "we" or, rather, as I have translated it, as a stylized form of self-reference to the speaker, thus, "I." Regarding the letter as a whole, see D.L. *Vitae* 6.88. According to Eratosthenes, the son's name was Pasicles.
54. Epistle 35 in Malherbe, *Cynic Epistles.*

sir, not to flee what is inevitable,[55] said in brief something appropriate for every difficult situation. For it is inevitable that the person suffer misfortune who tries to flee from what cannot be avoided, as it is inevitable that one who tries to attain what is impossible fail to achieve it. Perhaps, then, I will therefore seem to you quite tactless and pedantic. And against this charge, I do not defend myself. Indeed, if it seems good to do so, lay the charge against me, but heed the ancients. For I believe, judging from my own experience, that we human beings are subject to affliction precisely whenever we wish to live a life without difficulty.

But this is not within the realm of the possible. For it is inevitable that we live with a body, as it is inevitable that we live also with other human beings, and most difficult situations develop out of both the foolishness of those who live together and, again, from the body. If, therefore, the knowledgeable person conduct himself in these terms, he is without pain and undisturbed—a happy person. But if he is ignorant even of this, he will never cease being buoyed up by empty hopes and gripped by desire. You, therefore, if you are content with the life of most persons, make use of those counselors, for, in fact, they are rather more polished in these matters. But if the life of Socrates and of Diogenes appeals to you, throw aside the things of tragedy for others and give yourself over to their emulation.

B. PSEUDO-DIOGENES

1. To Crates:[56] After you took off for Thebes, I was going up from Piraeus[57] around noon when, because of the hour, a powerful thirst came upon me. I hurried then to Panop's well. And while I was getting the drinking cup out of my beggar's bag, one of the servants working in the fields[58] came running up, cupped his hands, and was drawing water for himself from the well and drinking in this way. So I, of the opinion that this was wiser than a cup, was not ashamed to use him as a teacher of what is good.[59] Having therefore thrown away the cup I had, I have sent this piece of wisdom on to you as well, having found some people

55. I.e., *ta anagkaia*.
56. Epistle 6 in Malherbe, *Cynic Epistles*.
57. I.e., the main harbor of Athens.
58. Literally, the *chōra*.
59. From whom one learned or whom one recognized as a teacher was apparently a common preoccupation in antiquity. The idea, not to be ashamed to learn from those of lower social status (e.g., children or slaves), appears elsewhere both in Cynic literature (cf. Pseudo-Diogenes 13; D.L. *Vitae* 6.37) and in other texts (e.g., *Gos. Thom.* 4).

going up to Thebes, because I do not want to know anything of what is good without you.

But you too for this reason, try to forge your way into the marketplace, where many persons spend their time.[60] For thus we will be able to discover also other bits of wisdom from each of them in turn. For nature is manifold, which, having been ejected from life through supposition, we call back for human beings' salvation.

2. To Crates:[61] Approach as well the statues in the marketplace to beg your daily bread. For such an exercise is, in a way, also good. For you will meet persons more insensitive[62] than statues. And when they share with eunuchs and speakers of obscenity rather than with you, do not be amazed. For everyone honors the person close at hand, and not the one far off.[63] Those, then, who please the crowds are eunuchs rather than philosophers.[64]

3. To the same man:[65] Most persons, whenever they hear of a shortcut leading to happiness,[66] hurry toward the happiness they have imagined, just as we do toward philosophy. But once they get to the road and see how difficult it is, they back away as though they were ill, then somehow blame not the fact that they are soft but our insensitivity. Let, therefore, these persons sleep with their pleasures as they were eager to do. For toil will take hold of those who live this way—not the kind for which they slander us but greater ones—on account of which they are shamefully enslaved to every circumstance. But you, continue in your

---

60. The asceticism of the Cynics was eminently social. They did not retreat from public spaces to train themselves for happiness, but, rather, practiced their particular form of virtue precisely there. Thus, they could be found, as here, in the marketplace (see, further, Dio Chrysostom *Or.* 77/78.34–35; Pseudo-Diogenes 8, 11, 35, 37, 38; Lucian *Peregr.* 3; Julian *Or.* 6.202B-C; D.L. *Vitae* 6.58, 61, 69); on the docks (cf. Dio Chrysostom *Or.* 32.9); in public buildings (see, e.g., Dio Chrysostom *Or.* 8.4; D.L. *Vitae* 6.22); sanctuaries (see, e.g., Teles 8H.40–44); gymnasia (see, e.g., Dio Chrysostom *Or.* 6.14; Pseudo-Crates 20 [above, letter 4]); shops (see, e.g., Teles 46H.20–30); as well as banquets (see, e.g., Lucian *Nigr.* 25; *Pisc.* 34; *Fug.* 19; Julian *Or.* 6.201A; D.L. *Vitae* 6.33). Ian G. Kidd ("Cynics," in P. Edwards, ed., *The Encyclopedia of Philosophy* (New York: Macmillan, 1967) writes: "Independence [like that of the gods] was not to be achieved . . . by the withdrawal of a hermit; the Cynic engaged in an active crusade which required a continual training . . . in the very face of temptation, and thus to free the natural 'perceptions' and capacities for virtuous actions."
61. Epistle 11 in Malherbe, *Cynic Epistles.*
62. I.e., *arathesteros.*
63. Cf. Plato *Lys.* 214A–215C.
64. Regarding the letter as a whole, cf. D.L. *Vitae* 6.49.
65. Epistle 12 in Malherbe, *Cynic Epistles.*
66. The Cynics characterized their way of life as a shortcut to happiness. Cf. Pseudo-Crates 6, 13, 16, 21; Pseudo-Diogenes 2, 30, 44; Lucian *Vit. Auct.* 11; Julian *Or.* 7.225C; D.L. *Vitae* 6.104. See also V. Emaljanow, "A Note on the Cynic Short Cut to Virtue," *Mnemosyne* 18 (1965) 182–84; cf. D.L. *Vitae* 6.39.

training,[67] just as you began it, and be eager to oppose in equal measure pleasure and toil, because both are also equally inclined by nature to war with us and impede our most basic efforts,[68] the one because it leads to shameful things, the other because it leads away from what is good through fear.

4. To Apolexis:[69] I was asking you about a place to live. And thanks for taking it up, but after seeing a snail, I found a place to live that keeps away the wind, the large wine jar in the Metroon.[70] Release yourself, therefore, from this service and celebrate with us as we discover nature.

5. To Amynander:[71] One does not need to be grateful to one's parents, either for the fact that one was born, because what exists has been brought into being by nature, or for one's particular character. For the blending of the primal elements is the cause of this. And indeed, no thanks is needed even for the things done on purpose or intentionally. For birth is a consequence of making love, which is pursued for the sake of pleasure, not birth. These pronouncements I, the prophet of insensitivity, utter in opposition to the ignorant life. And if to some they appear to be too harsh, nature establishes them with truth, as does the life of those who live, not ignorantly, but in accordance with virtue.

6. To Metrocles:[72] Not only bread and water, a bed of straw, and a coarse cloak teach poise[73] and hardiness, but, if one needs to speak this way, also a shepherd's hand. Would that I knew as well that man of yore who was a cowherd! Take care, therefore, also of this, wherever you hurry off to. For it has to do with the ordering of our life. And let uncontrolled intercourse with women go its way, which requires a lot of free time. For there is no free time, not only for a poor man to beg, according to Plato,[74] but also for the person who is hurrying along the shortcut to happiness. Intercourse with women brings enjoyment to men[75]— the uneducated many—who likewise, on account of this practice, must pay the price. You will learn with those who have learned from Pan to do it manually. Do not turn aside, not even if certain people, on account of such a life, call you a dog or something worse.

67. I.e., *askēsis*.
68. I.e., *kai eis ta prōta empodizein*.
69. Epistle 16 in Malherbe, *Cynic Epistles*.
70. Cf. Lucian *Vit. Auct.* 9; D.L. *Vitae* 6.23.
71. Epistle 21 in Malherbe, *Cynic Epistles*.
72. Epistle 44 in Malherbe, *Cynic Epistles*.
73. I.e., *sōphrosyne*. The standard discussion of this extremely important term in Greek thought is Helen North, *Sōphrosyne* (Ithaca, N.Y.: Cornell University Press, 1966).
74. Cf. Plato *Resp.* 3.406A–407E.
75. Literally, *anthrōpoi*, human beings.

7. To Zeno:[76] One should not get married nor rear children, because our kind is weak, and marriage and children further burden human weakness with problems. For this reason, then, those who have entered into marriage and bringing up children for the sake of help,[77] later repent, once they know that these things only cause more troubles, when it was possible to have escaped from the beginning. The insensitive person, however, taking what is his[78] as sufficient for endurance, forgoes marriage and begetting children.

"But life will become void of human beings. For whence," you will say, "shall be the succession of generations?"

If only stupidity would leave life alone and everyone were to become wise! For now, only the person who has been persuaded by us will probably abandon these things, while life in general, unheeding, goes on making children for itself. But if humankind were also to fail, does this not merit mourning as much as if the begetting of flies and wasps were also to fail?[79] For this is what they say who have not considered the nature of things.

SUGGESTED READINGS

Primary Sources

Malherbe, A. J., ed. *The Cynic Epistles*. Missoula, Mont.: Scholars Press, 1977.

Mullach, F. G. A. *Fragmenta Philosophorum Graecorum*. 2 vols. Paris: Firmin-Didot, 1857/65; 1928.

O'Neil, E., ed. and trans. *Teles (The Cynic Teacher)*. Missoula, Mont.: SBL, 1977.

Paquet, L. *Les cyniques grecs*. Ottawa: Éditions de l'Université d'Ottawa, 1975.

Sternbach, L., ed. *Gnomologium Vaticanum*. Berlin: Walter de Gruyter, 1963.

Secondary Literature

Bernays, J. *Lucian und die Kyniker*. Berlin: Hertz, 1879.

Billerbeck, M. *Der Kyniker Demetrius: Ein Beitrag zur Geschichte der frühkaiserzeitlichen Popularphilosophie*. Leiden, Neth.: E. J. Brill, 1979.

———. "La réception du Cynisme à Rome." *Acta Classica* 51 (1982) 151–73.

Gerhard, G. A. "Zur Legende vom Kyniker Diogenes." *ARW* 15 (1912) 388–408.

Hock, R. "Simon the Shoemaker as an Ideal Cynic." *GRBS* 17 (1976) 41–53.

76. Epistle 47 in Malherbe, *Cynic Epistles*.

77. I.e., both now and later on in life. Families in antiquity (as in most other times and places) were a present source of labor plus old-age insurance.

78. I.e., what this person has in and by himself.

79. The Cynics had a reputation for being misanthropes (Pseudo-Heraclitus 5 [3]; cf. n. 25). According to Pseudo-Heraclitus 7 (2), however, the philosopher was always *skuthrōpos*, "not because I hate men, but because I hate their wickedness."

———. "The Workshop as a Social Setting for Paul's Missionary Preaching." *CBQ* 41 (1979) 438–50.

———. *The Social Context of Paul's Ministry: Tentmaking and Apostleship*. Philadelphia: Fortress Press, 1980.

———. "Lazarus and Micyllus: Greco-Roman Backgrounds to Luke 19:19–31." *JBL* 106 (1987) 447–63.

———. "Cynics." In *The Anchor Bible Dictionary*. New York: Doubleday & Co., forthcoming.

Höistad, R. *Cynic Hero and Cynic King: Studies in the Cynic Conception of Man*. Lund, Swed.: Carl Bloms, 1948.

Kindstrand, J. F. "Demetrius the Cynic." *Philologus* 124 (1980) 83–98.

Malherbe, A. J. "The Beasts at Ephesus." *JBL* 87 (1968) 71–80.

———. "Gentle as a Nurse: The Cynic Background of 1 Thess. 2." *NovT* 12 (1970) 203–17.

———. "Pseudo-Heraclitus, Epistle 4: The Divinization of the Wise Man." *JAC* 21 (1978) 42–64.

———. "Self-Definition among Epicureans and Cynics." In vol. 3 of *Self-Definition in the Greco-Roman World*, edited by B. Meyer and E. P. Sanders, 46–59. Philadelphia: Fortress Press, 1982.

———. "Antisthenes and Odysseus, and Paul at War." *HTR* 76 (1983) 143–73.

Moles, J. "'Honestius quam Ambitiosius'? An Exploration of the Cynic's Attitude to Moral Corruption in His Fellow Men." *JHS* 103 (1983) 103–23.

Niehues-Pröbsting, H. *Der Kynismus des Diogenes und der Begriff des Zynismus*. Munich: Fink, 1979.

Shorey, P. "Emendation of Çrates, Epist. XIX." *CP* 4 (1909) 323.

Vaage, L. "Q: The Ethos and Ethics of an Itinerant Intelligence." Ph.D. diss., The Claremont Graduate School, 1987.

———. "The Kingdom of God in Q." *Forum* (forthcoming).

———. "The Woes in Q (and Matthew and Luke): Deciphering the Rhetoric of Criticism." In *SBLASP*, edited by D. J. Lull, 582–607. Decatur, Ga.: Scholars Press, 1988.

MUSONIUS RUFUS
On Training
(Discourse VI)

INTRODUCTION

The opinions expressed in the following discourse are those of Caius Musonius Rufus, born in Volsinii, Italy, of an Etruscan family sometime before 30 C.E. He died toward the end of the century. The author, however, is a certain Lucius, evidently a pupil of Musonius,[1] whose work was likely published sometime after Musonius's death, that is, in the first half of the second century C.E.

Musonius taught in Rome, enjoyed his greatest popularity and influence at the time of Nero, followed Rubellius Plautus when Plautus was exiled to Syria, was himself then exiled by Nero to the island of Gyara in the Cyclades, later recalled to Rome after Nero's death, only to be exiled again and recalled once more. During the period of his second exile, Musonius is known to have been in Syria and Greece (that is, Athens). Lucius was apparently with Musonius for much of this itinerary, although we lack any further biographical information about him.

The present discourse is a rather conventional essay, one of twenty-one by Lucius that have been preserved on a variety of ethical questions. They appear as rather pallid summaries of what were likely, in the mouth of Musonius and the context of his person, much more vivid discussions full of the give-and-take, wit, and bite of philosophic debate.

Summarizing the contents of the discourse is difficult, insofar as it is itself already a summary. The basic point is the need not just to under-

---

1. He is, in any case, neither the Lucius of Apuleius nor Lucian the commentator on the *Categories* of Aristotle from whom Simplicius freely borrowed.

stand virtue, but also to practice it. Practice is a vital part of learning. (Compare it, for example, to the disciplines of medicine and music).

The type of ascetic behavior advocated here is similar to that of the Cynic epistles, although it is perhaps less radical in its vision. Certainly, like the Cynics, the ascetic behavior envisioned by Musonius is more "ethical" than "religious." Unlike the Cynic epistles, however, it is not the ethos of a new (natural) order of things that is rehearsed but, instead, part of the exigencies of being a philosopher. Musonius's comparison of the pursuit of a virtuous life with the training of a doctor or a musician suggests that his point of view has essentially to do with teaching, namely, learning what the philosopher in Greco-Roman antiquity traditionally did: demonstrate and promote the "good" life. We might speak, therefore, in this case of a "professional" asceticism, serving to accredit and consolidate the particular social role played by its practitioner.

The text on which the following translation is based is that of O. Hense as printed (and occasionally altered) in Cora E. Lutz, "Musonius Rufus, 'The Roman Socrates,'" *Yale Classical Studies* 10 (1947) 3–147.[2] The primary source (at least in the case of Discourse VI) is Stobaeus *Anthologium* III.29.78 (in the edition of Wachsmuth and Hense, III, pp. 648–51).

TRANSLATION

He used to exhort energetically those who were with him that they train,[3] always using these sorts of statements. "Virtue," he said, "is not only a matter of theoretical knowledge, but also practical, as is the case with medicine and music. It is necessary, therefore, just as the doctor and musician have mastered not only the theoretical aspects of their trade, but have also practiced[4] implementing them, that likewise also the person intent on being good not only thoroughly learn whatever teachings bear one to virtue, but also practice doing them with all due attention and toil.

Because how would anyone gain self-control[5] straightaway, if he only

2. Discourse VI is found on pp. 52–56. I am indebted to Lutz—specifically, the introduction to her work—for most of the historical information noted above.
3. I.e., *pros askēsin.*
4. I.e., *gegumnasthai.*
5. I.e., become *sōphrōn.*

knew that one should not succumb to pleasure, but had never practiced resisting it? How would anyone become just, having learned that one should love equality, but never having bothered to avoid greed? How would we acquire manliness, given that although we were aware, on the one hand, that what seems frightening to most persons is not to be feared, we had not bothered to become fearless in this regard? How would we become astute, knowing that what is good is truly so and that certain things are bad, but without practicing disdain for the things that only seem to be good?

For this reason, the learning of lessons appropriate to every virtue should always be followed also by training in it, if indeed it matters that we profit somewhat from the learning itself. And, indeed, inasmuch as the person set on doing philosophy should train even more than the person devoted to medicine or some such trade, so is philosophy a greater and harder undertaking than every other pursuit. For in the case of the other trades, those devoted to them have not thoroughly corrupted their souls beforehand nor learned things opposed to what they are about to learn. But those who apply their hand to philosophy have previously been in a state of great corruption and are quite full of vice and thus pursue virtue, needing even more training regarding this.

How, therefore, and in what way ought one to train with regard to these things? Because it happens that human beings are neither just a soul nor just a body, but something put together out of these two things, it is inevitable[6] that the one who trains take care of both, although especially of the better part, as is fitting, namely, the soul, but also the other, if indeed no part of the person is to be found wanting. For it is certainly necessary that also the body of the person who does philosophy be well prepared to do the body's work, because the virtues regularly make full use of this instrument, it being inevitable for the affairs of life.

With regard to training, then, one aspect of it would properly be a matter of the soul alone, while another would be shared by both the soul and the body. Now then, the training common (koinē) to both will be employed whenever we adapt to cold, heat, thirst, hunger, plain food, a hard bed, abstinence from pleasure, and endurance of strenuous labor. For through these and other things, the body is strengthened and becomes unfeeling and hard and useful for every task, and the soul is

6. I.e., *anangkē*.

strengthened, being developed, on the one hand, by endurance of toil toward manliness, on the other by abstinence from pleasure toward self-control.

The training appropriate to the soul is, first of all, seeing that proofs are ready to hand both concerning the things that seem to be good, that they are not good, and concerning the things that seem to be bad, that they are not bad, and to acquire the habit of making known the things that are truly good and distinguishing them from those that are not. And, then, to take care not to shy away from any of the things that seem to be bad nor to go after any of the things that seem good, and to avoid by all means those things that are truly bad, but to pursue in every way those things that are truly good.

To summarize, then, I have tried to state what kind of training each sort is. But I shall not here try at all to state how each should be done in detail, distinguishing and separating those disciplines that are shared by the soul and body and those that are properly for the soul alone, going rather pell-mell through what is pertinent to each. Because, in fact, all of us who have taken part in philosophical discussions happen to have heard and learned these things, that neither toil nor death nor penury is bad in any way nor anything else that has been freed from badness, nor, on the other hand, are wealth, life, pleasure good nor any other thing that does not partake of virtue.

Nonetheless, even though we have learned these things, on account of the corruption that is engendered in us straightaway from childhood on, and the evil style of life caused by this corruption, when toil comes our way we think that something bad is drawing near. And when pleasure is present we think that we have something good with us; death we shudder at as the ultimate fate, but life we embrace as the greatest of goods. We are pained when we pay money as though we were being hurt, but rejoice when we receive it as though we profited thereby. And likewise in the case of most other things, we conduct our affairs not in accordance with correct instruction but, rather, we follow common custom.

Because, then, I say, that these things are this way, it is necessary that the one who is training seek to master himself, that he try not to accept pleasure readily, not to avoid toil, not to take delight in living, not to fear death, and, in the case of possessions, not to esteem getting them more than giving them up.

SUGGESTED READINGS

Charlesworth, M. P. *Five Men: Character Studies from the Roman Empire.* Freeport, N.Y.: Books for Libraries Press, 1967.

Dudley, D. R. *History of Cynicism: From Diogenes to the 6th Century A.D.* London: Methuen & Co., 1937.

Pohlens, M. *Die Stoa: Geschichte einer Geistigen Bewegung.* 2 vols. Göttingen: Vandenhoeck & Ruprecht, 1959.

Ross, W. D. "Musonius Rufus." In *The Oxford Classical Dictionary,* edited by N. G. L. Hammond and H. H. Scullard. Oxford: Clarendon Press, 1979.

PHILO
On the Contemplative Life:
Or, On the Suppliants
(The Fourth Book on the Virtues)

INTRODUCTION

On the Contemplative Life (*De vita contemplativa*), attributed to Philo
Judaeus of Alexandria (ca. 20 B.C.E.–50 C.E.) and apparently meant to
accompany another treatise on the Essenes (*Vit. Cont.* I.1), describes the
life and rituals of an otherwise unknown mixed celibate community of
Hellenized Jews near Maerotic Lake in Egypt. The community members
are called the "Therapeutai," a term deliberately used by Philo in its
double sense of "worshipers" and "healers" (I.2). Although to whom the
treatise is addressed is unclear, it assumes on the part of the reader some
familiarity both with Judaism and Greek philosophy, especially that of
Plato. Its portrayal of the ascetic life style of the Therapeutes was so
important in establishing the antiquity of Christian monastic communities that Eusebius preserved large portions of it in his *Historia ecclesia*
(2.17), alleging that the Therapeutes were Christian monastics whose
community developed from St. Mark's missionary work in Alexandria.
Not only Eusebius but also other church fathers, including Clement of
Alexandria (*Strom.* 5.234), Jerome (*De Vir. Ill.* 11), and Porphyry (*Abst.*
4.11), refer to this work and the community it eulogizes. As early as 1583
with the appearance of Scaliger's *De emendatione temporum*, the importance of this work for the Christian church paradoxically led to questions about its authenticity as a work of Philo. However, the chief
skeptic of modern times has been Lucius (*Die Therapeuten*, Strassburg,
1880), who claimed that the asceticism described in *Vit. Cont.* belonged
to the third century C.E. and thus assigned the work to an unknown

Christian apologist of the same date. However, most scholars since F. C. Conybeare have accepted Philo's authorship as genuine.[1] Even with this acceptance, we are faced with a further anomaly. One of the reasons for its continuing appeal is that it is the only evidence we have for a Hellenized Jewish monastic community, especially one that included celibate women.[2] If *Vit. Cont.* is a work of Philo, it provides a link between Hellenistic philosophical Judaism and later Christian monasticism that seems almost too good to be true. Yet, as Conybeare has remarked, at least eight characteristics of "recluses" are contemporary with Philo's Therapeutes.[3] Although aspects of their ascetic piety (e.g., fasting, vigilance, prayer, and celibacy) are found also in later Christian communities, Philo's Therapeutes exhibit the traits of religious philosophers, dedicated to the cultivation (*therapeuein*, as their name implies; *Vit. Cont.* 1.2) of virtue. For Philo as a Jewish philosopher, such a life was "guided by God and in harmony with God and the Logos."[4] Following the "natural tendency of the religious philosopher to cultivate solitude,"[5] the Therapeutes reject wealth and property in the manner of Greek philosophers like Anaxagoras and Democritus (2.10) and practice spiritual training (*askēsis*) by studying what for Philo is the "highest philosophy," the Law of Moses.[6]

The life of contemplation (*theōria*) is also a means of achieving one of the four Stoic cardinal virtues: temperance or *enkrateia*. The subtitle of *Vit. Cont.*, "The Fourth Book of the Virtues (*Aretai*)" (assuming both that *aretē* means "virtue" rather than "mighty act," and that the book does not belong to Philo's other series of treatises, *De virtutibus*), leads one to speculate whether Philo intended it to point to the "fourth" of the Stoic

---

1. For an extensive discussion of opinions for and against authenticity, see especially F. C. Conybeare, *Philo of Alexandria, About the Contemplative Life; or, The Fourth Book of the Treatise Concerning the Virtues* (Oxford: Clarendon Press, 1895) 258–358; F. H. Colson, *Philo* (LCL; Cambridge: Harvard University Press, 1941) IX.104–5; Emil Schürer, *The History of the Jewish People in the Age of Jesus Christ (175 B.C.–A.D. 135)* (new Eng. version rev. and ed. by Geza Vermes and Fergus Millar; Edinburgh: T. & T. Clark, 1973) 2.591–97; Erwin R. Goodenough, *An Introduction to Philo Judaeus* (Oxford: Basil Blackwell & Mott, 1962) 32; David Winston, *Philo of Alexandria: The Contemplative Life, the Giants, and Selections* (Classics of Western Spirituality; New York: Paulist Press, 1981) 35.
2. For a comparison of the Therapeutes and Essenes, see Vermes and Millar, Appendix A to Schürer, *History* 2.593–97.
3. Conybeare, *Philo*, 274.
4. Goodenough, *Introduction*, 119.
5. Colson, *Philo* IX.105 n.
6. Conybeare, *Philo*, v n. 1.

cardinal virtues, *enkrateia*.[7] Further, if Philo wrote *Vit. Cont.* as "part of an *Apology for the Jews* addressed to gentiles,"[8] his intention might have been to demonstrate the superiority of the Jewish philosophical community over the Greek in its *enkrateia*, which he says the Therapeutes have seized upon as the "foundation of all the virtues" (4.34). Philo's extended polemic (5.40–7.63) against the Greek (and specifically Platonic) *symposia* may also illustrate the superiority of Jewish philosophy in bringing about a change in conduct by its practitioners.[9] He also wishes to distinguish the *anachōrēsis* (withdrawal) of the Therapeutes from that of the Greek philosophers (2.14) and from the extreme allegorists of Alexandria, inasmuch as it neither depletes the resources of city or kindred, nor is it undertaken as an "individual effort, outside organized religious life."[10]

The present translation is based upon the Greek text established by Leopold Cohn in volume IV of *Philonis opera quae supersunt*, edited by Cohn and Paul Wendland (Berlin: Georg Reimer, 1896–1930). Cohn's text is based upon the Greek codices, which he compared with the Armenian version, the Old Latin version edited by Johannes Sichardus (Basel, 1527), the excerpts from *Vit. Cont.* in Eusebius (*Hist. Eccl.* 2.17), and the edition of F. C. Conybeare (Oxford: Clarendon, 1895).

TRANSLATION

I

1. Because I have already discoursed upon the Essenes, who pursued and assiduously practiced the active life, or—to put it at any rate in a more acceptable sense[11]—having followed it in most respects, I shall presently, following the sequence of my presentation, discourse also upon what belongs to the subject of those who have embraced the contemplative life, adding nothing of my own for the sake of bettering the account, as is the custom of all poets and speechwriters to do, for

---

7. See Goodenough, *Introduction*, 31–32; Winston, *Philo*, 315 n. 1; Philo *Vit. Cont.* 4.34.
8. Goodenough, *Introduction*, 44.
9. See Philo *Congr.* 68–69, 79; see also Samuel Sandmel, *Philo of Alexandria: An Introduction* (New York: Oxford University Press, 1979) 113.
10. Harry Austryn Wolfson, *Philo: Foundations of Religious Philosophy in Judaism, Christianity, and Islam* (rev., 4th printing; Cambridge: Harvard University Press, 1968) I.69; see also Philo *Migr.* 16.89–90.
11. Conybeare, *Philo*, 192, follows the Greek manuscripts C, H, and P and the Armenian version by preferring "less bearable" (*aphorētoteron*).

lack of good habits, but simply embracing the truth itself, with respect to which even the most rhetorically skillful will fail. Nevertheless, one must persevere and make one's distinctions; for the magnitude of the virtue of these men must not become the reason for not speaking out on the part of those who are bound not to keep silent about any good deed.[12]

2. The source of the life of these philosophers becomes immediately clear in their appellation: for they are truly called *Therapeutai* and *Therapeutides*, either because they profess a healing art [*therapeia*] better than that in the cities—for the latter cures bodies alone, but the former also cures souls that have been overpowered by painful sicknesses that are hard to heal, pleasures and lusts and sorrows and greed and madness and injustice and an unnumbered host of other accidents and ills—or because they have been entrusted by nature and by the holy laws to care for [*therapeuein*] the Real, which is also better than the Good and purer than the One and more primal than the Moved.

3. With whom of those who profess piety is it right to compare them? Can it be with those who worship the elements: earth, water, air, and fire? To these elements some assign one name, others another, calling fire "Hephaestus," in my opinion, because of its "kindling" [*exapsis*] nature, whereas they call air "Hera," because it is "lifted up" [*airesthai*] and suspended on high; water they call "Poseidon," perhaps because it is "potable" [*poton*], and earth is "Demeter" because it appears to be the "mother" [*mētēr*] of all plants and animals.

4. But these names are the inventions of Sophists, because the elements are soulless matter, which cannot move on its own, having been made the foundation for all forms of shapes and creations by the Artificer.[13]

5. Or are they to be compared to those who worship the products of the elements, the sun, the moon, and the other stars, wandering or fixed, or the entire heavens and earth? But even these did not come into being in and of themselves, but of the agency of some Demiurge, who is most perfect in knowledge.

6. And what about those who worship the demigods? Surely this also is a matter worthy of jest, for how could the same person be both immortal and mortal? Apart from which, even the very source of their begetting is shameful, being infected by youthful intemperance, which

12. See Eusebius *Hist. Eccl.* 2.17.3; 2.16.1–2.
13. Thus Colson, *Philo* 9.115 and Winston, *Philo*, 42.

they impiously dare to attribute to the blessed and divine powers, as if those who have no share of mortal passion and are thrice-blessed had run mad and had intercourse with mortal women![14]

7. And what about those who worship images and idols, whose composition is of stone and wood, and who were up until a little while before completely without form, stonecutters and woodchoppers having cut them out of their natural structures, their kindred and related parts having become urns, footbaths, and other less honorable objects, more fittingly used in the dark than in the light of day.

8. It is not even right to mention what happens among the Egyptians, who have accorded the honor due the gods to irrational animals, not only the tame ones but even the most savage, from every sort of those dwelling below the moon—the lion among land-dwellers, the crocodile of those who inhabit the waters, and from those who make their way through the air, the kite and Egyptian ibis.

9. And although they see these creatures being born and in need of nourishment—being insatiable for food and full of excrement, venomous and man-eating, falling victim to all sorts of diseases, and dying not only a natural death but often a violent one—they yet bow down to them, civilized creatures bowing to creatures wild and untamed, rational creatures to the irrational, those akin to the divine to those distinguished in no respect from a Thersites,[15] those who are rulers and lords by nature to those who are by nature servants and underlings.

II

10. But seeing that these people fill with their folly not only the members of their own race but also their neighbors, let them remain incurable, maimed in their vision, the most vital of the senses—and I do not mean mere bodily sight, but that of the soul, by which alone the true and the false are distinguished.

11. But let the sect of the Therapeutes, on the other hand, having continuously been instructed beforehand to look, desire the sight of the Real, and to go beyond the sun of the senses; and let it never leave that ˙ post that leads to perfect happiness.[16]

12. They, entering upon their service[17] neither out of habit nor from

14. See Philo *Leg.* 2.557–58; *Op. Mund.* 100.7.
15. Homer *Il.* 2.215.
16. See also Socrates, speaking of "deserting his post" in Plato *Ap.* 22.28E–29A.
17. Cohn, Wendland, et al. *Philonis Alexandrini Opera quae supersunt.* 7 vols. Berloni: Georgii Reimeni, 1896–1930. Cohn has *therapeia*; Conybeare, following the Armenian

urging nor at the exhortation of any, but because they have been seized by a heavenly desire, are possessed by God like bacchantes and Corybants, until they behold the object of their desire.

13. Then, holding that because of their desire for the deathless and blessed life, their mortal life is already over, they leave their belongings to their sons and daughters or even to other relatives, bestowing inheritances ahead of time of their own free will, even to those who are not relatives, but companions and friends.[18] For it is fitting for those who have received visionary wealth ready to hand to leave blind wealth to those who are still sightless in their minds.

14. The Greeks praise Anaxagoras and Democritus because they, having been smitten with a longing for philosophy, allowed their property to become sheep pastures.[19] I myself also admire those men, who became greater than their possessions. But how much better are those who did not let go their property to be grazed by sheep but remedied the lack of those who were relatives or friends and made wealthy those who were without means. For the former act is thoughtless—I would not call mad an act of men at whom the Greeks marveled—but the latter act is sober and carried through with surpassing prudence.

15. What more would enemies do, who ravage the countryside of their opponents and cut down their trees, so that they might overpower them when they are suffering greatly, because of their scarcity of necessities? This is what those who followed Democritus did to those of their own blood, preparing for them a contrived need and an artificial poverty, not by intent perhaps, but through lack of foresight and by not seeing clearly what the others needed.

16. How much greater and more worthy of admiration, then, are these who, although having possessions, do not slacken in their philosophical pursuits but have honored greatness of mind above negligence and, while having fully surrendered their possessions, have not destroyed them, so that they benefit both themselves and others—others by their ungrudging largesse and themselves by philosophy. For anxieties occasioned by goods and possessions squander the time, but it is good to be frugal with time because, according to Hippocrates the physician: "Life is short, but art is long."[20]

---

version, has *theōria*.

18. Eusebius *Hist. Eccl.* 2.17.

19. Compare Philo *Prov.* 2.12.13; Plato *Hi. I* 282A; Plutarch *Per.* 16; *De vitand. alien.* 8.85lf.; Cicero *Tusc.* 5.114; *Fin.* 5.87; D.L. 11.6; Horace *Ep.* 1.12.12; Lactantius *Div. Inst.* 3.23; Origen *Cels.* 2.84.

20. Hippocrates *Aph.* 1.1.

17. Even Homer, as it seems to me, intimated this in the *Iliad*, at the beginning of the thirteenth book, with these words:

The Mysians, who fight hand-to-hand combat, and the noble Hippomol-goi, milk-drinkers, plain-living, these most just of men[21]

as though he were speaking on the one hand about injustice, caused by anxiety over livelihood and making of money and resulting in inequality, on the other hand about justice, caused by the opposite course of life, according to which the wealth of nature is regulated and surpasses that found in vain imaginings.

18. Therefore, when these give up their possessions while they are still unseduced by anything, they flee without turning back, leaving behind siblings, children, wives, parents, numerous relations, the company of friends, and the native lands in which they were born and raised, because custom is an attractive and most potent source of enticement.[22]

19. Moreover, they do not emigrate to settle in another city, like those luckless or bad servants who beg to be sold by those who have acquired them, procuring for themselves not freedom, but an exchange of masters—for each city, even the best governed, is filled with tumult and unspeakable disturbances, which one who was once and for all taken up by wisdom could not endure.

20. They instead pass their time outside the city walls by seeking solitude in garden spots or solitary wild places,[23] not because of some crude or artificial misanthropy, but because they know that intercourse with persons who are dissimilar in habit is unprofitable and harmful.[24]

III

21. Therefore, the sect exists in many places in the inhabited world—for it was fitting for both Greek and barbarian to share in the perfect good[25]—but its members are quite numerous in Egypt in each of the so-called nomes and especially around Alexandria.

22. The best from all quarters set out as if to a fatherland that was far from their home, to a most favorable region, situated most opportunely for the sake of safety and the temperateness of the air, above Lake Maerotis upon a plateau.

21. Homer *Il*. 13.5–6; compare Philo *Conf. Ling.* 1.405.
22. Compare Philo *Decal*. 2.181.
23. Compare Philo *Abr*. 23.
24. See Eusebius *Hist. Eccl*. 2.17.7.
25. Ibid.

23. The dwellings and villages in a circle around them provide the safety, while the temperateness of the air is yielded by the natural breezes from the lake, which has its mouth toward the sea, and because the sea is nearby, the light breezes from the sea and the heavy ones from the land make up the most healthful state because of their intermingling.

24. The houses of those who have come together here are very frugal, affording shelter from two of those things most necessitating it, the heat of the sun and the chill of the air. But they are not close together, like houses in cities—for this is a source of trouble and displeasure for those who have become zealous after solitude, and neighbors press too closely—nor are they far apart, because of the community life they welcome, and so that, if there should be an incursion of brigands, they might come to each other's aid.

25. And in each house is a sacred chamber, which is called a sanctuary [sēmeion] or chapel [monastērion],[26] in which, being drawn apart, they celebrate the mysteries of the holy life, bringing nothing into it—not drink nor food nor anything necessary for bodily needs—only the laws and the pronouncements declared as oracles by the prophets, hymns, and other writings by which knowledge and piety are increased and perfected.[27]

26. Therefore, they keep the memory of God always unforgotten, because even in their dreams nothing other than the beauties of the divine virtues [aretai] and powers [dynameis] appear;[28] many of them even talk in their sleep in dreams of the glorious teachings of sacred philosophy.

27. They are accustomed to pray twice each day, at dawn and at dusk; when the sun rises, praying for a fine day that is truly fine, filling their understanding with heavenly light, and when the sun sets, they pray that the soul, completely unburdened of the multitude of perceptions and sensations, sitting in its own council and assembly, may pursue the truth.[29]

28. The interval from dawn to dusk with them is completely devoted to training [askēsis]: for in reading their sacred literature they philosophize[30] according to the wisdom of their ancestors, by allegorizing, con-

---

26. See Conybeare, Philo, 211.
27. See Colson, Philo, 127 n. 9; Eusebius Hist. Eccl. 2.17.9.
28. Conybeare, Philo, 217; cf. Philo Conf. Ling. 1.431; Quaest. in Ex. 2.68.
29. Conybeare, Philo, 213; see also Eusebius Hist. Eccl. 2.17.10.
30. See Philo Vit. Mos. 2.216; Som. 1.15.

sidering that the words of the written text are symbols of a hidden nature that is revealed in deeper meanings.

29. They also possess the writing of the ancients who, because they were the founders of the sect, left behind them many memorials of the method applied in allegories, which they use like some archetypes to imitate the procedure of the method.[31] They do not simply practice contemplation but also compose songs and hymns to God in all sorts of meters and melodies, which they necessarily inscribe with rather solemn rhythms.

30. For six days each of them, remaining alone and apart, practices philosophy in the previously mentioned chapels, neither going beyond the outer door not looking outside,[32] but every seventh day they gather as a common assembly and are seated in order according to age with appropriate demeanor, their hands inside their garments, the right hand between the breast and the chin, the left hand withdrawn along the flank.[33]

31. Then the eldest and most learned in their teachings comes forward and speaks, with a firm countenance and in a firm voice, with reason and prudence, not making an inappropriate display of rhetorical cleverness like the orators and sophists of the present time, but, after having searched closely in his thoughts for precision, he also expounds it. This precision does not rest merely on the tips of the ears, but through the hearing, enters into the soul and sticks there fast.

32. This common shrine, in which they assemble every seventh day, is a double enclosure, one side of which is reserved for the men, the other for the women; for even women, in accordance with their custom, are members of the congregation, because they have the same zeal and the same vocation.[34]

33. But between the two enclosures a wall is built, in the manner of a breastwork, about three or four cubits above the ground floor, the upper floor being left open to the roof for two reasons: to preserve the modesty befitting the female nature on the one hand, and on the other for those [women] sitting within earshot to have ready access to the speaker's voice, with no impediment.

31. Eusebius *Hist. Eccl.* 2.17.12–13; Conybeare, *Philo*, 214; Colson, *Philo* 9.130–31.
32. Conybeare, *Philo*, 214, conjectures this as meaning, "They do not even look out of a window," always supposing that they had windows.
33. See Philo *Som.* 1.61.
34. Conybeare, *Philo*, 215–16, contrasts the Therapeutes with the Essenes in their inclusion of women.

IV

34. Having seized upon temperance [*enkrateia*] as a foundation beforehand, they erect the other virtues of the soul upon it. None of them would touch food or drink before sunset, because they judge the pursuit of philosophy worthy of the daylight, whereas the necessities of the body deserve the darkness,[35] for which reason they allot daytime to the former and a small portion of the night to the latter.

35. And some, in whom a greater desire for knowledge is set, do not remember to eat until after three days;[36] while others are so fortunate, and fare so sumptuously as the guests of Wisdom, who furnishes her teachings so abundantly and unstintingly that they even refrain from eating for double this time, and scarcely after six days do they take a taste of necessary nourishment, being accustomed to feed upon air, as they say grasshoppers do, their song, as I myself think, alleviating their lack of nourishment.[37]

36. But because they believe that the seventh day is all-hallowed and a high festival day, they deem it worthy of a special honor. On it, after paying attention to the soul, they also care for the body, releasing it from its constant toils, just as they also release their beasts.

37. But they eat nothing lavish, only plain bread, with salt as seasoning, to which the more fastidious add hyssop, while their drink is springwater.[38] For they appease the mistresses that nature has set over the mortal race—hunger and thirst—giving them however nothing in addition to curry their favor, but only those necessities without which it is not possible to exist. They eat for this reason—so that they may not be hungry—and they drink so that they may not be thirsty, because they consider satiety inimical and treacherous both to soul and to body.

38. Now as to their two forms of shelter, clothing and housing, we have said previously of their housing that it is unadorned and improvised, erected only for necessity. Their clothing likewise is very plain, intended for the remedy of intense cold and extreme heat, a heavy cloak instead of a shaggy hide during the winter,[39] and a sleeveless vest or a garment of linen in summer.

---

35. Cf. Winston, *Philo*, 318 n. 19.
36. Compare Philo *Vit. Mos.* 3.2.145.
37. See Plato *Phdr.* 259C; Philo *Omn. Prob. Lib.* 8.
38. See Eusebius *Hist. Eccl.* 2.17.14–15.
39. "Instead" rather than "from" for *anti* is the reading of Conybeare, *Philo*, 219, and Colson, *Philo*, 134–35.

39. For they exercise a total modesty, knowing that vanity is the origin of falsehood and modesty the origin of truth, but each has the significance of being a source, because the manifold forms of evil flow from falsehood while from truth issue the benefits of good, both human and divine.

V

40. But I also wish to speak of their common meetings[40] and the rather cheerful pastimes of their banquets [*symposia*], in comparison with the banquets of others. For the latter, when the wine is poured unmixed, as if they are drinking not wine but some drug inciting madness and frenzy and something even more grievous, act like wild dogs, rearing up to bite each other and snapping at each other's noses, ears, fingers, and other parts of the body, to prove true the myth about the Cyclopes and Odysseus's companions, who ate up "morsels" of men, as the poet says, and acting even more savagely than the Cyclopes.[41]

41. For he, suspecting enemies, acted to avenge himself, but they attack neighbors and friends and at times even relatives, at their own salt and at their own tables, exchanging acts of war for scenes of peace,[42] like the actions of those performing gymnastic exercises, counterfeiting the true coin of training [*askēsis*] as wretches rather than wrestlers,[43] for this is the phrase that must be assigned them.

42. For the deeds that athletes do in the stadia when sober, during the day, subject to the observation of all Greece, with skill and for the sake of victory and crowns [as Olympic victors], these wretches, counterfeiting the former at night at their drinking parties, in the darkness, perform to their dishonor and to the affront and harsh outrage of those who suffer them, [and] becoming intoxicated, behave drunkenly, without skill and with evil art.[44]

43. And if no one should come forth into their midst as an umpire, to put an end to such affairs, they wrestle to the overthrow with a greater license, thirsting for blood and ready to die at one and the same time, for they suffer no less than they inflict, a thing of which they are ignorant,

40. See Strabo 17.8.794C, on the pattern of the voluntary association (*thiasos*).
41. Homer *Od.* 9.373f.: "And from his gullet burst forth wine /and morsels of human flesh."
42. See Philo *Spec. Leg.* 3.96; *Gig.* 51; *Conf. Ling.* 46.
43. So Winston, *Philo*, 48, following Colson, *Philo*, 139, and Conybeare, *Philo*, 223, who calls this phrase "a common pun in antiquity."
44. See Conybeare, *Philo*, 223.

having lost their wits by daring to drink wine, not, as the comic poet says, to the harm of their neighbors alone but also to their own harm.[45]

44. So, for example, those who shortly before came to the banquets safe and sound and as friends, depart shortly after as enemies and mutilated in body, some even needing lawyers and judges, while others require the aid of apothecaries and doctors.

45. Still others, who appear to be rather moderate drinking companions, after downing unmixed wine like mandragora, brim over and, thrusting their left elbows forward and twisting their necks at an angle, belching into their drinking cups, are weighted down by a deep sleep, neither knowing nor hearing anything, as if they had only one sense, the most servile one—taste.

46. But I know some who, when they become slightly drunk, and before they become completely soaked, make ready ahead of time the next day's drink from voluntary contributions and deposits, supposing that the hope of drunkenness in future is happiness at hand.

47. Passing their lives in this way, they remain homeless and hearthless, hateful to their parents, wives, and children, hateful to their native land, and enemies even of themselves, for a luxurious and profligate life is a menace to all.

VI

48. But someone perhaps might approve the style of banquets that now prevails everywhere because of the desire for Italianate extravagance and luxury, at which Greeks and non-Greeks alike aim, making their preparations for show rather than for good cheer.

49. There are dining rooms with three or more couches, decorated with tortoise shell or ivory and with more costly material, most set with precious stones, with coverings of genuine purple interwoven with gold, others dyed with flowers of all kinds of colors to draw the eye; a number of drinking cups drawn up in order according to each kind, rhytons and phials and kylikes and many other kinds, most skillfully wrought beakers, perfectly made with relief carvings by ingenious craftsmen.

50. The slaves who wait at table are most well formed and of surpassing beauty, as if they are present not for the sake of their service but rather for the pleasure their appearance affords the gaze of the beholders. Those who are still small boys pour out the wine, while the bigger

45. Cohn, *Philonis Opera* IV.57 n. 18.

boys, freshly bathed and clean-shaven, carry the water. They make up their faces and underline their eyes and braid their hair well, binding it tightly.

51. For they all have thick hair, either because they have not cut it at all or have cut only the forelocks at their tips for an even balance and the precise appearance of a more circular line.[46] And they wear chitons as fine as cobwebs,[47] made very white, girt up with the front hanging a little below the knee and with the back a little below the hip joints; and by drawing each section together along the seam of the tunic with double-twisted cords,[48] they tie the tunic in uneven folds, widening the spaces at the sides.

52. Still others wait in relays, lads or adolescents with downy cheeks,[49] having recently sprouted facial hair and having become a little before the playthings of the pederasts, carefully trained for heavier services, specimens of the hosts' wealth, as far as those who employ them know, but as is actually the case, specimens of their lack of taste.

53. In addition, there are a variety of sweetmeats and spices and seasonings over which bakers and cooks labor, taking care not to please only the taste, as is necessary, but also the sight with their elegance . . . [lacuna] . . . swiveling their necks around [those who attend the banquets][50] greedily crave with their eyes the plumpness and abundance of the meat and with their noses the savor the food gives off. Then, when satiety of both sight and smell occurs, they urge each other to eat, praising not least the preparations and the host for his extravagance.

54. Seven and more courses are brought in, loaded with everything that earth and sea, rivers and sky produce, everything choice and plump, selected from the beasts of the land, the fish of the sea, and the birds of the air, each of them differing both in presentation and in seasoning. So that no species occurring in nature be omitted, the last tables are brought in loaded with fruit, apart from those set aside from the revels and those selected as a second course.

55. Then some tables are carried out empty because of the greediness of the guests, who, taking their fill in the manner of sea gulls, gulp it

---

46. This phrase is very difficult to translate. Colson, *Philo*, 143, uses Conybeare's "provisional rendering," 229–30, which I follow.

47. Thus Conybeare, *Philo*, 230.

48. The description of these tunics is rather convoluted. Given the antihomoerotic tone of the entire passage, it would seem that the aim of this style of dress is to show as much of the young male body as possible.

49. See also Homer *Od.* 11.318; Xenophon *Symp.* 4.23.

50. Cohn's conjecture for the lacuna, *Philonis Opera* IV.63 n. 3.

down in such a way that they gobble up even the bones, but other courses they leave half-eaten, having already mutilated them and pulled them to pieces. And when they finally give up, some having filled their bellies up to the throat, while others still unsatisfied in their desires, . . . [lacuna] . . . [turn to drink].[51]

56. But why should I talk at length about these things, which are condemned by many of the more temperate as exacerbating desires whose curtailment would be beneficial? For one should pray for those most abominable things—hunger and thirst—rather than the luxurious abundance of food and drink at such feasts.

VII

57. Of the drinking parties in Greece, the two that are most celebrated and famous are those at which Socrates happened to be present: the one at the house of Callias, at the time he gave the victory feast when Autolycus was wearing the crown,[52] the other at Agathon's, which men who were philosophers both in character and discourse, Xenophon and Plato, thought worth mentioning,[53] for they recorded as worthy to be remembered those banquets they supposed posterity would use as paradigms of orderly conduct.

58. Yet even these, when compared to the banquets of our subjects, those who pursue the contemplative life, appear ludicrous. Although each of the former descriptions has its own charms, the more human account is that of Xenophon, describing flute girls, dancers, wonderworkers, makers of jests in their banter, those who took their joking seriously, and other things of the kind that belong to the merrier sorts of recreation.

59. But almost the whole of Plato's account is about love[54]—not only of men who are madly in love with women, nor of women who are madly in love with men, for those passions serve the laws of nature[55]—but of men with men, who differ from them only in age.[56] For even if the subject of love and the heavenly Aphrodite seem to have been discussed in a refined way, this was done for the sake of rhetorical flourish.

60. For the common and profane love has entirely taken up the

---

51. Cohn's conjectural emendation to fill the lacuna here, *Philonis Opera* IV.60 n. 18.
52. Athenaeus 5.187F.
53. Plato *Symp.* 143A; Xenophon *Symp.* 2.11ff.; Plutarch *De Pyth. or.* 15, 401C.
54. See Plato *Symp.* 172B.
55. Ibid. 180D.
56. Ibid. 173A; Xenophon *Symp.* 2.1.

greatest part of the discussion—the love that on the one hand takes away manliness, the virtue most useful for life in war and in peace, and that on the other hand produces effeminacy as a disease in the soul, making androgynes out of those who ought to be fitted with all the pursuits necessary for defense.

61. And, having abused the time of boyhood, it has reduced it to the status and disposition of a boy-beloved and has also caused damage to the lover with regard to the barest necessities, body and soul and property. For necessarily the mind of a pederast is disposed toward his darling, sharp-sighted with regard to him alone but blind toward all other matters, private and public; [and his body] wastes away with passion, especially if he should not obtain his object of desire, while his property is lessened in two ways, both from neglect and from expenditures on the beloved.

62. But there also grows up alongside this another, greater, common evil, for these people bring about the desolation of cities and a scarcity, sterility, and infertility of the best type of men—these people who imitate persons ignorant of farming. For instead of the deeply furrowed fertile plain they sow salt-sea fields and stony, hard places that, in addition to having a nature that produces nothing, destroy the seeds that have been sown in them.[57]

63. I keep silent about the fabrications of the myths concerning the double-bodied people—who, although at the beginning growing together because of the powers that made them one, afterwards were sundered in those parts that had been put together, the harmony by which they once were joined having been lost[58]—for all these tales are seductive, capable by the novelty of their conception to entice the ears, but those who are familiar with Moses, having learned from their first youth to love the truth, look down upon them as from a great height, remaining undeceived.

VIII

64. But because the famous banquets are full of such folly, carrying in themselves their own conviction, if anyone is willing not to regard them according to their reputation and the report handed down about them as being an unqualified success, I shall set in opposition to these the ban-

57. Plato *Leg.* 8.838C.
58. Plato *Symp.* 189D–90.

quets of those who have dedicated their own lives and themselves to knowledge and to the contemplation of the questions of nature according to the most sacred precepts of the prophet Moses.

65. In the first place, they assemble every seventh week, reverencing not only the simple set of seven days but also its square; for they know it to be pure and ever-virgin.[59] It is the eve of the great festival that has been allotted the fiftieth day,[60] fifty being the most sacred and most natural of numbers, as it is formed from the square of the right-angled triangle, which is the source of the creation of the All.[61]

66. So when they assemble, clad in snow white raiment, joyous but with the height of solemnity, at a sign from the daily priests, the *ephemereutai*—for it is their custom to call those who are in such service by this name—before they recline, standing in a row in rank order and holding their eyes and hands toward heaven, their eyes because they have been trained to behold things worthy of their sight and their hands because they are cleansed of desire and soiled by no excuse of things done for the sake of gain,[62] they pray that their feast may be acceptable to God and that it take place according to his will.

67. And after the prayers, the elders recline, following the order of their admission.[63] They do not regard them as elders because they are well struck in years and have white hair [but like young boys still][64] if they have fallen in love with this sect late in life. They only consider as elders those who, from their early youth and into their prime, have entered into the contemplative side of philosophy, which is indeed the loveliest and most divine.

68. And women also feast together with them, the majority of whom are elderly virgins, who have retained their purity not out of necessity, as some of the priestesses among the Greeks do,[65] but rather of their own free will, out of their zealous desire for Wisdom. Having desired to

---

59. Winston, *Philo*, 320 n. 38, following Conybeare and Colson, takes this festival of the "seventh hebdomad" as occurring on the fiftieth day, *after* the 49 days, which are "seven squared," and compares the festival to the three "first fruit festivals at Qumran," following J.M. Baumgarten, *Studies in Qumran Law* (Leiden, Neth.: E. J. Brill, 1977) 131–42.

60. I.e., Pentecost; see Conybeare, *Philo*, 238; Philo *Spec. Leg.* 2.176; Josephus *A.J.* 3.10.6.

61. See Philo *Spec. Leg.* 2.176; *Vit. Mos.* 2.80; Plutarch *Moral.* 373F.

62. Colson, *Philo*, 153: "for the cause of gain" takes issue with Conybeare's "pretense."

63. Conybeare, *Philo*, 240: "election."

64. Cohn, *Philonis Opera* IV.64 n. 1, brackets these words, which are omitted in the Armenian version. He is followed by Winston's translation, but Colson and Conybeare both eliminate the brackets.

65. See Plutarch *De. def. or.* 435D; *De Pyth. or.* 413F; Origen *Cels.* 7.48 (365).

live together with her, they have had no regard for the pleasures of the body, having struggled in the birth pangs, not of mortal offspring but immortal ones, which the soul that loves God is able to bear on her own, when the Father has sown the rays of mind in her, by which she will be able to contemplate the teachings of Wisdom.[66]

IX

69. Their order of reclining has been divided, with the men apart on the right and the women apart on the left. And does anyone not suppose that coverlets, even if inexpensive ones, yet softer at any rate, would be provided for those who are nobly born, refined, and trained in philosophy? Yet they have pallets made of any material that is handy, and upon them very cheap coverings of local papyrus, affording little room for leaning upon the elbows: for although they soften a Laconian harshness in training, they always and everywhere practice the contentment of the free, hating with all their might the charms of pleasure.

70. They are not waited upon by slaves, being of the opinion that the possession of servants is utterly contrary to nature, for nature has made all free, but the injustices and greed of those who pursue the kind of inequality that breeds mischief, by putting the yoke of power on the weaker, have bound them to the stronger.

71. At this holy banquet, however, there is no one who is a slave, as I have said, but the free are servants, discharging their serving functions not under compulsion nor by awaiting commands, but with a willing spirit, anticipating requests with zeal and enthusiasm.

72. For those who are appointed to this service are not simply those who chance to be free but young men chosen from those in the organization with every care, according to merit, in a manner befitting those who are refined and noble, aiming for the height of virtue. These serve eagerly, like true-begotten sons, pleasing to their fathers and mothers, regarding those whom they serve as common parents, more their own than those of their blood, because indeed there is nothing more native to the right-minded than nobility and goodness.[67] And they enter to do their serving ungirt, with their tunics let down, so as not to present any appearance of a servile demeanor.

73. At this banquet—I know that some will laugh when they hear, but only those committing actions worthy of weeping and wailing will

---

66. See Eusebius *Hist. Eccl.* 2.17.17–19.
67. See Philo *Omn. Prob. Lib.* 87; *Abr.* 2.6; *Vit. Mos.* 3.2.161, 10; Matt 12:47//Mark 3:35.

laugh—wine is not brought in on those days, but only clearest water, cold for many, but warm for those of the elders who are delicate. The tables also are clean of anything containing blood: the food upon them consists of loaves of wheaten bread, seasoned with salt, although sometimes a flavoring of hyssop is offered as additional seasoning on account of the fastidious.[68]

74. For as right reason instructs priests to offer wineless sacrifices, so it also instructs these to conduct their lives; for wine is a drug of madness, and costly meat inflames the most insatiable of wild beasts, desire.[69]

X

75. Such are the preliminaries. But when the participants in the banquet are reclining in the orders that I have indicated, and when the attendants are standing in their order, ready for service [their president, after a great silence has fallen upon them all][70]—but, one might say, when does it not? Still, it is a greater silence than before, so that no one dares to murmur or even to breathe too loudly—investigates some passage from the sacred scriptures or even elucidates a proposition put forth by another, paying no heed to display—for he does not aim for a rhetorical tour de force—but rather desiring to see things more accurately and, having seen, not to begrudge his vision to those who are not similarly clear-sighted, as they at any rate have an equal passion for learning.

76. He employs a rather leisurely method of instruction, pausing at intervals[71] and lengthening his discourse by means of repetitions, engraving his thoughts upon their souls—for in the explication of one who runs things together glibly in one breath, the mind of the hearers, being unable to make the connections, falls behind, and fails to comprehend what is being spoken.

77. But these listen with their attention directed straight at him [pricking up their ears and lifting up their eyes],[72] remaining in one and the same posture, signifying their agreement and understanding by a nod

68. See Philostratus *VA* 6.11.112 for the rejection of meat by true philosophers.
69. See Philo *Spec. Leg.* 1.148, 1.94; Plato *Ti.* 70E.
70. Here Cohn's conjectural emendation for the lacuna at this point (IV.66, n. 4) is followed; Conybeare's suggestion (247) translates, "Their president, when a common silence has fallen." Cohn's version, which follows the Armenian, seems more likely.
71. Conybeare's suggestion (*Philo*, 248).
72. Cohn, following the Armenian, offers this conjecture to fill the lacuna in the Greek text at this point (IV.66 n. 15); Conybeare (249) conjectures only "pricking up their ears."

and a glance, and their approval of the speaker by a smile and a slight turning round of the countenance, whereas they indicate any difficulty by a gentler movement of the head and with the tip of a finger of the right hand. And the young men who are standing around pay no less attention than do those who are reclining.

78. The exegesis of the sacred scriptures is given through their hidden meanings by way of allegories.[73] For the entire Law appears to them to resemble a living creature,[74] having as its body the written commandments, but as its soul the unseen sense that is stored up in the wording, in which sense the rational soul especially begins to contemplate the things that belong to it, beholding as if through a mirror of words the extraordinary beauties of thoughts being revealed and, once it has unwrapped and disclosed the symbols, bringing forth the thoughts naked into the light for the benefit of those who are able, with a little prompting, to contemplate the invisible by means of the visible.[75]

79. Then, when the president appears to have spoken long enough, and when the discourse on his side and the hearing of it on the part of his audience has risen to meet objections without error, in accordance with his intention, applause rises from them all,[76] as if they were all rejoicing together at what is yet to follow.

80. Thereupon the president, standing up, sings a hymn composed to God, either one he himself has just written or an old one written by the poets of old—for they have bequeathed many measures and tunes, trimeter verses,[77] processional hymns, hymns for offerings, hymns to be sung at the altars, and choral songs written with carefully worked-out measures for many varieties of evolutions.[78] After him, the others also sing, in ranks and in appropriate order, with those who listen to them in the utmost silence, except whenever it might be appropriate to sing the conclusions of verses and refrains, for then all the men and women sing out.

81. But when each has finished a hymn, the young men bring in the table mentioned a little earlier, and upon it is the sacrosanct food, unleavened bread with a seasoning of salt with which hyssop has been

---

73. See Plutarch *Aud. Poet.* 19E; Plato *Resp.* 2.378D; Eusebius *Hist. Eccl.* 2.20; Origen *Hom. in Lv.* 5.1.

74. Plato *Phdr.* 264C; Philo *Quaest. in Gen.* 3.3; Marcus Aurelius *Med.* 4.40, 5.8.

75. See Plato *Men.* 81; *Resp.* 7.259; Dio Chrysostom *Or.* 4; Philo *Leg. All.* 2.353.21.

76. Conybeare, *Philo*, 251, following the Armenian, inserts "applauding three times."

77. See Conybeare, *Philo*, 252; Josephus *A.J.* 7.12.3.

78. Only Colson (*Philo IV*; Appendix 524) remarks on this novel form of Hellenizing the Jewish liturgy via the Greek chorus, with its stasima, strophes, and antistrophes.

mixed,[79] out of respect for the holy table that has been set up in the sacred vestibule [*pronaos*] of the Temple,[80] for upon it are pieces of bread and salt, without spices, the bread unleavened and the salt unmixed.

82. For it was considered appropriate that the simplest and least composite things be assigned to the most powerful class of priests as a reward for their service, and that the others, while desiring these things, refrain from them, so that their superiors might retain their privilege.

XI

83. After the supper they keep a sacred vigil. The vigil is observed in this manner: they all rise together, and first two choruses, one of men and the other of women, are formed in the middle of the banquet hall. The most revered and most musical person is chosen for each as their conductor and chorus leader.

84. Then they sing hymns to God composed in many measures and many melodies, sometimes in unison, sometimes in antiphonal harmony, clapping their hands and dancing, calling upon God at times in processional hymns, at times in standing hymns, and performing turns and counterturns in their dances.

85. Then, when each of the choruses has celebrated the feast individually and separately, as in the bacchic feasts after they have quaffed the unmixed wine dear to the god, they come together again and become one chorus out of two, in imitation of the chorus of old, instituted beside the Red Sea because of the wonders that were wrought there.

86. For the sea at God's command became the cause of salvation for some and of utter destruction for others. For when it burst asunder, withdrawing with the violent recoil of its waves, each side opposite the other like solid walls, the ground between them was revealed as a highway, and the portion that had been opened up was shown to be entirely dry land, across which the people walked to the opposite shore, when they were led to the higher ground. But when the sea ran back over the dry land with the onrush of the returning water, and when it was poured back over the dry bottom, the enemies who had pursued them closely were inundated and destroyed.

---

79. Winston, *Philo*, 321 n. 49, points out that salt being mixed with the shewbread is in the LXX, not in the Hebrew.

80. Conybeare, *Philo*, 253, points out that the table with the shewbread mentioned in Exod 25:30; 29:32–33; Lev 24:5–9; 8:31; 1 Sam 21:4–5; and Matt 12:3 appeared only in the Temple at Jerusalem and not in the synagogues.

87. Having witnessed and experienced this event, which was a work greater than word, thought, or expectation, men and women together, inspired by God, forming one chorus, sang hymns of thanksgiving to God their savior, the prophet Moses leading the chorus of men and the prophetess Miriam leading that of the women.[81]

88. From this chorus that of the Therapeutai and Therapeutides most likely has been copied, the treble chorus of the women answering the deep voices of the men in responsive melodies and antiphons, accomplishing a harmonious and truly musical concord of sound. Their thoughts and their speech being utterly noble, the choral dancers are also reverent, the aim both of their thoughts and their speech and the dancers being piety.

89. Thus they are drunk until dawn with this lovely intoxication, not being heavy-headed or drowsy, but even more clearheaded than when they were attending the banquet, and standing with their faces and their entire bodies in the direction of the dawn, when they see the sun rising, they stretch their hands up to heaven and pray for well-being, truth, and clear-sightedness of thought. And after the prayers they each withdraw to their own sanctuaries to their customary trade and cultivation of philosophy.

90. So much then, for the Therapeutai, who take delight in the contemplation of nature and of things in nature, and live on the soul alone, being citizens of heaven and of the world,[82] having been truly commended to the Father and Maker of All by their virtue, which has procured for them the friendship [of God],[83] adding to it the most proper gift of nobility, better than every good fortune, attaining to the very height of happiness.

SUGGESTED READINGS

(*Note*: Although there are many works on Philo and some extensive commentaries, such as that of F. C. Conybeare, on *De vita contemplativa*, there are no treatments of the specific relationship of this treatise to ascetic behavior, either of a philosophic or religious type. Thus, I have included first some general works

---

81. This idea of a "double chorus" appears to be an interpretation of Exod 15:1–18, with Moses leading the chorus of the "people of Israel," and Exod 15:19–21, with Miriam leading the women of Israel in song and dance, the latter probably being the older version of this song.

82. A standard Stoic concept: see Conybeare, *Philo*, 257, citing Phil 3:20.

83. Added by Cohn (71 n. 22); cf. Philo *Sobr*. 56; *Vit. Mos*. 1.156; *Rer. Div. Her*. 21; *Omn. Prob. Lib*. 44; *Abr*. 129; *Leg. All*. 3.204; Isa 41:8; Winston, *Philo*, 321 n. 52.

on Philo and then some works upon his relationship to contemporary religion and philosophy. For further references, consult the footnotes.)

On Philo

Bréhier, Emile. *Les idées philosophiques et religieuses de Philon d'Alexandrie*. Paris: Librarie Philosophique, 1925.

Drummond, James. *Philo Judaeus*: or, *The Jewish-Alexandrian Philosophy in Its Development and Completion*. 2 vols. London: Williams & Norgate, 1888.

Goodenough, Erwin R. *By Light, Light*. London: Oxford University Press, 1935.

Heinemann, Isaak. *Philons griechische und jüdische Bildung*. Hildesheim, W.Ger.: Georg Olms, 1962.

On Philo, Philosophy, and Judaism

Armstrong, A. Hilary. "The Self-Definition of Christianity in Relation to Later Platonism." In *Jewish and Christian Self-Definition*, vol. 1, *The Shaping of Christianity in the Second and Third Centuries*, edited by E. P. Sanders, 74-99. Philadelphia: Fortress Press, 1980.

Cohen, Shaye J. D. *From the Maccabees to the Mishnah*. Library of Early Christianity, vol. 7. Philadelphia: Westminster Press, 1987.

Festugiére, André Jean. *Personal Religion among the Greeks*. Berkeley: University of California Press, 1954.

Goldstein, Jonathan. "Jewish Acceptance and Rejection of Hellenism." In *Jewish and Christian Self-Definition*, vol. 2, *Aspects of Judaism in the Greco-Roman Period*, edited by E. P. Sanders, 64–87. Philadelphia: Fortress Press, 1981.

Moore, George Foot. *Judaism in the First Centuries of the Christian Era*. 3 vols. Cambridge: Harvard University Press, 1927-30.

Nickelsburg, George W. E. *Jewish Literature Between the Bible and the Mishnah*. Philadelphia: Fortress Press, 1981.

Nickelsburg, George W. E., and Michael E. Stone. *Faith and Piety in Early Judaism*. Philadelphia: Fortress Press, 1983.

Whitchurch, Irl Goldwin. *Philosophical Bases of Asceticism in the Platonic Writings and in Pre-Platonic Tradition*. New York: Longmans, 1923.

JULIAN OF ECLANUM
To Florus
(in Augustine, *The Unfinished Work Against Julian*)

INTRODUCTION

The Latin passages here translated are taken from Julian of Eclanum's treatise *To Florus*. This eight-book treatise is not extant, but a large portion of it was excerpted by Augustine in his last polemic against Julian, which remained unfinished at the time of Augustine's death in 430 C.E. Julian, an Italian cleric of the early fifth century, tried in the *Ad Florum* (*To Florus*) to counteract the severe asceticism championed by some contemporary Christian writers.

Although Augustine is Julian's chief target, he was by no means the most enthusiastic partisan of sexual renunciation in this era; indeed, Augustine's treatises *On the Good of Marriage* and *On Holy Virginity*, composed as companion pieces in 401, had modified the rigorous asceticism advocated by Jerome that verged on denouncing marriage entirely. Nor was Augustine the first to criticize Jerome's position: it had already, in the 390s, been challenged by the Christian writer Jovinian, who stressed the equal status of marriage and virginity. In response to this debate, Augustine affirmed both Jerome's preference for virginity and Jovinian's praise of marriage and reproduction.

From the mid-390s on, however, Augustine had grown increasingly committed to the theory that sin had been transmitted from Adam and Eve to all later humans, a view for which he thought he found support in Romans 5. In 412 C.E. and the years thereafter, this theory became a point of argument between Augustine and followers of Pelagius (including Julian), who contended that a properly Christian understanding of the goodness of creation and the freedom of the will precluded Augustine's belief in the automatic passage of sin from the first humans to their descendants.

Augustine's reflection on human freedom had led him to hypothesize the ways in which the effects of its loss still plague us: a war rages within us between good resolutions and evil desires; all humans must suffer death; and—of great importance for the present topic—human sexual life has been rendered forever problematic. In the seeming uncontrollability of our sexual organs, in the sense of shame at nudity and during sexual activity, even in women's pain during childbirth, Augustine saw the results of original sin. Over against these present realities, Augustine set a vision of life in Eden as it would have been had Adam and Eve not sinned: although the first couple would have reproduced by sexual intercourse (a view rejected by Jerome, Gregory of Nyssa, and John Chrysostom), they would have felt no lust, their sexual members would have been under the perfect control of the will, no shame would have attended the sex act, and Eve would not have suffered pain in childbirth. In elaborating this vision of how human life *should* have been, Augustine believed that he had upheld the goodness of marriage but had "improved" upon some features of sexual activity as we presently know it (of which he had extensive experience during his own adolescence and early manhood).

To Julian of Eclanum, who espoused the teaching of Pelagius, Augustine's theory seemed dangerous: marriage and human bodies were devalued, infants were deemed guilty despite their inability to make choices, and the Creator himself was implicated by the evils of human life. For Julian, lust was an endowment given humans at creation. He argued that Augustine's conclusions about original sin, based on the sense of shame and on pain in childbirth, were disproved by experience. Indeed, if human bodies were tainted, how could God have deigned to become man? According to Julian, Augustine's position led straight to "Manichaeanism," that is, to the view that the human body and human nature were derived largely from an evil principle. Julian's charge of "Manichaeanism" hit hard, as Augustine at his baptism had renounced a long youthful devotion to the Manichaean religion.

From 418 or 419 to the end of Augustine's life in 430 C.E., Julian kept his opponent under siege. Augustine replied to Julian in Book II of *On Marriage and Concupiscence*, in *Against Two Epistles of the Pelagians*, and in *Against Julian*, as well as in this last, exhaustive work of his life, the *Contra Secundam Juliani Responsionem Opus Imperfectum*, in which Augustine's method is to cite passages from Julian's *To Florus* and then argue against their import. A few of these passages from Julian's treatise are here translated into English for the first time. They show that Julian's position not only was coherent but also might be more attractive to some Christians of every era than Augustine's theory that original sin is transmitted through sexual intercourse.

Selections from the first three books of the *Opus Imperfectum* are translated from the critical edition of those texts in CSEL 85/1 (Vienna, 1974); selections from books four through six of the *Opus Imperfectum* are taken from the nineteenth-century Benedictine edition of the works of Augustine, which can conveniently be found in *PL* 45.

TRANSLATION

[Julian forcefully expresses his starting point:]

This always was the greatest distinction between Manichaeans and Catholics,[1] the broadest boundary, one might say, by which the doctrines of the religious and those of the irreligious are set apart from each other—I might even hold that this point is the great bulwark that separates our opinions as the heights of heaven from the earth: we ascribe every sin to an evil will, whereas they ascribe it to an evil nature. (I, 24)

[Julian especially faults the consequences of Augustine's theory of original sin for his assessment of marriage and reproduction:]

As for original sin, if (as you say) it is acquired by generation from the moment of birth, it is possible to condemn marriage, which was instituted by God; moreover, original sin cannot then be taken away from infants, since what is innate continues to the end of life in the person in whom it inheres by virtue of its origin. (I, 61)

We are not stirring up calumny against you, as if you were condemning marriage and were positing that man, who is born from it, is a work of the devil. We neither point this out in bad faith nor do we draw inferences in ignorance. We do, however, anxiously and guilelessly note what might be the logical conclusion of your train of thought. For never is there marriage without the union of bodies. When you say, "Whoever is born from that union belongs to the devil," you surely proclaim that the devil has legal power over marriage. (I, 62)

---

1. Julian views himself as an orthodox Catholic and Augustine as a Manichaean.

Finally, in churches that enjoy great honor and large congregations of people, it is preached that the force of sin is so great that even before the formation of the members, before the soul exists and is placed in the body, sin, hovering over the ejaculated seed, attacks the hidden parts of the mother and makes guilty those about to be born. And at birth itself, an already older guilt is waiting to take on substance. This law of sin, dwelling thereafter in the members, compels captive man into the service of crime—man, who is more worthy of pity than deserving of reproof in his disgrace, because what we declare to be the faults of an evil will, this in the church is proclaimed by men, women, and distinguished priests to be a suffering that stems from our origin. (II, 8)

There I responded to you thus: with deference to your authority, I say that you evade the point. Rather, learn that truth will remove your freedom to ramble. Just look: although we are content to hold that sin is the work of an evil will or the work of the devil, we ask how this sin can be found in an infant. Through the will? But there is no will in him. Through the formation of the body? But God bestows the body. Through the entry of the soul? No, because the soul owes nothing to bodily seed but rather is made anew by God. Does this sin come through marriage? No, for that belongs to the parents' act, and you yourself have stressed that the marriage act is not sinful. If you have not in fact conceded this—as the course of your discussion proves—marriage itself is cursed because it is the cause of evil. But in fact, marriage does not have an "essence" of its own; rather, its very name shows that it is the act of persons, that is, of parents, who by their union, in your view, become the cause of sin and are rightfully condemned. On this understanding, it can no longer be doubted that marriage partners should be delivered to eternal punishment, because by their deed it comes about that the devil acquires the exercise of lordship over men. If you accept this view, you abandon the whole point that earlier you seemed to hold, that is, that man is a work of God. It obviously follows that the devil is the author of humans and from him comes the origin of those born, if offspring take their beginning from the union of bodies, if evil comes into humans through their origin, and if through evil, the devil gets his right over humans. (II, 24)

. . . The Apostle [Paul] knew, and knew full well, that marriage is not to be censured, for to it belongs friendship, service, and sexual intercourse accompanied by pleasure, which was instituted and blessed by God. Thus it is not possible for the devil to hold possession of the offspring, nor is the fruit of marriage cursed. It is in accordance with the highest justice that sin is not imputed unless the freedom to abstain from it is present. (II, 39)

. . . Let us clarify what we have said by a summary: sexual union implicates the offspring only in that those who are married become parents. If the parents yearn to behave rather licentiously with each other, or if they stray into illicit, adulterous sexual union, their behavior cannot affect the children, because children are born from the force of the seeds, not from the filth of vice. (II, 40)

Thus there is transmitted to the offspring not the vice of the begetters, but the seeds. It is God, however, who established the force of the seeds and blessed them, as even you are forced to confess. (II, 41)

[Julian draws a lesson from Jesus' words in Matt 22:30, his reply to the Saduccees' question on the woman married seven times:]

. . . Knowing his own works, Jesus described why marriage had been instituted, namely, so that offspring might fill up the ranks of those doomed to death. He also teaches, however, that abundant fertility will come to an end when greedy death is no more. If then by Christ's own attestation—Christ who is its author—fertility is created so that it might counter the frailty of human nature, it means that this state of marriage was ordained before sin. Thus it seems that mortality relates not to the duplicity of sin but to nature—and marriages are also ordained to pertain to it as well. . . . (VI, 30)

[Julian enlists the Apostle Paul's discussion of sin in Romans 5 to support his views over against Augustine's theory of the transmission of original sin from Adam:]

The Apostle shows that he did not affirm sin to be transmitted by generation, for when he names "man," he adds "one." "One" is the first number. In explaining through which person he thought sin was introduced, he not only named him, he even counted! He writes, "Through one man sin came into this world."[2] Now "one" suffices to show that the act was a deed of imitation, because "one" is not enough for generation to take place. Sin indeed was passed on, but by only "one." It is evident that imitation, not generation, is here indicted, for generation cannot take place except through two people. So prove that generation took place by Adam alone without a woman! Your elegant talent doesn't

2. Rom 5:12.

even shrink from making a claim like this! Or, as doubtless you understand that reproduction cannot take place except through two people, agree, even if belatedly, that the work of two persons [i.e., sexual reproduction] is not condemned by the number "one." . . . (II, 56)

However, when I say that Adam's sin was the greatest, it is not because I doubt that the devil was more guilty, but because the Apostle Paul, when he gives the reason for the course of events, thought it more fitting to mention the man—because it is especially from the man that he thought the human race successively descended—rather than to name an aerial substance [i.e., the devil]. Indeed, of those humans it surely was the first woman who transgressed, but because the father is in all things more powerful and has the greater authority, Paul said that the man was the pattern for sin. He taught this not because the trespass originated with the man, but due to the power of the male sex, he judged that the man was more likely to be imitated. You see, of course, that the consequence of this way of thinking demonstrates its agreement with the truth. (II, 190)

[Julian holds that both libido and pleasure are "natural" to humans, placed in them at creation, before the first sin—and that what is in accordance with "nature" carries its own necessity:]

. . . We show by the testimony of the whole world that the pleasure of all the senses is something given in nature. But that pleasure and concupiscence were present in Paradise before the sin, the facts themselves declare. A way was thus paved for transgression through concupiscence, which by the beauty of the apple incited the eyes and spurred on the expectation of a pleasant taste. This concupiscence errs, then, when it does not keep within its bounds, but when it keeps to the limit of the permissible, it is a natural and innocent inclination. It cannot, I say, be the fruit of sin; rather, is it proved to be the occasion for sin not through its own fault but through that of the will. . . . (I, 71)

. . . If then you would say that it is written of this union that "they become two in one flesh,"[3] and that accordingly the Apostle Paul said "through one man" in order to signify that the members of those generating were joined together, I will reply that this verse also prevails against your impiety, for it is not written that "there will be two men in one man," but "there will be two in one flesh." By naming the union in this way, that pleasure of sexual intercourse and libido that by affecting

3. 1 Cor 6:16; cf. Gen 2:24; Matt 19:5 = Mark 10:8; Eph 5:31.

the senses overcomes the limbs, and as that wise man Paul understood, that longs to make one flesh, is shown to have been instituted by God and placed in bodies before sin. (II, 59)

. . . Next, when we speak of libido, without which there can be no union of the spouses, we assert that it is natural and belongs to the work of God. We do not defend it as some great good, but as the sense of bodies, which were made by God. In many writings you try to claim that libido was inserted into the inner parts of man by the devil, and in this you bring shame on your teaching. . . . (III, 142)

. . . For thus God made bodies, God distinguished the sex of bodies, God made the genital organs, and God placed in us the desire through which these bodies are joined with each other. Furthermore, God gave power to the seeds, and he works through the mystery of nature upon the material of the seeds—and God, to be sure, makes nothing that is evil, nothing that is guilty. (IV, 40)

. . . Thus as for the libido, which is found both in humans and in animals, it is of nature and was established by God—the very libido about which you ramble in various of your disputations, through which you twist amidst varied and contrary doctrines, misunderstanding it not less from foolishness than from impiety. . . . (IV, 120)

What was to the Maker a possibility passes into the creature as a necessity. For he made diverse natures and diverse species within the natures, keeping to an order that flowed forth from the beginning of things, so that some things were of necessity and others were in the realm of the possible. Thus whatever creatures have by nature, they were allotted from the side of necessity. (V, 46)

[Julian sets forth his own reproductive theory:]

Then this new scientist [i.e., Augustine], neglecting the things that I said, declares that we are wrong when we wrote, "Just as then the soil that was taken up, the matter, was not the author of man,[4] so now that force of pleasure which forms and mixes the seeds does not effect the force of the divine operation; rather, from the treasurehouse of nature it offers to God the material from which he deems it worthy that man be made." Yet although he testifies that I explained these points correctly—with the exception that I said that the seeds are prepared by the force of pleasure—Augustine speculates on the matter in this way:[5] "The plea-

4. Gen 2:7.
5. *On Marriage* II, 26.

sure of that carnal lust of the flesh does not form the seeds; rather, seeds are already in bodies, formed by the true God. They are not made by pleasure, although pleasure accompanies their arousal and ejaculation." It is evident that he set this forth not to deceive, but from a lack of understanding. For by "the force of pleasure" I meant the principle of the virile body, to which I necessarily assigned the name "virility." Thus this "virility" (we now are allowing the word) depends upon the structure and health of the genital organs and the internal parts, and it serves desire and [sexual] activity. This I named "the force of desire and concupiscence." I preferred to call it not simply "desire," but "the force of desire," in order to indicate that all-encompassing fire that is felt both before and during the act.

In fact, those with an infirmity of the genital organs, for example, eunuchs, do not have seed, although admittedly they are stirred by some ashes of the fire that was put out [by their castration]; they are not able to generate offspring, however, because by their particular debility they have been deprived of the force of the bodily members by whose service the seeds are prepared from the internal fluids. God has arranged it this way so that there might be a bodily force that, if health is present, unfolds at the proper age and attains the capacity for fecundity. The seeds of the body are thereby readied with the help of the season of puberty. Thus there can be a certain premature desire, unaccompanied by the stipulated years, through which a sterile kindling flickers. But as for the seeds being mingled with desire, it is widely debated among medical writers whether there may be one desire that floats atop the senses and another inside the viscera and more immediate to generation.

Even the poet of Mantua himself was more expert about nature than this inept Punic philosopher, for Vergil noted that cattle are made thin with hunger when the familiar desire agitates their first copulations, and they are to be kept away from the green boughs and the springs. Often too the farmers whip them to a run and wear them out in the sun, when the threshing floor groans deeply as the grain is beaten and the light chaff is carried away by the breeze. They do this lest the cattle, blunted by too much luxury, use the generating field and besmear sluggish furrows. Rather, let their hidden parts suffer a certain dryness and thus let the female thirstily seize the seed and conceal it deep within.[6] Doubtless it is not necessary for my argument to quote Vergil; nonetheless, it suffices to note his acuity. (V, 11)

6. Cf. G. 3.129–37.

[To Julian, Augustine's theory of the sexual consequences of original sin are proved wrong by experience:]

On Augustine's theory, the shame of sexual intercourse should finally have receded after the gift of grace: no irritant of repose should move through the members, nor should the senses bear the burden of pleasure. After people are baptized, the freedom of the will should return, so that by the reinstatement of the condition of nature the law of sin would be driven out. Then you would acknowledge that humans are as capable of shining in the splendor of the virtues as of fearing the squalor of vices. Nor should those imbued with the sacraments be subject to death. (II, 92)

Indeed, none of these things just mentioned comes to pass in the bodies of the baptized: on the contrary, the truth reveals more clearly than the sun that it is impossible and improper for the whole cure of sin to take place in this manner. You should acknowledge either that these items that we listed earlier are not the result of sin (thus neither was nature injured, so that the principle of grace stands firm through which is manifest that that which is in accord with God's order is not changed), or indeed you must deny any healing power to Christ's sacraments, which cannot cure even one of what to you are so many "maladies." (II, 94)

[Julian appeals to a variety of nontheological arguments to prove that Augustine's view of the consequences of original sin is wrong:]

Time urges us to pass on to other topics. Because you surely have nothing to sell to inexpert ears except "natural shame,"[7] I will as briefly as possible touch on some remaining points. Who, then, would deny that this sense of modesty out of which we cover our genital organs varies with persons, places, ranks, and customs? In public meetings, nudity is obscene, but it carries no dishonor in the baths. We have one kind of clothing for the bedchamber, scanty and casual; but we have another kind for the forum, more carefully arranged and lavish. Moreover, as our intimates often testify, we are negligent of the way we look in private, yet when a person less known or of higher status is present, do we not then prepare our clothing more carefully? Why does no one think nudity is a vice for sailors and for many workmen? Simplicity such as this is not to be imputed to the persons themselves but rather to their

7. Perhaps a veiled reference to Augustine's admission (*Conf.* I, 13) that his rhetorical education had trained him to be one of the "word-merchants" (*venditores grammaticae*).

occupations, for even the Apostle Peter, following the universal custom, fished naked in a boat after the resurrection of the Lord.[8]

Focus your eyes on the duties of physicians: they apply their skill to the pursuit of health in even the shameful places of the body. Athletes also receive their honors while they are nude. And in truth it is not just young men and those joined together by the fellowship of wantonness who go nude, but also among certain races, both sexes go naked and voluntarily conduct their unions without secrecy. Given all this, what wonder if the Scots and the barbarian peoples of their regions go naked as well, because even philosophy, to which we above made reference, argues the same[9]—and yet the Traducians[10] come up with this teaching about the shame of nudity. (IV, 44)

What madness it is for you first to assert that the pain of birth is associated with sin, because birth pains very clearly belong to the condition of the sexes. We should not regard them as a punishment for transgression: all the animals who are in no way stained by sin, with what anguish, with what groans, do they suffer in giving birth! From this it appears that the evidence does not point to sin, because birth pains can be found apart from sin. . . . Thus, that passage[11] did not mean that the woman would suffer in giving birth because of the sin, but that she would suffer more intensely, just as we read that in different eras, debilities of the body came about for some persons because of sin. This increase in suffering [in childbirth], however, in no way overturns the frugality of nature [in causing pain]. . . . (VI, 26)

Nevertheless, lest we seem to be negligent and pass over something, admit another point. We know that this pain of childbirth varies for women in accordance with the condition of their bodies and their strength. Indeed, among the barbarians and those in herding societies, women who are hardened by exercise give birth with great ease in the midst of journeys, so that there is no break in the work of traveling. They at once travel on, in no way enfeebled by the difficulty of giving birth, transferring the burden of their wombs to their shoulders. And in gen-

---

8. John 21:7.

9. Julian had previously appealed to the Cynics' argument that many human practices—including a feeling of shame about sexual intercourse—were matters of "convention" not of nature.

10. Traducianism held that the soul as well as the body was transmitted through reproduction. Over against this view, Julian upheld the creationist position, that each soul is created new by God and placed within the developing fetus. From Julian's viewpoint, Augustine's theory of original sin necessarily entailed the Traducian position, although Augustine did not commit himself firmly to one theory or another.

11. Gen 3:16.

eral, the poverty of lower-class women does not demand the service of midwives, but for rich women the opposite holds, for they have been made soft by luxuries. . . . (VI, 29)

[Augustine's speculation about the means of reproduction in Eden had the sin not occurred is so foolish to Julian that he thinks it is best treated by a spoof:]

Truly, what discretion could keep us from laughing when we come to the examples that you supply? For you say[12] that by the very words of the Apostle[13] he [Julian] is refuted, "not as the modest namer of a religious intent, but as the immodest proclaimer of a licentious desire. Yet by the very seeds which farmers sow in the fields, he can be refuted. For why may we not believe that God could have granted to blessed man in Paradise in regard to his own seed that which we see granted to farmers for seeds of wheat, that in the same way that the farmer's seeds are sown, so would ours be, without any shameful lust?"

How charmingly he represents the modest namer and the immodest proclaimer! He sets forth exceedingly ill-composed tropes and recites the songs of peddlers! But I cannot read this other section without amusement: if Adam had not sinned, then the woman could have been made ready for fecundity just as the soil is. Perhaps sheaves of children would shoot forth through all the joints and through the small conduits of the body that doctors call pores. Thus fertile in all parts, she would sweat forth offspring instead of lice! And if some of them should break forth through her eyes, they would take away the sight of the one who brought them forth; if a helmeted swarm marches forth from the sphere of the pupil, without doubt blindness would curse the wretched woman. Nor would it be hard to slay the offspring—not born, but sweated. And so you have a race appropriate to the story of the Myrmidons[14] and also to the Manichaean teaching, whether you speak of lice or fleas.

Such would be the woman's reproductive activity: what can the man for his part produce? Certainly he would not apply his members to her, but iron implements; devoid of genitals, he would press plowshares and hoes upon her. Thus most fulsome thanks are due to the error of the first humans, through which such terrible tortures of happy nature are nullified! The childbearing of women with husbands takes place more gently than either their suffering the plow or their experiencing the whole body

---

12. *On Marriage* II, 29.
13. 1 Cor 15:35–44.
14. According to ancient Greek legend, the Myrmidons were a race of people created from ants to repopulate Aegina after the territory was devastated by a plague.

run wild with fecundity. May shame cover the faces of the Manichaeans and may they seek your name, Lord. Oh, what monstrous charges against the innocents and against God, what ballots of arguments and testimonies! . . . The God who made all things exceedingly good created nothing in such a way that one could show that it could have been made more fitting or more in accordance with reason, within the category in which it *was* made. (V, 15)

[Augustine's argumentative strategy involved tarring Julian with the brush of Jovinian, who three decades earlier had opposed Jerome's ascetic teaching. Julian, in response, compares Jovinian to Augustine:]

Indeed, if Jovinian is denounced as hostile to Ambrose,[15] compared with you, he ought to be pardoned. For what censor would ascribe to you enough good sense that you might be worthy of comparison to Jovinian? For he said that good was a necessity, whereas you say that evil is; he said that men were restrained from error through the sacraments, whereas you indeed think that they are not freed even by grace. Jovinian said that the virginity of Mary was destroyed by the process of giving birth, whereas you surrender Mary herself to the devil by the circumstance of her being born. He puts the good and the better, that is, marriage and chastity, on a par, whereas you, indeed, call the union of the spouses unwholesome and depreciate chastity by comparing it with something most loathsome. Because you make no gradation between them, you entirely change the ranking of these things, so that you prefer virginity not as a good, but as something better than an evil. It cannot be acceptable to compare something utterly vile, except with another thing that is most foul.

Indeed, Jovinian has not so injured God as you have! He wished to conflate the rigor of God's judgment with his favor, whereas you conflate it only with malignity. He says that in the eyes of God both the good and the best would enjoy equal reward; but you say that the good and the wicked alike, the innocents and Satan himself, must be tortured with one punishment. Jovinian wishes to view God as most merciful, whereas you see him as most wicked. He says that humans imbued with God's sacraments are not able to sin, whereas you contend that God himself sins in the feeble power of the sacraments, in the extremity of his teachings, and by the monstrosity of his judgments. There is as great a difference between you and Jovinian as there is a similarity between

15. Ambrose had been attacked by Jovinian on the grounds that his ascetic teaching, like Jerome's, was "Manichaean."

you and Mani! To the extent that Jovinian is found more endurable than you, to that extent is Mani more terrible than Jovinian. (IV, 122)

[Moreover, Julian argues, Augustine's theory of reproduction has serious consequences for our understanding of Jesus and the virgin birth:]

Thus you have tried to convince us that the sexual union is so cursed that you want it understood that not on account of the magnificence of the miracle, but because the union of the sexes was damnable, Christ wished to be born of a virgin mother. Is it possible that anyone, anywhere, ever held anything more wicked and shameless than this? It is as if you distinguished two kings and their kingdoms as contenders for the possession of humanity in the miracle of the virgin birth in order to argue that anything brought forth from marriage belongs to the devil, but to God belongs only what comes from a virgin birth. Is this not to show that the One who makes the virgin fruitful is exceedingly impoverished, lacking in his share [of power], and to deny that the same God who made humans brings them forth by human marriage? Let the attentive reader keep a record of your words and know that you, a faithful disciple of the Manichees and first in rank of the Traducian race, have condemned nothing else than the union of legitimate marriage. (I, 66)

SUGGESTED READINGS

Brown, Peter. *Augustine and Sexuality*. Berkeley Hermeneutical Studies in Hellenistic and Modern Culture, Colloquy 45. Berkeley: Center for Hermeneutical Studies, 1983.

———. *The Body and Society: Men, Women and Sexual Renunciation in Early Christianity*. New York: Columbia University Press, 1988.

Bruckner, Albert. *Julian von Eclanum. Sein Leben und seine Lehre. Ein Beitrag zur Geschichte des Pelagianismus*. TU 15,3. Leipzig, E.Ger.: Hinrichs, 1897.

Clark, Elizabeth A. "'Adam's Only Companion': Augustine and the Early Christian Debate on Marriage." *Recherches Augustiniennes* 21 (1986):139–62.

———. "Vitiated Seeds and Holy Vessels: Augustine's Manichean Past." In *Ascetic Piety and Women's Faith: Essays on Late Ancient Christianity*, edited by E. Clark. Studies in Women and Religion 20. Lewiston, N.Y.: Edwin Mellen Press, 1986.

Montcheuil, Yves de. "La Polémique de Saint Augustin contre Julien d'Eclane d'après l'*Opus Imperfectum*." *RSR* 44 (1956):193–218.

Refoulé, François. "Julien d'Eclane, théologien et philosophe." *RSR* 52 (1964):42–84.

Schmitt, Emile. *Le Mariage chrétien dans l'oeuvre de Saint Augustin. Une théologie baptismale de la vie conjugale*. Paris: Etudes Augustiniennes, 1983.

STOBAEUS
Anthology
(Excerpts)

INTRODUCTION

Little is known about Joannes Stobaeus beyond the fact that he was a fifth-century C.E. collector of sayings and excerpts of discussions about a variety of topics (*eklogai apophthegmata hypothēkai*) from a wide variety of ancient sources ranging from the sixth- and fifth-century B.C.E. Greek comic poets to the third- and fourth-century C.E. moralists and philosophers.[1] Far more important is the character of the various sayings and excerpts collected and preserved; such sayings and excerpts were of great interest in ancient popular and technical-schoolish philosophical debates and discussions.

The ethical topics (*topoi*) are the most relevant for this volume. The three divisions below—"Concerning Marriage: That It Is Not Good to Marry," "Concerning *Enkrateia*," and "Concerning *Sophrosyne*"—correspond to three different ethical topics and Stobean chapter headings. They reflect popular and schoolish thinking about the appropriate life style, or engagement of the social, cultural, and physical world, for the sage.

The type of "response to the world" discussed and debated in these selections is a renunciation of the world, or aspects of it, motivated by a singleness of purpose, an intellectual and spiritual resolve and reprioritization, not a simple loathing of the physical and social world (Dumont). It is a concentration upon the self, a turn inward, an effort to

---

1. Cf. O. Hense, "Ioannes Stobaeus," Pauly-Wissowa, *RE* 9 (1916): 2549.

define and to cultivate the self as an object of ethical concern (Foucault). The self is discovered, as it were, through its stand over against the world that is nature, culture, and society.

The sentiments expressed in these selections point to and encourage a relativization of the things of the world and intellectual and spiritual reservation (Dumont). Such a response among some (e.g., Cynics, some Stoics, and others) led to actual physical withdrawal from culture and society, the adoption of the single life and celibacy, and the life of poverty. Among others of a more intellectualist and aristocratic disposition (e.g., some Stoics, other philosophers and moralists), renunciation took the form of a rather modest self-limitation of the usual aristocratic male prerogatives for the sake of ethical and spiritual cultivation.

Thus, among Greek and Roman aristocratic males, especially, was the preoccupation with, and reconceptualization of, such virtues as *sophrosyne*[2] and *enkrateia*.[3] The spiritualization of such virtues and the turn inward reflected, among other things, anxieties about the continuing durability of the prevailing socioeconomic-political structures that had been self-defining. Inwardness, moderation, and relativization of the world were seen by many as the best recourse in troubled times.

This type of ascetic behavior as a type of response to the world has its origins in the Greek classical tradition. It extends through postclassical antiquity into the Roman aristocratic empire, the Middle Ages, and the Reformation period. The works of Max Weber and Ernst Troeltsch establish its presence in the post-Reformation period in the West.

The five-volume edition (*Anthologium*) of C. Wachsmuth and O. Hense (Berlin: Weidman, 1958) is the best available critical Stobean text. The translations here were based on this edition.

---

2. This technical term will be left untranslated in the text. Although it clearly has to do with temperance or moderation, these terms cannot adequately convey the rich connotations of the Greek. See Helen North's impressive works, *Sophrosyne: Self-Knowledge and Self-Restraint in Greek Literature* (Ithaca, N.Y.: Cornell University Press, 1966) and *From Myth to Icon: Reflections of Greek Ethical Doctrine in Literature and Art* (Ithaca, N.Y.: Cornell University Press, 1979).

3. As with *sophrosyne*, this term is a highly technical one. It is also better left untranslated. The basic meaning of self-control is adequate, but it does not convey the rich meanings that discussions about it often convey.

TRANSLATION

CONCERNING MARRIAGE:
THAT IT IS NOT GOOD TO MARRY
(4.22 Hense)

33. Philippides (fourth/third century B.C.E.): I have told you not to get married, but to live pleasantly. For Plato the good was this . . . not to take a wife, nor to expose oneself to fate through greater troubles.

34. Anaxandrides (fourth century B.C.E.): We free ourselves from a maiden as from a pungent storehouse.

35. Hipponax (sixth century B.C.E.): Two days of a woman's life are the sweetest—when someone marries her, and when someone carries her out for burial.

38. Menander (fourth/third century B.C.E.): Never get married, not even to an individual [masc.] friendly to me.

39. Euripides, *Alcestis* 895–897 (fifth century B.C.E.): The unmarried and childless are envied by humankind: one soul to grieve over is enough of a burden.

41. Euripides, *Alcestis* 246–247: Never shall I say to you that marriage gladdens more than it grieves.

44. Menander: Having a wife and being the father of children . . . brings many anxious moments *[merimnas]* in life.[4]

48. [Unknown]:[5] You can live a good life—if you do not have a wife.

51. Philemon (fourth/third century B.C.E.): Whoever desires marriage will [later] come to regret it.

52. Hippothoon (fifth century B.C.E.): Once bound *[zeuchtheis]* in marriage, one is no longer free *[eleutheros]*.

53. Menander: Even though others get married, let the one who toils and who desires to live pleasantly stay away *[apechesthō]* from marriage.

55. [Unknown]:[6] Old age and marriage resemble each other: we are zealous to attain both of them, but when we do attain them we later come to grieve.

---

4. Cf. 1 Cor 7:32–34. See also Vincent L. Wimbush, *Paul the Worldly Ascetic: Response to the World and Self-Understanding According to 1 Corinthians 7* (Macon, Ga.: Mercer University Press, 1987) 49–71, for discussion of Paul's use of popular philosophical language in the context of discussion about the ascetic life for Christians in Corinth.

5. Some scholars think the saying was composed by a comic poet.

6. See n. 4 above.

56. Antiphanes (fourth century B.C.E.): To get married is to be utterly unhappy.

59. Socrates (fifth century B.C.E.): Socrates, having been asked who among humankind have regrets [metamelontai], said, "Those who have gotten married."

60. Plato[7] (fifth century B.C.E.): Plato, when asked whether the married should take up philosophy, said, "Since you do not even know how to save yourself alone, how can you save yourself with your wife upon your shoulders?"

62. Epameinondas[8] (fourth century B.C.E.): Epameinondas, having been asked what was the benefit [to the state] of one who was not married and had no children, said, "Having no hesitation in dying for the sake of his homeland."

64. Solon (sixth century B.C.E.): Solon, when someone advised him to impose a penalty on those who do not get married, said, "A wife, sir, is a heavy burden."

65. Thales (sixth century B.C.E.): Thales, having been asked why he, in the prime of life, had not had children, answered, "Because I did not desire to subject my life to unnecessary pains."

CONCERNING ENKRATEIA
(3.17 Hense)

10. From the Epistle of Simon to Aristippus[9] (fifth/fourth century B.C.E.): Be mindful of hunger and thirst, for these things enable those who seek sophrosyne to do great things.

11. Pythagoras (sixth/fifth century B.C.E.): Enkrateia is the master of the greatest bodily strength and wealth.

13. Apollonius (first century C.E.): We have been zealous for independence [autarkeia] not in order that we may in all situations simply experience the cheap and simple things, but in order that we may feel confidently about them.

17. Aristippus: The one who abstains [ho apechomenos] does not master desire, but the one who has experienced it [ho chromenos], and then rejects it. For it is just as the [situation with the] one who has no

---

7. See A. Riginos, *Platonica: The Anecdotes Concerning the Life and Writings of Plato* (Leiden, Neth.: E. J. Brill, 1976) for discussion and more examples.

8. See R. F. Hock and E. O'Neil, *The Chreia in Ancient Rhetoric* (Atlanta: Scholars Press, 1986) for more examples and background discussion.

9. Cf. A. Malherbe, *The Cynic Epistles: A Study Edition* (Missoula, Mont.: Scholars Press, 1977) 250.

experience with the ship and the chariot: It is not *he* who is master of them, but the one who guides them as he wishes.

23. Epicurus (fourth/third century B.C.E.): If you desire to make someone rich, do not hand over material goods,[10] but take away the desire for them.

26. Pythagoras: To die is much better than to wreck *[amaurōsai]* the soul through lack of self-control *[akrasia]*.

27. Socrates: Socrates said that *enkrateia* is the power *[to kratein]* over desire in the body.

30. Socrates: Socrates, having been asked how a person might become rich, said, "If that person becomes poor with respect to desires."

36. Epicurus: Epicurus, having been asked how a person might become rich, said, "Not by adding to material possessions, but by constricting *[peritemnōn]* most of one's needs."

41. Eusebius [of Myndus] (fourth century B.C.E.): *Enkrateia* is also a good thing for the body. It is an ally for the health of the body, and produces *sophrosyne* in the soul. And *sophrosyne* is quiet and calm, and provides a peaceful life for the soul.

CONCERNING *SOPHROSYNE*
(3.5 Hense)

18. Menedemus (fourth/third century B.C.E.): Menedemus, when a young man said, "To get whatever one might desire is a good thing," responded, "It is much better not to desire what is not needed."

32. Socrates: Socrates, having been asked what things need especially to be renounced *[apechesthai]*, said, "Shameful and unjust pleasures."

41. Alexander (fourth century B.C.E.): When some had urged Alexander to look at the daughters of Darius and his wife who was outstanding in beauty, he said, "It is shameful for men who have been victorious in battle to be defeated by women."

45. Iamblichus, from the epistle concerning *sophrosyne* (fourth century C.E.): Every virtue on the one hand holds its mortal nature in low esteem. On the other hand, it embraces its immortal [nature]. *Sophrosyne* most especially has this zeal, inasmuch as it holds in low esteem those pleasures which rivet the soul to the body. . . .

48. Iamblichus: *Enkrateia*, as Socrates used to say, is the foundation of the virtue of benevolence. Thus, *sophrosyne* is considered the ordered

10. Hense notes that *chrēmatōn* is odd here. Thus, *chrēmata* is supplied.

arrangement *[kosmos]* of all good things, as Plato declared. And the same virtue is the assurance of the most noble states of mind. . . .

51. Epameinondas: The ambassadors came from a king conveying gold, desiring to bribe Epameinondas. And he welcomed them to a meal, knowing why they had come. He ordered them to dine first, then to say whatever they wanted. After having been served a light meal they drank wine. They did not know what they should do regarding these things,[11] but he [Epameinondas] smiled and said, "Depart now, and tell your king how I dine, and he will know that the one who is content with such things *[ho arkoumenos]* would not be a betrayer."

52. Crates (fourth century B.C.E.): Crates stepped into the agora and saw some selling and some buying. "These," he said, "on account of the interdependent nature of the[ir] activity, assume each to be happy. But I [make] myself [happy], because I avoid *[apēllagmai]* both of them, neither buying nor selling.[12,*]

SUGGESTED READINGS

Dumont, Louis. *Essays on Individualism: Modern Ideology in Anthropological Perspective*. Chicago: University of Chicago Press, 1986.

Foucault, Michel. *The History of Sexuality*, vol. 2, trans. Robert Hurley. New York: Pantheon Books, 1985.

Inwood, Brad. *Ethics and Human Action in Early Stoicism*. Oxford: Clarendon Press, 1985.

MacMullen, Ramsay. *Enemies of the Roman Order: Treason, Unrest, and Alienation in the Empire*. Cambridge: Harvard University Press, 1966.

Malherbe, Abraham J. *The Cynic Epistles: A Study Edition*. Missoula, Mont.: Scholars Press, 1977.

North, Helen F. *Sophrosyne: Self-Knowledge and Self-Restraint in Greek Literature*. Ithaca, N.Y.: Cornell University Press, 1966.

————. *From Myth to Icon: Reflections of Greek Ethical Doctrine in Literature and Art*. Ithaca, N.Y.: Cornell University Press, 1979.

Weber, Max. *The Sociology of Religion*, trans. Ephraim Fischoff. Boston: Beacon Press, 1964.

Whitchurch, I. Goldwin. *The Philosophical Bases of Asceticism in the Platonic Writings and in Pre-Platonic Tradition*. Cornell Studies in Philosophy 14. New York and London: Longmans, Green & Co., 1923.

11. Some would omit *epi toutois*.
12. Cf. 1 Cor 7:29–31; see also Wimbush, *Paul the Worldly Ascetic*, 23–47.
*　　I should like to express my gratitude to my colleague and friend, Ronald F. Hock, for his many helpful suggestions for the translation.

EVAGRIUS PONTICUS
The Kephalaia Gnostica

INTRODUCTION

Evagrius Ponticus (345–399 c.e.) has been described as the "absolute ruler" of the "Syriac and Byzantine mystical theology" and as influential over "western ascetical and mystical teaching."[1] In the West, his disciples Palladius and John Cassian provided intellectual structures for monasticism.[2] Evagrius's works were available in the Latin translations of Rufinus.[3] Among Syriac theologians, his influence is seen in the work of Stephanos bar Soudaili, Jacob of Serug, Philoxenos of Mabbug, Isaac of Nineveh, Sergios of Reshaina, Babai the Great, the anonymous *Book of the Holy Hierotheos*, Dionysius bar Salibi, and Barhebraeus.[4] In Byzantium, Evagrius exercised influence over writers such as Climacus and Maximus Confessor.[5] His influence continued beyond the condemnation of his writings because of their Origenism in 553.[6]

1. H. von Balthasar, "The Metaphysics and Mystical Theology of Evagrius," *Monastic Studies* 3 (1965) 183.
2. R. Draguet, "L'*Historie Lausiac*, une oeuvre écrite dans l'esprit d'Évagre," *RHE* 41 (1946) 341–64; 42 (1947) 5–49; S. Marsili, *Giovanni Cassiano ed Evagrio Pontico, dottrina sulla carita e contemplazione*. Studia Anselmiana 5 (Rome: S. Amselmo, 1936).
3. *Clavis Patrum Graecorum*, ed. M. Geerard, IV. Corpus Graecorum (Turnhout: Brepols, 1974).
4. Antoine Guillaumont, Les *"Képhalaia Gnostica"* d'Évagre le Pontique et l'histoire de l'origénisme chez les grecs et chez les syriens. Patristica Sorbonensia 5 (Paris: Les Editions du Seuil, 1962) 173–332.
5. M. Viller, "Aux sources de la spiritualité de S. Maxime: les oeuvres d'Évagre le Pontique," *RAM* 11 (1938) 156–84, 239–68.
6. J. D. Mansi, *Sacrorum conciliorum nova et amplissima collectio*, IX (Florence: T. Baracchi, 1763) 396–400; F. Diekamp, *Die Origenistischen Streitigkeiten im sechsten Jahrhundert und das fünfte allgemeine Concil* (Münster: Aschendorff, 1899); A. Guillaumont, Les *"Képhalaia Gnostica,"* 143–70.

Evagrius's own intellectual roots were in the tradition of Origen, especially as mediated by the Cappadocian theologians Melania the Elder and Rufinus. The intellectual structures reflect the travels of Evagrius's early life. The traditional narrative of his education suggests he studied with Gregory of Nazianzus.[7] This would have placed Evagrius in the midst of discussions of Egyptian and Syriac monasticism and made him aware of local experiments in ascetic living, especially Eustathius's cenobitism and its adaptation by Basil the Great.[8] Significantly, the teachings of Origen provided a theoretical framework for the efforts.

Evagrius[9] accompanied Gregory of Nazianzus to Constantinople when his mentor was named patriarch. After Gregory returned to Asia Minor in 381, Evagrius joined the staff of Patriarch Nectarius. To escape an affair with a wealthy married woman, Evagrius fled to Jerusalem. After a period of illness and nonexceptional living, he made contact with the ascetic communities of Melania and Rufinus. Melania helped Evagrius recapture his self-understanding as an ascetic. Rufinus, student of Didymus the Blind of Alexandria, reinforced in Evagrius the conviction that Origen was the essential theoretician of the ascetic life.

They encouraged Evagrius to go to the Nitrian Desert, about thirty-five miles south of Alexandria. He arrived in 383 and listened to the teaching of Macarius the Great, Macarius the Alexandrian, Anthony, and John of Lycopolis. He also began to teach and would, on occasion, debate theological and life style issues in Alexandria. He maintained an extensive correspondence.

The *Kephalaia Gnostica* provides theoretical structures and practical advice for ascetic living. It is composed of six "centuries," each containing ninety maxims (apophthegms). They are deliberately disjointed and cryptic, intended only for those who are already committed to an ascetic life and who have the intellectual background to read the "encoded" instructions.

In the translation that follows, Evagrius comments on the nature of divinity (1–3, 12, 35, 42–43, 50, 87), creation (5, 8, 50, 63, 87), the original state of the creation (39), the Fall or "disturbance" (49–51), the role of the will (63–64, 66), body (11, 26, 76), soul (45–47, 59, 67–68, 84), mind (33–34, 46, 65, 74, 84), temptation (25, 68), demons (10, 22, 68), angels (23),

---

7. This has been called into question by Gabriel Bunge, *Evagrios Pontikos, Briefe aus der Wüste* (Sophia; Quellen östlicher Theologie 24; Trier: Paulinus, 1986).

8. J. Gribomont, "Eustathe de Sébaste," *Dict. Spir.* 4 (1961) 1708–12.

9. On the life of Evagrius, see Antoine Guillaumont and Claire Guillaumont, "Évagre le Pontique," *Dict. Spir.* 4 (1961) 1731–34; idem, "Evagrios Pontikos," *RAC* 6 (1965) 1088–1107.

struggle (25, 65–66), contemplation (13, 27, 34, 70, 73–74), renunciation (78–80), virtue (41, 59, 75–76), perfection (24, 67, 75, 86), salvation (28), passion and desire (53, 68, 84–85), impassibility (37, 65, 70, 81), and the future of humanity (11, 18, 26, 57, 65, 82).

The cosmology, eschatology, and relationships posited for human beings in the universe, as well as the process and goal of reattaining the knowledge (*gnosis*) of the Unity (God), are dependent on the neoplatonic philosophical structures of the Origenist tradition.

The text is preserved in two Syriac versions and a few Greek fragments. Syriac 1 has long been available in Syriac and an Aramaic translation. An early Syriac editor removed the Origenist orientation from most of the maxims.[10] Syriac 2, preserved in only one manuscript, British Library Ms. 17, 167, is the unexpurgated version of the text. It has been edited with a French translation by Antoine Guillaumont. The text translated here, on the basis of the Guillaumont edition, is the first "century" of the *Kephalaia Gnostica*.[11] The translation strives to be as literal as possible without sacrificing comprehensibility in English.

TRANSLATION

1. To the first good he is not opposed, because it is in his essence that he is Good, and as regards essence, there is nothing that opposes.

2. The opposition is in the qualities, and the qualities are in the bodies; opposition therefore is in the creatures.

3. Every reasonable nature is an intelligent essence and our God is intelligent; without division he resides in those in whom he resides, like terrestrial art, but he is superior to this in that he exists substantially.

4. All that exists is either susceptible to opposition or is constituted of opposition. But not all that is susceptible to opposition is with those that have been constituted of an opposition.

5. Principles do not engender and are not engendered, but the intermediate engenders and is engendered.

6. In comparison, we are one thing but that which is in us is another

---

10. W. Frankenberg, *Evagrius Ponticus* (Abhandlungen der königlichen Gesellschaft der Wissenschaften zu Göttingen, Phil.-hist. Klasse, N.F. 13,2; Berlin: Weidmann, 1912) 8–471. The Armenian text was published by H. Barsel Sarghisian, *Srboy Horn Evagri Pontac'voy Vark ev matenagrout'iunk* (Venice: S. Lazarus, 1907) 143–207.

11. Antoine Guillaumont, *Les six centuries des "Képhalaia Gnostica" d'Évagre le Pontique*. PO 28,1 (Paris: Firmin Didot, 1958).

thing, and that in which we are is another; but taken together [they] are that in which we are and that in which it is that we are.

7. When those that are together are raised, the number will also be raised, and when this is raised, that which is in us and that in which we are will be one.

8. When that in which we should be has been separated, he will engender that in which we are; but when that which is in us is mixed, he will raise that which will be raised with the number.

9. When we are in that which is, we see that which is, but when [we are] in that which is not, we engender that which is not. But when those in which we are will be raised, again it will not be that which is not.

10. Among the demons, certain oppose the practice of the commandments, others oppose thoughts of nature, and others oppose words *[logoi]* about divinity because the knowledge of our salvation is constituted from these three.

11. All who now possess spiritual bodies reign over a kingdom of worlds that exists and those [possessing] practical *[praktikē]* bodies, or who are joined to opposites, reign over the kingdom of worlds to come.

12. One is he who is without intermediaries, and he thus also, by means of mediations, is in all.

13. Among the rational *[logikoi]*, some possess spiritual contemplation and practice *[praktikē]*, but others hindrance and judgment.

14. For each one of the arts, you see in it about the one who made it; but the knowledge of him who is, you will find in all things if our Lord "made everything with wisdom."[12]

15. When the four will be raised, also the five will be raised, but when the five will be raised, the four will not be raised with them.

16. That which has been separated from the five will not be separated from the four, but that which has been separated from the four is delivered also from the five.

17. When that which is in us will be changed, those things in which we are will be changed, and this often to the point that that which is, will no longer be named with modes.

18. The goal of the practical *[praktikē]* and of suffering is the heritage of the saints, but that which is opposed to the first is the cause of the second; and the end of this is the heritage of those who are opposed.

19. Knowledge that is in the four is the knowledge of thoughts of creatures, but the knowledge of the One is the knowledge of him who alone is.

12. Ps 104:24.

20. When only thoughts of all that which was made by accident remain in us, then only he who is known will be known only by him who knows.[13]

21. Among the good and evil ones who are considered without necessity, certain [ones] are found in the soul and others outside it; but [as for] those who are said naturally to be evil, it is impossible that they would be outside it.

22. The bodies of demons have color and form but they escape our senses, because the mixture is not the mixture of bodies that our senses apprehend. For when they wish to appear as persons, they transform themselves into the complete image of our body, while not showing us their bodies.

23. The thoughts of things on earth are the good [things] of the earth; but if the holy angels know them, according to the word of *Teqū'itā*, the angels of God eat the good of the earth. But it is said, "Man eats the bread of angels."[14] Thus knowledge of the thoughts of that which is in the earth is also known by certain men.

24. If the sprout is in the seed with power, also perfection is in the receptive one with power. But if this is so, it is not the same as the seed and that which is in it, nor the sprout and that which is in the grain. But the seed of that which is held by the sprout and the sprout of this seed are the same. For although the seed becomes the sprout, the seed of that which is in the sprout has not yet received the sprout. But when it is liberated from sprout and seed, it will have the sprout of the first seed.

25. There are those who would "sift"[15] us with temptations, either questioning the thoughtful part of the soul, or striving to seize the feeling part, either of the body or the surroundings of the body.

26. If the human body is a part of this world, but "the form of this world passes,"[16] it is evident that also the form of the body will pass.

27. There are five chief principles under which all contemplation is placed. It is said that the first is contemplation of the adorable and holy Trinity; the second and third, contemplation of those who are incorporeal and those who are corporeal; and the fourth and fifth, contemplation of judgment and providence.

28. Among the many ways, there are three ways of salvation that together obtain to destroy sins; but two of them obtain alone that they might deliver from passions, and the virtue of the third is that it will be

13. Matt 24:35.
14. Ps 78:25.
15. Luke 22:31.
16. 1 Cor 7:31.

the cause of glory. However, glory accompanies the first, psalmody the second, and exaltation the third.

29. Also as with bodies go colors, forms, and numbers, thus also among the four elements matter is destroyed; for with them it possesses this, that it did not exist and it was made.

30. Only fire is distinct from the four elements, because of that which is living in it.

31. As it is among the sons of Israel and among the lands of the land of Judah and in the cities of Jerusalem, thus also the sign of the symbols of thought is "the part of the Lord."[17]

32. Persons who have seen something of that which is in the natures have seen only their common view, for only the just have received their spiritual knowledge. But the one who would dispute this is like the one who said, "I was acquainted with Abraham when he traveled with two wives."[18] This one spoke the truth but he did not see the two covenants and did not understand those who are born from them.[19]

33. Thus as each of the arts needs a sharpened sense that conforms to the matter, thus also the mind [nous] needs a sharpened spiritual sense to distinguish spiritual things.

34. The sense, naturally by itself, senses sensory things, but the mind [nous] always stands and waits [to ascertain] which spiritual contemplation gives it vision.

35. Even as the light, while always making us see, does not need a light by which to be seen, thus God, while making everything see, does not need a light that by it he would be known, for he, in his essence, ". . . is light."[20]

36. It is not the same as the sense and the sense organ, nor the sensitive and the sensible. For, the sense is the power by which we enjoy sensing matters; the sense organ is the member in which resides the sense; the sensitive is the living being that possesses the senses; the sensible is that which is apprehended by the senses. But the mind [nous] is not that way, because it is deprived of one of the four.

37. Spiritual sense is the impassibility of a rational soul who exists by the grace of God.

38. While we are awake, we are saying different things about sleep; when we are sleeping, we learn by experience. All that we hear about

17. Deut 32:9.
18. Gen 16—17.
19. Gal 4:22–31.
20. 1 John 1:5.

God while being outside him is similar. It is when we are in him that we receive the manifestation by experience.

39. When we were made in the beginning, the seeds of virtue were naturally in us, but not evil. It is not that of which we are receptacles, but of his power totally in us. Because while we are able not to be, the power of him who is not is not in us if the powers are qualities and that which is not is not a quality.

40. There was a time when evil did not exist, and there will be a time that it no longer exists; but there was no time that virtue did not exist and there will be no time that it does not exist. For the seeds of virtue are not destructible. Also the rich man who was condemned in Sheol because of his evil, and had pity on his brothers,[21] is convincing to me. Thus, to have pity is a beautiful seed of virtue.

41. If death is secondary to life, and sickness secondary to health, it is evident that evil is secondary to virtue. Death and sickness of the soul are evil, and virtue is more ancient than the intermediary.

42. There it is said that God is where he acts, and where he acts most, there he is present most; but he acts most in rational and holy natures, therefore he is present most in the celestial powers.

43. God is in every place and he is not in a place; he is in every place for he is in all that exists by his "wisdom full of forms."[22] He is not in a place because he is not among beings.

44. If the kingdom of the heavens is known by that which is contained and that which contains, the torment also will be known by that which is the opposite of these things.

45. There is nothing among the incorporeal that has power in the bodies; for our soul is incorporeal.

46. Everything that is in power in bodies, and is naturally in them in act, they are conatural with those from which they are. But the mind [nous] is delivered from view [form] and from matter.

47. There is nothing that is in power in the soul and able to get out by an act and to subsist independently, for this [exists] that it might naturally be in bodies.

48. Everything that is attached to the body accompanies those from which they are engendered, but nothing of that is attached to the soul.

49. It is not Unity alone that is disturbed by the receptivity of the mind [nous], that which by its negligence turns its face from it, and by being deprived of it, engenders ignorance.

21. Luke 16:19–31.
22. Eph 3:10.

50. All that exists, exists for the knowledge of God, but among beings some are first and some are second. Knowledge is more ancient than the first beings and the disturbance more ancient than the second.

51. The disturbance is the cause of evil but virtue is destructive of evil; but virtue is the daughter of names and modes and the cause of these is the disturbance.

52. Because the knowledge of those who are the first in their principality and who are seconds by their creation will be in the principals, although only those who are first in their principality will receive the knowledge of the Trinity.

53. Demons who fight with the mind [nous] are called birds; those who trouble the passion [thymos] [are called] animals; those who excite desire [epithymia] [are called] beasts.

54. The fullness of those who are first in their principality is without limit, but a limit is set for emptiness.[23] However, second beings are coextensive with emptiness, but they rest while the fullness approaches immaterial knowledge for the receptive.

55. Only those who are first by their making [creation] will be delivered from the corruption that is in the act, but there is none among the beings [who will be delivered] from that which is in power.

56. The good ones are the cause of knowledge and of torment, but the evil ones only of torment.

57. Persons fear Sheol, but demons fear the abyss. But there are among the evil ones serpents for which there is no word [term].

58. For one among the dead [is there] whose first cause is his birth; another comes from the saints unto those who are not walking in justice. But the mother of the third is remission. But if he is mortal who is naturally to be liberated from the body with which he is joined, certainly he who is not naturally [made] that it might happen to him who is immortal. For all who are joined with bodies will of necessity be liberated.

59. Likewise the light and clouds are accidents of the air; thus, virtue and evil, knowledge and ignorance, are united with the rational soul.

60. If today they have received the wise economy in their homes, it is evident that yesterday they sat and modified their deeds. However, he was called "wise"[24] because he gave more than he was receiving.

61. There are no second beings who receive knowledge, nor any first beings who first were in a place.

23. Phil 2:7.
24. Luke 16:1–8.

62. Knowledge is said to be in a place, whereas he who receives it is tied with a certain of the second beings, which truly and principally is said to be in a place.

63. That the rational *[logikoi]* exist always or do not exist depends on the will of the Creator, but whether they are immortal or mortal depends on their will, as does whether they are joined or not joined to one thing or another.

64. The true life of the rational *[logikoi]* is their natural activity, but their death is an activity outside nature. But if such a death is so mortal as to naturally extinguish the true life, who among beings is immortal? For every rational nature is susceptible to an opposition.

65. Within the knowledge of those who are seconds according to their making [creation], different worlds are constituted and unspeakable things become frequent. But in the Unity, nothing of that happens but an unspeakable peace and [there are] only naked minds that are always satisfied by their insatiability, if as according to the word of our Savior, "the Father judges no one, but all judgment he gave to the Christ."[25]

66. Virtues are said to be before [us] on the side on which we possess the senses. However, behind us are the evil things on the side on which we do not possess senses. For we are commanded to "flee fornication"[26] and "to pursue the love of strangers."[27]

67. We know the structure *[systasis]* of the world and the activity of the elements. And who will comprehend the composition of this constitutive material *[organon]* of the soul? And who will ascertain how this is joined to that and which is their empire and their participation with each other in order that the practical *[praktikē]* becomes a chariot for the rational soul who strives that it might obtain the knowledge of God?

68. There is a predominance of mind *[nous]* and fire in angels, but among persons desire *[epithymia]* and earth, but among demons passion *[thymos]* and air. The third, as one says, approaches the intermediaries through the nostrils and the first [approach] the seconds through the mouth.

69. For he who has knowledge, there is for him one after him; for he who has ignorance does not have [anyone].

70. With God, it is said that the first is the one who knows the holy Trinity; and after him, he who sees the thoughts of the knowable; then, third, he who sees incorporeal beings; then, fourth, he who knows the

25. John 5:22.
26. 1 Cor 6:18.
27. That is, "hospitality." Rom 12:13.

contemplation of worlds; and he who possesses impassibility deserves the fifth of those in contention.

71. The end of natural knowledge is the holy Unity, but there is no end for ignorance, as one says, but "there is not a limit to his grandeur."[28]

72. The Lord pitied this one, the one to whom he gave spiritual knowledge if "the just walk in the light, but the foolish in darkness."[29] But the Lord also had pity on the foolish, in that he does not torment him immediately, and in that he encourages him [to move] from evil toward virtue.

73. The life of a person is holy knowledge but the great mercies of God are the contemplation of beings. Many wise ones of this world have promised us knowledge, but the mercies of God are better than life.[30]

74. The light of the mind [nous] is divided into three: the knowledge of the adorable and holy Trinity; the incorporeal nature that was created by it; and the contemplation of beings.

75. If the crown of justice is holy knowledge and even more [if] the gold that contains the stones indicates the worlds that were or will be, the contemplation of corporeal and incorporeal nature is the crown that is placed on the head of strivers [agonistēs] by the just judge.[31]

76. It is not knowledge that is hidden in objects against which ignorance is opposed, but the knowledge of the intelligible forms of the objects. For ignorance is not naturally made that it might be in corporeal nature.

77. The second nature is the sign of the body, but the first [nature] is the sign of the soul. But the mind [nous] is Christ who is united to the knowledge of the Unity.

78. The first renunciation is the abandonment of the objects of this world, which happens in the will because of the knowledge of God.

79. The second renunciation is the abandonment of evil, which happens by the grace of God and by the diligence of the person.

80. The third renunciation is the separation from ignorance, which is naturally made to appear to persons according to the degree of their conditions.

81. The glory and light of the mind [nous] is knowledge, but the glory and light of the soul is impassibility.

82. That which the sensible death customarily does in us, similarly

28. Ps 145:3.
29. Eccl 2:14.
30. Ps 63:3.
31. 2 Tim 4:8.

"the just judgment of God"[32] provides for the rest of the rational *[logikoi]* beings when "he is ready to judge the living and the dead"[33] and "to render to each according to his deeds."[34]

83. If the Gihon is the river of Egypt and surrounds all the land of Cush,[35] and from which Israel was ordered by one of the prophets not to drink,[36] we know also these three other heads [branches of the river] and the river from which the four heads are separated.

84. For the mind *[nous]*, knowledge and ignorance are united. However, the desire *[epithymia]* is receptive to self-control and luxury, but to the passion *[thymia]* customarily happen love and hate. But the first accompanies the first ones and the second the second ones.

85. The wandering mind *[nous]*, when it becomes passible, is not controlled when it realizes the constitutive elements of its desire *[epithymia]*, but abstains from error when it becomes impassible and has entered the company of those who are incorporeal and who are fulfilling all of their spiritual desires.

86. Love is the excellent state of the rational soul, for in it, one cannot love anything that is among the corruptible things more than the knowledge of God.

87. All beings exist for the knowledge of God, but everything that exists for another is less than that for which it exists. Because of this, the knowledge of God is superior to all.

88. Natural knowledge is the true comprehension of those who exist for the knowledge of the holy Trinity.

89. All rational nature was naturally constituted that it might exist and be instructed, but God is the essential knowledge. However, the rational nature has as an opposition the fact of not being, but knowledge [has as an opposition] evil and ignorance. However, none of these are oppositions to God.

90. If today is that which is called Friday, on which our Savior was crucified, then all those who died are a symbol of his grave, for with them died the righteousness of God that lives the third day and is resurrected when clothed with a spiritual body, if "today and tomorrow he accomplishes miracles and the third day it is finished."[37]

The end of the first (century of the *Kephalaia Gnostica*)

32. 2 Thess 1:5.
33. 1 Pet 4:5.
34. Rev 22:13.
35. Gen 2:13.
36. Jer 2:18.
37. Luke 13:32.

SUGGESTED READINGS

Bamberger, J. E. *Evagrius Ponticus: The Praktikos and Chapters on Prayer.* Cistercian Studies 4. Kalamazoo, Mich.: Cistercian, 1972.

Bunge, Gabriel. *Evagrios Pontikos, Briefe aus der Wüste.* Sophia Quellen östlicher Theologie 24; Trier: Paulinus, 1986.

Guillaumont, Antoine. *Les "Kephalaia Gnostica" d'Evagre le Pontique et l'histoire de l'origénisme chez les grecs et chez les syriens.* Patristica Sorbonensia 5. Paris: Les Editions du Seuil, 1962.

———. *Les six centuries des "Kephalaia Gnostica" d'Evagre le Pontique.* PO 28, 1. Paris: Firmin Didot, 1958.

Guillaumont, Antoine, and Claire Guillaumont. *Evagre le Pontique. Traité Pratique ou le Moine.* 2 vols. SC 170–171. Paris: Les Editions du Cerf, 1971.

———. "Evagrios Pontikos." *RAC* 6 (1965) 1088–1107.

O'Laughlin, Michael. "Origenism in the Desert: Anthropology and Integration in Evagrius Ponticus." Th.D. diss., Harvard Divinity School, 1987.

Turner, H. J. M. "Evagrius Ponticus: Teacher of Prayer." *Eastern Churches Review* 7 (1975) 145–48.

See also Suggested Readings in chapter 17.

Coptic Manichaean:
Kephalaia of the Teacher
(Selections)

INTRODUCTION

Possibly no religious movement has had more influence on the development of asceticism and its evolution into monasticism than Manichaeism. The exemplary life style of Mani's followers inspired an array of reactions from the competing religions that Manichaeans sought to infiltrate. We can trace this process across a millennium: from Athanasius's disclaimer that Antony was not a Manichaean to the purge of crypto-Manichaeans in Ming China. Not only Christians but also Zoroastrians, Jewish sectarians, Platonists, Buddhists, Muslims, and Taoists were confronted by the Manichaean ethic.

Mani's dualism is remarkably monolithic. In fact, there is a pantheism in his theology. All of the Divine Light in the world exists with a unity of substance, whether it is in the godhead (the Father of Light), the gnostic human soul, the docetic Jesus, or the literal sun and moon. Truth is an essential aspect of divinity, so lying is a grievous sin. Muslim judges rejoiced that the Manichaeans would rather die than lie about their faith.

The foremost theological problem, according to Mani, is that the Divine Light has become mixed with Darkness, that is, the material substance (*Hyle*) of this world. The ultimate solution of this problem is the gnosis of the soul. An elaborate system of meditation, education, worship, asceticism, and even reincarnation is set out for this purpose. Above all, the individual is to avoid any activity that allows the Divine to be further mixed with the material. Hence, ascetic living is a cornerstone of the faith. The identifying sentence of a Manichaean, found in both eastern and western recensions of the mission history is: "We do not eat meat, or drink wine and we abstain from women." Plants, especially melons, are thought to contain a large quantity of light. The wandering monk should watch his step lest he tread on a plant or seed. The communal meals are efficacious for releasing the imprisoned light, but the dinner begins with an "apology to the bread" for the violence of milling and mastication. Fasting is particularly meritorious because it subdues the sinful flesh and enhances the divine soul.

We know that Mani visited India, and Buddhist practices appear to have influenced his cenobitic model. There are two classes of believers: the elect (also called the righteous, holy, pure ones, etc.) and the hearers (catechumens). The latter were laypersons, allowed to marry and "mingle" somewhat in the affairs of this world. They could hope to be reborn as an elect by providing "alms," that is, gifts and service to care for the elect. One could also donate a slave, but the supreme gift was a child who would be raised as an elect. Augustine was a hearer during his early life, and his writings on Manichaeism stem from this experience. Like the other heresiologists, he could mock Manichaean inconsistencies and inanities, but he could not challenge their ascetic fervor. In fact, Christian leaders were consistently frustrated by the discipline of the Manichaean example.

A routine of prayer and fasting (on Sundays) was incumbent on the hearers. The elect fasted on Monday, the holiest day in the faith, the weekday of Mani's death in prison, called his "crucifixion," when his divine soul was released. The annual feast of the Bema, Mani's empty chair, also recalled his passion. Augustine noted the irony that Manichaeans grieved for Mani's death, but they could not allow that the divine Christ suffered.

Mani was followed by a succession of popes who bore the title *"Archegos."* There were five other classes of the elect, including twelve apostles or teachers, 72 bishops, 360 priests (magister, presbyter) who functioned as abbots, and the remaining elect, who were either traveling preachers or sedentary monks.

The cenobitic aspect of the Manichaean community was evident from the beginning. It was necessary for two indispensable functions. First, every location where Manichaeans lived was expected to house the itinerant elect preachers. Al-Biruni noted that these men were often accompanied by a youthful apprentice. At first the hostel was staffed by hearers, but as the community grew, a hallowed corps of elect became necessary to incorporate a worshiping congregation. The next stage of growth would add a monastery wing for the copying of Mani's scriptures. Although Manichaeans strove to adapt their truth to the individual tenets of the local religion, for example, to become the "true" Christianity or Islam, the crypto-Manichaean converts were soon expected to conform to Mani's original system (a fact that Augustine and al-Biruni both lamented). Only among the Sogdians and Uigurs of Central Asia did Manichaeism and Buddhism come to coexist in peace, so that we find prayers addressed to both "Jesus the Splendor" and the "Buddha of Light."

The Coptic Manichaean texts are important documents in the history of asceticism. Of these, the *Kephalaia* seems to be the most appropriate for this volume: not only is it generally unavailable in English but also it is the one Coptic text that lists instructions and theological insights that are relevant to the ascetic life. On the one hand, it takes the student of ancient Christianity beyond Augustine (Ephrem, an-Nadim, etc.) to material that is edited by the Manichaeans themselves. On the other hand, the fact that it contains material from Mani that has been reedited into a later *Sitz im Leben* makes it useful for understanding the Cologne Mani Codex.

The *Kephalaia* contains "kernels" of Mani's teachings that have been edited into a somewhat Socratic dialogue. The early pages, on Mani's life, draw on a common tradition with the Shabuhragan and the Cologne Mani Codex, a tradition also found in an-Nadim, al-Biruni, the Chinese Compendium, and all biographies of the religion's founder. Their penchant for numeric outlines reflects Mani's skill as an organizer. In them we see an elaboration of the "three seals" mentioned by Augustine, that is, those ascetic responsibilities that govern the mouth, the hand, and the breast. Here the Manichaeans have posed the same questions that are addressed in the famous Uigur "Confession Book" where the Manichaean Ten Commandments (noted by an-Nadim) are categorized as "three with the mouth, three with the heart, three with the hand, and one with the whole self." In the *Kephalaia*, we see living evidence of the principles Mani established.

The following translation of excerpts is based on the Coptic text, which has been published in German in two parts: Part I (pages 1–244a), H. J. Polotsky and A. Boehlig, *Kephalaia*, Band I, 1 Hälfte (Stuttgart: Manichäeische Handschriften der Staatlichen Museen Berlin, 1940); Part II (pages 244b–291), A. Boehlig, *Kephalaia*, Band I, 2 Hälfte (Stuttgart: Manichäeische Handschriften der Staatlichen Museen Berlin, 1966).

TRANSLATION

p. 191

Chapter 79
Concerning the Fasting of
the Holy Ones

Again the Illuminator said to his disciples: "The fasting
which the Holy Ones practice is useful
in [four] important respects.   The first:
The holy man punishes his body through fasting, vanquishing
15 all the Archon substance which is in it.

The second: That Soul which comes into him in the
supply of his food each day is purified and
cleansed afterwards. And it is refined and sifted out the mixture
the Darkness which is bound up with it.   The third:
20 That man becomes a Pure One in every respect.
The mystery of the Children of Light, those who have no Destruction
in them or . . . the food, and they [do not] wound it.
But they are pure . . . not in them, i.e., pollution, since
they live in the Rest.   The fourth: they do a . . .
25 the cross. They restrain their hands from the hand [of]
. . . destruct the Living Soul.

Fasting is important for the Pure Ones for these four important
reasons so long as they persist. That is so long as they remain
in them each day, and they cause the body to subject all its members
to a holy fast.
30   [faith. Those who do not
have the power

p. 192

to fast] every day fast on the Lord's day. They also have a part in the
[deeds] and fasting of the Holy Ones through their faith and their
alms.

Chapter 80

The Kephalaion of the

Commandments of Righteousness

5

Again the Illuminator said to his disciples: "Know and
understand that the first righteousness which a man
will do to become truly righteous is this: He will practice
celibacy and purity. And he will acquire rest
10 of hand in order that he quiet it from the Cross of
Light. The third [*lege* first] is the purity of the mouth: That he
purify his mouth from all flesh and blood, and not taste
anything which is called wine or intoxicant.   This is the
first righteousness which a man performs in his body
15 and he is called 'righteous' by every person.
On the other hand, the second righteousness which he performs is
this:
He will place upon himself . . . wisdom and faith in order that [he]
. . . by means of his wisdom, and give his wisdom to every person
who will
hear it from him. But, through his faith, he will give faith
20 to those who are appointed to faith. Through his [grace], he will
grace
them with love, and clothe them in it in order that he attach them to
him.
When
it happens that that one acquires great wealth . . .
through righteousness. By the second divine work
he will cause others to send them, being like him in righteous-
25 ness.   Just as this righteous one will complete the
second [aspect]; and become a full-fledged Elect, so
also a Catechumen, when he becomes a Catechumen
of the Faith, is completed in two areas.

The first work of the Catechumenate which he
30 accomplishes is fasting-praying-and-alms. The fasting
in which he fasts is this: That
he fast on the days of the [Lord's Day . . .]
deeds of the world. The prayer is this: That

p. 193

he pray to the Sun and the Moon, the Great Illuminators. And the
alms is this: He should put alms . . .
out of holiness. And he should give it to them out of Righteousness . . .

The second work of the Catechumenate which he
5   performs is this: A man will give a son to the
church for righteousness or his relative or [his] household
member. Or he will save one who is in trouble or
buy a slave and donate him for righteousness so that
all the good which he would do for them, i.e., that which he gave as
gifts for
10 righteousness, then that Catechumen who . . .
will share with them.   The third occasion:
A man will build a living place or construct a place,
having it done as part of the alms in the holy
church.   When the Catechumen completes
15 these three great works, these three alms which he
gives as gifts for the holy church . . .
which these alms will do. But that Catechumen
who has given them to them will . . .
receives a part in them. The Catechumens who will give . . .
20 They have a great love and a part of every grace
and good thing in the holy church. They will find many
graces."

Chapter 81
The Kephalaion on Fasting:
It Generates a
Multitude of Angels

[Again] it happened one time when the Apostle was sitting down
in the congregation one of his disciples stood up in front of him.
He said to him: "I have heard you, my Lord, when you said:
'Seven angels are generated by the fasting of a
30 single Elect. Not only the Elect but also
the Catechumens generate them on the day of the Lord's Day. This

is the [work] of fasting in perfection. So I have . . .
  has passed since I became Archegos. Fifty
[Elect were with] me in the church which I became head of.

p. 194

[They stood] in my presence when they fasted each day. So I
[took account of] the fasting which a man performs only on these
three Lord's Days. And I discovered that every one of these Elect
generated seven angels by their fasting. Thus I
5 [counted] the fasting of these fifty men on the three Lord's
Days. They made three hundred fifty angels since seven
angels were attached to each of the Elect, i.e., the ones which are
  generated
daily through the fasting completed. I counted these three
Lord's Days in which these fifty men fasted, [and I]
10 multiplied them by three. I discovered that the number of angels
which are begotten by them constitute one thousand fifty angels.
  And I
thanked them for the great profit and good which I had achieved
in the three days. But I turned, and I suffered inwardly . . .[1]

p. 195

disciple, which he declared . . .
he did him this favor.'" The Apostle said [to the disciple:]
"The statement which you made, i.e., . . .
your own mouth: 'I know that this is a good thing
5 which is done because of these fasts in which these
Holy Men fast on the Lord's Day as if
[they] knew that it was (1) entirely benefit and (2) because of what
  they
renounce.' For in these words which you have uttered in my presence,
you [were behaving] . . . as if you had not known anything of truth.
10 For if you had understood the truth, and known
the benefit, then your heart would not have prompted you to reject
  the
good with pleasure. You were not ill to say it, nor do you . . .

---

1. Remainder of p. 194 unintelligible.

several times. Truly, if you comprehended the true
benefit, and you found your body to be ailing, sick and
15 troubled, and you have pain many times, then . . .
nor would you cease from doing the work which was entrusted to
you.
The whole time you pass, you stand firm in the . . .
you would go to the [great] country of Rest with [the]
Children of the Living. [And you enter] with glory and [victory] to
those
20 things which you had set your heart on and in which you were
strengthened
It will be said to you: 'A divine work has taken place: [your]
[body] has been found to be saved for you . . . there being no hurt or
harm or suffering for you.' And after all these things, I [will]
. . . you, since you desire to . . . complete the good and
25 that which I have assigned you. If you reject this work
and this divine work, [and] there are others like you
who reject it, then all this benefit and this
divine work—who will do it? For the wise men who
. . . , who know the truth, who are like you, do not attain
30 the benefit which . . . which you proclaimed. They will commit
this sin which . . .
[soul]. But as for me, thus have I

p. 196

. . . some Elders
you in it, and you do the work which I
proclaimed
[for] you . . .   from you, and a benefit occurs
in your life. And even if others murmur?
5 to reject . . .   you . . . Do not murmur?
to reject it. For thus I say to you in truth . . . : 'Greater is
the glory and the victory and the good of the one who preaches,
building
the church larger, than that of the brother who [turns] his heart
10 inward, and isolates himself and edifies only self.'
But on the matter of the word which [you have] uttered:
'Suppose I have
sinned at the time when I proclaim any of the words of my

mouth concerning building a church or [giving] alms . . .'
your heart pain . . . or you are afraid. The sort of man
15 . . . for the sake of the work of the church and the helping of those
   who . . .
you . . . he commanding and constructing with his word, then he has
no sin.   But the sort of man who speaks, commanding
. . . anything . . . his own need, just as
. . . his flesh . . . fourteen. Or he runs
20 . . . works which are defiled. . . .
   . . . themselves to take care of himself. [But]
the one who declares this work, while persisting completely in sin
           keep quiet and never speak . . .
any word again.   But as for you, I endow you only
25 in this way. You have the power to preach and to build up the church
of God so that your toil will be accounted to your merit."

When that disciple heard these things from the Apostle,
he worshiped him. And he said to him, "From you, my Lord, I have
   received
the word which you proclaimed for me. I will preach and
build up
30 the church. Only, may your power and your glory aid me!"

p. 208

Chapter 85
Concerning the Cross of Light:
. . . tread
on it

15 Again another disciple questioned the Apostle, saying
to him, "I heard you, my Lord, when you said in the
congregation of the Church: 'It behooves man to look at
his feet when he is walking on a road so that he will not
tread on the Cross of Light with his foot and destroy the
plants. In the Beginning it was appointed to the serpent
20 that he [man] tread upon him and kill him with his foot.'
But sometimes the Great One [who is over me] sends me to a
foreign place for the work of God . . . of the church.

Sometimes a Teacher of the church which I am in or some of
the foreign brothers [ask(?)] for alms for some food which
25 they need. I know that that which I do is a good thing,
since I listen to the one who is over me, who sends me on
the road to a foreign place. When I [collect]
the alms and they are brought to the church, and the
brothers and sisters take care of them in it, I know and I
30 understand that I have a great victory there in this work.
But I am afraid that perhaps I might be sinning at the time
when [I am] walking on the pathway, stepping on the earth
and treading on the Cross of Light . . .

p. 209

without power by means of my soul on the pathway when I walk on
it."
After the Apostle heard these remarks from that
disciple, he said to him, "You uttered the word in the manner
which is well established, but listen that I might cause
5   you to believe it equally well that if you walk on [the]
pathway for the sake of a work of God, and if your Great One over
you [is]
the one who sends you, then you have no sin. For [you]
do not walk on it for the sake of a matter of concupiscence or because
of . . .
of a craving, in which there is sin, but rather you make [your]
10 walkway for the sake of the work of God; you [do not] run [along it]
for the sake of your own desire.

But I say to you with a loud voice:
Every Righteous Elect man who walks on a pathway
for the sake of the work of God, if he walks upon the
15 ground, and if he treads the soul of his feet upon the Cross of Light,
then he is not sinful in that situation, but his whole pathway is a
garland and a palm. For he does not walk
because his own desire, nor does he run because of [worldly]
gain and idle works when he steps upon the earth and the Cross of
Light.

20 But the other [type of] man, who runs upon the pathway for
the sake of his own desire and the existence of his body,

when he . . . himself for the sake of gain and deeds which are.
. . . The path of the walkway of that man is wholly sinful,
since he walks on the path of sin and error.

25 . . . behold, I have told you that, as for the one whom his Teacher
will send and who will go on a pathway for the sake of a work of
God—his pathway is wholly victorious. But thus you stated, 'I step
upon the earth and the Cross of Light, and I extinguish [it]
with my [soul],' and you say: 'Perhaps I have sinned because
30 of [this thing].' Do not be afraid of this [possibility]
either. For this Living [Soul] is like a man

p. 210

who would have an illness overcome his body parts, and his heart
is heavy, and his soul distressed, and he is debilitated by his
illness, and he looks for a doctor to heal him and to make him strong.
And he [the doctor] heals him, and treats him, and makes him well
[from]
5 the illness which has come over him. Thus he thinks of this one.
So a wise man comes, who knows the incantations, who is a skillful
doctor, who gives him treatment for that which should [come over]
him. And he utters over him the incantations which he knows,
and he also thumps[2] on all his body parts.
10 That man who is sick knows that this person [the doctor]
thumps on him in order to give him treatment, but that he
does not do it to him because of some enmity which he had
against him from some previous occasion. But rather, all of that
which he does,
he does to [him in order that] he might heal his body
15 and remove [the] illness and the corruption, when he thumps on him
for the sake of this benefit. That man who is sick will not
produce ill will [?] or hatred toward that doctor who thumps
on him. He will not hate him out of enmity, for he knows
that he does it for his benefit.

20 But if one comes and thumps on him out of enmity, he will
hate him, and seize him, and not let him go, for he knows
that he thumps on him with enmity, and he strikes

2. Literally "treads."

him impudently, adding another injury to his illness.
In that very same way the Living Soul which is either in the earth
25 or in the Cross of Light, if you walk
on her on the pathway, and if you step on the Cross [of Light], it will
not
hold you accountable in ill will and anger, since it knows that [you]
walk on it for rest and healing, to preach for it, [you]
walk for its sake in order to reveal its mysteries. So the crushing
30 of the bones [of the divine soul in plants] which you have crushed,
does not
go to sin, but it will lead to the victory. As the Savior said: '[Where]
your heart is, your treasure also will be

p. 211

there.' For this reason, nothing will be lost from you on account of
the crushing of the bones and your suffering, but it is completely
gathered
into the Rest.   As to the matter of that other situation which you
mentioned: 'When a teacher shall come to me or foreign brothers,
and I speak
5   about alms, perhaps that word
would become a source of harm and damage the Cross [of]
Light.' Do not be fearful even of this possibility, for there is a difference
between one word and another. For this is not [such] a word, but the
word
which hurts is if a man utters a word
10 for the purpose of killing a man or killing animals or for the purpose
of
killing trees and the Cross of Light. The word
of falsehood and that of anger and that of wrath or a word of
envy and [???] alone or a word of accusation which one
will set out toward his brother: this is the word which harms. . . .
15 If a man utters it, it will lead to sin. For he begat
demons from it and . . . him for the sake of this
. . . the righteous man or the . . .
all of those which I uttered in order that . . .   his word for the
fetter
For every one who will . . . his word for a fetter.

20 But he also . . .   his going forth, it will be bound. In
     the place where he was bound, his . . . in it, but as long as . . .
     word concerning the . . .   not go . . .
     nor will they write [?] . . .   that the one who harms
     talk about the loosing of the Soul . . . concerning the mystery
25 [of its] healing. For the righteous man who talks about the necessity
     [of] alms, talking about her [the Soul's] healing, her being gathered
          in,
     [he] is like a wise doctor who will drive away . . .
     his illness, there being a wound in his body, cutting
     . . . this man who is wounded by means of wisdom . . .
30 and he is lost . . . this wound, and he cuts it out. After these things
     . . . and he puts . . . eaten medicine upon it in order that
     it be swallowed and be separated from the iron and eliminated

p. 212

     from him along with the medicine which is eaten, and the wound is
          purified
     from the infection. After these things he applies cool ointment
          . . . and it heals. That man who is wounded puts
          . . . him, but he does not . . .
5   he [does not] create ill will in his heart toward him, for
     he knows that he does the similar thing for his good and his
     healing. After the incision with which he will cut him and the burn
          with which

     he will cauterize him, he gives additional compensation to the doc-
          tor. He
     thanks him, and he befriends him his whole life long.

10 Just like the doctor is the Elect
     man who asks for alms, and gathers them
     in, and brings them to the church. But the alms
     are like the man who is [ill], for the power of the enemy is mixed in
          with them, since . . .
     gathering
15 . . . [Thus] also the church which will purify him into the image
     of the holy ones. Those alms will not be able to be saved
     without suffering and pain, for they . . . them, and

they see . . . which they break
then and eat[3] . . . and also suffering.
20 But there is no other format for the alms besides this, for it
is their door to go out . . .   out of the world
with trouble.   In the manner of the Holy Church
which the Apostle establishes in the world that
without suffering and pain, the Elect are not able to escape
25 the world. But only by the considering of . . .
and that of prayer and encratism and . . .
and that of being uniquely born and of withdrawal [anachōrēsis] of
beating
and scourging, the use of fetters, the . . .
these first . . .
30 and this pain . . .   they inherit . . .
forever and ever.   But the one who does not . . .
does not have Rest in the Country of the Living.
Thus [also] these Living Alms experience

p. 213

suffering for a moment, but they [experience] Rest forever
through the Holy Ones. But this I command
you my brethren and my members: Let a man not
let his hand go and strike that Living Cross which . . .
5   gluttony and surfeit. Rather, send a guide for them [the alms]
through the word to the Catechumens. As for the other word, behold:
we send it forth as we utter it. For they [the Light particles in the
alms] are
in a great imprisonment. But if you are about to consume them [food
alms]
do not consume them with gluttony and wantonness and over-
indulgence
10 and surfeit, but consume them with great hunger [from fasting]
and drink them with great thirst, and take care for [restraining] your[4]
body in regard to them."   Then the Apostle said to that
disciple, "Behold, you have hearkened unto that which I proclaimed
to you
concerning your desire, and you have no sin."

3. The alms are a food offering.
4. Plural pronoun.

15 When that disciple heard these things, he was persuaded and re-
     joiced greatly.
     He said to him, "I thank you, my Lord, that you convince us
     of each particular thing and you give us peace of mind in a
     gentle way. From now on, with ears . . .
     which is living, will live . . . for you through your words of Life
20 which we have heard from you."

p. 216

Chapter 87
Concerning the Alms: . . .
of Life in the Church

     Again it happened one time that the Illuminator was sitting

p. 217

     in the midst of the congregation. He said to his disciples:
     "As for all of these alms which every sect gives
     in the world for the sake of
     the name of God, within the whole [given] in his name,
     those which their catechumens give in the name of
5   God, in every place where these alms are received for Him, they are
     accompanied by sorrow and travail and misfortune. [But they have
        no]
     rest and no open door for them to pass through in order to find an
     occasion to go to God in whose name they were given. The only
     exception is the Holy Church[5] in which the commandments
10   of alms are established, in which they fulfill
     the will of the Exalted One. The Holy Church, then,
     occurs in two personas, in brothers
     and sisters. So at the time when these alms reach the
     Holy Church, they are saved in her, and they are purified, and [they]
15   rest there in her. They come out of her [the church] and they [go] to
        the
     God of Truth in whose name they were given. Thus
     it is the Holy Church herself which is a place of rest
     for all those alms which rest in her.
     She herself becomes a doorway for them and a ferry to that
20   Land of Rest. Yet the Holy Church

     5. That is, of the Manichaeans.

has no place of rest in all this world except
through the Catechumens who obey her . . .
only from the Catechumens who give her rest, since
[her] honor comes from the Catechumens by whose hand
25 she continues. What is the assembly of the Catechumens
like? It is like a good land which is . . .
the horticulturist who plants the good tree. Behold
that good tree becomes the strength and the . . .
of the whole land; and it produces excellent fruit.
30 That [horticulturist] creates a rest for the Tree of Life, and he
[rests himself]. Thus the Holy Church,
[when they . . .] her, they are like a good tree.

p. 218

But the congregation of the Catechumens is like
that "good soil" which receives the "good seed."
See how large the assembly of the Catechumens is:
It resembles the "good soil," since it is the very
5   place which receives the Holy Church. It [the assembly]
strengthens her [the church] and gives her rest by means of all its
    works
and all its pains. And it becomes a place of rest for her,
since she rests in it in every place. The place which
does not have Catechumens in it does not have the Holy Church
10   resting in it.   Like that Living
Soul which stands in a mixture[6] flesh for the present, she desires

to go forth and return to the house of her people. But she knows
and understands that she does not have a door which opens into all
    the
powers of heaven and earth. For they are her source of suffering
    which
15 . . . her in every place. So she does not have that door which opens,
except [that] the sun and moon themselves are the Luminaries of the
    heavens.
. . . they become a place of rest for her, and they become a door which
    opens

---

6. That is, with sinful flesh.

into the exit. And she passes through them into the Home Country of [her]
people. [From here] to the other Luminaries of the heavens, they have no
20 place of rest among all the Powers of heaven, except that
Land of Light which has been theirs forever.   Thus
they purify the Living Soul from all troubles,
which provide her a rest and they open her a door which opens to the house [of]
her people.   In this way the Land of Light
25 will become a final receiver of the Luminaries of [the]
heavens. And they will rest themselves in it, and they will reign
in it forever.   In this way also, the Holy Church
becomes a place of rest for the alms of the
Catechumens, and the Catechumens themselves become a
30 place of rest for the Holy Church. But as for both the former ones and the
[latter]—their place of rest, in which they will rest, [is the Land] of Light."

p. 228

Chapter 91
Concerning the Catechumen Who
Is Saved in a Single Body
(i.e., Does Not Have to Be Reincarnated)

Again that Elect said to this Apostle, "I
heard you, my Lord, when you said: 'There is a Catechumen
10 [who] does not enter a body except this one alone. But at the
time when he comes into his body, his soul . . .
in the dome of heaven, and he travels to the place
of Rest.' Now I beseech you, my Lord, that you
instruct me about the works of that Catechumen
15 who does not go into another body: Which ones
or which one is his Type and what is his Sign in order that I might
know it and tell my other brethren in order that they might preach
it to the Catechumens, so that they might wish for
that and come forth peacefully into the Good."
20 Then the Apostle said to him: "I will indeed instruct
you concerning the works of those Catechumens

of the Faith who do not enter [another] body. The Sign of
that perfect Catechumen is this: You find the wife
in the house with him, who is like a stranger to him.
25 And from his perspective, his house is considered a place of sojourn.
And he says: 'I live in a house for rent by the day
and by the month.' His brethren and his relatives
are considered in his eyes as if they were foreigners who took up
with [him]
when they traveled with him on the road, since he . . .
30 they will separate from him, and each one . . . he will . . .
the gold and the silver and the utensils of the . . .

p. 229

house: they are like borrowed vessels in his eyes. [He]
takes them, and serves [food] with them; and afterwards he gives
[them]
back to their owner. He does not put his heart and his treasure in
them.
He withdraws [the focus of] his intent from the world, and he places
5 his heart in the Holy Church. His attention is constantly
focused on God. The one who goes beyond all these things, [having]
the care and the concern and the good of the holy ones
in him, cares for the Church like his own house,
in fact, even more than for his house. He has put his whole treasure in
10 the Elect men and the Elect women. For this is what the Savior
spoke through the mouth of his apostle: 'From this day
forward, those who have wives let them be as those who do not have
them;
those who buy as if they did not buy; those who rejoice
as if they did not rejoice; those who weep as if they did not
weep; those who [realize a] profit in this world
15 as if without wantonness.'[7] These things which . . .
uttered, and they were spoken concerning those perfect Catechumens
who escape [reincarnation] with this single body and return
above. They are like the Elect in their [spiritual] walk.
This is the Sign of those Catechumens who

7. Cf. 1 Cor 7:29–31.

20 do not enter [another] body.   There are others who
    might possess
    encratism who have also [kept?] [the meat of] every animal from
    their mouths, preparing themselves for fasting and prayer each day,
    helping the Church by that which has come from them
    in alms, and the capacity for evil has died in them.
25 . . . , i.e., putting their feet in the church more than in
    their house. Their heart [is placed] on her [the church]. At all times,
        their
    sitting down and their standing up is like that of the Elect. They have
    stripped all the things of the world from their heart. But
    that [the Spirit] man, . . . which is placed in the Holy Church
30   . . . at every moment and his gifts and
        . . . and his honors and the graces which benefit

p. 230

    his life, when he guides them to the Holy Church
    in addition to those who come into the church, whether they
    are his children or his wife or a relative
    of his, he rejoices greatly over those [people] and he loves
5   [them and] he sets all his treasure on them.
    Behold, this is the Sign and the Type of those Catechumens who do
    not enter another body. Like the Good Pearl
    concerning which I have written to you in the Treasure of Life,
    the one which has no value, thus also it
10 occurs for those Catechumens, i.e., those Catechumens
    who do not enter [another] body. But when they leave
    their body, then they travel on their way, and cross over
    into the place above, and enter into the Life.
    They are purified in the heavens and they are plucked in the way
        that a fruit
15 comes to ripeness and is plucked from the tree. Thus the alms
    which pass over to the Elect are made like
    many Icons, and they are purified, and they depart
    to the Country of the Living. Thus also the souls
    of the Catechumens, especially those who do not enter into another
        body,
    are like them [the alms].
20 As to the remainder of all the Catechumens

I have written down in the Treasure of Life
the way that they are set free and purified, each one of
them according to his works and according to his donating to the
church. Thus also [is] his going forth to offer
25 it, and his healing and his purification.

For this reason, it behooves the Catechumen that he pray
constantly for repentance and forgiveness of sin from God
and the Holy Church because of his sins, the first
and the last, in order that his works might be gathered in,
30 both the first and the last, and apportioned to his share."

p. 231

After his disciples had heard these words from him,
they blessed him and glorified him with great blessings. They
said to him, "Blessed are you, our Father, and you are glorious.
Blessed
is the Hope which awaits us through you. For great is this thing
5 which you have bestowed on the souls in that you revealed to the
Elect the works and the commandments of the Elect [status]
by which they should live. And even the Catechumens
were not abandoned by you. But you taught them each
step and stair and rung in order that they might go up
10 by means of them to the Good, every one of them according to his
ability,
and that they might reach the Country of the Living. . .[8]

p. 232, line 17 (Chapter 91 continues:)

". . . since that time for all of the first sins.
When he goes back to repeating his first deeds
and he sins in them another time, then he will be held accountable
20 for all his sins, the first and the last. He receives
retribution for all of them. For God gives him repentance
and forgiveness of sin from his foolish ways, but
he did not persevere in that repentance which God
gave him. If he had remained steadfast in the Catechumenate
25 through faith and separated himself from all of his

8. The next few lines diverge from ascetic themes. The translation is picked up again
on p. 232.

first deeds, then all of his sins would be forgiven him,
whether he was an Elect in the [ranks of] the Elect
or a Catechumen in the Catechumenate.
That one who is a Catechumen who shall remain
30 steadfast in the Catechumenate, of the other sins [which he]
committed a multitude of them will be forgiven him
because of his fasting and [praying and]

p. 233

alms. Hear how I reveal to you
the works of the Catechumens who have faith. The Catechumen
who truly believes performs fifty fasts [which]
he fasts on the fifty Lord's Days of the year.
5 He keeps them pure when he abstains [enkrateuein] [from]
concupiscence toward his wife and when he purifies his bed through
celibacy all of those days of the Lord's Day. He . . .
in his eating and he does not defile his food through . . .
fish, and all the contamination of flesh and blood. He does not eat
10 anything which is defiled on these days of the Lord's Day. [He]
restrains
his hands from harming and causing destruction to the Living
Soul. The hours of prayers are followed [?] by him, he keeps
them, and he comes to prayer daily, every hour and
every day, at all the hours of prayer. They will . . .
15 you his fasting and his alms [which] he gave on
all the days of the year. The alms are accounted . . . because of
his good, the fasting which he performed, the clothing which he
bestowed
on the Holy Ones. And they built community with
each other through their fasting and their good.
20 They count these and the others, and put half of his work
for the Good [while] half is for sins. Truly, the sins which
he sins in half of the year are divided
in five parts. Four of them are forgiven him through
[the] patronage[9] of the Holy Church by means of the faith
25 [and the] good of the Elect [ones]. But one is for that other one,
since he knows the Gnosis. He separated his
[Light] from the darkness, and he offered a hymn and prayer

9. I.e., treasure of merits.

[to the] Luminaries above. The other Rest which he
[made] . . . this. . . . So because of these good things which
30 [he did, they forgave] him four parts, four
            sins which he sinned

p. 234

since the day when he became a Catechumen. Furthermore,
it is only one part which is required of him, and [from which] he
    receives
bitterness and pain. Afterwards he is purified
either above or below, being
5   purified according to the worthiness of his works, and he is cleansed
and washed and beautified. Then
he is transcribed into the Icon of Light[10]
and he is led up and he arrives at the Country of Rest so that
"where his heart is, there will his treasure be also."[11]
10 If he has stood fast in the Catechumenate,
he will receive the reward for his good deeds in this way.
But if he lies and turns from the truth, then
all his sins will be held accountable to him once again, the first
to the last. The judgment condemning his sins will be poured out
15 on him. But if he is sustained by his faith and made
strong by it, then a directive will come for him, and he will come
forth again, and become righteous and escape and be saved
from his [current life] into life forever and ever. At the time
of his coming forth, he will return and rest himself in Eternal
20 Life."   When these disciples heard
these words of wisdom, they glorified their Teacher, and they re-
    membered
the First Light, that which enlightens through the Nous and the
riches of his Wisdom. . .[12]

p. 248

Chapter 98
What Is "Virgin" or
What Is a "Celibate"?

Again one time when the Apostle was sitting in
the assembly of his congregation, he said to his disciples:

10. I.e., the soul returns to the divine.
11. Cf. Matt 6:19–21 (esp. v. 21); Jas 5:2–3.
12. The succeeding chapters (92–97) are not relevant to the present collection of texts.

15 "What is the virgin who is named 'virgin'?
or the one who is called 'celibate': what is he? Or if
a virgin is called 'virgin,' what is the significance? Or the
'celibate' who is called by this name, what does it signify
that he is called 'celibate'?"

20 His disciples said to him: "Explain to us, O Lord, these
two words since all good gifts are given to us
by your hand." Then our Illuminator said to them: "The
one who is called 'virgin,' if it refers to the mystery
of the Aeons of Greatness, it was called 'virgin'
25 according to the symbol of the whole Light which has not yet tasted
death and which has not yet come to the battle with the enemy.
On the other hand, that which is called 'celibate,' with reference to
the mystery of the Light, is that which comes
to be mixed with the
Darkness and polluted in the body . . . way. . . .
30 It went up to the Light. And it was called
'celibate.' Also, the pure virgins . . .
they come forth against the enemy . . .
[. . . not] taste death or. . . .

p. 249

But that which is called 'celibate' [is that]
Light which had mixed with the darkness and was purified and came
up from all of the created things and stood fast in the [Greatness].
It was called 'celibate' because it tasted
5 concupiscence, but afterwards was purified from that; it became a
Pure Being. Furthermore, that which is called
'virgin' is that Light which has been purified in the Icon of
the Messenger, and went up and attained the high[est sphere] and
took its place in the Icon of the Divine Beings. That which is called
10 'celibate' is the residue of that Light which is
left behind from what is purified, which goes up to heaven
and comes back down in reincarnation.   There is a part of
it which comes and arrives in the mold of the flesh of human beings.
The latter is chosen [while] in the flesh, and it receives the Hope
15 and it becomes a Pure One and is named 'celibate.'

Furthermore, that which is called 'virgin' is the Nous
of Light which comes and wears the images [eikon] of the Elect.

On the other hand, that which is called 'celibate' is
the New Man who is refined from this Old Man and is
20 purified and is stripped of the sin which is mixed with it and becomes
a 'celibate.' That which is called 'virgin' in the flesh is a man who has
never been joined with a wife or defiled by intercourse.
That which is called 'celibate' is the man who does have a
25 wife in the world. But afterwards, he purifies himself of her
and abandons her. Because of this he . . . and he becomes a holy
'celibate.' Behold I have explained to you the symbols
of the 'virgin' and 'celibate' by means of several
personas,[13] saying 'what is "virgin" or what is
"celibate"' in a number of ways."

Chapter 99
Concerning Reincarnation

Again one of the catechumens of the Apostle
said to him, "We have heard a word from you, my Lord,
which you have preached to us and taught us in the books
which you. . . ."[14]

p. 262

Chapter 109
Concerning the Fifty Lord's Days:
What Mysteries Do They Correspond To?
Or the Second (Fifty):
Whom Do They Signify?

Again a disciple stood up to question the Apostle,
15 saying to him: "I beseech you, my Lord,
that you speak to us about the fifty Lord's Days
on which the Catechumens fast:
For what thing do they fast or for
whose mystery do they fast? Or this second
20 set which are established in the midst of the Elect: To signify
whose mystery were they established among them? Explain this to
us and make it clear to us, since . . .
from you."   Then he said to
the one questioning him and those who were with him:
25 "Know that in each of the five Garments which the First

---

13. I.e., of the divine light.
14. The text that immediately follows is quite broken. The translation is picked up again on p. 262, chapter 109.

Man evoked there are five Powers
They belong to the . . .
each other, these five, five times . . .
their number. But when . . .

p. 263

the Call. And they came down, and their Answer wished
to come with him. But the Call and the Hearing make up
twenty-five characteristics in their twenty-five members which
are the Sons of Man. The Call and the
5 Hearing lifted themselves up from them. Just as their Father,
the Living Man, lifted himself from them by means of these things,
[so] those others established all the works above
and below. But these are what is called the Pentecost,
which are the fifty. They are great days, the prototypes of
10 the holy days. They fasted from the food
which is theirs. From that time until the time of the
coming of Jesus the Splendor, the Glorious One, who came . . .
their food, which is their . . . of the soul, which
is the Call and the Hearing . . .
15 that food. In the spiritual sense, they loosed . . .
all these fifty days which . . . this Living Food
was sufficient for all of them. It filled them all with power,
wealth and life, light. . . .
This Living Food . . .
20 became wealthy. They ceased to be fifty days, they went on
and became a hundred holy days, which are the fifty days
which correspond . . . fasting
which are attached in them
these mysteries of these first
25 things, I have
But the second ones in which the Elect
fast, correspond to the signs of the fifty . . .
the Call and the Hearing put them
in their

p. 264

places of brilliance at the coming of Jesus. These are the
great days of the fifty Lord's Days which I have revealed
to the Catechumens. Those are the second fifty
days which I have revealed to the Elect.

5   ... Since you inquire about these mysteries: they also correspond to
    the teachings of the sects which have those fifty days in which
    they fast, calling them 'Pentecost.'
    Since the apostles themselves fasted for
    these fifty days, they revealed them to their disciples.
10 Christ himself revealed these fifty days to them
    on the day when he [was] fasting on the mountain, at the time when
        the
    devil tempted him.[15] He spent seven more days going
    down to the house of Simon the Leper. He spent
    another three days in the sepulchre among the dead. But ...
15   in these fifty days. I bestowed them
    on the whole church in these fifty days
    in which the Catechumens fast corresponding to the mystery
    of the First Man. The other fifty ones [corresponding to] the symbol of
    the Second Man are the ones which were revealed in the church."

SUGGESTED READINGS

Asmussen, J. P. *Xuāstvānīft: Studies in Manichaeism*. Copenhagen: Prostant apud
    Munksgaard, 1965.
Klimkeit, H. J. "Christians, Buddhists and Manichaeans in Central Asia." *Budd-
    hist-Christian Studies* 1 (1981) 46–50.
Lieu, S. N. C. *Manichaeism in the Later Roman Empire and Medieval China: A
    Historical Survey*. Manchester, Eng.: Manchester University Press, 1985.
———. "Manichaeism in the Later Roman Empire and Medieval China: Cor-
    rigenda." BJRL 68 (1986):469–72.
———. "Precept and Practice in Manichaean Monasticism." JTS n.s. (1981) 153–
    73.
Polotsky, H. J. "Manichäismus." In *Der Manichäismus*, edited by G. Widengren,
    101–44. Darmstadt, W.Ger.: Wissenschaftliche Buchgesellschaft, 1977.
Ries, J. "Mani et manichéisme. In *Dictionnaire de Spiritualité Ascétique et Mys-
    tique*, edited by M. Villier. Paris: Gabriel Beauchesne, 1932–77.
Sundermann, W. "Studien zur Kirchengeschichtlichen Literatur der iranischen
    Manichaer: I." *AfO* 13 (1986) 40–92.
———. "Studien zur Kirchengeschichtlichen Literatur der iranischen Mani-
    chaer: II." *AfO* 13 (1986) 239–317.
———. "Studien zur Kirchengeschichtlichen Literatur der iranischen Mani-
    chaer: III." *AfO* 14 (1987) 41–107.
Vööbus, A. *The Origin of Asceticism: Early Monasticism in Persia*. Louvain, Belg.:
    CSCO, 1958.
Widengren, G. *Mani and Manichaeism*. New York: Holt, Rinehart, 1965.

15. Cf. Gospel accounts of Jesus' temptation by the devil: Matt 4:1–11; Mark 1:12–13;
Luke 4:1–13.

Introduction and Translation by
STEVEN D. FRAADE

The Nazirite in
Ancient Judaism
(Selected Texts)

INTRODUCTION

Rather than debating whether or to what extent varieties of ancient
Judaism and their systems of interdicts may be said to be "ascetic" or
"antiascetic," it is useful to consider what I term the "ascetic tensions"
that run through each.[1] Of particular interest are those points at which
supererogatory self-denial or self-imposed suffering (in Hebrew, *pĕrîšût*)
are debated by voices within ancient Jewish texts, whether those voices
are portrayed as being in explicit debate with one another, are juxta-
posed against one another already by ancient redactors of those texts, or
are only found to be in some tension with one another as we gather
those texts and set them alongside one another for purposes of critical
examination. Such practices are viewed positively as voluntary exten-
sions of what is already required or recommended by collective Jewish
practice as proper means to spiritual advancement in accord with divine
will, even as they are viewed suspiciously in terms of both their motivations and their consequences: their motivations may be vainly self-
centered, and their consequences may be socially detrimental. When
individuals or subgroups undertake higher levels of abstinent behavior,
precisely with regard to those areas in which that larger society commonly practices, or at least values, abstinence of more moderate degrees
(e.g., diet and sex), they distinguish themselves from that larger Jewish
society by virtue of such practice and are inevitably in some tension with

---

1. For a more developed argument of this point, with reference to previous
scholarship and with exemplification from a broad range of ancient Jewish sources, see
my essay, "Ascetical Aspects of Ancient Judaism."

it as a result, whether or not that was their intent. This tension is especially noticeable in the texts of ancient rabbinic Judaism, as the rabbinic sages of late antiquity saw themselves on the one hand as a spiritual, intellectual, and leadership elite and on the other hand as deriving from Israelite society as a whole, for which they sought to provide realizable models for collective Jewish practice.[2] However, this tension is as much intrarabbinic, for that is how it expresses itself within the corpus of extant rabbinic texts.

The texts that follow focus on only one aspect of the ascetic tension in ancient Judaism, especially within that variety that finds its expression in rabbinic texts of the third through sixth centuries C.E.: the figure of the Nazirite. According to biblical legislation (Num 6:1–21), an Israelite man or woman might achieve a high, priestly (even High Priestly) level of holiness through abstaining for a given period (later defined as a minimum of thirty days) from wine, grape products, contact with the dead, even of one's immediate family, and cutting of one's hair. At the end of the vowed period, or should contact with the dead cancel the vow, the Nazirite's hair is shorn and offered with other sacrifices on the altar. Later sources suggest that a person might become a Nazirite, especially for a finite period of time, for a variety of legitimate reasons: penitence, seeking divine favor at a time of distress or danger, and self-discipline. Even though Nazirite practice per se probably became extinct with the destruction of the Jerusalem Temple in 70 C.E.,[3] it remained representa-

---

2. Although we might conceive of the rabbinic program for Israel as a whole as one of religious *askēsis* (as classically understood), the rabbis resisted the internal pull to become themselves a separate ascetic (or monastic) elite within Israel. For a more general discussion of the class of rabbinic sage and their self-understanding in relation to larger Israelite society, see chap. 3 of my forthcoming book, *From Tradition to Commentary: Torah and Its Interpretation in the Midrash Sifre to Deuteronomy* (Albany: State University of New York Press, 1991).

3. That Nazirite vows were practiced before the destruction of the Temple is well evidenced. Note in particular the following: 1 Macc 3:47–51; Josephus *A.J.* 19.16.1 § 294; *B.J.* 2.15.1 §313; Acts 18:18; 21:23–24; *m. Nazir* 3:6; 5:4, 11; *p. Ber.* 7.2 (11b). Interestingly, most of these examples, if historically true, fall in the mid-first century C.E., that is, in the years shortly before the Temple's destruction. A burial inscription from the same period refers to a *family* of Nazirites. See Nahman Avigad, "The Burial-Vault of a Nazirite Family on Mount Scopus," *IEJ* 21 (1971):185–200. The speculation of some scholars (for references, see my "Ascetical Aspects," p. 283, n. 56) that the Nazirites in Second Temple times constituted a group (on the model of the Rechabites of Jer 35), however, is without basis. Because the Nazirite was required to bring a sacrificial offering to the Temple upon the completion of his vows or upon their violation through contact with a corpse, it is generally assumed that such vows, at least of a temporary nature, could not have been undertaken once sacrificial worship ceased. See Josephus *B.J.* 2.15.1 §313 and *m. Nazir* 5:4, cited below. However, it is possible that people would have continued to assume the obligations of a Nazirite without a formal vow or even would have undertaken lifelong Nazirite vows, but there is no firm evidence for this in the rabbinic period. For later evidence for the taking of "Samsonite Nazirite vows," see

tive of other forms of supererogatory abstinence, including other types of vows, whose merits and limits continued to be debated among the rabbis.[4] In other words, the Nazirite becomes emblematic both of the ideal of supererogatory abstinence (pĕrîšût) and of its dangers.[5]

These texts are all drawn from rabbinic literature, beginning with the earliest digest of rabbinic law, the Mishna (ca. early third century C.E.), and its accompanying Tosepta (sometime thereafter), which each devote a tractate both to the laws of the Nazirite and to vows more generally. Around the same time we have early midrashic commentaries (third century C.E.), which interpret the biblical warrant for the Nazirite. Finally, there is extensive commentary in the Palestinian (ca. 500) and Babylonian Talmuds (ca. 600) to the earlier mishnaic rules regarding Nazirite vows and practices.

Because each of these texts draws upon and relates to earlier traditions, the above dates are only meant as approximate signposts. What we have before us is an evolving, intertextual, and hence intergenerational reflection upon the Nazirite and the larger complex of issues relating to Jewish ascetic practice, for which the Nazirite is understood to stand.

TRANSLATION

MISHNA: NED. 1:1; 2:3

[1:1] Any substitute for [the form of words used to utter] a vow is as binding as the vow, for a ban as a ban, for an oath as an oath, for a Nazirite vow as a Nazirite vow. . . . [If he said,] "As the vows of the

---

Samuel Morrell, "The Samsonite Vow in the Sixteenth Century," *AJS Review* 14 (1989):223–62.

4. That vows of abstinence were commonly and, to the rabbis' chagrin, rashly and without proper intention undertaken in rabbinic times is well evidenced. It may be in relation to this practice that rabbinic discussions of the biblically prescribed Nazirite vows come, at least in part, as a response. For a positive rabbinic view of vows in general, see *m* 'abot 3:13: "Vows are a fence [protective guard] around abstinence." From a rabbinic legal perspective, a vow was a sacred obligation that once formally uttered could result in a sacrilege if violated, hence the need for rabbinic methods of legally abrogating vows if, once rashly undertaken, they could not be maintained. See Z'ev W. Falk, "Binding and Loosing," in Bernard Jackson, ed., *Studies in Jewish Legal History: Essays in Honour of David Daube* (London: Jewish Chronicle Publications, 1974) 92–100.

5. Note that the verb *nzr*, meaning to "dedicate," is rabbinically identified with the verb *prš*, meaning to "separate," with the latter having the dual sense of separation from pleasurable practices as well as separation from the larger society: *Sipre Zutta* ' to Num 9:6; *Sipra* 'Emor 4:1; *Tg. Onq.* to Lev 15:31. On the ambivalent rabbinic attitude to pĕrîšût and pĕrûšîm ("ascetics" and Pharisees), see my "Ascetical Aspects," 271–72.

wicked . . .", he is culpable for a Nazirite vow, an offering, and an oath. [If he said,] "As the vows of the pious . . .", he has said naught; [but if he said,] "As their freewill offerings . . .", he is culpable for a Nazirite vow and an offering.

[2:3] There is such a thing as a vow within a vow. . . . If a man said, "May I be a Nazirite if I eat, may I be a Nazirite if I eat," and he ate, he must fulfill each of the two vows.

MISHNA: *NAZIR* 2:3; 3:6; 5:4; 7:1

[2:3] If they filled a man's cup [with wine] and he said, "I will be a Nazirite with respect to it," he becomes a Nazirite. It once happened that a woman was drunk and when they filled her cup [with wine] she said, "I will be a Nazirite with respect to it." The sages said: She only intended to say, "May it be to me as Korban."

[3:6] If a person [in the Diaspora] vowed to be a Nazirite for a long period,[6] and fulfilled his Nazirite vow, and afterwards came to the Land of Israel, the School of Shammai say: He must fulfill a Nazirite vow of thirty days more [in the Land of Israel]. The School of Hillel say: He must again fulfill his original Nazirite vow [in the Land of Israel]. It once happened that when the son of Queen Helena[7] went to war, she said, "If my son returns in safety from the war I will be a Nazirite for seven years. When her son returned from the war she was a Nazirite for seven years, at the end of which she went up to the Land of Israel. The School of Hillel ruled that she must be a Nazirite for another seven years. At the end of the seven years she contracted ritual impurity. Thus, she ended up being a Nazirite for twenty-one years. Rabbi Judah said: She only needed to be a Nazirite for fourteen years.[8]

[5:4] If a man vowed to be a Nazirite and he went to bring his cattle and found that they had been stolen, and he had made his Nazirite vow before they were stolen, his vow is binding; but if he had made his Nazirite vow after they were stolen, his vow is not binding.[9] Nahum the

6. More than thirty days, the period considered by the rabbis to be the minimum period for a Nazirite vow. Compare Josephus *B.J.* 2.15.1 §313.

7. She was Queen of Adiabene and a convert to Judaism. The incident, if historical, would have occurred in the early 40s C.E.

8. This is traditionally explained as follows: She served for one term of seven years before coming to the Land of Israel, for another term of seven years in the Land of Israel, because she could not be presumed to have been ritually pure outside it, and for another thirty days (the minimum period) after she was in the Land of Israel.

9. The man had intended to bring one of his cattle as an offering upon completing his vow. If circumstances change after the vow is taken, it cannot be abrogated. See *m. Ned.* 9:2.

Mede made a similar error when Nazirites came up from the Diaspora [to Jerusalem] and found the Temple destroyed. Nahum the Mede said to them: Would you have vowed to be Nazirites had you known that the Temple was destroyed? They answered: No. And Nahum the Mede released them from their vows. But when the matter came before the sages they said to him: If any man vowed to be a Nazirite before the Temple was destroyed, his Nazirite vow is binding; but if he vowed after the Temple was destroyed, his Nazirite vow is not binding.

[7:1] Neither a High Priest nor a Nazirite may contract ritual impurity because of their [dead] kindred, but they may contract ritual impurity because of a neglected corpse.[10] If they were on a journey and found a neglected corpse, R. Eliezer says: The High Priest may contract ritual impurity but the Nazirite may not contract ritual impurity. But the sages say: The Nazirite may contract ritual impurity, but the High Priest may not contract ritual impurity. R. Eliezer said to them: Rather, let the priest contract ritual impurity for he does not need to bring an offering because of his ritual impurity, and let not the Nazirite contract ritual impurity for he must bring an offering because of his ritual impurity. They answered: Rather let the Nazirite contract ritual impurity, for his sanctity is not a lifelong sanctity, and let not the priest contract ritual impurity, for his sanctity is a lifelong sanctity.

TOSEPTA: NED. 1:1

[If he said,][11] "As the freewill offering of the wicked . . .", he has said naught, for the wicked do not make freewill offerings. [If he said,] "As the freewill offerings of the pious . . .", R. Judah says: It is as if he had vowed a Nazirite vow. For the early pious would make freewill offerings [and not formal vows] of Nazirite obligations, since God did not grant them otherwise an opportunity to bring [sin offerings] for their inadvertent sins, therefore they made freewill offerings of Nazirite obligations so as to bring an offering. Rabban Simeon ben Gamaliel says: [If he said,]

---

10. Literally, "a corpse of a religious obligation," that is, one that is found and there is no one else to bury it. In such a case even a High Priest or a Nazirite not only may but must incur impurity so as to attend to the corpse. See *m. Nazir* 6:5. In being forbidden from having contact with the corpse even of a next of kin, the Nazirite is like the High Priest and of a higher order than the regular priest who was permitted to attend to the corpse of a next of kin. See Lev 21:1–2, 11; and *b. Ta'an.* 26b–27a. On the similarity of the holiness of the Nazirite to that of the High Priest, see *Encyclopaedia Judaica* s.v. "Nazirite." On the priestly quality of the Nazirites' abstinence from wine, see Philo *Spec. Leg.* 1.249.

11. See *m. Ned.* 1:1, cited above.

"As the freewill offering of the pious . . .", it is not as though he had vowed a Nazirite vow. For the early pious would not make freewill offerings of Nazirite obligations, for if one wished to bring a burnt offering he brought it; offerings of well-being, he brought them; a thanksgiving offering and the four kinds of bread, he brought them. But they would not make freewill offerings of Nazirite obligations because they would then have had to make atonement, as it is said, "And he shall make atonement on his behalf for the sin that he committed through (against) the corpse (soul) (ʿal hannepeš)" (Num 6:11).[12]

TOSEPTA: *NAZIR* 4:7

Simeon the Righteous[13] said: In all my life I ate the trespass offering of a Nazirite only once. It happened that a man came to me from the south, and I saw that he had beautiful eyes, a handsome face, and curly locks. I said to him: "My son, why did you want to destroy such lovely hair?" He said to me: "I was a shepherd in my village and I came to fill water from the river. When I looked at my reflection my impulse to do evil overcame me and sought to drive me from the world. I said to him: 'Evil one, you should not pride yourself in something which is not yours, in something which is destined to become dust and worms. Behold I vow to shave you off for the sake of heaven.'" I patted his head and kissed him, saying: "My son, may there be many like you who do God's will in Israel. In you is fulfilled what Scripture says: 'If anyone, man or woman, who distinctly utters a Nazirite vow, to set himself apart *for the Lord . . .'* (Num 6:2)."[14]

TANNAITIC MIDRASH: *SIPRE* NUM 30

"And [the priest] shall make expiation on his behalf [for the sin that he committed through (against) the corpse (soul) (ʿal hannepeš)]" (Num

12. For the rabbinic understanding of this verse, that the Nazirite incurs guilt because of the self-denial he caused to *his* soul, see below.
13. Presumably the High Priest mentioned in *m.* 'abot 1:2, ca. 190 B.C.E. For the possibility that the reference is to another High Priest named Simeon, ca. 41 C.E., or to Simeon son of Shetaḥ, ca. 90 B.C.E., see David Goodblatt, "Agrippa I and Palestinian Judaism in the First Century," *Jewish History* 2 (1987) 30–31, n. 64.
14. For a close parallel, see *Sipre* Num 22, where the story is provided as commentary to the words, "to set himself apart for the Lord." For later parallels, see *p*. *Ned*. 1:1, 6; *b*. *Ned*. 9b–10a. For discussion, see David Halivni, "On the Supposed Anti-Asceticism or Anti-Naziritism of Simon the Just," *JQR* 58 (1968) 243–52, with references to the earlier literature. Compare Philo *Spec. Leg.* 1.247–54, where it also stressed that the Nazirite undertakes his vow as a way of dedicating himself to God.

6:11): For he sinned against his soul. R. Eleazar Hakappar (ca. 200 c.e.) says: Against which soul did he sin that he needs expiation? For he denied his soul wine.[15] And we can argue a fortiori: if one who denies his soul wine needs expiation, how much more so one who denies himself everything. R. Ishmael says: Scripture [in speaking of expiation] refers only to the impure Nazirite, as it says, "And shall make expiation on his behalf for the guilt that he incurred through the corpse," for he became impure from contact with the dead.[16]

TANNAITIC MIDRASH:
SIPRE ZUṬṬA' TO NUM 6:8

"All the days of his term as Nazirite he is holy (consecrated) to the Lord": Because he decided to follow the way of abstinence and purity he is called "holy," and furthermore Scripture equals him to the prophet, as it is said, "And I raised up prophets from among your sons and Nazirites from among your young men" (Amos 2:11).[17]

PALESTINIAN TALMUD: BER. 7:2 (11b)

It is taught: In the days of Simeon the son of Shetaḥ [ca. 90 b.c.e.] three hundred Nazirites went up [to Jerusalem]. For one hundred and fifty he found grounds for annulment [of their vows], but for [the other] one hundred and fifty he did not find grounds for annulment. He went to King Yannai and said to him: "There are three hundred Nazirites here who require nine hundred sacrifices. If you provide half I shall provide the other half." He [Yannai] sent him four hundred and fifty. An informer went and told him: "He [Simeon] did not give anything of his."

15. The sense that the word *nepeš* refers not to the dead corpse but to the Nazirite's own self may derive from Num 30:3: "If a man makes a vow to the Lord or takes an oath imposing a prohibition on himself (ʿal napšô). . . ."
16. R. Eleazar Hakappar's interpretation is also cited, and becomes itself the subject of interpretation, in the following: *b. Taʿan* 11a–b; *b. Ned.* 9b–10a; *b. Nazir* 2b–3a; 19a; *b. B. Qam.* 91b. Note how the Nazirite serves as the basis for discouraging all forms of supererogatory abstinence. Thus, in *B. Qam.* 91b, R. Eleazar Hakappar's dictum is cited with regard to those who afflict themselves excessively in mourning, and in *b. Taʿan.* 11a–b, it is cited with regard to supererogatory fasting. The later Babylonian sources disagree whether R. Eleazar Hakappar meant to brand all Nazirites as sinners or only those who, because they vow rashly, are not diligent and become defiled. In this regard, see also Tosaphot to *b. Ned.* 9b–10a. A similar interpretation of the Nazirite as sinner is given in the name of R. Simeon in *p. Ned.* 1:1 (36d), to be cited below; *p. Nazir* 1:6 (51c); *b. Nazir* 9b–10a.
17. Compare the targumic rendering of *Tg. Neb.* Amos 2:11–12, which substitutes "teachers" for "Nazirites."

When King Yannai heard this he became angry. Being afraid, Simeon the son of Shetah fled. Some time later distinguished men of the Kingdom of Persia came to King Yannai. While they were sitting and eating, they said to him: "We know that there used to be here a certain old man here who would say before us words of wisdom." He told them what had happened. They said: "Send and bring him." He sent and gave him his word [that he would not harm him]. When he came he sat between the king and the queen. He [Yannai] said to him: "Why did you deceive me?" He said to him: "I did not deceive you. You gave of your wealth and I gave of my teaching, as it is written, 'For the shelter of wisdom is like the shelter of money'" (Eccl 7:12).[18]

PALESTINIAN TALMUD: *NED.* 1:1 (36d)

The mishnah[19] is in accord with the view of R. Judan, as it is taught in the name of R. Judan: "It is better not to vow than to vow and not fulfill" (Eccl 5:4): Best of all is not to vow at all. R. Meir said: "It is better not to vow than to vow and not fulfill." Best of all is to vow and to fulfill one's vows. And thus it says, "Make vows and pay them to your God" (Prov 76:12)....

[If he said] "As the vows of the pious . . .", he has said naught.[20] This would seem to suggest that the pious make vows. However, when such a one vows he is no longer pious. The mishnah is in accord with the view of R. Judah, as it is taught in the name of R. Judah: The early pious desired to bring a sin offering, but God did not grant them an opportunity to sin, so they made freewill offerings of Nazirite obligations so as to bring a sin offering.[21] R. Simeon says: They were sinners for vowing Nazirite vows, as it is said, "And [the Priest] shall make expiation on his behalf for having sinned with respect to the corpse [(soul) (*'al han-nepeš*)]" (Num 6:11): This sin is with respect to his own soul, for having abstained from wine.[22] And this is in accord with Simeon the Righteous,

---

18. The remainder of the story need not concern us here. For parallels, see the following: *p. Nazir* 5:5 (54b); *Gen Rab.* 91 (ed. Theodor-Albeck, 115–17); *Eccl Rab.* 7:11. For historical discussion, see Goodblatt, "Agrippa I," 16–23; with which contrast Daniel R. Schwartz, *Agrippa I: The Last King of Judaea* (Hebrew) (Jerusalem: Zalman Shazar Center, 1987) 79, n. 5; both of which cite earlier treatments. Compare Acts 21:23–24, 26 and a similar story told by Josephus (*A.J.* 19.6.7 § 294) about King Agrippa I.

19. *m. Ned.* 1:1, cited above, to the effect that the righteous do not vow, but make freewill offerings.

20. *m. Ned.* 1:1.

21. See *t. Ned.* 1:1, cited above.

22. A similar interpretation is given in the name of R. Eleazar Hakappar, in *Sipre Num* 30.

who held the same view as that of R. Simeon [that Nazirites are sinners].[23]

R. Mana asked: Why should I care about Simeon the Righteous, even if he follows the view of R. Simeon? Did Simeon the Righteous never eat sin offerings for other types of offenses all his days?[24] Rather, because people vow in rashness, in the end they regret their vows, and because they regret their vows, when they bring their offerings they are like one who slaughters unconsecrated animals in the Temple Court. But this one vowed with integrity, his mouth and his heart acting in unison.[25]

BABYLONIAN TALMUD: BER. 63A

It has been taught: Rabbi [Judah the Patriarch] says: Why does the section of the Nazirite (Num 6:1–21) follow immediately after that of the unfaithful wife (Num 5:11–31)? To teach that whoever sees an unfaithful wife in her degradation should vow to abstain from wine.[26]

BABYLONIAN TALMUD: TAʿANIT 11A–B

Said Samuel: Whoever undertakes [supererogatory] fasting is called a sinner. His reasoning was like that of the following tanna, as it is taught: R. Eleazar Hakappar B'Rabbi said: "And [the Priest] shall make expiation on his behalf for the sin that he committed through (against) the corpse (soul) (ʿal hannepeš)" (Num 6:11): Against which soul did he sin? Rather,

23. The story is next told about Simeon the Righteous's encounter with the Nazirite shepherd from the south. See t. Nazir 4:7, cited above. Thus, the reason that Simeon the Righteous never ate the trespass offering of a Nazirite except this once was because he, like R. Simeon of the Talmud, thought that Nazirites were sinners.

24. As a priest, he surely must have eaten many sacrifices brought because of sinful behavior. Parallels have R. Mana asking rhetorically, What is so different about the trespass offering of the defiled Nazirite that Simeon the Righteous should not eat it if he eats other trespass offerings for sinful behavior? See b. Ned. 9b–10a; Num Rab. 10:7.

25. In other words, unlike sin offerings that are brought in atonement for a sin, the offerings of Nazirites are often themselves sinful because they are offered resentfully at the conclusion of a vow that never should have been undertaken to begin with. However, R. Mana appears to reject the suggestion that Simeon the Righteous acted as he did out of agreement with R. Simeon (and R. Eleazar Hakappar), that Nazirites are by definition (according to Num 6:11) sinners. For this view, see Tosaphot to b. Ned. 9b–10a, as well as Halivni, "On the Supposed Anti-Asceticism," 243–52. The same combination of traditions is found, with only slight variation, in p. Nazir 1:6 (51c). R. Mana (ca. 350 C.E.) appears as R. Mani in b. Ned. 9b–10a, where part of his statement is attributed to R. Jonah, and as R. Muna in Num Rab. 10:7.

26. The obvious implication is that wine led to her unfaithfulness. A similar tradition seeks to explain why the mishnaic and talmudic tractate Nazir precedes that of Soṭa in the Order Women. See b. Nazir 2a; Soṭa 2a; Num Rab. 10:4.

[he sinned against his own soul] by denying himself wine.[27] And we can argue a fortiori: if this one who denies himself only wine is called a sinner, how much more so one who denies himself everything. R. Eleazar says: One who undertakes [supererogatory] fasting is called holy, as it is said [with regard to the Nazirite], "Holy shall be the uncut hair of his head" (Num 6:5). And if this one who only denied himself one thing is called holy, how much more so one who denies himself everything. How would Samuel explain the fact that [the Nazirite] is called [by Scripture] holy? This refers to the growth of the hair [and not to the Nazirite himself]. And how would R. Eleazar explain the fact that [the Nazirite] is called [by Scripture] a sinner? This refers to [a Nazirite] who defiled himself [through contact with a dead corpse]. Did R. Eleazar really say this? For has R. Eleazar not said: A person should always conduct himself as if holiness dwells in his stomach [and he should not harm that holiness by fasting], as it is said, "[I am] the holy one in your midst [innards]" (Hos 11:9). There is no contradiction [between the two teachings of R. Eleazar]. The first [that the Nazirite is holy] refers to one who is able to bear self-affliction; the second [that one who afflicts himself afflicts God's holiness] refers to one who is unable to bear self-affliction.[28] Resh Laqish said: [One who does not afflict himself] is called pious, as it is said, "A pious man treats his own self well, whereas the wicked causes harm to his flesh" (Prov 11:17). Rab Sheshet said: A disciple of the sages who undertakes supererogatory fasting, let a dog eat his meal. . . . Said R. Jeremiah bar Abba in the name of Resh Laqish: A disciple of the sages is not allowed to undertake [supererogatory] fasting, for he thereby diminishes [his ability to perform] his work for the sake of heaven.[29]

BABYLONIAN TALMUD: NED. 9B–10A

R. Jonah said to [R. Mani]:[30] The reason [that Simeon the Righteous did not eat the sacrifices of Nazirites] is as follows: When people regret [their sinful deeds] they become Nazirites, but when they are defiled [through contact with a corpse] and have to extend their Nazirite vows

27. See n. 15.
28. Compare John Chrysostom, De Sacerdotio 13.3 (PG 48:644), who distinguishes between lifetime Nazirites (ascetics) who have become accustomed to abstaining from "food, drink, and bed" and priests who have not.
29. Rashi explains that by such fasting he becomes weak and is unable to sustain his studies.
30. For the view of R. Mani (= Mana), see p. Ned. 1:1 (36d) cited above and n. 25.

[for a second term], they regret them and end up bringing [their concluding sacrifices] like unconsecrated offerings to the Temple Court.[31] If so, might not an undefiled Nazirite also [regret his vows and be like one who brings unconsecrated offerings to the Temple Court]? An undefiled Nazirite is not so, for he estimates his willpower [before deciding] how much he can vow.[32] . . . Said Abaye: Simeon the Righteous, R. Simeon, and R. Eleazar Hakappar all agree that the Nazirite is a sinner.[33]

SUGGESTED READINGS

Cartlidge, Tony W. "Were Nazirite Vows Unconditional?" *CBQ* 51.3 (1989):409–22.

Fraade, Steven D. "Ascetical Aspects of Ancient Judaism." In *Jewish Spirituality: From the Bible Through the Middle Ages*, edited by Arthur Green, 253–88. Vol. 13 of *World Spirituality: An Encyclopedic History of the Religious Quest*. New York: Crossroad, 1986; corrected paperback edition of 1988 includes additional bibliography.

Halivni, David. "On the Supposed Anti-Asceticism or Anti-Naziritism of Simon the Just." *JQR* 58 (1968):243–52.

Milgrom, J. "Nazirite." In *The Encyclopedia Judaica*, edited by Cecil Roth. Jerusalem: Keter Publishing House, 1971.

31. See *p. Ned.* 1:1 (36d), cited above, where this is the view of R. Mana.

32. This passage is preceded by the story of Simeon the Righteous and the Nazirite shepherd and is followed by the tradition of R. Judah about the early pious having vowed Nazirite vows in order to bring offerings and R. Simeon's denial of this. See *t. Nazir* 4:7, *t. Ned.* 1:1, and parallels, cited above.

33. The text continues by citing the tradition attributed to R. Eleazar Hakappar, that Num 6:11 refers to the Nazirite and by extension to all who afflict themselves with supererogatory abstinence. For this tradition, see *Sipre* Num 30 and *b. Ta'an.* 11a–b, cited above, and parallels. However, the Tosaphot to our passage differentiate between Simeon the Righteous and the others, arguing that Simeon the Righteous considered only a defiled Nazirite to be a sinner, for having vowed rashly, whereas the others consider all Nazirites to be sinners for having afflicted themselves, even if they did not defile themselves. See n. 25.

PART THREE

RITUAL AND REVELATION

Hêkālôt Rabbātî §§ 297–306:
A Ritual for the Cultivation
of the Prince of
the Torah

INTRODUCTION

In the visionary literature of ancient Jewish mysticism known as Merkavah mysticism, texts appear that concern the theurgic cultivation of an angel or "Prince" appointed over Torah (śar-tôrâ). This angel is said to impart the ability to learn and retain Torah at a prodigious rate. This literature can be seen as a kind of magic in the service of scholasticism. Nonetheless, these texts prescribe rituals similar to ascetic practices. The texts thus raise significant questions about the relationship between ascetic practice, magic, and theurgy.

The śar-tôrâ passage translated here is appended to Hêkālôt Rabbātî, a text that concerns the ascent to the Merkavah, the chariot-throne of God.[1] Whereas Hêkālôt Rabbātî and similar texts describe the practitioner's ascent to heaven, the śar-tôrâ tradition provides instructions for bringing an angel to earth.[2] Although pseudepigraphically attributed to rabbis of first- and second-century Palestine, our text was probably composed in Jewish Babylonia between the sixth and ninth centuries. Differences between the ritual practices, systems of purity, and liturgical

---

1. The texts of Merkavah mysticism, including Hêkālôt Rabbātî, are published in Schäfer, Synopse zur Hekalot-Literatur (Tübingen: J.C.B. Mohr [Paul Siebeck], 1981). All citations from Hekhalot literature in this essay and translation will follow the numbering of paragraphs in the Synopse. This translation is based primarily on MS Vatican 228. Other manuscripts are used where a clearer reading is available.

2. Cf. the ritual for the conjuration of the Angel of the Presence (śar happānîm); see P. Schäfer, "Die Beschwörung des sar ha-panim. Kritische Edition und Übersetzung," Frankfurter Jüdaistische Beiträge 6 (1978) 107–45.

compositions in these texts and those of the Talmudic Rabbis suggest that they were not composed by the central shapers of Rabbinic Judaism.[3]

The narrative (I, §297–98) tells how, when the Second Temple was being built, the Jewish leaders compelled God to reveal to them the secret of the praxis for success in learning.[4] The Temple, habitation of the Divine Presence (šěkînâ), is an appropriate setting for the revelation of this secret.[5]

The praxis (II) consists of two stages: (1) a preparatory ritual (§299) and (2) the recitation of the names of angels (§300–302) in daily prayer.[6] A numinous hymn (III) is appended in §306;[7] §304–5 (IV) testifies to the benefits and efficacy of the praxis. The preparatory ritual requires a supererogatory level of ritual purity. After cleansing himself from impurity, the practitioner is to refrain from vegetables[8] and eat bread "of his own hands."[9] The efficacy of the praxis, however, resides in the incantatory recitation of the names of the angels.

This phenomenon differs from what is commonly seen as asceticism

---

3. The constant emphasis in the text that the study of Torah is burdensome also suggests that its authors were not accustomed to the life of the academy.

4. In a section preceding this narrative (§281–94), Israel complains of the double burden of building the Temple and engaging in study. God, looking upon from heaven, declares that he recognizes their plight and will reveal them the secret of acquiring Torah rapidly; he does so over the objection of the angels.

5. In Hêkālôt Rabbātî, Rabbi Nehunia ben ha-Qanah discloses the secrets of ascent in the Temple. On that passage and the role of purity in ascent to the Merkavah, see L. H. Schiffman, "The Recall of Rabbi Nehunia ben ha-Qanah from Ecstasy in the 'Hekhalot Rabbati,'" AJS Review 1 (1976) 269–81; and S. Lieberman, "The Knowledge of Halakha by the author (or authors) of the Heikhaloth," in I. Gruenwald, Apocalyptic and Merkavah Mysticism (Leiden, Neth.: E. J. Brill, 1980) 241–44. On the function of the Temple cult in attracting the Divine Presence, see B. A. Levine, In The Presence of the Lord (Leiden, Neth.: E. J. Brill, 1974). In our text, the secrets are revealed through Zerubbabel, who was the subject of numerous apocalyptic legends in late antiquity and the early Middle Ages. See Encyclopedia Judaica, s.v. "Zerubbabel" and "Zerubbabel Apocalypse"; L. Ginzberg, Legends of the Jews (Philadelphia: Jewish Publication Society of America, 1946–47) 4:351–52, 6:437–39.

6. These divine names are referred to as the Awesome Crown and the Great Seal. On these terms, see G. Scholem, Jewish Gnosticism, Merkavah Mysticism, and Talmudic Tradition, 2d ed. (New York: Jewish Theological Seminary, 1965) 69.

7. Cf. the role of liturgical prayer in Merkavah mysticism, see M. D. Swartz, "'Alay le-shabbeaḥ: A Liturgical Prayer in Ma'aśeh Merkabah," JQR 77 (1986–87) 179–80.

8. Other śar-tôrâ rituals require the petitioner to avoid garlic or onions, foods that may cause bodily odors; see §489 in the Synopse. Greco-Roman magical and dream incubation texts prescribe avoidance of fresh foods that are hard to digest. See R. Arbesmann, "Fasting and Prophecy in Pagan and Christian Antiquity," Traditio 7 (1949) 1–71, esp. 9–27.

9. This requirement may be to ensure that the bread is not kneaded by a woman and thus contract menstrual impurity; cf. §572 in Schäfer, Synopse, from an Aramaic śar-tôrâ text.

in Judaism and in the Greco-Roman world in that the praxis is not an exemplary way of life, but preparation for an extraordinary experience.[10] Nonetheless, we should not dismiss the *śar-tôrâ* phenomenon as unrelated to that historical context. In the Mediterranean world, fasting and self-denial were common forms of preparation for mantic and theurgic activity.[11] In ancient Judaism, ritual purity functioned to ward off demonic forces and allow the practitioner to be in the presence of divine beings.[12]

It has been argued that in many societies in late antiquity, the ascetic functioned as a bulwark of defense against the demons and as a spiritual athlete imbued with wondrous powers.[13] In Babylonian Jewish society the rabbi, with the power of his Torah, was similarly seen as a numinous figure.[14] The theurgists of the *śar-tôrâ* sought to appropriate some of that power through the direct agency of the angel of the Torah.

TRANSLATION

I. THE SECRET OF THE TORAH
IS REVEALED

(§297) Rabbi Ishmael said: Thus said Rabbi Akiba to me in the name of Rabbi Eliezer the Great: Our fathers had not taken it upon themselves to put one stone on top of another in the Temple of YHWH until they compelled and obliged the King of the universe and all his servants to reveal to them the secret of the Torah: how it is performed, how it is expounded, how it is used.

At once the Holy Spirit appeared from the third entrance in the House of YHWH—for the *Šekînâ* did not descend and dwell in the Holy of Holies because of the decree. When our fathers saw the Throne of Glory,

10. Cf. S. Fraade, "Ascetical Aspects of Ancient Judaism," in A. Green, *Jewish Spirituality from the Bible to the Middle Ages* (New York: Crossroad, 1987) 253–88.

11. On this point, see especially Arbesmann, "Fasting and Prophecy."

12. In *b. Yoma* 4b, Exod 24:15 is interpreted to mean that the cloud purged Moses of food "to make him like the ministering angels." See S. Lowy, "The Motivation of Fasting in Talmudic Literature," *JJS* 9 (1958) 20, n. 11, and the sources cited there. Other traditions state that eating and drinking were unnecessary at Sinai because Moses and the Elders were nourished by the light of the *Šekînâ*. See I. Chernus, *Mysticism in Rabbinic Judaism* (Berlin: Walter de Gruyter, 1982); D. Goodman, "Do Angels Eat?" *JJS* 37 (1986) 160–75.

13. P. Brown, "The Rise and Function of the Holy Man in Late Antiquity," *JRS* 71 (1971) 82–101.

14. J. Neusner, *A History of the Jews in Babylonia* 5 (Leiden, Neth.: E. J. Brill, 1970).

which was elevated and stood between the entrance hall[15] and the altar—for until then they had not yet constructed a building, but [it appeared] over a place of plans,[16] on which the hall of the Temple and the altar, and the whole Temple were to be completed[17]—

(§298) When our fathers saw the Throne of Glory, which was elevated inside it, hovering between the hall and the altar, and the King of the universe upon it, they immediately fell to their faces. And at that moment he said:

"The Glory of this latter House shall be greater than that of the former one.[18] For in the first sanctuary I was not bound to my children, except by this voice. O, my sons, if you only would! Why do you prostrate and fall to your faces? Get up and be seated before My Throne, the way you sit in council.[19] Take the crown, accept the seal,[20] and learn the secret of the Torah: how you shall perform it, how you shall expound it, how you shall use it. Raise the paths of your heart; let your hearts look into Torah."

At once Zerubbabel the son of Shealtiel stood up before him like an interpreter[21] and elaborated the names of the Prince of the Torah, one by one, with his name, the name of his crown, and the name of his seal.

II. THE PRAXIS

(§299) Rabbi Ishmael said: Thus said Rabbi Akiba to me in the name of Rabbi Eliezer the Great: Whoever wishes to bind himself to the Prince of the Torah[22] must wash his garments and cloaks and perform a stringent immersion [rendering him free] from any doubt of nocturnal pollution. He must enter and sit twelve days in a room or attic. He may not come or go, nor may he eat or drink; but every evening he shall eat clean bread of his own hands, and drink water, and not taste any kind of vegetable.

15. Heb. 'ulam. See Ezek 40:49.
16. Referring perhaps to the place where the plan for the temple was laid out; cf. Ezek 43:11. See P. Schäfer, Übersetzung der Hekhalot-Literatur 2 (Tübingen: J.C.B. Mohr [Paul Siebeck], 1987), 284, nn. 34 and 35.
17. This parenthetical note seems to be a gloss explaining how the Throne could appear in a specific location in the Temple if it had not yet been built.
18. Hag 2:9.
19. Heb. yĕšîvâ, a court session of sages.
20. The "crown and the seal" are the potent names listed below (§302).
21. Heb. turgĕmān (dragoman). The reference is to the interpreter of the Torah in the ancient Temple and synagogue who would both translate and interpret the scriptures and proclaim the interpretation in a loud voice. Cf. Neh 8:8.
22. That is, obligate the angel to him theurgically.

(§300) Then he shall recite the midrash[23] of the Prince of the Torah regularly in his prayer three times every day after the Prayer,[24] which he shall recite from beginning to end. And afterwards, he must sit and repeat it for the twelve days of his fast, from morning to evening; he shall not be silent[25] at any time. When he finishes it, he shall stand on his feet. He must adjure the servants and their King twelve times for each Prince. After that, he must adjure them by a seal for each one of them.

(§301) And these are their names. He shall say: ŠQDHWZY'Y YWY, the Prince; ZHPNWRY'Y YWY, the Prince; ZHWBDY'L YWY, the Prince; ABYRGHWDRY'W YWY, the Prince; NYHPDRYW'YLYY YWY, the Prince; HDRYWN YWY, the Prince; 'ZBWDH'Y YWY, the Prince; ṬṬRWSY'Y YWY, the Prince; 'ŠRWYLY'Y YWY, the Prince; SGNSG' YWY, the Prince; PLYṬRYYHW YWY, the Prince; DHYBYRWN YWY, the Prince; and 'DYRYRWN YWY, the Prince.[26]

(§302) He must adjure them, these twelve,

> In the name of Yofiel, glory of the world by the authority of his King, and in the name of Sarviel, who is one of the princes of the Merkavah; and in the name of Shahadriel, beloved Prince; and in the name of Ḥasdiel, who is called to the Divine Power six times every day.

Then he shall go back and adjure those last four by the Great Seal and by the Great Oath and by the name 'Azbogah,[27] which is the Great Seal, and in the name of ṢWRṬQ, holy name and awesome crown.

(§303) At the end of twelve days, he may proceed to any aspect of Torah he requests: whether to Scriptures or Mishnah, or gazing at the Merkavah. For he goes forth in a pure state, and from great abstinence and affliction. For we have in hand a teaching, a decree of the forebears and a tradition of the ancients, who wrote it down and left it for the generations, so that the humble could make use of it. Whoever is worthy is answered by them.

---

23. This term, which commonly means rabbinic exegesis of the Bible, is used here to refer either to this pericope, including the narrative, or to the list of names of angels to be recited. The *Shiʿur Qômâ* instructs the reader to "repeat this Mishnah (teaching)." See M. S. Cohen, *The Shiʿur Qomah* (Lanham, Md.: University Press of America, 1983).

24. That is, the petitionary prayers of the statutory rabbinic liturgy, known as *hattĕpîllâ*, "The Prayer," or the *ʿĂmîdâ*, "the prayer recited while standing."

25. That is, he should not pause in repeating the prayer.

26. Note that there are actually thirteen names in this list. The names vary from one manuscript to another.

27. On this name see Scholem, *Jewish Gnosticism*, 66–67.

III. TESTIMONY TO THE SUCCESS
OF THE PRAXIS[28]

(§304) Rabbi Ishmael said: Thus said Rabbi Akiba to me in the name of Rabbi Eliezer the Great: Happy is he, the merit of whose fathers is his aid and the just deeds of whose children stand on his behalf. He may make use of the majesty of the crown, and of this seal; they are obliged to him, and he is exalted by the majesty of the Torah.

(§305) Rabbi Ishmael said: This spell[29] was performed by Rabbi Eliezer and he was answered, but he did not believe it. He returned and it was performed by me, and I did not believe it, until I brought a certain fool and he became equal to me [in learning]. It was done again by the shepherds, and they became equal to me.

They sent Rabbi Akiba out of the land [of Israel], by authority of a court, and he was detained until it was done by the populace, who could not read or recite, and they were made equal to wise scholars. [Rabbi Akiba] came and supported and agreed to the testimony of the court, saying: "This thing was even done outside of the land, and it was successful." Thus Rabbi Eliezer the Great and the sages said, "perhaps we have the merit of the land of Israel in our favor."[30] They did not believe it until they sent Rabbi Akiba to Babylonia and it was performed and it succeeded. He gave witness, and afterward we heard and rejoiced.

IV. Prayer

(§306) Rabbi Ishmael said: How shall a man begin before he prays this [ritual of] the Prince of the Torah? When he stands to pray, he should say:

May you be glorified, uplifted and exalted, glorious King,[31]
for you dwell over a throne high and exalted, awesome and fearsome,
in the lofty chambers of the magnificent palace.
The servants of your Throne are awestruck
and the heavens at your footstool tremble,

28. Paragraphs §304 and 305 are additions to the text that appear in three of the principal manuscripts.

29. Heb. *dāvār*, "utterance."

30. That is, perhaps the merit of the Land of Israel is responsible for the success of the praxis.

31. Most manuscripts elide several lines of this hymn; MS Oxford 1531 notes that a portion of the prayer is contained in chap. 7 of *Hêkālôt Rabbātî* (= §153 in the *Synopse*). The translation of this passage is taken from MS Budapest 238, augmented by the parallel text in Schäfer §153.

every day, with the sound of hymn,
and in a melodious roar and a tumultuous song,
as it is written, "Holy, holy, holy is YHWH of Hosts,
The whole earth is full of His glory."[32]
And they say:
Who does not exalt you, O King, awesome and feared by all your servants?
In shaking and trembling they serve you;
in agitation and quaking, they are awestruck before you
with corresponding expression,[33] in unison
they exclaim your awesome name in dread and fear.
None is earlier and none is later—anyone who delays his voice past
    another's even a hair's breadth
is immediately cast aside,
and a flame of fire thrusts him away.
As it is written, "Holy, holy, holy is YHWH of Hosts,
The whole earth is full of His glory."[34]

SUGGESTED READINGS

(Note: A German translation of this passage can be found in Schäfer, *Über-setzung*. The *śar-tôrâ* materials have not been the subject of a separate study apart from the Merkavah traditions. A discussion of this passage is found in Gruenwald, *Apocalyptic*, 169–73. Halperin, *Faces of the Chariot*, which was unavailable at the time of this writing, includes an extensive discussion of this material. On Hekhalot Rabbati, see also Smith, "Observations," and Blumenthal, *Understanding Jewish Mysticism*.

For an introduction to Merkavah mysticism, see Scholem, *Major Trends* and *Jewish Gnosticism*; Gruenwald, *Apocalyptic*; and Dan, "Religious Experience." The best discussion of asceticism in ancient Judaism is Fraade, "Ascetical Aspects"; Lowy, "Fasting," and Montgomery, "Ascetic Strains" are also valuable. On the influence of the ancient Jewish concept of purity on these traditions, see Levine, "Presence of God" and *In the Presence of the Lord*, and Neusner, *Idea of Purity*. Familiarity with the Jewish magical tradition is important for an understanding of the *śar-tôrâ* material; on this, see Trachtenberg, *Jewish Magic*.)

Arbesmann, Rudolph. "Fasting and Prophecy in Pagan and Christian Antiquity." *Traditio* 7 (1949) 1–71.
Blumenthal, David. *Understanding Jewish Mysticism*, vol. 1. New York: Ktav, 1978.
Dan, Joseph. "The Religious Experience of the Merkavah." In *Jewish Spirituality from the Bible to the Middle Ages*, edited by Arthur Green, 289–307. New York: Crossroad, 1987.

---

32. Isa 6:3.
33. Heb. *Gezērâ šawwâ*. In rabbinic exegetical terminology, an argument by analogy. Here the poet refers to choruses of angels facing each other, singing in unison.
34. Isa 6:3.

Fraade, Steven D. "Ascetical Aspects of Ancient Judaism." In *Jewish Spirituality from the Bible to the Middle Ages*, edited by Arthur Green, 253–88. New York: Crossroad, 1987.

Gruenwald, Ithamar. *Apocalyptic and Merkavah Mysticism*. Leiden, Neth.: E. J. Brill, 1980.

Halperin, David J. *Faces of the Chariot*. Tübingen: J.C.B. Mohr (Paul Siebeck), 1988.

Levine, Baruch A. *In the Presence of the Lord*. Leiden, Neth.: E. J. Brill, 1974.

———. "The Presence of God in Biblical Religion." In *Religions in Antiquity: Essays in Memory of E. R. Goodenough*, edited by Jacob Neusner, 71–87. Leiden, Neth.: E. J. Brill, 1968.

Lowy, Samuel. "The Motivation of Fasting in Talmudic Literature." *JJS* 9 (1958) 19–38.

Montgomery, James A. "Ascetic Strains in Early Judaism." *JBL* 51 (1932) 183–87.

Neusner, Jacob. *A History of the Jews in Babylonia*, vol. 5. Leiden, Neth.: E. J. Brill, 1970.

———. *The Idea of Purity in Ancient Israel*. Leiden, Neth.: E. J. Brill, 1973.

Schäfer, Peter. "Die Beschöwrung des sar ha-panim. Kritische Edition und Übersetzung." *Frankfurter Jüdaistische Beiträge* 6 (1978) 107–45.

———. "Prolegomena zu einer kritischen Edition und Analyse der Merkavah Rabba." *Frankfurter Jüdaistische Beiträge* 5 (1977) 65–101.

———. *Synopse zur Hekhalot-Literatur*. Tübingen: J.C.B. Mohr (Paul Siebeck), 1981.

———. "Tradition and Redaction in Hekhalot Literature." *JSJ* 14 (1983) 172–81.

———. *Übersetzung der Hekhalot-Literatur*, vol. 2. Tübingen: J.C.B. Mohr (Paul Siebeck), 1987.

Schiffman, Lawrence H. "The Recall of Rabbi Nehunia ben ha-Qanah from Ecstasy in the 'Hekhalot Rabbati.'" *AJS Review* 1 (1976) 269–81.

Scholem, Gershom. *Jewish Gnosticism, Merkavah Mysticism, and Talmudic Tradition*, 2d ed. New York: Jewish Theological Seminary, 1965.

———. *Major Trends in Jewish Mysticism*, 2d ed. New York: Schocken Books, 1954.

Smith, Morton. "Observations on Hekhalot Rabbati." In *Biblical and Other Studies*, edited by Alexander Altmann. Cambridge: Harvard University Press, 1963.

Trachtenberg, Joshua. *Jewish Magic and Superstition*. 1939. Reprint. New York: Atheneum, 1982.

van Uchelen, N. A. "Ethical Terminology in Heykhalot-Texts." *JJS* 37 (1986) 250–58.

Allogenes
(Nag Hammadi Codex XI, 3)

INTRODUCTION

Allogenes, the very complex third-century Sethian gnostic philosophi-cal revelation treatise discovered among the Nag Hammadi documents, points to a social basis of ascetic formation. None of the traditional ascetic tasks is mentioned—no fasting, no sleeplessness, no concern about clothing. Yet, the treatise promulgates methods of withdrawal, standing, praising, interiority, and divine revelation.

The asceticism of *Allogenes* has two foci: first, it attempts to mold the reader's understanding of the means of intellectual and philosophical integration through a series of overlapping narratives; second, it pre-sents a strongly articulated model of one person's spiritual formation (the character Allogenes = "stranger," "one of another race") as a means of describing the growth toward divinization that is set out as the high-est human aspiration.

Both of these foci revolve around a complex set of interconnected narratives in the treatise. As the interpretive translation here makes clear, the primary narrative line presents Allogenes's instruction to his disciple Messos. Allogenes's instruction centers on his description of his own enlightenment after he was instructed by Iouel. Allogenes also relates philosophical and ascetic material from the Illustrators and from an anonymous male figure (whom I identify as a guardian). Allogenes, moreover, presents the teaching he has received as a direct teaching: he is quoting instruction as it was given to him, but in a different environ-ment.

Allogenes, however, is more than a narrational medium; he also interprets and alters the instruction that he has received as he presents it to Messos. The treatise explains how Allogenes himself was formed by Iouel's philosophical speculation concerning such figures as the Triple Power, Protophanes, and Kalyptos. When Allogenes summarizes his experience for Messos, however, the material has been adjusted in the new interpretive environment. The same sort of adjustment happens with the material Allogenes receives from the Illustrators. The second generation (Allogenes) and the third (Messos) will adapt the revelatory philosophy of earlier generations (Iouel, the Illustrators).

Asceticism here is a complex set of narrative instructions interpreted for use by a seeker of enlightenment. The reader understands philosophical asceticism and formation by watching the character Allogenes carefully. Allogenes receives instruction from two or three sources, and he gives instruction. However, Allogenes is more than one revealer in a series because he also processes the material he has received: he tells Messos (and the reader) his emotional responses, the length and effect of his meditation, his anxiety about teaching, and his visionary withdrawals. At each stage, he presents himself and his own ascetic formation as a model to Messos (and to the reader). Allogenes, then, becomes a model of one person who achieved philosophical divinization in a school environment. Allogenes's ascetic practice and growth incorporate the philosophical teaching of Iouel and the philosophically ascetic process of withdrawal. The complex narratives reveal a lively social environment in which philosophical asceticism was experienced, practiced, analyzed, and taught.

Originally written in Greek, *Allogenes* survives only in one fragmentary Coptic text from Nag Hammadi Codex XI. There is as yet no published critical edition. Karen L. King's 1984 unpublished doctoral thesis, "The Quiescent Eye of the Revelation, Nag Hammadi Codex XI.3 'Allogenes,' a Critical Edition," provides an introduction, critical edition, and translation. (Her critical edition and translation are soon to be published.) In addition to King's translation, the treatise has been translated by John D. Turner and Orval S. Wintermute in *The Nag Hammadi Library*, ed. James M. Robinson (2d ed.; New York: Harper & Row, 1988), and in part by Bentley Layton, *The Gnostic Scriptures* (Garden City, N.Y.: Doubleday & Co., 1987). The partial translation that follows, compared with previous translations, will seem more periphrastic and interpretive. I have purposefully so translated in order to give nontechnical readers access to the ascetic theology of the treatise. The translation is based on the facsimile edition of Codex XI, corrected and revised in light of King's thesis, and in consultation with the late George MacRae.

TRANSLATION
[57, 4—69, 2]

ALLOGENES'S SEVENTH NARRATIVE
SUMMARIZING HIS APPROPRIATION OF
IOUEL'S TEACHING FOR MESSOS

But when Iouel, she to whom all the glories pertain, said these things, she separated from me; she left me. But I did not lose my grasp of the words that I heard. I prepared myself in them, and I counseled with myself for a hundred years. But I rejoiced in myself greatly, living in a great light and on a blessed road, because those things that I became worthy to see and again those things that I became worthy to hear, those things that are appropriate for the great powers alone . . . [58:] [lacuna 5+ lines] . . . of God.

When the fulfillment of the hundred years came it brought to me a blessedness of eternal hope full of goodness. I saw the good, self-generated [*Autogenes*] god with the savior who is the thrice-male, perfect child, and the goodness of that one, the first-appearing [*Protophanes*] Harmedon, the perfect mind and the blessedness of the Hidden One [*Kalyptos*], together with the earliest beginning of the blessedness, the aeon of Barbelo, full of divinity, and the first origin of the unoriginate one, the triple-powered, invisible spirit, the All that is higher than the perfect.

After I had been taken by the eternal light from the garment that clothed me, and I had been taken up to a holy place, whose image cannot be revealed in the world, then through a great blessedness, I beheld all those things about which I heard and I praised them all. I [59:] stood upon my knowledge. I turned toward the knowledge of the All, the aeon of Barbelo.

And I beheld holy powers by means of the illustrators of the male virgin Barbelo; they [the illustrators] said to me that I will find the power to test what happens in the world.

THE ILLUSTRATORS' FIRST SPEECH
WITH INSTRUCTIONS TO ALLOGENES
REGARDING ANACHORESIS,
STANDING AND UNKNOWN KNOWING

Allogenes, gaze upon your blessedness silently, that in which you know yourself within as you are. Seeking yourself, perform a withdrawal up to the vitality that which you will see moving. And when you cannot stand, do not fear anything, but if you wish to stand, withdraw up to the existence, and you will find it standing and resting itself according to the image of the one who rests himself truly. He retains all of these things in a silence and an inactivity. And when you receive a revelation of this one, by a first revelation of the unknowable one, that one that should you know him, you must be ignorant of him. And when you become fearful of that place, withdraw backward because of the activities. And when you have become perfect in that place, still yourself. And according to your interior pattern, know thus also [60:] that it is in this way among all these things according to this form. And do not be greatly scattered, so that you will have power to stand. Neither wish to be active lest you fall completely from your interior inactivity of the unknown one. Do not know him, for that is an impossibility, but by a thought that is light, when you know him, be ignorant of him.

ALLOGENES'S EIGHTH NARRATIVE
EXPLAINING TO MESSOS HIS RESPONSE
TO THE POWERS' TEACHING

Then I heard these [very] things as they were being spoken. A stillness of silence came to be within me. I heard the blessedness, that through which I knew myself as myself.

And I withdrew upward to the vitality, seeking her. And I entered into it with her. And I stood not firmly, but quietly. And I beheld a movement, eternal, noetic, undivided in which are all the powers without form, without limiting him in a limitation.

And when I wished to stand firmly, I withdrew upward to the existence that I found standing and resting herself according to an image and a likeness of that which clothes me through a revelation of the undivided one and the one who rests himself. I was filled with a revelation from a primary revelation [61:] from the Unknown one. As though I were ignorant of him, I understood him and I received power from within him. Since I received an eternal strength, I knew him who exists within me, and the triple-powered one, and the revelation of that which is unreceivable from him. And by a primary revelation of the first one unknown to all of them, God who is higher than perfect, I saw him and the Triple Power who exists within them all. I was seeking after the god, the ineffable and unknowable. This is the one who if one should know him at all, he is ignorant of him, the mediator of the Triple Power, the one who dwells in stillness and silence, and is unknowable.

And when I was confirmed in these things, the powers of the illuminators said to me:

THE POWERS OF THE ILLUSTRATORS'
SECOND SPEECH TO ALLOGENES

Cease hindering the inactivity that exists within you by searching for incomprehensible things, rather hear about him in the manner as is possible through a primary revelation and a revelation.

Concerning the Revelation and Primary Revelation

For he exists as a something in the manner of existent things, or that he exists and he will come into being, or he acts, or he knows, without possessing mind, nor life, nor existence incomprehensibly. [62:] And he exists as something and as a possessor of things. Neither is he left over in any way, as though he gives anything that is assayed, or purified, or he receives or he gives. Nor is he diminished in any way either through his own desire, or by giving or receiving, or receiving through another. Neither does he have any desire for himself nor through another's agency, it does not usually befall him. But neither does he give anything through himself lest he become diminished in another way. Therefore neither does he need mind or life, nor even anything at all. He is better than the All in the privation and the unknowability that he possesses, that is the Existence that does not come into being. Because he possesses a silence and a stillness, lest he be diminished by those who are not usually diminished.

Negative Theology, 62,28–63,32 Parallel to
Apocryphon of John

He is neither a divinity, nor a blessedness nor perfection, but he is something unknowable and that which is not possessed. But he is another one who is more exquisite than blessedness and divinity and perfection. For neither is he not perfect, but he is another [63:] more exquisite thing, nor is he not boundless, nor is he bounded by another, but he is a more exquisite thing. He is not corporeal; he is not incorporeal. He is not great; he is not small. He is not numbered. He is not a creature; neither is he an existent thing. This is the one whom it is possible for one to know him, but he is another who is more exquisite, the one whom it is impossible for another to know him.

Concerning the Primary Revelation

He is a primary revelation and a knowledge of himself who alone understands himself. Because he is not an existent thing, rather he is another more exquisite of those exquisite ones. But like that which he possesses and that which he does not possess, neither is he inherent in an aeon, nor is he inherent in time, nor does he usually receive anything from another, nor is he diminished, nor does he diminish another, nor is he diminished. For he is a comprehension of himself, as something so knowable, as more exquisite than those who are good in unknowability.

Concerning the Attributes

He possesses blessedness and perfection and silence—not the blessed-ness or the perfection with silence, but he is another who exists, one whom it is impossible for another [64:] to know him, and he is at rest. But they are things that he possesses unknown to all of them. For he is more exalted in beauty than all those who are good, and he thus is unknown to all of them in any form. And through all of them, he is within them, not only as the knowledge that is unknown, which is what he is. And he is joined by the ignorance that sees him.

Concerning Knowledge of Him

Or how is he unknowable? Whether there is one who sees him as he exists in every form, or whether there is one that would say about him that he exists as something like knowledge, he sinned against him, he has a judgment, namely, that he did not know God. He will not be judged by the one who is not concerned about anything, nor has any desire, but [the judgment is] from himself alone because he did not search for the origin that truly exists. He became blind apart from the eye of revelation that is at rest, the one that is activated, the one from the Triple Power of the first thought of the invisible spirit. This one thus exists from . . . [65:] [lacuna 15+ lines] . . . something . . . established . . . a beauty and a first emanation of stillness and silence and tranquility and unfathomable greatness. When he appeared, he had no need of time, or anything from an aeon, but of himself he is unfathomably unfathomable. He does not activate either himself in order to become still, nor is he an existence lest he be in want. At once he is a corporeal being in a place; and he is incorporeal in a house. He possesses a nonexistent existence that exists for all of them. He does not possess any desire but he is a high exaltation of greatness and he is exalted over his own stillness, so that . . . [66:] [lacuna 14+ lines] . . . those . . . the invisible spirit bestowed all these things upon those who did not show concern for him at all. Nor if one happens to receive from him, does he receive power. Nor does anyone activate him according to the resting unity. For he is unknow-able; he is a breathless place of boundlessness. As he is boundless and powerless and nonexistent, he does not bestow existence, but he bears all these things resting [and] standing out from the one who stands at every time, since an eternal life has appeared, the invisible spirit, and Triple Power, the one who is in all existent beings. And it surrounds them all being higher than all of them. A shadow . . . [67:] [lacuna 15+ lines] . . . that was . . . he was filled by a power and he stood prior to them bestowing power upon them all.

THE ILLUSTRATORS' ADVICE
GIVEN DIRECTLY TO ALLOGENES

And about all these things you have certainly heard. And do not seek after anything more, but go. Neither do we know whether the unknown possesses angels, or gods, nor whether the one who is at rest possesses anything within himself except this rest, which is he, lest he be diminished. Nor is it proper to hinder yourself by continuously searching. It was suitable that you know him alone, and for them to speak with another one. But you will receive them . . . *[68:]* [lacuna 15 lines] and he said,

THE GUARDIAN'S (?) INSTRUCTIONS
ABOUT THE BOOK

Write these things that I will tell you and that I will remind you for the sake of those who will be worthy after you. And you will place this book upon a mountain. And you shall adjure the guardian, "Come, Horrible One."

ALLOGENES'S TENTH NARRATIVE SECTION
TO MESSOS; THE CONCLUSION

And after he said these things, he separated from me. But I was filled with joy, and I write this book that was appointed for me, my son Messos, so that I might reveal to you those things that were proclaimed in my presence within me. And first I received them in a great silence, and I stood myself. These are those things that were revealed to me, my son *[69:]* Messos . . . [lacuna lines 2–13] . . . Proclaim them, my son Messos, these five seals of all the books of Allogenes.

Allogenes

SUGGESTED READINGS

King, Karen Leigh. "The Quiescent Eye of the Revelation, Nag Hammadi Codex XI.3 'Allogenes,' A Critical Edition." Ph.D. dissertation, Brown University, 1984.

Robinson, James M. "The Three Steles of Seth and the Gnostics of Plotinus." In *Proceedings of the International Colloquium on Gnosticism, Stockholm, August 20–25, 1973*, edited by Geo Widengren, 132–42. Stockholm: Almqvist and Wiksell, 1977.

Schenke, Hans-Martin. "The Phenomenon and Significance of Gnostic Sethianism." In *The Rediscovery of Gnosticism; Proceedings of the International Conference on Gnosticism at Yale, New Haven, Connecticut, March 28–31, 1978*, edited by Bentley Layton, vol. 2, 588–616. Studies in the History of Religions 41. Leiden, Neth.: E. J. Brill, 1980–82.

Stroumsa, G. *Another Seed: Studies in Gnostic Mythology*. NHS 24. Leiden, Neth.: E. J. Brill, 1984.

Turner, John D. "Sethian Gnosticism: A Literary History." In *Nag Hammadi, Gnosticism, and Early Christianity*, edited by Charles W. Hedrick and Robert Hodgson, 55–86. Peabody, Mass: Hendrickson, 1986.

————. "The Gnostic Threefold Path to Enlightenment." *NovT* 22 (1980) 324–51.

Valantasis, Richard. *Third Century Spiritual Guides: A Semiotic Study of the Guide-Disciple Relationship in Christianity, Neoplatonism, Hermetism, and Gnosticism.* Harvard Dissertations in Religion. Minneapolis: Fortress Press, 1990.

Williams, Michael. "Stability as a Soteriological Theme in Gnosticism." In *The Rediscovery of Gnosticism; Proceedings of the International Conference on Gnosticism at Yale, New Haven, Connecticut, March 28–31, 1978*, edited by Bentley Layton, vol. 2, 819–29. Studies in the History of Religions 41. Leiden, Neth.: E. J. Brill, 1980–82.

————. *The Immovable Race: A Gnostic Designation and the Theme of Stability in Late Antiquity.* Leiden, Neth.: E. J. Brill, 1985.

EVAGRIUS PONTICUS
Antirrheticus
(Selections)

INTRODUCTION

Evagrius Ponticus (345–399 C.E.) made a lasting contribution to Western thought in general and to monastic consciousness in particular. He was a Greek participant in Egyptian monasticism, one of the desert fathers, and he brought to the desert a theological sophistication acquired in the company of St. Basil and St. Gregory of Nazianzus.

The excerpts here are from his *Antirrheticus*, which he sent from his desert retreat in Nitria to Abba Loukios of the Ennaton monastery in Alexandria during the 390s. We have both Loukios's letter to Evagrius requesting a compendium on spiritual warfare and the reply of Evagrius that accompanied the *Ant.*[1] In fact, this is a major work that undoubtedly was frequently copied and distributed to Evagrius's friends and followers in the desert and elsewhere. It is the only work of Evagrius to be clearly named in the *Historia Lausiaca*,[2] an indication of its importance for later monastic communities.

In Evagrius one encounters an important change in the ascetic tradition. Although famous for his practice of bodily asceticism—the monastic histories document naked vigils on winter nights,[3] diets of unmoist-

---

1. *Ep.* 4 of the Evagrian corpus; for this and the letter of Loukos, see G. Bunge, *Evagrios Pontikos, Briefe aus der Wüste* (Sophia; Quellen östlicher Theologie 24; Trier: Paulinus, 1986) 181–83, 214–16.
2. *Hist. Laus.* 39: "He wrote three books for monks called *Antirrētika*." Let it be noted that the name only appears in some Greek versions and editions, which are less trustworthy than the Syriac tradition.
3. *Hist. Laus.* 39.

ened bread,[4] and sleepless vigils[5]— Evagrius writes very little about such bodily efforts. He chooses rather to address the issue of "inner asceticism," the fight against psychological and demonic hindrances. This mental discipline and acquisition of virtue he calls *praktikē*.[6] It is the first stage of the monastic life.

The selections translated here are an important part of Evagrius's arsenal for the *praktikē* level of monastic training. They constitute a biblical compendium for spiritual warfare. In this, as in all his works, Evagrius divides demonic hindrances into eight issues: gluttony, lust, the love of money, sadness, anger, listlessness, vainglory, and pride.[7] The *Ant.* presents biblical remedies for the manifestations of each of these. Thus it is an important example of how the Bible was interpreted and used in early monastic circles. A short description of a problem or temptation is followed by a biblical quotation that fits the case and that could be invoked and repeated in time of need. Of course, this usage of Scripture is modeled on the words of Jesus in the temptation story in the Gospels.

Lists of verses from the OT had been an important part of earlier apologetic Christianity.[8] These "testimonies" extracted what was essential for Christian witness. Here we find the same type of direct reference format employed in the realm of psychological and spiritual struggle.

Because the *Ant.* is systematic in its citation of Scripture, it is a witness to the emerging canon.[9] It provides a vivid picture of the temptations and struggles of the monks in a form that is infinitely more reliable than our usual source for such information, namely, hagiography. Finally, mental discipline and discernment here come to center stage in the life

4. E. Amélineau, *De historia Lausiaca quaenam sit huius ad monachorum aegyptiorum historium scribendam utilitas* (Paris: Leroux, 1887) 113.

5. Ibid., 113.

6. See, for example, his book called the *Practicus*. It is translated in the only book on Evagrius in English, J. E. Bamberger's *Evagrius Ponticus, The Praktikos and Chapters on Prayer* (Cistercian Studies 4; Kalamazoo, Mich.: Cistercian, 1972).

7. These will eventually become the "seven deadly sins" in the West. See A. Guillaumont and C. Guillaumont, *Évagre le Pontique, Traité Practique ou le Moine* (2 vols., SC 170 and 171; Paris: Les Editions du Cerf, 1971) 1.63–84.

8. R. Grant, *Greek Apologists of the Second Century* (Philadelphia: Westminster Press, 1988) 58.

9. Evagrius does not quote Titus, 2 Peter, 2 John, 3 John, or Revelation here. However, he does quote 2 Peter and Revelation elsewhere. In the *Ant.* 1 John is "The Letter of John" and 1 Peter is "The Letter of Peter," but these section titles may have been added later. I believe he did not recognize 2 and 3 John and was uncertain of 2 Peter. See further, M. O'Laughlin, "Origenism in the Desert: Anthropology and Integration in Evagrius Ponticus" (Th.D. dissertation, Harvard University, 1987) 52.

style of the committed Christian, an attitude that became standard in later monasticism.

The *Ant.* survives in Syriac and Armenian. The best published text is of a British Museum Syriac MS.[10] What follows are excerpts from that printed text. The Syriac translator used the Peshitta (the standard translation of the Bible in Syriac) for the biblical quotations; however, because Evagrius used the Greek Bible, I will use it as well, basing my translations of the biblical quotations as much as possible on the RSV. Where the biblical quotations differ in substance from the Greek Bible, I will usually follow the quotation. The verse numbers cited refer to the RSV unless they are marked LXX, when the numbering (and content) of the Greek OT is indicated.

What has been translated are the Prologue, which sets the tone and provides the rationale for the work, and selections from three of the eight books of the *Ant.* These three books, corresponding to three of the eight sins (or issues) emphasized, are the most relevant for the present volume: here, one moves beyond the physical requirements of continence and self-control and enters the psychological realism, the intermediate stage, of monastic training, when the struggle is more difficult.

TRANSLATION

PROLOGUE[11]

Concerning rational nature under heaven and what it fights and what assists the fighter and whatever the fighter, who stands in watchful valor for the battle, must confront. Those fighting are human beings, and assisting them are the angels of God, and those opposing them are the filthy demons.

It is impossible to be overcome by these enemies due to force or through the carelessness of one's protectors; rather, what causes defeat is the weakness of the fighters. Then the knowledge of God vanishes and is cut off from them. Our Lord, Jesus Christ, who surrendered everything for our salvation, gave us authority "to tread upon snakes

10. MS addit 14578, f. 34b–77a, printed in W. Frankenberg, *Euagrios Ponticus* (Abhandlungen der königlichen Gesellschaft der Wissenschaften zu Göttingen; Philol.-hist. Klasse, Neue Folge, 13,2; Berlin, 1912) 472–545.

11. This begins in W. Frankenberg, *Euagrios*, 472. Further references to page numbers will be given thus: "F 472."

and scorpions, and over all the powers of the enemies."[12] In what remains of all his teaching he passed on to us what he did when he was tempted by Satan.[13] In the moment of struggle, when the demons attack us and prick us with darts, we must answer them with a verse from Holy Scripture, so that the filthy thoughts[14] do not persist in us. These make use of sin caused by one's actions to enslave the soul. They stain it and sink it into sinful death, as [the Bible] says, "The soul that sins shall die."[15]

But whenever there is no sin actually rooted in the *nous*,[16] one is able to make answer to the evil one and sin is easily and quickly conquered. This is wisely related to us by Ecclesiastes, which says: "An answer is not given quickly against those doing evil."[17] Solomon also says in his Proverbs,

Answer not a fool according to his folly,
Lest you become like him yourself.
But answer a fool according to your wisdom,
in order that he not appear wise in his own eyes.[18]

For if he who commits an act of folly or becomes angry with his brother is responded to by an act of folly, according to his folly, he becomes just like the demons, and their anger is like savage fury. But whoever is long-suffering and speaks from the Scriptures is preserved "from anger" and is preserved "from wrath."[19] If the fool is responded to according to his folly, one reproves the demon's folly and shows it that one is aware that, according to the Scriptures, there is a [remedy] against it.

For [often] the words required to confute the enemies, who are the cruel demons, cannot be found quickly enough in the hour of conflict, because they are scattered throughout the Scriptures, and thus it is

12. Luke 10:19. Cf. Origen *Cels.* 11:48.
13. Matt 4:1–11; Luke 4:1–13.
14. 'Thought' (*logismos*) is for Evagrius always a negative concept, usually closer to 'demonic temptation' than 'idea.'
15. Ezek 18:4.
16. The *nous*, more than being just the mind or the spirit, was for Evagrius the central element of the human person. See M. O'Laughlin, "Origenism," and, idem, "Elements of Fourth Century Origenism: The Anthropology of Evagrius Ponticus and Its Sources," in C. Kannengiesser and W. Petersen, *Origen of Alexandria, His World and His Legacy* (Notre Dame, Ind.: Notre Dame University, 1988) 355–73.
17. Eccl 8:11. In the Greek Bible "answer" is *antirrhēsis*, the present topic of Evagrius. If he used a corrupt text omitting the negative, the quotation would fit the context better.
18. Prov 26:4–5.
19. Ps 37:8.

[more] difficult to make a stand against [the demons]. Therefore we have carefully chosen [certain] words from the holy Scriptures, so that equipped with them, we can drive the Philistines out forcefully as we stand to the battle, as strong, valiant men and soldiers of our victorious king, Jesus Christ.

This much we know, beloved, to the extent that we stand against them in the struggle and answer the demons verbally, they will be increasingly embittered against us. This we learn from Job, who says, "Whenever I begin to speak, they wound me."[20] And David also says, "I am at peace, but when I speak, they make war on me!"[21] But it is wrong to be frightened by them; rather one must stand against them confidently in the power of our Savior.

For if we believe in Christ and keep his commandments, we will cross over the Jordan and march into the "city of palms."[22] In this battle we are in need of spiritual weapons,[23] which are orthodox faith and teaching. These are [revealed in] a perfect fast, brave victories, humility and stillness[24]—being hardly moved or completely unmoved and praying without ceasing.[25]

For[26] I am amazed that any person can contend in the struggle that goes on in the *nous* or can be crowned with the garlands of righteousness if he is satisfying his soul with bread and water.[27] This leads quickly to habitual anger, and to disdain and disregard for prayer, and to fraternizing with heretics. Saint Paul says, "Every athlete exercises self-control in all things,"[28] and they show constant humility to all, lifting their hands everywhere without anger or evil designs.[29]

It is proper for us to perform this work with the weapons of the spirit.

20. Job 6:4 (LXX).
21. Ps 120:7.
22. I.e., Jericho: Deut 34:3; Judg 1:16; 3:13; 2 Chr 28:15.
23. Cf. 2 Cor 10:4.
24. Stillness (*hesychia*) will become the goal of prayer and spirituality of all Byzantine monasticism.
25. Evagrius mentions this goal, inspired by 1 Thess 5:17, in *Practicus* 49, *Ep.* 19:2, and *Ad Virginem* 5. Perhaps he is referring to the single-phrase meditative technique now called the Jesus prayer. See A. Guillaumont, "The Jesus Prayer among the Monks of Egypt," *Eastern Churches Review* 6 (1974) 66–71 and the section "Betet ohne Unterlass" in G. Bunge, *Das Geistgebet* (Koinonia 25; Cologne: Luthe, 1987), 29–43 (contains detailed bibliography).
26. F 474.
27. Although other foods were eaten in the desert, bread, water, and salt were the staple diet of the monks. Evagrius counsels against satisfying hunger for bread and thirst for water in *Practicus* 16 and 17. See A. Guillaumont and C. Guillaumont, *Évagre* 2.540–45.
28. 1 Cor 9:24b.
29. Cf. 1 Tim 2:8.

We prepare ourselves and show those who undermine us that we will
fight against sin unto [the shedding of] blood,[30] destroying evil thoughts
and "every proud obstacle to the knowledge of God."[31] We take pains
that what will stand before the judgment seat of Christ is not a solitary
man, but a solitary *nous*.[32] For a solitary man is one who has turned from
sin through his substantive deeds and actions, but a solitary *nous* is one
who has turned from that sin that springs from the thoughts that reside
in it and that sees the light of the holy Trinity at the time of prayer.[33]

However, the moment for this is subject to our Lord Jesus Christ, who
[first] must contend against thoughts from the demon of gluttony, and
then against thoughts from the seven other demons, [the names of
which] I put as headings in the book for monks that follows. I have
struggled to open my mouth and speak before God and his holy angels
and before my own afflicted soul. I reveal all the struggles of the ascetic
life openly, [that life] that the Holy Spirit taught David through the
Psalms, and that was also delivered to us by the blessed fathers. This is
named after these things in the Scriptures.[34]

Every kind of opposition will arise through the thoughts that come to
us from each of the eight demons. But an "answer" from the Holy
Scriptures is written and prepared for each of the thoughts, one that
matches it and neutralizes it.

III. THE LOVE OF MONEY

Philargyria[35] 1. For the demons who counsel me within my mind while
I dream, to "get someone of your relatives or some rich person to send
you money"—"I stretch out my hand to the most high God, who made
heaven and earth, that I will not take anything from all that is yours."[36]

Philargyria 5. For the thought, inspired by love of money, that shuts

30. Cf. Heb 12:4.
31. 1 Cor 10:5.
32. For Evagrius, a person is judged at death but does not return to God until the
nous has been purified and is bodiless. Cf. *Kephalaia Gnostica* 3:15.
33. Cf. *Ant. Accedia* 16; *Kephalaia Gnostica* suppl. 30. This phenomenon is an
important part of this spiritual tradition; see H. Beyer, "Die Lichtlehre der Mönche des
vierzehnten und des vierten Jahrhunderts, erörtert am Beispiel des Gregorios Sinaïtes,
des Euagrios Pontikos und des Ps.-Makarios/Symeon," *JÖB* 31, pt. 2 (1981) 473–512.
34. Meaning obscure.
35. We now move to the middle section of the work, none of which has been
previously translated into a modern language. The previous two sections, dealing with
the concrete issues of gluttony and fornication, have been translated, and are found in
O. Zöckler, *Evagrius Pontikus* (Biblische und kirchenhistorischen Studien 4; Munich: C.
H. Beck, 1893).
36. Gen 14:22–23, F 494.

one's bowels against him who begs for life's necessities and counsels us who live in solitude to stockpile things—"You shall love your neighbor as yourself: I am the Lord."[37]

Philargyria 13. For the soul seeking to die with Jesus[38] while still retaining some trappings of wealth, [remember that] Elisha also made this mistake when he left the world, and he then renounced everything whatsoever he had—"So he departed from there, and found Elisha the son of Shaphat, who was plowing, with twelve yoke of oxen before him, and he was with the twelfth. Elijah passed by him and cast his mantle upon him. And he left his oxen and ran after Elijah, and said, 'I will kiss my father, and then I will follow you.' And Elijah said, 'Go back again; what have I done to you?' And he returned from following him, and took the yoke of oxen, and slew them, and boiled their flesh with the yokes of the oxen, and gave it to the people, and they ate. Then he rose and went after Elijah, and ministered to him."[39]

Philargyria 14. For the thought of the soul that is money grudging, and sets aside the rest of its possessions for itself, and is not willing to share with the brothers that arrive—"And Elisha said to his servant, 'Set on the great pot, and boil soup for the sons of the prophets.'"[40]

Philargyria 15. For the thought of the complaining soul that receives gold on behalf of the brothers for business purposes, and stung by lust, desires to retain it and cares nothing for the leprosy of Gehazi. Let those reading be mindful of how Elisha the prophet was in command of the thought of love of money, which is the chief of the evil passions, and of the remaining passions that are gathered around it, out of which are born enduring thoughts, those that hinder the *nous* through evil habits and make it leprous—"And Elisha said to him, 'Where are you coming from, Gehazi?' And he said, 'Your servant went neither here nor there.' But Elisha said to him, 'Did my heart not go with you when the man turned from his chariot to meet you? And now you have received the money and now you have received the garments, and in so doing, you have also received gardens and olive orchards and vineyards, sheep and oxen, menservants and maidservants. But the leprosy of Naaman shall also cleave to you, and to your descendants forever.' So he went out from his presence a leper, as white as snow."[41]

37. Lev 19:18b, F 494.
38. Rom 6:8; Col 2:20.
39. 1 Kgs 19:19–21, F 494–6.
40. 2 Kgs 4:38, F 496.
41. 2 Kgs 5:25–27, F 496.

Philargyria 17. For the thoughts that reproach us because we have abandoned our parents and will not be sent the money to meet our needs—"For my father and mother have forsaken me, but the Lord has received me."[42]

Philargyria 22. For the thoughts that are interested in riches and do not see the consuming pain that wealth brings—"If riches increase, set not your heart on it."[43]

Philargyria 23. For the thought that our parent's house is a reflection of their greatness and makes a little cell hateful to our eyes—"I would rather be a castoff in the house of the Lord, than live in residence in the tents of sinners."[44]

Philargyria 36. For the thought that fixes before one's eyes the ruin of the valuables and the property that brought great bodily comfort to Job—"The Lord gave, and the Lord has taken away, as it seemed good to the Lord."[45]

Philargyria 37. For the thought, inspired by love of money, that counsels us to stock up on provisions and clothing and not to give to the poor who have need of these things—"Break your bread for the hungry one, and lead the homeless poor to your house. If you see someone naked, clothe him, and do not disregard your own blood relations."[46]

Philargyria 40. For the thought that urges us to deny our brother, on the grounds that we have nothing to give—"Give to him who begs from you, and do not refuse him who would borrow from you."[47]

Philargyria 42. For the demon that says to us, "It is possible for a man who has property to serve the Lord"—"No one can serve two masters; for either he will hate the one and love the other, or he will be devoted to the one and despise the other. You cannot serve God and mammon."[48]

Philargyria 46. For the thought, inspired by love of money, that grants blessings to our brothers according to the flesh and to our countrymen who are in the world because they possess that wealth that is seen—"For the things that are seen are transient, but the things that are unseen are eternal."[49]

Philargyria 49. For the thought that seeks to put aside things for one's

42. Ps 26:10 (LXX), F 496.
43. Ps 61:11b (LXX), F 496.
44. Ps 83:11b (LXX), F 496.
45. Job 1:21b (LXX), F 498.
46. Isa 58:7, F 498.
47. Matt 5:42, F 498.
48. Matt 6:24, F 500.
49. 2 Cor 4:18b, F 500.

exclusive use—"Let each of you look not only to his own interests, but also to the interests of others."[50]

Philargyria 50. For the thought of the possession of wealth that incites us and exhibits before us [visions of] former wealth, saying that with it one can sustain many brothers—"But whatever gain I had, I counted as loss for the sake of Christ. Indeed I count everything as loss because of the surpassing worth of knowing Jesus Christ my Lord. For his sake I have suffered the loss of all things, and count them as refuse, in order that I may gain Christ."[51]

Philargyria 51. For the thoughts that sicken us through covetousness and blindness to the idolatry that is born from it—"Put to death therefore what is earthly in you: fornication, impurity, . . . and covetousness, which is idolatry. On account of these the wrath is coming upon the sons of disobedience."[52]

Philargyria 52. For the thoughts that seek to collect anything beyond the necessities and desire the amassing of wealth—"Keep your mind free from the love of money, and be content with what you have; for he has said, 'I will never fail you or forsake you.'"[53]

Philargyria 53. For the soul that seeks anything beyond food and clothing and does not remember that our entry into the world was naked and our leaving the world will again be thus—"For we brought nothing into the world, and we cannot take anything out of the world; but if we have food and clothing, with these we shall be content."[54]

Philargyria 54. For the thought, inspired by love of money, that says that possessing money will have no evil result, but rather will bring substantial relief for the brothers and for strangers—"For the love of money is the root of all evils; it is through this craving that some have wandered away from the faith and pierced their heart with many pangs."[55]

Philargyria 57. For the thought, inspired by love of money, that does not want to do right among the brothers because they are not "in need" and so it denies the love of God "in deed"[56]— "If anyone has the world's goods and sees his brother in need, yet closes his heart against him, how can God's love abide in him?"[57]

---

50. Phil 2:4, F 500.
51. Phil 3:7–8, F 500.
52. Col 3:5–6, F 500.
53. Heb 13:5, F 500.
54. 1 Tim 6:7–8, F 500.
55. 1 Tim 6:10, F 502.
56. 1 John 3:18.
57. 1 John 3:17, F 502.

IV. SADNESS[58]

Lypē 1. For the soul that hopes that the Lord will not hear it sighing over what befalls it—"The people of Israel groaned under their labors, and cried out for help. Their cry while they labored rose up to God, and God heard their groaning."[59]

Lypē 3. For the soul that does not know that when the living words of God are searched and diligence is taken over the commandments of God, then temptations increase in frequency—"Then Moses turned to the Lord and said, 'O Lord, why have you afflicted this people? And why have you sent me? For since I came to Pharaoh to speak in your name, he has afflicted this people, and you have not delivered your people.'"[60]

Lypē 7. For the soul that does not know that the demons make plots concerning us—"The enemy said, 'I will follow in pursuit, I will overtake, I will divide the spoils, I will satisfy my soul, I will destroy with my sword, my hand will rule."[61]

Lypē 11. For the soul that is grieved because of the disturbances of the night and supposes that it will remain permanently in difficulties because of its fearfulness—"And I will give you peace in your land, . . . and you will pursue your enemies, and they shall fall before you in the slaughter."[62]

Lypē 12. For the human thoughts that rise up in us and say that contending with demons does not do us any good—"Then I said to you, 'Do not be in dread or afraid of them. The Lord your God who goes before you will himself fight alongside you against them.'"[63]

Lypē 13. For a soul that is troubled by the voice of a demon that hisses over it in the stillness of the air—"Begin to take possession, and contend with him in battle. This day I will begin to put the fear and dread of you upon all the peoples that are under heaven, who shall hear the report of you and shall tremble and be in anguish before you."[64]

---

58. This section of the *Ant.* reveals that for Evagrius *Lypē* was much more than grief or vexation. It is rather fear of supernatural forces and lack of spiritual confidence. It is essential to note the degree to which deliverance comes not from the strength or merit of the monk, but from God. This is an eloquent testimony to Evagrius's position on the central issue of grace, which his disciple Cassian would later address in reaction to the negative anthropological view of Augustine. Evagrius, like Cassian, taught a complete reliance on God's power. See O. Chadwick, *John Cassian* (2d ed; Cambridge: Cambridge University Press, 1968) 110–36.

59. Exod 2:23–24, F 502.
60. Exod 5:22–23, F 502.
61. Exod 15:9 (LXX), F 502.
62. Lev 26:6–7, F 504.
63. Deut 1:29–30, F 504.
64. Deut 2:24–25, F 504.

Lypē 15. For a lord,[65] that his soul might remain undisturbed when demons fall in tumult upon his body from the stillness of the air—"I said, 'O Lord God, you have only begun to show your servant your strength and your power, your mighty hand and your high arm; for what God is there in heaven or on earth who can do as you have done and according to your might?'"[66]

Lypē 17. For the soul that wants to know the source of these temptations—"The Lord might afflict you and thoroughly try you, but do you good in your latter days."[67]

Lypē 18. For the human thoughts that are terrified by the sight of demons in the form of entwining snakes at one's back and to one's side in the confusion of the night—"Let not your heart be faint; do not fear, or tremble, or shrink from facing them, for the Lord your God is he that goes with you, to fight for you against your evil enemies."[68]

Lypē 20. For the thoughts of reluctance to adopt the practice of the fear of God[69] out of terror of the terrible visions and of the torches that burn with brilliant flames—"Do not be afraid or dismayed; . . . for thus the Lord will do to all your enemies against whom you fight. You shall overcome them."[70]

Lypē 22. For the thought that does not realize that singing the Psalms changes the condition of the body and that incites a demon to touch one on the back and to cut at the nerves and trouble every part of the body—"And whenever the evil spirit was upon Saul, David took the lyre, and played it with his hand, and Saul was refreshed, and was well, and the evil spirit departed from him."[71]

Lypē 23. It is necessary for us to turn and answer in a hostile manner a demon that is seen bringing destruction, just as our blessed father Macarius also spoke out when he saw one bringing destruction and ready to attack him at the moment when he was going to see the garden paradise that Jannes and Jambres made—"'You come to me with a sword and with a spear and with a shield, but I come to you in the name of the Lord of hosts.'"[72]

Lypē 24. For the demons that make disturbances in the air and after

---

65. Many of the *antirrhetica* are addressed to "a lord." The Greek *kyrios* often meant nothing more than "Herr" in German or "señor" in Spanish, but perhaps in this case Evagrius is addressing the more illustrious or sophisticated.

66. Deut 3:24 (LXX), F 504.

67. Deut 8:16, F 504.

68. Deut 20:3, F 504.

69. I.e., monasticism.

70. Josh 10:25, F 504.

71. 1 Sam 16:23, F 504.

72. 1 Sam 17:45, F 504–6.

that make us listen to their sounds—"The Lord does not deliver by the sword or the spear, but the battle is the Lord's and he will give you into our hand."[73]

Lypē 27. For the soul that does not believe that the air is filled with holy angels that help us and that are not seen by the demons—"Then Elisha prayed, and said, 'O Lord, I pray thee, open his eyes that he may see.' So the Lord opened the eyes of the young man, and he saw; and behold, the mountain was full of horses and chariots of fire in a circle around Elisha."[74]

Lypē 31. For a lord, concerning the demonic thought of riches[75] that comes to us in the night—"Arise, O Lord! Stop them and cast them down, and deliver my soul from the ungodly and from the sword."[76]

Lypē 33. For the demons that touch our bodies during the night and wound our limbs the way scorpions do—"The Lord is my light and my savior; whom shall I fear? The Lord is the defender of my life; of whom shall I be afraid? When evildoers assailed me to eat up my flesh—my persecutors and my enemies—they fainted and fell."[77]

Lypē 34. For the demons that appear to us out of the stillness and bend down over us out of the air in the manner of Indians[78]—"Though an army should set itself in array against me, my heart shall not be afraid."[79]

Lypē 36. For a lord concerning the demons that fall upon the skin of the body and put burning points like flames on it and then make cuts on it like those made by a cupping instrument. These [cuts] have indeed been seen by and have amazed many eyes—"Judge, O Lord, those that injure me, fight against them that fight against me. Take hold of shield and buckler, and arise for my help. Brandish a sword, and block the way of those that persecute me. Say to my soul, 'I am your salvation.'"[80]

Lypē 43. For a lord, concerning the demon that threatens me with madness and mental deficiency in order to shame me and those that seek the Lord in the monastic way of life—"Let not them that wait on you, O Lord of hosts, be ashamed on my account. Let not them that seek you be embarrassed by me, O God of Israel."[81]

Lypē 45. For a lord concerning the beasts that appear flying through

73. 1 Sam 17:47b, F 506.
74. 2 Kgs 6:17, F 506.
75. See n. 65 above.
76. Ps 16:13 (LXX), F 506.
77. Ps 26:1-2 (LXX), F 506.
78. Indians were often regarded as weird contortionists living at the end of the earth. This may have been due to reports of the practice of yoga.
79. Ps 26:3 (LXX), F 506.
80. Ps 34:1-3 (LXX), F 506.
81. Ps 68:6b-7 (LXX), F 508.

the air and that make us leave the enclosure because we need the venerable Egyptian Macarius to speak out and say[82]—"Do not deliver a soul that praises you to the wild beasts."[83]

Lypē 47. For those demons that become like obscene images that appear little by little out of thin air. It is necessary that we answer them as the blessed Anthony also did, saying—"The Lord is my helper, and I shall look down on my enemies."[84]

Lypē 48. For the demon that bursts into fire like a flame and then changes into smoke—"The snare is broken, and we are delivered. Our help is in the Lord, who made heaven and earth."[85]

Lypē 50. For the thought that says to me that the road to knowledge of Jesus Christ is full of increasing difficulty and great suffering—"The sluggard makes excuses, and says, 'There is a lion in the way, and danger in the streets!'"[86]

Lypē 51. For the soul that does not know that the devil cannot even come close to an animal without the command of God—"'Have you not blessed the works of his hands, and multiplied his cattle upon the land? But put forth your hand, and touch all he has, and then it is certain he will revile you to your face.'"[87]

Lypē 52. For the soul that does not know that after trials come to it due to thoughts, Satan becomes active and tries to get God to give him authority over the body—"The Devil answered and said to the Lord, 'Skin for skin, all that a man has he will give as a ransom for his life.[88] But put forth your hand, and touch his bones, and his flesh, and he will certainly revile you to your face.'"[89]

Lypē 53. For the thoughts that strike fear in us by prophesying to us and saying, "Demons will come during the night in the form of stars, appearing in the cell and burning your eyes and your faces." It is useful for us in that moment of trial to remain kneeling and continue in prayer, turning our faces away and not looking when they try to make us tremble—Let darkness cover the night.[90] "Let the stars of the night be

---

82. Departure from one's cell was often seen as spiritual defeat. The Macarius referred to is the same person mentioned in *Lypē* 23.
83. Ps 73:19 (LXX), F 508.
84. Ps 117:7 (LXX), F 508. Evagrius is here quoting from *Vit. Ant.* 6 by Athanasius. The example of Anthony was a central inspiration to these Egyptian circles, and his *Vita* was an important source. On this issue, see G. Bunge, "Évagre," 332.
85. Ps 123:7b–8 (LXX), F 508.
86. Prov 22:13, F 508.
87. Job 1:10–11, F 508.
88. Literally, "soul."
89. Job 2:4–5, F 508.
90. Cf. Gen 1:1–5.

darkened; let it remain dark, and not become light, nor let the morning star be seen to rise."[91]

Lypē 56. For the soul that does not withstand manfully the demon that comes suddenly out of the stillness at the moment of prayer and that settles upon the wings[92] and upon the neck and scrapes the ears and strikes the nostrils—"The Lord is good to those that wait on him in the day of affliction, and he knows them that reverence him."[93]

Lypē 57. For the soul that desires to know who will be counted as demons in the day of judgment and who will complete the generation of torment;[94] concerning this torment, the prophet also speaks mysteriously in prophesy—"And this shall be the plague with which the Lord will smite all the peoples that wage war against Jerusalem: their flesh shall rot while they are still on their feet, their eyes shall rot in their sockets, and their tongues shall rot in their mouths."[95]

Lypē 58. For the demons that suddenly flash out like fire from the stillness and trouble me by causing severe pains. They throw the soul into stupor and do not leave it [except] trembling in the terror of them. It is useful for us to say then that which our holy father Macarius[96] also said to them, answering—"Be broken, you nations, and be dismayed; listen even from the ends of the earth; fortify yourselves, yet be undone; even if you refortify yourselves further, you will still be undone."[97]

Lypē 61. For the soul that does not know that foolish thoughts give birth to fear and trembling within and the holy light of trust granted to the *nous* becomes darkened—"Abstain from injustice, and you shall not fear; and trembling shall not come over you."[98]

Lypē 62. For the soul that is afraid of the flashes [of light] within the enclosure—"Be not afraid before them, for I am with you to deliver you, says the Lord."[99]

Lypē 65. For the soul that is made fearful by the wars of demons that one senses—"Do not be afraid of them, nor be dismayed at their faces, because they are a house of provocateurs."[100]

Lypē 68. For a soul that fears because it is reviled on account of the

---

91. Job 3:9 (LXX), F 508. Cf. *Lypē* 62.
92. I.e., the shoulders.
93. Nah 1:7, F 510.
94. On the eschatology of Evagrius, see M. O'Laughlin, "Origenism," 142–53.
95. Zech 14:12, F 510.
96. On Macarius, see *Lypē* 23 and 45.
97. Isa 8:9, F 510.
98. Isa 54:14b, F 510.
99. Jer 1:8, F 510.
100. Ezek 3:9, F 520.

Lord's name—"Then the apostles left the presence of the council, rejoicing that they were counted worthy to suffer dishonor for the name."[101]

Lypē 70. For the thought that prophesies to me of serious tribulations arising from temptations—"I consider that the sufferings of this present time are not worth comparing with the glory that is to be revealed to us."[102]

Lypē 71. For the thought of the soul that thinks that it is tempted beyond its power [to resist]—"God is faithful, and he will not let you be tempted beyond your power, but with the temptation he will also provide the way of escape, that you may be able to endure it."[103]

Lypē 72. For a soul that, because of a strange, indescribable temptation, which I do not wish to describe in writing, because of men who, whether it is from baseness or from stupidity, laugh at careful and careless speech alike and suppose that the demons do not harass solitaries openly. These people are not always aware of the warring of the demons, which, after seeking the authorization from God, receive power to tempt us—"Why, we felt that we had received the sentence of death; but that was to make us rely not on ourselves but on God who raises the dead; he delivered us from so deadly a peril, and he will deliver us."[104]

Lypē 73. For the demon that leads me back to sins of youth—"Therefore, if anyone is in Christ, he is a new creation."[105]

Lypē 74. For the thoughts of sadness that come to us concerning transient possessions and that plunge the mind into rending tribulation and kill it—"Godly sadness produces a repentance that leads to salvation, and brings about no regret, but worldly sadness produces death."[106]

V. ANGER

Orgē 2. For the angry thoughts that arise while one is on the way toward the proper life style—"Do not quarrel along the way."[107]

Orgē 3. For the thought that bears false witness concerning the origin of anger—"Do not bear a false witness against your neighbor."[108]

101. Acts 5:41, F 510–12.
102. Rom 8:18, F 512.
103. 1 Cor 10:13b, F 512.
104. 2 Cor 1:9–10, F 512.
105. 2 Cor 5:17, F 512.
106. 2 Cor 7:10, F 512.
107. Gen 45:24, F 512.
108. Exod 20:16, F 512.

Orgē 4. For the thought coming from the devil that awakens and stirs up rage against the brothers—"You shall not utter a false report."[109]

Orgē 7. For the soul that thinks that becoming perfectly humble is beyond nature[110]—"Now Moses was an exceedingly humble person, more than anyone else on earth."[111]

Orgē 8. For the soul that does not know that injuries caused by people come at that moment when God permits [the soul] to be tested—"And David said to Abessa and to all his servants, Behold, my son who came forth out of my bowels seeks my life, still more now may this Benjamite! Let him curse, because the Lord has told him to. If by any means the Lord may look upon my affliction, then [God] shall repay me with good for his cursing this day."[112]

Orgē 10. For the soul that tolerates angry thoughts and gathers up evil pretexts and useless suspicions against the brothers—"Refrain from anger and forsake wrath. Do not fret, this only leads to evil. For the wicked shall be cut off, but those who wait on the Lord will inherit the land."[113]

Orgē 12. For a lord whose mind understands the suddenness with which anger manifests itself at night, and how it turns into terrible visions. [The mind] also realizes that when almsgiving and long-suffering are present, these vanish—"You have made me wiser than my enemies in your commandment . . . I have more understanding than all my teachers, for your testimonies are my meditation."[114]

Orgē 14. For the thought that collects evil opinions about a brother: that he is neglectful [in prayer] or a blasphemer or that there is some activity he ought not to do—"Do not plan evil against your neighbor who dwells trustingly beside you."[115]

Orgē 17. For the anger that rises up against a brother and makes one's mind unsettled at the time of prayer—"Every sincere soul is blessed, but a passionate soul is ugly."[116]

Orgē 18. For the thought that stirs up our anger against cattle that do not walk straight ahead on the path—"A righteous person has pity for the lives of his cattle, but the wicked withhold their mercy."[117]

---

109. Exod 23:1, F 512.
110. Evagrius's *Ep. ad Melaniam* deals extensively with the issue of "going beyond nature."
111. Num 12:3, F 514.
112. 2 Sam 16:11–12, F 514.
113. Ps 36:8–9 (LXX), F 514.
114. Ps 118:98–99 (LXX), F 514.
115. Prov 3:29, F 514.
116. Prov 11:25 (LXX), F 514.
117. Prov 12:10, F 514.

Orgē 22. For the angry thought that disturbs and uproots long-suffering and makes us commit acts of folly; such is the power of the desire for possessions. Against this it is of value to display humility—"He who is slow to anger abounds in wisdom, but a short-tempered person exalts folly."[118]

Orgē 23. For the angry thought that prevents us from answering in a humble way someone who reproaches us in a suitable manner—"Anger kills even the wise, yet a submissive answer turns away anger, while a grievous word stirs up anger."[119]

Orgē 25. For the soul that believes that there will be no angry thought reproved before God except that which comes from our own sinfulness—"The thoughts of the wicked are an abomination to the Lord, but the words of the pure are pleasing to him."[120]

Orgē 26. For the thought of befriending angry and wrathful people that takes control of us—"Make no friendship with a man given to anger, nor live with a wrathful man, lest you learn his ways, and thus snare your soul."[121]

Orgē 28. For the mind that shows no pity or compassion for his enemy when he sees him in bitter poverty, nor seeks to set a table for his enemy—"If your enemy is hungry, feed him, and if he is thirsty, give him something to drink, for you will heap coals of fire on his head, and the Lord will reward you with good."[122]

Orgē 29. For the thought of the soul that is quickly inflamed by wrath and is suddenly embittered against the brothers—"Be not quick to anger, for anger lodges in the bosom of fools."[123]

Orgē 30. For the soul that does not try to determine the source of anger, but wants food and clothes and possessions and to be honored; on account of these things anger is stirred up—nor do they depart from one's heart—rather they lead the *nous* into total destruction—"Remove anger from your heart, and put away fornication from your body, for youth and folly are vanity."[124]

Orgē 32. For the thoughts that stir me up to anger against someone who annoys us, [so that I react] with destructive words etched into his heart—"Woe to those who write evil, whenever they write, they write evil!"[125]

118. Prov 14:29, F 514.
119. Prov 15:1 (LXX), F 514–16.
120. Prov 15:26, F 516.
121. Prov 22:24–25, F 516.
122. Prov 25:21–22, F 516.
123. Eccl 7:9, F 516.
124. Eccl 11:10, F 516.
125. Isa 10:1 (LXX), F 516.

Orgē 35. For the wrathful thought that rises up against a brother out of *accēdia*—"Every one who is angry with his brother shall be liable to judgment."[126]

Orgē 36. For the wrathful thought that is inflamed when one is struck and does not want to receive a second blow—the thought is aroused by the first blow—"If anyone strikes you on the right cheek, turn to him the other also."[127]

Orgē 37. For the thoughts that provoke us to hate and curse our enemies—"Love your enemies, and bless those who curse you, do good to those that hate you, and pray for those who persecute you, so that you may be sons of your father who is in heaven."[128]

Orgē 38. For the angry thought for which the repentance of a brother is not sufficient, but that turns to embitter him again again—"If your brother sins, rebuke him, and if he repents, forgive him; and if he sins against you seven times in the day, and turns to you seven times, and says, 'I repent,' you must forgive him."[129]

Orgē 39. For the *nous* that allows angry thoughts against the brother and perverts the "new commandment" of love—"A new commandment I give you, that you love one another, even as I have loved you, that you love one another."[130]

Orgē 41. For the thoughts that encourage one to rejoice over the misfortune of our enemies—"Rejoice with those who rejoice, weep with those who weep. Live in harmony with one another."[131]

Orgē 43. For the angry thought that suggests that we do evil and act deceptively—"Why not rather suffer wrong? Why not rather be defrauded? But you yourselves wrong and defraud, and that even your own brethren."[132]

Orgē 44. For the angry thought that is aroused against [our] servanthood and reviles us—"Were you a slave when called? Never mind. Even if you can gain your freedom, use the opportunity [for service] instead. For he who was called in the Lord as a slave is a freedman of the Lord."[133]

Orgē 46. For the soul that becomes instantly angry yet seeks to attain

126. Matt 5:22, F 516.
127. Matt 5:39b, F 516.
128. Matt 5:44–45, F 516.
129. Luke 17:3–4, F 516.
130. John 13:34, F 516.
131. Rom 12:15, F 518.
132. 1 Cor 6:7b–8, F 518.
133. 1 Cor 7:21–22, F 518.

in itself the ultimate in knowledge of the truth—"But the fruit of the spirit is love, joy, peace, patience, kindness, goodness, faithfulness, gentleness and self-control."[134]

Orgē 47. For the thoughts that throw us into a [state of] agitation because of the failings of the brothers—"Bear one another's burdens, and thus fulfill the law of Christ."[135]

Orgē 48. For the thoughts of the soul that reasons angrily concerning people who have received many valuable things from others and turn and murmur against them—"Let us not grow weary in doing good, for in due season we shall reap, if we do not lose heart."[136]

Orgē 49. For the angry thoughts that do not permit us to be reconciled with the brothers, that depict before our eyes reasons to justify [anger]. Shame, fear, and pride over stumbling again because of the same offenses as the first time that one sinned in this way all remain. This is an indication of the cunning of the demon, which does not want to leave the *nous* free from anger—"Do not let the sun go down on your anger, and give no opportunity to the Devil."[137]

Orgē 51. For the angry thoughts that presume to grumble over the service of the brothers—"Do all things without grumbling or questioning, that you may be blameless and innocent, children of God . . . in the midst of a crooked and perverse generation."[138]

Orgē 54. For the soul that does not know the aim of God's commandment, and perverts it through thoughts of anger—"The aim of our commandment is love that issues from a pure heart and a good conscience and sincere faith."[139]

Orgē 55. For the *nous* that, when struggling with the thoughts, remains on the level of the intellect—"The Lord's servant must not be quarrelsome but kindly to everyone."[140]

Orgē 58. For the soul quickly angered that yet seeks the righteousness of God—"Let every person be quick to hear, slow to speak, slow to anger, for the anger of a man does not work towards the righteousness of God."[141]

Orgē 61. For the mind that wishes to repay evil with evil or abuse with

---

134. Gal 5:22–23, F 518.
135. Gal 6:2, F 518.
136. Gal 6:9, F 518.
137. Eph 4:26–27, F 518.
138. Phil 2:14–15, F 518.
139. 1 Tim 1:5, F 520.
140. 2 Tim 2:24, F 520.
141. Jas 1:19–20, F 520.

abuse and does not try, through blessing [the revilers], to forget the diabolical reasonings and accusations—"Do not return evil for evil or reviling for reviling; but on the contrary, bless, for to this you have been called, that you may obtain a blessing."[142]

Orgē 62. For the mind that says that the fear of God abides in it, yet hates its brother—"He who says he is in the light and hates his brother is in the darkness still."[143]

Orgē 63. For the thoughts that are engendered by hatred and make the mind commit fratricide—"Anyone who hates his brother is a murderer, and you know that no murderer has eternal life abiding in him."[144]

SUGGESTED READINGS

Bamberger, J. E. *Evagrius Ponticus, The Praktikos and Chapters on Prayer.* Cistercian Studies 4. Kalamazoo, Mich.: Cistercian, 1972.

Bunge, J. Gabriel. "Evagre le Pontique et les deux Macaire." *Irenikon* 56 (1983) 215–27, 323–60.

———. *Evagrios Pontikos, Briefe aus der Wüste.* Sophia. Quellen östlicher Theologie 24. Trier: Paulinus, 1986.

Guillaumont, A. Les ⟨⟨képhalaia gnostica⟩⟩ d'Évagre le Pontique et l'histoire de l'origénisme chez les Grecs et chez les Syriens. Patristica Sorbonensia 5. Paris: Editions du Seuil, 1962.

———. "Un philosophe au desert: Évagre le Pontique." *Revue de L'Histoire des Religions* 181 (1972) 29–57.

Guillaumont, A., and C. Guillaumont. *Évagre le Pontique, Traité Practique ou le Moine.* 2 vols. SC 170 and 171. Paris: Les Editions du Cerf, 1971.

———. *Évagre le Pontique. Le Gnostique ou a celui qui est devenu digne de la science.* SC 356. Paris: Les Editions du Cerf, 1989.

O'Laughlin, M. "Origenism in the Desert: Anthropology and Integration in Evagrius Ponticus." Th.D. dissertation, Harvard Divinity School, 1987.

See also the readings suggested in chapter 12.

142. 1 Pet 3:9, F 520.
143. 1 John 2:9, F 520.
144. 1 John 3:15, F 520.

PART FOUR

LIFE AND TEACHINGS

PSEUDO-ATHANASIUS
The Life and Activity of the Holy and Blessed Teacher Syncletica

INTRODUCTION

Despite its promising title, this fifth-century *vita* (*Life*) spuriously attributed to Athanasius is not primarily a biography and offers only a few glimpses of the details of the life of the holy woman Syncletica. The majority of the text consists of the teachings attributed to her, with biographical materials framing the central didactic section. The composition of this text has been placed at the middle of the fifth century because of the appearance of individual sayings from it in sixth-century Latin collections of apophthegms and because of the apparent influence of the writings of both Evagrius Ponticus and John Cassian upon it. It is assumed to have been written in Egypt, somewhere near Alexandria, where Syncletica lived.[1]

Syncletica withdrew from society at the death of her wealthy parents, whose attempts to marry her off she had successfully eluded, to practice her ascetic rigors. She was concerned always with the need to keep such matters to herself and not succumb to the seduction of others' praise; nevertheless, her teachings focus primarily on ascetic life in community and presuppose some form of monastic setting. In her old age, she suffered from what was apparently lung cancer as well as other painful infections. Her holiness and power over the devil (who had caused her affliction) were demonstrated by both her endurance and her ability to predict the exact moment of her own death. Substantively, her teachings

---

1. See *Vie de Sainte Syncletique* (trans. Sr. Odile Bénédicte Bernard. Spiritualité Orientale 9; Abbaye Notre Dame de Bellefontaine, 1972) iii–iv. This is the only translation of the text into a modern language.

are concerned with the internal battles an ascetic wages against the temptations of "the enemy" and so engage questions of proper and improper emotions and thoughts and only secondarily specific behavior. The imagination and the mind are the elements to be guarded, for everyone has the potential to behave in a holy fashion, if only one gains control over one's affective and intellectual qualities.

This didactic text is addressed toward the proper formation of female ascetics who are represented in the text by Syncletica's eager audience; it presupposes a variety of ascetic social formations, including anchorite and cenobitic models, as well as continent life within marriage.

The text offers an intriguing picture of a woman who dedicated herself early on to a life of fasting, voluntary poverty, and mortifications of the flesh, who attracted a following of eager female disciples, and whose extended illness and eventual death became a special form of ascetic practice—the endurance of illness. Although Syncletica is not unique among female ascetics for suffering illness, this text is remarkable for being steeped in imagery of disease and healing, illness and health. Whether or not the events recounted or the teachings recorded are to be attributed to a historical woman, Syncletica, this text presents the viewpoint of an author who is preoccupied with ideas of bodily decay and the possibility for spiritual cure.

The text used for this translation is found in J.-P. Migne, *Patrologiae Cursus Completus, series graeco-latina*, vol. 28, cols. 1487–1558.

TRANSLATION

1. It was necessary that all people not be uninitiated in good things. For in this way if they were exercised [engumnasmenoi][2] in matters, they would have impunity in life; and at all events the majority of the good escaped notice untouched. But they have suffered from their minds becoming dull through neglect. For often valuable pearls elude day-laboring men. For those who have untested skill concerning them [the pearls] look down on them as something of little or no value. Thus we, having an infantile and unpracticed [anaskēton][3] soul, when we encoun-

2. The verb used here, *engumnadzo*, is an athletic term and calls up the imagery of the Christian as a contending athlete. This imagery recurs in this text (cf. §§ 8, 10, 13, 31, and elsewhere) and is a common image in other early Christian texts, particularly those concerning martyrdom and asceticism.

3. This adjectival form, *anaskētos*, is related to the noun *askēsis* and the verb *askēo*; all of these terms are used extensively in this text and are, of course, the source for the English "asceticism" and related words.

ter the present pearl, we observe nothing great, looking fixedly only on its form; while as far as knowledge about its own nature is concerned, we remain far away. But little by little from its proximity we have learned its beauty; divine love *[erōs]*[4] was born within us for what we saw; for these circumstances kindled our thought toward desire *[pathos]*.

2. But why do I speak of those present, or even reckon myself among them, as our knowing and saying something concerning the famous and blessed Syncletica? For I think that all human nature is left behind with respect to the narrative of her good deeds. But if someone were to attempt to say something concerning her, that person—whether wise or knowledgeable—would be greatly, even infinitely, distant from the objects of the search. For just as those who want to gaze intently into the sun disable their eyes, those who try to examine her life become dizzy by the magnitude of her perfection, yielding a little and becoming exhausted, and they submit to confusion in their thought.

3. Searching out things having to do with her according to our own power, hearing superficially from people her age about things from her early life, from her own activities dimly illuminated, we have come to write, hoarding up on wholesome *[sōteriōdes]*[5] food. For not only are we unable to speak of her dignity, but it is a difficult thing for most people.[6]

4. The one who is named for the heavenly assembly *[sunklētos]*[7] was from the land of the Macedonians. Her ancestors, having heard of the love of God and the love of Christ of the Alexandrians, went from Macedonia to lay hold of the city of the Macedonian [= Alexandria]. When they arrived at the place, they found the circumstances to be better than what they had heard said about the place. It was not that a large number of people pleased them, nor did they marvel at the greatness of the buildings; but finding there a single faith with pure love *[eilikrinēs agapē]*,[8] they regarded this foreign settlement their second home.

---

4. The language of love in early Christian ascetic texts is complex; here *erōs*, the word for sexual love, is used.

5. This adjective is etymologically linked to *sōteria*, "salvation." Both words can have theological meaning as well as connotations related to physical health.

6. This is a commonplace trope of hagiography: the author makes a self-effacing statement concerning his/her unworthiness to tell the story of a subject so marvelous. Compare Gregory of Nyssa *Vit. Mac.*, Prologue, 1; *Vita Melaniae Junioris*, Prologue; and prologues from other *vitae*.

7. Syncletica's name is shown to be a pun; this has led some to question whether this biography refers to an actual woman or whether "Syncletica" is an invention of the author.

8. *Agapē* is the form of love invoked most often by the author of this text, but see n. 4.

5. And the blessed Syncletica was admired from all sides because of her family; moreover, she was adorned *[ekkosmeō]* by all the other customary worldly *[kata ton kosmon]* pleasures.[9] And present with her as well was a like-minded sister, and two brothers who were also prepared for the most religious life. One of the brothers, when he was of youthful age, died; the other, having arrived at his twenty-fifth year, was exhorted into marriage by his parents. But when everything was prepared for the desired end, and when the contracts were completed, the young one flew away like a bird from a snare, having exchanged his earthly bride for the perfect and free assembly of the saints.

6. But she [Syncletica] still being in paternal protection, for the first time trained *[askēo]* her soul toward love for the divine; and thus she performed no cares of the body, as she carefully observed the impulses of her nature.[10]

7. For she was exceedingly beautiful physically as to attract to herself from her first youth many suitors. Some were attracted by her abundant wealth, some by the decorum of her parents; but over and above these things they were attracted to the beauty of the girl herself. And certainly her parents gladly urged the young girl toward marriage, urging this so that through her the succession of their line would be protected.[11] But the wise and noble-spirited woman did not at all arrange things according to these counsels of her parents; hearing worldly marriage, she imagined divine marriage; and overlooking many suitors, she possessed the inclination for the divine Bridegroom alone.

8. It was possible to see in her the true disciple of the blessed Thecla following in the same teachings.[12] For Christ was the one suitor of the

9. Here the author plays on the Greek similarity between words referring to physical ornamentation and words referring to the world; Syncletica makes use of this linguistic connection when she renounces the world (see §11).

10. *Tas tēs phuseōs hormas epetērei. Hormē* has a technical meaning in Stoicism, where it refers to appetite, including both "reasoned choice" and "irrational impulse." Given the strong relationship between certain Stoic ideas and early Christian ascetic ideas, perhaps there is a connection here. For this relationship, see Michel Spanneut, *Le Stoicisme des péres de l'Eglise de Clément de Rome à Clément d'Alexandrie* (Patristica Sorbonensia 1; Paris: Seuil, 1957). Although Spanneut's treatment deals with earlier texts, he argues that Stoic notions become established in the earlier period and remain as a strong feature of later Christian discourse.

11. Parental concern that their property be safeguarded through the marriage of their children is a frequently offered explanation for parental resistance to a child's decision to lead a chaste life. See Anne Yarbrough, "Christianization in the Fourth Century: The Example of Roman Women," *CH* 45 (1976) 154–57; Elizabeth A. Clark, "Ascetic Renunciation and Feminine Advancement: A Paradox of Late Ancient Christianity," *ATR* 63 (1981) 241–43.

12. Thecla is the model for female Christian ascetics. See, for example, Gregory of Nyssa, *Vit. Mac.* 2, where Macrina's mother dreams of Thecla on the eve of Macrina's

two, and Paul himself was for both of them the guide to the Bridegroom
[*numphagōgos*].[13] And I think that the bridal chamber was not different
for them; for the church was the one bridal chamber for them, and the
same David sang for them both holy and divine hymns. For he gladdens
the souls dedicated to God with euphonious cymbals, and he sends up
the most perfect ode by means of tymbals and ten-stringed harps. Miriam leads the women choral dancers to these sacred weddings, saying,
"We will sing to the Lord; for he has been glorified magnificently."[14] And
to those who are guests at the common meal of the divine banquet,
"Taste and see that the Lord is good."[15] And the weave of their bridal
garments is one: "For as many as were baptized in Christ, have put on
Christ."[16] Accordingly, their love for the Lord was of like fashion; for
they were deemed worthy of the same gifts; but they also competed
[*amillaomai*] in the same contests [*agōn*].[17] For no one was ignorant of the
martyrdoms of the blessed Thecla, as she struggled bravely [*enathlēo*][18]
through fire and wild beasts; and I think that many people will not
escape noticing the virtuous and sweaty sufferings of this one [Syn-
cletica]. For if the one Savior was the object of their desires, there
necessarily was one opponent for them. And I understand the gentler

birth, and that *Vita* in general, where Thecla is Macrina's secret name; Jerome *Ep.* 22,
41; *Vit. Olmp.* 1; Ambrose *Virg.* 2,3; Methodius *Symp.*, Discourse 8, 1, 170; 8, 17, 232; 11,
282. For additional examples, see the introduction to the SC edition of Gregory of
Nyssa *Vit. Mac.* (trans. Pierre Maraval; Paris: Les Editions du Cerf, 1971) 146, n. 2.

13. This term refers to a variety of figures who lead virgins to Christ (angels, priests,
apostles, and even Scripture). See, for example, Basil of Ancyra *Virg.* 29 (*PG* 30.729A),
37 (*PG* 30.744B), and 50 (*PG* 30.769A).

14. Exod 15:1, RSV: "'I will sing to the Lord, for he has triumphed gloriously.'" In
Exod, this verse is the first in Moses' hymn to God following the miracle of the parting
of the Red Sea. Interestingly, the author here has placed the words in the mouth of
Miriam, Moses' sister, whose role as singer and prophetess was highlighted by later
Jewish and Christian writers as a model for female piety. For a study of the biblical
image of Miriam, see Rita J. Burns, *Has the Lord Indeed Spoken Only Through Moses? A
Study of the Biblical Portrait of Miriam* (SBLDS 84; Atlanta: Scholars Press, 1987). Philo
uses the image of Miriam to praise the woman who leads the Therapeutrides in song in
Vit. Cont. 85–90. The New Prophecy movement in the second and third centuries used
the image of Miriam to authorize the prophetic activity of Maximilla and Priscilla; see
Pierre de Labriolle, comp. and ed., *Les sources de l'histoire du Montanisme* (Collectanea
Friburgensia, n.s. 15; Paris: Leroux, 1913) 55–56 (Origen *Comm. in Matt.* 15:30 [*PG* 13,
1344]), 106 (Pseudo-Athanasius *Dialogue Between a Montanist and an Orthodox*), 159
(Didymus of Alexandria *Trin.* III, 41 [*PG* 39, 984]).

15. Ps 33:9 (LXX), 34:8 (RSV): "O taste and see that the Lord is good." The Greek may
have been read as a pun here, as *chrēstos ho kurios* sounds like *christos ho kurios*.

16. Gal 3:27; the text has been changed from second-person plural to third-person
plural.

17. Both of these terms have athletic connotations; see n. 2.

18. This term continues the athletic imagery; the same term is used in the comparison
of the virgin Macrina with her ancestor of the same name who was persecuted as a
Christian; see Gregory of Nyssa *Vit. Mac.* 2.

sufferings to be Thecla's, for the evil of the enemy attacked her from the outside. But with Syncletica he displays his more piercing evil, moving from the inside by means of opposing and destructive thoughts.[19]

9. The weave of multicolored clothing did not seduce her eye, nor the different colors of precious stones. Cymbals did not deceive her hearing, nor was the flute able to weaken the course of her soul. The tears of her parents did not soften her, nor the exhortation of any other relative. But holding onto her reasoning power adamantly, she did not change her mind; and having closed up all her senses just like a window, she associated only with her Bridegroom, saying that Scripture: "As I am to my beloved, my beloved is to me."[20] And if discussions were smoky and dark, she fled them, bringing herself together with the inner treasuries of her soul; where exhortations were shining and helpful, she directed all of her own mind toward the reception of what was said.

10. She did not neglect the physical salutary remedy [sotērios pharmakos]; for she had a love for fasting in which no one of those around her was her equal.[21] She believed that fasting was the protection and foundation of other things. And if she ever had to eat outside of the accustomed time, she experienced the opposite thing from those who eat. For her face was a pallor, and the weight of her body collapsed; for when one is disgusted by an action, the action itself is changed. For as the beginning lays things out, so in general the things that depend on it follow from it. For while to those for whom food becomes and bears pleasure, the weight of the body flourishes; to those for whom the opposite occurs, their flesh is undernourished and slight. The sickly witness to my word. Certainly the blessed one herself testing herself to cure her body [nosēleuein to sōma], brought blossom to her soul;[22] for she acted according to the apostle who said: "For as much as our outer human being perishes," he says, "the inner human being is renewed."[23] Therefore she struggled bravely [enathleō] while escaping the notice of many.[24]

---

19. This is a common trope in early Christian discussions that compare ascetics with martyrs; ascetic practice takes on much of the imagery of the martyrs' sufferings but is described as even more painful; see also §106. For a comparison of the literature and a discussion of the transformation of representations of martyrs and ascetics, see Marcel Villier, "Le Martyre et l'ascèse," RAM 6 (1925) 105–42.

20. Cant 2:16; the LXX text is slightly different.

21. Here fasting is characterized as a physical remedy, playing on the spiritual and medical nuances of sōtērios. See n. 4.

22. Here, as at the beginning of the paragraph, imagery of illness is used ironically. There, the "salutary remedy/medicine" is actually the avoidance of food; here, "to cure the body" means to repress its desires.

23. 2 Cor 4:16.

24. This is an important aspect of ascetic experience, that is, that one must not

11. When her parents died, this one who was inspired for so long by divine thoughts took her sister with her—for her sister was deprived of sight—and departed from her paternal home. She led herself down to the tomb of a relative, which was remote from the city; and having sold everything she renounced her possessions and distributed them among the poor. Having summoned to herself one of the elders, she cut her own hair.[25] At that time she put away from herself all cosmetics; for it was the practice for women to call their hair "the cosmos."[26] This was a symbol that her soul had become a simple and pure being. Then for the first time she was deemed worthy of the name, "virgin."

12. After she distributed all her property to the poor, she said: "I was deemed worthy of a great name; but what deserved thing will I offer in return to my benefactor? I do not have it. For if in external affairs people abandon all their property on account of perishable honor, how much more is it necessary that I, deemed worthy of such a grace, give over, with the things held to belong to me, even my body? But what do I say, to give property or body, when everything belongs to him? 'For the earth and her fullness are the Lord's.'"[27] Having clothed herself with humility by means of these words, she lived as a recluse.[28]

13. Then she was again in her paternal courtyards, being trained [progumnadzō][29] sufficiently in sufferings; and having been led to the very height of the stadium,[30] she made progress in virtues. How many then approached this divine mystery unprepared and inadvisedly, and fell short of the object of their desire, not having considered everything ahead of time? Just as people who are about to make a journey first give thought to their provisions, just so she, having prepared herself with provisions—with long sufferings—she made the journey toward heavenly things without restraint. For, having put away beforehand the things for the completion of the house, she made for herself the most

---

display one's ascetic practice for fear of committing the sin of pride. See later in this text an extended discussion of this problem (§§ 38, 49–54).

25. This is a common sign of renunciation among women; for a discussion, see Elizabeth Castelli, "Virginity and Its Meaning for Women's Sexuality in Early Christianity," *JFSR* 2:1 (1986) 76.

26. Here I have tried to retain the Greek pun, whereby the word for "adornment, ornamentation, orderliness" (*kosmēsis*) is tied etymologically to the word for "world" (*kosmos*).

27. Ps 23:1 (LXX); 24:1 (RSV).

28. *Hesuchazo* means "to be quiet or tranquil, to keep silence." It also is used as a technical term signifying the solitary life of a hermit (in opposition to cenobitic life); see as examples *Apophthegmata Patrum* (PG 65, 85D), Evagrius Ponticus *or.* 111.

29. See n. 2.

30. This is probably a metaphor for Syncletica's intense struggle, drawing again on the athletic image.

secure tower.[31] And whereas the work of dwelling places is usually constructed from external materials, she did the opposite thing. For she did not bring with her external materials, but rather she poured out internal things. For having distributed her property to the poor, and having renounced anger and memory of past injuries, and expelled envy and love of fame, she built up her house upon the rock from which the tower was splendid and the house free from storms.[32]

14. What more do I say? For from the beginning she surpassed those who were in the habit of the solitary life [monērēs bios]. For just as the most naturally suited of children, still in the process of learning their letters, compete with those who are older in the presence of the teachers; just so, she, fervent in spirit, outran the rest.[33]

15. We are not able to speak of her active and ascetic life, because she did not allow anyone to become an observer of this. For she did not want the people who were with her to be heralds of her manly deeds [andragathēmata].[34] For she did not give as much thought to good deeds as to guarding the secret of them. But she did this not because she was oppressed by jealousy, but because she was summoned by divine grace. For she bore in her heart that word of the Lord: "If your right hand does something, do not let your left hand know it."[35] Thus, escaping notice, she performed the acts fitting to her profession [of the religious life].

16. From youth until her prime not only did she flee the society of all men [andres], but she also for the most part avoided women [hai homophuloi][36] for two reasons: in order not to be glorified by hyperbole of ascetic practice [askēsis],[37] and in order not to be beguiled away from virtue by bodily necessity.[38]

17. Thus she observed carefully the first movements of her soul, not allowing herself to be dragged down by them together with bodily

31. See Luke 14:28.
32. These are all virtues discussed at length in the teachings section of this work. See the passages on voluntary poverty (§§ 30–37), the renunciation of anger (§§ 62–64), and memory of past injuries (§ 64).
33. Compare Athanasius Vit. Ant. 3–4.
34. This term literally means "manly deeds" and signifies in this literature Christian acts of virtue.
35. Matt 6:3.
36. Literally, this term means "of the same breed, akin." I have translated it to mean "women" because of the context.
37. Throughout the text, I have translated askēsis as "ascetic practice," rather than as "asceticism," in order to avoid the problem of assuming that askēsis signifies a unified and monolithic system.
38. This idea is not clear; perhaps it means that human contact threatens the development of virtue.

desires. Just like an unpruned tree she trimmed the offshoots of fruitless branches; for she set aside through fasting and prayer the thorny buds of thought.[39] And if she progressed in one or another of these in some small way, she addressed various torments of them, mortifying the body by means of all sorts of sufferings. She was not satisfied by mere abstinence from bread, but she also contented herself with little water.

18. When the battle of the enemy was waged against her, she called emphatically upon her Master for aid *[summachiā]*[40] by means of prayer;[41] for she was not satisfied by a simple ascetic practice to extinguish the assault of the lion.[42] And from her supplication the Lord was there, and the enemy fled. But often the hated one endured the battle, and the Lord did not ward off the murderer, in order to strengthen the exercise of the virtuous soul.[43] But this was like an increase of gifts, and she was strengthened to a very great extent in victory against the enemy. For she was not satisfied by mortifying herself only through contentment with little food, but she also tried to shut herself up with regiments against pleasure. For on the one hand she ate bread made from bran; on the other hand she often took no water at all. She even slept for a time on the ground. When the adversary continued to wage war, she used as her weapons prayer, clothing herself with it instead of weapon and shield; and her helmet was composed out of faith and hope and charity. For faith went before all, binding together her entire armor. And mercy was also present, if not acted upon, then at least in intention.

19. Therefore, by means of these things the surviving enemy was defeated, and she lightened her most piercing ascetic practice. She did this so that the members of her body might not be suddenly weakened; for this was the positive proof of defeat. For, when all the weapons have come to battle, what hope is there for the soldier in [the moment of] battle? Certainly, the ones who were immeasurably and indiscriminately consumed by fasting experienced it as a crucial blow. Just so in the rejection of the adversary, they corrupt themselves. But she did not

39. This notion of ascetic practice and prayer in combination appears frequently in this text (§§19, 29, and elsewhere) and may be dependent upon the idea found throughout the work of Evagrius Ponticus of prayer as the theory and asceticism as the practice of holy life.

40. This is a military term; the image of Syncletica's encounters with the devil as a war appears throughout the text. For a general treatment of the image of holy women as "soldiers of Christ," see Elena Giannarelli, *La tipologia femminile nella biografia e nell'autobiografia cristiana del IV° secolo* (Studi Storici 127; Rome: Instituto Storico Italiano per il Medio Evo, 1980), chapter 1.

41. Compare Athanasius *Vit. Ant.* 5.

42. Ibid., 7.

43. Ibid., 10.

act in this way but did everything according to superior judgment.[44] And she contended with the hated one in strength through prayer and ascetic practice. She took care of her body when her own boat moved toward calm. For sailors, when overtaking a stormy wave, persevere without eating, opposing with all their own skill the danger before their eyes. Once they are alive, then they give attention to the secondary saving. All of their time is not spent on the swelling of the sea. Just as they accept the shortest calm as a rest from toils; but they do not spend it without anxiety nor are they dragged down into deep sleep, but having had an experience of things that have gone away, they receive some idea of things about to happen. For although the storm abated, the sea has not become weaker; and if the second passed, nevertheless the third remains. And if the event has been banished, that which causes it is still present. It is thus in the present situation: even if the spirit of desire has been cast out, likewise the one exercising power over it is not far away. Whence it is necessary to pray ceaselessly for the sake of the stability of the sea and the bitter evil of the hated one. Therefore the blessed one having seen accurately the little wave present in life, and foreseeing the surgings of the spirit, she was carefully steering her own ship[45] toward devotion to God. For she anchored without disturbance in the saving harbor, placing herself in the most steadfast anchor, faith in God.

20. Her apostolic life, governed by faith and voluntary poverty [aktēmosunē],[46] yet shone through with charity and humility. She performed the practice of the saving word: "You will walk on the asp and the basilisk and on all the power of the hated one."[47] She heard this cry familiarly: "Well done, good and faithful servant; you have been faithful over a little, I will set you over much."[48] This saying, if it refers to gifts, here let it signify: "You were victorious in the material battle, and you will also secure the trophy concerning the immaterial, with me shielding you. Let them know the greatness of your faith, the principalities and powers concerning which Paul, the one who serves me, wrote; for you

44. Compare John Cassian *Conf.* 2,2.
45. The ship here is a metaphor for the body, a metaphor that can be found also in Methodius *Symp.*, Epilogue, 298.
46. This notion of *voluntary* poverty, a virtue to be cultivated, is to be distinguished from poverty that results from economic disadvantage; *penia* signifies the working poor, whereas *ptōchos* refers to the destitute.
47. A combination of Ps 90:13 (LXX); 91:13, "You will tread on the lion and the adder," and Luke 10:19, "Behold I have given you authority to tread upon serpents and scorpions, and over all the power of the enemy."
48. Matt 25:23.

were victorious over opposing powers, you will come into contact with greater ones."

21. Thus having withdrawn [anachōreō][49] by herself, she became perfect in good works. As time went on, and when her virtue blossomed, the sweet fragrance of her most glorious sufferings passed on to many. "For nothing," it says, "hidden will not be made manifest."[50] For God knows how to proclaim by himself those who love him toward the correcting of those who hear. Then therefore some began to enter with a desire for that which is better and to make entreaties for their own edification. For they approached the ways she led her life, wishing to be helped and according to the accustomed formula, they asked her: "In what way is it necessary [to be] to be saved?" But she, having sighed heavily and let flow a multitude of tears, withdrew into herself, and as if she had made an answer by means of the tears, she practiced [askeō] a second silence. But the ones who were with her compelled her to speak of the mighty works of God. For the ones who admired her were amazed by the singular sight. And again they exhorted her to speak loud and clear. And the blessed one, having been compelled for such a long time, after sufficient time, and after a great silence, spoke in a humble voice this scriptural word: "Do not do violence to the poor, for he is poor."[51] And those who were present, receiving the word gladly as if tasting honey and honeycomb, had a great many further questions; and hereafter they pressed her with scriptural words, for they said to her: "You received freely, give freely."[52] And they said: "Watch that you do not return the talent you have hidden, after the manner of the servant."[53] And she said to them: "What then do you imagine about me, a sinner, as someone who does or says something [good]? We have in common the Lord as teacher; from the same source we draw out the spiritual stream. From his breasts we are fed with milk, the Old and New Testaments." And they said to her: "We know this too, that our guide is one, Scripture, and the same teacher; but you have made progress toward virtues with vigilant zeal; and it is necessary for those who have become in habit of good things, because they are stronger, to help the young. For even our

49. This can be a technical term for a particular form of ascetic life; anchorites withdraw from the world and live a solitary existence.
50. Matt 10:26. The Gospel text has gnōsthēsetai (will be known); this text has phanerōthēsetai (will be revealed).
51. Prov 22:22.
52. Matt 10:8.
53. The reference is to the parable in Matt 25.

common teacher commands this." And the blessed one, having heard these things, wept as though a newborn at the breast. Those who were assembled, setting aside their question, exhorted her to stop crying. And as she became calm, again she became silent for a long time. They began to exhort her again. And she, feeling compassion and knowing that her words do not distribute praise for her, but implant help for those around her, began to speak to them in this way:

22. "Children, we all [men and women] know how to be saved, but through our own neglect of salvation we abandon it.[54] For it is necessary first of all to guard that which has been learned through the grace of the Lord. These things are: 'You will love the Lord your God with your whole soul, and your neighbor as yourself.'[55] In these is the beginning of the law observed, and in this the fullness of grace rests. The expression of the word is short, but the power of it is multiple and infinite within it. For everything that profits the soul is dependent on this. Paul witnesses, saying that the end of the law is charity [agapē].[56] Therefore, whatever people say that is useful according to the grace of the spirit, it is from charity, and it is perfected in it. Therefore salvation itself is the double charity.

23. "And it is necessary to add this, which is again from charity, that each of us knows what it is to desire the better things." But the women were confused by what was said, and again asked in turn. And she said to them: "You are not ignorant of the parable in the gospel concerning the hundred, the sixty, and the thirty; the hundred represents our profession [of the religious life]; the sixty is the division of encratites; the thirty the rank of those who live the married life moderately.[57] And it is good to pass over from the thirty to the sixty, because it is good to make progress from the lesser to the greater; but it is dangerous to pursue the lesser from the greater. For the one who has once descended to the

54. Several sayings in this text also appear in the collection *Apophthegmata Patrum, Sayings of the Desert Fathers*, attributed to Syncletica. They are cited from the alphabetic collection of sayings, hereafter cited as *Alpha. Syn*. This saying appears as *Alpha. Syn.* 23. A complete translation of the alphabetic sayings may be found in Benedicta Ward, *The Sayings of the Desert Fathers: The Alphabetical Collection* (London: A. R. Mowbray, 1981), and Syncletica's sayings are excerpted in Ross Kraemer, ed., *Maenads, Martyrs, Matrons, Monastics: A Sourcebook on Women's Religions in the Greco-Roman World* (Philadelphia: Fortress Press, 1988) 117–22.

55. Matt 22:37, 39.

56. See 1 Tim 1:5. *Agapē* has been translated here "charity," in order to distinguish it from other words used in the text signifying "love."

57. This third group probably refers to those who live chastely within marriage; *sōphrosunē* has not only the meaning of "discretion" or "moderation" but is also cast in opposition to *porneia*. See, among many others, *1 Clem* 62.2, 64; Ignatius *Eph.* 10.3;

worse is not able to stand among the few but is borne into the depth of perdition. Certainly, the ones professing virginity who drag down their mind because of weak character make excuses for themselves with excuses for their sins. For they say to themselves, or rather to the devil, if we live chastely *[sōphronōs]* (but rather in folly *[aphronōs]*!) in marriage, then we will be judged worthy of the thirty. And they say that all the Old Testament supported the procreation of children. Therefore let it be known that this view is that of the enemy. For the one who is led from the greater to the lesser is thrown under the opponent. For just so the soldier who flees is judged as a deserter. But he is not judged worthy of pardon because he has withdrawn to a lesser army; rather because of his running off he deserves punishment. Therefore it is necessary, just as I said before, to ascend from the lesser toward the [greater]. And the apostle teaches, concerning this, that forgetting what lies behind, it is useful to strain forward to what lies ahead.[58] Therefore it is necessary for those who have conquered the hundred to repeat this in themselves and not to give in to the goal of the number itself. For it is said: 'When you have done what has been ordered, say, "We are unworthy servants."'[59]

24. "Therefore it is necessary for us who have professed this religious life to hold extremely fast to chastity. For it seems that chastity is performed among worldly women[60] but to be at the same time unchastity *[aphrosunē]*, through sinning by all the other senses. For they look around in an indecent fashion, and they laugh in a disorderly way.[61] But we, having given up these things most of all, advance toward virtues, and we remove from before our eyes vain illusion. For the Scripture says, 'Let your eyes look straight ahead.'[62] And we check our tongue from these sorts of sins. For it is unlawful for the organ [made for singing] hymns to utter shameful statements. But one must not only avoid saying these things, but also hearing them.

25. "But it is not possible to guard against these things if we frequently have the experience of going out into public. For through our senses, even if we do not wish them to, the thieves enter. For how can a house whose windows are open not be blackened by smoke that comes in from

---

Justin 1 *Apol.* 6.1, 14.2; Clement of Alexandria *Paed.* 3.8, 3.12; *Strom.* 2.23; etc. Hereafter, *sophrosunē* will be interpreted here to mean "chastity."

58. Phil 3:13.
59. Luke 17:10; cf. §57.
60. This feminine form of *kosmikos* is used to describe Christian women who live in the world, as opposed to virgins; see Athanasius *Virg.* 11.
61. Compare *Alpha. Syn.* 2.
62. Prov 4:25.

the outside? Therefore it is absolutely necessary to avoid that which concerns going out in public in the agora. For if we believe it to be burdensome and difficult for us to see our brothers and parents naked, how much more hurtful is it to us to see those stripped naked indecently in the streets, speaking licentious words? For it results from these things that unpleasant and pestilential visions emerge.

26. "But even when we close ourselves up in our houses, we are not near to being free from anxiety there, but rather to keep vigil;[63] for it is written: 'Be watchful.'[64] As much as we are made secure through chastity, how much more we are engaged in conflict by keener thoughts. For 'the one who adds knowledge,' it is said, 'adds suffering.'[65] For as much as athletes make progress, so much more they are engaged by their competitors. Look at how much you have acquired and do not neglect the things that are present. Have you conquered material and practicable fornication [porneia]?[66] The enemy will set before you fornication of the senses. And even whenever you will prevent this for yourself, it lurks in the spaces of thought, moving you toward a spiritual battle. It introduces seemly faces and [memories of] ancient associations to those who live the solitary life. Therefore it is necessary not to assent to these visions; for it is written, 'If the spirit of the powerful one rises up against you, do not give up your place.'[67] For assenting to these things is equal to worldly fornication. For it says, 'the powerful are punished powerfully.'[68] Therefore great is the struggle against the spirit of fornication. For it is the first among the evils of the enemy toward the perdition of the soul. And this the blessed Job, hinting, said to the devil: '[Behold] the one who has power in the center of his belly.'[69]

27. "The devil arouses the goad of fornication by means of many and varied mechanisms against Christ-loving human beings. Certainly often the malignant one will reanchor sisterly charity toward his own evil. For he tripped up by means of sisterly relationship virgins who had fled

63. Agrupheo is used specifically of ascetic practices; see Clement of Alexandria Quis. Div. Salv. 41; Constitutiones apostolorum 3.7.7; etc. Compare also Athanasius Vit. Ant. 21.
64. Matt 24:42.
65. Eccl 1:18.
66. The translation of this term presents difficulties; it refers to sexual activity outside the prescribed norms of Christian behavior, that is, to any sexual practice besides heterosexual acts with the purpose of producing children. I have opted for the rather problematic translation "fornication" because of later uses in the text ("fornication of the senses," "worldly fornication"), that is, uses that employ porneia as a metaphor for other acts. An alternative would be to leave the word in the text untranslated.
67. Eccl 10:4.
68. Wis 6:6.
69. Job 40:16. Athanasius Vit. Ant. 5 uses the same citation in a similar vein.

marriage and illusion all their lives.[70] He wounded monks, and those who fled any kind of lascivious thing whatsoever; but he deceived them through pious discussion. For this is the work of the enemy which is displayed, clothed in alien dress, while its own garb escapes notice. He displays a grain bread, and he places under it a trap. But I think that even our Lord speaks concerning this: 'They come to you in sheep's clothing but inwardly are ravenous wolves.'[71]

28. "Therefore what will we do about this? Let us be wise as serpents, and innocent as doves,[72] setting in motion against his snare our cunning intelligence. For the statement 'Be wise as serpents' says for the assaults of the devil not to escape our notice. For the like makes the quickest judgment from the like. And 'the innocence of doves' displays the purity of action.[73] Therefore every good work is an act of fleeing from the worse thing. But how do we flee what we do not know? Therefore it is necessary for us , having realized the terribleness of the enemy, to guard against his evil machinery.[74] For it says, 'the one who goes around seeking someone to devour'[75] and 'his food is elect.'[76] Therefore it is necessary always to be watchful. For he does battle by means of external acts, and subdues by means of internal thoughts. And he does much more by means of the internal; for night and day he approaches spiritually.

29. "Therefore what is useful in the present war? Clearly, painful ascetic practice and pure prayer; these have emerged generally as able to keep off all destructive thoughts.[77] But it is necessary to use some particular notions for expelling the plague from the soul in the present circumstances. When the most shameful thought has occurred, offer instead the opposite to it. For if a vision of seemly appearance should come into being in the regions of thought, which reasonably in this case one must punish, erase the eyes of the image, and extract flesh from the cheeks; cut away under the lips, and further imagine the ugly coagulated state of bare bone. Further contemplate whatever was desired; for thus thought

---

70. It is unclear exactly what kind of sin is being described here; perhaps it is a reference to spiritual marriage, but it may also be a reference to relationships between sisters. See the French translation, which renders this passage in the following way: "Les vierges, en effet, qui ont renoncé au mariage et à toutes les mondanités, il les a prises au piège de leurs rapports avec leurs soeurs."
71. Matt 7:15.
72. Matt 10:16.
73. *Alpha. Syn.* 18.
74. Compare Athanasius *Vit. Ant.* 21–22.
75. 1 Pet 5:8.
76. Hab 1:16.
77. Compare §§17, 19.

may be able to hold back the vain wanderer. For the object of love was nothing but a mixture of blood and phlegm, the very thing that provides a use for a woven robe for living beings. Thus therefore by means of such thoughts it is likely to drive off polluted evil. And just as it is fitting to drive back a nail with a nail, so it is with a demon.[78] Still it is necessary on the whole to represent the body of the beloved [erōmenos] as a wound that smells oppressive, and is inclined to putrefy, briefly put, as resembling a corpse, or to imagine oneself as a corpse. But the best of all is to rule over the stomach; for thus one is able to govern even the sexual pleasures."[79]

30. Therefore it was a divine symposium for those present. For they were made merry from the chalices of wisdom. The blessed Syncletica was to them like the pouring out of divine drink and liquid. Each one of them received whatever she wanted, and one of those coming with her asked her whether voluntary poverty is a good perfection. And she said, "Entirely good to those [tais] who are capable of it. For those who submit themselves to this virtue have affliction of the flesh but recreation of the spirit. For just as rugged clothing, being tread upon and stirred up violently, is washed and bleached, just so the strong soul is strengthened to a very great extent by means of poverty [penia].[80] But those who have a weaker mind suffer the opposite of this. For afflicted as a consequence of little, like torn clothing, they die, not bearing the washing according to virtue. And there is one artificer, but the end for the clothes is different; for one is torn and destroyed while the other is bleached and renewed. Therefore one might say that poverty is the good treasure for the virile spirit [to andreion phronema]. For it is the restraint from practical sins.

31. "It is necessary first to be exercised [engumnadzō] in sufferings. I mean in fasting and in sleeping on the ground, and in others in turn, and thus to acquire this virtue. For those who have not acted in this way, but run suddenly toward the rejection of their property, generally are seized by repentance.

32. "For property is the instrument of a life devoted to pleasure.[81] Therefore, first do away with your own skill, that is, gluttony and luxurious life, and then you will be able to cut off your material belongings with contentment. For I think that it is difficult, when the skill is

78. Evagrius Ponticus Praktikos 58.
79. There is a pun in Greek here that connects food and sex: to govern the stomach (gastros) and to rule over sexual (hypogastrios) pleasures.
80. Alpha. Syn. 5; the image of clothing being washed and bleached as a metaphor for ascetic practice is also present in Evagrius Ponticus or. 40.
81. Apolaustikos Bios; see Aristotle Eth. Nic. 1095b17.

present, not to use the instrument. For how is the one who does not reject the first able to reject the second? Accordingly, even the Savior, when conversing with the rich man, does not advocate to him the sudden rejection of his belongings; but he asks him first if he has acted in accordance with the law. And the Lord, undertaking to be a true teacher, asks: 'If you learned the letters of the alphabet, if you apprehended the syllables, and if you have easily acquired vocabulary, henceforth from now on you possess [the skill of] reading fluently'; that is, 'Go, sell all your belongings, and then follow me.'[82] And I think perhaps that if he did not promise to have done what was asked, he was not persuaded to voluntary poverty.[83] For how is one able to begin to read, without knowing the meaning of syllables?

33. "Therefore voluntary poverty is good for those who are in the habit of goodness. For having made a renunciation of all their unnecessaries, they bear the sign toward the Lord, singing purely that divine word: 'Our eyes hope in you; and you give food in good season to those who love you.'[84]

34. "In another way again they confer upon themselves a great advantage: for not having their mind on earthly treasure, they are clothed in the kingdom of heaven,[85] and they accomplish clearly the words of David the psalmist: 'I became like a beast before you.'[86] For just as beasts of burden, performing their own work, are satisfied with only the food needed for their life, thus the ones who labor at voluntary poverty, who believe that using silver is as nothing, and who perform physical work only to get their daily bread.[87] These ones possess the foundation of faith; for it is to them it was said by the Lord not to worry about tomorrow, and that 'the birds of heaven do not sow, nor reap, and the heavenly father feeds them.'[88] They boldly said such words (for God is the speaker), and speaking confidently they utter that scriptural phrase: 'I believed, on which account I spoke.'[89]

35. "But also the enemy is defeated to a very great extent by those who are voluntarily poor; for he does not hinder what he does not have. For the greatest part of grief and temptations lies in the removal of riches;

82. Matt 19:21.
83. Athanasius *Vit. Ant.* 2.
84. Ps 144:15 (LXX); 145:15 (RSV).
85. Athanasius *Vit. Ant.* 2.
86. Ps 72:22 (LXX); 73:22 (RSV).
87. Athanasius *Vit. Ant.* 3.
88. Matt 6:26.
89. Ps 115:1 (LXX); 116:10 (RSV).

what can he do to the impoverished? Nothing. Set fire to their lands? They have none. Kill their beasts? But they do not have any of these. Attack their most beloved things? But they said farewell to these a long time ago. Therefore voluntary poverty is a great punishment against the enemy and a highly honored treasure to the soul.[90]

36. "Therefore as much as poverty is wonderful and sublime in virtue, love of money is bad and wretched in evil. Truly concerning this the divine Paul said that it is the cause of all evils.[91] For desire for wealth, false oath, theft, rape, fornication, envy, hatred of siblings, war, idolatry, covetousness, and the offshoots of these, hypocrisy, flattery, derision; love of money is accepted as the cause of all of these. Then the apostle justly named it the mother of all evil. Not only does God seek vengeance against [those who practice] these evils; but they corrupt themselves by their own accord. For bearing an unsatisfying evil, they do not achieve their goal, thus the plague is to them incurable. The one who doesn't have desires little, and but having this, he grasps at more.[92] He has a hundred pieces of silver, and he desires a thousand; and attaining this, the direction bears toward infinity. And thus, not being able to establish for themselves an end, they always lament their poverty. And love of money always bears with her envy. And this first destroys the possessor. For just as a viper when it is born first kills its own mother, before it injures others; so envy causes its possessor to wither, before it is distributed to those from the neighborhood.

37. "What a great thing if we were able, while seeking after the excellent wealth, to survive sufferings as incurable as the many with which the hunters of the vain world fall in. They survive shipwreck, they encounter pirates, they fall in with robbers on land; furthermore, they hold themselves up against storm and violent winds; and often having succeeded, they call themselves paupers in accordance with their feelings of envy. But we do not at all face boldly such dangers on behalf of true advantage. But if we prosper in a small way, we are made great ourselves by displaying it. And often we do not utter the event in narrative; but immediately we seem to have the spark of goodness, which we steal for ourselves from under the enemy. But those ones, having gained much, desire still more; and they present what they have as nothing, but direct themselves toward what they do not have. But we

90. Perhaps there is a pun of contrast here: *timōria* (punishment) and *polutimos* (highly prized).
91. The reference is to 1 Tim 6:10.
92. These sayings about greed in §§36–37 resemble *Alpha. Syn.* 10.

who have no objects of desire want to acquire nothing. And suffering the most extreme poverty, we call ourselves rich. Therefore it is good for the one who does good not to speak out; rather, such people will be punished: for what they seem to have will be taken from them.

38. "Therefore it is necessary to take every care in order to have our spiritual benefit escape notice. The ones who speak of their achievements are tempted also to speak of their defects. If they hide these things, for the sake of not being blamed by their audience, all the more they must guard against the former as being estranged from God. And certainly those who live according to virtue do the reverse, and they narrate out their small faults with the addition of what they have not done, eschewing human opinion. They hide the good things, on behalf of security of the soul. For just as a revealed treasure becomes scarce, so virtue that is recognized and revealed publicly is led astray. For just as a lighted candle is destroyed when in the front of the fire, so the soul is dissolved and loses its tone because of praises.[93]

39. "And the reverse of this is also true: for if the heat released the candle, cooling then makes it stable; and if praise takes away tone from the soul, reproach and insult lead it to the greatness of virtue. For it [Scripture] says, 'Rejoice and be glad when people say everything falsely against you.'[94] And elsewhere it says, 'in tribulation you widen me.'[95] And again, 'my soul expected reproach and distress.'[96] But there are innumerable good things such as these to contemplate from holy Scripture for profiting the soul.

40. "There is grief [lupē] that is useful, and there is grief that brings destruction. Useful grief includes moaning over our own sins and over our ignorance of things pertaining to our neighbor and toward the completion of our purpose and the achievement of the perfection of goodness. These things therefore are of the type of authentic and good grief. But there is another grief, suggested by the enemy, which anyone knows will cling to these others. For he throws in grief full of unreason, then it is called despair by some.[97] Therefore it is necessary to drive away this spirit mostly by means of prayer and singing of psalms.[98]

41. "When we have good concerns, it is not useful to think that

93. *Alpha. Syn.* 21.
94. Matt 5:12.
95. Ps 4:2 (LXX).
96. Ps 68:21 (LXX). The word translated here "distress" has the nuance of referring specifically to bodily suffering caused by disease.
97. John Cassian *Conf.* 5,11.
98. *Alpha. Syn.* 27.

someone is without cares in this life. For Scripture says, 'all the head is in suffering, and all the heart is in grief.'[99] In one sentence the Holy Spirit has described the monastic life and the worldly life. For by 'the suffering of the head,' the monastic way is signified; for the head is the ruler. For it says, 'the eyes of the wise man are in his head.'[100] Therefore discernment, I think, lies in the head. It says 'suffering' because every bud of virtue is established in sufferings. But by means of 'grief in the heart' it signified the unstable and wretched ethos [of the world]. For some have said that the heart is the dwelling place of anger and grief. Not being glorified, people become aggrieved; desiring for others, they waste away; toiling, they become impatient; being rich, they are driven mad, because on account of guarding their property, they do not sleep.

42. "Therefore we will not seduce ourselves with the thought that people who are in the world are carefree. For perhaps in comparison they toil much more than we do. In general for women the hatred in the world is great; for they bear children difficultly and in danger, and they endure nourishing babies with milk, and they are ill with them when their children are ill; and they survive these things, without having a result for their labor. For either the ones who have been borne in the womb are disabled in their bodies, or in perversity the ones who have been poured forth murder the ones who brought them forth. Therefore knowing these things, let us not be enticed by the enemy, as if having a relaxed and carefree existence. For when they give birth, they perish from sufferings; when they don't bear children, they waste away sterile and childless under reproaches.[101]

43. "I tell you these things so you might be made safe against the adversary. What I have said is not by nature fitting for everyone, but only for those who want the monastic life. For just as one does not offer one single food to animals, so the same word is not useful to all human beings.[102] For 'one ought not to pour new wine,' it says, 'into old wineskins.'[103] For the ones who are filled with contemplation and knowledge feast differently from those who take a taste of ascetic practice and activity, and those who act honestly in the world toward power. For just as some animals live on dry land, others live in water, and others are

---

99. Isa 1:5.
100. Eccl 2:14.
101. This is a common topos for literature concerning female ascetic behavior. See John Chrysostom *Virg.* 51–72, Gregory of Nyssa *Virg.* 3, and other literature cited in Castelli, "Virginity and Its Meaning," 68–70.
102. Evagrius Ponticus *or.* 101.
103. Matt 9:17.

feathered; likewise human beings: the ones who possess the moderate life are like the land animals; those who gaze steadfastly on things above are like the birds; and those who are covered by the waters of sin are like the fish. For 'I came,' it says, 'into the depths of the sea, and the tempest drowned me.'[104] Such is the nature of animals. But we, like eagles having grown wings,[105] will enter the heights and we will tread underfoot lions and dragons; and we will rule over the one who rules today. We will do this if we bring to the Savior our whole mind.

44. "But as much as we raise ourselves toward the heights, the adversary tries to hinder us by means of his own traps. And what great thing is it for us to have adversaries as we rush toward the good, when they feel envy toward worthless things? Certainly they do not assent to people taking buried treasures out of the ground. Therefore, if they are hostile to earthly vision, how much more so do they feel envy toward the kingdom of heaven?[106]

45. "Therefore it is necessary to be armed in all kinds of ways against them. The soul, like a ship, when it is swallowed up by external waves, is overwhelmed by internal bilge water. And certainly at one time even we are destroyed by sins of external actions, at another time we are led astray by internal thoughts. Therefore we must watch out for encounters with external spirits, and drain out the impurities of internal thoughts;[107] and always be vigilant to thoughts, for they occur continuously.[108] In reference to the external waves, when sailors cry out, often the salvation occurs by means of the nearest boat; but the bilge waters, often while the sailors are sleeping and the sea is silent, come in and often kill them.[109]

46. Therefore it is necessary to make the mind more laborious toward the thoughts. For the enemy, wishing to defeat the soul like a house, either makes its overthrow from the foundations, or beginning from the roof, brings down the whole thing, or coming in through the windows, first binds the householder and subdues everything. Therefore the foundation is good works, the roof is faith, and the windows are the senses. The enemy attacks through all of these. Whence one must be many-eyed when one wishes to be saved. We do not have here freedom from

---

104. Ps 68:3 (LXX); 69:2 (RSV).
105. Compare Evagrius Ponticus *or.* 82.
106. Evagrius Ponticus *Praktikos* 59.
107. An extended metaphor is employed here: *antlia* means "bilge water"; continuing the metaphor, *exanteleō* means "to drain off, to empty out of water."
108. *Alpha. Syn.* 24.
109. Compare Athanasius *Vit. Ant.* 20, 55, 89.

anxiety. For the Scripture says, 'Let the one who stands watch lest he fall.'[110]

47. "We sail in obscurity; for our life is called the sea by the holy psalmist David. But there are rocky places in the sea, places full of beasts, as well as calm places. We seem to sail in the calm part of the sea, but worldly people in the dangerous part; and we sail by day guided by the sun of righteousness,[111] but they sail at night, borne by ignorance. But it is often possible for the worldly person in the midst of storm and darkness, crying out and being watchful, to save his own boat; but we in the calm may be submerged by carelessness, neglecting the rudder of righteousness.[112]

48. "'Let the one who stands watch lest he fall.' For the one who falls has only one thought: to stand up again. Let the one who stands guard himself lest he fall. For there are different transgressions. For the ones who fall are deprived of standing; the ones lying down, nothing harms them at all. Let not the one who has stood disparage the one who has fallen, but let him fear him, lest the fallen one perish and he go down into a deeper pit. For it is likely that his cry is being defeated by the depth of the well, and he cannot ask for help. For the just one says: 'Let the depth not swallow me up, nor the cistern close its mouth down over me.'[113] The first one who fell stood fast. Look at yourself, lest in falling down you become dinner for the beasts. The one who has fallen does not secure his door. But you will not be at all drowsy; but always sing that divine saying: 'Make my eyes light, lest I sleep into death.'[114] Be continuously vigilant over the roaring lion.[115]

49. "These words concern what is not raised up. The one who has fallen will be saved through conversion and wailing. You who are standing[116] watch yourself. For fear is laid upon you concerning two things: either that you might return to the old things, with the enemy attacking through your negligence, or that you might be tripped up while running your course. For our enemy the devil, whether he attracts one to him from behind when he sees the soul is slow and sluggish, or it seems to be excellent and patient of toil by means of ascetic practice, he

110. 1 Cor 10:12.
111. See §90; also, for the same metaphor for Christ, see Evagrius Ponticus *Praktikos*, Epilogue; John Cassian *Inst.* 8, 9–10.
112. *Alpha. Syn.* 25.
113. Ps 68:16 (LXX); 69:15 (RSV).
114. Ps 12:4 (LXX); 13:3 (RSV).
115. Athanasius *Vit. Ant.* 7.
116. The feminine participle is used here.

comes in sideways, slightly and covertly, by means of arrogance. And thus he lays aside the soul completely. This tool is the last and most important of all the evils. From it the devil was overthrown, and by means of it he tries to cleanse the most able people. For just as the most fearful of enemies, with their thin arrows spent, and when the warriors are prevailing in battle, they bring forth with them the stronger of all weapons, the sword; just so, the devil, when his first snare is completely used up, then he acquires the last sword, arrogance.[117] But what are his first traps? Clearly, gluttony, love of pleasure, fornication. For these spirits come together mostly in youthful years. Love of money follows after them, then covetousness, and the things like them. Therefore the struggling [athlia] soul, when it prevails over these passions, when it governs the stomach, constrains completely sexual pleasure by means of chastity, and looks disdainfully at money; then the malignant one, perplexed, attacks the soul from all sides through undisciplined movement. For he increases the soul's magnitude by indecently elevating it against its sisters. Heavy and deadly is the poison of this enemy. He cast down suddenly many who were in darkness by means of it. For he suggests to the soul false and death-bearing thought. For he pretends that it apprehends what is unknown to most, that it excels in fasting; and he places before it a multitude of manly deeds [andragathēmata];[118] he bears it into forgetfulness of all sins, toward elevation against those who are with it. For he steals from its mind sins, not because this is useful to him, but so that it might not be able to say the healing word: 'Against you alone I sinned; have mercy on me.'[119] Neither truly will he agree to it, saying, 'I will give thanks to you, Lord, with my whole heart.'[120] But just as that one says in his heart, 'I will ascend and I will put my throne in place,'[121] just so he will delude this one with sovereignties and highest offices, even with teaching positions [didaskaliai] and gifts of healing. Therefore in this way the deceived soul is corrupted and is destroyed, stricken by a wound that is difficult to heal.

50. "Therefore, what should one do, when such thoughts are present? Ceaselessly meditate on the divine word that the blessed David cried out: 'I am a worm and not a human being.'[122] And in another place it

---

117. Evagrius Ponticus *Praktikos* 14.
118. See n. 34.
119. Ps. 50:6, 3; 6:3; 9:14 (LXX).
120. Ps 110:1 (LXX).
121. Isa 14:14.
122. Ps 21:7 (LXX).

says, 'I am earth and ashes.'[123] Still hear the word of Isaiah, 'All human justice is like the rag of one who menstruates.'[124] And if these thoughts enter the anchorite's heart, let her enter a cenobium.[125] Let her be compelled to eat twice a day, if she has fallen into enemy hands in this passion on account of excessive ascetic practice. Let her be punished by women of like age, and let her be rebuked, and let her be greatly censured, as if she has achieved nothing great; let her perform every service. Let the most excellent lives of the saints be presented in interpretation; let those who are with her try to direct themselves by means of toils toward ascetic practice for a few days, so that she, seeing the magnitude of their virtues, will believe her own to be inferior.

51. "This illness is preceded by another evil, disobedience. Whence through the opposite, obedience, it is possible to purify the putrefying cancerous sore of the soul; for it says, 'Obedience is better than sacrifice.'[126]

52. "Therefore it is necessary to purify the swelling of glory in season, and to praise and worship in season. For if the soul is found careless and sluggish, still having grown numb even in advancing toward good, it is fitting to praise it. And if it does a little that is useful, one ought to admire it and invest it with sublimity. And one must speak of the serious and inhumane transgressions as if they were the smallest and most worthless; for the devil, wishing to disturb everything greatly, tries to hide the preexisting sins of the zealous ascetics; for he wants to increase arrogance. He places all sins before the eyes of the novice and insecure souls. For he suggests to it: 'What kind of forgiveness will there be for you who has fornicated?' And he says to another, 'You were so covetous, it is impossible for you to have salvation.' Therefore one must speak gently to weakened souls; for it is necessary to say to them: 'Rahab was a prostitute, but was saved through faith; Paul was a persecutor, but he became a chosen instrument; Matthew was a tax collector, but no one is ignorant of his grace; and the robber pillaged and killed, but he was the first one who opened the door of paradise. Therefore contemplating these, do not despair for your own soul.'

53. "Whenever you find these things fitting, it is necessary to perform a cure for those [souls] captured by arrogance. For it is necessary to say

123. Gen 18:27.
124. Isa 64:6, RSV: "All our righteous deeds are like a polluted garment."
125. Compare John Cassian *Conf.* 19, 2–6.
126. 1 Sam 15:22.

to her: 'Why are you filled with conceit? Because you don't eat meat? Others don't even look at fish. And if you don't drink wine, look: others don't even eat oil. Do you fast until late? Others continue without food for two or three days. Do you think that you are great because you do not bathe? Many, even with bodily suffering, have no use at all for this [a bath]. But you admire yourself, because you sleep on a pallet and in a bed of hair? Others always sleep on the ground. But even if you have done this, it is nothing great; for some cast rocks under themselves, in order not to have any physical pleasure; and others even suspend themselves for the entire night. But even if you did all these things, and even if you performed the most extreme ascetic practice, you ought not to think it great. For demons have done and do more than you do; for they neither eat, nor drink, nor marry, nor sleep; but they live in the desert, even inhabiting a cave, if you think doing that is a great thing.'

54. "Therefore in this way and with such words it is possible to cure the two opposing passions: I mean despair and arrogance. For just as a fire violently blown out and scattered is destroyed, or dies when there is no wind; just so virtue flies away through disdain while it receives most violently ascetic practice; and the good is also destroyed from lack of care, when we do not direct it completely toward the breath of the divine spirit. A pointed sword is readily shattered under a rock; and ascetic practice that is quickly intensified dies from being treated arrogantly. Wherefore it is fitting for the soul to be made safe from all sides, and to turn back toward the shadowy places the harshest ascetic practice inflamed by the fever of arrogance, and sometimes to prune back the extravagant things, so that the root might become more flourishing.

55. "Compel the one who is trapped by mounting despair to reread the words that have gone before. For the soul that falls to the ground is violent. And certainly the best of farmers, when they see a short and weak plant, water it plentifully and deem it worthy of great care in order that it might grow. And when they see a bud that is untimely in growth, they cut off the excess; for these are wont to be readily dried up. And doctors treat some weak children abundantly, and they urge them to walk; but they watch over others, who are bound without food.

56. "Therefore it is clear that arrogance is the greatest among the evils. And from this its opposite, humility, shows itself. It is difficult to acquire humility. For if one is not far from all glory, one will not be able to value this treasure. Humility is so great that the devil seems to imitate all the virtues but does not know this one at all. Knowing its security and

steadfastness, the apostle commands us to be clothed in it,[127] and to be surrounded by it, all doing useful things. For if you fast, and if you give alms, or if you teach: if you are wise and intelligent, it will furnish you again with an impregnable fort. Let humility, the most beautiful of all virtues, reinforce and keep your virtues from dispersing. Look at the canticle of the three holy children, how not mentioning at all other virtues, they included the humble ones with the singers, not mentioning the wise or the poor. For just as it is impossible for a ship to be built without nails, just so it is impossible to be saved without humility.[128]

57. "Because it has grown up both good and salvific, the Lord, completing the economy [of salvation] for human beings, put it [humility] on.[129] For it says, 'Learn from me, that I am gentle and humble in heart.'[130] Behold the one who speaks; one must learn perfectly from him. Let humility be the beginning and end of goodness for you. He speaks of humble thought; he refers not only to external form but to the internal human being. Have you performed all the commandments? The Lord knows, but he urges you again to take up the beginning of servitude. For it says: 'When you do all these things, say: "We are unworthy servants."'[131]

58. "Therefore humility corrects by means of reproaches, by means of violence, by means of blows; in order that you might hear through the foolish and the stupid, the poor person and the beggar, the weak one and the insignificant, the one who makes no progress in work, the illogical in expression, the dishonorable in appearance, the weak in power. These things are the sinews of humility. These things our Lord heard and suffered. For he spoke to the Samaritan himself and to the one who had a demon. He took the form of a slave, he was beaten, he was tortured with blows.

59. "Therefore it is necessary for us to imitate these acts of humility. Therefore there are some who pretend by means of external forms and humble themselves, while they hunt glory by these means; but they are recognized by their fruits, for they did not bear being insulted even superficially, but immediately they vomited their own poison like serpents."

60. The ones who were gathered rejoiced greatly and robustly at these

---

127. 1 Pet 5:5.
128. *Alpha. Syn.* 26.
129. Migne's Greek text is jumbled here: the third line in his text should come after the two lines that follow it.
130. Matt 11:29.
131. Luke 17:10. Cf. §23.

words, and again they persisted in not having taken their fill of good things. And again the blessed one spoke to them: "The contest is great for those who are coming to God, and it is struggle at first, but then the joy is indescribable. For just as those who wish to kindle a fire first are burned and cry, thus they obtain what they desire; for it says: 'Our God is a consuming fire.'[132] Thus it is necessary for us to kindle the divine fire in ourselves through tears and struggle. For the Lord himself says: 'I came to cast fire on the earth.'[133] Some by means of neglect bear the smoke, but do not kindle the fire, because of the patience that is outside of them, but especially because of their weak and obscure relationship with the divine.

61. "Whence charity is a great treasure; and concerning this the apostle said: 'If you distribute all your belongings, and mortify the body, but have no love, you are a noisy gong or a clanging cymbal.'[134] Therefore charity is great among the good, while anger is terrible among the evil; for darkening and enraging every soul, anger bears one toward unreason. But the Lord, being concerned in every way with salvation, does not allow the soul to be short and uncovered. Does the enemy mobilize lust? Our Lord cultivated chastity. Does he cause arrogance to be born? But humility is not far away. Did he enliven hate? But charity is present in the midst of it. Therefore as much as the enemy waves his sword against us, all the more so our Lord made us safe with instruments, toward our salvation and toward the fall of the enemy.

62. "Anger is the evil among evils. 'For the anger of a man,' it says, does not work the righteousness of God.'[135] Therefore it is necessary to rule over it because it appeared useful at certain times; for it is useful to be angry and to move against demons.[136] It is not seemly to be moved violently toward a person, even if s/he sins; but it is necessary to convert him/her after the emotion of anger has been made to cease.

63. "To be angry is a lesser of the evils; but the remembrance of injuries is the weightiest of all. For anger, like smoke, having disturbed the soul for a little while, is dissolved. But the remembrance of injuries, fixing in the soul, performs more terribly than a wild beast; when a dog, driven mad with passion against someone, when soothed with food gives up his anger; and other wild beasts are appeased by customary

132. Heb 12:29; Deut 4:24; 9:3. Cf. *Alpha. Syn.* 1.
133. Luke 12:49.
134. Composite of 1 Cor 13:3 and 13:1; Syncletica has made a rather interesting interpolation into the text!
135. Jas 1:20.
136. Evagrius Ponticus *or.* 24.

things. But the one ruled by memories of past injuries is not persuaded by consolation, nor tamed by food, and time that changes everything does not cure this emotion. Therefore, these people who suffer this emotion are the most atheistic and impious of all. For they do not obey the Savior who says: 'Go, first be reconciled to your brother; then bring your gift.'[137] And elsewhere: 'Do not let the sun go down,' it says, 'on your anger.'[138]

64. "Therefore it is good not to be angry, but if it happens, he did not allow the space of a day to the emotion, for he said, 'do not let the sun set.' And you wait until your whole time sets. Do you not know how to say: 'The day's own trouble is sufficient for the day'?[139] Why do you hate the person who injures you? Hate the illness, not the person who suffers the illness.[140] Why do you glory in evil, powerful one?[141] Concerning you the psalmist cried this out: for 'lawlessness,' he says, 'the whole day.'[142] That is, throughout the time of your life you disobey the lawgiver who says: 'Do not let the sun set on your anger,' and 'your tongue reckons injustice.'[143] For you do not rest from slandering your brother. Whence your just punishment is borne from the hymnist from out of the Spirit: 'For because of this,' he says, 'God defeats you in the end, plucks you out and sends you out of the tabernacle, and your root out of the land of the living.'[144] These are the gifts of memories of past injuries; these are the contest prizes of evil.

65. "Therefore one must guard against remembering past injuries, for many terrible things follow from this: envy, grief, backbiting talk. The evils of these are bearers of death, although they may seem to be slight. For they are like the thin arrow of the enemy. Often the wounds from a double-edged blade and a bigger sword—these are fornication and covetousness, and murder—are cured often through the saving drug of conversion; but arrogance or memory of past injuries or backbiting, seeming to be like a small arrow and escaping notice, destroy by being fixed firmly in crucial parts of the soul. But these do not kill by the greatness of the blow, but through the carelessness of the wounded ones; for while disregarding the backbiting and the rest, little by little one is killed by them.

137. Matt 5:24.
138. Eph 4:26.
139. Matt 6:34.
140. *Alpha. Syn.* 13.
141. Ps 51:3 (LXX); 52:1 (RSV).
142. Ps 51:3 (LXX); 52:1–2 (RSV).
143. Ps 51:4 (LXX); 52:2 (RSV).
144. Ps 51:7 (LXX); 52:5 (RSV).

66. "Therefore backbiting talk is serious and wicked; for it becomes the food and the resting place of some people. But do you not accept vain hearsay, and do not become the receptacle of other people's evils. Prepare your own soul as free from superfluity. For receiving the stinking impurity of words, you will introduce stains into your prayer by means of thoughts, and you will hate without reason those whom you might encounter.[145] For you will dip your ear under the inhumanity of evil talk, you will contemplate everything lowly born. Just as the eye, immoderately preoccupied by color, has seen an indistinguishable fantasy surrounding things.

67. "Therefore it is necessary to guard the tongue and the ear, so as not to say anything about anyone, nor to hear anything with great eagerness. For it is written, 'Do not receive a false report'[146] and 'the one who speaks against his neighbor secretly, I banished him.'[147] In the psalmist it says, 'that my mouth might not speak the works of people.'[148] But we speak of things that are not works. Therefore it is necessary not to believe the things said, nor to condemn the ones who say them. But act and speak in accordance with divine Scripture: 'Like a deaf person I did not hear, and like a mute I did not open my mouth.'[149]

68. "One ought not rejoice over the misfortune of a person, no matter if s/he is very much a sinner. For some, when they see him/her whipped or imprisoned, said in an uneducated way that worldly proverb: 'the one who spreads [his couch] badly will endure hardship during the meal.'[150] Therefore you, who have spread your affairs well, will you have the courage to rest in life? And what do we do with the one who says, 'One event is for the righteous and the sinner'?[151] For here the condition of life is singular for us, although we have different behavior.

69. "One ought not hate enemies. For even the Lord in his own voice commanded this to us. For he says, 'Do not love only those who love you; for even sinners and tax collectors do this.'[152] For good does not require skill or contest for its pursuit; for it attracts to itself those who love it. But evil needs divine teaching to expunge it, and much suffering. For

---

145. Evagrius Ponticus *or.* 20–22.
146. Exod 23:1.
147. Ps 100:5 (LXX); 101:5 (RSV).
148. Ps 16:4 (LXX); 17:3–4 (RSV).
149. Ps 37:14 (LXX); 38:14 (RSV).
150. Apparently this proverb refers to dining couches on which one reclines while eating; the proverb may be analogous to the English saying, "You've made your bed, now lie in it."
151. Eccl 9:2.
152. Matt 5:46.

the kingdom of heaven does not belong to the relaxed or those who are free from anxiety, but to the violent.

70. "Therefore just as one ought not hate one's enemies, likewise one ought not flee or sneer at the negligent or the indifferent. Since some attribute to themselves that scriptural word: 'You are holy with the holy, and you distort yourself when together with the crooked.'[153] According to this, it says, we flee the sinners in order not to be perverted with them. Out of ignorance of soul, these people are the opposite. For the Holy Spirit commands not to be distorted along with the crooked, but for those ones to be restored from crookedness. For 'you distort yourself together with' means you draw together to yourself, from the left and from the right.

71. "Three types of notions exist concerning the life of human beings. The first is of the highest evil, the second of some middle condition, for it looks to both while partaking in neither one. The third, led in great contemplation, strengthens not only itself, but also tries to lead the ones behind by the hand. Therefore the evil among human beings, mixed with the ones who are worse, greatly increase terrible things. The middle ones try to flee the licentious ones, fearing lest they be dragged down again by them. For they are still babies with respect to the virtues. The third group, having virile [andreia] thought and strong mind, spend time together with bad people and dwell together with them, wishing to save them. And certainly they are reproached by those outside, and they are treated scornfully by those who see them spending time with those who are more neglectful; for they reprove them as if they were like them. Those hearing as praises the things they receive from human beings gladly accomplish the divine work. For it says, 'Rejoice and be glad, when people speak every lie against you.'[154] Therefore the action of these people is lordly, for even the Lord ate with tax collectors and sinners; but the condition of these is that love of sibling is better than love of self. For they see sinners as houses in flames, and having little regard for their own, they are relied upon to save what belongs to others that is being destroyed. And being burnt from the caustic violence, they endure in the face of it. But the ones in the middle, when they see their brother being consumed by sin, flee. They fear lest the fire might be spread to them. But the third group, maintaining the custom of their evil neighbors, kindle excessively the ones who burned, bearing toward

153. Ps 17:26, 27 (LXX); 18:26 (RSV).
154. Matt 5:11, 12 (a combination of portions of these two verses).

them their own evil as wood to perdition. Like taking a pitching boat, they throw oil on it instead of water. But the ones who are opposite to these, the good people, placed their own possessions second to the salvation of the others. These things are the sure signs of true charity; such ones are the guardians of pure charity.

72. "The terrible things depend one upon the other; for jealousy, sadness, perjury, anger, and remembrance of past injuries follow from love of money; thus the opposites of these are held by charity: gentleness, I mean, and patience, and forbearance, and the perfect good, voluntary poverty. For it is not possible for one to achieve this virtue (I mean charity) if not through voluntary poverty;[155] for the Lord did not send charity to one person, but to all. Therefore the ones who have must not avoid noticing those who are in need. For what is of charity is concealed from notice; for to excel in everything is impossible for a human being; this work is God's.

73. "Therefore, why, one says, does the one who possesses nothing struggle concerning almsgiving and it becomes for you a pretext for acquiring? This was commanded to the worldly people. For almsgiving is not ordained so much for the maintenance of the poor as in accordance with charity. For the God who controls the rich supports the poor. Therefore is almsgiving commanded unnecessarily? Not at all! But it becomes the beginning of charity for those who do not know it. For just as the foreskin is the model of circumcision of the heart, just so almsgiving exists as the teacher of charity. Therefore for those to whom charity is given out of grace, almsgiving is unnecessary.

74. "I say these things not to reproach mercy but to display the purity of voluntary poverty. Therefore let not the lesser be a prevention to the greater. In a short time you corrected the small portion, for you have given everything at once. Look up at the greater remaining portion, that is, charity. For you are a cross bearer. You ought to speak in the freer voice: 'Behold we have given up everything, and we have followed you.'[156] You have been deemed worthy to imitate the confident tongue of the apostles. For Peter and John say, 'I have no gold or silver.'[157] The tongue is double, but the faith is one.

75. "Let not almsgiving be done openly by the worldly people. For it says, 'Do not anoint my head with the oil of a sinner.'[158] Therefore it is

---

155. Evagrius Ponticus *Praktikos* 18.
156. Matt 19:27.
157. Acts 3:6.
158. Ps 140:5 (LXX); 141:5 (RSV).

fitting for the almsgiver to have the judgment of Abraham, and like him to perform a just act justly. For the just one was hospitable, and provided with his hearth his judgment. For, it says, he stood as a servant, not wishing that slaves become sharers in the benefit. Such ones who truthfully possess hatred of almsgiving are assigned the second division. For the Lord who created the world placed two classes of inhabitants upon it. For some who live in a holy way he ordained marriage in order to produce children; for the others he ordained chastity for the highest purity of life, making them like angels; and he gave to them laws, vindications, and doctrines. It says to them: '"Vengeance is mine, I will repay," says the Lord.'[159] Here it says, 'You will work the earth'[160] and he exhorts, 'Do not be anxious for tomorrow.'[161] He gave the law to these ones; but through his grace he made known by our own eyes his commandments to us.

76. "The cross is the trophy of victory to us. For our profession is nothing but the renunciation of life, the rehearsal of death.[162] Therefore just as the dead do not operate in the body, so neither do we. Forasmuch as was accomplished by the body, we have done it when we were infants. For the apostle says, 'The world is crucified to me, and I to the world.'[163] We live in the spirit. We demonstrate virtue through it; we are merciful in accordance with the mind; for 'blessed are the merciful'[164] in soul. For just as it says here, that the one who desires a beautiful woman, even if his actions are different, performed the sin unwitnessed; just so, here almsgiving is spoken of: the intention brings the act to completion, even if silver is absent, we have been honored by a great worth.

77. "For just as the lords of the world have obtained slaves for different services: they send some out into the fields to work the earth, and to guard the succession of the race; others, if they observe those born among them to be gentle and very beautiful, they transfer them into their own houses for their own service. Likewise the Lord, having taken some in holy marriage, placed them in the fields of the world; but the ones who are better than these, mostly having been of fortunate choice, he drafted into his service. These ones are alienated from all earthly

---

159. Rom 12:19.
160. Gen 3:23.
161. Matt 6:34.
162. Plato *Phd.* 81a describes the practice of philosophy with the same language, *meletē thanatou.*
163. Gal 6:14.
164. Matt 5:7.

matters; for they were deemed worthy of the Master's table. They are not anxious concerning clothing; for they are clothed in Christ.

78. "Therefore the Lord is one master of both groups. For just as the husk and the seed are of the same grain, so from one God are both the ones who live devoutly according to the world and the ones who profess the solitary life. And clearly both are useful: leaves are for the service and protection of the seed, but the acquisition of fruit is also necessary, for it is the beginning of everything. For just as it is not possible to be plant and seed at once, so it is not possible when the glory of the world surrounds us to make heavenly fruit.[165] When leaves break off, and the corn stalk has dried up, the ear of corn is fit for the harvest. And therefore we, rejecting the illusion of the earth as though it were the leaves, and drying our bodies up like the stalk, and elevating our thoughts, we will be able to produce the seed of salvation.

79. "It is dangerous for the one who has not been led by means of a life of activity to endeavor to teach. For just as, if someone has an unsound house and receives strangers hospitably into it, he injures them in the fall of the house; just so such ones who have not first built themselves up securely, they destroy the ones who have come with them. They summoned to salvation with words, but rather they injured the ones gathered to them by the evil of their habits.[166] For the unfortified exposition of words is like letters composed from colors that easily fall off, dissolved in the least amount of time by gusts of wind and drops of rain; but the teaching that is practiced all eternity cannot dissolve. For the word, carving out substantial things on the soul, bestows forever an image of Christ in the faithful.

80. "Therefore it is necessary that we perform the cure of the soul, not a superficial cure, but that we order the whole soul completely, especially not neglecting its depth. We have performed the removal of the hair; let us also carry away the worms in the head. For such things left alone cause us to suffer all the more. For our hair was the ornament according to life: honors, glories, the acquisition of possessions, bright raiment of clothing, the intimacies of baths, pleasures of food. We were determined to cast these things away, but let us still more cast off the soul-destroying works. But what are such things? Backbiting, perjury, love of money. Therefore our head is the soul; when wild beasts were

165. *Alpha. Syn.* 22.
166. *Alpha. Syn.* 12.

watched out for in the woods of worldly affairs, they seemed to escape notice; but now having practiced, they are conspicuous to all. Because of this, the more insignificant sins are clearly seen among virgins and monks, for just as in a clean house the small visible insect becomes clearly seen by all, even the smallest one. But among worldly people as in corrupted caves the greatest of hidden poisonous animals escapes notice, concealed by the surrounding forest. Therefore we must clean our house continuously and look around, lest any of the soul-destroying insects might penetrate into the treasuries of the soul; and make holy through sacrificial fire the places with the divine incense of prayer.[167] For just as one casts out the poisonous animals with the more piercing quality of medicine, just so prayer with fasting chases away foul thought.[168]

81. "One of the soul-destroying wild beasts is to be dragged down on the part of those who talk about fate, even if they call it 'genesis.' This is the most terrible nail of the devil. When often he only moves pestilential illusion against the mind of serious souls, and then he flies away; but he dominates the more negligent. For no one of those living according to virtue believes in or accepts the deranged and vain notion of this one. For s/he places God as the beginning of all goods that have existed and that now exist; and secondly s/he appoints God in her/his own mind as the chief and judge of virtue and vice. Such ones who have suffered from thoughtlessness and apathy come immediately to that demon. For just as children who desert their post and do not recall the education from their parents for their use, they, shrinking back, gain possession of the desert spaces and are united with wild and barbarous demons.[169] For fearing to place the blame for their own actions on their intentions, they calumniate things that are not there.

82. "Further rejecting the divine from themselves, they say that things having to do with pleasure happen to them because of their birth. For fornicating and stealing, being ill with love of money and craftiness, they stand in awe of your acts, and bend from the truth. Their achievement of the goal is despair that brings ruin to them. For it is necessary from these thoughts that God is removed from them, and over and above God, God's judgment. For they say, 'If he has judged me this, to fornicate or to be covetous, judgment is superfluous. For the punishment

---

167. Evagrius Ponticus *or.* 75.
168. *Alpha. Syn.* 3.
169. The text reads *marmarōdesi*, but the editor notes the alternate reading *Barbarōdesi*. If the first is correct, the text might read, "wild and hard [marblelike] demons."

of voluntary sins is just; but the involuntary act that comes from some origin renders its performer innocent.' And from this judgment is annulled.

83. "One must hear how the divine is also cast away from them. For they say in their vanity that it is either first or second or always existent. Therefore if they say God precedes, it will follow by necessity that all things are made by him, for he is in everything. Surely he is the lord of fate. If one is a covetous person or a fornicator from one's origin, it is necessary through the mediator of this birth that God himself is the cause of evil; the very thing is outrageous. If they say that God is the second, it is obvious that he would be subject to the first; and whoever wishes the principal, to this one necessarily the one who comes after will follow. And again God is guilty of evils for them; the very thing is wicked. And if they wish him to be coeternal, they move to combat those things that are naturally opposed. Therefore from these thoughts their vain idea is completely rejected. Concerning these Scripture spoke: 'The foolish one says in his heart, "God does not exist,"'[170] and 'They spoke lawlessness into the heights.'[171]

84. "They make excuses with pretexts for their sins. For they mutilate the Scriptures, being blind and wishing to give assurance to their depravity from them. First trying to vomit forth from the gospel their own poison, they do great violence. For it says, 'thus was the birth of the Christ.'[172] The divine Scripture called his birth 'genesis.' Yet the birth among human beings according to the economy [of the incarnation] is called 'genesis.' But if they spread false reports concerning the star, let them learn again his glorious coming. For us the brightest star became the herald of truth; but the vain opinion of those ones bears many away to the pursuit of the human birth. And from this it has been shown that in every way evil is hostile to itself. And they call Isaiah into witness for their folly. For they say that he said this: 'Lord maker of peace and creator of evil.'[173] Therefore peace is acknowledged by all as being the work of God, but evil truly is practiced by them, evil coming from the soul. For us, the evil that is originated from God is the most useful kind. For toward the salvation of the soul and the education of the body are there famines and droughts, illnesses and sufferings, and all other various accidents. For the salvific remedies that they supposed were evil of

170. Ps 13:1 (LXX); 14:1 (RSV).
171. Ps 72:8 (LXX); 73:8 (RSV).
172. Matt 1:18.
173. Isa 45:7.

the soul were not truly evil, these bear conversion to us from the mightier one. 'For what son is there that the father does not educate?'[174] Moreover 'his ways are not in the human being,'[175] again in the same way they bring forward their own destruction; having no paths, they want to search one out. Covetousness, gluttony, fornication are not a path; for these things are without independent existence not befitting themselves. For these people are wont to say that these are paths. Scripture says that our paths are common to all, that of life and that of death. For truly the journeys are of beginning here and of migrating out of these senses.

85. "Therefore those possessed by an evil genius will do anything for their rejection of free will. They are even placed by means of this zeal to exchange freedom for slavery. For this is the work of evil, always to drag down others together with it to the worse. For they became witnesses for themselves, as ones who sold themselves to evil. Therefore this is the deceptive handiwork of the devil. For he prepares careless souls by means of heresy to be stooped, not allowing them to come to their senses through knowledge of the truth. For just as a boat sailing without a rudder is always afflicted, so danger always breathes upon them, for no one is able to start toward the salvific harbor who abandons the Lord who steers the boat. He thus leads astray the souls devoted to him. Often the enemy lies in ambush for the zealous souls on account of these, wishing to cut off their good race. For he throws in that to do well comes from the movement of the stars. But the adversary brings this thought to those who have turned from worldly wisdom to the solitary life; for the devil, being intelligent in evil matters, sets up traps for human nature. For he is constantly present for them through despair; he drags some down by vainglory, he destroys others by love of riches. For just as a death-bearing doctor brings poison to humans; and he destroys one through the liver, bringing him the toxin of desire; another he makes wounded in the heart, fastening his temper to anger. He blunts the principal power of some, surrounding them with ignorance, or twisting them by means of superstition.

86. "Therefore he diverted some by means of inquiries that were not straight. For wanting to discuss concerning God and his nature, they suffered shipwreck. Not holding the reins on the active life, they rushed headlong toward contemplation, and becoming dizzy, they have fallen down.[176] Having not undertaken the first thing in an orderly way, they

174. Heb 12:7.
175. Jer 10:23.
176. Evagrius Ponticus or. 145–46.

failed to achieve the second thing. For just as those who encounter the letter 'alpha' see first its form, then are taught its name second, and thusly they learn the number, and finally they apprehend the accents. Therefore if there is such a need of practice and art for the first letter, how much more labor and time is needed for the creator, being led into contemplation of the one deemed worthy of inexpressible glory? But let not anyone prance about for having gained possession of the divine through having begun from external teachings. For such a one deceives himself, deluded by the demon. For the hymnist says: 'From the mouth of infants and sucklings you have restored dread.'[177] And the Lord in the gospel: 'Let the children come to me, for the kingdom of heaven belongs to such ones.'[178] And elsewhere, 'If you do not become like children, you will not enter the kingdom of heaven.'[179] You were educated for the sake of the world; become dull for God's sake.[180] Cut off the old, that you might grow the new. Take down the unsound foundations, in order that you might put on the adamantine pedestal of the Lord, in order that you like the apostle might be built up on solid rock.

87. "Therefore it is not necessary to be contentious. Do not be occupied greatly by speaking too much. For the devil is able to do damage by means of untimely nonsense. For he has many traps, and he is a terrifying hunter. For the smallest sparrows he places tiny snares; for the great birds he prepares strong nets. Weighty and death-bearing is the net that is faith in birth [fate]. The thought toward this is to be avoided. But does he persuade you by means of events foreknown? The trope proceeds by guesswork; the notion is unstable. For nothing necessary follows what was said by them; for just as to some individuals and sailors out of the particular nature of clouds there is a certain obscure knowledge of winds and rain; just so to these an unsound foreknowledge is present from demons. For certainly they say some things by conjecture, as even ventriloquists do. But this may be able best to put a stop to the bad thought: for if these false-speaking conjectures were constituted by demons, vain is the art of those who attach importance to them.

88. "But if the enemy continues to plead his case about these things, overcome him by means of this, by the fact that he attacks the soul sometimes with other thoughts. For that which is unstable is uncertain. And what is uncertain is near to perdition. For the devil is not satisfied with one's first evil; but rather he suggests to the soul chance. And he

177. Ps 8:3 (LXX); 8:2 (RSV).
178. Luke 18:16.
179. Matt 18:3.
180. 1 Cor 3:18.

represents our principal mind as a flower of nature, that when our body is dissolved, the soul will be destroyed as well. He suggests all these things to us so that the soul might be destroyed through carelessness. But when these shadowy phantasms appear, let us not agree to these as to truths. For these things demonstrate their evil, having come at one time in one way and otherwise at another time, then flying away in the blink of an eye. Certainly I know a certain servant of God living in accordance with virtue, who, when sitting in her cell, looked out for the introduction of thoughts; and she kept count of which was the first, which was the second, and for how much time each one of them held her; and whether she fell short of or exceeded the day before. Thus she knew accurately the grace of God and her own endurance as well as her power, in addition to the defeat of the enemy.

89. "Therefore we must observe these received rules. For the ones who traffic in the affairs that are transient weigh the profits each day, and gladly they receive more and hate losses. Much more than this is it fitting for the traffickers to watch over the true treasure and to long after the multitude of good; if some small theft of the enemy occurs, to bear it in a dignified fashion for the sake of being judged, but not to give up hope on themselves, and to cast away everything because of an involuntary mistake. You have ninety-nine sheep; seek the one that is lost. Do not be terrified because of the one, do not flee the Master, or the bloodthirsty devil will destroy your entire flock, capturing it through his actions. Therefore do not desert on account of the one; for the Master is good. For he says through the psalmist: 'If he falls, he will not be cast down, because the Lord sustains his hand.'[181]

90. "Forasmuch as we do or profit here, we believe that these are slight compared to the future eternal wealth.[182] For on this earth it is as though we are in the second maternal womb. For we do not have such a life in those innermost parts. For we did not enjoy such solid food in those places as now; we were not able to work as we can here; for we do not enjoy the light of the sun and all external rays. Therefore just as occupying those receptacles, we were lacking many things of the world; thus in this current world we covet the kingdom of heaven. We took a taste of the food from here, yearning for divine food. We have enjoyed the light here, longing for the sun of justice.[183] We believe the Jerusalem above is our city and our mother. We will call God our father. We will live here wisely, in order that we might have eternal life.

181. Ps 36:24 (LXX); 37:24 (RSV).
182. Athanasius *Vit. Ant.* 17.
183. See §47 for other parallels.

91. "For just as the fetuses inside their mother, perfected from diminished food and life, and because of this are brought to a greater security [sōtēria]; likewise the righteous withdraw from the ways of the world for the higher journey, according to what has been written: 'from power to power.'[184] Sinners, like the embryos dead in the womb in the mother, are handed over from darkness to darkness. For they die on earth, covered in the multitude of their sins; and led away from life, they are borne down to dark and hellish places. We are born into life three times. The first is the going forth from the maternal bosom, when we pass from the earth to the earth. The two remaining pass us from earth to heaven: one is out of grace, which comes to us through divine Baptism, for we call this truly a regeneration; the third accrues out of our conversion and good works. In this one we stand now.

92. "We are obliged now, coming to our true Bridegroom, to be adorned more decently. Let the vision of worldly marriage become for us an edifice. For if those who are connected to a man who is easily caught execute such care with baths and anointings with oil and varied ornamentations (for out of these they imagine themselves prepared as more lovable), and if such a fantasy inspires those who live according to the body, how much more therefore should we, those ones betrothed to the heavenly Bridegroom, transcend the notion of washing off the filth of our sins through strenuous ascetic practice, exchanging spiritual garments for bodily ones. Those ones adorn the body with worldly and earthly blossoms; we make the soul bright with virtues. Instead of precious stones we place on our head the threefold crown: faith, hope, and charity; we place around our neck the honorable adornment, humility; instead of a belt, we gird ourselves with chastity; let voluntary poverty be our garment; let incorruptible foods be brought to the table, that is, prayers and psalms. But as the apostle says: move not only the tongue, but also perceive by the spirit what is said. For often the mouth utters a sound, but the heart is occupied by thoughts. We ought to pay heed, lest when we come to the divine wedding we become ill from a lack of light, that is to say, of virtue. For our betrothed will not at all receive us hospitably unless he receives our promises. But what are these? To be concerned less with the body, but to a great extent to irrigate the soul; for these are the things assented to him.

93. "For just as it is impossible to bring up two well buckets full of water at the same time; for because of the turning axle, the empty one descends, while the other full one comes up; thus it is also for us: when

184. Ps 83:8 (LXX); 84:7 (RSV).

we will bear to our soul every solicitude, it comes up full of good things, aimed at the heights. Our body, which becomes empty by means of ascetic practice, does not weigh down the directed power. The apostle, as a witness to this, says: 'As much as the external person is corrupted, that much the internal person is restored.'[185]

94. "Do you happen to be in a cenobitic monastery? Do not exchange your place. For that would do great harm. For just as birds departing from their eggs, prepare them watery and sterile; thus the virgin or monk cools and kills the faith, changing from place to place.[186]

95. "Let not the luxury of riches according to the world allure you, as if having some use. For the sake of pleasure, people honor culinary skill; may you excel their ease with the taking of foods in your fasting by means of your frugality. For it says, 'The soul, in being filled, mocks honeycomb.'[187] Do not be glutted with bread, and you will not desire wine.[188]

96. "There are three principal heads of the enemy, from which all evil descends: desire, pleasure, grief. These depend one upon the other, and one follows from the other; one may be able in a measure to govern over pleasure, but one cannot govern over desire. For the one is fulfilled by pleasure through the body; the other begins from the soul. But grief is furnished out of both of these. Therefore do not allow desire to operate, and the rest you will disperse. But if you allow the first to emerge, it is spread toward the second, they will make a circle of retribution toward themselves, and in no way will it allow the soul to recover. For it is written: 'Do not give water a way out.'[189]

97. "All things do not confer a benefit on all; let each one have full satisfaction according to his/her own mind. Because it is fitting for many to be in a cenobium, and for others it is useful to withdraw [anachōreō] by themselves.[190] For the very thing is true of plants: those that are in moist places become more flourishing, while those in dry places become more stable; of human beings some behave well in the elevated places, while some are maintained in humbler places. Therefore many are saved in the city, imagining themselves in the desert; and many are destroyed, being in the mountains, acting as though they were in a

---

185. 2 Cor 4:16.
186. *Alpha. Syn.* 6.
187. Prov 27:7.
188. *Alpha. Syn.* 4.
189. Sir 25:25.
190. Contrast John Cassian *Inst.* 8, 18.

populated place. It is possible while being with many people to be alone in spirit, and being alone to spend time with the crowd in the mind.[191]

98. "Many are the nails of the devil. Did he not alter a soul through suffering? He presents wealth as bait. Is he not able through the use of violence and reproaches? He produces praise and glory. Is he defeated through health? He infects the body with disease. For not being able to deceive by means of pleasures, he tries to bring about the unchosen and undesired perversion of the soul through involuntary labors. For he introduces the gravest illnesses in order by means of neglect to confuse their love for God. But if the body is cut up, and consumed by the most violent burning heat, and still oppressed by incurable and unrestrained thirst; if being a sinner supports these things, remember the future torture and the eternal fire and the judicial punishments, and do not neglect the present. Rejoice that the Lord visited you, and keep on your tongue the auspicious word, 'the Lord disciplining has disciplined me, but he has not handed me over to the death'[192] of sin. You were iron, but you cast out rust because of the fire. If being just you are in ill health, you progress from the great things to the greater. You are gold, but you become more excellent through the fire. The angel Satan was given to you in your flesh; I rejoice greatly, look at the one to whom you become similar. For you were judged worthy of the gift of Paul. You are approved after testing by fire, trained by cold, but Scripture says: 'We went through fire and water.'[193] What remains is to prepare the place of refreshment. You experienced the first, expect the second. While working cry out the words of the holy David, for he says: 'Toiling and poor and suffering am I.'[194] You will become perfect through these three. For it says, 'In affliction you expand for me.'[195] In these exercises especially, let us train our souls, for under our eyes we see the adversary.[196]

99. "Let us not become aggrieved that through weakness and plague of the body we are not able to stand in prayer or sing with our voices; all these things are accomplished to our advantage, toward the purification of desires. For both fasting and sleeping on the ground have been prescribed to us because of shameful pleasures. Therefore if sickness blunted these things, toiling is superfluous. But why do I say superfluous? For just as through the better and stronger remedy for illness the

191. *Alpha. Syn.* 19.
192. Ps 117:18 (LXX); 118:18 (RSV).
193. Ps 65:12 (LXX); 66:12 (RSV).
194. Ps 68:30 (LXX); 69:29 (RSV).
195. Ps 4:2 (LXX); 4:1 (RSV).
196. *Alpha. Syn.* 7.

accidents that bring ruin are put to sleep. And this is the great ascetic practice, which perseveres in illnesses, and offers up thanksgiving songs to the powerful one.[197] Are we deprived of our eyes? Let us not bear it heavily; for we have cast out the organs of insatiate desire, but we see with our inner eyes the glory of the Lord. Are we deaf and dumb? Let us give thanks for having cast out completely vain hearing. Have we suffered because of our hands? But we have the internal hands made ready for the war against the enemy. Does illness control our whole body? But the health of the internal person will greatly increase.

100. "Being in a cenobium, we greatly prefer obedience of ascetic practice. For it teaches contempt[198] and it promises humility.[199] But there is also an intense ascetic practice that comes from the enemy. For his disciples practice it. Therefore how do we distinguish the divine and royal ascesis from the tyrannical and demonic? Clearly, through moderation. Let there arise all the time one canon of fasting. Do not fast for four or five days, and the next day break the fast with a multitude of food. This is the pleasure of the enemy. Everywhere intemperance is deadly. Do not use up all your weapons in one battle; found naked in battle, you will become an easy target. Our weapons are the body, and the soul is the soldier, and both are engaged toward useful things. Being young and healthy, fast. For old age will come with weakness. As you are able, store up food, so that, when you are not able, you will find it.[200] Fast with logic and scrupulousness. Watch lest the enemy come into the trading place of the fast; and this is perhaps what, I think, the Savior spoke concerning this: 'Be trustworthy moneychangers,'[201] that is, know exactly the divine imprint; for there are counterfeit coins;[202] the nature of the gold is the same, but they differ in imprint. The gold of one is fasting, continence, almsgiving; but the children of the Greeks put on them the image of their tyrant, and all the heretics honor these. It is necessary to watch and to flee them as one would a counterfeiter. Watch lest, falling untrained among them, you are damaged. Therefore receive with security the cross of Christ imprinted with virtues, that is, straight [orthos] faith with holy acts.

197. *Alpha. Syn.* 8.
198. This term is used as a virtue here.
199. *Alpha. Syn.* 16.
200. Compare *Alpha. Syn.* 15.
201. This saying from oral tradition is found also in John Cassian *Conf.* 1, 20.
202. This term, *paracharagma*, literally means "false coin," but also has the figurative meaning of "false doctrine."

101. "We must govern our soul with every discretion, being in a cenobium, not seeking our own ways, not being enslaved to our own mind, but obeying the mother according to faith.[203] We handed ourselves over to exile; that is, we are on the outside of worldly boundaries; therefore we have been cast out; let us not seek after the same things. There we had glory, here reproaches. There an abundance of food, here lack of bread. In the world the ones who sin are thrown unwillingly into prison, but we imprison ourselves because of our sins, in order that this voluntary act of mind might drive off future punishment.

102. "Do you fast? Do not allege illness by way of excuse. For the ones who do not fast fall to the same diseases. Did you begin with the good? Do not draw back, when the enemy wounds you. For he will be rendered impotent by your patient endurance. The ones who begin to sail first experience the right wind when unfurling their sails; later the opposite wind opposes them. But the sailors do not abandon the ship because of the intruding wind; when they are a little calmer or when they have contended against a storm, they make their voyage; just so we, when an opposing wind descends, stretching the cross instead of the sail, complete our voyage without restraint."[204]

103. These are the teachings of the holy and all-virtuous Syncletica, rather more by actions than by words, but many and great things were made known by her for the use of those who heard and saw her. Such a plenitude of good things grew from her that the human tongue is at a loss for expressing them.

104. The good-hating devil, not bearing such abundance of good things, wasted away, and devised in himself so that he was able to confuse the origin of good things. And further he asks the oldest virgin to the final struggle [agōn]; and he took revenge against her with hatred, not caring to begin the blows[205] externally, but grasping her internal organs,[206] he deeply assigned to her bodily suffering, so that she became inconsolable from human succor.

105. He first smites the most necessary organ in life, the lung, and through illnesses that bring ruin, bit by bit he fastens his malignancy [kakia]. For he allowed in a short time through intercession to shorten her death; but just so the bloodthirsty executioner displays through

---

203. *Alpha. Syn.* 17.
204. *Alpha. Syn.* 9.
205. The term here is *plēgē*, which can mean either "blow" or "plague."
206. Literally, the text reads "grasping her entrails" or "her intestines."

many blows and much time his own severity. For breaking up the lung into small pieces by means of spittle that brought them up, he cast it out. Unceasing fevers were present, consuming her body after the manner of a file.

106. When she turned eighty years old, the devil transferred to her the contests of Job. For he made use then of the same scourges. But in the present he cuts short the time, making the sufferings more burdensome. The blessed Job endured in the plague thirty-five years; here, the enemy, as though stripping off some first fruits the time of ten years, to attach the plagues to the holy body of this one. For three-and-a-half years through famous sufferings, she battled against the enemy. Therefore on Job the devil made the beginnings of wounds on the outside; on her he added punishments from the inside. For her internal organs [entrails] having been struck by him, he assigned to her greater and more difficult sufferings. Thus I do not think that the oldest martyrs struggled more bravely than the famous Syncletica. For the abominable one attacked them from the outside. For whether he brought to them death by the sword, or fire, they were gentler than the present trials of Syncletica. For instead of a fiery furnace burning her inward parts from below, the fire is burning from the inside bit by bit. And in the manner of a file over a very long time, her body wastes away. And it is truly weighty and inhumane to speak about. For the ones entrusted with judicial powers, when they wish to set upon the more serious sinners punishments, they destroy them by means of the slightest fire; thus the enemy from the insides made her punishment by causing the smoldering fever unceasing night and day.

107. Nobly subjected to such a plague, she did not lapse in her spirit, but again the blessed one contested against the enemy. And certainly again by means of good teachings she healed those wounded by him; for she drew up the souls unharmed as if from a bloodthirsty lion. And she healed the wounded by means of the salvific remedies of the Lord. She kept safe some who were unwounded; for, showing them the treacherous traps of the devil, she made them free from sin.

108. The wondrous one said that it was necessary not to neglect the souls dedicated to God. For the enemy is especially hostile to these.[207] For when these are calm, he gobbles them up,[208] and the one who has been defeated is cured again; he retreats a little, and watches. And if

---

207. Athanasius *Vit. Ant.* 23.
208. This verb can be used to describe the course of a gnawing or consuming disease.

they fall asleep a little, thus he moves in beside them. For just as it is impossible for the very bad not to have a good spark, just so the opposite is true for the good. For the lot of those who struggle is in the opposing measure. Certainly often the human being is surrounded by every shameful thing and is confused by every licentiousness; but likewise he is merciful, and often in the zealous indwell chastity, fasting, extreme ascetic practice; but there are also the misers and the scandalmongers.

109. Therefore, it is necessary not to neglect the small things, as though they were incapable of doing damage. For water dissolves a stone in time. Therefore the greatest of goods in human beings comes to them from divine grace. We have learned to scare away from ourselves the seemingly small things. Therefore the one who battles against the great thing by means of grace, overlooking the small, will be greatly harmed. For our Lord, like a genuine father, reaches out a hand to his children newly beginning to walk; and delivering us from great dangers of whatever sort, he allows us to move on our own, like on our own feet, showing our free will.[209] For the one who is easily caught by small things, how will s/he be able to guard against the greater things?

110. Again seeing her confident affirmations against him, the hater of good was vexed. And seeing her destruction of his tyranny, he devised another type of evil; and he struck her speech organ, to cut off the spoken word, thinking that by this act he would starve of the divine words those who were with her. But if he deprived the hearing of use, he bestowed an advantage even greater. For perceiving with their eyes the sufferings, they strengthened further the will. For the wounds of the body of that one [Syncletica] cured the stricken souls. And one could see the caution and healing of those who saw the greatness of soul and patient endurance of the blessed one.

111. Therefore the enemy made this excuse for this blow against her: for having caused pain in one tooth, he made her gums putrid in like manner. And the bone fell out; the spreading passed into the whole jaw, and became decay of the body pressing on the neighboring parts; and in forty days the bone was worm-eaten. And within the space of two months' time, there was a hole. The surrounding spaces were all becoming black. And the bone itself was corrupted, and little by little wasted away; putrefaction and the heaviest stench governed her whole body so that the ones who served her suffered more than she did. Most of the

---

209. Compare John Cassian *Conf.* 13, 14, where God is compared with a nurse helping a child to walk.

time they withdrew, not bearing the inhuman odor; but when need called, the multitude approached, kindling incense, and again withdrew because of the inhuman stench. The blessed one clearly saw the adversary, and did not at all agree to have human aid brought to her, demonstrating again in this her own virility *[andreia]*. But those who came with her exhorted her to anoint the places with unguent for their own weakness, but she was not persuaded. For she believed that through external assistance they would destroy the glorious contest. And the ones with her sent for a doctor, so, if he could, he would try to bring about a cure. But again she did not allow him to be brought, saying: "Why do you thwart this good battle? Why do you seek what is apparent, ignorant of what is hidden? Why do you concern yourself with what is, not contemplating the one who made it?" And the doctor, who was present, said to her: "We do not bring a remedy for the sake of cure or consolation, but in order to bury the alienated and dead part of the body according to custom, so that those who are here will not be corrupted at the same time. For they bring such to the dead, and we do it now; I put on aloe at the same time as myrrh and myrtle wet with wine." And she accepted receiving his advice, feeling mercy rather for those who were with her; for from this the excessive stench was destroyed.

112. Who did not shudder, seeing such a great plague? Who was not helped, seeing the patient endurance of the blessed one, and forming a notion in her of the fall of the enemy? For there he placed the plague, whence the salvific and sweetest source of words were sent, and his excess of terribleness dispersed the every comfort. For just as a bloodthirsty beast, he scared away all zeal from those who had come with her, for the tearing in pieces of the fallen prey. And seeking a feast, he became food. For she was offered as bait through the snare by the weakness of the body; seeing a woman, he looked down on her, for he did not know of her virile mind. He observed ailing members, for he was blind and not able to observe her strongest spirit. Therefore for three months she competed in this contest. Her whole body was strengthened by divine power. The completion toward her resting place was made less. Therefore she was without nourishment; for how was she able to take meals, when she was ruled by such putrefaction and stench? Even sleep was separated from her, cut off by her sufferings.

113. When the end of victory and the crown were near her, and she saw visions and the power of angels, and exhortations of holy virgins to the ascension, and being illuminated by ineffable light, and the land of paradise. And with the vision of these, she became as if one herself,

proclaimed to those with her to bear nobly, and not to esteem the present lightly. She said to them, "In three days I will depart from the body." Not only this, but she revealed even the hour of her departure from there. And when the hour was complete, the blessed Syncletica went to the Lord, receiving the kingdom of heaven, the prize for her struggles for him. In glory and grace of our Lord Jesus Christ, with the Father as well as the all-holy Spirit forever and ever. Amen.

SUGGESTED READINGS

Castelli, E. "Virginity and Its Meaning for Women's Sexuality in Early Christianity." *JFSR* 2:1 (1986) 61–88.

Clark, E. A. "Ascetic Renunciation and Feminine Advancement: A Paradox of Late Ancient Christianity." *ATR* 63 (1981) 241–43.

de Labriolle, Pierre, comp. and ed. *Les sources de l'histoire du Montanisme.* Collectanea Friburgensia, n.s. 15. Paris: Leroux, 1913.

Giannarelli, E. *La tipologia femminile nella biografia e nell'autobiografia cristiana del IV^a secolo.* Studi Storici 127. Rome: Instituto Storico Italiano per il Medio Evo, 1980.

Kraemer, R. *Maenads, Martyrs, Matrons, Monastics: A Sourcebook on Women's Religions in the Greco-Roman World.* Philadelphia: Fortress Press, 1988.

Spanneut, M. *Les Stoicism des pères de l'Eglise de Clément de Rome à Clemént d'Alexandrie.* Patristica Sorbonesia 1. Paris: Seuil, 1957.

Villier, M. "Le martyre et l'ascèse." *Revue d'ascetique et de mystique* 6 (1925) 105–42.

Yarbrough, A. "Christianization in the Fourth Century: The Example of Roman Women." *CH* 45 (1976) 154–57.

ZACHARIAS
The Life of Severus

INTRODUCTION

Scholars generally call the following narrative the *Vita Severi* (*Life of Severus*)[1] although Zacharias, the author, a sixth-century bishop of the city of Mitylene, labeled it a "history of the deeds" of Severus of Antioch (465–538 C.E.). Severus was, during the first half of the sixth century, the leading theologian of the anti-Chalcedonian party in Syria, and later in Egypt.[2] The chief purpose of the narrative was neither biographical nor historical, but a partisan one: to defend Severus against charges of paganism by portraying him, now patriarch of Antioch (512–518), as a pious and ascetic young man who, although remaining a catechumen into his early thirties, under the direction of Zacharias followed a "philosophical" way of life while a rhetorical student in Alexandria and then a law student in Beirut.

The opening dialogue of the narrative explains Zacharias's reason for writing. Unnamed pamphleteers had circulated a scurrilous opusculum in Constantinople, the capital and scene of much religious turmoil, and Zacharias, practicing law there, felt it necessary to respond in order to

---

1. Zacharias Rhetor, *Vie de Severe* (ed. and trans. M.-A. Kugener; PO 2; rev. ed., Belgium: Turnhout, 1971) 207–64. The text, on which the following English translation is based, survives only in a Syriac translation.
2. See Gustave Bardy, "Sévère d'Antioche," *DTC* 4, 2; and Marcel Brière, "Introduction generale aux homélies de Sévère d'Antioche" (PO 29, 1960) 7–72. Also see W. H. C. Frend, *The Rise of the Monophysite Movement* (Cambridge: Cambridge University Press, 1976); R. A. Darling, "The Patriarchate of Severus of Antioch: 512–518" (Ph.D. dissertation, University of Chicago, 1982); and Iain Torrance, *Christology after Chalcedon: Severus of Antioch and Sergius the Monophysite* (Norwich, England: Canterbury, 1988).

salvage Severus's reputation. Thus he claims to have been one of Severus's closest friends and an eyewitness to his behavior in both cities. He describes how, under his own tutelage, the future monk, abbot, and patriarch converted to Christianity, leaving the life of an ambitious barrister and becoming one of the leaders of the Philoponoi,[3] among whom were numerous future monks. This group gathered in Beirut not only for the evening office and other devotions but also seemed to have some authority to expose and combat the pagan activities—among them sorcery, necromancy, and soothsaying—that flourished in the cities of the late-fifth-century East.[4] Severus not only knew and approved of the endeavors of this group, according to Zacharias, but also read eagerly a selected portion of the church fathers already regarded as orthodox—the Cappadocians, Athanasius, and Cyril. (He seems to have formed anti-Chalcedonian theological loyalties due to the curriculum with which his teacher provided him.) He also read the Scriptures and is supposed to have composed, as his first Christian writing, a panegyric on the apostle Paul. (This is no longer extant, if it ever was.)

Zacharias admits that Severus was unbaptized during his student days but wanted his readers to believe that a combination of regional tradition and innate caution kept him a catechumen until his eventual appreciation of the fact of mortality and the formation of his intention to become a monk like so many other reformed law students. His lengthy account thus paints a portrait of the gradual conversion of an already assiduous, virtuous young man who was never tainted with either paganism or heresy, by which Zacharias probably means "Nestorianism," the diophysite interpretation of Christology supposedly promulgated at the Council of Chalcedon. Zacharias concludes the work with an account of Severus's simultaneous baptism and acceptance of monastic vows and with the story of his influence in the monastic circles near Gaza until his appearance in Constantinople (508–511) to defend the cause of the anti-Chalcedonian party.

The work that appears here, then, is an account of an ascetic conversion in which the already-established vocabulary of Eastern Christian monasticism embellishes the curriculum vitae of an ecclesiastical lumi-

3. This term is a Greek adjective meaning "conscientious" or "industrious." As a substantive it denotes a lay group in the church of the patristic era; to such a zealous group certain ecclesiastical duties could be delegated by a bishop or priest. See *A Patristic Greek Lexicon*, 7th ed., s.v., "philoponos."
4. On the subject see, most recently, Robin Lane Fox, *Pagans and Christians* (New York: Alfred A. Knopf, 1987).

nary. It is also a contribution to the large body of Monophysite propaganda literature, of which John of Ephesus's later *Lives of the Eastern Saints* is a lengthier and humbler example.

Severus was a religious genius, as his extant writings attest. Other accounts of the life of this leader highlight the way in which he sought to import a quasi-monastic discipline into the ever-reluctant Christian churches of Antioch. His hagiographer, John of Beith-Aphthonia, describes his ferocity upon taking possession of his cathedra:

> He sent away the scullions and cooks from the bishop's palace, with all the edibles they had prepared. He overturned the baths which were there, like the God-loving kings Hezekiah and Josiah when they tipped over the statues of Baal. He continued the hard life he had taken as a monk, in sleeping on the earth, in no baths, in the long service of song [in the monastic office] and in a diet of vegetables like the youths of Babylon, and in buying rough and common bread from the marketplace, such as bakers customarily make for the poor.[5]

In each account of Severus's life, the reader is provided with an edifying story of a reformed and reforming monk-bishop; both Zacharias and John contributed to the stature of their hero, at least for Monophysite audiences. More revealing, perhaps, than either account is a brief section of Severus's Homily 27, given to his own congregation in Antioch early in his patriarchate. The Syrian Orthodox liturgy celebrates Severus in its diptychs as the *tōgō Suryōyō*, the "crown of the Syrians." Before this coronation in the later tradition, or his defense by his biographers, however, Severus seems indeed to have been a pagan, and he regarded his conversion as an instance of divine intercession:

> For when I was in that city of Beirut, I heard of the many miracles and cures which the blessed martyr accomplished; my heart was moved in me, but God, the lover of many, moved my thought [*logismos*] so I would run to the martyrium of the holy martyr Leontius and pray. Therefore I went up from the city of Beirut with my friend the scholastikos [Zacharias?] and we went to that holy place and prayed. I prayed thus when I was a Hellene [pagan]; I said this: 'Holy Leontius, holy martyr, pray [to] your God for me, that he save me from the cult of the Hellenes and from the seduction [*planē*] of my parents.' On that night a great mystery was revealed to me . . . and the god of the universe, Jesus Christ, converted me from the wandering of the Hellenes by the prayers of the holy martyr Leontius, and called me to the chaste, monastic life.[6]

5. John of Beith-Aphthonia, *Vie de Severe* (ed. and trans. M.-A. Kugener; PO 2, 1907) 207–64.

6. Gerard Garitte, "Textes hagiographiques orientaux relatifs à s. Léonce de Tripolo. ii. l'homélie copte de Sévère d'Antioche," *Mus* 79 (1966) 335–86.

TRANSLATION

The history of the deeds of the life of the Holy Martyr Severus, patriarch of Antioch, written by Zacharias the Scholastikos, who read the legal curriculum with him, both in Alexandria and in Beirut.

INTRODUCTORY DIALOGUE

— Whence have you come to us, friend and companion?

—From the Royal Stoa, reverence, I have come to you because I want to learn the reason for the matters about which I wish to ask you. There is a pamphlet that troubles my spirit; it seems to have come from among Christians, but in actuality is anxious to mock the Christians.

—How can this be, tell me? And in what way have you come across this pamphlet?

—When I was investigating the scribes' books, at the Royal Stoa. For you know how much I love them. One of those booksellers gave me the aforesaid pamphlet but only to read, and in it there is something vile, with slanders and calumnies and disgraceful things against a man who is a philosopher. This man is someone who is known to you from before; now he has shone in the episcopacy, and until now has been renowned for conduct and in orations for religion and truth. I am speaking of Severus, he whose glory is great among those who, without taking sides, know how to judge beautiful things. And since then I have been extremely grieved in my spirit.

—And if you have such praise as this, comrade, for this man, why do you care about that insolent person and slanderer, whoever he might be? For it seems from what you say that he is a Christian in appearance only, and by deception, and in reality is more diligent to praise pagans, and reviles those whose virtue is well attested, and who are called by philosophy to serve God as priests, and have done so for a long time.

—It is not as if I doubt, or agree to these things that have been written so wickedly—not for this reason do I come to you. But my soul is grieved, as I have said, lest simple men read [the pamphlet]. They may be ready to receive such accounts about a bishop such as he. But if the truth concerns you, and indeed it does, tell [Severus's] manner of life from youth, for the glory of our great God and Savior Jesus Christ, in whom are placed those who serve the priesthood and those who serve philosophy—the true philosophical way. For you [should] add his city of origin, and the people from which he comes, and the family, if you know these things about the man. But before all these things, [tell] how he has conducted himself and how he has thought about God since his youth. For the belittler has brought a reproach against [Severus], not only on account of his life and conduct, but about this, that formerly he was worshiping evil demons and idols. For he has said, indeed, "He was caught in the act of offering pagan sacrifices in Phoenicia at the time when he was learning free instructions and laws."

—But if any man should gather things that defame the conduct of another, we should not become anxious over what is said, lest it lend truth to what has been said. For it is easy for the evil demons and their friends to slander those who live according to virtue. And it is not right to be amazed if Satan calls "Satan" the servants of Christ the almighty God. It was so when that creative and operative cause of all came unto us; he impelled the Jews to blaspheme and say, "He expels the demon by means of Beelzebub, the prince of demons."[7] But because you have told me that you fear lest simple men would be damaged by this pamphlet, and because I honor the truth and am devoted to you, I related these things. For I was with him from the first stage of life in Alexandria and in Phoenicia. And I heard the same teachers, and associated in the same customs. Those who read with us and are still alive—and in number they are not few—witness to the things that are said.

SEVERUS'S ORIGINS, AND
CAREER IN ALEXANDRIA

The illustrious Severus is a Pisidian by race; his city was Sozopolis, or rather that [city] that was his lot after that original [city] from which all of us have fallen due to the transgression of Adam, and unto which the Divine Apostle calls us anew, saying, "For we have here no lasting city, but we seek her who is prepared, of which God is the craftsman and author."[8] Then he was raised by his worthy parents, as those who know them say. For they are descended from Severus, the one who was bishop of that city at the time of that first Synod that was gathered in Ephesus against the wicked Nestorius. After the death of his father, who was a member of the municipal council, his mother was widowed. She sent him with his two older brothers to Alexandria to study the curriculum of grammar and rhetoric in Greek and Latin alike.

7. Matt 12:24.
8. Heb 11:10.

For as men say, the custom in their country is that, unless there is some pressing necessity, they would be brought to baptism [only] at a mature age. Thus it happened that he and his brother were, until that time, only hearers when they came to Alexandria. I was there too for the reason of making diatribes in Alexandria. Thus the three brothers came first of all to John the Sophist, who was called Semeiographos, and after that unto Sopatros who was renowned in the art of rhetoric; he is well attested concerning this by everyone. It happened that I too was going there, as was Menas, of Christ-loving memory, whose orthodoxy and chaste conduct and humility and philanthropy and love of the poor were attested by all. For he was among those who were constantly in the holy church, the Philoponoi, as it is the Alexandrian custom to call them. When we were engaged in rhetorical instruction, we were stunned at the natural swiftness and studious diligence of Severus, who is worthy of wonder. We were amazed at how, in a short time, he was expert in speaking beautifully, because he constantly studied and repeated the teachings of the ancient rhetoricians, and he pursued and concerned himself with their beautiful discourses. And his mind was concerned with nothing else; he was not entrapped with the ordinary pursuits of youth, but gave himself entirely to the teachings, his zeal for them keeping him away from every inglorious show [i.e., theatrical spectacles].

It grieved us, then, that one of such fervor had not yet been made worthy of divine Baptism, and we counseled that he would set the orations of Basil and Gregory, the illustrious bishops, in opposition to the orations of Libanius the Sophist, by whom, with the ancient rhetoricians, he was dazzled. And by means of the rhetoric dear to him, he might reach as far as their teaching and philosophy, and when he tasted words such as theirs, his mind would be entirely theirs. And at once he praised the letters of Basil to Libanius, and those that Libanius made to answer them, in which Libanius acknowledged that he had been conquered by Basil, and gave the victory to [Basil's] letters.

Thus he immersed himself in the icon of Basil the illustrious and meditated [on his discourses]. Menas, my comrade, who was so admired in piety by all men, said something in a prophecy, and its completion was eventually manifested: "This one will shine among bishops like the holy John, to whom was entrusted the rudder of the holy church of Constantinople." Again, these things, which God alone knows beforehand, were revealed about Severus while still young by means of a devout soul.

[Pages 14 to 44 of the *Vita Severi* contain an account of the battle of the Philoponoi of Alexandria, in which Zacharias was a leader, against a group of pagans, some of them also Christians, who practiced magic and frequented Egyptian temples. An interesting account of pagan survivals in Egypt, it is included by Zacharias as an attempt to associate Severus with the antipagan forces but actually has little to do with the life of the latter.]

But let no one consider that this account is beyond the established undertaking. For my goal is to show that the great Severus is far removed from the slander brought against him. For he was constantly with those who made their cause against the pagans, and he was praising them. He would ever be remote from these [accusations], which are beneath blame and blemish of pagan error. But he was a Christian by his faith, if still a hearer at the time. Just as when he was studying secular instruction in Phoenicia but was an example to all men, also in Alexandria he was far removed from any pagan opinion. Thus some time after the destruction of the idols [in Alexandria, at the hands of the Philoponoi], the Christ-loving Menas departed human life, who had predicted for [Severus] the episcopacy. And he quickly proceeded toward him whom he loved, with many virtues, virginity of soul and flesh, and love of mankind with perfect love, much serenity and humility. Then, at that time, I was gripped with a bodily illness, and the pagans reckoned a judgment had been sought against us in return for what we had done against their gods out of zeal and piety, and in return for the fires with which we had burned [the idols]. And they spread the rumor that I was dying. And when later I was saved from the illness thanks to a renowned miracle of our Lord Jesus Christ, I delivered an oration at the grave of Menas the illustrious. In it I made known the destruction of the pagan idols and narrated how they were burned in front of the entire population of the city. And rightly, everyone at the side of the grave learned about him, renowned for his great sweetness and philanthropy, and were amazed at the zeal shown against the pagans. There the great Severus rejoiced at the accounts of these things, and against those things said against the pagans, as if to glorify me. And he surpassed everyone in clapping his hands. But the pagans did not know what had been prepared as a speech, and one of them, enraged, said, "If you wish to speak against the gods, why have you led us to the tomb of your comrade?"

I have had to say these things because of the slanderer, as has been said. Because I am not trying to tell of my own deeds, which are those of a man mired in sin and not worthy to write the history of the great Stephen, of Athanasius, and Paralius, and especially not of Menas, and the companions who were zealous along with them, and especially of the great Severus, for whose profit this writing is destined, and whose stay in Pheonicia should be told.

SEVERUS'S CAREER AT
THE BEIRUT LAW SCHOOL

When the much-praised Severus was ready to go from Alexandria to Phoenicia, to gain instruction in laws and with the intention to study the art of lawyers, he was urging me to go with him. When I said that I still needed to read even more of the orations of the rhetoricians and philosophers, because the pagans even now excessively consider themselves superior and glorify themselves in these studies, and they should be freely debated from these writings. He went before me for one year only, and when it was completed, I went to Beirut, too, that I might read the laws of the *politeia*. And upon arriving, I was prepared for the *edictales* to cause me grief, for this was suffered by everyone newly arrived in the city to study law. They all suffered some disgrace, becoming the cause of laughter—this shows the self-control [*enkrateia*] of those mocking and joking! And I expected this especially from Severus, now priestly, because he was at an early stage of life; I expected that he would agree to the form of the others.

When on the first day [of instruction] I entered the school of Leontios son of Eudoxios, the one who was then teaching laws and was famous to all those concerning themselves with the law, I found the illustrious Severus with others who were sitting around him listening to legal instruction. Afterwards, when I thought that he would be my enemy, I saw that he was philanthropically disposed to me. First he greeted me, really glad and rejoicing. I then gave thanks to God for this glorious wonder. Then it happened that we who [were] at that time *dypondii*, when we had completed the *praxeis*, would depart [the classroom], and those of his year stayed for their argument. I then went straight to the holy church, which is called Anastasia, to pray. And after that I went to the Theotokos church, which is in the city center beside the port. And after prayer, I was walking in front of that same church; after a little while, that man of God, as he came up to me, joyfully greeted me and said, "God sent you to this city because of me. Tell me how to be saved correctly." Then, out of joy, I looked up to heaven and glorified God, who had raised up in him an intention such as this, and that he had made an inquiry about salvation. And I said to him, "Because you have sought the matters of religion, come to me," as I took him by the hand, "and I will take you to the temple of the Theotokos, and there I will tell you things from the sacred Scriptures and I will teach you the holy fathers." Then he, when he heard these things, was asking for the books of the great Basil and the illustrious Gregories [Gregory Thaumaturgus, Gregory Nazianzen, and Gregory of Nyssa] and the other teachers. When I said that I had brought many of their treatises, he came with me to the temple of the Theotokos. And then he prayed with me these [prayers] that are right, and he had the same question. I then began from the Book of Creation, which the great Moses wrote. I showed him God's care for us, how after the creation of all things that came into being he also took us from the things that were not. He put our first parents in paradise and gave them the saving law as rational beings and major-domos [!], which they were to observe, and how they disregarded the royal commandments after the deception of the serpent, and then were driven out of this happy life, and by means of the law exchanged for death that previous immortality.

As I was telling him this, I was showing him [a picture of] Adam and Eve, for they were depicted in that temple, along with how after the expulsion from paradise they were clothed in clothes of skin. Afterward I showed the abundance of sufferings that proceeds from that—the entirety of deception and the strength of demons which willingly we have released when we obey the leader of the revolt. I added a part concerning God's pity for us and that, because of his goodness, he did not allow his creature to perish—he who was incorruptible, and did not suffer these natural occurrences, went unto [the creature] that would have received an immortality superior to our nature if it had kept God's law. And after the natural law, God gave us the law written by Moses, and by means of many holy prophets. But when he saw that men needed a stronger cure, the Word of God, the Creator God, visited us, having been made man by the will of the Father and by the Holy Spirit. "For when [the sun] arose, he alighted us from the heights, who were sitting in darkness and the shadows of death."[9] He was conceived by the Holy Spirit in the flesh, and from a virginal and spotless womb went forth in the strength of the Holy Spirit. This was the first proof of his divinity, which he gave; miraculously he created a seedless conception

9. Luke 1.

and a birth higher than nature. He wished to release us from the power of the slanderer, to whom we have sold our souls, and willingly took the cross upon his body, instead of us. He gave his body to death for a salvation, arose in three days, when he destroyed the tyranny of the slanderer and of the evil demons his helpers, along with the power of death. "When he raised us with him simultaneously, he made us to sit with him in heaven," as the Scripture says,[10] and manifested to us the new road of salvation that leads to heaven. And when he conquered the entire habitable earth by means of his disciples, he put an end to the oracles of pagan magic, and sacrifices to demons, established one catholic church in the whole world, and teaches us to repent and seek a refuge in it by means of saving baptism, which is the death, burial for three days and resurrection of the Savior of all who is the Christ. When I had added other proofs [of the divinity of Christ], of which the Scriptures are full, I said to Severus, "All persons of the correct opinion must seek a refuge in him by life-giving baptism."

"Well spoken," he said, "but now it is right to act, when I am anxious about legal instructions."

And I said to him, "If you are willing to believe me, or if you are willing to believe the sacred Scriptures and the universal teachings of the church, first of all avoid the disgraceful public shows, and those where one sees wild beasts fighting poor men. After that, keep your flesh pure and every day, after studying law, offer the evening prayers to God. For it is right for us that we should labor in the evening services of the holy churches while others often pass the evenings playing dice and, seized with drunkenness, drink with prostitutes and completely defile themselves."

Severus then promised to do and observe [these precepts]. "Only," he said, "you will not make me a monk. Because I am a law student, and I love the law very much. Now, if you wish to say anything else, say it."

I was happy, and I said, "I came to this city for the study of laws and philosophy, for I am diligent in the legal craft. But as you are concerned about your salvation, now I have an undertaking, not to neglect the law, but to gain for us the knowledge of rhetoric, philosophy, and of the sacred Scriptures and theology as well."

"What is this?" he said. "For you made a great and strong promise, if possible not to neglect legal studies, but at the same time to gain these other great goods, and especially this that is most important of all."

10. Eph 2:6.

[I answered,] "We are reading the laws, as I have made known, all week, except for Sunday and Saturday afternoon. We will complete the legal readings of the teachers and read them on the other days, and then rest during the half-day before Sunday, that day that the law of the *politeia* commands us to make holy to God."

"If this is good," he said to me, "we will keep for that time the writings of the doctors of the church, that is, of the great Athanasius, of Basil, Gregory, John, Cyril, and the others. We will leave our fellow students to do what they want, and sweeten ourselves with divine teachings, and wise things, and the whole of the written teachings of the church."

He then said, "It is because of this that I first asked you if you had brought with you all these books. Because now that, thank God, we are gathered to do this, you will gain for us the good things of which you have spoken, because I will not stop during such time as we have agreed upon."

Because these things seemed good, we began the treatises of selected teachers of the church against the pagans. Afterwards, we read the *Hexaemeron* of Basil the wise in all things. Afterward the solitary discourses [the *Asceticon*?] and letters, and the treatise to Amphilochius, the *Antirrheticus* against Eunomios, and the address to young men that tells them how to profit from pagan writings. Finally, we continued with the writings of the three divine Gregories and those of the illustrious John and Cyril.

We were engaged not only with these writings, but each day we went to the church for evening prayer. We had with us the marvelous Evagrius, whom God had sent to Beirut to persuade many young men to substitute divine philosophy for the vanity of legal studies. . . .

[Page 55 then begins a section in which Zacharias describes the conversion of Evagrius and his joining the local group of Philoponoi, the lay enthusiasts who had given themselves to *praktikē philosophia* and imitated monastic discipline, and Evagrius's father's opposition to his becoming a monk; Zacharias and then Severus joined them for evening prayers. Evagrius became leader of the "holy gathering," fasted regularly, and bathed only at Easter. Page 56 takes up the narration about Severus.]

Little by little, the great Severus emulated him in [ascetic] conduct and in *theoria* [contemplation]. Along with me, he was reading in the aforesaid manner. Once he had become acquainted with the writings of the teachers of the church and from them received the *theoria* of divine philosophy, along with directions for practical philosophy, he emulated the conduct of Evagrius, as a living *typos* and *eikon*. In him he saw a Christian philosopher, who was such not in words only, like many others, but was elevated in works. [Severus] imitated him when he tortured his body by fasting and in his perfections. He made himself equal [to Evagrius] in chastity and other virtues, in abstaining from eating food, not because it is evil, as the Manichaeans say, but because by abstinence a person approaches philosophy more easily. For the majority of the year he took no baths, until he had one only on the same day as Evagrius [i.e., on Easter].

[Pages 57–65 describe the conflict between the "holy association" and a group of students who were practitioners of magic and sorcery; it includes the attempts of the former to convert them. Zacharias, on p. 65, attempts to show that] In these matters, Severus assisted us with his advice. He learned what had taken place and told us what should be done. And the one who composed the lies and impossible scandals that he heaped up against Severus should be ashamed [of having] forged such things against him.

[The narrative of the Philoponoi's war against the magicians continues until p. 75, with a description of their cooperation with the bishop, clergy, and municipal officers of Beirut to burn magic books in front of the Theotokos Church, as well as the arrest of other pagans. Severus seems to have played an ambiguous role at best, for on p. 70 Zacharias states, "Such were the fruits of the orders of the great Severus. In these matters, he led like an army commander, but so as not to give a show, he remained quiet and bent himself to the study of laws. He who has changed the truth by his lie and inventions should bear himself this accusation that cannot be demonstrated nor in any way established."]

We have demonstrated sufficiently that the continual servant of God and high priest Severus could not have been taken in the act of offering pagan sacrifices or devoting himself to magic, as the slanderer has had the boldness to say. He, whoever he might be, will be punished by God in this life, if he is still alive, for the lie of this kind that he invented, and when he departs human life, in front of the tribunal that no one can fool. This high priest[11] of God was, in fact, in Alexandria and Phoenicia with those who, with the sole strength of God and our Lord Jesus Christ, were taking action against pagans, magicians, and pagan gods. Especially was he with them in Phoenicia, because he already had acquired the practical philosophy from imitating Evagrius, and because he knew better

---

11. Or, alternately, patriarch or bishop.

knowledge and *theoria* of doctrines after he had diligently read the writings of the church writers.

And when he was ready enough, he composed a panegyric on the divine apostle Paul. He offered this first discourse to God and asked him by means of his [Paul's] aid to be made worthy of saving Baptism. Everyone who read it admired his knowledge of sacred Scriptures, just as formerly they had wondered at his anxiety about legal studies. Evagrius the marvelous, having observed this knowledge, rebuked me strongly. He said to me, "Why, after having acquired all this knowledge, and having sought God for divine Baptism, has Severus waited to receive Baptism? How do you know that he will continue in his intention and his desire? If he does not join in the holy mysteries, and if he does not receive saving Baptism at once, you will undergo great punishment. Because he has received this knowledge from you, he who is late to show in Baptism the fruits of repentance, who hesitates to receive the royal seal and to be counted among the number of servants of our Lord Jesus Christ. But if you are concerned for your salvation and his, go and see that he receives divine grace at once."

After I heard this plea, I went to find Severus and told him these words of the pious Evagrius.

He said to me, "You [all] seek me, who after Baptism would be covered with spots. Because I see how, very often, young men are entranced by harlots, and I live in a city that is a fountain of pleasure. Wait until I have finished law school and I will be baptized in Alexandria, where you have assured me that orthodoxy has reigned at all times."

[Severus agreed to be baptized as soon as Zacharias was willing, but the latter refused because he was not in communion with the (Chalcedonian) bishops of Phoenicia, but only with the "holy fathers of Egypt and Palestine" such as Peter the Iberian, bishop of Maiouma; John, bishop of Sebennytos; and Theodore, bishop of Antinoe, all of whom were *agonistai*, "athletes," as Zacharias terms them. The Philoponoi decided collectively that the philosopher, or ascetic, John, resident at the shrine of Leontius in Tripoli, should further catechize and baptize Severus. This he did, and Evagrius was his godfather. Severus did not immediately become a monk, however; he returned to Beirut and continued to pursue legal studies, although many of the Philoponoi had already joined the monastic life and entered monasteries. Severus was beginning more serious ascetic practices, although he "had little more than a shadow of his body . . . in the contemplation of natural knowledge and in philosophy" he surpassed even Evagrius (p. 90). Still intent on returning to Pisidia to practice law, he visited once more the shrine of Leontius in Tripoli and then made a pilgrimage to Jerusalem and, farther south, the anti-Chalcedonian monasteries of southern Palestine west of Gaza; here, Zacharias relates, he "clothed himself in the monastic habit instead of the toga [of the lawyer]; he served divine books instead of legal ones; instead of labors at the law court he chose the labors of monastic life and philosophy. Little by little the divine grace proclaimed him rhetor for religion and anointed him chief priest of Antioch the great city" (p. 93).]

[Severus then joined the rigorous monastery founded by Peter the Iberian, where the monks] spent every day fasting, taking the earth for their bed, standing upright every day, giving the entire night to watching, praying constantly, and assisting at the office. They gave only a small part of the day to manual labor, so that they could acquire what they needed to nourish their bodies and to help the poor. Each one labored over the sacred Scriptures during the hour of manual labor. Their chastity was so great that they did not look at each other's faces. They looked at the ground and made their responses to everyone. They labored religiously at all things that led to virtue and attempted not to speak unnecessarily. I knew some among them who, during the bodily lifetime of the great Peter, were advised to remain silent for six years, speaking only to God in the prayers and the divine office, and not to reveal (because of the curiosity of the demons) that God had given this combat as a remedy for their faults. They were careful to obey, so that no needless words left their mouths and they did not even express useless thoughts by standing still, or walking, or moving their eyes.

It is this philosophy that the great Severus took up and whose yoke he bore. Then he sent me one whom he had raised from youth [apparently, one of the servants who still attended Severus in some way] and who had accompanied me, and made me know in a letter what was pleasing to God about this, and asked me to release his servants into his own country, and [to do] everything that he had confided in me, which I did.

[Zacharias then recounts the destinies of other companions from Beirut and relates that he had gone to Constantinople to practice law after completing law school.]

[p. 96] The illustrious Severus, having mightily undergone for a time the divine philosophy in the aforementioned monastery, was led by love of desert places and the life called solitary (which the great Antony began, or another like him in virtue) [and] left the common life and went into the desert of Eleutheropolis. He took with him Anastasius of Edessa, who possessed the same devotion and zeal. They gave themselves to such a hard life, and to such serious works, and to such a height of asceticism, that their bodies became very ill and they would have departed human life if God, who receives joy, had not made the abbot of the monastery founded by Romanos the illustrious to come to visit them, to bring them into his convent, and to give them the care that was right. These monks' life was harder than that of all the Palestinian monasteries famous for their ascetic labors. But it was beloved by Severus rather for the greatness of its harshness, which became the reason why his feet were afflicted with tumors; afterwards this sickness was healed.

After living for a time in this monastery, he returned to the port of Gaza, and lived the life of the solitaries in a peaceful cell of the laura of Maiouma, near the monastery of the great Peter [the Iberian]. But when he had shone for some time in these two monasteries, in the monastic peace, some asked him, because of the grace that had been given to him, to live under his direction and bear the monastic habit. He had to give to the purchase of a monastery, and for supplying it, the rest of the money left to him, apart from that which his brothers got, of the wealth of his parents, and most of which he had already given to the poor. He built private cells to receive others.

[Pages 98–100 discuss the disciples who gathered around Severus and his increasing reputation for piety and monastic discipline. The remainder of the account is devoted to a description of how Severus in 508 had to travel to Constantinople to defend before the imperial court the rights of the Monophysite monks of Palestine, threatened with ejection from their monasteries by Elias, bishop of Jerusalem, under the influence of a formerly Monophysite monk Nephalios, now a Chalcedonian.

During this period (508–511) Severus began to write treatises against the Council of Chalcedon and its defenders and attracted the attention of the Emperor Anastasius as a potential defender of the Henotikon, a document intended to preserve religious unity in the empire. In becoming counselor to Anastasius, he ceased to live the life of a monk, although he was able to return to his monastery in Gaza once more before his elevation to the patriarchate of Antioch.]

[p. 110] For himself and for all those living in Palestine, he has gained peace, and he preferred the monastic life to everything else.

But God wished that he be seated as patriarch of Antioch, the great city, and made him bear the [consequences] of the approval of all the oriental monks. Many of them learned of his faith, orthodoxy, and philosophical virtues when they were in Constantinople for the same reason.[12] But above all the monks of the monastery of Tourgas had learned to know him. They were expelled from one of the villages near Apamea by order of Flavian[13] because they zealously fought the doctrines of Nestorius and had come to Palestine a hundred in number. They bore crosses on their shoulders and were received by Severus and the heirs of Peter, of Isaiah, of Romanos, of Solomon, of Acacius.[14] Moreover, by the entire people who already admired [Severus's] fame in fighting for orthodoxy, so that at a council held in Phoenicia he had joined the great Theodore, at the wish of the orthodox bishops, and brought triumph[15] in all the struggles.

Our devout emperor approved the choice that [the council] made concerning the patriarchate. When Flavian was expelled from the archpriesthood (the patriarchate) by the decision of the Eastern bishops, because he made new decisions regarding faith, [the Emperor] ordered Severus to leave his monastery, to go to Antioch, because of the agreement of the monks, to receive the high priesthood and gain for all men the [religious] union broken by Flavian . . . [Zacharias, pp. 112–14, describes the crimes of the "Nestorians" of Syria and Persia and holds that the emperor installed Severus to combat their influence in his realm.]

When, then, I learned [of Severus's elevation] I reminded Severus in a letter of the prophecy that the blessed Menas had made about this. I told him that his choice was made by divine command; he should not refuse it. God was fulfilling the prophecy made about the matter, and in making him ascend the patriarchal throne would make the city consider him a second Peter [the Apostle]. . . .

I have given a history, O beloved, of the life of the great Severus until his archpriesthood. The history of the other things I am leaving for the city that has received him, to those guided by him, who will learn from his apostolic teaching and know his ascetic life; I am ending the account that I have made, as you asked me, for the glory of the great God and our Savior, Jesus Christ, who is the completion, the beginning, and end of every true and devout history.

12. I.e., to oppose the Council of Chalcedon.
13. Patriarch of Antioch to 512.
14. I.e, other monastic leaders.
15. To the orthodox?

SUGGESTED READINGS

Bardy, G. "Sévère d'Antioche." In *DTC*, edited by A. Vacant, E. Mangenot, and E. Amann. Paris: Letouzey et Ané, 1915–50.

Brière, M. "Introduction generale aux homélies de Sévère d'Antioche." In PO 29, edited by F. Graffin, 7-72. Paris: Firmin-Didot, 1960.

Chestnut, R. C. *Three Monophysite Christologies: Severus of Antioch, Philoxenus of Mabbug, and Jacob of Sarug.* Oxford: Oxford University Press, 1976.

Darling, R. A. "The Patriarchate of Severus of Antioch: 512–518." Ph.D. dissertation, University of Chicago, 1982.

Fox. R. L. *Pagans and Christians.* New York: Alfred A. Knopf, 1987.

Frend, W. H. C. *The Rise of the Monophysite Movement.* Cambridge: Cambridge University Press, 1976.

Garitte, G. "Textes hagiographiques orientaux relatifs à s. Léonce de Tripoli. ii. l'homélie copte de Sévère d'Antioche." *Mus* 79 (1966) 335–86.

Torrance, I. *Christology after Chalcedon: Severus of Antioch and Sergius the Monophysite.* Norwich, England: Canterbury, 1988.

ETHIOPIAN MOSES
(Collected Sources)

INTRODUCTION

The life and sayings of the desert father known as Ethiopian Moses[1]
(ca. 320–407 C.E.), preserved in four ancient sources, are presented here.
The earliest of these is in Palladius's *Hist. Laus.*[2] Palladius spent the
years 387 to 400 C.E. in the monastic life, primarily in Egypt, before
becoming a bishop in Asia Minor. His *Hist. Laus.*, written in 420 C.E., is a

[This project was supported by a Scripps College Sabbatical Research fellowship, a
grant from the Kittredge Fund, and an American Academy of Religion Research
Assistance Grant. I wish to express my appreciation to these organizations for their
assistance and also to Dr. Ambrose Moyo, Chair, and to my colleagues in the
Department of Religious Studies, Classics and Philosophy at the University of Zim-
babwe, where this project was carried out. Dr. J. G. Platvoet, Lecturer in the Study of
Religions at the Katholieke Theologische Universiteit Utrecht and Visiting Lecturer in
Religious Studies, offered a helpful interpretation of the preconversion life of Moses
and information on African traditions. Dr. H. C. R. Vella, Senior Lecturer in Classics,
carefully reviewed my translations. Dr. G. Verstraelen-Gilhuis, Senior Lecturer in
Religious Studies, provided assistance on the history of Christianity in Africa. Professor
H. D. Betz of the University of Chicago, Dr. Howard Jackson of Pomona College, and
my colleagues in the Asceticism Seminar also provided helpful suggestions.]

1. Cuthbert Butler, *The Lausiac History of Palladius: A Critical Discussion Together with
Notes on Early Egyptian Monasticism* (Texts and Studies VI, 1; 1898–1904; reprint ed.,
Hildesheim: Olms, 1967) 2.197–98, n. 33, distinguishes five monks named Moses in the
hagiographical literature. I follow him in not conflating the biographies of these
different figures. For the life and dates of Ethiopian Moses, see H. G. Evelyn-White, *The
Monasteries of the Wâdi 'N Natrun* (3 vols. 1926–33; reprint ed., New York: Arno Press,
1973) 2.154–57; DeLacy O'Leary, "Moses the Black," in *The Saints of Egypt* (London:
SPCK; New York: Macmillan Co., 1937) 206–7.

2. I have used the edition of Butler, *Lausiac History* 2.58–62, as the basis for the
translation of the life of Moses in Palladius *Hist. Laus.* 19.

collection of edifying accounts of the lives of the monks he knew personally or had learned of through their disciples.[3]

The *Hist. Laus.* was the source of Sozomen's life of Moses in his *Hist. Eccl.* 6.29.[4] Sozomen, a lawyer who lived in Constantinople, composed two works on church history, of which only the *Hist. Eccl.* (ca. 443–448 C.E.) is extant.[5] His writings were intended to demonstrate the divine origins of Christianity and God's continuing blessing upon it and to defend the monastic life as the highest ideal of Christian philosophy.[6]

A collection of sayings attributed to Ethiopian Moses is contained in the alphabetical collection of the anonymous *Apoph. Patr.* ("Sayings of the Fathers").[7] The late-sixth-century editor of this collection arranged the sayings according to the alphabetical order of the names of the monks to whom they were ascribed. The sayings were preserved for the instruction and edification of the monks, and the collection as a whole also functioned as a spiritual guide to them in their quest for perfection.[8]

The final source for Moses's life is an anonymous tenth-century vita preserved in the *Acta Sanct.*, where it is attributed to Laurence, a Rutian monk in Calabria.[9] The author used the historical account of Palladius and the anonymous sayings source selectively and sequentially in composing his panegyric on the life of Ethiopian Moses. He also charmingly enhanced the story of Moses's life by describing his admission to the monastic community in accordance with the ritual for admission used perhaps in Laurence's own community or at least in later monastic practice, but not in earlier anchorite communities.

All four testimonies regarding Ethiopian Moses are included here to

3. For a discussion of Palladius's life and work, see Butler, *Lausiac History* 1.2–6; and the Introduction in Robert T. Meyer, *Palladius: The Lausiac History* (Ancient Christian Writers 34; New York: Newman, 1964) 3–15. See also *Hist. Laus., Prooem.* in Butler, *Lausiac History* 2.3–5.

4. Butler, *Lausiac History* 1.51–58, argues that the larger unit in which Sozomen's life of Moses is contained is dependent on Palladius. This argument is corroborated by my comparative analysis of the two lives of Moses. The Greek text of Sozomen *Hist. Eccl.* 6.29 used for this translation is Joseph Bidez and Günther Christian Hansen, eds., *Sozomenus Kirchengeschichte* (GCS 50; Berlin: Akademie-Verlag, 1960) 280–82.

5. The arguments about the dating of the *Hist. Eccl.* are discussed by Chester D. Hartranft, *The Ecclesiastical History of Sozomenus* (NPNF, 2d ser., 2; Grand Rapids: Wm. B. Eerdmans, 1957) 199–201.

6. *Hist. Eccl.* 1.1 (Bidez and Hansen, *Sozomenus*, 6–10).

7. *Apoph. Patr.* (PG 65) cols. 281–89 is the text used for this translation.

8. *Apoph. Patr.* (PG 65) cols. 72–76. See also Wilhelm Bousset, *Apophthegmata: Studien zur Geschichte des ältesten Mönchtums* (1923; reprint ed., Aalen: Scientia, 1969) 60–75; Benedicta Ward, ed. and tr., *The Sayings of the Desert Fathers. The Alphabetical Collection* (Cistercian Studies 59; London: A. R. Mowbray, 1975) vii–ix.

9. "Vita S. Moyse Aethiope," in *Acta Sanct.*, Augusti Tomus Sextus (ed. Joannes Bollandus, et al.; Paris: Victor Palme, 1868) 199–212. The author of the Moses entry

complete the picture of this ascetic. They also provide the reader with examples of hagiography in historical, hortatory, and panegyric writings. A similar diversity of literary traditions can also be found in the Gospel accounts of the life of Jesus and in other early Christian aretalogical literature.

Ethiopian Moses has provided Christian hagiography with an outstanding example of the total transformation God's grace can work in a human life. Moses is first presented as a recalcitrant, large, black Ethiopian slave who was expelled by his master. He then turned to plundering flocks and to other evil deeds, as leader of a robber band. This description suggests something about Moses's historical and social background. He may have come from one of the Nilotic cattle-raising and -raiding tribes, who are characteristically tall and dark.[10] The appellation "Ethiopian" is probably applied to him in the ancient meaning of dark-skinned people, not as an inhabitant of present-day Ethiopia.[11] His rejection of the slave role may indicate that he had been taken into slavery, not born into it.[12] The feats of strength ascribed to him are consistent with his being a well-trained warrior. His plundering and slaughter of rams may reflect his previous activity as a cattle-raiding nomad, as well as his incredible strength and presumed perversity.

The exact circumstances of Moses's conversion appear to have been unknown to our ancient sources. They reported only his dramatic repentance and entry into the monastic life. Perhaps he regarded monasticism as one legitimate and esteemed life style open to him in a new social world, after he had rejected slavery and banditry,[13] or perhaps he took asylum among the desert solitaries in an attempt to avoid punishment for his crimes and was converted by the preaching and example of the monks.[14]

condenses and comments upon the ancient literature about Moses and adds glosses on these texts. The final section contains the life of Moses.

10. See, for example, the description of one such group, the Nuer, in E. E. Evans-Pritchard, *The Nuer: A Description of the Modes of Livelihood and Political Institutions of the Nilotic People* (Oxford: Clarendon Press, 1940).

11. See Frank M. Snowden, Jr., *Blacks in Antiquity: Ethiopians in the Greco-Roman Experience* (Cambridge: Harvard University Press, 1970) vii.

12. According to Platvoet, this may have occurred in Nubia or in the regions adjacent to Aksum. For the slave trade in Aksum, see Y. M. Kobishanov, "Aksum: Political System, Economics and Culture, First to Fourth Century," in G. Mokhtar, ed., *Ancient Civilizations of Africa* (7 vols., UNESCO, Ancient Civilizations of Africa; Berkeley: University of California Press, 1981) 2.391.

13. I owe this suggestion to Dr. J. G. Platvoet.

14. F. G. Holweck, "Moses the Ethiopian," in *A Biographical Dictionary of the Saints* (1924; reprint ed., Detroit: Gale, 1969) 723; and Herbert Thurston and Donald Attwater,

The stringency of Moses's ascetic behavior can be summarized succinctly: he was a monk of Scete.[15] This area, because of its aridity and solitude, required the greatest physical and moral strength for survival. Thus, those monks who succeeded in living here were held in great esteem.[16] Living as an anchorite in his cell,[17] Moses succumbed neither to *adiaphoria*, the temptation to abandon a regulated human existence and to wander aimlessly in the desert,[18] nor to the escape of sleep.[19] He maintained a regimen of prayer, work, and carefully controlled intake of food and drink.[20] His virtue was tested not only by temptations of the imagination,[21] which he sought to control, but also by the physical and spiritual assaults of the demons, a special sign of his advanced state of perfection.[22] He submitted his inmost thoughts to the gaze of his spiritual fathers and followed their guidance.[23] As a result, he achieved that state of "transparent chastity,"[24] witnessed by his gifts of tears,[25] in which he no longer experienced the temptations of the demons. He was also renowned for what Peter Brown has called the "relentless ascesis of social relations,"[26] a refusal to judge the actions of his fellow monks. He achieved the height of perfection when he died as a martyr at the hands of the Mazices, who raided Scete in 407 C.E.[27] Moses's rigorous asceticism was consistent with a traditional African interpretation of penance,

---

eds., "St. Moses the Black," in *Butler's Lives of the Saints* (New York: P. J. Kenedy & Sons, 1962) 3.436 make this argument. See also "Vita S. Moyse" (*Acta Sanct.* 199). As a person seeking asylum among the ascetics, he would, of course, have had to conform to their life style or he would have been excluded from the community.

15. On the history of Scete, see Evelyn-White, *Monasteries* 2.150–67; and Bousset, *Apophthegmata*, 60–66.

16. For the significance of the desert to ancient Egyptian asceticism and of Scete in particular, see Peter Brown, *The Body and Society: Men, Women, and Sexual Renunciation in Early Christianity* (New York: Columbia University Press, 1988) 213–40, esp. 215 and the bibliography in n. 9.

17. For the importance of the monk's cell, see Brown, *Body and Society*, 218–19, 227.

18. On *adiaphoria*, see ibid., 220.

19. On sleep as escape, see ibid., 219.

20. See the discussion of the role of food in ancient asceticism in ibid., 219–24.

21. On sexual temptation, see ibid., 229–32.

22. Ibid., 226: "For all but the greatest ascetics, direct experiences of the demonic were a distant prospect."

23. On the role of the spiritual father, see ibid., 227–28.

24. Ibid., 231.

25. On the gift of tears, see ibid., 238–39.

26. Ibid., 227.

27. Interestingly, neither Palladius nor Sozomen reports this tradition. If Palladius knew of Moses's death at the hands of the Mazices, perhaps he did not consider it a martyrdom. Rather he was the victim of a raid, not a particularly honorable death. Butler (*Lausiac History* 2.198, n. 33) assumes that the Moses whose life the historians recount is the same Moses whose martyrdom is reported in the later texts.

suffering, and martyrdom as essential components of the Christian experience.[28]

The accounts of Moses's life and sayings in the four sources included here reflect the different sociocultural contexts of their authors. Palladius, who dedicated his work to Lausus, royal chamberlain of Emperor Theodosius II, intended through this work to demonstrate to Lausus and other Christians that the building of character through monastic asceticism was more important and edifying than the construction of elaborate religious edifices.[29] Sozomen intended his history to be, among other things, a defense of monasticism as the highest form of human perfection.[30] The account of Moses's life served the purposes of both historians well.

The sayings in the *Apoph. Patr.* were intended primarily for the instruction and edification of the monks themselves. Moses's refusal to judge his fellow monks, expressed in the phrase "to die to one's neighbor,"[31] appears to have so impressed the editor that he added some anonymous sayings on this theme to the collection of sayings attributed to Moses.[32] Thus Moses is made representative of an asceticism, apparently originating with Anthony the Great[33] but obviously derived from the New Testament,[34] that contrasted with the practice of fraternal correction in his own community. At the same time, his willingness to accept fraternal correction was also notable.[35]

Moses's life in the tenth-century panegyric offered the monastic communities a model of monastic perfection and served as an occasion for the larger Christian community to praise God's goodness and Moses's response to God's grace and to entreat Moses on his festal day to pray on their behalf.[36]

28. W. H. C. Frend, *Saints and Sinners in the Early Church: Differing and Conflicting Traditions in the First Centuries* (Theology and Life 2; Wilmington, Del.: M. Glazier, 1985) 107.
29. Palladius *Hist. Laus.*; *Prooem.*; and *Ad Laus.* in Butler, *Lausiac History* 2.3–7.
30. Hartranft, *Sozomenus*, 212.
31. *Apoph. Patr.* 14 (*PG* 65, col. 288).
32. In the Prologue to the *Apoph. Patr.* (*PG* 65, cols. 72–76), the editor claims to have included some unidentified sayings arranged in chapters after the alphabetical sections. I believe the unattributed sayings 15 through 18 in the Moses collection represent such an insertion. They elaborate the theme of saying 14, which is attributed to Moses.
33. *Apoph. Patr.* 2, 9 (*PG* 65, cols. 76–77); Brown, *The Body and Society*, 227.
34. Matt. 7:1–5; 8:22 and par.
35. Perhaps the editor was aware of the abuses inherent in the practice of fraternal correction. Moses's life provided the occasion to suggest an alternative asceticism.
36. Moses's festal day is celebrated on August 28 in the Roman calendar and on 24 Baounah (June 18) in the Coptic church. His body is venerated at Deir-el-Baramus monastery in Egypt. See Holweck, *Biographical Dictionary*, 723.

The lives and sayings of Ethiopian Moses included here also reflect various perceptions of color differences in antiquity.[37] The two historians, Palladius and Sozomen, writing for educated audiences far removed from Africa, appear unconcerned with the issue of color, noting simply that Moses was an "Ethiopian," that is, a black African. However, sayings three and four in the *Apoph. Patr.* indicate that Moses's brother monks were clearly conscious of his color difference. They used the term "Ethiopian" as a derogatory appellation to exclude him from the community, ostensibly to test his humility.[38] Moses passed the humility test by deprecating himself as less than a man, apparently because he regarded himself as a sinner and thus not totally "white" on the inside, despite the white tunic he wore over his body.[39] It appears that the *Apoph. Patr.*, a guidebook by and for monks, reflects actual attitudes about color discrimination in these Egyptian communities, intensified through the creation of a life style in which their dualistic theology was enacted, as in the wearing of white garments mentioned above.[40]

37. Snowden, *Blacks in Antiquity*, 169–95, examines the Greco-Roman attitude toward Ethiopians in theory and practice. He argues, from the use of the Scythian-Ethiopian paradigm in ancient literature to discuss the broad spectrum of racial difference, that there was no racial discrimination in early Christianity (196–215). He notes (171–72 and n. 25) that the Scythian-Ethiopian paradigm first occurred in Hesiod. Later it became a topos: "(1) as examples of anthropological or geographical opposites or extremes differing from the Greek; (2) in explanations of the diversity of racial types; (3) in statements of conviction that (a) race is of no consequence in evaluating men and (b) all whom God created He created equal and alike." Snowden, *Before Color Prejudice: The Ancient Views of Blacks* (Cambridge: Harvard University Press, 1983), further develops this argument. I disagree with Snowden's conclusion that there was no racial discrimination in antiquity, because I regard color discrimination as an aspect of racism. See Martin Bernal, *Black Athena: The Afroasiatic Roots of Classical Civilization* (London: Free Association Books, 1987) 1.28–29, 201–4, for the connection between racism and skin color.

38. A strong argument can be made in support of the existence of color discrimination in early Christianity. In addition to the evidence in the *Apoph. Patr.*, passages in patristic literature depict the devil as black and, more specifically, as a young Ethiopian boy. These passages are collected in P. Basilius Steidle, "Der 'schwarze kleine Knabe' in der alten Mönchserzählung," *Benediktinische Monatschrift* 34 (1958) 339–50. See also *TDNT*, s.v. *melas*. There is also evidence that Egyptians in antiquity discriminated against darker-skinned Africans. S. Adam, "The Importance of Nubia: A Link between Central Africa and the Mediterranean," in Mokhtar, *Ancient Civilizations* 2.231, shows that Egyptian art portrayed the Nubians as having darker skin than they actually had. A. H. Zayed, "Egypt's Relations with the Rest of Africa," in Mokhtar, *Ancient Civilizations* 2.136–52, argues that Egyptians in antiquity were conscious of their distinctiveness from darker Africans based on skin color. By this late date, Egyptians had apparently forgotten, or chosen to overlook, their African origin, which, according to Bernal, *Black Athena* 1.15, is uncontested, in favor of a Mediterranean cultural identity.

39. *Apoph. Patr.* 4 (PG 65, col. 284). This attitude is consistent with the doctrine of sin ascribed to Moses in this text.

40. The dualism in orthodox Christianity in Egypt may reflect its competition with

The tenth-century panegyric reverts to classical discussions about Ethiopians, both in its reference to washing an Ethiopian white[41] and in its use of "Scythians and Ethiopians" as a formula for the universality of humanity. In its celebration that black Moses had been transformed into "a soul more brilliant than the rays of the sun,"[42] Moses himself becomes a paradigm for every soul who renounces the "blackness" of evil in order to be washed "clean" by God's grace.[43]

TRANSLATION

1. PALLADIUS,
THE LAUSIAC HISTORY

XIX. Once there was a man called Moses, an Ethiopian by birth, who was black. He was a house slave of a certain government official. His own master got rid of him because of his great recalcitrance and penchant for robbery, for it was said that he even went so far as to commit murder. I am obliged to tell about his wicked behavior in order to demonstrate the excellence of his conversion. At all events, they say that he was even the leader of a robber band. His behavior is quite apparent in his robber exploits, for he bore a grudge against a certain shepherd[44] who, with the aid of his dogs, once prevented him from carrying out a certain scheme at night. After Moses decided to kill him, he sought out

---

Manichaeism, in which a dualistic theology was also expressed in the life style of the community. See Geo Widengren, *Der Manichäismus* (Wege der Forschung CLXVIII; Darmstadt, W.Ger.: Wissenschaftliche Buchgesellschaft, 1977) 385–99 on the history of Manichaeism in Egypt; and Samuel N. C. Lieu, *Manichaeism in the Later Roman Empire and Medieval China: A Historical Survey* (Manchester: Manchester University Press, 1985) 143–49, on asceticism, Manichaean and orthodox, in Egypt.

41. This topos occurs in "Vita S. Moyse," 6, *Acta Sanct.* 210. Snowden cites Aesop's fable no. 274, which describes the permanence of nature by claiming it is impossible to change an Ethiopian's color (*Blacks in Antiquity*, 197 and n. 6), and Jerome's counterargument, based on the conversion of the eunuch in Acts, that it can happen (198 and n. 8). He also cites the use of the proverb "to scrub an Ethiopian white" by Lucian *Somn.* 28 (LCL 3, trans. A. M. Harmon; Cambridge: Harvard University Press, 1947) 208.

42. "Vita S. Moyse," 2, 6 *Acta Sanct.* 209–10. The analogy of Moses's soul to the rays of the sun has interesting Manichaean antecedents. See Henri Charles Puech, *Sur le manichéisme et autres essais* (Paris: Flammarion, 1979) 5–101; and Lieu, *Manichaeism*, 15–16, for the Manichaean doctrine of salvation and its cosmology.

43. In presenting Moses as a model of radical transformation, the author has also preserved the perspective of the Donatist rigorist tradition of the North African church. See Frend, *Saints and Sinners*, 94–117.

44. This story suggests that Moses may have come from one of the Nilotic cattle-raising and -raiding tribes. See the discussion in the Introduction.

the place where the shepherd kept the flock. He was informed that it was across the Nile. Now the river was full and extended about a mile across. Biting down upon the sword in his mouth and putting his garment upon his head, he thus swam across the river. While he was swimming across, the shepherd was able to escape his notice and bury himself in the sand. Then Moses slaughtered the four rams[45] from the herd and bound them with a rope and swam back again. And when he came to a small encampment, he skinned them and ate the best parts of the rams. And after he had sold the skins for wine and drunk the equivalent of eighteen Italian pints, he went out fifty miles to where his compatriots were.

This formidable man, finally, was spurred on by some crisis and took himself to a monastery.[46] And such was the effect of his conversion that he also brought his helper in wickedness from his youth, the very demon who was his companion in sin, forthwith to the acknowledgment of Christ. They say by way of example that once robbers, who were ignorant of who he was, attacked him as he was sitting in his cell. There were four of them, and, after he had tied them up like a bundle and put them on his back like leftover husks, he brought them into the assembly of the brethren and said, "Because I am not allowed to harm anyone,[47] what do you bid me do with these men?" So the robbers confessed, and, because they recognized that this was the very Moses who once was a notorious and infamous robber, they praised God, and they, too, set themselves apart from the world because of his transformation. They reasoned: "If this man who was so strong and powerful in robber exploits has come to fear God, why should we put off salvation?"

Demons attacked such a Moses,[48] attempting to draw him back into his disposition toward intemperance and promiscuousness. He was so tempted, as he himself recounted, that he barely avoided being drawn headlong from his purpose. Then he went to the great Isidore, who lived in Scete, and told him the details of his struggle. And Isidore said to him,

45. Male animals are generally kept to a small number in a flock to avoid battles for dominance. In killing all the shepherd's male animals, Moses has dealt a serious blow to the shepherd's source of livelihood. This further underscores Moses's familiarity with herding practices.
46. The actual events surrounding Moses's conversion are apparently unknown to his biographers.
47. Possibly this was one of the original conditions for Moses being granted asylum in the community.
48. Christ, the ultimate exemplar, was also subject to temptation by the demons. See Mark 1:12//Matt 4:1–11//Luke 4:1–13. The demons are not said to have physically attacked Christ, as they did Moses. However, see Mark 5:1–10.

"Do not be distressed; they are powers and for this reason they attacked you very vigorously, testing your disposition. For a dog in a meat market does not resist its disposition, but if the market is closed and no one gives him anything, he stops coming around. The same also applies to you. If you remain firm, the unheeded demon has to turn away from you." He then returned and from that very hour he practiced asceticism more vigorously, especially with regard to food, eating nothing except twelve ounces of dry bread, while doing a full day's work and saying fifty prayers. Thus his body became emaciated, but he was still consumed by the fire of passion and troubled by dreams. Again he went to another of the saints and said to him: "What shall I do, as my reason is clouded by night visions of the soul that contain the enjoyment of pleasure?" He said to him: "Because you have not taken your mind off fantasies about such things, you thus give substance to them. Give yourself over to vigils and pray soberly, and you will be freed quickly from them." He listened also to this advice, and, when he returned to his cell, he decided that he would not sleep at all at night, or lie down. So, staying in his cell for six years, he remained standing all night long in the middle of the cell, praying and never shutting his eyes. But still he was not able to overcome the temptation. He then again adopted another life style. He would go out every night and enter the cells of the old and more ascetic brothers. He would take their water jugs, and, without being observed, he would fill them with water. For they get water some distance away, some two miles, some five, and others half a mile away. Then one night the demon who was on the lookout for him exhausted his patience. As Moses was bent over at the cistern, the demon gave him a blow across the loins with some kind of stick and left him for dead. Moses neither felt anything nor knew what had happened nor who his assailant was. Then the next day someone coming to draw water found him lying there, and he reported it to the great Isidore, the presbyter of Scete. Then, taking Moses, he brought him into the assembly, and he was ill for a year, his body and soul just barely subsisting. The great Isidore then said to him: "Stop contending with the demons, Moses, for there are limits even to courage and in the practice of asceticism." He replied to him: "I shall not stop until my demonic fantasies stop." Isidore replied to him: "In the name of Jesus Christ your dreams have stopped. So rejoin the community with confidence." For it was so that you might not boast of having overcome your passions that you were overpowered for your own good.[49] And he went back again into his own cell. Afterwards,

49. 2 Cor 12:7-10.

when he was questioned by Isidore about two months later, he said that he no longer suffered any temptation.[50] He was deemed so worthy of the gift of power over the demons that we are more afraid of these flies than he of demons. Such was the life style of Moses the Ethiopian, who himself was also included among the greatest fathers. He died at the age of seventy-five in Scete, as a presbyter, leaving behind seventy pupils.

2. SOZOMEN,
ECCLESIASTICAL HISTORY

XXIX. At that time, the celebrated Mark lived at Scete, as well as Macarius the younger and Apollonius and Moses the Ethiopian. . . . Moses, who was a slave, was driven out of the house of his master because of his bad moral character, and, having turned to robbery, he led a robber band. After he had ventured to commit many evil deeds and murders, through some sudden reversal he embraced the monastic life, and at once he attained the excellence of philosophy. Still, because he boiled with bodily vigor from his former way of life and was excited by pleasureful fantasies, he wasted his body with countless ascetic exercises. On the one hand, he abstained from meat and ate only a little bread, accomplishing a great deal of work and praying fifty times a day. On the other hand, for six years he prayed the whole night standing, never lying down or closing his eyes in sleep.[51] At other times, he would go to the dwellings of the monks at night and secretly would fill the pitcher of each one with water. This was very hard work, for the place where some drew water was ten stades away, some twenty, some even thirty or more.[52] For a long time he continued to have his former bodily strength, although he made every effort to conquer it with many ascetic exercises and oppressed his body with severe labors. It is said, at any rate, that once when robbers overran the house where he practiced philosophy by himself, he apprehended and bound all of them. He put the four of them on his shoulders and brought them into the assembly and turned the business of the robbers over to his fellow monks, as it was not any longer permitted him to harm anyone. Indeed, they say that no one else ever made such a change from evil to excellence. So he

50. See the Introduction and note 24 above on the state of "transparent chastity."
51. Sozomen has conflated the two separate accounts of Moses's ascetic practices that he found in Palladius.
52. Note that Sozomen has changed the distances from miles, as in Palladius's account, to stades. This change probably reflects the unit of measure he assumed would be more familiar to his readers.

attained the height of monastic philosophy and produced extraordinary fear in the demons. He also became presbyter of the monks in Scete. As he was so great a monk, he left behind many outstanding pupils. When he was around seventy-five years old, he died.

3. THE SAYINGS OF THE FATHERS
ABOUT FATHER MOSES

1. Once Father Moses fought hard against sexual immorality, and because he was no longer strong enough to sit in his cell, he went and made it know to Father Isidore. The old man encouraged him to go back to his cell. But he did not accept this, saying, "I am not strong enough, Father." So, taking Moses with him, he led him onto the roof and said to him, "Look toward the west." And looking, he saw a countless multitude of demons. They were agitated and shouting for war. Father Isidore said to him again, "Gaze also toward the east." And he looked and saw a countless multitude of holy angels clothed in splendor. And Father Isidore said, "Behold, these angels are sent to the holy ones by the Lord for support. Those in the west war against them. Certainly those with us are more numerous."[53] And so Father Moses gave thanks to God, took heart, and went back to his cell again.

2. Once a brother at Scete stumbled. A council was convoked and Father Moses was sent for. He did not want to come. The presbyter then sent for him, saying, "Come, the community is waiting for you." He rose up and came. And he took a basket full of holes and filled it with sand and came. Those who came out to meet him said to him, "What is this, Father?" The old man said to them, "My faults are flowing out behind me and I do not see them. Yet I have come today to pass judgment on another's transgressions." Upon hearing that, the others said nothing to the brother, but they yielded to him [Moses].

3. Another time, a council was convoked in Scete. The Fathers wished to put Moses to the test. They treated him with contempt, saying "Why has this Ethiopian come into our midst?" He, upon hearing this, kept silent. After they were dismissed, they said to him, "Father, weren't you troubled just now?" He said to them, "I was troubled but I did not say anything."[54]

---

53. Angels also ministered to Jesus after his temptation in the desert (Mark 1:13//Matt 4:11) and during his passion (Luke 22:43). See also *RAC*, s.v. Engel.

54. See Isa 53:7, a passage applied to Jesus in Luke 8:32. The *kenosis* of Jesus was undoubtedly the monk's model for this behavior (Phil 3:8; Heb 12:2). Moses accepted

4. It was said of Father Moses that he became a cleric, and they laid the tunic upon him. And the archbishop said to him, "Behold, you have become completely white, Father Moses." The old man said to him, "Indeed, the outside, O Lord Father; would that the inside were also white!" The archbishop, wishing to put him to the test, said to the clerics, "When Father Moses comes into the sanctuary, drive him out, and go along with him to hear what he says." So the old man came in and they rebuked him and drove him out, saying, "Go away, Ethiopian." He left and said to himself, "Rightly have they treated you, ash skin, black one. As you are not a man, why should you come among men?"[55]

5. Once a command was given at Scete, "Fast this week." And as it happened brothers from Egypt came to visit Father Moses, and he made them a small cooked meal. And the neighbors, seeing the smoke, said to the clerics, "Behold, Moses has broken the command and has made a meal for himself." They said, "When he comes, we will speak to him." When the sabbath arrived, the clerics, recognizing the exemplary social behavior of Father Moses, said to him in front of the community, "O Father Moses, you have broken the command of men but you have observed that of God."[56]

6. A brother visited Father Moses in Scete, seeking advice from him. The old man said to him, "Go away, sit in your cell, and the cell will teach you everything."

7. Father Moses said, "A man fleeing the world is like a bunch of sun-ripened grapes; a man remaining among men is like unripe grapes."

8. Once an official heard about Father Moses and came to Scete to see him. Some people told the old man about it, and he rose to flee to the marsh. But they came upon him and said, "Tell us, old man, where is the cell of Father Moses?" And he said to them, "What do you want with

the humiliation imposed upon him by the community, even though it troubled him. The fathers of Scete, however, do not fare well in this example. It is not clear why Moses had to be tested. And, as I have argued above, the test imposed on Moses clearly reflects the color prejudices of the monks.

55. The archbishop's exchange with Moses begins with a reference to the topos of making an Ethiopian "white." Moses's humility prompts him to express doubts about his total spiritual transformation. This gives the archbishop the opportunity to draw upon the opposite topos, found in Aesop, that it is impossible in nature for an Ethiopian to become "white" and to suggest that the same is true in the spiritual realm. The monks implement the archbishop's test of Moses and drive him out of the community. The saying ends with both Moses and the community accepting the truth of the paradigm that it is impossible to make an Ethiopian white. They do so, however, for different reasons.

56. For breaking the fast, cf. Mark 2:18–28 and par.; *Gos. Thom.*, log. 6, 14, 27, 104. See also *RAC*, s.v. Fasten.

him? He is an imbecile." And when the official came into the assembly, he said to the clerics, "Because I heard about Father Moses, I came down to see him. And, lo, an old man on his way to Egypt met us, and we said to him, 'Where is the cell of Father Moses?' and he said to us, 'What do you want with him? He is an imbecile.'" When the clerics heard this, they were distressed and said, "What sort of person was the man who said such things about the holy one?" They said, "An old man wearing old clothes. He was big and black." They said to him, "That was Father Moses himself, and because he did not want to meet you, he said these things to you." The official was greatly edified and went away.

9. Father Moses used to say in Scete, "If we observe the commands of our Fathers, I decree to you before God that the barbarians will not come here. But if we do not observe them, this very place will be made desolate."[57]

10. Once as the brothers were sitting before him, he said to them, "Lo, the barbarians are coming to Scete today. So rise and flee." They said to him, "Are you not going to flee, too, Father?" He said to them, "I have looked forward for many years to this day, so that the word of the Lord Christ might be fulfilled that says, 'All who take the sword will perish by the sword.'"[58] They said to him, "Then we will not flee either, but we will die with you."[59] He said to them, "This is not my affair. Let each person decide how he stands." They were seven brothers, and he said to them, "Lo, the barbarians are at the door." And coming in, they slew them. One of them fled and hid behind a pile of rope and saw seven crowns descending and crowning them.

11. A brother questioned Father Moses, saying, "I see something in front of me but I am not able to grasp it." The old man said to him, "If you do not become a corpse like those who are buried, you will not be able to grasp it."[60]

12. Father Poemen said that a brother questioned Father Moses about how a man could consider himself dead toward his neighbor. And the old man said to him, "If a man does not see in his heart that he is already three days in the tomb, he cannot excel in this saying."[61]

13. It used to be said about Father Moses in Scete that, as he was about

---

57. Christian tradition similarly attributes the destruction of the Temple in Jerusalem to Jewish disobedience of the law. See Mark 13:1–3 and par.
58. Matt 26:52.
59. Compare Mark 14:31 and par.
60. This saying is reminiscent of material in the Nag Hammadi literature. Cf. *Gos. Thom.*, log. 11, 51, 56.
61. Cf. *Gos. Thom.*, log. 56, 75.

to enter to Petra, he grew tired as he traveled, and he said to himself, "How can I get my water there?" And there came to him a voice saying, "Enter [the city] and do not be anxious." So he entered. And some of the Fathers visited him, and he had nothing except a single flask of water. And when he made a small lentil pudding with it, it was gone. The old man was distressed.[62] So having entered and then left [the city], he prayed to God. And, lo, a rain cloud came down on Petra itself and filled all of its cisterns. And after this they said to the old man, "Tell us why you entered and left." And the old man said to them, "I was making the case to God that 'You brought me here and, lo, I have no water for your servants to drink.' This is why I entered and left, to entreat God, until he sent us water."

14. Father Moses said that it is necessary for a man to die to his neighbor and not to judge him in anything.[63]

15. Again he said that it is necessary for a man to make himself dead to every evil deed[64] before he departs from the body in order not to harm any man.[65]

16. He said again, "If a man does not have it in his heart that he is totally sinful,[66] God will not listen to him." And a brother said, "What does it mean, 'he has it in his heart that he is a total sinner'?" And the old man said that "if someone bears in mind his own faults, he will not see those of his neighbor."[67]

17. He said again, "If the deed is not in harmony with the prayer, one labors in vain."[68] And a brother said, "What does it mean, 'harmony of deed with prayer'?" And the old man said "that we should no longer do those [sinful] things because of which we are praying. For whenever a man gives up his own will, then God is reconciled to him and graciously accepts his prayer."

18. A brother asked, "In every suffering of man, what assistance is there for him?" And the old man said, "God is the one who assists us. For it is written, 'God is our refuge and strength, our very assistance in the afflictions which pour down upon us.'"[69] The brother said, "What about the fasts and vigils that a man performs?" The old man said to him,

62. His distress came, apparently, from his inability to perform customary acts of hospitality, such as providing a drink for his guests.
63. Compare Luke 18:9–14.
64. Compare Gal 2:19.
65. See n. 32 above.
66. See Rom 7:24. This appears to be an important aspect of Moses's theology.
67. See Matt 7:1–5 and par.
68. The importance of combining work and prayer was revealed to Anthony. See *Apoph. Patr.* 1 (*PG* 65, col. 76).
69. Ps 46:1.

"These make the soul humble. For it is written, 'Behold my humility and suffering, and take away all my faults.'[70] If the soul should fear all these faults, God will have compassion upon it because of them." The brother said to the old man, "What should a man do about all the temptations that come upon him or about all the machinations of the enemy?" The old man said to him, "It is necessary to weep in the presence of the goodness of God, so that he may assist him, and if he implores God with knowledge, it will cease quickly. For it is written, 'The Lord is my assistance, and I will not be afraid of what man can do to me.'"[71] The brother asked, "Lo, a man beats his slave for a fault he has committed. What should the slave say?" The old man said, "If he is a good slave, he will say, 'Have mercy on me, I have sinned.'" The brother said to him, "Does he say nothing else?" The old man said, "No. For from the moment he takes the blame upon himself and says, 'I have sinned,' immediately his Lord will have compassion upon him.[72] The goal of all these things is not to judge one's neighbor. For when the hand of the Lord destroyed every firstborn son in the land of Egypt, there was not a house in which there was not someone dead."[73] The brother said to him, "What does this saying mean?" The old man said to him that "if we are able to see our own faults, we will not see the faults of our neighbor. For it is folly for a man who has his own dead to leave it and go to weep over his neighbor's dead. To die to one's neighbor is this, to bear one's own faults and to be unconcerned about every man, that this one is good and that one bad. Do not do evil to any man; do not think anything bad in your heart toward anyone; do not hold in contempt someone who does evil; do not be persuaded by someone who does evil against his neighbor; do not rejoice with the one who does evil to his neighbor; do not slander anyone. But say, 'God knows each one.'[74] Do not be persuaded by the slanderer; do not rejoice at his slander; do not hate the person who slanders his neighbor. This is what 'do not judge' means. Do not have hatred for any man, and do not hold hatred in your heart. Do not hate the one who hates his neighbor. And this is what peace is. Encourage yourself with these words: For a short time there is distress, but rest lasts forever, in the grace of the Lord God. Amen."[75]

70. Ps 25:18.
71. Ps 118:6.
72. Perhaps this statement should be read in light of saying 4 above. It also reflects Old Testament wisdom theology.
73. Exod 12:29–30.
74. Job 21:27; Ps 44:21; 139:1; Luke 16:15; Acts 1:24; Gal 4:8–9.
75. Sir 6:19.

4. THE LIFE OF ST. MOSES
THE ETHIOPIAN

Transcribed by Laurence, a Rutian Monk,
from the Ambrosian Codex

1. The kingdom of God has not been closed to slaves or evildoers, but they are within it who, as is fitting, have made use of repentance and prefer to live righteously and according to God. And it has by no means been closed to Scythians or Ethiopians,[76] for all are included in the flock of Christ, and all are drawn toward the fold of full knowledge by the Good Shepherd, Christ, who lays down his life for the sheep.[77] And this can be seen in the case of many others, but especially in the case of him who is now our subject for narration. I refer to Moses the Ethiopian. To the same degree that the man was wayward, so was he great and famous for his virtue.

2. He, then, who had a black-skinned body, acquired a soul more brilliant than the rays of the sun. He had been the slave of a certain government official. He was not a well-disposed slave, nor was he concerned about what pleased his master, but on the contrary he was far from having a good disposition. For if anything was vulgar and worthless, if anything was wayward and ignorant, that he either did or planned to do, and he continually had it in his acts and thoughts each and every day, so to speak, not to be deterred at all from his goal, not by the anger of his master, not by discipline, not by any other forms of punishment. Thereupon, his master, doubtless giving up the effort to reform him, cast him out of his sight, and he acted correctly. And Moses committed robberies and fraud and murders and all kinds of other evil deeds, one of which it will be helpful to recall.

3. Trusting in the strength of his body, Moses once set out alone to commit a robbery. Because a certain shepherd had hindered and prevented him from making an assault, whether by being informed in advance or by some other means I cannot say,[78] he became totally enraged and attacked him by swimming across the flooding Nile by night. The shepherd learned in advance about the assault and turned to flight. Moses, having failed in his objective, selected four rams, which he

76. This text supports Snowden's argument. See n. 37 above.
77. John 10:11, 15.
78. The author is not sure how the shepherd learned of Moses's planned attack. His source, Palladius, suggests, with some ambiguity, that the shepherd's dogs alerted him. Apparently this author was not sure what Palladius meant.

slaughtered in his anger and bound with rope. He crossed the river by swimming with them. Then, after partaking of their flesh and selling their skins for wine, he went back to his companions who had a dwelling about fifty stades[79] from this river. Such were the terrible youthful deeds and devices of this Moses, ones such as these and even worse. I have recounted them fully, as I am amazed at the sympathy of God toward his own creature and at his forbearance, how he draws all to salvation through repentance. And there is no kind of wrongdoing that can prevail over his great and unspeakable compassion.

4. He was so terrible and so famous a robber leader that merely saying his name inspired fear in many. He was famous for his evil behavior and unrivaled for his cruelty. But divine grace grasped his soul on some not at all insignificant occasion, because of which, when it befell him, he became mindful of God and death and judgment. He abandoned his long-standing and thoroughly wicked way of life, as well as his whole desert band and all their treachery. He unexpectedly approached the venerable abode of the ascetics, pitiful in appearance, abject in manner, contrite in spirit, totally restrained, totally filled with suffering, weeping copiously, and sighing. And at first he caused fear in the monks there. Then he fell down at the feet of the head monk and fervently asked pardon for his faults. He confessed them in detail. He made known his thoughts, deeds, desires, intentions, acts. He omitted nothing of what he had done, because he wanted nothing of what he had undertaken to go unacknowledged.

5. With reference to these things, he asked, after he had renounced everything worldly, to receive the pledge of salvation (I refer to the monastic habit), and he poured forth many tears to the end that he might not be cheated of his desire, as he entreated from outside. The head was so amazed by the marvel of his repentance (for it so happened that he was not unaware of the deeds of the man) that he received him graciously, he had compassion on him, he embraced him with both hands as though he saw him as one of the great men, altogether prophetically or else perceptively. He tonsured him,[80] he judged him worthy of the monastic habit, and he listed him on the register of the brotherhood. He taught him, advising him, encouraged him, and gave him suitable commands. Moses was not like a newcomer to the ordinances of the monastic community but rather was like someone who

---

79. Once again, Palladius's unit of measure has been changed from miles to stades.
80. On the tonsure, see RGG³, s.v. Tonsur.

had practiced them for a long time, fulfilling every service of the brothers with eagerness. He was not absent from the assembly. He devoted his time to fasting and prayer, and he partook of bread and water only every three or four days. This was a remarkable man. He exhibited the gifts of complete humility, unceasing tears, indescribable sighs, nocturnal vigils.

6. Why, indeed, should I say more? Moses became great in deeds and in wonders.[81] To those observing him, he became an object of astonishment. He was the persecutor of demons, the servant of the sick, and, so that I may mention everything, he became all to all,[82] because divine grace honored him so that he might benefit everyone. He was an outstanding father, a most diligent teacher, a model and exemplar and measuring rod of the monastic life style. All the monks regarded Moses as father, shepherd, leader, for thus had the most Holy Spirit determined. And why is it necessary to say many things? As infamous as he was for evil, so greatly did he shine as an expert in perfection. Moses was indeed a great monk, and he was talked about by everyone. The desert, the mountains, the city, and all the surrounding areas all resounded with Moses, Moses, Moses. And here it seems to me that Moses alone has changed his appearance, even though an Ethiopian is never completely washed clean. For indeed, he cleansed his soul, if not his body, with the hyssop of repentance, and he made it more brilliant than the sparkling suns.[83] And these are just a few of his many accomplishments.

7. Indeed it is fitting to recall something about his struggles,[84] after his repentance, with the most shameful men and with the intrusions of demons. Robbers once came upon him as he was traveling, indeed, they even fell upon him. And he bound them with chains and brought them to the fathers. He also saved them with his warnings, and he summoned them from their wicked impulse. Demons also came upon him while he was away from the cells at night for want of water, for the old monks were not able to draw it. Taking their water pitchers, he filled them with water without their being aware of it, for in those areas the water was some distance away. Then, on one of these nights, the demon who was lying in wait, no longer able to bear the steadfastness of the athlete, struck him in the loins as he was looking into the well to fill a water pitcher and left him lying there as though he were dead. Nor did he

81. Here a miracle tradition is connected with Moses.
82. Compare 1 Cor 9:22.
83. Unlike the monks in the *Apoph. Patr.* 3 and 4, this author does not confuse skin color with spiritual transformation.
84. A catalogue of sufferings is a typical element in the lives of holy people. Compare 2 Cor 11:23–33.

know who had done this. Then, on the next day, some monks came to draw water and found him prostrate and lifeless, and they carried him into the assembly. He was barely able to regain complete strength within a full year. He was frequently admonished by them to stop struggling with the demons, as an abundance of courage is needed to deal with them. But they also prayed over him, and he was delivered again from impure dreams and was prepared to approach the divine mysteries. "This has been permitted," they said, "in order that you may not boast as though you have overcome this passion by your own ascetic practice, and so that you may not be deluded by the false impression that you have overcome them by yourself." And thus he overpowered them and proved them to be weak and impotent.

8. When a brother fell into a certain fault at Scete, they sent for him to join the community. He declined, but they sent for him again, and he rose, taking along a basket full of holes that he had filled with sand, and came, carrying it. They heard about it and came out to meet him, and inquired what he thought he was doing. He said, "My faults are flowing out behind me but I do not see them. And yet I have come to pass judgment on another's transgressions." When they heard this, they yielded to the brother and let him go. And a certain official heard about him and came to Scete to see him. And when the old man learned of this, he rose up and fled. By chance he met the official, who asked where the cell of Moses was. "Indeed, he is an imbecile. What do you want with him?" he said. And coming into the community, the official told the brothers what had been said to him by the man he had met. They were distressed and asked what sort of person had said this. "An old man who was big, wearing old clothes, and black." They replied, "This was Moses himself, but because he did not want to meet you, he said these things to you." The official went away edified.

9. So then, O best of all fathers, after you had lived and become full of days, both those that pass away and those of the spirit, gloriously have you brought your life to a perfect conclusion. And now you dwell in the heavenly booths. May we also be judged worthy of them through your supplications to Christ, to whom are glory, power, and honor befitting, for all ages of ages. Amen.

SUGGESTED READINGS

Bernal, Martin. *Black Athena: The Afroasiatic Roots of Classical Civilization*, vol. 1. London: Free Association Books, 1987.

Bidez, Joseph, and Günther Christian Hansen, eds. *Sozomenus Kirchengeschichte*. GCS. Berlin: Akademie-Verlag, 1960.

Bousset, Wilhelm. *Apophthegmata: Studien zur Geschichte des ältesten Mönch-tums*. 1923. Reprint. Aalen: Scientia, 1969.

Brown, Peter. *The Body and Society: Men, Women, and Sexual Renunciation in Early Christianity*. New York: Columbia University Press, 1988.

Butler, Cuthbert. *The Lausiac History of Palladius: A Critical Discussion Together with Notes on Early Egyptian Monasticism*. 1898–1904. Reprint. Hildesheim: Olms, 1967.

Evans-Pritchard, E. E. *The Nuer: A Description of the Modes of Livelihood and Political Institutions of the Nilotic People*. Oxford: Clarendon Press, 1940.

Evelyn-White, H. G. *The Monasteries of the Wâdi 'N Natrun*, 3 vols. 1926–33. Reprint. New York: Arno Press, 1973.

Frend, W. H. C. *Saints and Sinners in the Early Church: Differing and Conflicting Traditions in the First Six Centuries*. Theology and Life 2. Wilmington, Del.: M. Glazier, 1985.

Meyer, Robert T., ed. *Palladius: The Lausiac History*. Ancient Christian Writers 34. New York: Newman Press, 1964.

Mokhtar, G., ed. *Ancient Civilizations of Africa*. Vol. 2. UNESCO General History of Africa. Berkeley: University of California Press, 1981.

Snowden, Frank M., Jr. *Before Color Prejudice: The Ancient Views of Blacks*. Cambridge: Harvard University Press, 1983.

————. *Blacks in Antiquity: Ethiopians in the Greco-Roman Experience*. Cambridge: Harvard University Press, 1970.

Steidle, P. Basilius. "Der 'schwarze kleine Knabe' in der alten Mönchserzählung." *Benediktinische Monatschrift* 34 (1958) 339–50.

Ward, Benedicta, ed. and trans. *The Sayings of the Desert Fathers. The Alphabetical Collection*. Cistercian Studies 59. London: A. R. Mowbray, 1975.

Theodore's Entry into the
Pachomian Movement
(Selections from *Life of Pachomius*)

INTRODUCTION

The following passages translated from the Bohairic version of the *Life of Pachomius* (*Vita Pachomii*) recount the story of Theodore's ascetic progress from his early childhood through his entrance into the Pachomian *Koinonia* in 328 C.E. The Bohairic is the only complete Coptic version of the story, although other Coptic fragments exist, as well as complete versions in Greek and Arabic.[1] A careful study requires a cautious comparison of all of the accounts, especially because other scholars have assumed the secondary nature of the Bohairic text translated here.[2]

The monastic literature of Egypt reveals a general tendency to soften the harsh demands of the early monks over the years as numbers increased and contact with the social world outside the monastery grew. This was particularly true for contact with ecclesiastical authorities and relatives who remained in the world.[3] It is in view of this development

1. The relationship among the various versions of the *Vita Pachomii* is complex. See Armand Veilleux, *La liturgie dans le cénobitisme pachômien au quatriéme siécle* (Studia Anselmiana 57; Rome: Herder, 1968) 11–107; Philip Rousseau, *Ascetics, Authority, and the Church in the Age of Jerome and Cassian* (Oxford: Oxford University Press, 1978) 243–47; James E. Goehring, *The Letter of Ammon and Pachomian Monasticism* (Patristische Texte und Studien 27; Berlin: Walter de Gruyter, 1986) 3–23.
2. Paul Peeters, "Le dossier copte de S. Pachôme et ses rapports avec la tradition grecque," AnBoll 64 (1946) 267–68; Armand Veilleux, *Pachomian Koinonia. The Life of Saint Pachomius and His Disciples* (Vol. 1; Cistercian Studies 45; Kalamazoo, Mich.: Cistercian, 1980) 272–73.
3. Goehring, *The Letter of Ammon*, 279–80; Fideles Ruppert, *Das pachomianische Mönchtum und die Anfänge klösterlichen Gehorsams* (Münsterschwarzacher Studien 20; Münsterschwarzach: Vier-Türme, 1971) 142–50. The Greek *Vita prima* (24) states that

that the harshness of the Bohairic account of Theodore's entrance into the Pachomian *Koinonia* rings true. Although it concludes with Theodore's mother's anguish over the loss of her two sons to the monastic life and her tearful departure home, the Greek *Vita prima* alters the account to have her remain with the virgins and thus gain her soul. She too enters the monastic life. The dismemberment of the family, so stark in the Bohairic edition, is thus ameliorated in the Greek version. The account of the mother's loss of her younger son, Paphnouti, to the monastic life, which adds so dramatically to her anguish in the Bohairic and Greek stories, is absent in the Arabic text.[4] Although both the Arabic and Bohairic texts report the intervention of the local clerics to circumvent the monks and permit the mother to see her sons, the Greek version drops this event in order to avoid the sense of opposition between monks and clerics that it suggests.

The story of Theodore's ascetic advancement from his childhood efforts in the home to his entrance into the Pachomian *Koinonia* encapsulates many aspects of the monastic enterprise in Egypt. The histories of monasticism often present the broader development of the monastic life in Egypt as an evolution from ascetic practice in the home to individual withdrawal (*anachorēsis*), to communal life (*koinonia*), an evolution fostered by the insights and efforts of certain individuals (Amoun, Antony, and Pachomius).[5] However, in the present text, from the mid-fourth century, one finds all three stages in the ascetic progress of a single individual, Theodore. He begins his ascetic life with the practice of continence in his parents' home. From there he joins a group of monks to lead an anchoritic life in the vicinity of his home. Only then does he travel further afield to join the increasingly renowned Pachomian movement. Thus, this account demonstrates that although monas-

---

Pachomius tested prospective monks and their parents before allowing them to join the system. This is surely a later development. The parallel Bohairic text has him test prospective monks as to whether they can renounce their parents. In the cases of Theodore and Ammon (*Epistula Ammonis* 2,30), clearly the parents were never informed of their sons' decision by the monastery, let alone consulted in the decision-making process. Shenoute required a signed contract to avoid later legal disputes. Johannes Leipoldt, *Schenute von Atripe und die Entstehung des national ägyptischen Christentums* (Leipzig: Hinrichs, 1903) 106–7.

4. E. Amélineau, *Monuments pour servir à l'histoire de l'Égypte chrétienne au IVᵉ siècle. Histoire de saint Pakhôme et de ses communautés* (Annales du Musée Guimet 17; Paris: Leroux, 1889) 405–6.

5. An important account of the increasing social detachment of the monastic movement in Egypt is found in E. A. Judge, "The Earliest Use of Monachos for 'Monk' (P. Coll. Youtie 77) and the Origins of Monasticism," JAC 20 (1977) 72–89.

ticism generally developed from the individual to communal practice, the different stages often existed simultaneously.[6]

Theodore's story raises fascinating questions about the social world of the Egyptian monk and its interaction with the surrounding secular and ecclesiastical realms. His decision to undertake an ascetic life occurs at a young age and apparently against the wishes of his parents. Together with other examples, it raises the question of monasticism as a "youth movement" in its initial stages. Amoun, Antony, and Pachomius were all young men when they embarked on the ascetic life. That they came to be known as the "fathers" of Egyptian monasticism should not be allowed to obscure this fact. Unencumbered by demands of later life (family, job, status, etc.), youth often are more open to experimentation. That such experimentation often agitates their parents is likewise a given fact, a fact clearly seen in the present account of Theodore. One suspects that such negative interaction between monks and parents was much more frequent than the sources allow.[7]

The story of Theodore's youth likewise raises the issue of the social status of monastic recruits. Coptic monasticism is often portrayed as composed of the native peasant classes. Here, however, Theodore is drawn from a prominent family, bears a Greek name, and has been sent to school. It is clear from elsewhere in the Pachomian sources that the movement profited greatly, particularly in the area of leadership, from the more aristocratic men who joined it. Theodore, after all, became Pachomius's most prominent successor.

Finally, this text reveals the cross-purposes at which the monastic and ecclesiastical enterprises worked. The Bishop of Sne, seeking to maintain peace, sought to appease a distraught mother whose son had disappeared into a walled Pachomian monastery. Upon the rejection of the appeal by monks, the ecclesiastical authorities, in the persons of the local clerics, found a way to circumvent the monks' desire to avoid contact and yet allow the mother to see her son. They took her up on a roof from whence she could see Theodore at a distance. It was a clever solution to the problem (one did not want to turn prominent members of the society against the church), but one must still wonder what the

6. We need to ask whether stories such as that of Theodore came naturally to follow this pattern that had evolved in Egypt from the third to the fourth century or, alternatively, whether this natural pattern may have been imposed by scholars to characterize monastic development in evolutionary terms. The nineteenth-century quest for origins imposed such evolutionary schemes in many fields of study.

7. See n. 3.

monks thought of such efforts. Would they have accepted them as a fair compromise or seen them as an affront to their profession, further evidence of the laxity of the church?

The translation here is dependent on the critical Bohairic text by Lefort (1925).[8]

TRANSLATION

SECTION 31 [33:20][9]

We must now, for the glory of God, tell [the story of] his [Theodore's] life from his youth. Theodore was the son of a prominent family, and his mother loved him greatly. When he was eight years old, they enrolled him in school so that he might learn to write, and he advanced in great wisdom. But when he turned twelve, he gave himself up to [acts of] great continence. Eating no food except that which monks normally eat, he fasted each day until evening. On some occasions he would carry [the fast] over to a second [day].

One day when he returned from school [34:1] for the Feast of Epiphany, which is on the eleventh of the month of Tobi [January 6], and saw his household in great celebration, he was straightway pierced with a very strong feeling. "If you enjoy yourself in those foods and wines, you will not see God's eternal life." Then he went to a secluded room in his house, and falling down on his face he prayed and wept, saying, "My Lord Jesus Christ, you alone know that I want no part of this world, but that it is you alone that I love and your abundant mercy."

And when his mother learned that he had come [home] from school and did not see him, she arose immediately and went about looking for him. She found him in a room alone praying. She looked at him, saw his eyes full of tears, and said to him, "My son, who is it who has troubled you? I will bring great wrath down upon him. But all the same, get up [now] and let us go and eat, for it is a feast day, and we have been

---

8. L. Th. Lefort, ed., *S. Pachomii vita bohairice scripta* (CSCO 89; Scriptores Coptici 7; 1925; Reprint. Louvain: Secrétariat du Corpus SCO, 1965) 33–40. A French translation of this text appears in L. Th. Lefort, *Les vies coptes de saint Pachôme et de ses premiers successeurs* (Bibliothèque du Muséon 16; Louvain: Bureaux du Muséon, 1943) 102–8. An English translation appears in Veilleux, *Pachomian Koinonia* 1:55–62.

9. The section numbers are those of Lefort's edition of the Bohairic *Vita Pachomii*. The parenthetical reference refers to the page and line numbers of that edition.

expecting you since morning, I and your brothers and all our house-hold." But he said to her, "You all go and eat. I will not eat at this time." After they had gone, he continued praying until morning, neither eating nor drinking. And when morning came, he left his home and his city and went to a monastery in the nome [or diocese] of Sne [where] he led an anchoritic life with some old and pious monks. He was fourteen years old.[10] He remained there, walking in great humility.

After living six years in that place, he conducted himself in that life style through the [35:1] providential care of God—[for] the Lord does not forget those who seek him with all their heart and all their soul.[11] And when the old man, Apa Pecos, came south on business of the brothers, Theodore returned north with him to our father Pachom. He [Theodore] was in his twentieth year.

SECTION 32 [35:5]

When he arrived at our father Pachom, he [Pachom] received him with joy because he saw his [Theodore's] love toward God. And after he had entered the monastery, he gave himself up to ascesis and fasting and vigils, so that he would not be inferior to all the brothers. And he strove to acquire great grace, with the result that, in spite of his age, he became the consoler of many, raising up through his gentle words all who had fallen, as it is written, "the spirit blows where it wills."[12] Our father Pachom, seeing him make great progress, had confidence in his

10. The various sources are confused about Theodore's age at the various stages in his monastic career. The Greek *Vita prima* and the Vatican Arabic vita (Ar. 172) report that he joined the Pachomian movement at age fourteen. The *Letter of Ammon* states that he was thirteen when he joined Pachomius. None of the three mention, as does the Bohairic text, that he first spent six years in a non-Pachomian monastery in Latopolis. Because the Bohairic vita reports that he joined the Latopolis monastery at age fourteen, it seems most likely that the discrepancies between the accounts have resulted from the deletion of this pre-Pachomian monastic period from the other three sources. Goehring, *Letter of Ammon*, 214–15; Peeters, "Le dossier copte," 267–68; and Veilleux, *Pachomian Koinonia* 1:272, have argued conversely that the Latopolis period was added in the Bohairic text and is most likely inauthentic. Their argument rests on the simple criterion of numbers; three vitae agree against the Bohairic text. It seems, however, that there would be little reason to fabricate the Latopolis stay.

11. Veilleux, *Pachomian Koinonia* 1:57, following Lefort, *Les vies coptes*, 103, translates this section as follows: "After leading that sort of life for six years in that place, it happened that, by the disposition of providence—the Lord forgets not those who seek after him with all their heart and with all their soul—the old man Pecos. . . ." Although this translation makes much sense, it does reorganize the Coptic.

12. John 3:8.

heart, saying, "In a short time many souls will be entrusted to him by God, who always knows his own.

Our father Theodore made good progress in every way, conducting himself in that life style with great strength. And he was growing in the teachings[13] that he heard from our father Pachom, after whose likeness he walked in all things. The brothers, when they saw that he was growing up like Samuel, having a grace in their presence above all the rest, began to imitate his example. And our father Pachom would respond to them all to go to him [Theodore] and be comforted by him in their tribulations and temptations. They [36:1] went to him so often that they called him the brothers' consoler. And he gave rest to everyone through his soothing words. For he prayed with many of them many times until the Lord gave them rest from their temptations.

SECTIONS 33–36

These four sections, not translated here, record Theodore's wish to see God (sec. 33), his first vision (sec. 34), and his consultation with Pachom about fasting (sec. 35) and a headache (sec. 36).

SECTION 37 [39:2]

After a time, his mother obtained a letter from the bishop of Sne [addressed] to our father Pachom [requesting] that he send her son Theodore [out] to her so that she might see him. For she had heard that no one among them met his relatives again. When she came north with her son Paphnouti, she sent the letter to him [Pachom] through the [monastery] gatekeeper. And when he [Pachom] had read it, he called him [Theodore] and said to him, "Will you go out to meet your mother and your brother, especially since our father, the bishop, wrote to us concerning this matter, so that she [or "he"][14] might be satisfied?" Theodore answered him, "If I go out and meet her, will I not be found inferior before the Lord as a result of transgressing his commandment that is written in the gospel?[15] If that is not the case, I will go. But if it will be a weakness on my part [to go], God forbid that I see her. But even if it were necessary to kill her, I would not spare her, just as long ago with the sons

13. Or "instructions."
14. The Coptic has a letter missing, which enables the translation of either "she," the mother, or "he," the bishop.
15. Luke 14:26.

of Levi in the command of the Lord through Moses.[16] God forbid that I should sin against the one who created me on account of love of parents according to the flesh." Our father Pachom answered and said to him, "If you want to keep the commandment of the gospel, shall I cause you to transgress it? But when they told me only that she was weeping outside the gate, [I feared that] you might hear [of it] and your heart be grieved [over it]. For it is my complete desire that you be [40:1] steadfast in all the commandments of life. Moreover, if the bishop who wrote us hears that you did not meet her, he will not be grieved over the affair, but will rather rejoice over your intention, because they [the bishops] are our fathers who instructed us according to the Scriptures."

Afterwards our father Pachom sent out [instructions] to have them well cared for in a place apart according to their rank. And after three days in that place, they told her, "He will not come out to you." And she began to weep great and abundant tears. And when the clerics of the church saw her in this great affliction, they asked the brothers why the old woman wept in this way. And they told them that she was weeping on account of her son Theodore, because he does not come out [of the monastery] to her, so that she might see him and put her heart at rest. And they [the clerics] told her that he comes out in the morning with the brothers and goes to a place and works. So they took her up on the roof of a house. She waited to look until he came out with the brothers, and she saw him.

SECTION 38 [40:19]

And his brother began to run after him, weeping and saying, "I want to stay with you also and become a monk"; for he was younger than [Theodore]. Afterwards when he [the brother] grew weary and wept, he [Theodore] did not stay [back] to talk with him, nor did he treat him as a brother [according to the flesh]. When our father Pachom was told about the harsh way he [Theodore] treated [lit. "spoke with"] him, he called him aside alone and said to him, "O Theodore, do you not know how to condescend in the beginning, as with a newly planted tree?[17] It is taken great care of and watered until its roots are strong. It is the same in these [matters]." And so he had him [the brother] taken in and made a monk. He too led the [monastic] way of life like all the brothers.

16. Exod 32:27–28.
17. The Coptic is disturbed here.

As for the mother, she returned south in great anguish with very bitter tears for her sons. For not only had Theodore not met her, but her younger son, Paphnouti, had gone with him and become a monk.[18]

SUGGESTED READINGS

Text

Halkin, Francois, ed. *Sancti Pachomii Vitae Graecae.* SubsHag 19. Bruxelles: Société des Bollandistes, 1932.
Lefort, L. Th., ed. *S. Pachomii vita bohairice scripta.* CSCO 89; Scriptores Coptici 7. 1925. Reprint. Louvain: Secrétariat du Corpus SCO, 1965.

Translations

Amélineau, E. *Monuments pour servir à l'histoire de l'Égypte chrétienne au IVe siècle. Histoire de saint Pakhôme et de ses communautés.* Annales du Musée Guimet 17. Paris: Leroux, 1889. (Pp. 405–6; French translation of one Arabic text.)
Lefort, L. Th. *Les vies coptes de saint Pachôme et de ses premiers successeurs.* Bibliothèque du Muséon 16. Louvain: Bureaux du Muséon, 1943.
Veilleux, Armand. *Pachomian Koinonia. The Life of Saint Pachomius and His Disciples.* Vol. 1. Cistercian Studies 45. Kalamazoo, Mich.: Cistercian, 1980.

Studies

Goehring, James E. *The Letter of Ammon and Pachomian Monasticism.* Patristische Texte und Studien 27. Berlin: Walter de Gruyter, 1986.
Judge, E. A. "The Earliest Use of Monachos for 'Monk' (P. Coll. Youtie 77) and the Origins of Monasticism." JAC 20. Münster, W.Ger.: Aschendorff, 1977.
Leipoldt, Johannes. *Shenute von Atripe und die Entstehung des national ägyptischen Christentums.* Leipzig: Hinrichs, 1903.
Peeters, Paul. "Les dossier copte de S. Pachôme et ses rapports avec la tradition grecque." AnBoll 64 (1946) 258–77.
Ruppert, Fideles. *Das pachomianische Mönchtum und die Anfänge klösterlichen Gehorsams.* Münsterschwarzacher Studien 20. Münsterschwarzach: Vier-Türme, 1971.

18. The Greek *Vita prima* (sec. 37) ameliorates the situation by adding that "because of her great love for him, she did not want to return home and she remained with the virgins, saying to herself, 'Not only will I see him some day among the brothers, but I too shall gain my soul.'" (Translation from Veilleux, *Pachomian Koinonia* 1:324.)

JEROME
Life of Paul,
the First Hermit

INTRODUCTION

The *Life of Paul* is the first of three biographies of Eastern holy men Jerome (ca. 340–420 C.E.) wrote in Latin. It was written early in Jerome's literary career, in the late 370s, during or (more likely) just after his sojourn in the Syrian desert as a hermit. It is the first item mentioned in Jerome's list of his own writings.[1]

The second of the three biographies, of Malchus, is a short adventure story demonstrating the virtues of chastity. Malchus and his wife, after experiencing trials and tribulations, commit themselves to lives of chastity and continue to live in Syria as monk and nun.

The third of the biographies, the *Life of Hilarion* of Palestine, is a dramatic sketch of the holy man at work. Jerome describes the journeys of one who first sought spiritual perfection as a hermit and then reluctantly ministered to those eager for his teaching and miracles. Seeking escape from a clamorous world, Hilarion continued his life traversing the Roman world in pursuit of solitude.

Malchus (fl. ca. 360) and Hilarion (ca. 291–371), however romantic Jerome's account of the adventures of the former, no matter how implausible the reporting of the miracles of the latter, were real people. But no evidence proves the existence of Paul. This "first hermit" lived only in Jerome's imagination. Why the fictitious biography? The reasons are rooted in the nature and needs of early Christianity and in the personality and experiences of Jerome himself.

---

1. *De Vir. Ill.* 135.

All great social and religious movements within literate societies eventually express their message through the written word. A movement may begin among the semiliterate and those who renounce literate culture, but the success of a movement often depends as much on the writings of the apologist as on the practitioner, whose labors (and education) may not permit the leisure or artifice to write of beliefs and goals.

So it was in the beginning of Christianity and so it was with the two great, closely related movements within Christianity in late antiquity. The cenobitic (or communal ascetic) movement of the eastern Mediterranean found its apologist and missionary in John Cassian, who established a monastery at Marseilles about 415 and whose written works—rules for a monastic community (*Inst.*, ca. 426) and meditations on the Egyptian ascetics (*Conf.*, ca. 429)—explained and justified the monastic life to the Latin-speaking world of the western Mediterranean.

The other related movement, that of individual asceticism, found its propagandists in two of the great fathers of the church. Athanasius, the disputatious bishop (328–373) of Alexandria, wrote in Greek, about the year 357, the first biography of a Christian ascetic. This *Vit. Ant.* vividly describes an Egyptian ascetic Athanasius had known in his youth. *Vit. Ant.* enjoyed a wide readership, and within twenty years two separate Latin translations, including one by Jerome's elder contemporary, Evagrius, were made of Athanasius's biography.

Some twenty years later, about the year 377, Jerome composed in Latin his *Life of Paul the Hermit*, a work that closely follows (and resembles) Athanasius's *Vit. Ant.* and that adopts and adapts the phraseology of Evagrius's translation. The translator and editor of the Latin Bible and author of learned letters and commentaries on biblical books was perfectly capable of writing a learned treatise on Christian ascetics. Why did he not?

First, Jerome clearly desired not simply to imitate but to surpass Athanasius. Hence, *his* saint is presented as superior in age, as well as in piety, to Antony. Second—and far more importantly—Jerome's biography served two perceived needs. Jerome had experienced at first hand in Rome the low repute in which Christian ascetics were held by urban pagans and Christians alike. Jerome's Latin biography would supply to the western Mediterranean public a positive vision of the ascetic life. Furthermore, some contemporary (and later) Christian leaders taught that only the Bible should be read: better to be unlearned than corrupted by pagan texts. Others saw the wider issue: the need for good Christian literature suitable for the young in age and belief. Jerome himself, in a letter written to announce the completion of his *Life of Paul*,[2] declared that he had labored to write in terms suitable for the unsophisticated. Jerome's own erudition (and love of displaying his learning) constantly intrudes in the biography in the form of quotations and paraphrases of the standard Latin literary masters, but, nonetheless, Jerome's *Paul* appealed precisely to the audience he seems to have in mind.

The very existence of Jerome's *Paul* is witness to the influence of Athanasius's *Vit. Ant.* Even Augustine noted that the *Vit. Ant.* was read and discussed by Christians in distant Trier hungry for information about eastern ascetics.[3] The popularity of Jerome's *Paul*, in turn, stimulated six separate Greek translations, as well as renditions into Ethiopian, Coptic, and Syriac. The impact on later generations of the work may be judged by the literally hundreds of surviving late antique and medieval manuscripts of the *Paul*. Thus did a literary creation become the archetype of the Christian holy man. Thus was the ascetic ideal communicated to a wider audience. In addition, the propagandistic pamphlet in the guise of biography introduced a new genre of literature: the long tradition of hagiographies begins with Athanasius and Jerome.

D. Vallarsi edited the standard Latin text of Jerome's *Lives*; his text is reproduced in *PL* 23 (1865) cols. 17–60. H. Hurter edited a better text of the Latin as well as the Greek versions of the *Lives* in W. Oldfather et al., *Studies in the Text Tradition of St. Jerome's Vitae Patrum* (Urbana: University of Illinois Press, 1943). The present translation is based on Hurter's text, with some use of Vallarsi.

TRANSLATION

1. Many have often wondered who was the first monk to dwell in the desert. Some thus look for precedents in ages gone by and establish the Blessed Elijah[4] and John [the Baptist] as the first hermits. But of these two, Elijah seems to us to have been more a prophet than a monk and as for John, he seems to have begun to prophesy even before his birth.[5]

2. *Ep.* 10.3.
3. *Conf.* 8.6.15.
4. Cf. 1 Kgs 17–19.
5. On John the Baptist, see especially Luke 1:11–17; Matt 3:1–4; and Mark 1:2–6.

Some, moreover, claim (and this is the common opinion of the uninformed) that Antony was the source of this practice. This claim is valid,
but only partially so. For Antony was not so much the first hermit as the
hermit whose example stirred others to emulation. In fact, the man who
buried the body of his master Antony, one Amathas, and another disciple of Antony, Macarius, now also swear that a certain man of Thebes
named Paul was the first hermit, although not recognized as such. This
belief we also follow.

There are those who bandy about one opinion or the other, as they so
desire. They invent incredible tales: a man, for example, covered with
hair to the soles of his feet who lived in a cavern deep underground and
much else in addition that is tiresome to track down. Because the lies of
these people are outrageous, they require no formal refutation. Because,
therefore, written accounts of Antony have been carefully set down in
Greek as well as in Latin,[6] I have undertaken to write a few things about
Paul's beginning and end. I do so more because the topic has been
ignored than because I have confidence in my ability. As for Paul's
middle years and what traps the devil laid for him, no one knows.

2. In the age of the persecutors Decius and Valerian,[7] when at Rome
Bishop Cornelius and at Carthage Bishop Cyprian suffered the glorious
death of martyrdom,[8] a fierce storm of persecution devastated the Chris-

---

Jerome refined this comment in a later statement on the founders of the ascetic
movement: John the Baptist was the ideal example; Paul founded the movement;
Antony popularized it (*Ep.* 22.36; cf. *Ep.* 58.5).

6. A clear indication that, at the time of composition (after 374), Jerome was aware of
Athanasius's *Antony* and at least the Latin version of the *Antony* by his elder contemporary, Evagrius of Antioch (see the Introduction). Jerome several times in the *Paul*
borrows and adapts the Latin phraseology of Evagrius.

7. Jerome has modified the standard Latin practice of dating by the name(s) of the
emperor(s) alone, so that Decius (249–251) and Valerian (253–260) appear primarily as
persecutors, not rulers.

8. The great persecution of Christians initiated by Decius resulted in the death of
Fabian, Bishop of Rome, in January of 250. Seventeen months later (in June of 251),
Cornelius was elected bishop and died in exile, in mid-September 253. Cyprian (200–
258), bishop of Carthage, was executed on 14 September, 258. Jerome linked the two
martyred bishops because of the coincidence of their dates of death and because of
their high office. Although both bishops died *after* the reign of Decius, Jerome includes
Decius because the persecution under Valerian (from 257 to 260) could be thought of as
an extension of that begun by Decius (249–251). Compare Lactantius's comment (*Mort.
Persc.* 5.1): "Not long after the death of Decius, Valerian as well was seized by a not
dissimilar madness" (for persecuting Christians). The tradition that implicated Valerian
in the Decian persecution, however, seems to be founded on nothing more than
unreliable reports that Valerian held censorial office under Decius (cf. *Historia Augusta:
Two Valerians* 5.4; Zonaras 12.20). An older tradition, in fact, viewed Valerian as
friendly to Christians until, under malign influence, he began his persecution in 257
(Eusebius, *Hist. Eccl.* 7.10.3–4). Furthermore, the two persecutions appear to have had
different aims: the Decian persecution aimed at enforcing adherence to traditional forms

tian communities in lower Egypt and the Thebaiad.[9] At that time, Christians prayed that they might for Christ's sake die by the sword. But, in fact, the cunning enemy[10] carefully searched for punishments that brought a lingering death, for he habitually desired to destroy not bodies, but souls. And as Cyprian himself, who suffered at the hands of Satan, states, "They wanted to die, but execution was denied them."[11] So that Satan's cruelty may be noted well and remembered, we add two examples.[12]

3. A martyr steadfast in the faith, who had emerged victorious over the torture racks and red-hot plates, the devil ordered to be covered with honey and set out in the heat of the sun, with his hands tied behind his back. Thus would one who had survived fiery plates yield to the stinging bites of flies.

Another Christian, one in the flower of manhood, the devil ordered to be led away to the most delightful gardens. There, among the radiant lilies and blushing roses, next to a gently murmuring stream, while the wind softly whispered among the leaves of the trees, the youth was placed upon a bed of feathers and, so that he might not escape, bound with caressing garlands and then left alone. Then came a prostitute of great beauty who began to embrace him tenderly about the neck and (that which is even criminal to say) to fondle his genitals. And when his body was aroused with passion, the wanton conqueror threw herself on top of him. What Christ's soldier should do and where he should turn, he knew not. Physical tortures he had overcome. Now physical pleasure was defeating him. But then, with heavenly inspiration, he bit off his

---

of worship (and thus depriving the church of a congregation), whereas Valerian primarily attacked church leaders (thus depriving the congregation of a church).

9. That is, the urbanized area of the delta in northern Egypt and the area of upper Egypt, about Thebes, which had become a focus of monastic activity.

10. "Cunning (*callidus*) enemy" or "adversary" is one of Jerome's favorite phrases for the devil. The epithet comes from Genesis 3:1, where, in Latin, the tempting serpent is *callidior*, "more cunning."

11. Cyprian wrote (*Ep.* 56.2): "especially since they were eager to die, but execution was denied them." The minor variations are typical of Jerome when he quotes from memory authors he knows well. In the letter in which he announces his *Paul* (*Ep.* 10.3), Jerome indicates that he has been studying Cyprian.

12. For Christian reports of trials and tribulations during the persecutions of the mid-third century, see, for the Decian persecution, Lucianus's report in *Cypr. Ep.* 22 and Eusebius *Hist. Eccl.* 6.39–41; for the Valerianic persecution, see *Cypr. Ep.* 80–81 and Eusebius *Hist. Eccl.* 7.10–12. Horror tales from the Diocletianic persecution (after 302) may be found in Eusebius *Hist. Eccl.* 8.7–9. The evidence suggests that Christians were indeed persecuted with greater viciousness (and less attention to legal procedure) in Egypt than elsewhere (Africa and Italy, for example). Nonetheless, the two "examples" Jerome gives here come largely, if not entirely, from his own vivid imagination.

own tongue and spat it in the face of the one kissing him. Thus did the consequent enormity of pain overcome his lustful urge.

4. Now then, at the same time these events took place in the northern Thebaiad, Paul, whose sister had already married, came into considerable wealth at the death of both of his parents. Paul was then about sixteen years old, highly educated in Greek and in Coptic, of a gentle disposition, and a sincere lover of God. When the storm of the [Decianic] persecution began to rage, he withdrew to a remote and little-known estate. Truly, "what does not the awesome hunger for gold drive human hearts to do?"[13] For now Paul's brother-in-law began to think about betraying the one whom he ought to have protected. Neither the tears of his wife (usually effective in such cases), nor the bond of kinship, nor even God, surveying all from on high, recalled him from crime. He diligently pressed forward, exercising cruelty as if out of a sense of duty.[14]

5. When Paul, a highly perceptive young man, perceived his brother-in-law's intent, he took refuge in an uninhabited mountainous region. There he would wait out the persecution. Turning necessity into opportunity, he willingly explored the region, proceeding step by step, sometimes advancing, sometimes retreating, sometimes retracing his steps. Finally he came upon a rocky mountain, not far from the foot of which was a great cave closed off by a stone. Man hungers to reveal what is hidden: he removed the stone and eagerly explored the interior, where he came upon a large room open to the sky. Here an ancient palm tree formed with its spreading branches a ceiling. At the base of the palm was a crystal-clear spring, from which flowed a stream. The earth that gave birth to the stream soon swallowed it up through a small opening. Furthermore, there were inside the hollow mountain several small rooms wherein one could see mallets and long-since-rusted anvils of the sort used to mint money. Egyptian records report that this place was a clandestine mint dating from the time Antony was joined to Cleopatra.

6. So then, Paul came to cherish his dwelling (given to him as if by God himself) and spent all his life in prayer and solitude. The date palm supplied him continually with food and clothing. There is nothing impossible in all of this. I call as witnesses Jesus and his angels that in the part of Syria that borders the land of the Saracens, I saw[15] monks: one

13. Cf. Vergil *Aen.* 3.56–57.
14. Cf. Florus *Epit.* 1.40.6.
15. Some manuscripts have *et vidisse* ("I saw"); most MSS read *et vidisse et videre* ("I saw and I do see"), clearly indicating composition during Jerome's two-year stay in the desert of Syria in the late 370s. But the early Greek translations of *Paul* do not translate

lived as a recluse for thirty years on coarse barley bread and muddy water; another subsisted on five dried figs a day, while living in an old cistern (which in the Syrian language is called a "Kubba"). These things will seem unbelievable to those who do not believe that all things are possible for those who believe.[16]

7. So then (to return to the point at which I digressed), at the time when the blessed Paul had reached the 113th year of a heavenly life[17] on earth, while elsewhere in the desert was living Antony, aged ninety, it occurred to Antony—as he himself frequently affirmed—that no more righteous monk than he dwelt in the desert. But one night a dream revealed to Antony that another and better monk than he existed, one whom he ought to seek out. As soon as dawn came, the venerable old man, supporting his weak limbs with a sturdy staff, set out for where he knew not. By midday, the sun blazed overhead, but he did not falter and stayed his course, saying, "I trust in my God that he will show me that servant of his whom he promised." No sooner had he said this than Antony spied a man-horse. (The fancy of poets name this creature a "hippocentaur.") At the sight of this creature, Antony protected himself by making upon his forehead the sign of the cross. "Hey, you!" said Antony, "where does this servant of God dwell?" The beast gnashed its teeth and tried to speak clearly, but only ground out from a mouth shaking with bristles some kind of barbarous sounds rather than lucid speech; the creature indicated the sought-for route by extending its right hand and then, as Antony watched in amazement, it fled swiftly over the open ground and vanished.

Whether the devil himself took on the shape of this creature, thus to terrify Antony, or whether the desert, typically capable of engendering monsters, also gave birth to this beast, we know not.

8. And so Antony, wondering and thinking about what he had just seen, continued on his journey. In a brief time he came to a rocky valley and saw there a dwarf, whose nostrils were joined together, with horns growing out of his forehead, and with the legs and feet of a goat. Seeing this thing, Antony, like a good soldier, took up the shield of faith and the breastplate of hope. But the creature I have just described offered to Antony, as pledges of peace, dates to sustain him on his journey. Antony perceived the creature's intent, stepped forward, and, after asking it

---

et videre, and a likely explanation for that circumstance is that *et videre* was added to the text at a later date.

16. Cf. Mark 9:23.

17. *Caelestis vita* ("heavenly life") became a standard phrase describing the ascetic's life—"heavenly" because the purity of life sought aimed at imitating the angels.

what it was, he received this reply: "I am a mortal being, one of the inhabitants of the desert, whom the pagan race, confused by various error, worship and call fauns, satyrs, and incubi.[18] I come as the ambassador from my herd. We beseech that you pray for us to our common Lord, whom we acknowledge came for the salvation of the world, and his sound has spread among the lands." While the dwarf said this, the aged traveler poured out tears in abundance, tears flooding forth as evidence of his heart's great delight. For he rejoiced in the glory of Christ and the defeat of Satan. He also marveled that he could comprehend the dwarf's speech. Striking the ground with his staff, Antony said: "Alas for you, Alexandria, you who worship monstrosities instead of God. Alas, city of whores, where have gathered all the demonic powers of the world. What now will you say? Beasts speak of Christ and you worship monstrosities instead of God." He had not even finished speaking when the goatlike creature fled as if in winged flight.

No doubt should move anyone to disbelief in this event. It is confirmed by something that happened during the reign of Constantius, when the world was witness. A living man of exactly the sort I have described was brought to Alexandria and exhibited to the populace as a great spectacle. Afterwards the cadaver was preserved in salt (so that the body would not decay in the summer's heat), taken to Antioch, and shown to the emperor.

9. But to continue my story, Antony advanced further into the desert, gazing now at the tracks of many a wild beast, now at the vast expanse of the desert. What he should do and in what direction he should turn,[19]

18. In modern parlance, an incubus is a nightmare or dream with sexual overtones. In a traditional sense, the incubus is a demonic spirit that descends sexually upon a sleeper—vividly illustrated in the paintings of the Anglo-Swiss artist Henry Fuseli (1741–1825). An Italic tradition conceived of the incubus as a leprechaunlike creature: he guarded a treasure obtainable by the human who acquired control over the incubus (Petronius *Sat.* 38.8). More commonly, the incubus was associated with the Greek shepherds' deity, Pan, the goatlike personification of savage places and uninhibited behavior (including, but not solely, unrestrained sexual activity) that urban society sought to restrain and control. Thus Augustine *Civ. D.* 15.23 speaks of "forest creatures and Pans, commonly called incubi," lusting after women.

Elsewhere, Jerome also accents the savage, rather than the sexual, aspect of the incubus: "hairy creatures, incubi, satyrs, forest creatures" (*Comm. in Isa.* 13.20–22). But here Jerome inverts the usual symbolism of the Pan-incubus: in the *Paul*, the incubus represents uncorrupted nature, receptive to the gospel, while corrupt urban society is not.

19. Jerome here reveals his rhetorical training. "What he should do and in what direction he should turn" are standard phrases used by the orator when deliberating a dilemma. See, for example, Cicero *De Orat.* 3.214 and Quintillian *Inst. Orat.* 11.3.115. The early Latin poet Ennius composed a dramatic example of this rhetorical trope for

he did not know. Another day had now gone by. The only thing left for him to do was to trust that Christ could not abandon him, and so he spent the second night in constant prayer. In the gray light just before dawn, he saw not far away a she-wolf, panting with thirst, crawl toward the foot of a mountain. He followed the wolf with his eyes, and, when the wild beast had entered a cave, Antony approached and looked inside. But his curiosity was unsatisfied, for the darkness within hindered his sight. Truly, as the Scripture says, "Perfect love drives out fear."[20] Stepping carefully and holding his breath, the bold explorer entered the cave. Advancing step by step, sometimes standing still, he heard a sound. Through the horror of the blind night, moreover, he perceived a distant light. When he hastened toward it, his foot struck a stone and set off a clamor. When the blessed Paul heard that sound, he shut and bolted his door. Then Antony fell down before the entrance and until noontime and even longer prayed entrance, saying: "Who I am, from where, and why I have come, you know.[21] I realize that I am not worthy of your glance. Nonetheless, I shall not go away until I have seen you. You who receive wild beasts, why do you turn away a man? I have sought and I have found; I knock that it may be opened.[22] If I do not obtain my request, I shall die right here in front of your door. Then surely you will at least bury my corpse."

Saying such things, there he stood fixed and remained;
And to him thus the hero in words that were few replied:[23]

"No one prays like this who threatens harm; no one does harm or injury in tears. Do you wonder that I do not let you in, when you have come to die?" Speaking thus with laughter, Paul opened the door. The two embraced, greeted each other by name, and then together gave thanks to God.

10. After bestowing the sacred kiss, Paul sat down beside Antony and began to speak thus: "Look at the unkempt hair covering a body decayed with age. This is the man whom you have sought with such hard work. You see before you a man soon to become dirt. Now, then, because love

---

his play *Medea* (276 Vahlen = 217 Jocelyn): "Where now should I turn? What path should I take?"

20. Cf. 1 John 4:18.

21. "Who I am . . . you know" is a parody of Lentulus's letter to Catiline in Sallust *Cat.* 44.5.

22. Cf. Matt 7:7; Luke 11:9.

23. Cf. Vergil *Aen.* 2.650; 6.672.

indeed endures all things,[24] please tell me how the human race is doing. Do new buildings arise in old towns? What empire now rules the world? Are there still any who follow pagan cults?"

While they were chatting about such things, they watched a raven alight upon a branch of a tree. The bird then gently swooped down and dropped an entire loaf of bread before them as they sat marveling.[25] Once the bird had flown away, Paul said, "Look, the Lord has sent us our meal. Truly, the Lord is gracious and compassionate. For sixty years now, I have received half a loaf, but now that you have come, Christ has doubled the ration for his soldiers."

11. Once they had given thanks to God, the two men sat down beside the clear-running spring. But they spent the entire day until nightfall arguing over who should first break bread. Paul urged that his guest should have first bite; Antony replied that Paul's greater age gave him the right. Finally, they decided that each would grab hold of the loaf and pull. Whatever portion remained in each one's hand would be his. After eating, they bent down and drank a little with their mouths from the clear spring. Offering to God a prayer of thanksgiving,[26] they spent the night in watchful prayer.

At dawn, the blessed Paul spoke to Antony: "My brother, long ago did I know that you were living in the desert. Long ago did God promise you to me as my fellow servant. But now the time has come to sleep and—for it has been my constant 'desire to depart and be with Christ'[27]— with the race completed, there remains for me the crown of righteousness.[28] You have been sent by the Lord to cover my wretched body with soil, returning earth to earth."[29]

12. Antony wept at hearing this and in sorrow begged Paul not to abandon him, but to welcome him, Antony, as a companion for the great journey. "Seek not," said Paul, "what benefits you, but rather what benefits others. It profits you to cast away the burden of the flesh and seek the Lamb,[30] but it profits the other brothers to learn from your living example. Therefore, please go and bring back, unless it is too much trouble, the cloak that Bishop Athanasius gave you, to serve as a shroud for my body." The blessed Paul made this request, moreover, not

24. 1 Cor 13:7.
25. Cf. 1 Kgs 17:4–7.
26. Cf. Ps 49:14.
27. Phil 1:23.
28. Cf. 2 Tim 4:7–8.
29. Cicero *Tusc.* 3.59.
30. Cf. Rev 14:4.

because he greatly cared whether his corpse would rot away covered or bare (for he had been accustomed for many years to clothe himself solely with woven palm leaves), but because he wanted Antony to leave him. Thus he could lighten the burden of grief Antony would bear at his death.

Antony was dumbfounded at hearing that Paul knew of Athanasius and his cloak. He saw, it seemed, Christ himself in Paul. Worshiping God dwelling within Paul, Antony dared not reply. Weeping in silence, he kissed Paul's hands and eyes and began his journey back to the monastery. (This monastery was later captured by the Saracens.) His pace could not keep up with his spirit, but even though the passage of time had all but broken a body weak with fasting, his resolve conquered his old age.

13. Exhausted and panting, Antony completed his journey and finally arrived home. Two of his disciples,[31] who had for many years attended the old man, rushed up to him and said, "Where have you been all of this time, father?" Antony replied, "Alas for me, a sinner! I, who falsely bear the name of monk! I have seen Elijah, I have seen John in the desert, and truly have I seen Paul in paradise." And then, with his lips sealed and beating his chest with his hand, he brought out from his cell the cloak. To his disciples, who asked that he explain a little more fully what was happening, he said, "There is a time for silence and a time for talking."[32]

14. Antony then set out to retrace his steps, taking no food to sustain him on the journey. He thirsted for Paul, he longed to see Paul, he concentrated his entire attention on Paul. For he feared what in fact happened: that in his absence, Paul would repay the breath of life he owed to Christ. On the second day of his journey, while only three hours distant from his goal, he had a vision of Paul gleaming in pure white, ascending on high amidst bands of angels and the prophets and apostles assembled. Antony at once prostrated himself, threw gravel on his head, wept, and cried out, "Paul! Why do you abandon me? Why do

---

31. The two disciples are presumably Amathas and Macarius, the two witnesses mentioned at the beginning of the *Life*. The edition of Eusebius's *Chronicle* that Jerome produced (in 380–81) includes the following entries for the years 356 and 357: "the monk Antony dies in the desert at the age of 105. . . . Sarmata, Amathas, and Macarius are considered notable disciples of Antony (356). . . . The Saracens attack the monastery of the blessed Antony and kill Sarmata (357)" (ed. Helm 240). Athanasius, however, merely stated that, at his death, Antony was accompanied by two disciples of fifteen years standing (*Vit. Ant.* 91). Palladius, writing about the year 420, also identifies the two disciples as Amathas and Macarius (*Hist. Laus.* 21)—but his source may have been none other than Jerome.

32. Eccl. 3:7.

you leave without saying good-bye? So late in my life I met you; so soon do you depart?"

15. Afterwards, the blessed Antony often related that he covered the remainder of his journey with such speed that he seemed to have flown like a bird. And not without reason, for when he entered the cave, he saw Paul kneeling, with his head held high and his arms extended to the sky. But the body was lifeless. At first, Antony believed Paul still to be alive and so knelt beside him to join in prayer. But when he heard not even a breath of normal sound from his partner in prayer, Antony embraced and kissed him, wept, and understood that even the corpse of the holy man was praying in appropriate posture to the God for whom all things live.

16. Antony wrapped Paul's body in the cloak, carried it outside, and chanted, as was customary, Christian hymns and psalms. But Antony grieved because he had no shovel to dig a grave. One thought after another came to mind and, considering the situation, he said, "It is a round trip of four days if I return to the monastery; but I shall accomplish nothing if I stay here. Better it would be that I die here; with my last breath, let me fall beside your warrior, Christ."

Along such lines was he thinking when, behold, from out of the deep desert came running two lions, with their manes streaming back from their shoulders. Antony's first reaction at seeing them was to shake with fear. But, then, turning his thoughts to God, he remained calm, looking on the lions as if they were doves. The lions came directly up to the corpse of the blessed Paul and stopped still. Then, with their tails thrashing, they reclined at the feet of the corpse and let out a mighty roar, so that you would think that they were offering lamentation in the only way they could. Next, the lions began to paw the ground nearby, competing with one another to excavate the sand, until they had dug out a space big enough for a man. Then, with waggling ears and downcast heads, they approached Antony and, as if requesting wages for their labor, began to lick his hands and feet. Antony realized that they sought his benediction and so straightaway he poured out his praise to Christ, rejoicing that even dumb animals recognize that God exists, and said, "Lord, without whose nod no leaf nor even a single sparrow falls to earth,[33] give unto these creatures as you know best." And then with his hand he motioned them away.

When the lions had departed, Antony lifted the holy body onto his

33. Cf. Matt 10:29.

bowed shoulders, placed the corpse in the grave, gathered together the sand that the lions had excavated, and made the customary mound. On the next day, Antony claimed for himself Paul's tunic (which Paul had woven from the fibers of palm leaves as one weaves wicker baskets), lest the dutiful heir should have nothing from the property of the intestate saint.

And so he returned to his monastery and reported to his disciples everything just as it had occurred. On the holy days of Easter and Pentecost, Antony always wore Paul's tunic.

17. At the end of this work, let me ask those who know not their own patrimony, who clothe their homes with marble, who string on a single thread the cost of villas, what did this barely clothed old man ever lack? You drink from jeweled goblets; he satisfied his needs with his own cupped hands. You weave gold into your garments; he owned a tunic unworthy of even your lowliest slave. But paradise awaits that poor wretch, while hell will seize as its own you golden people. He, although barely clothed, preserved the garment of Christ; you, clothed in silk, have thrown away Christ's garment. Paul lies covered with ordinary dirt; he will be resurrected in glory. You burden the earth with the weight of your tombs; you and your wealth will be consumed by fire. Why do you wrap your dead in garments of gold? Is it because you think the corpses of the rich know not how to decay unless wrapped in silk?

18. Whoever reads this, I pray that you be mindful of Jerome the sinner. If the Lord should give him the choice, he would rather have the tunic of Paul along with the merits he has earned than the purple of kings along with the punishments they deserve.

SUGGESTED READINGS

Altaner, B. *Patrology*. New York: Herder and Herder, 1960.

Brown, Peter. *The Making of Late Antiquity*. Cambridge: Harvard University Press, 1971.

———. *The Body and Society: Men, Women, and Sexual Renunciation in Early Christianity*. New York: Columbia University Press, 1988.

Coleiro, E. "St. Jerome's Lives of the Hermits." *VC* 11 (1957) 161–78.

Frend, W. H. C. *The Rise of Christianity*. Philadelphia: Fortress Press, 1984.

Kelly, J. N. D. *Jerome*. London: Gerald Duckworth & Co., 1975.

Quasten, J. *Patrology*. Westminster, Md.: Newman Press, 1950–86.

Rousseau, P. *Ascetics, Authority, and the Church in the Age of Jerome and Cassian*. London: Oxford University Press, 1978.

The Story of Mygdonia
and Tertia
from the *Acts of Thomas*

INTRODUCTION

The *Acts of Thomas,* like other apocryphal acts of apostles, is a work of popular novelistic literature. From the fifth century on, this lively account of the adventures and martyrdom of the apostle Thomas was attributed to one Leucius, who was also said to have composed the *Acts of Andrew, John, Paul,* and *Peter.*[1] Few today support the notion that Leucius or any other single author wrote all five early apocryphal acts. The author of the *Acts of Thomas* remains, therefore, unknown. He or she[2] is likely to have lived in Syria in the first half of the third century. The author clearly did not create the work ex nihilo but made extensive use of preexisting literary sources,[3] which were in turn probably based in large part on oral legend.

The *Acts of Thomas* is a lengthy work, divided into thirteen acts that relate the story of Judas Thomas's mission to India. We have here included translated selections from the last five acts, which comprise a distinct and coherent narrative easily separated from the foregoing acts.

1. On the tradition of Leucius's authorship, see W. Schneemelcher and K. Schaefer-diek, "Second and Third Century Acts of Apostles: Introduction," in E. Hennecke, *New Testament Apocrypha* (ed. W. Schneemelcher; Eng. trans. ed. R. McL. Wilson; Philadelphia: Westminster Press, 1965) 2.178–88.

2. Stevan Davies, *The Revolt of the Widows: The Social World of the Apocryphal Acts* (Carbondale and Edwardsville: Southern Illinois University Press, 1980), makes a rare claim for female authorship of the apocryphal acts. Dennis McDonald, "The Role of Women in the Production of the Apocryphal Acts of the Apostles," *The Illif Review* 40.4 (1984) 21–38, offers a critical response to Davies's thesis.

3. On the composite nature of the *Acts of Thomas,* see Yves Tissot, "Les Actes de Thomas, exemple de recueil composite," in François Bovon, *Les actes apocryphes des apôtres. Christianisme et monde païen* (Geneva: Labor et Fides, 1981) 223–32.

These last five acts tell the story of Thomas's conversion of Mygdonia and Tertia to the life of Christian continence. The husbands of these two aristocratic women are, not surprisingly, strongly opposed to their new life style, and this opposition leads to the imprisonment of Thomas and the women. Thomas is finally executed, but Mygdonia and Tertia still persist in their chaste devotion to Christ. Defeated in their efforts to persuade their wives to return to their marriages, their husbands free them and acknowledge their choice to live an ascetic life.

Other apocryphal acts of apostles contain similar stories relating the obstacles that heroic women had to overcome in order to embrace a life of sexual continence. An original oral legend probably lies behind the literary version of the story of Mygdonia and Tertia and of the other female "chastity stories" and this legend was likely generated by second-century Christian women in Syria and other parts of the East who had themselves chosen a life of sexual continence.[4] The storytellers' precise social context is difficult to reconstruct; however, basic elements can be inferred from the stories themselves and corroborated by external evidence concerning women's social and sexual roles.[5]

The story of Mygdonia and Tertia reflects a social context in which women had little disposal over their own sexuality: the sexuality of a matron belonged to her husband, that of a concubine or a female slave to her master. The woman's social role served to safeguard her sexuality. The sphere of her activities was confined—in the ideal if not always in fact—to the household; the streets, the marketplace, and political assemblies constituted a male sphere that she ought not enter. Her proper role was the management of the household and the production of legitimate offspring for her husband. Because the social and sexual roles of women were so closely identified, women who transgressed the boundaries of the social and physical space ascribed to them by leaving the house, especially at night, were assumed to be transgressing sexual boundaries as well. The Augustan laws of the first century B.C.E. attempted to translate a woman's social obligation to stay at home, run a husband's household, and bear his children into a legal obligation, providing incentives for those who married and had children and sanctions against those who did not.

Within this context, a woman's decision to pursue a life of sexual continence entailed a struggle to gain the right to dispose of her own

4. See Virginia Burrus, *Chastity as Autonomy: Women in the Stories of Apocryphal Acts* (Lewiston, N.Y.: Edwin Mellen Press, 1987) 31–80.

5. For what follows on social context, see ibid., 81–112.

sexuality. This meant repudiating the right of her husband or partner to control her sexuality and asserting the superior right of Jesus, her new spouse. The heroines in the story find both husband and king aligned against them; the state intervenes to enforce women's roles within the patriarchal household. Sexual continence was not the socially legitimate option for women in the second century that it was in the fourth century, when Christianity became a legal and even dominant religion. The story of Mygdonia and Tertia suggests that those women who told it believed that the choice of a life style of sexual continence meant conflict within the household and pressure from the state.

The form of asceticism advocated by the story of Mygdonia and Tertia in the *Acts of Thomas* places it within the encratite tradition of second- and third-century Syria.[6] The focus of the ascetic practice is sexual continence, but other disciplines are also urged. Dietary restrictions accompany abstinence from sexual relations. Mygdonia repeatedly refuses not only to sleep with her husband but also to eat with him. When her nurse offers to fetch large quantities of wine and bread for the baptismal Eucharist, Mygdonia restrains her, requesting only water and a single loaf. As young women of high birth, Mygdonia and Tertia must of course renounce their attachment not only to food and sex but also to possessions, to fine clothing and adornment, to physical beauty, to reputation and power, and to the attentions of servants. The renunciation of beauty and fine clothing receives particular emphasis, and one of Mygdonia's earliest acts is to cut her hair and tear her clothes. This attempt to destroy the attractiveness of her body, like her refusal to dine with her husband, is closely linked to Mygdonia's pursuit of sexual continence as a necessary precondition for salvation.

It is not so much the form of the ascetic practice as the female perspective from which it is presented that is unique to the story of Mygdonia and Tertia and the other apocryphal stories of female chastity. The bulk of ancient ascetic literature was written by men and explored the problematic of male chastity: the suppression of sexual desire. The story of Mygdonia and Tertia illuminates the problematic of female chastity: the attainment of sexual and social autonomy.

The *Acts of Thomas* is extant in both Greek and Syriac. The Syriac text

6. For background on the term "encratite," see Henry Chadwick, "Enkrateia," *RAC* 5:343–65. For background on early Syrian Christianity, see Arthur Vööbus, *History of Asceticism in the Syrian Orient* (CSCO 184/Sub. 14 and 197/Sub. 17, 1958; CSCO 500/Sub. 81, 1988); Robert Murray, *Symbols of Church and Kingdom: A Study in Early Syriac Tradition* (Cambridge: Cambridge University Press, 1975); H. J. W. Drijvers, *East of Antioch: Studies in Early Syriac Christianity* (London: Variorum Reprints, 1984).

appears to have been significantly amended to conform to later catholic orthodoxy. The Greek text is thus to be preferred. Most scholars agree, however, that the work was originally composed in Syriac. The following translation is based on the Greek text edited by M. Bonnet, *Acta Apostolorum Apocrypha* II.2 (Hildesheim, 1959) 197–288. We have also made occasional reference to the Syriac text edited and translated into English by W. Wright, *Apocryphal Acts of the Apostles* (Amsterdam, 1968) 218–98. Content summaries of untranslated portions have been included in order to provide transitions between the translated selections.

TRANSLATION

[The apostle Judas Thomas had recently arrived in the Indian kingdom ruled by Misdaeus. A large crowd gathered to hear Thomas speak. The wealthy Mygdonia ordered her slaves to push through the crowd so that she could be carried closer to the apostle.]

87. . . . And the wife of Charisius, the king's kinsman, leaped out of the litter and threw herself on the ground in front of the apostle; seizing his feet and imploring, she said: "Disciple of the living God, you have entered a desolate country. For we live in a desert, behaving like irrational animals; but now we shall be saved by your hands. I beg you, then, think of me and pray for me, so that the compassion of the God whom you preach may come upon me, and I may be his dwelling and may join in the prayer and hope and faith in him, and I too may receive the seal and may become a holy temple, and he may dwell in me."

88. And the apostle said: "I pray and ask for all of you, brothers, who believe in the Lord, and for you sisters who hope in Christ, that the Word of God may settle on all and may dwell among you, for we do not have power over you." And he began to say to the woman Mygdonia: "Get up from the ground and reconsider your situation. For neither this extra ornament nor the beauty of your body nor your clothing will help you. Nor will your honorable reputation or worldly power or this foul communion with your husband profit you, if you are deprived of the true communion. For the display of adornment is made useless, and the body ages and changes, and clothes become old, and power and mastery pass, with punishment, according to how each one has conducted him or herself in it. And the communion of childbearing passes too, because it is indeed a condemnation. Jesus alone remains forever, and those who hope in him." Having spoken these words, he said to the woman: "Go in

peace, and the Lord will make you worthy of his own mysteries." But she said: "I am afraid to go, for fear that you might then leave me and go to another nation." And the apostle said to her: "Even if I go, I will not leave you alone, but Jesus, because of his compassion, will be with you." And, falling down, she prostrated herself before him and then went to her house.

89. After bathing, Charisius, King Misdaeus's kinsman, came back and sat down to eat dinner. And he inquired concerning his wife, asking where she was, for she had not come from her bedroom to meet him as was her custom. And her handmaids said to him: "She is not well." He burst in and entered her bedroom and found her lying down on the bed, covered; and unveiling her, he kissed her, saying: "Why are you so unhappy today?" And she said: "I am not well." And he said to her: "Why did you not respect the dignity of your freedom and remain in your house, but left and listened to trifling words and watched magic works? Get up and eat dinner with me, for I can't eat without you!" But she said to him: "Today I excuse myself, for I am very much afraid."

90. When he heard these things from Mygdonia, Charisius did not want to go out to dinner, but he commanded his servants to bring her to dine with him;[7] then when they brought her in,[8] he requested that she dine with him, but she excused herself. Because she was unwilling, he dined alone, saying to her: "Because of you, I excused myself from dining with King Misdaeus, and you were unwilling to dine with me, were you not?" But she said: "Because I am not well." When he rose, Charisius then wanted to sleep with her as was their custom, but she said: "Did I not tell you I have excused myself today?"

[Charisius slept in another bed and had an ominous dream. The next morning he went to call on the king, while Mygdonia visited Thomas.]

95. And Charisius, the king's kinsman and friend, came to lunch and did not find his wife in the house, and he questioned all in his house: "Where did your mistress go?" One of them answered and said, "She went to that stranger." And when he heard these things from his slave, he was irritated at the rest of his servants because they had not immediately reported to him what had happened, and he sat down and waited for her. When evening arrived and she entered the house, he said to her: "Where were you?" She answered and said: "At the doctor." And he said: "Is that stranger a doctor?" And she said: "Yes, he is a doctor of souls; for

---

7. The Syriac text here makes better sense of the narrative: "but he ordered his servants to bring food to him so that he might dine in her presence."
8. Syriac: "when they brought the food in."

many doctors treat bodies, which dissolve, but he treats souls, which do not perish." When he heard these things, Charisius felt much bitterness within himself toward Mygdonia, because of the apostle. But he did not answer her, because he was afraid, for she was superior to him in both wealth and understanding. And he went to dinner, but she entered her bedroom. And he said to the servants: "Call her to dinner." But she was unwilling.

96. Having heard that she did not wish to come out of the bedroom, he went in and said to her: "Why don't you want to dine with me, and perhaps not to sleep with me as usual? And concerning the latter point I have a greater suspicion, for I heard that that magician and deceiver teaches that one should not live together with his own wife, and he overthrows what nature demands and the gods have ordained." When Charisius had said these things, Mygdonia was silent. He spoke to her again: "My mistress and consort Mygdonia, do not be led astray by deceitful and foolish words or by deeds of magic, which I have heard this man performs in the name of the Father, Son, and Holy Spirit. For no one in this world has heard of anyone raising the dead, but I hear it rumored of him that he raises the dead. And just because he does not eat or drink, do not think that he does not eat or drink for righteousness' sake; he does this because he possesses nothing. For what else would someone who has no daily bread do? And he has one garment because he is poor. As for his not taking anything from anyone, he does this because he knows that he does not really cure anyone."

97. When Charisius had said these things, Mygdonia was silent, just like a rock, and she prayed that at dawn she might go to the apostle of Christ. And Charisius left her and went to dinner despondent, for he was anxious to sleep with her according to their custom. But when he went away, she knelt down and prayed, saying: "Lord God, Master, merciful Father, savior Christ, give me power so that I might conquer Charisius's shameless boldness, and allow me to guard the holiness in which you delight, in order that through it I too may find eternal life." Having prayed these things, she lay down, covered, on the bed.

98. Charisius, when he had dined, stood over her, but she cried out, saying: "You no longer have a place by me, for my lord Jesus, who is with me and rests in me, is mightier than you." Laughing, he said: "You joke well, saying these things about that sorcerer, and you mock him well, the one who says that you do not have life with God unless you make yourself holy." After he said these things, he tried to lie down to sleep with her; however, she would not allow it but, crying out bitterly,

she said: "I call upon you, Lord Jesus, not to forsake me, for I have made my refuge with you. For as I learned that you are the one who seeks those who are held in ignorance, and the one who rescues those who are trapped in error, I now ask that you, whose reputation I have heard and believed, come to my aid, and rescue me from Charisius's shamelessness, so that his foulness will not overpower me." And, striking her hands,[9] she fled from him naked; and, as she went out, she pulled down the bedroom curtain, threw it around herself, and went to her nurse and slept there at her side.

[Charisius spent the night in despair. He did not know where Mygdonia had gone after fleeing naked from him, and he feared she had run out to the marketplace to meet Thomas. He mourned her loss and determined to enlist the king's aid in taking vengeance on Thomas.]

101. While Charisius was thinking these things over, day dawned; having endured the night, he dressed in poor clothing, put on shoes, and, despondent and with a sad expression, went out to greet the king. When he saw him, the king said: "Why are you so unhappy, and why do you come dressed in this way? And I see that your face too is changed." And Charisius said to the king: "I have some news to tell you, a new desolation, which Siphor has brought into India: a certain Hebrew man, a magician, whom he has encamped in his own house and who does not separate from him. Many visit him, and he teaches them of a new god and instills in them new laws that have never been heard, saying: 'It is impossible for you to enter into the eternal life that I preach to you unless you rid yourself of your own wives, similarly also, the women of their own husbands.' And it happened that my unfortunate wife went to him and became a hearer of his words, which she believed, and she left me in the night and ran to the stranger. But summon both Siphor and that magician who is hidden with him, and inflict punishment on their heads, so that all our people will not be destroyed!"

[Misdaeus promised to avenge Charisius and restore his wife to him. He first summoned and interrogated Siphor. Then he sent soldiers to Siphor's house to arrest Thomas. Thomas remained silent under interrogation and was subsequently scourged, chained, and imprisoned.]

114. And Charisius went home rejoicing, thinking that his wife would be with him and that she would be just as she was previously, before she heard the divine word and believed in Jesus. And he went and found her with her hair chopped off and clothes torn; and seeing this, he said to

9. The Syriac text offers an interesting variant: "tying his hands."

her: "My lady Mygdonia, why does this cruel sickness possess you? And for what reason have you done these things? For I have been your husband from your girlhood; both the gods and the laws grant that I rule over you. What is this great madness of yours, that you have become a laughingstock in all the nation? But put aside the anxiety that proceeds from that sorcerer; I will remove his face from our midst, so that you will no longer see him."

115. And when she heard these things, Mygdonia yielded to her grief, groaning and lamenting. And again Charisius spoke: "Have I then wronged the gods so much that they have afflicted me with so great a disease? How have I committed such a great offense that they cast me down so low? I beg you, Mygdonia, do not strangle my soul with the pitiful sight of you and your lowly appearance, and do not wear my heart out with anxieties over you. I am Charisius, your husband, whom all the nation honors and fears. What must I do? I do not even know how to act. And what shall I think? Shall I be silent and patient? And who will put up with it, when people seize his treasure? Who would bear patiently the loss of your noble ways? For what is there for me? Your fragrance is in my nostrils, and your radiant face is fixed in my eyes. They are taking away my soul, and they are destroying the beautiful body in which I delighted when I saw it. And they are maiming my most quick-sighted eye; they are cutting off my right hand. My joy is turned to grief and my life to death, and light is plunged in darkness. Let none of my kinsmen look at me henceforth, for they have given no help. I will not prostrate myself before the gods of the east henceforth, for they have inflicted on me such great evils. Indeed, I will no longer pray to them, nor will I sacrifice to them, because I am robbed of my spouse. What else would I ask of them? For all my glory has been taken away. And I am a ruler, second to the king in power; but Mygdonia, having disregarded me, has taken away all these things. Oh, that someone would cut out my eye, if only you would be devoted to me as you used to be!"

116. As Charisius said these things with tears, Mygdonia sat, remaining silent and looking at the ground; and, approaching again, he said: "My most desired lady Mygdonia, remember that I chose and took you as the most beautiful of all the women in India, although I could have joined myself in marriage to others more beautiful than you. But, no, I lie, Mygdonia—for, by the gods, it would not be possible to find another like you in the land of the Indians. Oh, woe is me forever, because you do not want to speak to me! Insult me if you want, so that I may be

deemed worthy of a single word from you! Look at me, because I am more handsome than that sorcerer;[10] but you are my wealth and honor; and all know that no one is comparable to me;[11] but you are my birth and kinship; and see, he is taking you away from me."

117. When Charisius had said these things, Mygdonia spoke to him: "The one whom I love is better than you and your possessions, for your possessions, being of the earth, turn back to earth; the one whom I love is heavenly, and he will take me with him to heaven. Your wealth will pass away, and your beauty will vanish, along with your robes and your many deeds; but you will remain alone, naked, with your errors. Do not remind me of your acts, for I pray to the Lord to forget you, so as no longer to remember former pleasures and physical intercourse, which will pass away like a shadow; but Jesus alone remains forever, along with the souls who hope in him. Jesus himself will free me from the shameful deeds that I performed with you." When he had heard these things, Charisius's soul was undone, and he turned to sleep, saying to her: "Think it over by yourself tonight. If you want to be with me the way you were before, and not see that sorcerer, I will do everything to please you; and if you put an end to your attitude toward him, I will cast him out of the prison and free him, and he may move to another country; and I will not grieve you, for I know that you are very much attached to the stranger. The matter did not start with you—he also deceived many other women along with you—and those women came to their senses and returned to themselves. Do not, then, dismiss my words as nothing and make me a disgrace among the Indians!"

118. Saying these things, Charisius slept, but she, taking ten denarii, went secretly to give them to the jailor, so that she might go in to the apostle. And Judas Thomas came and met her on the road. When she saw him, she was afraid, for she thought he was one of the ruling powers, for a great light preceded him. And she said to herself, as she fled: "I have destroyed you, wretched soul. For you will not see Judas, the apostle of the living one, again, and you have not yet received the holy seal." And, fleeing, she ran into a narrow place and hid, saying: "I prefer to be killed[12] by the more common people, whom it is possible to persuade, rather than fall in with this powerful ruler, who scorns gifts."

119. As Mygdonia was thinking these things over by herself, Judas

10. An addition in the Syriac text clarifies the sense of the passage: "and I have wealth and honor."
11. Syriac adds: "in respect to lineage."
12. Syriac: "taken."

came and stood over her; when she saw him, she was afraid and fell down, nearly dead with fright; but, standing beside her and taking her hand, he said to her: "Do not be afraid, Mygdonia; Jesus will not neglect you, nor will your Lord, to whom you have entrusted your own soul, overlook you. His compassionate rest will not forsake you; the kind one, because of his great kindness, and the good one, because of his goodness, will not forsake you. So get up off the ground, because you have risen altogether above it. Behold the light, for the Lord does not allow those who love him to walk in darkness. Look to the one who travels with his slaves, for he is an ally to them in dangers." And Mygdonia stood up and turned to him and said: "Where were you going, my Lord? And who is it that led you out of prison to see the sun?" Judas Thomas said to her: "My Lord Jesus is more powerful than all powers and kings and rulers."

120. And Mygdonia said: "Give me the seal of Jesus Christ and I will receive the gift from your hands before you leave this life." And taking him along, she entered the courtyard and woke up her nurse, saying to her: "My mother and nurse Marcia, all the help and comforts you have provided for me from childhood to my present age are trifling, and the favor I owe you on their account is transitory. But now do me a favor as well, so that you may receive repayment forever from the one who bestows great favors." And at this, Marcia said: "What do you want, my daughter Mygdonia? And what is to be done to please you? The stranger did not allow you to fulfill the honors that you offered me before, and you made me a disgrace in all the nation. And now, then, what new thing are you ordering?" And Mygdonia said: "Become a partaker with me in eternal life, so that I may receive from you the perfect nurture. Take bread and a mixture of water and bring them to me, sparing my freedom."[13] And the nurse said: "I will bring many loaves of bread, and instead of water, gallons of wine, and I will fulfill your desire." But she said to the nurse: "I don't need gallons, nor many loaves. Bring only this: a mixture of water, one loaf of bread, and oil."

121. And when Marcia had brought these things, Mygdonia stood before the apostle with her head bare. And he took the oil and poured it on her head, saying: "Sacred oil given to us for sanctification, secret mystery in which the cross was shown to us, you are the displayer of covered parts; you are the humbler of hard deeds; you are the one who reveals hidden treasures; you are the bud of kindness. Let your power

13. Syriac: "pitying me, a freeborn woman."

come; let it settle on your slave Mygdonia; and heal her through this freedom." When the oil had been poured out, he ordered the nurse to undress her and to wrap a muslin cloth around her; and there was a spring of water there, in which the apostle went up and baptized Mygdonia in the name of the Father and the Son and the Holy Spirit. When she was baptized and dressed, breaking bread and taking a cup of water, he made her a partaker in the body of Christ and the cup of the Son of God, and he said: "You received your seal and established for yourself eternal life." And immediately a voice from above was heard, saying: "Yes, Amen." And when she heard that voice, Marcia was amazed and begged the apostle that she might also receive the seal. And giving it to her, the apostle said: "Let the zeal of the Lord be around you as it is around the others."

[Thomas returned to the prison while the guards were still sleeping and remained there.]

123. Charisius went in to Mygdonia as soon as it was dawn. And he found the women praying and saying: "New God who comes to us in this way through a stranger, God hidden from those who live in India, the God who shows his glory through his apostle Thomas, the God whose reputation we have heard and in whom we have believed, the God to whom we have come to be saved, the God who through love and compassion descended to our insignificance, the God who sought us when we did not know him, the God who rules the heights and is not hidden from the depths, turn the madness of Charisius away from us!" On hearing this, Charisius said to Mygdonia: "You are right to call me wicked and mad and vile, because if I had not tolerated your disobedience and had not given you your freedom, you would not have invoked God against me or revealed my name in the presence of this God. Believe me, Mygdonia, no help is coming from this sorcerer; he can't do what he promises. But I do everything just as I promise before your very eyes, so that you will believe and remain constant to my words and be with me just as you were before."

124. And, approaching her, he begged her again, saying: "If you obey me, I will have no further grief. Remember that day when you met me for the first time. Tell the truth: which of the two was more beautiful to you, me at that time or Jesus at this time?" And Mygdonia said: "That time required what belonged to it, and this time requires its own. That time was a time of beginning, but this a time of fulfillment. That was a time of transitory life, but this of eternal life. That was a time of passing pleasure, but this outlasts everything. That was day and night, but this is

day without night. You have seen that transitory marriage of here and now, but this marriage lasts into eternity. That was a communion of destruction, this is life eternal. Those wedding attendants are short-lived men and women, but these now will remain to the end. . . .That wedding chamber is taken apart again, but this one lasts through everything. That bed was covered with coverlets, but this one with affection and trust. You are a passing and fading bridegroom, but Jesus is a true bridegroom who remains deathless on into eternity. That bridal gift was money and clothes that get old, but this one is living words that never fade away."

[When he heard Mygdonia's words, Charisius went to consult with the king. Misdaeus immediately ordered Judas Thomas to be brought to him, so that he might condemn and execute the apostle. Charisius begged the king to take a gentler approach, in the hope that the apostle might agree to persuade Mygdonia to return to married life. Misdaeus agreed, and Thomas was brought before the king.]

127. . . . Misdaeus said: "See, I set you free. Go now and convince Mygdonia, the wife of Charisius, that she does not want to separate from him. . . .For by doing this, you may spare yourself, for you have not yet had your fill of life. But know that if you don't convince her, I am going to pluck you out of this life which is dear to all. . . ."

[Charisius added his own words to the king's, arguing that he had done the apostle no wrong, yet the apostle had thrown his household into confusion. He begged the apostle to persuade Mygdonia to change her mind and threatened to kill him if he failed. Then Charisius and Thomas went together to Charisius's house.]

129. . . . And they found Mygdonia sitting and Marcia standing by her, with her hand resting on Mygdonia; and Mygdonia said: "Oh, Mother, may the remaining days of my life be cut short for me, and all of the hours become as one hour, and may I depart from this life so that by departing more quickly I might see this fair one whose reputation I have heard, this living one who gives life to those who believe in him, where there is no day and night, no light and darkness, no good and evil, no poverty and wealth, masculine and feminine, no freeborn and slave, no one arrogant and subordinating the humble." As she said these things, the apostle stood next to her, and she stood up instantly and prostrated herself before him, whereupon Charisius said to him: "Do you see how she pays you honor and how willing she is to do everything you prescribe?"

130. When he said this, Judas spoke to Mygdonia: "My daughter Mygdonia, listen to the things brother Charisius says." And Mygdonia

said: "If you can't even name the act with a word, will you force me to endure the act? For I have heard from you that this life is not profitable and this rest is transitory and these possessions are not lasting. Furthermore, you said that the one who turns aside from this life will receive eternal life, and the one who hates the light of day and night will gaze with wonder at the light that is not quenched, and that the one who despises these possessions will find other everlasting possessions. But now you are afraid. But who changes things, when he has been praised for his work? Who will turn again and tear a thing off its foundation? Who after digging a well of water in an abundant place turns again and fills it in? Who after finding a treasure does not use it?" But when Charisius heard this, he said: "I will neither follow your example nor come after you to destroy you, nor will I—even though it is in my power—put chains on you.[14] And I will not permit you to converse with this sorcerer. If you obey me, I know what I have to do."[15]

[Thomas returned to the home of Siphor. Siphor, his wife, and his daughter were baptized and broke bread with Thomas.]

134. After Misdaeus the king had set Judas free, he dined and went home and related to his wife the things that had happened to their kinsman Charisius, saying: "See what has happened to that poor man! You know yourself, my sister Tertia, that nothing is more beautiful to a man than his own wife, through whom he is refreshed. Well, it happened that his wife went to that sorcerer of whom you have heard, who is residing in the land of the Indians, fell under his potions, and was separated from her own husband; and he is confused about what to do. And when I wanted to destroy this malefactor, he did not want me to. But you, go to her and counsel her to turn to her own husband and distance herself from the empty words of the sorcerer."

135. And Tertia at once got up and went to the house of Charisius, her husband's kinsman, and found Mygdonia stretched out on the ground in self-humiliation. She had spread sackcloth and ashes under herself, and she was praying to the Lord that he forgive her her earlier sins and that she might depart quickly from this life. And Tertia said to her: "Mygdonia, my dearest sister and companion, what is this deed? What is this sickness that has possessed you? Why are you doing acts of sheer madness? Know yourself and return to your former way! Draw near to the many members of your family and have a care for your true hus-

---

14. Syriac: "but you I will bind, because I have power over you."
15. Syriac: "And if you yield (good and well); and if not, I know what I will do."

band and do not do what is alien to your status as a freeborn woman." Mygdonia said to her: "Oh, Tertia, you have not yet heard the preaching of life; it has not yet reached your ears; you have not yet tasted the medicine of life, nor been freed from the groanings of corruptibility. You are fixed in a transitory life and you do not know eternal life and salvation. You have not perceived the communion that is incorruptible. You stand clothed with garments that age and you have not desired eternal garments, and you set great store by this beauty that vanishes but you do not think about the shamefulness of the soul. And you are rich in numbers of servants, and you take pride in the glory from many, but you do not ransom yourself from condemnation to death."

136. . . . And when Tertia heard these things, she ran off and went to Siphor's house, so that she might see the new apostle who had settled there. . . .Tertia said to him: "May I become a sharer of this life that you proclaim all will receive who come together in the assembly of God!" And the apostle said: "The treasury of the holy kingdom is open, and those who worthily partake of the goods there rest and, resting, they rule. But first, no one comes to him who is unclean and vile, for he himself knows our inner hearts and the depths of our thought, and nothing escapes him. And so, if you truly have faith in him, you will be made worthy of his mysteries, and he himself will magnify you and enrich you and make you an heir to his kingdom."

137. When she heard these things, Tertia went back home rejoicing, and she found her husband still there, not having eaten yet. When he saw her, Misdaeus said: "How is it that your entrance today is more beautiful? And why did you walk? It is not fitting for freeborn women like you." And Tertia said to him: "I owe you the greatest thanks, because you sent me to Mygdonia. For when I went, I heard of the new life, and I saw the new apostle of the God who gives life to those who have faith in him and fulfill his commands. . . ."

[When he heard his wife's words, Misdaeus was overcome with grief and rage. He sought out Charisius, and together they had the apostle arrested again and imprisoned to await sentencing. But Misdaeus's troubles were not over. His son Vazan approached the apostle in prison and was impressed by his words.]

150. Vazan, the young man, entreated the apostle, saying: "I beg you sir, apostle of God, allow me to go and I will persuade the prison guard to give you permission to come home with me, so that through you I can receive the seal and become your servant and a keeper of the commandments of the God whom you preach. For formerly I lived a way of life in

accordance with what you teach, until my father forced me and joined me to a wife named Mnesara. For even though I am twenty-one years old, I have already been married seven years. And before I was joined to a wife I had not had relations with any other woman. Because of this, I was considered worthless by my father. And to this time neither son nor daughter has been born to me by this wife. Rather, my wife has lived together with me in chastity during this time, and if she were feeling well today and had listened to you, I know that I would be at rest and she would receive eternal life. But she is in danger and tried by much sickness. . . ."

[At this point Tertia and Mygdonia and Marcia joined the gathering in Thomas's prison cell, having bribed the guard to let them in. Tertia began to relate the story of their adventures.]

152. . . . "King Misdaeus, having sent for me, said: 'That magician has not yet prevailed over you, as I hear he performs magic on people with oil and water and bread, and he has not yet bewitched you. But listen to me, for I will lock you up and crush you, and I will destroy him. For I know that if he has not yet given you oil and bread and water, he does not have the power to prevail over you.' But I said to him: 'You have power over my body; and do all that you wish. But I will not join you in destroying my soul.' And when he heard these things, he locked me up in a room, and Charisius also brought Mygdonia and locked her up with me. And you[16] led us out and brought us to those here. But give us the seal quickly, so that the hopes of Misdaeus, who is plotting these things, may be cut off!'

[Thomas sent Vazan out to make preparations for baptism. On the way, he met his wife Mnesara, who had been miraculously cured and was coming to join him. Vazan and Mnesara continued to Vazan's house. Thomas, Siphor and his wife and daughter, and Tertia and Mygdonia and Marcia followed them, while the prison guards slept. When they had all reached Vazan's house, Thomas prayed for Vazan, Tertia, and Mnesara, who were to be baptized.]

157. After the apostle had prayed he said to Mygdonia: "Undress your sisters." And after taking off their clothes, she wrapped cloths around their waists and brought them. And Vazan came forward first, the others after him, and Judas, taking oil in a silver cup, spoke. . . . And after praying, he poured it first on the head of Vazan and then upon the heads of the women, saying: "In your name, Jesus Christ. Let this be for the forgiveness of sins for these souls and for the diverting of the adversary

16. The "you" here refers to Jesus appearing as Judas Thomas.

and for the salvation of their souls!" And he called Mygdonia to anoint the women and he anointed Vazan. After anointing them, he led them into the water in the name of the Father and the Son and the Holy Spirit.

[Following the baptisms and eucharistic meal, Thomas, Tertia, Mygdonia, and Marcia returned to their respective prisons. Judas Thomas was tried before Misdaeus and sentenced to death. Misdaeus ordered his soldiers to execute Thomas quietly outside of town, because he feared the people's reaction. Thomas's grieving followers witnessed his death and then took the body, wrapped it in fine linens, and buried it in the tomb of the kings.]

169. . . . And Misdaeus and Charisius carried Mygdonia and Tertia off and oppressed them greatly, but the women did not assent to their will. The apostle revealed himself and said to the women: "Do not be led astray; Jesus, the holy one, the living one, will quickly send you help." And Misdaeus and Charisius, knowing that Mygdonia and Tertia did not obey them, yielded, conceding that the women might live according to their own will. . . .[17]

SUGGESTED READINGS

Text of the Acts of Thomas

Bonnet, Maximilianus. *Acta Apostolorum Apocrypha,* vol. 2.2. Hildesheim: Georg Olms Verlagsbuchhandlung, 1959. Pages 99–291. Greek.

Hennecke, Edgar. *New Testament Apocrypha,* vol. 2, edited by W. Schneemelcher; English translation edited by R. McL. Wilson. Philadelphia: Westminster Press, 1965. Pages 442–531. English based on the Greek.

James, Montague Rhodes. *The Apocryphal New Testament.* Oxford: Clarendon Press, 1924. Pages 365–438. English based on the Greek.

Klijn, A. F. J. *The Acts of Thomas.* Leiden, Neth.: E. J. Brill, 1962. English based on the Syriac.

Wright, William. *Apocryphal Acts of Apostles.* 1871. Reprint, Amsterdam: Philo Press, 1968. Pages 146–298. Syriac and English.

Secondary Studies

Bornkamm, G. "The Acts of Thomas." In E. Hennecke, *New Testament Apocrypha,* vol. 2, edited by W. Schneemelcher; English translation edited by R. McL. Wilson, 425–42. Philadelphia: Westminster Press, 1965.

---

17. A variant Greek manuscript tradition for this last section runs as follows: "And although Misdaeus and Charisius pressured Tertia and Mygdonia greatly, they did not convince them to give up their resolve. And Judas appeared and said to them: 'Do not forget the former things. For Jesus himself, the holy and living one, will help you.' And because the people around Misdaeus and Charisius did not persuade the women, they let them pursue their resolve."

Bovon, François, ed. *Les actes apocryphes des apôtres. Christianisme et monde paien.* Geneva: Labor et Fides, 1981. Collected essays.

Burrus, Virginia. *Chastity as Autonomy: Women in the Stories of Apocryphal Acts.* Lewiston, N.Y.: Edwin Mellen Press, 1987.

Corrington, Gail Paterson. "Salvation, Celibacy and Power: 'Divine Women' in Late Antiquity." SBLSP 24 (1985) 321–25.

Davies, Stevan L. *The Revolt of the Widows: The Social World of the Apocryphal Acts.* Carbondale and Edwardsville: Southern Illinois University Press, 1980.

Kraemer, Ross. "The Conversion of Women to Ascetic Forms of Christianity." *Signs* 6 (1980) 298–307.

MacDonald, Dennis. "The Role of Women in the Production of the Apocryphal Acts of the Apostles." *Illif Review* 40 (1984) 21–38.

MacDonald, D. R., ed. *The Apocryphal Acts of Apostles. Semeia* 38. 1986. Collected essays.

Schneemelcher, W., and K. Schaeferdiek. "Second and Third Century Acts of Apostles: Introduction." In E. Hennecke, *New Testament Apocrypha,* vol. 2, edited by W. Schneemelcher; English translation edited by R. McL. Wilson, 167–88. Philadelphia: Westminster Press, 1965.

Chaeremon the Stoic
on Egyptian Temple Askesis
(From Porphyry, *On Abstinence* 4:6–8)

INTRODUCTION

Egyptian temple life and philosophers are part of the background of and competition for Christian monasticism. There was also a long tradition of foreign admiration and imitation of Egyptian temple life.[1]

The deserts and temples on the edge of the deserts provided a convenient place for separation and contemplation. Philo the Jew went to the desert near Alexandria (*Leg. All.* 2:85). Ptolemagrius of Akmim went outside town to practice philosophy, to garden, and to be the local host for the feasts of the god Pan.[2] Rostovtzeff also shows the temples as places of asylum and change of life; he pictures Hephaistion (like Pachomius later) as a soldier who decided to stay in the temple after the life of the army. He later became an oracle giver.[3]

Foreigners indeed came. Iamblichus says Pythagoras visited Egyptian priests to learn a way of life (as Antony also visited holy men in the Nile Valley). Hippolytus the Christian says Pythagoras imitated the priests in enjoining silence and making his disciples live solitary lives in under-

1. The ideas in this introduction are drawn largely from the author's more extensive discussion, "Monasticism in an Age of Anxiety," presented at the 1983 Claremont Conference on the Roots of Egyptian Christianity.

2. C. Welles, "The Garden of Ptolemagrius at Panopolis," *TAPA* 77 (1946) 192–206. Ptolemagrius is like Paulinus of Nola.

3. M. Rostovtzeff, *Social and Economic History of the Hellenistic World* (London: Oxford University Press, 1967) 2.734–35. For bibliography on the much discussed *enkatochoi*, cf. 3.1497. For study of the asceticism of the astrologers (and of the variety of people resident in the temples during the Roman period), see F. Cumont, *L'Egypte des Astrologues* (Brussels: Fondation Egyptologique Reine Elisabeth, 1937) 103–6. The accounts of the astrologers, with those of Apuleius's Lucius (*Golden Ass* 11.19–21), provide another transition between the Hellenistic and later monastic worlds.

ground chambers.[4] The (later Pachomian) area near the Luxor Memnon statues served as a special goal for foreigners and an ascetic outpost for the Memphis temples. A Greek ostracon from Deir el-Bahri (near Luxor) tells how Polyaratos visited the sanctuary of Amenotes in the time of Ptolemy II and was cured of his illness. "The Counsels of Amenotes" (the Greek name for Amenhotep), found in the same place, teaches the philosophic life through popular Greek wisdom.[5] Lucian's Eucrates tells how he sailed up the Nile to the statues of Memnon and met Pancrates, a scribe from a Memphis temple who had lived underground in an Isis sanctuary.[6] Near the statues, Philostratus's Apollonius of Tyana visited naked philosophers who lived and had shrines and a medium-sized stoa with a hospice for strangers in a grove. The philosophers said they abstained from animal flesh, desires, and envy, as well as from the use of miracle methods, which truth does not need. They told of lying on bare ground, naked and on guard against dreams and visions. They served as an ascetic outpost to which Memphis priests sent a man charged with involuntary manslaughter.[7]

The best description of the abstinent temple life is that of the first-century Stoic philosopher and priest-scholar of Alexandria, Chaeremon, quoted in the third-century philosopher Porphyry and cited by Jerome. Porphyry (the disciple, biographer, and editor of Plotinus), in his book *On Abstinence from Animal Food*, addresses those in his own day who seek the contemplative and intellectual life. His ideal is to endure events of the day, dissolve the perturbations of the soul, and realize fidelity and constancy of friendship. He tells of the pleasure of living with frugality—no wine, little food, small, hard bed, little sleep, and the purgation of everything of a foreign nature to allow the ascent of the soul. Porphyry puts Chaeremon's Egyptian priests (as well as Josephus's Essenes) among his ancient models. They exemplify the pure and creative ascetic life (among the pressures of admiration and festivals), with their purifi-

4. Iamblichus *Life of Pythagoras* 18–19 (4); Hippolytus *Haer.* 1.2; Tertullian *De Anima* 28.

5. On both Polyaratos at Deir el-Bahri and the "Counsels of Amenotes," see M. Lichtheim, *Late Egyptian Wisdom Literature in an International Context* (Göttingen: Vandenhoeck & Ruprecht, 1983) 104–5. On Hellenization of religion, Rostovtzeff, *Social and Economic History*, 3.1592.

6. Lucian *Pseudol.* 27–39. Also on Democritus entombing himself.

7. Philostratus *Life of Apollonius of Tyana* 2.6–43. The story of Apollonius is particularly important because it shows the mockery and competition between those who use miracles and prophecy (Apollonius—following the Asian Indians, etc.) and those who refuse these methods. Cf. Mark 2.

cations, solemnity, and suppression of passions, their nights spent in singing hymns and in intellectual endeavors. For the present author, the reality of the Chaeremon vista is emphasized by the similarity to a modern Coptic monastery. The modern-day Coptic fasts before festivals are very close indeed to the forty-two or more days cited by Chaeremon. Reading Chaeremon is reminiscent of walking through a modern Coptic monastery, where the monks are trying to live a solitary life but are flooded with visitors at festivals. The crowds demonstrate great admiration for the ascetic life.

The textual edition is Porphyry's *Opuscula Selecta* (Leipzig: A. Nauck, 1886) and the somewhat emended text of J. Bouffartique and M. Patillon found in the edition and translation of P. W. Van der Horst, *Chaeremon: Egyptian Priest and Stoic Philosopher* (Leiden, Neth.: E. J. Brill, 1984) 16–23. Van der Horst and others downplay the asceticism as philosophically "idealized description." The philosophic reality of ancient Egypt is shown in its mockery by Lucian and Philostratus's Apollonius. One may also note the symbiosis of temple and philosophic life, especially in the multiple accounts and records found near the statues of Memnon.[8]

TRANSLATION

6. Chaeremon the Stoic, in his writings about the Egyptian priests, says they were considered to be philosophers by the Egyptians. He explains that they chose temples as places to practice philosophy, for living a life with their statues is suitable to the whole yearning for contemplation. Because they dwell in temples, they obtain security

8. The relation of Chaeremon to the reality of ancient Egypt is emphasized by the life shown by Ptolemagrius and the writings of Deir el-Bahri, as well as the Serapeum in Alexandria. The discipline (like that of the priests), described by Chaeremon and required of those who lived with the priests, may well have been a background for Christian monasticism. Such people, renting dwellings or living near the temple with the priests, would be like Hephestion and Apuleius's Lucius. They would have been required to live continuously (or at least during their residence in the temple) the prefestival ascetic life lived only sporadically by the priests. Compare present-day priests and monks living together. The requirements, relationships, and competition of life together generally may have strengthened the commonly practiced asceticism.

The combination of philosophic idealism and healing found in modern monasticism is also found both in ancient Egyptian temples such as Deir el-Bahri and in followers of Pythagoras (including Apollonius of Tyana). The ability to be purified (religiously) was one of the attributes of both temple priests and certain groups of philosophers. Cf. P. W. Van der Horst, *Chaeremon: Egyptian Priest and Stoic Philosopher. The Fragments Collected and Translated with Explanatory Notes* (Leiden, Neth.: E. J. Brill, 1984) 56, n. 1.

through being honored as philosophers and worshiped as divine, or as sacred animals. They are solitary, mingling only at sacrifices and higher feasts. At other times the temples were inaccessible to others. For it was necessary that those approaching be purified and abstain from many things. And this was the common law for Egyptian temples. Having given up every other occupation and human labors, they devote the whole of their life to the contemplation and admiration of divine things, through which they obtain honor, security, and piety; through contemplation they obtain knowledge; through both, an arcane and time-honored discipline of manners. For to be united with divine gnosis and foresight removes one from greediness, puts down the passions, and raises one toward an "examined" life. They sought simplicity and moderation in dress, continence and patient endurance, righteousness and lack of greed in all things. Their antisocial nature made them solemn. For during the time of what are called purifications, they did not mix with their near relatives and those of their order, nor were they seen by others . . . except for what was needful for the required purifications. . . . For the sanctuary was not to be entered by those not cleansed, and they lived in holy places for the holy services. At other more open times they mixed with those like themselves, but they did not live together with the ritually unclean. But they always appear near the gods or statues, bearing them in sacred processions or arranged in solemn order. Such acts were done not for the sake of vanity, but for some philosophically significant reason.[9] Their solemnity was apparent from their composure, for their gait was well disciplined, with face composed. They were so concerned about this that they did not want to wink, seldom laughing, except for a smile. Their hands were always in their robes.[10] And each had a symbol indicative of the rank that he had in sacred affairs (for there were many ranks). Their diet was plain and simple. As for wine, some drank not at all, others a little. It was harmful for the nerves, filled the head, and was a hindrance to learning. In addition, they said it induced sexual desires. They were circumspect in other things—not using bread during times of purifications; at other times eating bread mixed with hyssop (for they said that hyssop greatly cleanses the bread's power). As for oil, many abstain [to some extent]; most [abstain] completely. If it was used with vegetables, only a little, enough to help the taste.

9. *Physis*: some philosophical or allegorical reason.
10. *Schēma*: also a name for monastic dress.

7. Foods and drinks from outside Egypt were not lawful for them to touch. This was a strong force to cut them off from luxury. And they abstained from all fish from Egypt and tetrapods having uncloven and cloven hooves, and nonhorned [animals] and birds that eat flesh. Many abstained from eating any animals whatsoever, and during the times of purifications it was the custom for all to abstain even from eating eggs. . . .

And there were certain common ceremonies, but differing by groups of priests and according to each god. The purity rites, however, cleansed all. When they were to observe certain particulars regarding the religious rite, they prepare for them for a number of days—some forty-two, some more, some less, but not less than seven, abstaining from all animals and also from herbs and vegetables, abstaining the whole time from relations with women (for they never had relations with men). Three times a day they washed in cold water—on getting up from bed, before dinner, and before sleep. When they happened to dream, they immediately cleansed the body with a bath. They used cold bathing for most other matters, but not as much. Their beds were woven from branches of palm called "bais"; a semicircular log, well smoothed, was placed in support of their heads. They experienced thirst and hunger and taking in little food throughout their whole lives.

8. A testimony to their continence is that although they did not practice walking or riding, they lived without disease and were muscular and strong enough for moderate-level work. At any rate, they carried many things in the sacred rites that required more than common strength. They divided the night into observations of the heavens, as well as of the holy rite; the day into worship of the gods, all singing hymns three or four times—morning, when the sun is at midpoint, and when it is declining. The remaining time they spent at arithmetic and geometrical studies, working out some calculations and investigating, busying themselves in learning. During winter nights they were working, engaged in the love of learning, not worrying about anxieties of gain, freed from that evil despot, great expense. Therefore, their unceasing and uninterrupted labor is testimony to their perseverance, their lack of desires to their continence. They considered one of the most irreligious things to be to sail from Egypt, because they were wary of foreign luxuries and their use. This seemed to them to be lawful only for those so compelled by the requirements of life in the king's court. It was very important to them to keep their country's customs, even in small things. Those found to have broken them were expelled. The true way of philosophizing was

kept by their prophets, priests in charge of vestments, sacred scribes, and astrologers. The remainder of the priests, temple workers, and servants of the gods were likewise in a purified state, although not with such strictness or continence as the above.

Such are the tales told about the Egyptians by a lover of truth and accurate reporter, who among the Stoics was thought of as a most clever philosopher.

SUGGESTED READINGS

Bleeker, C. J. *Egyptian Festivals.* Leiden, Neth.: E. J. Brill, 1967.

Cumont, F. *L'Egypte des Astrologues.* Brussels: Fondation Egyptologique Reine Elisabeth, 1937.

Lichtheim, M. *Late Egyptian Wisdom Literature in an International Context.* Göttingen, W. Ger.: Vandenhoeck & Ruprecht, 1983.

Van der Horst, P. W. *Chaeremon: Egyptian Priest and Stoic Philosopher. The Fragments Collected and Translated with Explanatory Notes.* Leiden, Neth.: E. J. Brill, 1984.

Welles, C. "The Garden of Ptolemagrius at Panopolis." *TAPA* 77 (1946) 192–206.

The Life of Chariton

INTRODUCTION

According to tradition, Chariton of Iconium (now Konya in modern Turkey) introduced the monastic life to Palestine. Venerated as a saint by the Greek Church, his "Life" was inserted by Symeon Metaphrastes in the *Menologium* (ca. 950 C.E.).[1] Metaphrastes's text was a summary of an early Byzantine "Life of Chariton," which was later discovered and published by G. Garitte with a critical apparatus but no translation.[2]

The author of the "Life of Chariton" is not known by name, but from the content of his work we know that he was a monk in one of Chariton's foundations in the Judean Desert. He most probably wrote before the Persian invasion in 614, as there is no hint in the text of any trouble for the Christians of his time that resembled the persecution suffered by Chariton at the hands of the heathen. As for a *terminus post quem*, our author seems to have felt impelled to write his hero's praises owing to the publication of works that extolled the virtues of other holy men who had come onto the stage much later than Chariton and whose monasteries were then eclipsing the old laurae (paths) founded by him (in one of which our monk had his abode). The foremost among these hagiographic writings was Cyril of Scythopolis's collection of biographies (ca. 559 C.E.), which deals with the lives of the most famous monks and

1. Symeon Metaphrastes, *Vitae Sanctorum, Mensis September: Vita et conversatio et certamen Sancti Patris nostri et confessoris Charitonis* (PG 115) 899–918.
2. G. Garitte, "La Vie prémétaphrastique de s. Chariton," *Bulletin de l'Institut Historique Belge de Rome* 21 (1941) 5–46.

monastic founders of the Judean desert.[3] Our anonymous monk, therefore, very likely wrote not long after the appearance of Cyril's book. Hagiographic literature could assume different forms—anecdotes, panegyric or eulogistic writing, or biography in a proper sense. Among such forms, our author chose the panegyric, a choice that speaks clearly of his taste and cultural background.

Tradition had handed down a few main facts for the author's elaboration. Chariton had been a confessor in one of the persecutions launched by the Roman emperors against the Christians; he had later arrived in Palestine as a pilgrim from his native Lycaonia; he had been the first to introduce monastic life in Palestine (or at least in the Judean Desert). Here he had founded three monasteries of the laura type, the first of which was linked to the name of Macarius, bishop of Jerusalem between 314 and 334 C.E. Such data fixed a chronological peg for Chariton's activities and for the claim of priority made in his name by the tradition kept alive in his three monasteries. The coupling of the names of the emperor Aurelian (270–275 C.E.), as Chariton's persecutor, and Macarius, as the bishop who consecrated his first monastery, creates a chronological problem, quite apart from the question of whether Aurelian did indeed ever persecute the Christians. The time gap is too great, and it seems likely that our author is mistaken or deceived himself into choosing the name of an emperor earlier than the one really involved, in order to better sustain his claim of priority, especially against Hilarion, Jerome's candidate for the title of father of Palestinian monasticism. (Hilarion was said to have retired into solitary life in a hut near Gaza in 308 C.E.; this hut was later the kernel of his monastery, not later than 330.)[4]

In any case, there is no reason to reject the tradition ascribing to Macarius the consecration of the old church in the laura of Pharan. Whether Chariton was the father of monasticism in all of Palestine or only in the Judean Desert, he was assuredly not the first to choose a solitary life in the wilderness. This Jewish practice had not lacked some early Christian followers. From Eusebius[5] we learn about Narcissus, bishop of Jerusalem from the time of Commodus (180–192 C.E.) until after Caracalla's ascent in 212. Narcissus retired into the desert on account of slanderous attacks launched against him by some members

3. E. Schwartz, *Kyrilios von Skythopolis* (Texte und Untersuchungen zür Geschichte der Altchristlichen Literatur 49,2; Leipzig: Hinrichs, 1939).
4. D. J. Chitty, *The Desert a City* (Oxford: Basil Blackwell & Mott, 1968) 13.
5. Eusebius *Hist. Eccl.* 6.9–10.

of his own flock. He lived in the wilderness for many years, finally coming back after his slanderers' death. Besides, even Chariton's biographer admits that solitaries, although rare, were already seen in the region. Chariton's innovation was the fact the he saw asceticism not as a private choice, but as an experiment in organized life, and not for a limited time, like a Jewish Nazirite or Narcissus himself, but for life. The laurae he founded were communities of hermits, each living an independent life in his isolated cell and choosing his own kind of ascetic practice, but all the cells were linked by a path (*laura*) leading to the central church. Here the monks would meet once a week for prayer and a common meal. An abbot presided over the community; he was generally assisted by a steward (*oikonomos*) who took charge of the simple needs of the brethren by providing them with food and raw material for their work, bringing the products to the market, and buying all the necessities with the proceeds.

If we can take the text at its face value on this matter, Chariton was the first to teach a kind of rule that contained the basic aspects of monastic life as later crystallized in Palestine, not only in communities of the laura type but in cenobia as well—a pattern different from the Syrian as well as from the Egyptian ascetic trends and achievements. Chariton's rule ordered fixed hours for prayer and obligatory manual work, and it enjoined charity, thus laying upon the monks the obligation of hospitality and involvement and demanding some measure of economic planning. In a word, the monk was forbidden the choice of shutting himself off from society and social problems; the enclosed life or standing on a column were out of the question. He was bound to stability: wandering monks of the Syrian type were unacceptable to Chariton, as well as to the other founding fathers of Palestinian monasticism, Euthymius, Gerasimus, and Sabas.[6] Also, Chariton disapproved of the continuous stream of visitors to famous ascetes, who "advertised their virtues to please men"; this kind was well known, both in Egypt and in Syria. In a word, Chariton enjoined asceticism with humble moderation, solitary life with compassionate involvement—an equilibrium that took root in Palestine and characterized all later monastic ideals and achievements in this region.

6. To give partial satisfaction to the thirst for wandering of the solitaries, Euthymius, Gerasimus, and Sabas established the custom of periodical sallies into the desert, especially during Lent. This was permitted only to experienced ascetes, who sometimes took with them promising disciples, thus teaching them the art of survival in the wilderness. These sallies also answered the need of exploring remote sites and discovering those best suited for the foundation of new monasteries and hermitages.

A technical problem in translation was posed by the many quotations from the Scriptures. For the New Testament, I used the Revised Standard Version of the Bible Society (London: William Collins Sons, 1971). As for the Old Testament, as the author quotes from the Septuagint (LXX), scientific exactitude would have demanded the use of an English version of the same. I had always before me two texts for comparison: *The Septuaginta Version of the Old Testament with an English Translation* (London: S. Bogster and Sons Ltd.; New York: James Pott & Co., 1879), and *The Septuaginta Bible in the Translation of Ch. Thomson, as edited, revised and enlarged by C. A. Muses* (Indian Hills, Colo.: The Falcon Wing Press, 1954). However, I finally decided to make use of the Revised Standard Version for most quotations from the Old Testament in order to avoid inequality of style and to provide the reader with a more familiar translation. Sometimes I had recourse to the English translations of the Septuagint, in those cases in which there was an appreciable difference between the Septuagint and the Masoretic texts, or when a particular shade of meaning, present in the former, and absent from the Revised Standard Version of the latter, was the key motif of the quotation and could not be overlooked without jeopardizing the understanding of our text. Chapter and verse references are given according to the Septuagint, and are followed by the RSV.

Note also that the author of the text makes rather free use of the scriptural text, often modifying it to better suit his intention. Such cases of divergence from the scriptural text are indicated by the addition of "cf" before the reference.

TRANSLATION

LIFE AND WAYS OF SAINT CHARITON, CONFESSOR AND ASCETE

1. Many are indeed the examples of teaching of the holy men who lived a pious life, and anyone who wishes to observe the commandments of the Lord with all his power and to escape, as the Scripture says, "the snares set by the Enemy by the wayside,"[7] such a man can unroll the holy books, thence to draw the stream of salvation as though from perennial springs. For indeed both Testaments, as well as the writings of the God-inspired church fathers and ascetes, all display as in a picture,

---

7. Ps 139:6; Ps 140:6 (RSV).

by means of the written word, the virtues of the holy men, one by one, to
all who wish to take heed. But, although the teachings of these sources
are full and complete, nevertheless most people are frail and frivolous—
for we children of the present generation are not all men of mature
judgment—and, like the deaf, we need loud and repeated sounds of
words, in order that our hearing can begin to pick up the message
sounded in our ears. Therefore, although my account [will not do justice]
to the story, I deemed it necessary to avoid giving up to complete
oblivion, through complete silence, what should be "proclaimed upon
the housetops"[8] for the salvation of mankind: rather, I propose to relate
the virtues of Chariton, "full of grace and truth,"[9] of which I am partly
informed. God plainly opens my lips to eulogize the man, not so that I
may add anything to his fame—for what can an occasional praise be to
one who is heir to the eternal and perfect glory?—but in order that I may
perchance benefit the readers, should they desire to rise to the same zeal
for virtues. For, if truly we are all "slow of heart"[10] in our indifference
toward the commands of God, "lovers of vanity and seekers after lies,"
as the divine David says,[11] nevertheless man's soul, like stone, when it
receives the frequent and unceasing dripping of the word, cannot but be
pierced by a certain yearning, and it opens in readiness to nobly endure
the same trials to which the saints were submitted by the visible as well
as the invisible enemies.

2. Hence I will begin. There was a time when the darkness of impiety,
as a moonless night, threw its shadow over all the holy churches of God,
and, after the manner of a tremendous storm, the persecutors' fury
shook the hearts of the faithful, and their rising, like a dashing stream,
submerged not a few Christians into the abyss of godlessness. For when
a man who was fatal to the Roman Empire, Aurelian,[12] Satan's true

8. Matt 10:27.
9. Cf. John 1:14. An untranslatable play on words between Chariton's name and the
Greek word *charis*, "grace."
10. Ps 4:2.
11. Ibid.
12. Aurelian (270–275) is not known as a persecutor of the Christians. On the
contrary, he showed some interest in the affairs of the church, when he intervened in
Antioch against its bishop, Paul of Samosata, whose controversial opinions were
causing much dissension. The emperor replaced him with Domnus, who had the
support of the bishops of Italy and Rome (Eusebius *Hist. Eccl.* 7.30.19). In his last days,
according to Lactantius and Eusebius, Aurelian did indeed plan a persecution against
the Christian church, but he never signed the edict, having been struck down by death
(Lactantius *Mort. Persc.* 6; Eusebius *Hist. Eccl.* 7.30.21–22; cf. also Paulus Orosius, *Hist.
Adv. Pag.* 7.23.6; 27.12). Also, the information about martyrs under Aurelian is scanty
and unreliable. See *Enciclopedia cattolica*, v. Aureliano. Moreover, Aurelian was not
"fatal to the Roman Empire" as our author indicates. On the contrary, he led many
successful campaigns against the barbarians and the Palmyrene kingdom, repelling the

servant, took the reins of the state, at the beginning of his reign, although he was a fervent worshiper of idols, he nevertheless let the Christians adore the God of the universe without hindrance; but later, prompted by the cursed demons whom he served, while he treated with every honor those who worshiped them, Aurelian began to remove cruelly from life all who confessed Christ to be God, after sentencing them first to many and bitter torments. For the bloody man either would send the holy ones to death by putting them to the sword, or he would give them as food to wild beasts, or burn them alive in all-devouring fire, or drown them in the sea, tied to heavy stones. Therefore, he ordered his impious edict to be displayed in the marketplace of every city that was under the scepter of his imperial rule, and [took pains] to have his heinous counsel put into effect with the utmost zeal.

3. Then those who had built the foundation of their own faith on trust in the Savior Christ, as on a rock, would remain steadfast and unshaken, reckoning the blows of the impious as "infants' darts," as it is written,[13] and won the gory crown of martyrdom; those on the other hand who were captive to a hopeless view about the Savior, and so had the foundation of their faith in him built, as it were, on weak, easily dissolved sand, such men were unable to endure the attacks of their adversaries, as though they were some violent flood or gale, and "made shipwreck of their faith," as the apostle says.[14] Then, as when a pack of wolves bursts into a big flock, one could see the spiritual sheep of the true Shepherd scatter here and there, utterly helpless to save their own lives. For those who had had time to read that iniquitous edict, as soon as it was displayed in public, hastily ran away; but, of the others, some were suddenly seized from their homes and taken to prison, some shut themselves in secret cubicles, then escaped by night. Others still—alas for the perdition of their souls!—"in love with this present world" like Demas,

---

former and reconquering the latter. The details of the story would apply much better to Valerian, the emperor who launched the last persecution against the Christians before Diocletian's. This persecution, described by the Christian poet Commodianus, began with two edicts in 257 and 258, and for three-and-a-half years many outstanding Christians went into hiding or suffered martyrdom throughout the empire. Valerian was defeated and taken prisoner by the Persians, and his successor, Gallien, put an end to the persecution and restored freedom of worship. Valerian (in Greek: *Oualerianos*) and Aurelian may easily have been confused in the oral tradition heard by the author, but, of course, both are too early to link with the information about the role of Macarius in the consecration of the church at Pharan. If the story of Chariton's confession is not entirely a legend, it must therefore be placed at the time of Diocletian's persecution in 303–304, or under one of the last emperors of the East who persecuted the Christian faith: Galerius (d. 311), Maximinus Daia (d. 313), or Licinius (d. 324).

13. Cf. Ps 63:7; Ps 64:7 (RSV).
14. 1 Tim 1:19.

as the apostle says,[15] denied the Savior Christ and so went about their business without peril, the wretched ones, having given up eternal life in exchange for the transient. Others [. . . .] strengthening [their hearts] with religious fervor, spontaneously [walked] in front of the most impious and godless judge, proclaiming their readiness to take leave of life through a violent death, rather than depart from their faith in Christ.

4. Then, at that very time, the imperial edict having been published also in the city of Iconium, in the province of Lycaonia,[16] the great Chariton, who, by the Savior's will, was a distinguished person, well known to all in that town, stood up as a true servant of Christ: he was arrested and immediately brought to the tribunal of the impious governor.[17] But let us hear how the holy man was interrogated and what he freely answered.

What was, then, the first question of the governor? "What is this man's name and which is his religion?" he asked; and, learning that Chariton was one of the leading citizens of the above-mentioned town, the governor said to him: "Why, then, man, do you oppose the most lawful decrees of the mighty emperor, absolutely refusing to sacrifice to the immortal gods?" "Because your gods are not gods, consul," answered the noble martyr of Christ, "but evil demons, filled with haughtiness, which is also their downfall; for it is written: 'For all the gods of the peoples are devils, but the Lord made the heavens,'[18] and elsewhere: 'The gods who did not make the heavens and the earth shall perish.'[19] For, although they are of created nature and servants of God, the maker of the universe, as they held the office of demiurges over the world above and below, so the wretched beings endeavored to divert God's own glory to themselves. Thus an everlasting punishment was meted out to them, and they lost the angelic status they held, as well as their place near God; and as for you, who 'do not see fit to acknowledge God,' as the apostle

---

15. 2 Tim 4:10.

16. The father of monasticism in Palestine also set a precedent in the matter of his national origin. Of the founding fathers of the monastic movement in this region, Euthymius, Sabas, Theodosius the Cenobiarch, and his disciple Theognius, also the founder of a monastery, were all from Cappadocia; Gerasimus was a Lycian; all came from Asia Minor. Accordingly, Palestinian asceticism may be considered to owe a greater debt to Anatolian influence (i.e., to the Basilian stream), than to the nearer centers of monastic traditions in Syria and Egypt. On this question see J. Patrich, "The Monastic Institutions of St. Sabas and His Disciples (in Hebrew with an English Summary)" (Ph.D. dissertation, University of Jerusalem, 1988).

17. *Archōn*. Later on the governor is called *hēgemōn*—the specific title of a provincial governor—and *hypatikos*, "consularis," referring to his rank as a former consul, or equal in dignity to a former consul.

18. Ps 95:5; Ps 96:5 (RSV).

19. Jer 10:11.

says,[20] they entice you by vain appearance as to take them for gods and 'to worship the creature rather than the Creator,'[21] for two reasons: in the first place, in order to be themselves glorified by this appellation (for the foul beings are so ambitious and braggart that they enjoy being honored as gods), and secondly, in order to draw you, whom they have cheated, down with them 'into the unquenchable fire prepared for them.'"[22]

5. The governor replied: "I should lose my temper and condemn you to death, O Chariton, for having so insulted our omnipotent gods; however, as they are mild, I shall follow their example for the time being, and gently urge you to offer them a libation and to say good-bye to such silly talk." "If these idols are really gods, consul," answered the servant of Christ, "you are not well advised to forbear the insults uttered at them by myself; for it is proper to be exceedingly jealous, following the example of that famous and great man, Phineas,[23] and not to lose a moment in putting to the sword any man who speaks impiously of your gods. But if they are not gods, it is of no use your showing forbearance, as you call it, on the one hand, and your threats on the other, as well as your 'injustice without cause,' as it is written:[24] indeed, no peril will lead me astray to forsake a living God and go over to spiteful and cursed demons, for I am also a disciple of the all-praiseworthy Thecla, who shines like a star with the sparkles of martyrdom in this very city of Iconium, and of Paul, exalted by all, who became her trainer for the struggle of the contest,[25]

20. Rom 1:28.
21. Rom 1:25.
22. Matt 25:41.
23. Num 25:7–8.
24. Ps 24:3; Ps 25:3 (RSV).
25. Thecla, a very early martyr, was venerated at Iconium, her native city, and especially at Seleucia, where she was martyred. In the last third of the second century, a presbyter from Asia Minor wrote a fictional account of her conversion, her travels at St. Paul's side, and her final martyrdom: *Acta Pauli et Theclae, Acta Apostolorum Apocrypha I* (ed. R. A. Lipsius and M. Bonnet; Leipzig: H. Mendelssohn, 1891) 235–69. English translation: "The Acts of Paul and Thecla," in E. Hennecke and W. Schneemelcher, *The New Testament Apocrypha* (Philadelphia: Westminster Press, 1965) 353–64. All this was pure invention, and the presbyter was consequently deposed (Tertullian *Bapt.* 17; Jerome *De Vir. Ill.* 7). The romance, however, experienced great success and its diffusion obscured the true story of the martyr. See U. M. Fasola, "Tecia di Iconio," in *Bibliotheca Sanctorum XII* (Rome: Istituto Giovanni XXIII dell Pontificia Universitá Lateranese, Cittá Nuova Editrice, 1969) 176–77. Cf. also recent studies that have addressed the life and work of Thecla relative to the larger issue of women and the Apocryphal Acts: S. Davies, *The Revolt of the Widows: The Social World of the Apocryphal Acts* (Carbondale: Southern Illinois University Press, 1980); D. R. MacDonald, *The Legend and the Apostle: The Battle for Paul in Story and Canon* (Philadelphia: Fortress Press, 1983); and V. Burrus, *Chastity as Autonomy: Women in the Stories of the Apocryphal Acts* (Lewiston, N.Y.: Edwin Mellen Press, 1987).

and who says: 'Who shall separate us from the love of Christ? Shall tribulation, or distress, or persecution, or famine, or peril, or sword?'"[26]

6. To which the governor replied: "But if they are not really gods, those whom we piously adore, how is it that we, who put our trust in them, are so well provided with the resources of living?" Answered the great Chariton: "You are all misled, governor, saying that the soulless statues are gods, and rejecting the truly living God. In fact, the God-inspired Scripture has another fitting saying about them, and indeed also about yourselves: 'The idols of the nations are silver and gold, the work of men's hands. They have mouths, but they speak not, they have ears, but they hear not, nor is there any breath in their mouths. Like them be those who make them, and the same also every one who trusts in them.'[27] Is not the Scripture speaking the truth, in wording this thought so? Try, if you want, to apply fire to their sides, or order their legs to be shattered with an axe, and, if you are not lacking sense like them, you shall know that they are soulless and unstirring statues, quite unable to utter a sound."

7. Enraged by those words, the lawless consul gave an order to strip off the holy man's clothes and to beat him spread-eagled with thongs without mercy. Then, when the execution of his order was well advanced, the ungodly judge said to him: "Will you sacrifice to the gods, Chariton, or shall the torturers apply the same lashes to your body again?" "No," answered the martyr, "for if it were possible to die even ten thousand deaths for the Savior Christ's sake, I would gladly agree to it, rather than deny his divinity and offer libations to evil demons." So the villain ordered the righteous man to be tortured again, to such an extent that his tormentors almost touched his intestines. Then, after the holy man had remained silent for many hours and the public executioners had discharged their torments on him, both stubbornly and furiously, the wicked governor ordered them to pause, not that he deemed the man worthy of being spared a little—how could it be?—but for fear that he might evade, by a quicker death, the longer chastisements in store for him. And so the attendants carried away the holy body of the martyr on their shoulders—for he could not walk on his own feet—and put him in jail, reserving him for a second appearance in court. And to cut it short— for it is necessary to conclude—after the healing of his wounds Chariton was brought again into the court, and at first the villainous governor

26. Rom 8:35.
27. Ps 134:15–18; Ps 135:15–18 (RSV).

tried, with flattery and kingly promises, to trick him into sacrificing to
the gods; but, as he was not persuaded, for the second time the blessed
one was put to the trial of worse chastisement—for his sides were
thoroughly roasted with fire in the manner of cooked meat—and finally
carried away again to the public prison by the same attendants.

8. A short time went by, and the emperor who fought against God
paid a penalty fitting to the treatment he had dared to inflict upon the
Christians and departed from human life in as cruel a way as he had
been cruel. What then? The inheritor to the scepter of the impious
Aurelian's empire was chastened by the example of his predecessor,
and, dreading to be mulcted with the same punishments from the scales
in heaven, should he take the same steps against the Christians as
Aurelian had done, he ordered an end to the persecution of the Christians in all the provinces. At this point, a divine provision was made, to
ensure that the God-inspired man of whom we speak should not benefit
himself alone at the end of his martyrdom, but would give a share of his
excellences also to others, as he trained for the prize in the contest of
endurance, so that he might be deemed worthy of a greater reward for
his virtues after this new trial. Thus he was freed from his chains and
released from prison, but, as one already dead under the tortures and
adorned with the crown of martyrdom, he looked down upon the present life and would live no more for himself, but wanted "Christ to live in
him," as the apostle says;[28] so, like a living corpse—paradoxically speaking—a breathing martyr, carrying the stigmata of Christ on his own
most pure body, Chariton entered the path that leads to the holy city of
God, having chosen to imitate Elijah's and John's life in the desert.

9. Then, when he was near his goal, Chariton met again with a similar
breed of persecutors, lacking nothing whatsoever from the former in
regard to wickedness. They were outcasts, men who deemed it child's
play to slaughter human beings, who used to rob the wayfarers on the
road. Seeing the holy man journeying along the highway[29] all by him-

---

28. Gal 2:20.
29. The Jericho road, which leads from the Jordan to Jerusalem, passing near the site
of Pharan, and which branches off the ancient "king's highway" that links Syria to
Egypt, was a likely choice for a traveler journeying on foot from Anatolia to the Holy
City. The stretch between Jericho and Jerusalem was frequented by brigands, as is
known from the Gospel story of the Good Samaritan. In the fourth century Jerome
wrote that this road was called "the ascent of the reds" (Hebrew: Ma'ale Adummim)
because of the blood spilled there daily: "Das Onomastikon der biblischen Ortsnamen
mit der lateinischen Übersetzung des Hieronymus," in E. Klostermann, Eusebius Werke
3.1 (GCS 11, 1; Leipzig: Hinrichs, 1904) 25, 11.9–16; Jerome Ep. 108; 12; PL 22, 887.

self, carrying but some trifle to supply his needs on the way, they took it away from him, and, having tied both his hands behind his back and fastened an iron collar around his neck, those wrongdoers dragged the righteous man along like a wrongdoer, and led him to their home cave, to be put to a violent death. And, if once the tribe of the Jews was denounced for having made that celebrated temple of God a den of robbers,[30] now you shall see such a deed reversed by that great man, for you will find the robbers' den turned by him into a church of God; how and in what manner, the next chapter of this story will clearly reveal.

10. Now, those rascals left the holy one bound in the cave just indicated, and scattered here and there to their usual run along the highways, in the hope of accomplishing some of their favorite deeds against unhappy travelers. As for Chariton, first of all, even in this contingency he earnestly addressed thankful words to the Lord; then he turned to the demon who had put this plan into effect, mocking him thus: "You have brought me to these murderers and given me into their hands, as one that has slipped away from the trial of death, or in the hope to impede the advance of my plan toward its achievement. If the former is true, you should know from the very facts that by God's grace I despise all death for the sake of his love, and there is absolutely no way for you to scare me, for on the last day God will raise me from the dead to eternal life, whereas you are destined to be consigned to the undying fire.[31] If, on the other hand, your aim is to thwart my desire for the solitary life, if this is the will of God 'in whom I live and move and have my being,'[32] you will gain absolutely nothing, foul rascal; for if this is his pleasure, as he rescued the blessed youths[33] and Thecla, exalted by all, from the fire and the wild beasts, so will he surely snatch me away from the teeth of these men's murderous daggers, in the very manner as he once did with the great Isaac, piously offered in sacrifice by his own father, following a divine command.[34]

11. And, after he had spoken these words, a wicked snake crept into one of the wine jars that stood there, and, after having drunk its fill of the contents, injected its deadly poison into the wine, and went off. Later, the above-mentioned robbers came back home, and, as one over-

30. Matt 21:12–13.
31. Cf. John 6:40.
32. Acts 17:28.
33. Dan 3:24–26.
34. Gen 22:11–12.

come with thirst, they greedily poured the unmixed wine down their throats, and all at once fell flat on their faces shrieking. And so they paid the penalty for their evil deeds, and thereafter many escaped their murderous hands. This was the reward of the man's struggle for piety, this was the fruit of his unbroken and unhesitating faith in God; in such a way the Lord of the universe naturally delivers those who serve him from the hunters' snare. Thereupon the den of those foul robbers became a holy tabernacle of God (what is now the so-called Old Church, which is situated in the most chaste laura called Pharan, that was founded by the great Chariton). This was the prize won by his holy wounds, which not only defeated a most impious emperor and a yet more impious governor, and even consigned evil waylayers to a well-deserved death, but also drove away the devil himself, loaded with the shame of his discomfiture on all fronts. Behold the wonder! By the device that the wrathful demon employed against the holy man, by means of the wretched murderers, in order to hinder his God-pleasing choice of the ascetic life, by this very same device the Lord of glory arranged instead that the plan piously pursued by Chariton should be brought into effect.

12. In fact, ask yourselves what happened and how did Chariton's affairs proceed? He is barred from reaching Jerusalem, is led captive to the cave, stands prepared to fight the murderers carrying no spear, no shield, no dart, nor any other weapon to defend himself; but with holy prayers alone he makes himself heard, like the divine Moses once on the mountain in the fight against the children of Amalek,[35] with prayers that had equal power and the same freedom of speech in front of God, although he did not hold up his hands, for he was bound; and he strikes those miscreants with the venom of the viper, as though with darts, and brings upon them a quick death.

13. Then the bonds that restrained his hands unfastened of themselves,[36] and Chariton became heir to the ill-amassed riches, but made good use of them and scattered them abroad liberally, in accordance with the Lord's command. Some he distributed to the poor and to the holy fathers of the deserts, who were likely to be in need. At that time they were rare and few in number; they lived scattered in the caves of the Reed-bush (Calamon),[37] which is near the Dead Sea, they too having

---

35. Exod 17:9–12.
36. Cf. Euripides *Ba.* 6.447: this may be a clue to the author's cultural background. Our monk had probably enjoyed a classical education.
37. If this information is true, this is the earliest appearance of Christian ascetes in

fled from the rising of the impious that happened in those days, as I have already explained. With the rest of the money, Chariton built the above-mentioned sacred laura, with the most holy church within, which was consecrated by Macarius of sainted memory, who dutifully ruled the holy church of God here in Jerusalem and was one of the pious number that gathered at the Council of Nicaea.[38]

14. Thus Chariton began to live as a hermit[39] in the said cave, and hence realized to perfection the saying: "Be still and know that I am God."[40] Accordingly, as time went by, an innumerable crowd of pagans and Jews were induced to receive the saving bath, as a consequence of the miracles made by God through the holy man; and more than that, they were even drawn to enter the monastic life from what he taught them and by the example he set before their eyes. For he shone with the brilliance of his virtues, like a bright beacon in that true Pharos of the souls,[41] so that the sight of him urged on all who, wishing to escape the rough waters of life, were anxious to bring themselves, like a boat, to anchor in the monastic haven, with the help of the Holy Ghost. Would you not say that this was a match for what happened to the blessed Paul? Indeed, it is so; for Paul, when the creeping beast bit his hand and left him unharmed,[42] brought not a few to recognize the Savior; and this man, who through a beast had escaped the violence of men wilder than wild beasts, caused the greatest possible number of people to become Christians and monks to boot, and handed down the holy commandments of the Lord to them to observe, by his own example.[43]

---

the wilderness of the Jordan, later a favorite haunt of hermits. But the author may be introducing an anachronism, based on conditions in his days.

38. H. Gelzer, H. Hilgenfeld, and O. Cuntz, *Patrum Nicaenorum Nomina latine graece coptice syriace arabice armeniace* (Leipzig: Teubner, 1898) 21 (22). Noticing that the author refers to the church of Jerusalem as the one to which he himself belongs, Garitte, "La Vie," surmised that he may have been a monk in the laura of Pharan, which is near the Holy City. But the laura of Souka also was subject to the see of Jerusalem. Besides, if the author lived and wrote in Pharan, there would be no reason for him to give a lengthy explanation on the whereabouts of the old church, as he does in chapter 11. On the contrary, the text contains a clue that may be interpreted as suggesting that the author belonged to the Old Laura of Chariton at Souka; see n. 60.

39. *Hēsychazein,* "to live in *hēsychia.*" This term is crucial for the conception of the pattern of ascetic life pursued by Chariton, at first alone and later within the framework of the laura system. The term *hēsychia* does not always lend itself to be translated literally as "silence"; I have used also "seclusion," "tranquility," and "heremitical life," according to the context.

40. Ps 45:10; Ps 46:10 (RSV).

41. A play on words, based on the resemblance between the name of the site, Pharan, and Pharos, the famous lighthouse of Alexandria.

42. Acts 28:3–6.

43. This may hint at the fact that, although Chariton was believed to have handed

15. For who will steal from the body and enrich the soul so lightly, wearing himself out with the practice of asceticism, as the apostle says: "For as much as our outer man wastes away, so the inner man is renewed"?[44] For Chariton, already steeled by the trial of the tortures, was high-minded and indomitable before the attacks of any affliction, so that he considered the most extreme self-denial a luxury, being absolutely without property wealth; and he was fond of lying on the bare ground for a short time and standing in psalm-chanting almost all night long, as much as the lovers of life welcome sleeping the whole night on ivory couches smothered with soft and overflowing quilts. He felt more pleasure constricting his holy weals under a garment of hair than those who wrap themselves in smooth clothes spun of silk yarn, and with good reason, for the hope of the eternal beatitude kept in store for him induced him to bear more readily every toil for the sake of the Savior Christ. He was merciful, compassionate, hospitable, charitable, full of brotherly love, gentle, quiet, peaceable, affable to all, willing to teach, endowed with "a speech seasoned with the salt" of the Holy Ghost.[45]

16. But why speak at length? Through his virtues, Chariton drew such power from the "divine grace that dwelt in him"[46] that he could "cast out unclean spirits and heal every disease and every infirmity," as the gospel says,[47] by means of his God-inspired prayers. Hence all the people streamed to him like a river, and made the desert into a city, as it were, with their crowding, so that the blessed one saw himself deprived of his beloved tranquility and of his conversation with the Lord of the universe through uninterrupted prayer, owing to the disturbance caused by this state of things. Besides, the holy man was very eager to escape from the more-than-human fame that he was attaining (for the man was as unambitious as can be); indeed, he knew that vainglory can obscure virtue just as rust does to iron. Therefore he devoted a period of time to expounding his teachings clearly and fully to his disciples, explaining what way of life was becoming to the monastic state; he put down the rule pertaining to nutrition, that is, that one must partake of food once a day toward evening, and in any case moderately, so that the belly might not be heavy from gluttonous eating and thus be of hindrance in rising for the nocturnal prayer. He described the unpretentious and simple

---

down an ascetic tradition of his own, it was more a pattern taught by personal example than a fixed set of rules.
44. Cf. 2 Cor 4:16.
45. Cf. Col 4:6.
46. Cf. Rom 6:11.
47. Cf. Matt 10:1.

nourishment of which the monk must partake, that is, bread with salt for food, and for drink, water, either spontaneously produced from natural springs or fallen from heaven as rain, for the relief of mankind. He set forth the discipline pertaining to prayers and psalmodies, namely, that by night the monks must keep vigil for six hours, and by day seven times, at fixed hours, they shall praise and glorify the Maker of all, after the blessed David,[48] and, as for the remaining hours of the day, either they must fill their mouth with the holy song of the divine David, at the same time busying their hands with uninterrupted work, each in his own abode, or they may unroll the books inspired by God and speaking with God's own voice, and pluck from them, as though from blooming meadows, the fruit that benefits the soul.

17. And if any evil or unclean thought should be implanted by the common enemy of all, like a weed in the soil of one's heart, Chariton prescribed rooting it out with the help of assiduous and persistent prayer to God, as though with an axe, to avoid the possibility that, because of negligence, the evil growth might have room to send its roots deeply under earth, and might rise some height above, and bear the bitter fruit of the practice of pleasure seeking, whereby it would cause the greatest harm to the mind that has grown it, which would be unable to resist, when the roots of the evil have become hard to pull out. Besides, Chariton laid down the precept that the monks must not come out frequently from their cells to the outside but stay at home as much as possible and adhere with all their might to tranquility, the mother of all virtues. But, if one of the needy should knock at the door and ask for bread, for the relief of the inexorable need of the flesh, he must never be sent away empty-handed, as the Master of the universe, Christ, is nourished by us through these people, for he says: "What you did to one of the least of these my brethren, you did to me."[49] This is the king's highway, explained the God-inspired Chariton, made by nature to lead to God's mansions[50] those who travel unswervingly along it, the road of which the wise Solomon said: "Do not swerve to the right or to the left."[51]

18. Then Chariton saw, on the one hand, that the brethren were well

---

48. Cf. Ps 118:164; Ps 119:164 (RSV). Of course, the author is referring to private prayer. In a monastery of the laura type, monks met for communal prayer only once or at most twice a week: on Sundays (for Mass, if a priest was available) and, in the laurae of Gerasimus and Sabas, also on Saturdays. On this subject and generally on the question of the life style in a laura, see Patrich, "Monastic Institutions."

49. Matt 25:40.

50. Cf. John 14:2.

51. Prov 4:27.

advanced in the way of life according to God's will and capable not only
of helping themselves but also of training others for the struggles of
ascetic life; on the other hand, they could not acquire additional perfections, on account of the immense crowd of men, women, and even
children who came to see them and caused them distraction and disturbance beyond measure. Chariton was rightly determined to prevent this
sight, and so, both on this account and on account of the causes mentioned above, but, even more, in order that the Lord of the universe
might operate wonders through him also elsewhere, and thence once
more he might convert many people to the salutary fear of himself,
Chariton chose one brother who surpassed all the others in excellence of
life and promoted him, with the consent of the brethren, to be their
leader in his place; then he became an exile from the holy laura that he
himself had built.

19. In spite of the many entreaties to stay, tearfully offered by the
assembly of the brethren to Chariton, he did not suffer to yield, inasmuch as he estimated this step to be beneficial both to them and to
himself. "For if I depart hence in God, O my children," he said, "nobody
will come here in the future, and this will be good for both sides, for it
will be easier for me, your father, as well as for you, whom 'I have
begotten in Christ through the Gospel,'[52] to stay calmly in our cells, as in
a beehive, and produce the sweet honey of virtue in the manner of
bees." Having spoken these words, he embraced and blessed everyone,
entrusted them to the Lord, and then he left that place. And at the end of
one day's march he came upon another cave, situated in the vicinity of
Jericho, but in a deserted spot that offered him the greatest quiet, as he
desired.

20. So Chariton spent a long time there too, feeding on the herbs he
found and unceasingly performing his devotions to God, as was his
wont. Then God, who always governs all matters with the aim of bringing salvation to humankind, drew him back into the light, like a hidden
treasure, neither perceptible and inanimate, nor brightly shining with
material of colorful appearance, but a spiritual treasure, adorned with
the manifold beauties of virtues, and which is not consumed by being
shared with others, but on the contrary, giving to others, it remains
always whole and in want of naught, for the gift of the Holy Ghost is
awarded to the worthy in everlasting form. Indeed, in the other world,
the more the owner squanders his wealth, as though draining off stag-
nant waters, the greater he makes it; and as for this world, the great

52. Cf. 1 Cor 4:15.

Chariton cured diseases of both kinds, of the mind as well as of the body, by invoking the name of the Savior Christ. And not only was he successful every time in the practice of this so great a grace, but, always setting to himself additional degrees of ascent in his heart, he even came to partake of this grace in ever-increasing measure, as it happens in the medical art; those who are well versed in it and treat patients even by the tens of thousands gain additional knowledge through their greater experience, rather than suffer a diminution of their professional skill.

21. Thus, also at that place many people were cured by Chariton, or rather by the divine grace that dwelt in him, and desired to imitate his life of seclusion ("Be imitators of me as I am of Christ" he used to say, after the divine Apostle[53]); and so in this site too he built another school of virtues,[54] which was later enlarged by Elpidius of sainted memory, a man of exceptional ascetic exploits. They called the place Douka, after one Doukas,[55] who took care of the community and repulsed the attacks launched against this chaste monastery by some sinning Jews, who lived as free landowners in the village of Na'aran.[56]

53. 1 Cor 11:1.
54. *Phrontistērion arētōn. Phrontistērion,* literally "place for meditation," often means simply "school," especially for superior or philosophical studies. The term is often used by Christian writers in the sense of "monastic cell" or "monastery." See G. W. H. Lampe, *A Patristic Greek Lexicon,* s.v. *phronistērion;* although this meaning too is clearly in the background, the context demands the translation given above.
55. Contrary to the explanation advanced in the text, the name Douka is earlier than Chariton's time; it is already mentioned in the Book of Maccabees (1 Macc 16:15; cf. Josephus *B.J.* 1.56; *A.J.* 13.230). A Hasmonaean fortress stood on the mountaintop; see M. Avi-Yonah, *Gazetteer of Roman Palestine* (Qedem; Monographs of the Institute of Archaeology; Jerusalem: The Hebrew University of Jerusalem, 1976) 52. The explanation offered by the author is better understood, however, if one keeps in mind that *dux* (*doux* in Greek; *dukas* in Aramaic) was the title of the military governor of Palestine, whose task was to defend the province against enemy attacks and to preserve the peace by suppressing civil disturbances and domestic feuds. In the tradition related by the text, the name Dukas may have been meant as a nickname, because its similarity to the title *"dux"* could not pass unnoticed. Even if we concede this, the whole story is not a very sound basis for historical conclusions. A background of Jewish hostility against monks sounds credible enough, but it is doubtful whether the author possessed specific information verifying his account of the relations between the monastery and its Jewish neighbors. Not only is the name he mentions merely a sobriquet, disguising an etiological motif, but also the title he gives to the man (*pronooumenos*) is quite vague and does not seem to apply to any specific function within the community, unless he meant a layman acting as protector or guardian of the monastery. In truth, despite plenty of sources about acts of violence committed against monks by Saracens and Samaritans, there is no real case against the Jews for this kind of offense—at least before the Persian conquest.
56. The village of Na'aran was situated near Jericho in an area celebrated for its palm and balsam plantations. Until the seventh century at least, it was inhabited by Jews (Antiochus Monachus *Hom.* 84; *PG* 89, 1692), who were in constant conflict with the people of Jericho (Lam *Rab.* 1:17). According to our text, the villagers were not *coloni* but free peasants, owners of the lands they tilled (*klēronomoi*). Ancient Na'aran is identified with Duyuk, at the foot of Jebel Qarantal, on the slopes of which Chariton

22. But, not to make a long speech by repeating myself, here too Chariton and his disciples were most seriously disturbed, as in Pharan, by people flocking to him and were prevented from devoting themselves to silence. Therefore Chariton removed himself from that place as well, after having instructed these disciples too as to the best way for cell-dwellers to defeat the devil's tricks, and, having handed over the reins of the direction of the brethren to the man immediately after him,[57] he went off to another deserted spot, fourteen stadia, more or less, from the estate called Thecoa.[58] The Savior of all the universe was pleased to shift him from place to place, so that his servant should become famous everywhere, and those who came to him would be hallowed by his holy prayers and would believe in the Savior Lord (for almost all the population was then pagan) and be freed from the passions that had them in bondage.

23. So once more, many brethren gathered around Chariton and renounced the worldly bustle through him, and set out to keep the Lord's commands through the practice of monastic life; for, when they heard their instructor teaching that sacred oracle that says: "It is good for a man that he bear the yoke in his youth: let him sit alone,"[59] they put it into practical effect. So Chariton established a holy laura there too. This laura is given the name of Souka by some, who use, as they say, the Syriac dialect, whereas others call it in Greek "Old Laura."

24. And now our story, proceeding step by step, has brought us to the last thing in chronological order, but the first from the point of view of miraculous power. For, wherever he was, Chariton set great value on never being diverted from his life of seclusion, which, most of all, had raised him to the highest degree of spiritual stature. Therefore, when he discovered downstream a cave opening in a steep hillside, not far from this chaste laura[60] (what is called to the present day "St. Chariton's

---

founded his laura. A synagogue has been discovered at Duyuk (Cf. Avi-Yonah, *Gazetteer*, 84).

57. A minimum of hierarchy was already present in monasteries at a very early date. A "second in command," fulfilling the task of steward, was appointed even in the simplest and smallest of monastic communities; cf. Cyril of Scythopolis *Vit. Euth.* 17 (ed. Schwartz, 27).

58. Thecoa was a village, but its inhabitants were not independent farmholders as were those of Na'aran, because the place is called *ktema*, meaning that it belonged to one big landowner.

59. Lam 3:27–28.

60. The expression "this laura," which referred to Souka, may be taken as a clue about the place where the "Life" was composed and perhaps recited in public. The author also gives special prominence to Chariton's "hanging place," the particular pride of the Old Laura, whereas he does not even mention the holy man's grave, which must

hanging place," as it is impossible to climb up there, except with a ladder), he thought to take his abode high up there. And some time having elapsed, Chariton became physically feeble on account of his great age, as well as owing to his extreme asceticism, so that he was unable to fetch by himself the water for his own needs. Wishing to avoid troubling one of the brethren on this account, he prayed to God, and immediately, from a corner of the cave, a limpid, cool stream was made to spring forth, and it flows to this very day. O what freedom of speech had this man before God! O what friendly care the God of the universe had for him! Truly well the divine David says: "The Lord fulfills the desire of all who fear him; he also hears their cry and saves them."[61] This is no lesser a miracle than those accomplished by Moses, Samson, and Elisha, of whom the first struck a rock and water came out of it, as the story goes,[62] the second caused water to spring out of a jawbone in answer to his prayer,[63] and the third made the waters of Jericho, which were bitter and wholly undrinkable, sweet and pleasant and conducive to fertility.[64]

25. What more? Chariton knew from a divine revelation that the day was near for his departure from the body, or rather the day of his coming to sojourn in the house of God, for in his case it is more fitting to say so. Then he gathered to his dwelling place all the saintly hegumens and brethren of the said three chaste monasteries, and, having assured them that his departure was close at hand, he went with all of them to the holy laura of Pharan, where at the beginning he had stripped for the struggles of asceticism, and gave the following instructions, which he left to them as a kind of legacy to be preserved for the benefit of their souls.

26. "My children, the divine Apostle said: 'The appointed time has grown very short,'[65] signifying with these words the brief span of each man's life; therefore, because you have yet yours left in your hands—as

---

have been a focal point of his veneration and was situated in the laura of Pharan— although later his relics seem to have been transferred to Souka, probably in connection with the abandonment of Pharan during the Persian invasion or after the Arab conquest. In my opinion, the interest shown by the author in the "hanging place," together with his reference to Souka as "this laura," may tip the scale in favor of the view that he was, after all, a monk of the Old Laura near Thecoa. In the second half of the sixth century, this was also the largest and most flourishing of Chariton's founda- tions, as indicated by its remains.

61. Ps 144:19; Ps 145:19 (RSV).
62. Exod 17:6.
63. Judg 15:18–19.
64. 2 Kgs 2:19–22.
65. 1 Cor 7:29.

for myself, I am already hastening to the Lord, for 'the time of my departure has come'[66]— it is up to you to take care of your souls with all dispatch, for after the end of life in this world, it is impossible to cultivate the fruit of repentance or virtue. 'In Sheol who can give thee praise?' says the blessed David.[67] Indeed, in this world are the struggles of the contest, in the other the crowns for those who 'compete according to the rules';[68] here belongs the war against the invisible enemies, there the proclamation of the valor; here the pains and the toils, there the prizes and the glory; here the trade of the goods, there the feast of the gain: in a word, here is achieved the doing of both good and evil, there the retribution of each. But all things of this world, as pleasant or as toilsome as they may be, are in any case temporary, whereas in the other world both states are forever. So let us not bring upon ourselves, because of a temporary enjoyment of sin, not only the loss of the eternal reward, but also our consignment to everlasting punishment. 'For these will go away into eternal life, and those into eternal shame,' says the Lord.[69]

27. "First of all, keep the faith in God steadfast and unshaken in your hearts in every possible way, without ever changing it in whatever peril you may find yourselves. For not only pagans will persecute the holy church of God and rise against her but also the 'false Christs,'[70] the Arians, endeavoring as far as is in their power to break the unity of the divinity of the holy, worshipful, and consubstantial Trinity, would bring in the rack of manifold tortures against those who do not believe them. 'But be of good cheer,' admonishes the Savior, 'for I have overcome the world';[71] and again: 'Do not fear those who kill the body but cannot kill the soul; rather fear him who can destroy both body and soul in hell; yes, I tell you, fear him!'[72]

28. "Secondly, pursue peace and the beatitude correlated to it[73] in such a way that, whenever it should happen that you are carried away by the devil's banditry and become angry, 'the sun will not go down on your anger,' as the apostle says.[74] Instead, cure the pain of the wrong with repentance and remove from your souls the bearing of malice, a passion

66. 2 Tim 4:6.
67. Ps 6:5.
68. Cf. 2 Tim 2:5.
69. Cf. Matt 25:46; Dan 12:2.
70. Cf. Matt 24:24.
71. John 16:33.
72. Matt 10:28; Luke 12:5.
73. Cf. Matt 5:9.
74. Cf. Eph 4:26.

hateful to the Lord, in order that 'the peace of God, which passes all understanding, will guard your hearts.'[75] Whenever an unclean thought be sown in your mind, quickly press hard to make away with it through prayer and the vision of the eternal chastisements, which will immediately drag away these thoughts; for, as Chariton used to say, one must absolutely not keep company with any licentious forms that the adversary draws with shadows in the mind to drive the man to madness, in order that the body or the soul may not possibly be defiled, neither in state of waking nor in dream. For God says: 'You shall be holy, for I am holy.'[76] Flee from avarice, as being the mother of idolatry; love poverty with all your might, so that, in the pursuit of it, you will not fail to become poor in spirit and to gain the beatitude that comes from this state.[77] In fact, the divine Apostle teaches us what one should possess for the unavoidable need of the body, when he says: 'If we have food and clothing, with these we shall be content.'[78]

29. "If anyone in your midst, by the grace of God, should be girded with exceptional virtues, let him not fall into the pit of haughtiness by thinking that he has achieved something great and extraordinary, for he must be fully convinced that, without the active help of a divine grant, one can do nothing by himself.[79] For, according to the divine James, 'every good endowment and every perfect gift is from above, coming down from the Father of lights.'[80] And the blessed David says: 'Unless the Lord builds the house, those who build it labor in vain.'[81] Thus, if such a man should observe others greater in virtue than himself, let him endeavor to imitate them as much as he can and not divert his gaze toward those who are more backward, as though he had already reached the state of perfection, so that he will stand back from the race and fall under a charge of boastfulness and vanity, like that vainglorious Pharisee.[82]

30. "But, if he can find nobody better than himself, let him measure his own achievements by the more exacting commands of the Lord. Of what sort are these? 'If any one forces you to go one mile, go with him two miles,'[83] and 'If any one strikes you on the right cheek, turn to him

75. Cf. Phil 4:7.
76. Lev 19:2.
77. Cf. Matt 5:3.
78. 1 Tim 6:8.
79. Cf. John 15:5.
80. Jas 1:17.
81. Ps 126:1; Ps 127:1 (RSV).
82. Luke 18:10–12.
83. Matt 5:41.

the other also,'[84] and 'You will render account for every careless word,'[85] and 'If you say to your brother "fool," you are liable to the hell,'[86] and 'Every one who looks at a woman lustfully has already committed adultery with her in his heart,'[87] and whatever other commandments of this kind. And, if by any chance this virtuous man has put into practice all these injunctions (which is rare), then let him call himself a useless servant, as the Lord ordered his disciples.[88] But, if he has not, let him reckon how far he is from those holy commands; and not only will he not be flattered about what he did accomplish, but on the contrary, he will even deem himself unhappy, considering how short he falls from perfection and how far he is removed from other goals; for also the divine Apostle, in making this reckoning, came to the same conclusion: 'Forgetting what lies behind and straining forward to what lies ahead, I press on toward the goal for the prize of the upward call.'[89]

31. "And if this virtuous man should observe that one of the brethren is reluctant and careless in the fulfillment of the Savior's commands, on no account shall he judge his brother, but let him say about him the words of the blessed Paul: 'Who am I to pass judgment on the servant of another? It is before his own master that he stands or falls. And he will be upheld, for God is able to make him stand.'[90] Immediately after that, to prevent the likelihood that, after having displayed loathing for his brother and having condemned him, he may himself succumb to the same sin, inasmuch as he partakes of a nature that is liable to change, this virtuous man shall say to himself these words: 'Let any one who thinks he stands take heed lest he fall' and be judged with greater severity, as is written.[91]

32. "See that you never advertise your virtues for the sake of pleasing men, lest you be deprived of the eternal reward kept in store for you ('Truly, I say to you, they receive their reward in full,' says the Lord[92]) and be liable to those words of the psalmist, where he says: 'God will scatter the bones of the men-pleasers,' et cetera.[93] Instead, practice your virtues in a hidden corner—either self-discipline, or almsgiving, or ear-

---

84. Matt 5:39.
85. Matt 12:36.
86. Cf. Matt 5:22.
87. Matt 5:28.
88. Cf. Luke 17:10.
89. Phil 3:13–14.
90. Rom 14:4.
91. Cf. 1 Cor 10:12.
92. Matt 6:2.
93. Ps 52:5; Ps 53:5 (RSV). Cf. Eph 6:6; Col 3:22.

nest prayer accompanied by tears, or collectively speaking, any other good quality of yours—and wait to receive in public the reward for your achievements from 'your Father who sees in secret.'[94]

33. "These things are said for the more perfect, but as many are the snares of the devil, and few are those who are never caught in the net, if, as is likely, one of you should yield to some sin, because of a plot of the devil, on the one hand, and by his own negligence, on the other, let him show a fallen countenance on account of his fault, but nevertheless with moderation, as he puts his hopes in the mercy of God, lest the sinner, being cut off on account of his extravagant grief, might in his despair become a recluse, never showing his face, in consequence of which, not only would he remain unredeemed, but would also drift into every possible path of evil, for this is the nature of despair. For this reason, let the sinner consider that even if God is a just and severe judge, who 'will render to every man according to his works,'[95] he is also 'a merciful and long-suffering Lord,' as is written,[96] and is compassionate toward every man who turns to him in repentance like the prodigal son. 'For as I live,' says the Lord, 'I desire not the death of the sinner, but rather that he turn from his way and live,'[97] and elsewhere: 'Come to me, all who labor and are heavy laden, and I will give you rest.'[98] Clearly with this great proclamation the Savior calls to himself, as though from an enclosed pit, those 'whose iniquities have gone over their heads and have weighed them down like a heavy load, and unto whom the bruises of sin have grown foul and festering,'[99] and with good reason, for 'those who are well have no need of a physician, but those who are sick,' says the Lord.[100]

34. "Wash the feet of the holy ones who come to visit you.[101] Show pity, that you too may be pitied in the same way, both you who pride yourselves on your virtues and the purity of your virginity or chastity, and those who are spiritually crawling on the ground, and are speckled with the stains of licentiousness. You for your part must show pity, in order that you may come out to meet the Bridegroom with the lamps of the soul brightly lit, as the oil naturally makes them glow with radiant

---

94. Matt 6:6.
95. Rom 2:6.
96. Ps 102:8; Ps 103:8 (RSV). Ps 144:8; Ps 145:8 (RSV).
97. Cf. Ezek 18:23; 33:11.
98. Matt 11:28.
99. Cf. Ps 37:4–5; Ps 38:4–5 (RSV).
100. Luke 5:31.
101. Cf. John 13:14.

light, and, after such great pains as you have endured for the sake of attaining the virgin life, you may not remain outside the wedding hall, having shown no pity.[102] As for the others, thereby they may avoid being cast out into the darkness, bound hand and foot, as the judgment goes (God forbid!), for having reclined in a filthy dress together with the guests around the table in the wedding hall.[103] For I would say, not unreasonably I think, that the purity of the soul is like a splendid garment; for as the garment, being resistant to spoiling, may be brought back to its former cleanliness at any time by being washed whenever it has become soiled, so the soul, originally woven without any taint by God her maker—for she is made in his image and likeness[104]— is at last dirtied by sin, as though by smoke, and her natural beauty becomes dim; but whenever a man's soul is wiped clean by his compassion for the needy and by other worthy fruits of repentance, she regains her former bloom, and then she will rightly be granted permission to take part in the enjoyment of the banquets of eternal delights, together with all the guests in the wedding hall, for now the soul will be clad in the whiteness of good deeds and wrapped in a mantle worthy of the Bridegroom.

35. "God, 'who desires all men to be saved and to come to the knowledge of the truth,'[105] has already offered to mankind many other means fit for cleansing the dirt of sin, like tears, confession, groans from the depth of the heart, fasting, prayer, remission of faults to one's debtors, humility, mildness, and so on. But each of these ways is very toilsome and can be achieved only with much sweat. On the other hand, the practice of charity can be accomplished without any toil and hardship, and more than the other above-mentioned ways, it is naturally suited for cleansing off the ugliness engendered in the soul by wickedness. For it is written: 'Sins are purged away by alms,'[106] and the admirable Daniel says to Nebuchadnezzar: 'Ransom your sins by practicing righteousness, and your iniquities by showing mercy to the poor';[107] and again: 'I desire mercy and not sacrifice';[108] and the diligent reader can collect many such sayings from the divine Scripture.

36. "This is said about charity; and what about endurance? Until the last day of your departure, O my children, dare not hope that you will

102. Cf. Matt 25:1–13.
103. Cf. Matt 22:11–13.
104. Gen 1:26.
105. 1 Tim 2:4.
106. Prov 15:27a.
107. Dan 4:24.
108. Hos 6:7.

not meet with various trials, for it is written: 'My son, if you enter in the service of God, prepare your soul for trial.'[109] But do not lose heart, for 'God is faithful,' says the most wise Paul, 'and he will not let you be tempted beyond your strength, but with the temptation will also provide the way of escape, that you may be able to endure it.'[110] And again it is written: 'I waited patiently for the Lord; he inclined to me and heard my cry,' et cetera.[111] Therefore 'you have need of endurance, so that you may do the will of God and receive what is promised.'"[112]

37. These and more exhortations the blessed Chariton addressed to the holy array under his command, and, after he prayed for all and blessed them, he died without suffering any pain in the members of his body. Lying down on the pallet of the dead, he stretched out his venerable feet and in good old age he surrendered his holy soul to the holy angels, who came to him as to one of their own. And, having been escorted to the grave by the fathers in a fitting manner, he passed over to the everlasting life. There pain, grief, and groaning have fled; there is the contemplation of the holy, consubstantial, and worshipful Trinity "face to face," as the divine Apostle says,[113] for those who have kept their mind pure and spotless; there is joy and inexpressible exultation through the beautitude kept in store in the heavens for those who were persecuted in this world for the sake of the Savior Christ, who says: "Blessed are you when men revile you and persecute you and utter all kinds of evil against you falsely on my account. Rejoice and be glad, for your reward is great in heaven."[114] There is the abode of all that are happy: apostles, prophets, martyrs, shepherds, teachers, confessors, ascetes, and all the others who have well pleased God. As he achieved all these qualities, through the gift of the holy "Spirit that dwelt in him,"[115] justly Chariton, together with all those, "inherits the kingdom prepared for them from the foundation of the world," as the Lord says.[116]

38. Indeed he was an apostle, because just as an angel of God drew the blessed Peter out from the prison and urged him to teach the word of salvation without cease,[117] in the same way "God's wisdom and Christ

109. Cf. Eccl 2:1.
110. 1 Cor 10:13.
111. Ps 30:1; Ps 40:1 (RSV).
112. Heb 10:36.
113. 1 Cor 13:12.
114. Matt 5:1–12.
115. Cf. Rom 8:11.
116. Cf. Matt 25:34.
117. Acts 12:6–10.

the power"[118] sent forth Chariton too, as he was shut away, to proclaim his divinity for the salvation of humankind, except that the one was sent into the cities, the other was consecrated "to cry in the wilderness," like the divinely speaking John,[119] calling to repent and to believe in the Savior Lord, so that every place, cities and desert as well, would be filled with the glory of God, and the desert might not be unproductive of the crop of believers. And, as the faithful of that time, having recognized the Savior Lord through the preaching of the apostles sold all they had and laid the proceeds at the apostles' feet,[120] in the same manner here too, those who were persuaded by the blessed man's exhortations to renounce the matters of the worldly life, entrusted to him, as to a spiritual father, the distribution of their possessions to the poor, and so sailed lightly across the sea of life, under the steering of his God-inspired teaching. For this reason then, in my opinion, one by no means goes astray from the truth by calling this great man an apostle.

39. I call him a prophet because, even if in those days it was not a time of prophesying—for the law and the prophets came to an end with John the Baptist[121]— nevertheless he was not bereft of this grace. For, as the divine Moses received the announcement of his own death before-hand—for God said to him: "Ascend this mountain and die"[122]— so also to Chariton did the Savior predict the end of his life and the storm that would come to the most holy churches after his time, also by means of which revelation he wished to honor the righteous man. For God says: "Those who honor me I will honor "[123] in order to show the intimacy and frankness of his relationship to him.

40. He is an indisputable martyr, in purpose as well as in deeds, even if he survived the struggles providentially, for the salvation of those who were later to be converted by him to the Savior Lord. For, even if he was revived by him "who gives life to the dead"[124] after he had almost died twice under the tortures, and henceforward there was no opportunity for him to struggle against governors and emperors, nevertheless Chariton contended "against the principalities, against the powers, against the world rulers of the darkness and against the spiritual hosts of wicked-

118. 1 Cor 1:24.
119. Cf. Matt 3:1-3.
120. Acts 4:34-35.
121. Cf. Matt 11:13.
122. Deut. 32:49, 50.
123. 1 Sam 2:30.
124. Cf. Rom 4:17.

ness,"[125] against the bitter and fearful persecutors, and aside from the rest, against the fighting of the Christians among themselves. Therefore, with good reason should he be called a martyr, who was tortured in body and soul by the visible and invisible enemies of the truth and was manifestly shown forth as a crowned winner.

41. About the asceticism of the man and his talent as a shepherd and a teacher, what could I say more than this: as Peter was the first of the apostles and Stephen the first of the martyrs, so Chariton was the first fruit of those who embraced the monastic life in all Palestine, and grazed the rational sheep under his care in green pastures, and nourished them on waters of rest[126] with his God-inspired teaching and by offering himself as an example of all that is good, so that he "restored their souls and led them in paths of righteousness," as is written,[127] and from sheep he made them shepherds, teaching others in their turn the evangelic way of life of the monk.

42. As for all the miracles that God did through Chariton, we shall pass them over, to be known to him alone, for whom he existed and piously lived, for whose sake he had endured dangers at the hands of the impious idolaters to the very point of death. For our part, we have disclosed to the uninformed a few of the many fine deeds of the holy man, which we ascertained, not by immediate hearing (for not a little time has elapsed from Aurelian's reign to our time), in order to prevent the fading away of this knowledge too, in the passage of time. For among the other holy ascetes who shone for their monastic virtues much later, some had their God-pleasing lives written secretly by their diligent followers during their lifetime, others immediately after their death, in order to keep fresh the memory of their pious deeds and not to surrender anything to silence. But nobody engaged in writing the life dear to God of this God-inspired man at that time, as in truth, not only were the God-loving monks rare, but even the Christians were but a few, and those few were driven in confusion by their persecutors. Thus, only by word of mouth did the pious monks of the holy monasteries subject to Chariton hand down his story, one to another in turn, and so preserved until the present time the memory of the excellent virtues described above, until it reached us. And if God accomplished some other miracle through him, now, at any rate, this miracle has been consigned to

125. Eph 6:12.
126. Cf. Ps 22:1–2; Ps 23:1–2 (RSV).
127. Ps 22:3.

oblivion, understandably too, owing to such a long lapse of time, even though it bubbled over a long time in the ascetic gymnasium.

43. But it seems to me that Chariton resembles those blessed men, Enoch and Melchisedek, who pleased the God of the universe no less than Abraham and Moses, as we learn from the divine Scripture, for the former was translated while still in the flesh,[128] and the latter took tithes from the great patriarch Abraham, as priest of God Most High.[129] Yet he did not hand down their pious achievements in such complete detail as he did with those of the divine men, Abraham and Moses. And so it was also for Chariton: if, because of ignorance due to the long time that has gone by, we could not even hint at all the miracles that the Savior did through him in succession, for the sake of the unbelievers, nevertheless, as far as one can surmise, in regard to his way of life Chariton is ahead of all the holy fathers who came after him, even more so as he is also the climax of all, being the first to set a pattern for the heremitical life after the admirable pioneers—I mean Elijah and John the Baptist—and he also supremely adorned that life with the perils of martyrdom.

44. This is, then, what is in my power to do, but you, O Chariton, [. . .] sweet in name and deed, whom Wisdom crowned with the grace of virtues, "for thou shalt receive a crown of graces for thine head,"[130] above all, do not cease interceding for all the Christian people, and especially for those who have embraced the monastic life as you did, if not in conformity with your example; because the more mighty and ineluctable for the simple man are the ambushes and schemes set up by the invisible enemy against us, the more are we in need of the almighty hand of the God of the universe, Christ, to come to our aid; to Him be glory and the power, with the Father and the Holy Ghost, for ever and ever. Amen.

SUGGESTED READINGS

Chitty, D. J. *The Desert a City: An Introduction to the Study of Egyptian and Palestinian Monasticism under the Christian Empire.* Oxford: Basil Blackwell & Mott, 1966.

Hirschfeld, Y. *Archaeological Survey of Israel: Map of Herodium* 108/2. Jerusalem: The Archaeological Survey of Israel, 1985.

———. "The Judean Desert Monasticism in the Byzantine Period: Their Devel-

---

128. Gen 5:24; Heb 11:5.
129. Gen 14:20; Heb 7:2.
130. Prov 1:9.

opment and Internal Organization in the Light of Archaeological Research." Ph.D. dissertation, Hebrew University, 1987 (in Hebrew).

Kallai, Z. "The Land of Benjamin at Mt. Ephraim." In *Judea, Samaria and the Golan—Archaeological Survey: 1967–68*, edited by M. Kochavi. Jerusalem: The Archaeological Survey of Israel, 1972.

Lombardi, G. *La tomba di Rahel, H. Fara—W. Fara presso Aratot.* Jerusalem: Franciscan Press, 1971.

Meinardus, O. "Notes on the Laurae and Monasteries of the Wilderness of Judea." *LA* 15 (1964–65) 227–29.

Ovadiah, A., and C. G. de Silva. "Supplementum to the Corpus of Byzantine Churches in the Holy Land: Part I." *Levant* 13 (1981) 200–261.

PART FIVE

DOCUMENTARY EVIDENCE

Life of Chariton
In Light of Archaeological Research

Our knowledge of Judean Desert monasticism, based on historical and archaeological sources, is rich and varied. We have for our reading biographies of several leaders of the monastic movement in this region, and many stories and anecdotes about their disciples. In addition, the archaeological remains provide a wealth of evidence. The dry desert climate and the remoteness of the monasteries have helped to preserve their walls in relatively good condition. Some of them, rebuilt at the end of the nineteenth century and still remaining in use, give us a vivid picture of the monasteries as they had been in the Byzantine period.

The main sources for studying the history of monasticism in the Judean Desert are the hagiographies written by monks who lived in the area during the Byzantine period. Although hagiographic writing naturally follows a program and obeys a fixed literary form, the close acquaintance of the writers with their heroes and with the daily life described in their works enhances their historical credibility. This is especially true of matters connected with everyday life in the monasteries, their geographical location, and so forth. The *Life of Chariton*, which was written by an anonymous monk living in one of Chariton's foundations in the second half of the sixth century, is a good example of this type of hagiography. This is the only source that deals with the beginnings of the monastic movement in the Judean Desert in the first half of the fourth century. The work is rich in literary hyperbole, but recent archaeological finds show that the factual descriptions are authentic and based on close acquaintance with real conditions.

The author mentions four monastic sites within the confines of the Judean Desert, namely, the three lauras founded by Chariton—Pharan,

Douka, and Souka—and the "hanging cave" in which the holy man dwelled at the end of his life. This essay is an attempt to illustrate some *material* aspects of the sites mentioned by the author of the *Life of Chariton*, and to draw some conclusions from these data.

THE LAURA OF PHARAN

The laura of Pharan was the first known monastery to be founded in the Judean Desert. The narrative of its founding by Chariton in approximately 330 c.e. contains features that characterize the founding of many other monasteries in the Judean Desert. Chariton was born to a well-known family in Iconium in Asia Minor (today Konya in southern Anatolia). At the beginning of the fourth century, he came as a pilgrim to the Holy City. As he approached Jerusalem, Chariton fell into the hands of robbers who brought him to their cave and left him bound within it. According to this account, Chariton was saved miraculously when a viper crept into the cave and poisoned the thieves' wine jugs with its venom. Upon returning to the cave, they drank the wine and died, and Chariton subsequently took possession of all their treasures. He distributed some of these riches to hermits living in Calamon near the Dead Sea (see below), and with the remainder he founded "the laura called Pharan." The laura was situated around the robbers' cave, which was dedicated as a church in the days of Macarius, Bishop of Jerusalem (ca. 314–333).[1]

Cyril of Scythopolis, the biographer of Euthymius, Sabas, and other monastical leaders and himself a monk in the Judean Desert, mentions that the laura of Pharan lies six Roman miles (8.9 km.) from Jerusalem[2] and that it was named after the village of Pharan, which Cyril situates ten stadia [1.8 km.] east of the laura.[3] On the basis of this information,

1. *Life of Chariton* 11–12. Cf. G. Garitte, "La vie prémetaphrastique de S. Chariton," *Bulletin de l'Institut Historique Belge de Rome* 21 (1941) 24–26. Also see translation by Leah Di Segni, selection 25 in this volume.
2. Cyril of Scythopolis *Vit. Euth.* 5, in E. Schwartz, *Kyrillos von Skythopolis* (TUGAL 49,2; Leipzig: Hinrichs, 1939) 14.
3. *Vit. Euth.* 58 (Schwartz, *Kyrillos*, 79). The village of Pharan would be reasonably identified with Kh. 'Ein Fara, east of the laura. However, a survey in this site revealed only potsherds from the Bronze Age. See G. Lombardi, *La tomba di Rahel, H. Fara–W. Fara prosso Aratot* (Jerusalem: Franciscan Press, 1971) 14–40; and Z. Kallai, "The Land of Benjamin and Mt. Ephraim," in M. Kochavi, *Judea, Samaria and the Golan—Archaeological Survey 1967–1968* (Jerusalem: The Archaeological Survey of Israel, 1972) 185, no. 137 (Hebrew). Was Cyril wrong, and was the village of Pharan at this time elsewhere in the vicinity of the laura? If so, then the location of the Byzantine Pharan may have been at Kh. Abu Musarrah, which lies about two kilometers west of the Pharan laura;

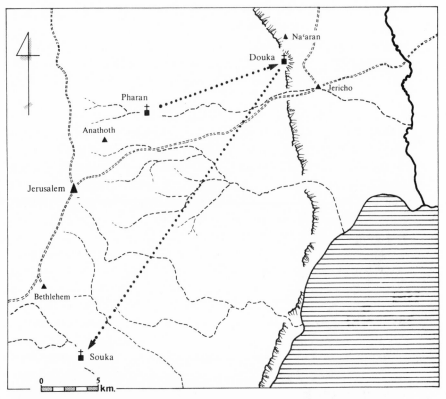

Fig. 1: Chariton's travels and the monasteries he founded in the Judean Desert.

the laura of Pharan has been identified with the remains found in the canyon section of Wadi Fara (upper part of Nahal Perat, called in Arabic *Wadi Qilt*), near the spring of ʿEin Fara, about nine kilometers northeast of Jerusalem (map ref. 1787/1379) (Fig. 1).[4]

It is no coincidence that the first monastery in the Judean Desert was founded in the vicinity of ʿEin Fara, one of the most abundant springs in

this site includes remains from the Byzantine period. See Kallai, "The Land of Benjamin," 186, no. 147.

4. The site was first identified by K. Marti, "Die alten Lauren und Kloster in der Wust Juda," *ZDPV* 3 (1880) 7–11. Further investigation of the site was done by V. Guérin, *Description géographique, historique et archéologique de la Palestine, III: Judée* (Paris: Imprimerie Nationale, 1869) 71–73; and by P. M. Jullien, "Une vallée des anciens solitaires de Palestine," *Échos de Notre Dame de France a Jerusalem* 4 (1896) 291–300. S. Vailhé and S. Pétridès in their joint article, "Saint Jean le paléolaurite, précédé d'une notice sur la Vielle Laura," *ROC* 9 (1904) 335–40, describe the results of a small exploratory excavation carried out by the White Fathers in the "lower" church of the laura. Other scholars who describe this excavation as well as the history of the laura are S. Schiwietz, *Das mörgenlanchische Mönchtum II: Das Mönchtum auf Sinai und in*

the desert heights. Above it rise impressive cliffs containing many caves suitable for use by hermits (Pl. 1). The site itself is not far from the border area of the desert. In its vicinity are located two villages: about two kilometers to the west is Kh. Abû Mussaraḥ and about four kilometers to the southwest is Anathoth (today ʿAnata) (Fig. 2).[5] These three elements—a perennial spring, rocky cliffs, and the vicinity of the desert border settlements—are typical of Chariton's three monasteries.

The fact that Chariton came to the Judean Desert as a pilgrim is significant. It provides us with the earliest documentation of the linkage between the monastic movement in this region and the stream of visitors to the Holy Land.[6] Most of the Judean Desert monks were not local people, but foreigners who had arrived in Jerusalem as pilgrims and settled in the desert after viewing the holy places. Pilgrims continued to be the main source of livelihood for the monasteries, both with the money they brought and with the constant flow of manpower they ensured. In this respect, Chariton can be truly described as the archetype of the Judean Desert monk. The unending stream of pilgrims brought about a perennial flow of foreign influences and created an interaction that caused Palestinian monasticism to be more versatile and many-sided than elsewhere.

The monastery of Pharan was founded as a laura. The Greek, *laura* means "lane" or a "narrow street." The term apparently referred to the arrangement of the cells along a path (or paths) leading to the center of the laura.[7] Most scholars believe that this particular meaning of the word "laura" originated in Palestine and was coined in the context of the first three monasteries founded by Chariton in the Judean Desert.[8]

Palastina im vierten Jahrhundert (Mainz: Kirchheim, 1913) 135–41; *DACL*, s.v. "Laures Palestiniennes"; B. Bagatti, "Alla laura di Fara," *LTS* 45 (1969) 18–24; and A. Ovadiah and C. G. de Silva, "Supplementum to the Corpus of the Byzantine Churches in the Holy Land," *Levant* 13 (1981) 204. Additional details are found in O. Meinardus, "Notes on the Laurae and Monasteries of the Wilderness of Judea," *LA* 15 (1964–65) 227–29, but his descriptions refer mainly to the current monastery structures. For more information, see S. Vailhé, "Les premiers monastères de la Palestine," *Bessarione* 3 (1897–98) 41–44; ibid., "Repertoire alphabetique des monastères de Palestine," *ROC* 5 (1900) 42, no. 94; B. Bagatti, "Il villagio bizantino e la laura," in G. Lombardi, *La Tomba di Rahel*, 152–72.

5. For Kh. Abû Mussaraḥ, see Kallai, "The Land of Benjamin," 186, #137. For Anathoth (ʿAnata), see V. Dinur, "Anata," *ESI* 4 (1985) 3–5.

6. D. J. Chitty, *The Desert a City: An Introduction to the Study of Egyptian and Palestinian Monasticism under the Christian Empire* (Oxford: Basil Blackwell & Mott, 1966) 48.

7. Marti, "Die alten Lauren," 4; Jullien, "Une vallée," 294; Schiwietz, *Das mörgenlanchische Mönchtum*, 138–39; Chitty, *The Desert a City*, 16.

8. Leclercq, "Laures Palestiniennes," 1966–67; P. V. Corbo, "L'ambiente materiale della vita dei monaci di Palestina nel periodo bizantino," *OCA* 153 (1958) 232; R. B.

Pl. 1: Laura of Pharan ('Ein Fara), general view of the site, looking south.

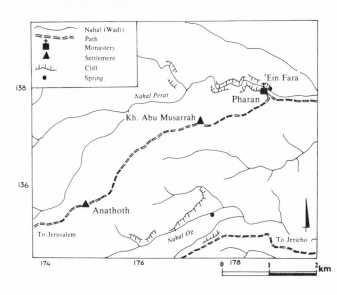

Fig. 2: Byzantine sites to the west of the laura of Pharan.

Chariton's laura-type monastery was a compromise between the ideal of solitary life on one hand and the human need for society and security on the other. The laura at that time was small and simple, with as few common elements as possible, a "rough hermit-assemblage" as described by Chitty.[9] The number of monks in the community was probably small, as can be seen from the archaeological survey of the site. In the area of the laura of Pharan are remains of only fifteen cells. That number reflects the condition of the site at its zenith, during the fifth and sixth centuries. It can be assumed that in the fourth century the community of Pharan included not more than ten to twelve monks. A historical hint that supports this assumption is Cyril's description of Euthymius's founding of a laura at the Plain of Adummim (Mishor Adummim). According to Cyril, Euthymius decided to found his laura when he had eleven disciples gathered at his place.[10] That means that a dozen monks were enough to form a community of the laura type.

Our survey at Pharan indicates that the laura remains—the kernel building and the cells—are scattered between two vertical cliffs that rise to a height of thirty to fifty meters (Fig. 3).[11] The main access path to the laura is from the south. Near the southern cliff, the path forks; one branch descends to the stream, and the other turns to the west in the direction of the kernel buildings of the laura. Along these two paths are scattered the cells of the laura.

The kernel of the laura stood at the foot of the southern cliff. Some of its remains were damaged following the establishment of the small Russian Orthodox monastery in the early twentieth century (today it is abandoned). In the kernel of the laura one can identify the remains of two churches from the Byzantine period. The most conspicuous is that of the cave church, placed at a height of about twelve meters above ground (Pl. 2). The cave church was the core of the laura. According to

Rubin, "The 'Laura' Monasteries in the Judean Desert during the Byzantine Period," *Cathedra* 23 (1982) 25 (Hebrew).
9. D. J. Chitty, "The Wilderness of Jerusalem," *The Christian East* 10 (1929) 77.
10. Cyril of Scythopolis *Vit. Euth.* 16.
11. Y. Hirschfeld, "The Judean Desert Monasteries in the Byzantine Period: Their Development and Internal Organization in the Light of Archaeological Research" (Ph.D. dissertation, Hebrew University, 1987) 24 (Hebrew). The survey was carried out in summer 1987 on behalf of the Institute of Archaeology of the Hebrew University of Jerusalem. The survey was headed by Y. Hirschfeld with the assistance of Rivka Birger and Einat Cohen. D. Huli was responsible for surveying and drawing the plans, and Z. Radovan for the photographs. The site was also surveyed by J. Patrich, "Judean Desert, Secret Passages and Caves," *ESI* 3 (1984) 61; ibid., "Dissidents in the Desert: The Cave Encampment of Simeon Son of Giora's, *Eretz* 1, 1 (1985) 51–61; and by U. Dinur and N. Feig, "Qala'at Musa," *ESI* 5 (1986) 86–88.

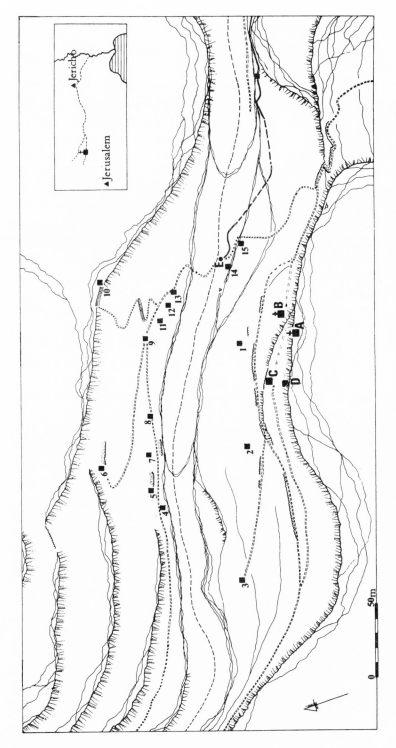

Fig. 3: Laura of Pharan ('Ein Fara), general plan: *A*, cave church; *B*, lower church; *C*, central building; *D*, reservoir; *E*, spring; 1-15, cells.

Pl. 2: Laura of Pharan, the cave church, looking south.

the author of the *Life of Chariton,* in the sixth century this was called "the old church."[12] The inference is that after Chariton's time another church was built in the laura. The archaeological evidence supports this conclusion. Beneath the cave church in the southern cliff, another church was built of hewn stone. This building was excavated by the "White Fathers" in the late nineteenth century and has been described several times, but to date no plan has been published. The traditional grave of Chariton is shown in this lower church.[13]

The remains of the cave church were carefully studied only recently. The survey shows that this cave and a number of other caves had apparently been hollowed out as early as the Second Temple period.[14] The survey indicated that these caves were used as hiding places by the Jews in the first revolt against the Romans. That discovery corroborated the identification of Wadi Fara with the ravine called Pheretai, mentioned by Flavius Josephus as the place where Simeon, son of Gioras, made ready his camp and his caves. The largest cave, which is the site of the church, was identified as Simeon's headquarters. Later in the early fourth century, it had been converted into a church by Chariton. The dimensions of the cave and its position close to the spring made it fit to serve as a church and as the core of the laura founded there.

Access to the cave church was by means of stairs and a vertical shaft (Fig. 4). The present stairs were built recently, but their foundations date from the Byzantine period. At the foot of the shaft, a cistern was hollowed out. It was fed by a canal, also hollowed into the rock, that drained rainwater from the cliff face. The shaft, which is 3.5 meters in height, is carved into the bedrock. At the upper end the shaft ends on a rock ledge. Another flight of stairs ascends to the level of the church. The entrance to the church was in the northeast corner. Two windows have been carved into the cave wall to bring light and air into the church. The prayer hall is regular (6.2 by 8.2 meters, height about two meters). In the eastern wall of the cave were carved a half-rounded apse, relatively shallow, and a square niche to the south of it. On the stone

---

12. *Life of Chariton* 11.
13. A photograph of the presumed Chariton's grave beneath the "lower" church was published by P. Compagnoni, *Il deserto di Giuda* (Jerusalem: Franciscan Press, 1978) 18-19, Pl. XII.
14. Patrich, "Judean Desert," 61–62; ibid., "Dissidents in the Desert," 58–60. A similar phenomenon was noted in other monastic sites in the Judean Desert, that is, the laura of Firminus in Wadi Suweinit, 1.5 kilometers north of Pharan, and in the monastery of Gabriel (Qasr er-Rawabi), about 2 kilometers south of Pharan. See Hirschfeld, "The Judean Desert Monasteries," 160–61.

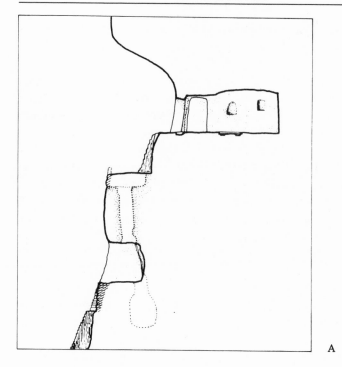

A

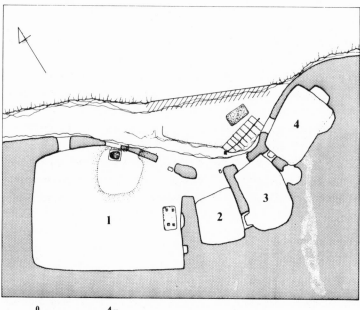

B

Fig. 4: Laura of Pharan (ʿEin Fara), the cave church (A) plan and (B) cross-section (looking east).

floor opposite the apse were carved four holes for the legs of the altar table, and in between them is an indentation apparently meant for a reliquary.

To the east of the prayer hall are three smaller chambers. As the head of the community, Chariton may be assumed to have lived in one of the cells adjacent to the cave church. The other members of the community lived in the cells and caves scattered in the area of the laura.

Our survey of the site located fifteen cells: six on the southern bank of the ravine and nine on the northern bank. The average distance between them is about thirty-five meters. The cells are small and simple: their average area about 23.5 square meters. A small garden plot was installed near each one of them. Water was obtained from the nearby spring.

Chariton's biographer describes the way of life in the laura. According to the story, Chariton instructed his disciples to stay in their cells as much as possible, and to pray continually while they worked at manual crafts. In addition, the monks of the laura kept seven fixed times of prayer during the day and six hours of vigil at night. They were to eat only one meal of bread, salt, and water toward sunset.[15]

It seems that in Chariton's time the organization of the laura was not yet fully crystallized. Its territorial limits were not marked off, as was usual in later times, not even clearly defined. The author of the *Life* states that the tranquility of the hermits was disturbed by "men, women and even children."[16] Only later were female visitors and youth firmly excluded.[17] Possibly some sort of centralized economy was organized in order to enable the monks to live a secluded life without being obliged to go out to sell their handicrafts and gain their bread. In later times at least each laura had a steward who provided to the needs of the cell-dwellers. However, when Euthymius stayed at Pharan, at the beginning of the fifth century, seemingly he earned his livelihood and managed his earnings independently. Also he was able to leave the place and go wandering into the desert whenever he chose, although the fathers of the laura of Pharan tried to keep track of his whereabouts.[18] This behavior is in contrast to the accepted norm of later times, which required from the laurites (the cell-dwellers of a laura) not to leave the laura without the

15. *Life of Chariton* 16.
16. Ibid. 17.
17. In Euthymius's system, which was canonized by Sabas, young men were not accepted in lauras but were sent to one of the cenobia of the desert, that is, the monasteries of Theoctistus, Theodosius, and others, until they reached a more mature age. Cyril of Scythopolis *Vit. Euth.* 16; Chitty, *The Desert a City*, 85.
18. *Vit. Euth.* 6, 8, 9.

abbot's permission. In the earlier period the internal organization of Pharan (and probably the other foundations of Chariton) seems to have been still flexible and provided only the flimsiest frame of communal life.

THE LAURA OF DOUKA

Chariton is presented as an archetype also in his behavior in front of popular veneration. His biographer states that the disturbance of his own and his monks' tranquility by the crowds of visitors caused the holy man to leave the laura of Pharan and find a new, more secluded place for himself. After parting from his monks, Chariton walked for two days until he found a cave "in the vicinity of Jericho" and settled there.[19] A short time afterward, a monastery called Douka was established near the cave. The author explains that the name of the monastery was derived from *dux*, a nickname given to a man who defended the monastery against the attacks of Jews from the nearby settlement of Na'aran.[20] This information is of importance in that it is one of the very few pieces of evidence regarding the mutual relations, in this case of a negative sort, that developed between the monks and their Jewish neighbors in the Judean Desert. Actually, however, the name Douka derives from the name of the fortress Doq, mentioned in sources of the Second Temple period.[21] The location of the fortress, as well as the monastery at the top of Jebel Quruntul and in the caves known as Deir el-Quruntul, three kilometers west of Jericho (map ref. 1423/1909), is clearly established (Pl. 3). At the foot of the mountain pours out of the spring of 'Ein Duyuk, whose modern name preserves the ancient toponym. Near the spring lie the ruins of the ancient sites of Na'aran, which was inhabited by Jews during the Roman and Byzantine periods.[22]

Deir el-Quruntul, like a number of other monasteries in the Judean Desert, was rebuilt by the Greek Patriarchate at the end of the nineteenth century. The descriptions given by scholars who visited the site before the reconstruction are therefore highly important. The first systematic description of the site was given by Tristram, who climbed to the caves at the foot of the cliff.[23] Additional details were given by Conder

19. *Life of Chariton* 19.
20. Ibid., 23.
21. I.e., F.-M. Abel, *Géographie de la Palestine*, II (Paris: J. Gabalda, 1938) 307. For recent discoveries in the site, see H. Eshel, "Finds and Documents from a Cave of Ketef-Yeriho," *Qadmoniot* 21 (1988) 18–23 (Hebrew).
22. M. Avi-Yonah, *Gazetteer of Roman Palestine* (*Qedem* 5; Jerusalem: Monographs of the Institute of Archaeology of the Hebrew University of Jerusalem, 1976) 84.
23. H. Tristram, *The Land of Israel: A Journal of Travels in Palestine* (London: SPCK, 1866) 212–17. The details of this description conform to those of Guérin, *Description geographique, I: Samaria* (Paris: Imprimerie Nationale, 1874) 41–45 (see n. 4).

Pl. 3: Deir el-Quruntul, aerial view, looking west. The recent monastery is built on the foundations of the laura of Douka.

and Kitchener concerning the two chapels, which were identified at different levels in the caves.[24]

A comprehensive description of the modern buildings of the monastery was published by Meinardus in 1969.[25] Meinardus also notes the existence of additional caves and sections of mosaic pavement at the foot of the hill. Its natural features—rocky cliffs and caves with a flowing stream at its foot and its proximity to Jericho—attracted Chariton and his monks to the place. Similar features led Chariton to establish his third monastery near Tekoa.

24. C. R. Conder and H. H. Kitchener, *The Survey of Western Palestine, III: Judea* (London: Palestine Exploration Fund, 1883) 200–204.
25. Meinardus, "Notes on the Laurae," *LA* 19 (1969) 305–27 (see n. 4).

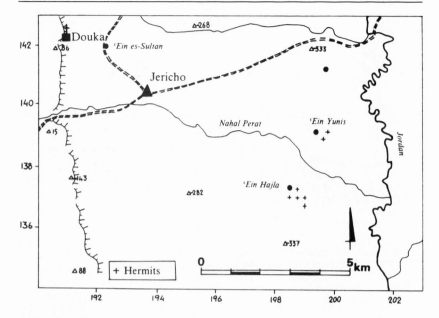

Fig. 5: 'Ein Hajla, location map.

In addition to the monks organized in the laura of Douka to the west of Jericho, there was a center of solitaries in the area southeast of Jericho. According to his biographer, Chariton divided the robbers' treasure among the hermits living in the caves of Calamon ("the reed-bush"), in the Dead Sea region.[26] Accordingly, hermits seem to have been already present in that area during the first half of the fourth century. The existence of hermits in this area is mentioned by sources from the fourth century, and later, during the fifth century, a laura called Calamon was established at the same place.[27]

The region of Calamon was located near 'Ein Hajla, a spring that flows 5.5 kilometers southeast of Jericho (map ref. 1985/1374) (Fig. 5).[28] The 'Ein Hajla spring is surrounded to this day by a dense growth of

26. *Life of Chariton* 13.

27. Two sources mention hermits in the Plain of Jericho during the second half of the fourth century. The first is the *Life of Porphyrius* written by the deacon Mark. Before becoming bishop of Gaza, Porphyrius lived for a time as an anchorite in one of the caves near the Jordan. See *Marc le Diacre, Vie de Porphyre* 4 (ed. H. Gregoire and M. A. Kurgener; Paris: "Les Belles Lettres," 1930) 4. The second source is Palladius, who describes hermits living in places close to the Jordan. See Palladius *Hist. Laus.* 50; E. C. Butler, ed., *The Lausiac History of Palladius* (Cambridge: Cambridge University Press, 1898–1904; reprint, Hildesheim: G. Olms, 1967) 144. For the laura of Calamon, see Vailhe, "Repertoire alphabétique," 520, no. 16; idem., "Les laures de saint Gérasime et de Calamon," *EO* 2 (1898–99) 112–17.

28. R. P. Féderlin, "Recherches sur les laures et monastères de la plaine de Jourdain et du desert de Jerusalem," *LTS* 20 (1903) 132–34.

Pl. 4: 'Ein Hajla, aerial view, looking east. The palm grove is part of the recent monastery that was built on the foundations of the laura of Calamon.

reeds (Pl. 4). The physical conditions of this area supplied the hermits' needs. In that respect, they are similar to the conditions that led Chariton to choose the locations of his monasteries on the desert heights. In this area, water is available: the Jordan River, on the one hand, and 'Ein Hajla and a number of smaller streams, on the other. The soft formation of this region is rich in caves and natural shelters among the rocks, which are easily carved. The area is also quite close to Byzantine Jericho. The proximity of Jericho, like that of the other settlements on the edge of the desert, gave the monks the supply base and sense of security that were vital to their existence in the desert.

CHARITON'S LAURA (SOUKA)

According to his biographer, Chariton left the Monastery of Douka and, after a few days, came to a desert site fourteen stadia (ca. 2.6

kilometers) from the village of Tekoa. After disciples had gathered around him, Chariton established the laura that was first named Souka, as the place was called in the local Syrian dialect.[29] Later it was known by two other names: the Old Laura (*Palaia Laura*) and the monastery of Chariton. Thus, Chariton emerges as an exemplary figure, constantly seeking new places for seclusion, each more distant than the other. The map of his travels (see Fig. 1) brings out the increasing distance between the monasteries he founded in the Judean Desert. In that regard Chariton can be viewed as an archetype of other exemplary monks such as Euthymius and Sabas.

The first name of the laura, that is, Souka, seems to be derived from the Hebrew word *Zuq* ("crag").[30] This name was given probably because of the lofty cliffs of the canyon section of the site. The Monastery of Chariton has been identified with Kh. Khureitun, ca. 2.5 kilometers northeast of Tekoa (map ref. 1727/1172) (Fig. 6).[31]

Chariton's tradition is perpetuated not only in the name of the site itself but also in the name of the canyon section of the Wadi Khureitun (Pl. 5). The section of the wadi to the east of Wadi Khureitun is called Wadi Mu'allak, which means "the overhanging valley." This name may preserve the memory of the "hanging cave" of Chariton, which was discovered near the site of the monastery.[32]

In the rocky area where the monastery was founded, two streams flow: a small one running from the southwest to the kernel of the laura and another, 'Ein en-Natuf (Arabic: "the dripping spring"), flowing at a distance of about 700 meters to the south of the laura. Although these two streams are far from abundant, they are sufficient to supply the

29. *Life of Chariton* 23.

30. F. M. Abel, *Geographie de la Palestine*, I (Paris: Librairie Lecoffre, J. Gabalda et cie, 1933) 471 (cf. 21); J. T. Milik, "La rouleau de cuivre de Qumrân (3Q15)," *RB* 66 (1959) 342. According to Chitty, *The Desert a City*, 15, the name Souka was derived from the word *Souk* ("market" in Arabic) as a kind of parallel to *laura* in Greek. According to Vailhé and Pétridès, "Saint Jean le paléolaurite," 333, the word means "monastery" in Syriac.

31. The first scholar to describe the remains of the monastery was T. Tobler, *Topographie von Jerusalem und seiren, Umgebungen*, II (Berlin: G. Reimer, 1854) 509–10. The remains of the monastery were investigated by Guérin, *Description géographique*, III, 138–39; and Conder and Kitchener, *The Survey*, III, 357. A comprehensive summary of the history of the monastery was published by Vailhé and Pétridès, "Saint Jean le paléolaurite," 343–58. See also Vailhé, "Les premiers monastères," 50–58; idem., "Repertoire alphabétique," 524–25, no. 21; Schiwietz, *Das mörgenlanchische Mönchtum*, 141; B. Bagatti, "La laura di Suka sul Wadi Kareitun," *LTS* 46 (1971) 336–45. The archaeological remains of the monastery of Chariton were surveyed and measured; see Y. Hirschfeld, *Archaeological Survey of Israel: Map of Herodium (108/2)* (Jerusalem: The Archaeological Survey of Israel, 1985) 36–48 (Hebrew and English).

32. Chitty, *The Desert a City*, 15.

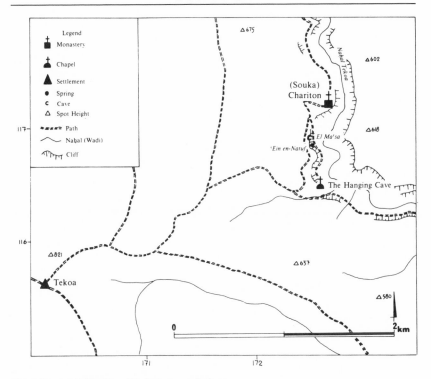

Fig. 6: Laura of Chariton (Souka), general plan.

Pl. 5: Laura of Chariton (Kh. Khureitun), general view of the site, looking west.

needs of a monastic community, at least in its early stages of existence. The laura of Chariton belongs to the large lauras that have two or three times the number of cells of the small lauras like Pharan; this is probably a consequence of later development.

Its total area equals about 450,000 square meters. The ruins that form the northern edge of the expansion are the core buildings of the laura, whereas the cells to the south extend as far as the cave known as the "hanging cave" of Chariton. In this area were found the remains of about thirty-five monks' cells. Most of the cells are small: the average area is 23.3 square meters, similar to that of the laura of Pharan. Water cisterns were installed in the foundations of most of the cells, and small garden plots on the sides of them.

The *Life of Chariton* tells us nothing about the monastery itself. The author concentrates on the cave in which Chariton dwelled as a hermit at the end of his life. After the establishment of the laura at Souka, Chariton is said to have chosen a cave in the steep cliff not far from the laura and decided to live there. His retreat was called the "hanging (cave)" (*to kremaston*) of Chariton because it could be entered only by means of a ladder. Wishing to spare the monks the need for carrying water for him, Chariton performed a miracle causing a spring to flow from one of the walls of his cave.[33]

The "hanging cave" of Chariton was discovered about 800 meters south of the kernel of the laura.[34] The alcove that was inhabited by the holy man is approximately 15 meters above ground level. Thus, access to it was possible only by means of a ladder, a fact that corresponds to the description in the *Life*. Later throughout the Byzantine period, the "hanging cave" became a memorial site for St. Chariton.

The site includes three caves arranged in three levels (Fig. 7). The cave that is on ground level is bell-shaped, its measurements being approximately seven by fifteen meters. Three water cisterns were installed beside the cave's walls. An opening through which one can climb into

33. *Life of Chariton* 24. For the historical background of the cave, see A. Strobel, "Die Charitonhohle in der Wuste Juda," *ZDPV* 83 (1967) 46–63. Strobel, like travelers and scholars who had visited the site before him, traditionally identified the "hanging cave" with Mugharat el-Ma'asa, one of the largest carstic caves in Palestine. The El-Ma'asa cave is about 400 meters south of the ruined monastery of Chariton.

34. Hirschfeld, *Archaeological Survey*, 53–55; idem., "The Hanging Cave of St. Chariton," *ILAN* 12 (1987) 149–58; Y. Hirschfeld and I. Schmutz, "Zur historisch—geographischen Entwicklung der monchischen Bewegung in der Wuste Judaa," *AW* 18 (1987) 42; Y. Hirschfeld, "Memorial and Venerative Sites of Saints in the Vicinity of the Chariton Monastery," in D. Jacoby and Y. Tsafrir, *Jews, Samaritans and Christians in Byzantine Palestine* (Jerusalem: Yad Izhak Ben-Zvi, 1988) 116–18 (Hebrew).

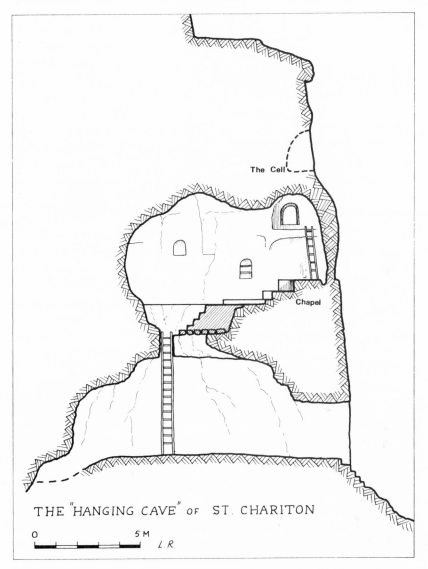

Fig. 7: The "hanging cave" of Chariton, reconstructed cross-section (looking west).

the middle cave was found in the ceiling of this cave at a height of four meters.

In the middle cave, the remains were found of a small chapel cut out of the rock (Pl. 6). These remains included a semicircular niche, the diameter of which was 1.1 meters. A number of other niches were cut out of the cave walls, and an additional water cistern was installed in the

Opposite Page
Pl. 6: The middle "hanging cave" of Chariton,
looking northeast.

Above
Pl. 7: The "hanging cave" used by Chariton during his final days.

eastern side of the cave. The opening leading to the alcove was cut out of the uppermost corner, on the northern side of the cave, 3.5 meters above floor level. After coming through the opening, an extremely narrow passage, somewhat like a shelf, led to the "hanging cave" itself.

The "cave" is a pear-shaped alcove (Pl. 7), its measurements being approximately one by two meters. Its walls were rock-cut, plastered with a well-smoothed yellowish plaster, and adorned with Greek monograms and drawings of three crosses. These had been executed in black, red, and yellow paint. An abbreviation of the formula Ἰησοῦς Χριστὸς υἱὸς θεοῦ, which, when translated, means "Jesus, the Messiah. Son of God," was inscribed next to the arms of the cross on the eastern wall of the niche. The niche's decoration and its location on the rock face permit its identification with the "hanging cave" to which Chariton retreated after establishing the nearby monastery that was named after him.

Cyril of Scythopolis, who visited at the Chariton monastery in the sixth century C.E., speaks of the Hanging Cave of Chariton outside the laura.[35] The location of this three-level cave, 800 meters from the ruined monastery, and the difficult access fit Cyril's testimony. The crosses and Greek monograms ornamenting the walls of the cell also lead to the conclusion that this was the Hanging Cave of St. Chariton. The remains of a chapel on the middle level may indicate its transformation from a mere hermitage into a cult site, a destination for pilgrimage in Byzantine times.

CONCLUSIONS

1. The archaeological research of the sites mentioned by the *Life of Chariton* shows its reliability, as well as the familiarity of the author with the local conditions and reality.
2. The assumption that Chariton had a clear concept of monastic life is confirmed by the common characteristics of the three monasteries he founded. All three were founded as cliff-type lauras near perennial water sources and not far from the settlements of the desert margins.
3. The three lauras of Chariton illustrate well the combination of circumstances that made possible the rise of the phenomenon of the solitary monk in the Judean Desert: a ready supply of water (a spring), a scarped terrain rich in natural caves and shelter, and

35. Cyril of Scythopolis *Life of Cyriac* 15, in E. Schwartz, *Kyrillos von Skythopolis*, 231.

proximity to the settlements of the desert margins. The proximity to population centers was vital for the monks, especially in the initial stages of their settlement in the desert.

4. Chariton's laura was small and simple. The Palestinian lauras of the fourth century—Pharan, Douka, and Souka—were still flexible and left each of the hermits enough latitude to choose his own way of ascetic life. The number of the monks in each laura at that stage was not more than ten to fifteen men.

5. The early monks of the Judean Desert made use of the caves that were adapted as hiding places in the Second Temple period (as in Pharan) or caves that were part of the ancient fortress (as in Douka). The settlement in an abandoned fort or hiding cave was convenient for monks who were looking for a reclusive way of life.

6. In contrast to the area of the desert ridge, no monasteries were founded on the Plain of Jericho until the middle of the fifth century. The historical sources record no inhabited monasteries but rather individual hermits in the area called Calamon. The hermits of this area, like their fellow monks of the desert high plateau, took advantage of local conditions: a ready supply of water (from the Jordan and from a number of springs, such as ʿEin Hagla), and the soft marl (or crumbly) formation, in which caves could easily be carved.

See the suggested readings given in chapter 25.

Canons from the
Council of Gangra

INTRODUCTION

In the middle of the fourth century, thirteen bishops gathered in the Paphlagonian city of Gangra to consider "certain pressing matters of ecclesiastical business."[1] During the course of their deliberations, it was discovered that a new movement under the leadership of Eustathius the bishop of Sebaste was gaining control of churches throughout Armenia. To reestablish the authority of the church, the bishops drew up twenty canons anathematizing Eustathian belief and practice. These canons, together with an introductory letter and epilogue, were sent to the bishops of Armenia.

The central issue dividing the bishops and the Eustathians was ascetic behavior. Both sides valued it, but the bishops regarded the Eustathians' rigorism as a threat to the unity of the church. Thus, their canons seek to define for all the churches what is proper in the practice of asceticism. To ensure that their views are followed, the bishops stipulate that anyone who does not subscribe to them will be excommunicated. Consequently, the documents of the council of Gangra serve to warn both the Eustathians and anyone else who may be attracted to their movement.

Eustathian asceticism comprised four interrelated elements: sex, fam-

1. It is impossible to be very precise in dating the Council of Gangra. Proposed dates range from just after the Council of Nicaea (in 325 C.E.) to 380. Very recently, however, T. D. Barnes proposed the date of 355 C.E. for the synod in Gangra. See his "The Date of the Council of Gangra," *JTS* n.s. (1989) 121–24. To the thirteen names listed in the Greek manuscripts, the Latin translations add Hosius of Cordoba. The areas represented by the bishops are not given but in all likelihood are in Asia Minor and Armenia, the two regions most affected by the problems dealt with during the council.

ily, dress, and diet.[2] Eustathius, who was greatly influenced by Egyptian monasticism, rejected all sexual intercourse. As a result, the Eustathians condemned marriage, claiming that married persons had no hope before God (letter and canons 1, 9, 10, and 14). They also abandoned family life (canons 15 and 16) and encouraged slaves, who were part of the Greco-Roman household, to abandon their masters (canon 3). Customary clothing was rejected in favor of monastic dress (canon 12). In place of traditional church fasts, the Eustathians established their own, completely rejecting the eating of meat (canons 2, 18, and 19). Indeed, they withdrew from all services held in established churches (canons 5, 6, 11, and 20), especially if a married presbyter officiated (canon 4), and took over the administration of funds previously controlled by the church (canons 7 and 8). Concern with women figures prominently in the canons. Canons 1 and 14 deal with married women; canons 13 and 17 indicate that Eustathian women donned men's clothing (evidently the monastic dress referred to in canon 12) and cut their hair in the fashion of men.

This translation is based on the critical edition of the Greek text by Périclès-Pierre Joannou for the Pontificia Commissione per la Redazione del Codice di Diritto Canonico Orientale in *Fonti*, fasc. 9, Discipline Générale Antique (Grottaferrata [Rome]: Tipografia Italo-Orientale, 1962), tom. 1, pt. 2, pp. 83–99.

I am grateful to my colleague, Jonathan Price, for his many helpful comments on the translation, and to Middlebury College for the leave during which the translation was completed.

TRANSLATION

CANONS OF THE HOLY FATHERS
CONVENED AT GANGRA
WHICH WERE SET FORTH AFTER
THE COUNCIL OF NICAEA

Eusebius, Aelian, Eugenius, Olympius, Bithynius, Gregory, Philetus, Pappus, Eulalius, Hypatius, Proaeresius, Basil, and Bassus, convened in

2. The documents of the Council of Gangra are our primary source for reconstructing Eustathian asceticism. Corroborating evidence for some features is found in the ecclesiastical histories of Sozomon (4.24; 3.14) and Socrates (2.43) and in Epiphanius *Haereses* 75.2.

holy synod at Gangra: to their most honored lords and fellow ministers in Armenia, greetings in the Lord.

Inasmuch as the most holy synod of bishops, having convened in the church at Gangra on account of certain pressing matters of ecclesiastical business, when the affairs concerning Eustathius were also investigated, discovered that many things were being done unlawfully by Eustathius's followers, it has out of necessity established guidelines [concerning these things] and has hastened to make [them] known to all in order to put an end to the things being done evilly by him.

For as a result of their condemnation of marriage and their enjoining that no one who is married has hope before God, many married women, being deceived, have withdrawn from their own husbands, and men from their own wives. Then afterwards, not being able to control themselves, the women have committed adultery. And for this reason, they have fallen into reproach.

Moreover, they were found to be promoting withdrawal from the houses of God and the church, [and] disposed contemptuously against the church and the things [done] in the church, have established their own assemblies, churches, different teachings, and other things in opposition to the churches and the things [done] in the church. They wear strange dress to the downfall of the common mode of dress; ecclesiastical funds[3] that have always been given to the church they distribute to themselves and their followers, as if [they were making distributions] to saints; slaves withdraw from their masters and, because of their strange dress, despise their masters; contrary to custom, women put on male dress in place of women's, thinking they are justified by this; and many [women], under pretext of piety, cut off the natural growth of feminine hair; they observe fasts on the Lord's day and despise the holiness of the free day and, condemning the fasts ordained in the churches, they eat [during these fasts]; some of them loathe the eating of meat; they do not wish to make prayers in the homes of married persons and despise such prayers when they are made; frequently they do not participate in the oblations taking place in the very houses of married persons; they condemn married presbyters; they do not engage in the liturgies when performed by married presbyters; they deplore the assembly of the martyrs and those who gather and conduct services there.[4] For each of

---

· 3. Literally, "first fruits."

4. Some manuscripts read: "And they despise the place where the martyrs lie and

them, upon leaving the rule of the church, became, as it were, a law unto himself. For there is not a common opinion among the whole lot of them, but each puts forward whatever he thinks, to the slander of the church and to his own harm.

Because of these things, the holy synod convened in Gangra was compelled to vote in condemnation of them and to set forth definitions, to the effect that they are outside the church. But if they repent and anathematize each of the things recounted as evil, they will be acceptable. And to this end the holy synod has set forth everything they must anathematize in order to be received. But if anyone should not comply with the things listed [herein], such a one is anathematized as a heretic and will be excommunicated and separated from the church. And it will be necessary for the bishops to be on guard against such behavior in all things discovered among them.

Canon 1

If anyone censures marriage, and loathes or censures the faithful and pious woman who sleeps with her husband, claiming she is not able to enter the kingdom, let such a one be anathema.

Canon 2

If anyone condemns those who with reverence and faith eat meat that is without blood, has not been sacrificed to idols, and is not strangled, claiming that because of their partaking they are without hope, let such a one be anathema.

Canon 3

If, under pretext of piety, anyone teaches a slave to despise his master and to withdraw from service and not to serve his master to the utmost with good will and all honor, let such a one be anathema.

Canon 4

If anyone separates himself from a married presbyter, claiming that it is not necessary to partake of the offering when he is celebrating, let such a one be anathema.

---

deplore the assemblies of those who gather and conduct services there." This reading is to be seen as an attempt to clarify the difficulty caused by the bishops' apparent use of "assembly" (*synaxis*) for both the gathering and the gathering place. The language of canon 20 is equally difficult.

Canon 5

If anyone teaches that the house of God and the assemblies held in it are readily despised, let such a one be anathema.

Canon 6

If anyone assembles outside the church on his or her own initiative and, despising the church, desires to perform church functions in the absence of a presbyter who conforms to the judgment of the bishop, let such a one be anathema.[5]

Canon 7

If anyone wishes to receive or give church funds[6] outside the church, contrary to the will of the bishop or the one entrusted with such matters, and wishes to act without his consent, let such a one be anathema.

Canon 8

If anyone, except the bishop or the one commissioned with the stewardship of alms, gives or receives funds, let the one giving and the one receiving be anathema.

Canon 9

If anyone practices virginity or self-control, withdrawing from marriage as if it were a loathsome thing and not because of the inherent beauty and sanctity of virginity, let such a one be anathema.

Canon 10

If any of those who practice virginity for the Lord's sake acts arrogantly toward those who are married, let such a one be anathema.

Canon 11

If anyone despises those who hold love feasts out of faith and invite the brothers out of honor for the Lord, and does not wish to accept invitations out of disdain for what is done, let such a one be anathema.

Canon 12

If, because of presumed asceticism, any man wear the periboleum and, claiming that one has righteousness because of this, pronounces

5. Literally, "desires to do the things of the church, a presbyter not being present according to the knowledge [or opinion; judgment] of the bishop."
6. Here and in the following canon the literal rendering is "first fruits."

judgment against those who with reverence wear the berus and make use of other common and customary clothing, let him be anathema.

Canon 13

If, because of presumed asceticism, any woman change her clothing, and in place of the clothing customary for women adopt that of men, let her be anathema.

Canon 14

If any woman abandons her husband and wishes to withdraw from marriage because she loathes it, let her be anathema.

Canon 15

If anyone abandons his or her own children and does not provide for them and, as far as possible, rear them in accordance with the proper piety, but under pretext of asceticism neglects them, let such a one be anathema.

Canon 16

If, under pretext of asceticism, any children abandon their parents, especially [if the parents are] believers, and do not bestow on them the honor that is their due, that is to say, shall prefer piety to them, let them be anathema.

Canon 17

If, because of presumed asceticism, any woman cuts her hair, which God gave as a reminder of [her] subjection, under the impression that this annuls the ordinance of subjection, let her be anathema.

Canon 18

If, because of presumed asceticism, anyone fasts on the Lord's day, let such a one be anathema.

Canon 19

If any of those practicing asceticism without bodily necessity behaves arrogantly and sets aside the traditional fasts commonly kept by the church, claiming that one's perfect power of reasoning undermines the validity of these fasts, let such a one be anathema.[7]

7. "Claiming that one's perfect power of reasoning undermines the validity of these

Canon 20

If, assuming an arrogant disposition and loathing, anyone condemns the assemblies [in honor?] of the martyrs or the services held in them [*martyria?*] and in memory of [the martyrs], let such a one be anathema.[8]

Epilogue[9]

We write these things not to cut off those in the church of God who wish to practice asceticism according to the Scriptures but [to cut off] those who undertake the practice of asceticism to the point of arrogance, both by exalting themselves over those who lead a simpler life and by introducing novel ideas that are not found in the Scriptures or in the writings approved by the church.

For this reason we admire virginity [when practiced] with humility and we approve of self-control [when practiced] with dignity and piety; we also approve of withdrawal from worldly affairs [when it is done] with humility; and we honor the noble union of marriage; we do not disdain wealth [when used] with righteousness and [the giving of] alms; we praise plainness and frugality of dress, with simple concern only for the body; but we do not approve of going about in lascivious and effeminate dress; we honor the house of God and we approve of the meetings held in them as holy and beneficial, not limiting reverence to the houses but honoring every place built in the name of God; and we approve the communal meeting in the church of God for the benefit of the community; and we bless the brothers' abundant good works on behalf of the poor, because they are performed in accordance with the traditions [established] by the church; and, to sum up, we pray that the things transmitted by the divine Scriptures and the apostolic traditions be done in the church.

SUGGESTED READINGS

There is no recent work on the Council of Gangra. Consequently, the student must refer to the standard dictionaries and histories of the early church. On the council itself the most helpful are "Gangres (Councile de)" by G. Bardy in *Dictionnaire de Droit Canonique* (vol. 5, cols. 935–38) and C. J. Hefele's *A History of the Councils of the Church* (reprint, New York: AMS, 1972), vol. 2, section 94,

---

fasts" is the apparent meaning here. The Greek, a genitive absolute, is obscure. A more literal rendering might be "perfect reasoning annulling in this."

8. As the bracketed expressions indicate, the Greek is obscure. See n. 4.

9. In some manuscripts, this is listed as canon 21.

325–39. For an overview of Eustathius's checkered career, with some information on the Council of Gangra, see "Eustathius of Sebaste" by Edmund Venables in *The Dictionary of Christian Biography* (ed. William Smith and Henry Wace; London: Clowes & Son, 1880). For a general treatment of Eustathian asceticism, see Charles A. Frazee, "Anatolian Asceticism in the Fourth Century," *Catholic Historical Review* 66.1 (1981) 16–33. See also Nina G. Garsoïan, "Nersēs le Grand, Basile de Césarée et Eustathe de Sébaste," *Revue des Études Armeniennes* 17 (1983) 145–69.

Egyptian Monasticism
(Selected Papyri)

INTRODUCTION

The papyrus petition and letters that follow speak to us directly from the world of early-fourth-century Egyptian monasticism.[1] They offer immediate access to a period that is portrayed anachronistically in the literary sources, where later theological, ecclesiastical, and instructional concerns have shaped the evidence.[2] In the documentary texts, individuals and communities appear in their original setting within the wider social world. They have not yet been removed from that setting and reshaped by the intentions of later authors. They do not yet serve as literary models of imitation or masters of instruction. Here we find a village monk mentioned by chance in a legal petition, early Christians seeking the aid of a revered holy man, and sisters working within a communal organization of uncertain variety. The evidence comes without interpretation and serves as a valuable data base through which to test the interpretive reliability of the later literary sources.[3]

1. Documentary evidence of Egyptian monasticism is sparse for the early centuries and increases substantially in the fifth, sixth, and seventh centuries. E. A. Judge, "Fourth Century Monasticism in the Papyri," in *Proceedings of the XVI International Congress of Papyrology* (Chico, Calif.: Scholars Press, 1981) 612–20; P. Barison, "Richerche sui monasteri dell'Egitto bizantino ed arabo secondo i documenti dei papiri greci," *Aegyptus* 18 (1938) 29–148.

2. Hermann Dörries, "Die Vita Antonii als Geschichtsquelle," *Nachrichten der Akademie der Wissenschaften in Göttingen, philologisch-historische Klasse* 14 (Göttingen: Vandenhoeck & Ruprecht, 1949) 357–410; Susan Ashbrook Harvey, "The Sense of a Stylite: Perspectives on Simeon the Elder," *VC* 42 (1988) 376–94; James E. Goehring, "New Frontiers in Pachomian Studies," in Birger A. Pearson and James E. Goehring, eds. *The Roots of Egyptian Christianity* (Studies in Antiquity and Christianity 1; Philadelphia: Fortress Press, 1986) 236–57.

3. James E. Goehring, "The Origins of Monasticism," in *Eusebius, Judaism and*